For Reference

Not to be taken from this room

W9-APZ-003

DISCARD

The Appraisal of Real Estate

Twelfth Edition

Estate

Readers of this text may be interested in the following publications from the Appraisal Institute:

- *Appraising Residential Properties,* third edition
- *The Dictionary of Real Estate Appraisal,* third edition
- *The Appraisal of Rural Property,* second edition

The Appraisal of Real Estate

Twelfth Edition

Appraisal Institute

Professionals Providing Real Estate Solutions

875 North Michigan Avenue • Chicago, Illinois 60611-1980

www.appraisalinstitute.org

Vice President, Educational
Programs and Publications: Larisa Phillips
Director, Content Development &
Quality Assurance: Margo T. Wright
Manager, Book Development: Stephanie Shea-Joyce
Technical Writer: Michael McKinley
Book Editor: Mary Elizabeth Geraci
Supervisor, Book
Design/Production: Michael Landis
Book Production Specialist: Lynne Mattick

For Educational Purposes Only

The opinions set forth herein reflect the viewpoint of the Appraisal Institute at the time of publication but do not necessarily reflect the viewpoint of each individual member. While a great deal of care has been taken to provide accurate and current information, neither the Appraisal Institute nor its editors and staff assume responsibility for the accuracy of the data contained herein. Further, the general principles and conclusions presented in this text are subject to local, state, and federal laws and regulations, court cases, and any revisions of the same. This publication is sold for educational purposes with the understanding that the publisher is not engaged in rendering legal, accounting, or other professional service.

Nondiscrimination Policy

The Appraisal Institute advocates equal opportunity and nondiscrimination in the appraisal profession and conducts its activities in accordance with applicable federal, state, and local laws.

© 2001 by the Appraisal Institute, an Illinois not for profit corporation. All rights reserved. No part of this publication may be reproduced, modified, rewritten, or distributed, either electronically or by any other means, without the express written permission of the Appraisal Institute.

Printed in the United States of America

Library of Congress Cataloging-in-Publication Data

The appraisal of real estate.— 12th ed.
     p. cm.
   Includes bibliographical references and index.
   ISBN 0-922154-67-8
       1. Real property—Valuation. 2. Personal property—Valuation. I. Appraisal Institute (U.S.)

HD1387 .A663 2001
333.33'2—dc21

2001022867

LIBRAR┆
┆AMI-DADE COMMUN┆   ┆LEGE
MIAMI, FLOR┆DA

TABLE OF CONTENTS

FOREWORD

For more than 50 years, *The Appraisal of Real Estate* has served generations of appraisers and their clients as the comprehensive repository of appraisal knowledge. The twelfth edition of the textbook continues that tradition and renews the focus on fundamentals to provide a solid foundation on which to build a broad and substantial understanding of real property valuation. The extensive revisions to the new edition have made the text a more powerful and persuasive tool for novice appraisers and established practitioners alike.

While this edition of *The Appraisal of Real Estate* has been reorganized significantly for clarity, coherence, and consistency, the text retains its distinction as the authoritative work on emerging issues such as the impact of automated valuation models on the appraisal industry, the new emphasis on extraordinary assumptions and hypothetical conditions in recent revisions of standards of professional practice, and important data sources. Readers will also find a clearer discussion of building description, style, and function and their interrelationship; greater emphasis on the relationship of market analysis and highest and best use analysis, with clearer explanations of the goals of both; and a more straightforward and rigorous explanation of the process of estimating depreciation. The new edition also features separate chapters on the theory, techniques, and applications of the sales comparison approach; a consistent set of terms for use in the income capitalization approach; succinct discussions of appraisal specialties and topics of contention within the industry; and topical bibliographies at the end of each chapter with additional references to related literature

The Appraisal Institute would like to acknowledge the significant contributions of John A. Schwartz, MAI, Chair of the Educational Publications Committee; Peter D. Bowes, MAI; John D. Dorchester, Jr., MAI; and Frank E. Harrison, MAI, SRA, who reviewed the entire manuscript. In addition, special recognition goes to Don M. Emerson, MAI, SRA, Jeffrey A. Johnson, MAI, and Stephen A. Manning, MAI, SRA, who served with Schwartz and Harrison on the development team that guided the decision-making process. The leadership of Michael S. MaRous, MAI, SRA, former Chair of the Educational Publications Committee, was also instrumental in the 18 months of the textbook's development. Many others assisted in the development of the twelfth edition of *The Appraisal of Real Estate,* and the Appraisal Institute would like to thank the following contributors, reviewers, and consultants: Charles B. Akerson, MAI; Sherryl V. Andrus, SRA; William

L. Christensen, MAI, SRA; Stephanie Coleman, MAI, SRA; Winfield L. Cooper, SRA; Larry O. Dybvig, MAI; James D. Eaton, MAI, SRA; Stephen F. Fanning, MAI; Ken G. Foltz, MAI, SRA; W. West Foster, MAI; Mark R. Freitag, SRA; Howard C. Gelbtuch, MAI; Maggie Hambleton, SRA; Robert Jones, MAI; David M. Keating, MAI; David C. Lennhoff, MAI, SRA; George R. Mann, MAI, SRA; Richard Marchitelli, MAI; Maureen Mastroieni, MAI; J. Virginia Messick, MAI; Arlen C. Mills, MAI, SRA; Dan P. Mueller, MAI; Bill Mundy, MAI; Joseph Rabianski; Steve D. Roach, MAI; Lee B. Smith, MAI; Gary P. Taylor, MAI, SRA; James D. Vernor, MAI; and Marvin L. Wolverton, MAI.

Brian A. Glanville, MAI
2001 President
Appraisal Institute

PART

I

FUNDAMENTALS

Part I of the text covers the fundamentals of real property, value, appraisal principles, interests and ownership in real property, and the competition between real estate and other investments for capital. **Chapter 1, Real Property and Its Appraisal,** introduces the distinct concepts of *real estate* and *real property* and outlines the services that professional real estate appraisers commonly perform for their clients. **Chapter 2, The Nature of Value,** discusses the various types of value appraisers deal with and how these types of value are defined. **Chapter 3, Foundations of Appraisal,** explains the economic principles on which the discipline of appraisal is based and discusses the forces that influence the value of real property. **Chapter 4, The Valuation Process,** illustrates the step-by-step process that appraisers follow to develop and report an opinion of value. **Chapter 5, Real Property Ownership and Interests,** explains the various interests and forms of ownership that make up the bundle of rights and discusses how less-than-complete ownership of real property affects the valuation process. **Chapter 6, Real Estate Markets, Money Markets, and Capital Markets,** defines how real estate markets work in relation to the other investment options that compete for investors' funds.

CHAPTER 1

REAL PROPERTY AND ITS APPRAISAL

Land provides the foundation for the social and economic activities of people. It is both a tangible physical commodity and a source of wealth. Because land is essential to life and society, it is important to many disciplines, including law, economics, sociology, and geography. Each of these disciplines may employ a somewhat different concept of real property.

Within the vast domain of the law, issues such as the ownership and the use of land are considered. In economics, land is regarded as one of the four agents of production, along with labor, capital, and entrepreneurial coordination. Land provides many of the natural elements that contribute to a nation's wealth. Sociology focuses on the dual nature of land:

- As a resource to be shared by all people
- As a commodity that can be owned, traded, and used by individuals

Geography focuses on describing the physical elements of land and the activities of the people who use it.

Lawyers, economists, sociologists, and geographers have a common understanding of the attributes of land:

> **Land** is investigated and analyzed in a variety of disciplines—government, the law, economics, geography, and environmental studies.

- Each parcel of land is unique in its location and composition.
- Land is physically immobile.
- Land is durable.
- The supply of land is finite.
- Land is useful to people.

Real estate appraisers view these attributes as the foundation of real estate's value. Contrasted with the physical character of land, value is an economic concept. Appraisers recognize the concepts of land used in other disciplines but are most concerned with how the market measures value. Markets reflect the attitudes and actions of people in response to social and economic forces.

Concepts of Land

Although land and improvements to land can be viewed in a physical sense, there are other concepts of land that are less obvious. These concepts help to characterize the importance of land and provide the foundation for land value systems.

Governmental and Legal

Land use derives from the mandates of organized society. In countries where the ownership and marketability of land are not free, government often dictates the use of land. In free market economies, land use is regulated within a framework of laws. To understand how the various forces affecting land operate, the basic role of law must be recognized.

The cultural, political, governmental, and economic attitudes of a society are reflected in its laws. The law does not focus on the physical characteristics of land but on the rights and obligations associated with various interests in land. In the United States, the right of individuals to own and use land for material gain is maintained, while the right of all people to use the land is protected. In other words, the law recognizes the possible conflict between private ownership and public use.

"Whose is the land, his it is, to the sky and the depths." This ancient maxim is the basis of the following legal definition:

> Land ... includes not only the ground, or soil, but everything that is attached to the earth, whether by course of nature, as are trees and herbage, or by the hand of man, as are houses and other buildings. It includes not only the surface of the earth but everything under it and over it. Thus in legal theory, the surface of the earth is just part of an inverted pyramid having its tip, or apex, at the center of the earth, extending outward through the surface of the earth at the boundary lines of the tract, and continuing on upward to the heavens.[1]

This definition suggests that land ownership includes complete possession of land from the center of the earth to the ends of the universe. In practice, however, land ownership is limited.

The U.S. Congress has declared that the federal government has complete and exclusive sovereignty over the nation's airspace and that every citizen has "a public right to freedom of transit in air commerce through the navigable air space of the United States."[2] Many states restrict ownership and use of subsurface areas such as underground aquifers. Because land ownership can be limited, ownership rights are the subject of law; the value of these rights is the focus of real estate appraisal.

The laws that govern the use and development of land in the United States give landowners great freedom in deciding how to use their land. However, this freedom is not without restrictions. The basic concept of private ownership calls for unrestricted use so long as such use does not unreasonably harm the rights of others. In the past, the test of harm focused

---

1.   Raymond J. Werner and Robert Kratovil, *Real Estate Law*, 10th ed. (Englewood Cliffs, N.J.: Prentice-Hall, Inc., 1993), 4.

2.   The Air Commerce Act of 1926 (formerly 49 USC 171 *et seq.*); the Civil Aeronautics Act of 1938 (formerly 49 USC 401 *et seq.*); and the Federal Aviation Act of 1958 (see 49 USC 401).

on owners of adjacent properties. The concept of harm has recently been expanded to encompass broader social and geographic concerns. The definition of reasonable use has been argued in many court cases.

Legal matters of particular concern to appraisers include the following:

- Easements
- Access regulations
- Use restrictions
- The recording and conveyance of titles

Also, appraisers must be familiar with local and state laws, which have primary jurisdiction over land.

Economic

Land is a physical entity with inherent ownership rights that can be legally limited for the good of society. Land is also a major source of wealth, which, in economic terms, can be measured in money or exchange value. Land and its products have economic value only when they are converted into goods or services that are useful, desirable, paid for by consumers, and limited in supply. The economic concept of land as a source of wealth and an object of value is central to appraisal theory.

The economic concept of land reflects a long history of thought on the sources and bases of value, which is referred to as *value theory*.[3] Value theory contributes to the value definitions used in appraisal reports and appraisal literature, and it is an important part of the philosophy on which professional appraisal practice is founded.

Social

Modern society has become increasingly concerned with how land is used and how rights are distributed. The supply of land is fixed, so increased demand for land exerts pressure for land to be used more intensively. Conflicts often arise between groups that hold different views on proper land use. Those who believe that land is a resource to be shared by all want to preserve the land's scenic beauty and important ecological functions. Others view land primarily as a marketable commodity. They believe society is best served by private, unrestricted ownership.

For example, environmental preservationist groups value the natural amenities of old-growth or virgin forest differently than logging companies do. Similarly, the developer of a proposed shopping center or a business park may view a particular parcel of land as developable green space in a desirable and affordable location serving a definable market area. On the other hand, local residents may argue that, as the site of a significant Civil War battle, the

---

3.   Paul F. Wendt, *Real Estate Appraisal: Review and Outlook* (Athens, Ga.: University of Georgia Press, 1974), 17.

parcel deserves government protection (if taxpayers could be persuaded to support such a public investment in historical preservation). These conflicting views do not alter the constitutional rights of ownership or market concepts of land. Rather, they reflect controversies that arise between the property rights of the individual and those of society. As a resource, land is protected for the good of society. As a marketable commodity, the ownership, use, and disposal of land are regulated so that individual rights are not violated.[4]

In 1876 the U.S. Supreme Court established the government's right to regulate "the manner in which [a citizen] shall own his own property when such regulation becomes necessary for the public good." The court quoted the words of England's Lord Chief Justice Hale: "When private property is 'affected with a public interest,' it ceases to be *juris privati* only."[5] Throughout American history, land ownership has been recognized as fundamental. John Adams wrote, "If the multitude is possessed of real estate, the multitude will take care of the liberty, virtue, and interest of the multitude in all acts of government."[6]

All laws and operations of government are intended to serve the public. Thus, in the public interest, society may impose building restrictions, zoning and building ordinances, development and subdivision regulations, and other land use controls. These controls affect what may be developed, where development may occur, and what activities may be permitted subsequent to development. In recent decades, the U.S. Government has increased its efforts to regulate the air and water emissions from manufacturing processes and to reduce pollution caused by dirt, chemicals, and noise. Protective controls over land use extend to wetlands, beaches, and navigable waters and to the preservation of the habitats of endangered species.[7]

As the nature and extent of land use controls change, so do the nature and extent of private land ownership. Such changes impact markets and ultimately real estate values. Consequently, real estate appraisers must be familiar with the regulations and restrictions that apply to land use and understand how these regulations affect a specific property.

Geographic and Environmental

The study of land includes consideration of its diverse physical characteristics and how these characteristics combine in a particular area. Each land parcel is unique, and location is a very important attribute. The utility of land and the highest and best use to which land can be put are significantly affected by the

---

4.   See also Charles E. Roe, "Land Use: The Second Battle of Gettysburg," *The Appraisal Journal* (October 2000): 441-449.

5.   94 U.S. 113 (1896). Quoted in "Land as a Commodity Affected with a Public Interest" by Richard F. Babcock and Duane A. Feurer in Richard N. L. Andrews, *Land in America* (Lexington, Mass.: D.C. Heath and Company, 1979), 110.

6.   Ibid., 31.

7.   For more information on the government's control of land use, see J.D. Eaton, *Real Estate Valuation in Litigation,* 2d ed. (Chicago, Appraisal Institute, 1995).

physical and locational characteristics of the land and other related considerations, broadly referred to as *geography*.

Land is affected by a number of processes. Ongoing physical and chemical processes modify the land's surface, biological processes determine the distribution of life forms, and socioeconomic processes direct human habitation and activity on the land. Together, these processes influence the characteristics of land use.

Land can be used for many purposes:

- Agriculture
- Commerce
- Industry
- Habitation
- Recreation

And land use decisions may be influenced by many factors:

- Climate
- Topography
- The distribution of natural resources, population centers, and industry
- Trends in economics, population, technology, and culture

The influence of each of these factors on a particular parcel of land varies.

Geographic considerations are particularly significant to appraisers. The importance of physical characteristics such as topography, soils, water, and vegetation is obvious, but the distribution of population, facilities, and services and the movement of people and goods are equally important. The geographic concept of land, which emphasizes natural resources, the location of industry, and actual and potential markets, provides much of the background knowledge required in real estate appraisal.

Real Estate, Real Property, and Personal Property

In real estate appraisal, an important distinction is made between the terms *real estate* and *real property*.[8] Although these concepts are different, some state laws and court decisions treat them as synonymous for legal purposes.

Real estate is the physical land and appurtenances affixed to the land—e.g., structures. Real estate is immobile and tangible. The legal definition of *real estate* includes the following tangible components:

- Land
- All things that are a natural part of land, such as trees and minerals
- All things that are attached to land by people, such as buildings and site improvements

---

8. The definitions of *real estate* and *real property* used in the Uniform Standards of Professional Appraisal Practice (USPAP) promulgated by The Appraisal Foundation can be found in Appendix A.

The distinction between **real estate** and **real property** is fundamental to appraisal.

real estate: Physical land and appurtenances attached to the land, e.g., structures. An identified parcel or tract of land, including any improvements.

real property: All interests, benefits, and rights inherent in the ownership of physical real estate; the bundle of rights with which the ownership of the real estate is endowed. In some states, real property is defined by statute and is synonymous with real estate.

In addition, all permanent building attachments (for example, plumbing, electrical wiring, and heating systems) as well as built-in items (such as cabinets and elevators) are usually considered part of the real estate. Real estate includes all attachments, both above and below the ground.

Real property includes all interests, benefits, and rights inherent in the ownership of physical real estate. A right or interest in real estate is also referred to as an *estate*. Specifically, an estate in land is the degree, nature, or extent of interest that a person has in it.

The total range of ownership interests in real property is called the *bundle of rights*. Imagine a bundle of sticks where each "stick" represents a distinct and separate right or interest. The bundle of rights contains all the interests in real property, including the right to use the real estate, sell it, lease it, enter it, and give it away, and each "stick" can be separated from the bundle and traded in the market. The U.S. Constitution guarantees the private enjoyment of these rights, subject to certain limitations and restrictions, which are discussed in Chapter 5.

Appraisers not only distinguish between real estate and real property, they also differentiate between *real estate, personal property*, and *trade fixtures*, as illustrated in Tables 1.1 and 1.2. Appraisers must know whether an item is personal property or a fixture to determine whether it will be included in the property value indication. If an item is classified as a fixture, it is part of the real estate, and its contribution to value is included in the reported opinion of value.[9] Because the distinction between fixtures and personal property is not always obvious, appraisers should read leases carefully and know how these items are treated in their areas. It is sometimes impossible to exclude personal property from an opinion of value. Personal property that is related to real estate and is to be included in the opinion of value should be identified and described in the appraisal (see Chapter 26).

9. In 1999 the Appraisal Standards Board replaced the term *estimate* of value in the Uniform Standards of Professional Appraisal Practice with the term *opinion* of value. One reason for this change was to better clarify the difference between the output of an automated valuation model (which provides an *estimate* of value) and the result of an appraisal performed by a person (who applies judgment and experience in the process of rendering an *opinion* of value). This text has been revised to reflect the evolution of the terminology used in USPAP.

Table 1.1	Distinctions Between Real Estate, Personal Property, and Trade Fixtures

Real Estate

Characteristics Items that have been installed or attached to the land or building in a rather permanent manner. All real estate improvements were once personal property; when attached to the land, they become real estate.

Examples
- Land
- Buildings
- Fixtures—e.g., plumbing, lighting, heating, and air-conditioning in a residential property

Personal Property

Characteristics Movable items of property that are not permanently affixed to, or part of, the real estate. Personal property is not endowed with the rights of real property ownership.

Examples
- Furniture and furnishings not built into the structure such as refrigerators and freestanding shelves
- Items such as bookshelves and window treatments installed by a tenant that, under specific lease terms, may be removed at the termination of the lease

Trade Fixtures

Characteristics Unlike fixtures, which are regarded in law as part of the real estate, trade fixtures are not real estate endowed with the rights of real property ownership. They are personal property regardless of how they are affixed. A trade fixture is to be removed by the tenant when the lease expires unless this right has been surrendered in the lease. Also known as a *chattel fixture*.

Examples
- Restaurant booths
- Gasoline station pumps
- Storage tanks
- Fitness equipment in a health club
- Plumbing, lighting, heating, and air-conditioning in an industrial building
- Industrial equipment such as air hoses, water pipelines, craneways, and bus ducts

Table 1.2	Criteria for Distinguishing Between Personal Property and Fixtures

Criteria	Explanation
The manner in which the item is affixed	Generally an item is considered personal property if it can be removed without serious injury to the real estate or to itself. There are exceptions to this rule.
The character of the item and its adaptation to the real estate	Items that are specifically constructed for use in a particular building or installed to carry out the purpose for which the building was erected are generally considered permanent parts of the building.
The intention of the party who attached the item	Frequently the terms of the lease reveal whether the item is permanent or is to be removed at some future time.

Source: Raymond J. Werner and Robert J. Kratovil, *Real Estate Law,* 10th ed. (Englewood Cliffs, N.J.: Prentice-Hall, Inc., 1993), 11–17.

Appraisal Practice

In our complex society, the words *appraiser* and *appraisal* can take on many meanings. It is important to use these terms correctly and to distinguish among the individuals involved in the appraisal process.

Buyers and *sellers* purchase and sell real estate and make decisions relating to prices and other real estate matters. Home buyers often have little or no background in real estate and must rely on others to make their decisions. The only "appraisal" they make is an evaluation of the conditions they observe or facts that are made known to them. At the opposite end of the spectrum, institutional investors may have personnel who are trained in appraising.

Real estate salespeople are licensed to sell real estate. They have training in their field but may or may not have extensive appraisal training. They are generally familiar with properties in a given locale and have access to historical market information. Some may develop appraisal expertise. As a group, real estate salespeople evaluate specific properties, but they typically do not necessarily consider all the factors that professional appraisers do.

Real estate financial officers and *executives* include loan officers, closing agents, agents at title companies, relocation officers and agents, and others. This group also includes government officials who deal with land or land values in the private marketplace. These professionals vary in their ability to understand market forces in a given locale, develop opinions of value, and apply appraisal concepts. Real estate investment advisors may have extensive training in understanding appraisals even if they do not develop appraisals themselves. Members of this group work with or review appraisals developed by others. While they are knowledgeable about appraisals, they are rarely trained appraisers.

Licensed and certified real estate appraisers meet educational, experience, and testing requirements set by the state and can perform appraisals in the jurisdiction covered by their licenses or certifications.[10] The types of properties that can be appraised are dependent on the type of license or certification held. Licensed and certified real estate appraisers are required to meet continuing education requirements and must adhere to the Uniform Standards of Professional Appraisal Practice (USPAP) or risk disciplinary action, including possible loss of license.

Full-time professional real estate appraisers are often licensed and certified in more than one state and spend the majority of their time appraising. These individuals have extensive training and experience and are committed to the

---

10. Although the federal government mandated that all states establish licensing or certification programs to regulate appraisals for federally related transactions, some states established laws requiring licensing/certification only for appraisals performed for these purposes. Other states require licensing/certification for appraisals performed for any (or almost any) purpose. In general, the courts do not require an appraiser to be licensed or certified; however, possession of a state-issued license or certification has become a basic indication of appraiser competency.

profession. This group includes those who perform and review real property appraisals. Professional appraisers are bound to strict compliance with regulatory requirements, and many are members of appraisal organizations such as the Appraisal Institute, which fosters participation in professional activities and educational development. Members agree to peer review of their ethical conduct or work performance, which reflects their strong commitment to professionalism.

Continuing education is the cornerstone of professional development. By pursuing continuing education, appraisers demonstrate their commitment to maintaining their skills at a level far above the bare minimum required to satisfy state licensing requirements. Individuals who complete a rigorous educational program and earn recognized professional designations find that their employment and business prospects are considerably enhanced. A commitment to professionalism helps regulate the industry and ensures quality appraisal work.

According to USPAP, appraisal practice encompasses three type of activities:

1. Appraisal
2. Appraisal consulting
3. Appraisal review

The nature of the real estate problem will indicate whether the task is an appraisal (valuation) or an appraisal consulting assignment (analysis or counseling).[11] In both types of assignments, conclusions are derived from appropriate analysis performed in conformance with accepted standards of professional practice (see Table 1.3).

The application of appraisal procedures and the report that communicates the appraiser's conclusions are guided by the nature of the assignment, i.e., its purpose and intended use. To avoid misunderstandings, it is advisable for the client and the appraiser to agree upon the scope of work for the assignment at the outset.

Appraisal Assignments and Reporting Formats

In the Uniform Standards of Professional Appraisal Practice (USPAP), complete appraisals and limited appraisals are differentiated based on whether or not the appraiser invokes the Departure Rule of the Uniform Standards. Complete appraisals are performed without invoking the Departure Rule; limited appraisals are opinions of value developed under the Departure Rule. The Departure Rule states that an appraiser may enter into an agreement to perform an assignment that calls for something less than, or different from, the work that would otherwise be required by the specific guidelines, pro-

---

11. See also Advisory Opinion 21, "When Does USPAP Apply in Valuation Services?" *Uniform Standards of Professional Appraisal Practice* (Washington, D.C.: The Appraisal Foundation, 2001).

Table 1.3	Comparison of Appraisal, Consulting, and Review

Appraisal

Definition*   The act or process of developing an opinion of value.

Characteristics   Appraisal involves selective research into appropriate market areas, the assemblage of pertinent data, the use of appropriate analytical techniques, and the application of knowledge, experience, and professional judgment to develop an appropriate solution to an appraisal problem. The appraiser provides the client with an opinion of real property value that reflects all pertinent market evidence.

Examples
- An opinion of market value for a fee simple estate, leasehold estate, preservation easement, or other estate (to assist in mortgage lending decisions, to assist in purchase or sale decisions, etc.)
- An opinion of investment value or some other properly defined value of an identified interest in real estate as of a given date (for insurance purposes, for relocation purposes, for property tax appeals, etc.)

Appraisal Consulting

Definition*   The act or process of developing an analysis, recommendation, or opinion to solve a problem, where an opinion of value is a component of the analysis leading to the assignment results.

Characteristics   Current market activity and evidence are studied to form a conclusion that may not focus on a specific value indication. An appraiser develops a value opinion in an appraisal consulting assignment as part of the process of answering some other question about real estate, such as whether a proposed use of a given property is economically feasible.

Examples
- Economic feasibility studies
- Marketability or investment considerations that relate to proposed or existing developments
- Land utilization studies
- Supply and demand studies
- Absorption analyses

Appraisal Review

Definition*   The act or process of developing and communicating an opinion about the quality of another appraiser's work.

Characteristics   Appraisal review procedures may be likened to a quality control or auditing function. A review appraiser examines the reports of other appraisers to determine whether their conclusions are consistent with the data reported and other generally known information.

Examples
- Field review
- Desk review

* From the Definitions section of the Uniform Standards of Professional Appraisal Practice (2001 edition)

vided that prior to entering into such an agreement the following conditions are met:

1. The appraiser has determined that the service to be performed is not so limited in scope that the resulting assignment would tend to mislead or confuse the client and the intended users of the report.

2. The appraiser has advised the client that the assignment calls for something less than, or different from, the work required by the specific guidelines and that the report will identify and explain the departure(s).

3. The client has agreed that performance of a limited appraisal or consulting service would be appropriate.

Appraisal reports communicating both complete or limited appraisals may be presented in three formats:

1. Self-contained appraisal reports
2. Summary appraisal reports
3. Restricted use appraisal reports

> The Uniform Standards of Professional Appraisal Practice (USPAP) define **two types of appraisal assignments**—complete and limited—and **three reporting formats**—self-contained, summary, and restricted use.

A self-contained appraisal report fully describes the data and analyses used in the assignment. All appropriate information is contained within the report and not referenced to the appraiser's files. A summary appraisal report summarizes the data and analyses used in the assignment. A restricted use appraisal report simply states the conclusions of the appraisal.

Appraisal reports can be delivered to a client as oral reports or in writing, either as a form report or a narrative report. (Further information on appraisal reporting formats is included in Chapter 26.)

Purpose and Intended Use of an Appraisal

The purpose of an appraisal is the stated reason and scope of the appraisal assignment. It is established by the client, and it points to the information that the client needs to answer specific questions pertaining to real property. If the client's questions are clearly understood, the purpose of the appraisal can be described in terms of the information requested.

When an opinion of value is required in an appraisal, the type of value sought must be defined at the outset. The defined value may be

•   Market value
•   Going-concern value
•   Assessed value
•   Use value
•   Investment value
•   Other types of value

Distinctions among these terms are discussed in Chapter 2.

The purpose of the appraisal establishes the foundation for the final value conclusion, which does not change to accommodate the use of the appraisal. The structure of an appraisal report may be adapted to the intended use of the opinion of value, but the value itself will not change. For example, the appraisal of a single-family property might be reported on a form to facilitate a sale or mort-

The **purpose and the intended use** of an appraisal are related, but distinct, concepts.

purpose of an appraisal: The stated reason for an appraisal assignment, i.e., to develop an opinion of the defined value of any real property interest or to conduct an evaluation study (consulting assignment) pertaining to real property decisions.

intended use of an appraisal: The manner in which a client will employ the information contained in an appraisal report.

Appraisals are **commonly used** in situations involving the transfer of ownership, financing and credit, litigation, taxation, and investment counseling and in other business decision making.

gage financing, in a restricted use report for rehabilitation decisions, or in a self-contained report for use in litigation. Whatever the circumstances, the dollar figure or figures associated with the defined value will be the same.

The intended use of an appraisal is the manner in which a client will employ the information contained in the appraisal report. The intended use or function of an appraisal is determined by the client's needs. For example, a client may want to know the market value of a residence to avoid paying too much for it or accepting too little for it in a sale. Corporate clients may need to ascertain the rent levels or demographic trends in an area to determine the advisability of relocating there. Or a developer may need to understand the supply and demand factors at work in a community before constructing an apartment complex.

Because an appraisal provides a basis for a decision concerning real property, the intended use of an appraisal depends on the decision the client wishes to make. In defining the appraisal problem, the appraiser should consider the client's requirements and reach an understanding that is acceptable to the client and the appraiser and is consistent with accepted standards of professional appraisal practice.

An appraisal may be requested in a number of situations. Table 1.4 does not reflect all possible uses for appraisals, but it does provide a broad sampling of professional appraisal activities.

Appraiser Liability

As the appraisal industry strives for greater professionalism, the scope of appraiser responsibility and potential liability grows. Appraisers may be held liable for negligence, misrepresentation, fraud, breach of contract, or lack of compliance with the standards imposed by government agencies, The Appraisal Foundation, and the Appraisal Institute. Areas of potential exposure include matters involving privity of contract,[12] disclosure, and litigation (e.g., discovery proceedings, interrogatories, and depositions).

---

12.   Privity of contract concerns the relationship between two parties, e.g., an appraiser who has entered into an agreement to perform an assignment and a client such as a bank or accounting firm. The client may allege that the appraiser acted improperly and, as a result, a third party (an investor) was harmed.

Table 1.4	**Typical Uses of Appraisals**

Transfer of ownership
- To help prospective buyers set offering prices
- To help prospective sellers determine acceptable selling prices
- To establish a basis for real property exchanges
- To establish a basis for reorganizing or merging the ownership of multiple properties
- To determine the terms of a sale price for a proposed transaction

Financing and credit
- To develop an opinion of the value of the security offered for a proposed mortgage loan
- To provide an investor with a sound basis for deciding whether to purchase real estate mortgages, bonds, or other types of securities
- To establish a basis for a decision to insure or underwrite a loan on real property

Litigation

Eminent domain proceedings
- To develop an opinion of the market value of a property as a whole—i.e., before a taking
- To develop an opinion of the market value of the remainder after a taking
- To estimate the damages to a property created by a taking

Property divisions
- To develop an opinion of the market value of a property in contract disputes
- To develop an opinion of the market value of real estate as part of a portfolio
- To develop an opinion of the market value of partnership interests

Environmental litigation
- To estimate damages created by violations of environmental laws
- To estimate damages created by environmental accidents

Tax matters
- To develop an opinion of assessed value
- To separate assets into depreciable (or capital recapture) items such as buildings and nondepreciable items such as land, and to estimate applicable depreciation (or capital recapture) rates
- To develop an opinion of the value of the real estate component of an estate plan that represents the foundation for future capital gains and inheritance taxes
- To determine gift or inheritance taxes

Investment counseling, decision making, and accounting
- To set rent schedules and lease provisions
- To determine the feasibility of a construction or renovation program
- To help corporations or third parties purchase homes for transferred employees
- To serve the needs of insurers, adjusters, and policyholders
- To facilitate corporate mergers, the issuance of stock, or the revision of book value
- To develop an opinion of liquidation value for forced sale or auction proceedings
- To counsel clients by considering their investment goals, alternatives, resources, and constraints and the timing of their activities
- To advise zoning boards, courts, and planners, among others, on the probable effects of proposed actions
- To assist in arbitrating valuation issues
- To analyze supply and demand trends in a market
- To ascertain the status of real estate markets
- To value fixed assets and assist in asset value allocations

> Appraisers may be held **liable** for professional violations or related misconduct.

> **liability:** In appraisal, a legal obligation to render services in compliance with professional standards and to refrain from malpractice, which includes negligence, misrepresentation, fraud, and breach of contract.
>
> **Uniform Standards of Professional Appraisal Practice (USPAP):** Current standards of the appraisal profession, developed for appraisers and the users of appraisal services by the Appraisal Standards Board of The Appraisal Foundation. USPAP sets forth the procedures to be followed in developing an appraisal, analysis, or opinion and the manner in which an appraisal, analysis, or opinion is communicated. The standards are endorsed by the Appraisal Institute and by other professional appraisal organizations.

Appraisers are advised to take measures to safeguard themselves from unintentional or involuntary malpractice. Ensuring competency through continuing education, the use of checklists and backup reviews, and strict adherence to the Uniform Standards of Professional Appraisal Practice can help reduce an appraiser's exposure to civil action.[13] Professional liability insurance is available and required by many lenders. Appraisers are advised to review all exclusions and retroactive dates in their insurance policies and to take normal precautions in their business practices.

Contested opinions of value may result from rapid changes in market conditions, the presence of contaminated materials on appraised properties, enforcement of environmental and preservation easements, and changes in legal and regulatory guidelines. The proliferation of legal proceedings suggests that litigation will continue to increase in the appraisal field as it has in other professions.

FURTHER READING

American Institute of Real Estate Appraisers. *Appraisal Thought: A 50-Year Beginning.* Chicago, 1982.

Andrews, Richard N. L. *Land in America.* Lexington, Mass.: D.C. Heath, 1979.

Appraisal Institute. *Appraising Residential Properties.* 3d ed. Chicago, 1999.

Benjamin, John D. "The Legal Liability of Real Estate Appraisers." *The Appraisal Journal* (April 1995).

Davies, Pearl Janet. *Real Estate in American History.* Washington, D.C.: Public Affairs Press, 1958.

Derbes, Max J., Jr. "When Are Appraisers Not Liable?" *The Appraisal Journal* (October 1995).

Finch, J. Howard. "The Role of Professional Designations as Quality Signals." *The Appraisal Journal* (April 1999).

Gaglione, Claudia L. "Third-Party Liability: Does Privity Matter." *Valuation Insights & Perspectives,* vol. 2, no. 3 (Third Quarter 1997).

Kinnard, William N., Jr., ed. *1984 Real Estate Valuation Colloquium: A Redefinition of Real Estate Appraisal Precepts and Practices.* Boston: Oelgeschlager, Gunn & Hain and Lincoln Institute of Land Policy, 1986.

---

13. For more information on appraiser liability, see Mark Lee Levine, *Real Estate Appraisers' Liability* (New York: Clark Boardman Callaghan, 1995). The bibliography of this text contains useful articles on areas of potential exposure for appraisers.

FURTHER READING *(continued)*

Kratovil, Robert, and Raymond J. Werner. *Real Estate Law*. 8th ed. Englewood Cliffs, N.J.: Prentice-Hall, 1983.

Levine, Mark Lee. "The Death of Privity: Recent Decisions." *The Appraisal Journal* (July 1998).

____. *Real Estate Appraisers' Liability*. New York: Clark Boardman Callaghan, 1991.

Love, Terrence L. *The Guide to Appraisal Office Policies and Procedures*. Chicago: Appraisal Institute, 1991.

Martin, Michael M. "The Ethics of Desire." *The Appraisal Journal* (July 1997).

Noyes, C. Reinold. *The Institution of Property*. London: Longmans, Green and Company, 1936.

Smalley, Steven P. "Appraisal: Science or Art?" *The Appraisal Journal* (April 1995).

Weinberg, Norman, Paul J. Colletti, William A. Colavito, and Frank A. Melchior. *Guide to the New York Real Estate Salespersons Course*. New York: John Wiley & Sons, Inc., 1983.

CHAPTER

2 THE NATURE OF VALUE

Value considerations are a central concern in a broad range of real estate activities. The term *value* is often used imprecisely in common speech, but in economics it has a specific meaning that distinguishes it from the related concepts of price and cost.

Distinctions Among Price, Cost, and Value

Appraisers make careful distinctions among the terms *price, cost,* and *value.* The term *price* represents the amount a particular purchaser agrees to pay and a particular seller agrees to accept under the circumstances surrounding their transaction. A price, once finalized, refers to a sale or transaction price and implies an exchange; a price is an accomplished fact.

> The **terms** *price, cost,* and *value* are used and **defined carefully** by appraisers.

Generally the circumstances of a transaction reflect conditions within one or several markets. A *market* is a set of arrangements in which buyers and sellers are brought together through the price mechanism. A market may be defined in terms of geography, products or product features, the number of available buyers and sellers, or some other arrangement of circumstances.

> A **market** is a set of arrangements in which buyer and seller are brought together through the price mechanism. A **real estate market** is the interaction of individuals who exchange real property rights for other assets such as money.

A *real estate market* is created by the interaction of individuals who exchange real property rights for other assets such as money. Specific real estate markets are defined on the basis of various attributes:

- Property type
- Location
- Income-producing potential
- Typical investor characteristics
- Typical tenant characteristics
- Other attributes recognized by those participating in the exchange of real property

The market for new, single-family residences selling for $150,000 in a well-defined neighborhood and the market for older apartment buildings located near the central business district and available for renovation are examples of specific real estate markets.

Many people use *cost* and *value* synonymously, but appraisal practice requires more precise definitions. The term *cost* is used by appraisers in relation to production, not exchange; cost may be either an accomplished fact or a current estimate.

Costs may be identified with the project phase to which they pertain—i.e., either actual construction cost or overall development cost. Construction cost normally includes the direct costs of labor and materials, as well as indirect costs. Development cost is the cost to create a property, including the land, and bring it to an efficient operating state. Development cost includes acquisition costs, actual expenditures, and the profit required to compensate the developer or entrepreneur for the time and risk involved in creating the project.

Real estate-related expenditures are directly linked to the price of goods and services in competitive markets. For example, the costs of roofing materials, masonry, architectural plans, and rented scaffolding are determined by the interaction of supply and demand in specific areas. Thus, they are subject to the influence of social, economic, governmental, and environmental forces.

Value can have many meanings in real estate appraisal; the applicable definition depends on the context and usage.[1] In the marketplace, value is commonly perceived as the anticipation of benefits to be obtained in the future. Because value changes over time, an appraisal reflects value at a particular point in time. Value as of a given time represents the monetary worth of property, goods, or services to buyers and sellers. To avoid confusion, appraisers do not use the word *value* alone; instead they refer to *market value, use value, investment value, assessed value,* and other specific kinds of value. Market value is the focus of most real property appraisal assignments, and its estimation is the purpose of most appraisals.

price: The amount a particular purchaser agrees to pay and a particular seller agrees to accept under the circumstances surrounding their transaction.

cost: The total dollar expenditure for an improvement (structure); applies to production, not exchange (price). Appraisers distinguish among direct (hard) costs, indirect (soft) costs, and the cost of entrepreneurial coordination.

value:
1. The monetary worth of a property, good, or service to buyers and sellers at a given time.
2. The present worth of the future benefits that accrue to real property ownership.

For appraisers the term *value* can be misleading. Appraisers typically refer to a **particular type of value** rather than use the word *value* alone.

---

1.   See Halbert C. Smith, "Value Concepts as a Source of Disparity Among Appraisals," *The Appraisal Journal* (April 1977): 203–208 and Jared Shlaes, "Value: More than Ever, In Your Eye," *The Appraisal Journal* (January 1993): 71–78.

Market Value and Other Types of Value
Market Value

The concept of market value is of paramount importance to business and real estate communities. Vast sums of debt and equity capital are committed each year to real estate investments and mortgage loans, which are based on opinions of market value. Real estate taxation, litigation, and legislation also reflect an ongoing, active concern with market value issues. In virtually every aspect of the real estate industry and its regulation at local, state, and federal levels, market value considerations are essential to economic stability.

Most Widely Accepted Components of Market Value Definition

There are a number of definitions of *market value* in the United States and in other countries. Although the wording differs, most definitions are similar in concept. Because most appraisals are used by third parties rather than the client alone, the intended use, not the user, of an appraisal determines which definition of market value is applicable to a specific assignment. Client wishes or instructions do not change the basic requirement that the appraiser must identify an appraisal's intended use and cite an appropriate definition of market value for that use. Appraisers must understand why a particular definition of market value should be used, apply that definition according to established standards, and communicate these requirements clearly to the clients they serve.

> **Market value** is the major focus of most real property appraisal assignments. Both economic and legal definitions of market value have been developed and refined. Continual refinement is essential to the appraisal profession.

> **Various definitions** of market value have been developed by The Appraisal Foundation, the federal government, the International Valuation Standards Committee, the Appraisal Institute, and others.

Despite differing opinions on individual aspects of the market value definition, it is generally agreed that market value results from the collective value judgments of market participants. An opinion of market value must be based on objective observation of the collective actions of the market. Because the standard measure of these activities is cash, the increases or diminutions in market value caused by financing and other terms of sale are measured against an all-cash value.

The definition that follows incorporates the concepts that are most widely accepted, such as willing, able, and knowledgeable buyers and sellers who act prudently as of a given date, and this definition gives the appraiser a choice among three bases: all cash, terms equivalent to cash, or other precisely revealed terms. The definition also requires increments or diminutions from the all-cash market value to be quantified in terms of cash.

Market Value

The most probable price, as of a specified date, in cash, or in terms equivalent to cash, or in other precisely revealed terms, for which the specified property rights should sell after reasonable exposure in a competitive market under all conditions requisite to a fair sale, with the buyer and seller each acting prudently, knowledgeably, and for self-interest, and assuming that neither is under undue duress.

Some appraisers cite this definition verbatim in their appraisal reports and state separately that the value is stated in cash, in terms equivalent to cash, or in other terms. Other appraisers simply change one phrase in the value definition—i.e., they may substitute "in cash" with "in terms arithmetically equivalent to cash" or "in terms precisely revealed below" as appropriate. Use of this definition represents the concept of value in exchange.

Market Value in USPAP

The Uniform Standards of Professional Appraisal Practice (USPAP) of The Appraisal Foundation require that certain items be included in every appraisal report. Among these items, the following are directly related to the definition of market value:

1. Identification of the specific property rights to be appraised.
2. Statement of the effective date of the value opinion.
3. Specification as to whether cash, terms equivalent to cash, or other precisely described financing terms are assumed as the basis of the appraisal.
4. If the appraisal is conditioned upon financing or other terms, specification as to whether the financing or terms are at, below or above market interest rates and/or contain unusual conditions or incentives. The terms of above- or below-market interest rates and/or other special incentives must be clearly set forth; their contribution to, or negative influence on, value must be described and estimated; and the market data supporting the opinion of value must be described and explained.

> The Uniform Standards of Professional Appraisal Practice (USPAP) include several **requirements for appraisal** reports that are directly related to the definition of market value.

Although this definition includes non–cash equivalent financing terms within the scope of the market value of appraised property rights, these rights are valued in relation to cash. Increments or diminutions in market value attributable to financing terms are measured against an all-cash standard, and the dollar amount of variance from the cash standard must be reported.

Market Value for Federally Insured Financial Institutions

The following definition of market value is used by agencies that regulate federally insured financial institutions in the United States:

The most probable price which a property should bring in a competitive and open market under all conditions requisite to a fair sale, the buyer and seller each acting prudently and knowledgeably and assuming the price is not affected by undue stimulus. Implicit in this definition is the consummation of a sale as of a specified date and the passing of title from seller to buyer under conditions whereby:

1. buyer and seller are typically motivated;
2. both parties are well informed or well advised, and acting in what they consider their best interests;
3. a reasonable time is allowed for exposure in the open market;
4. payment is made in terms of cash in United States dollars or in terms of financial arrangements comparable thereto; and
5. the price represents the normal consideration for the property sold unaffected by special or creative financing or sales concessions granted by anyone associated with the sale.[2]

This federal definition is compatible with the definition of market value cited in the current edition of *The Dictionary of Real Estate Appraisal*. The federal definition requires that the effect on property value of any special or creative financing or sales concessions be determined and that the opinion of value reflect cash equivalent terms. Special financing or sales concessions often characterize transactions in depressed markets. This definition was developed to address select categories of appraisal assignments in a real estate market characterized by unique circumstances.

Market Value in International Standards

According to the International Valuation Standards Committee, *market value* is defined for the purpose of international standards as follows:

> Market value is the estimated amount for which a property should exchange on the date of valuation between a willing buyer and a willing seller in an arm's-length transaction after proper marketing wherein the parties had each acted knowledgeably, prudently, and without compulsion.[3]

International Valuation Standards Committee (IVSC): International valuation standards were established in 1984 by the International Valuation Standards Committee (IVSC), a non-government organization member of the United Nations. The Appraisal Institute was a founding member of the IVSC, which now comprises more than 50 member nations.

---

2. *Federal Register,* vol. 55, no. 163, August 22, 1990, pages 34228 and 34229; also quoted in the Glossary of the Uniform Standards of Professional Appraisal Practice, 2000 edition. Note that the federal government's definition of *market value* quoted in USPAP was moved from the Definitions section in the 1996 edition to the Glossary section in more recent editions. In the 2001 edition of USPAP, a simplified definition of *market value* was moved from the Glossary back into the Definitions section of the document.

3. International Valuation Standards Committee, *International Valuation Standards 2000:* (London, 2000), 92-93.

Appraisal Institute Definition

In 1993 the Appraisal Institute adopted the following definition of market value, which was developed by the Appraisal Institute Special Task Force on Value Definitions to clarify distinctions among market value, disposition value, and liquidation value:

> The most probable price which a specified interest in real property is likely to bring under all the following conditions:
>
> 1. Consummation of a sale occurs as of a specified date.
> 2. An open and competitive market exists for the property interest appraised.
> 3. The buyer and seller are each acting prudently and knowledgeably.
> 4. The price is not affected by undue stimulus.
> 5. The buyer and seller are typically motivated.
> 6. Both parties are acting in what they consider their best interest.
> 7. Marketing efforts were adequate and a reasonable time was allowed for exposure in the open market.
> 8. Payment was made in cash in U.S. dollars or in terms of financial arrangements comparable thereto.
> 9. The price represents the normal consideration for the property sold, unaffected by special or creative financing or sales concessions granted by anyone associated with the sale.

This definition can be modified to provide for valuation with specified financing terms.

Other Definitions of Market Value

Market value definitions can be found in a variety of sources, including appraisal texts, real estate dictionaries, and court decisions. The Uniform Standards caution appraisers to use the exact definition of market value that applies in the jurisdiction in which the services are being performed. International standards further emphasize that appraisers should recognize the jurisdiction in which the appraisal will be used. Government and regulatory agencies redefine or reinterpret market value from time to time, so individuals performing appraisal services for these agencies or for institutions under their control must be sure to use the applicable definition.

Use Value

The realities of current real estate practice frequently require appraisers to consider other types of value in addition to market value. One of these, use value, is a concept based on the productivity of an economic good. Use value is the value a specific property has for a specific use. In estimating use value, the appraiser focuses on the value the real estate contributes to the enterprise of which it is a part, without regard to the highest and best use of the property or the monetary amount that might be realized from its sale. Use value may vary depending on the management of the property and external conditions such as changes in business operations. For example, a manufacturing plant designed around a particular assembly process may have one use value before a major change in assembly technology and another use value afterward.

Real property may have a use value and a market value. An older factory that is still used by the original firm may have considerable use value to that firm but only a nominal market value for another use.

Use value appraisal assignments may be performed to value assets (including real property) for mergers, acquisitions, or security issues. This type of assignment is sometimes encountered in appraising industrial real estate when the existing business enterprises include real property.

Court decisions and specific statutes may also create the need for use value appraisals. For instance, many states require agricultural use appraisals of farmland for property tax purposes rather than opinions of value based on highest and best use. The current IRS regulation on estate taxes allows land under an interim agricultural use to be valued according to this alternative use even though the land has development potential.[4]

Limited-Market and Special-Purpose Properties

When appraising a type of property that is not commonly exchanged or rented, it may be difficult to determine whether an opinion of market value can be reasonably supported. Such limited-market properties can cause special problems for appraisers. A limited-market property is a property that has relatively few potential buyers at a particular time, sometimes because of unique design features or changing market conditions. Large manufacturing plants, railroad sidings, and research and development properties are examples of limited-market properties that typically appeal to relatively few potential purchasers.

Many limited-market properties include structures with unique designs, special construction materials, or layouts that restrict their utility to the use for which they were originally built. These properties usually have limited conversion potential and, consequently, are often called *special-purpose* or *special-design*

> **use value:** The value of a property as it is currently used, not its value considering alternative uses; may be used where legislation has been enacted to preserve farmland, timberland, or other open space land on urban fringes; also known as *value in use*.
>
> **limited-market property:** A property that has relatively few potential buyers at a particular time.
>
> **special-purpose property:** A limited-market property with a unique physical design, special construction materials, or a layout that restricts its utility to the use for which it was built; also called *special-design property*.

---

4. The section on special use valuation in United States Estate (and Generation-Skipping Transfer) Tax Return (IRS Instructions for Form 706) states: "Under section 2032A, you may elect to value certain farm and closely held business real property at its farm or business use value rather than its fair market value. You may elect both special use valuation and alternate valuation."

properties. Examples of such properties include houses of worship, museums, schools, public buildings, and clubhouses.

Limited-market properties may be appraised based on their current use or the most likely alternative use. Due to the relatively small markets and lengthy market exposure needed to sell such properties, there may be little evidence to support an opinion of market value based on their current use. The distinction between market properties and limited-market properties is subject to the availability of relevant market data. If a market exists for a limited-market property, the appraiser must search diligently for whatever evidence of market value is available.

If a property's current use is so specialized that there is no demonstrable market for it but the use is viable and likely to continue, the appraiser may render an opinion of use value if the assignment reasonably permits a type of value other than market value. Such an estimate should not be confused with an opinion of market value. If no market can be demonstrated or if data is not available, the appraiser cannot develop an opinion of market value and should state so in the appraisal report. It is sometimes necessary to render an opinion of market value in these situations for legal purposes, however. In these cases, the appraiser must comply with the legal requirement, relying on personal judgment and whatever direct market evidence is available. Note that the type of value developed is not dictated by the property type, the size or viability of the market, or the ease with which that value can be developed; rather, the intended use of the appraisal determines the type of value to be developed. If the client needs a market value opinion, the appraiser must develop an opinion of market value, not use value.

Investment Value

While use value focuses on the specific use of a property, investment value represents the value of a specific property to a particular investor. As used in appraisal assignments, investment value is the value of a property to a particular investor based on that person's (or entity's) investment requirements. In contrast to market value, investment value is value to an individual, not necessarily value in the marketplace.

Investment value reflects the subjective relationship between a particular investor and a given investment. It differs in concept from market value, although investment value and market value indications sometimes may be similar. If the investor's requirements are typical of the market, investment value will be the same as market value.

investment value: The specific value of a property to a particular investor or class of investors based on individual investment requirements; distinguished from market value, which is impersonal and detached.

When measured in dollars, investment value is the price an investor would pay for an investment in light of its

perceived capacity to satisfy that
individual's desires, needs, or investment
goals. To render an opinion of investment
value, specific investment criteria must be
known. Criteria to evaluate a real estate
investment are not necessarily set down by

> **going-concern value:** The market value of all the tangible and intangible assets of an established and operating business with an indefinite life, as if sold in aggregate.

the individual investor; they may be established by an expert on real estate
and investment value, i.e., an appraiser.

Going-Concern Value

A going concern is an established and operating business with an indefinite
future life. For certain types of properties (e.g., hotels and motels, restaurants,
bowling alleys, manufacturing enterprises, athletic clubs, landfills), the
physical real estate assets are integral parts of an ongoing business. The
market value of a such a property (including all the tangible and intangible
assets of the going concern, as if sold in aggregate) is commonly called its
going-concern value. (See Figure 2.1.) Appraisers may be called upon to
develop an opinion of the investment value, use value, or some other type of
value of a going concern, but most appraisals of going-concern value relate to
market value.

Traditionally, going-concern value has been defined as the value of a
proven property operation. The emerging definition of the term highlights
the assumption that the business enterprise is expected to continue operating
well into the future (usually indefinitely); in contrast, liquidation value
assumes that the enterprise will cease operations. Going-concern value
includes the incremental value associated with the business concern, which is
distinct from the value of the real property. The value of the going concern
includes an intangible enhancement of the value of the operating business
enterprise, which is produced by the assemblage of the land, buildings, labor,
equipment, and the marketing operation. This assemblage creates an economically viable business that is expected to continue. The value of the going
concern refers to the total value of the property, including both the real
property and the intangible personal property attributed to business enterprise value (see Figure 2.2).

It may be difficult to separate the market value of the land and the
building from the total value of the business, but such a division of realty and
non-realty components of value is often required by federal regulations.
When an appraiser cannot effectively separate the market value of the real
estate from its business enterprise value, it is appropriate to state that the
reported opinion of value includes both market value and business enterprise
value and that the appraiser has not been able to distinguish between them.
Only qualified practitioners should undertake these kinds of assignments,
which must be performed in compliance with appropriate USPAP standards.
(Business enterprise value is discussed in Chapter 27.)

Figure 2.1   Components of a Going Concern

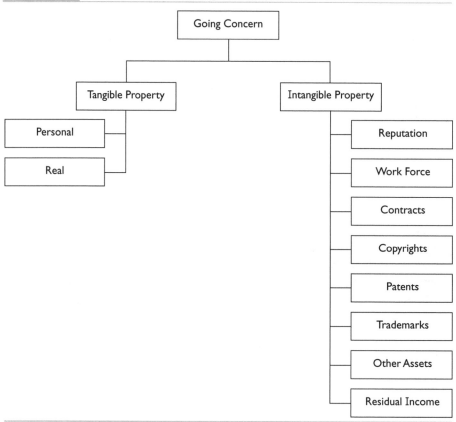

Figure 2.2   Components of Going-Concern Value

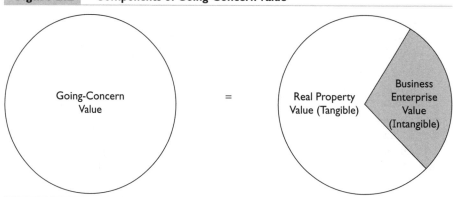

Assessed Value

Assessed value applies in ad valorem taxation and refers to the value of a property according to the tax rolls. Assessed value may not conform to market value, but it is usually calculated in relation to a market value base.

> **assessed value:** The value of a property according to the tax rolls in ad valorem taxation; may be higher or lower than market value, or based on an assessment ratio that is a percentage of market value.

Factors of Value

The economic concept of value is not inherent in the commodity, good, or service to which it is ascribed; it is created in the minds of the individuals who make up the market. The relationships that create value are complex, and values change when the factors that influence value change. Typically, four interdependent economic factors create value:

1. Utility
2. Scarcity
3. Desire
4. Effective purchasing power

> **Four interdependent factors** create value: utility, scarcity, desire, and effective purchasing power. Utility and scarcity are supply factors. Desire and effective purchasing power are demand factors.

All four factors must be present for a property to have value.

Utility

Utility is the ability of a product to satisfy a human want, need, or desire. All properties must have utility to tenants, owner-investors, or owner-occupants. Residential properties satisfy the need for shelter, and commercial properties generate income. Both may have design features that enhance their attractiveness. These features are called *amenities*. The value of amenities is related to their desirability and utility to an owner-occupant or tenant-occupant. The value to a tenant can be converted into income in the form of rent. The benefits derived from income-producing properties can usually be measured in terms of cash flow. The influence of utility on value depends on the characteristics of the property. Size utility, design utility, location utility, and other specific forms of utility can significantly influence property value.

> **utility:** The ability of a product to satisfy a human want, need, or desire.
>
> **amenity:** A tangible or intangible benefit of real property that enhances its attractiveness or increases the satisfaction of the user, but is not essential to its use. Natural amenities may include a pleasant location near water or a scenic view of the surrounding area; man-made amenities include swimming pools, tennis courts, community buildings, and other recreational facilities.

The benefits of real property ownership are derived from the bundle of rights that an owner possesses. Restrictions on ownership rights may inhibit the flow of benefits and, therefore, lower the property's value. Similarly, a property can only achieve its highest value if it can legally perform its most useful function. Environmental regulations, zoning regulations, deed restrictions, and other limitations on the rights of ownership can enhance or detract from a property's utility and value.

Scarcity

Scarcity is the present or anticipated supply of an item relative to the demand for it. In general, if demand is constant, the scarcity of a commodity makes it more valuable. Land, for example, is still generally abundant, but useful, desirable land is relatively scarce and, therefore, has greater value. No object, including real property, can have value unless scarcity is coupled with utility. Air, which has a high level of utility, has no definable economic value because it is abundant.

Desire

Desire is a purchaser's wish for an item to satisfy human needs (e.g., shelter, clothing, food, companionship) or individual wants beyond the essentials required to support life.

Effective Purchasing Power

Effective purchasing power is the ability of an individual or group to participate in a market—that is, to acquire goods and services with cash or its equivalent. A valid opinion of the value of a property includes an accurate assessment of the market's ability to pay for the property.

scarcity: The present or anticipated undersupply of an item relative to the demand for it. Conditions of scarcity contribute to value.

desire: A purchaser's wish for an item to satisfy human needs (e.g., shelter, clothing, food, companionship) or individual wants beyond essential life-support needs.

effective purchasing power: The ability of an individual or group to participate in a market, i.e., to acquire goods and services with cash or its equivalent.

supply: In real estate, the amount of a type of property available for sale or lease at various prices in a given market at a given time.

demand: In real estate, the amounts of a type of property desired for purchase or rent at various prices in a given market at a given time.

Supply and Demand

The complex interaction of the four factors that create value is reflected in the basic economic principle of supply and demand. The utility of a commodity, its scarcity or abundance, the intensity of the human desire to acquire it, and the effective power to purchase it all affect the supply of and demand for the commodity in any given situation.

Demand for a commodity is created by its utility and affected by its scarcity. Demand is also influenced by desire and the forces that create and stimulate desire. Although human longing for things may be unlimited, desire is restrained by effective purchasing power. Thus, the inability to buy expensive things affects demand.

Similarly, the supply of a commodity is influenced by its utility and limited by its scarcity. The availability of a commodity is affected by its desirability. Land is a limited commodity, and the land in an area that is suitable for a specific use will be in especially short supply if the perceived need for it is great. Sluggish purchasing power keeps the pressure on supply in check. If purchasing power expands, the supply of a relatively fixed commodity will dwindle and create a market-driven demand to increase the supply.

FURTHER READING

American Institute of Real Estate Appraisers. *Appraisal Thought: A 50-Year Beginning.* Chicago, 1982.

Davies, Pearl Janet. *Real Estate in American History.* Washington, D.C.: Public Affairs Press, 1958.

Harrison, Frank E. *Appraising the Tough Ones: Creative Ways to Value Complex Residential Properties.* Chicago: Appraisal Institute, 1996.

Heilbroner, Robert L. *The Worldly Philosophers.* Rev. ed. New York: Simon and Schuster, 1964.

Hodges, McCloud B., Jr. "Three Approaches?" *The Appraisal Journal* (October 1993).

Jevons, W. Stanley. *The Theory of Political Economy.* 5th ed. New York: Augustus M. Kelley, 1965.

Noyes, C. Reinold. *The Institution of Property.* London: Longmans, Green and Company, 1936.

Roll, Eric. *A History of Economic Thought.* 3d ed. Englewood Cliffs, N.J.: Prentice-Hall, 1964.

Samuelson, Paul A. and William D. Nordhaus. *Economics.* 13th ed. New York: McGraw-Hill, 1989.

Solot, Sanders K. "The First Appraisal." *The Real Estate Appraiser & Analyst* (April 1987).

Vane, Howard R. and John L. Thompson. *Monetarism—Theory, Evidence, and Policy.* New York: Halsted Press, 1979.

Wilson, Donald C. "How Tactical Utility Influences Price and Value." *The Appraisal Journal* (January 1998).

Yovino-Young, Michael. "Appraising from the Middle Ages to the Millennium." *Valuation Insights & Perspectives, vol. 4, no. 3* (Third Quarter 1999).

3 FOUNDATIONS OF APPRAISAL

Real property is the focus of real estate appraisal activity. Society generally perceives real property to be a good investment, allowing individuals to achieve economic goals through the ownership and successful management of real estate. In recent years, real estate markets have been turbulent. Lax underwriting in the 1980s contributed to an abundance of distressed properties and brought on federal intervention, such as the Financial Institutions Reform, Recovery and Enforcement Act (FIRREA) of 1989. Developers often perceive public controls as excessive. Some property owners decry the taking of private property rights and act on that perception by filing inverse condemnation claims. Nevertheless, real estate markets remain an important investment vehicle and a generator of economic activity.

In determining their level of participation in the real estate market, individuals consider their wants and needs as well as the variety of options available to them at different times. Their choices help support a free market economy. Thus, both individual and collective decisions contribute to the nation's economic success. Similarly, the production of goods, services, and income depends on the combined effects of four essential economic ingredients, commonly referred to as the *four agents of production*:

1. Land
2. Labor
3. Capital
4. Entrepreneurial coordination

Agents of Production

Traditional economic theory holds that four agents of production are combined to create real estate and that the sum of the costs to develop a property is one of the basic measures of real property value available to appraisers. In other words, a finished real estate product is created by combining land, labor, capital, and entrepreneurial coordination, and a well-supported opinion of value can be derived through systematic analysis of each of these components, their interrelationships, and their relationship to the property as a whole.

The first thing an entrepreneur generally considers in developing a property is the cost of acquiring the land. The cost of a vacant site or parcel of raw land is the cost of acquisition. The appraiser anticipates that improvements will be added and the property will be marketed to tenants or multiple end users.

land: The earth's surface, both land and water, and anything that is attached to it whether by the course of nature or human hands; all natural resources in their original state, e.g., mineral deposits, wildlife, timber, fish, water, coal deposits, soil.

labor: Direct and indirect costs required to construct and market improvements on a site.

capital: Accumulated wealth; a sum of money available for investment.

entrepreneurial coordination: The ability of an entrepreneur to combine land, labor, and capital in the development of real property; a component of real estate value that represents the investment of time, expertise, and equity by an entrepreneur (or developer) in the development of a property.

The labor component comprises all direct and indirect costs required to construct and market the product as land alone or with improvements. Direct costs include not only the wages paid to individuals, but also the cost of materials used in construction. Indirect costs consist of permit fees, marketing expenses, taxes, overhead, maintenance after construction is completed, the cost of project coordination or supervision, and financing costs that are not included in the rate paid to the lender over the development period.

Because real property is expensive to develop, most projects involve some sort of financing arrangement, which makes the availability of capital a significant part of the development equation. The cost of capital is the return on both the borrowed capital and the equity capital invested in the project. (The influence of debt and equity markets on the value of real property is covered more fully in Chapter 6.)

No legitimate developer will undertake to construct and market a property without anticipating receipt of a profit in addition to the return of the equity investment. The purchaser who continues an existing land use is not creating value, only maintaining value through proper management of the property. A developer, on the other hand, invests not only equity in a development but also time and expertise. Accordingly, an entrepreneur expects a reward—known as *entrepreneurial incentive* or *profit*—for creating and marketing a real estate product through the coordination of land, labor, and capital.[1] The fourth agent of production, entrepreneurial coordination, accounts for that investment of time and expertise. (The estimation of entrepreneurial incentive or profit is discussed in Chapter 14.)

Anticipation and Change

The human actions that collectively shape market operations reflect the pursuit of economic goals. To analyze the many dynamic and interactive factors that influence people's attitudes and beliefs about value, the fundamental principles of anticipation and change must be addressed.

---

1.   More precisely, *entrepreneurial incentive* is a forecast of the amount the developer expects to receive. This forecast is developed before construction is complete. *Entrepreneurial profit* is the actual amount received after the property is complete. The distinction between *entrepreneurial incentive* and *entrepreneurial profit* is examined in more detail in Chapter 14.

Value is created by the anticipation of benefits to be derived in the future. In real estate markets, the current value of a property is usually not based on its historical prices or the cost of its creation; rather, value is based on the market participant's perceptions of the future benefits of acquisition.

The value of owner-occupied residential property is based primarily on the expected future advantages, amenities, and pleasures of ownership and occupancy. Prior to the property's sale, the primary investment return is measured in these amenities, not in the receipt of income. The value of income-producing real estate is based on the income it will produce in the future. As a result, real property appraisers must be aware of local, regional, and national real estate trends that affect the perceptions of buyers and sellers and their anticipations of the future. Historical data on a property or a market is relevant only insofar as it helps interpret current market anticipations.

> The principles of anticipation, change, supply and demand, competition, and substitution are fundamental to understanding the **dynamics of value**.

> **anticipation:** The perception that value is created by the expectation of benefits to be derived in the future.
>
> **change:** The result of the cause and effect relationship among the forces that influence real property value.

> Value is created by the **anticipation** of future benefits.

The dynamic nature of the social, economic, governmental, and environmental forces that influence real property value accounts for change. Although change is inevitable and continuous, the process may be gradual and not easily discernible. In active markets, change may occur rapidly, with new properties put up for sale and others sold on a daily basis. Abrupt changes may be precipitated by plant or military base closures, tax law revisions, or the start of new construction. The pervasiveness of change is evident in the real estate market, where the social, economic, governmental, and environmental forces that affect real estate are in constant transition. Changes in these forces influence the demand for and supply of realty and, therefore, individual property values. Appraisers attempt to identify current and anticipated changes in the market that could affect current property values, but, because change is not always predictable, opinions of value may be valid only for a relatively brief period after the date specified in the appraisal report.

Shifts in market preferences also provide evidence of change. Real estate is not readily adaptable to new consumer preferences and thus often suffers obsolescence. The physical, functional, and economic impairments observed in buildings as they age result in depreciation, which is defined as a loss in property value from any cause. Depreciation may be seen as the difference between the cost to reproduce or replace a property and its present value. In general, losses in property value are caused by deterioration or obsolescence. Because obsolescence can begin in the design phase and deterioration may start while a building or improvement is still being constructed, the different types of deterioration and obsolescence found in a property have unique implications in appraisal. (A detailed discussion of deterioration and obsolescence is presented in Chapter 16.)

Supply and Demand, Substitution, Balance, and Externalities

The appraisal principles of supply and demand, substitution, balance, and externalities can be applied to the unique physical and legal characteristics of a particular parcel of real property. When these basic economic principles are in proper accord, they indicate highest and best use, which has great significance in real property appraisal. (Highest and best use is discussed in detail in Chapter 12.)

Supply and Demand

In economic theory, the principle of supply and demand states that the price of a commodity, good, or service (or, in a real estate context, the price of real property) varies directly, but not necessarily proportionately, with demand and inversely, but not necessarily proportionately, with supply. Thus, an increase in the supply of an item or a decrease in the demand for an item tends to reduce the equilibrium price; the opposite conditions produce an opposite effect. The relationship between supply and demand may not be directly proportional, but the interaction of these forces is fundamental to economic theory. The interaction of suppliers and demanders, or sellers and buyers, constitutes a market.

Supply

Usually property values vary inversely with changes in supply. If properties for a particular use become more abundant than they were relative to demand in the past, their equilibrium value declines. By contrast, if properties become more scarce and supply declines relative to demand, the equilibrium price of the properties increases. The supply of and demand for commodities always tend to move toward equilibrium. At this theoretical point (which almost never occurs), market value, price, and cost are equal.

In real estate, supply is the amount of a type of real estate available for sale or lease at various prices in a given market at a given time. Typically, more of an item will be supplied at a higher price and less at a lower price. Therefore, the supply of an item at a particular price, at a particular time, and in a particular place indicates that item's relative scarcity, which is a basic factor of value.

> **supply and demand:** In economic theory, the principle that states that the price of a commodity, good, or service varies directly, but not necessarily proportionately, with demand, and inversely, but not necessarily proportionately, with supply. In a real estate appraisal context, the principle of supply and demand states that the price of real property varies directly, but not necessarily proportionately, with demand and inversely, but not necessarily proportionately, with supply.

The supply of real estate is dependent on the costs of the four agents of production, which are brought together to produce a product that is offered for sale. When demand in a particular market increases, property values are driven up and the quantity of new properties offered for sale generally increases. When the supply of the agents of production declines, property values again tend to rise. On the other hand, increases in the productivity of labor, greater technological efficiency, improvements in capital goods, or the utilization of more capital goods per worker tend to reduce development costs. A building boom set in motion by developer's rising expectations of profit may result in an oversupply of properties.

Because real property is both a physical commodity and a service, the supply of real estate refers to the amount of service, or the usability of the space, as well as the quantity of physical space. Consequently, those involved in real estate are primarily concerned with the supply of land suitable for a specific use, not the total number of acres available. The supply of real estate incorporates both the quality and quantity of service space provided. Direct comparisons can be made only between properties that are similar both qualitatively and quantitatively. The quality of space may affect property value even more than its quantity. Quality is a function of the tangible attributes of a property such as its condition and its intangible attributes or amenities such as its design. The supply of a specific property type may be inventoried to reflect existing improvements on the resale market and new construction entering the market.

Generally the quantity of space supplied for a given use is slow to adjust to changes in price levels. The length of time needed to build new structures, the large amount of capital required, and government regulations often hamper a supplier's ability to meet changes in the market. The quality of space, however, can change more rapidly because suppliers can convert nonproductive space to alternative uses, cure deferred maintenance, and partition existing space into smaller units.

Demand

Demand is the desire and ability to purchase or lease goods and services. In real estate, demand is the amount of a type of real estate desired for purchase or rent at various prices in a given market for a given period of time. Typically less of an item will be demanded at a higher price, and more will be demanded at a lower price.

Because it is difficult to augment the supply of real property for a specific use in a short time, values are strongly affected by current demand. Demand, like supply, can be characterized in terms of both quantity and quality. For example, demand in a residential market may be defined by the number of households in the market area and the household incomes as well as the size and characteristics of the households and specific housing preferences. Demand that is supported by purchasing power results in effective demand, which is the type of demand considered by the market. Appraisers must interpret market behavior to ascertain the existing relationship between the supply of and the demand for the type of property being appraised.

Competition

Competition between buyers or tenants represents the interactive efforts of two or more potential buyers or tenants to make a purchase or secure a lease. Between sellers or landlords, competition represents the interactive efforts of two or more potential sellers or landlords to effect a sale or lease. Competition is fundamental to the dynamics of supply and demand in a free enterprise, profit-maximizing economic system.

Buyers and sellers of real property operate in a competitive market setting. In essence, each property competes with all other properties suitable for the same use in a particular market segment and often with properties from other market segments. For example:

- A profitable motel faces competition from newer motels nearby.
- Existing residential subdivisions compete with new subdivisions.
- Downtown retail properties compete with suburban shopping centers.

Over time, competitive market forces tend to reduce unusually high profits. Profit encourages competition, but excess profits tend to breed ruinous competition. For example, the first retail store to open in a new and expanding area may generate more profit than is considered typical for that type of enterprise. If no barriers to entry exist, owners of similar retail enterprises will likely gravitate to the area to compete for the surplus profits. Eventually there may not be enough business to support all the retailers. A few stores may profit, but others will fail. The effects of competition and market trends on profit levels are especially evident to appraisers making income projections as part of the income capitalization approach to value.

competition: Between purchasers or tenants, the interactive efforts of two or more potential purchasers or tenants to make a sale or secure a lease; between sellers or landlords, the interactive efforts of two or more potential sellers or landlords to complete a sale or lease; among competitive properties, the level of productivity and amenities or benefits characteristic of each property considering the advantageous or disadvantageous position of the property relative to the competitors.

substitution: The appraisal principle that states that when several similar or commensurate commodities, goods, or services are available, the one with the lowest price will attract the greatest demand and widest distribution. This is the primary principle upon which the cost and sales comparison approaches are based.

Substitution

The principle of substitution states that when several similar or commensurate commodities, goods, or services are available, the one with the lowest price attracts the greatest demand and widest distribution. This principle assumes rational, prudent market behavior with no undue cost due to delay. According to the principle of substitution, a buyer will not pay more for one property than for another that is equally desirable.

Property values tend to be set by the price of acquiring an equally desirable substitute property. The principle of substitution recognizes that buyers and sellers of real property have options, i.e., other properties are available for similar uses. The substitution of one property for another may be considered in terms of use, structural design, or earnings. The cost of acquisition may be the cost to purchase a similar site and construct a building of equivalent utility, assuming no undue cost due to delay; this is the basis of the cost approach. On the other hand, the cost of acquisition may be the price of acquiring an existing property of equal utility, again assuming no undue cost due to delay; this is the basis of the sales comparison approach.

The principle of substitution is equally applicable to properties such as houses, which are purchased for their amenity-producing attributes, and properties purchased for their income-producing capabilities. The amenity-producing attributes of residential properties may include excellence of design, quality of workmanship, or superior construction materials. For an income-producing property, an equally desirable substitute might be an alternative investment property that produces equivalent investment returns with equivalent risk. The limits of property prices, rents, and rates tend to be set by the prevailing prices, rents, and rates of equally desirable substitutes. The principle of substitution is fundamental to all three traditional approaches to value—sales comparison, cost, and income capitalization.

Although the principle of substitution applies in most situations, sometimes the characteristics of a product are perceived by the market to be unique. The demand generated for such products may result in unique pricing.[2]

Balance

The principle of balance holds that real property value is created and sustained when contrasting, opposing, or interacting elements are in a state of equilibrium. This principle applies to relationships among various property components as well as the relationship between the costs of production and the property's productivity. Land, labor, capital, and entrepreneurship are the agents of production, but for most real property the critical combination is the land and improvements. Economic balance is achieved when the combination of land and improvements is optimal—i.e., when no marginal benefit or utility is achieved by adding another unit of capital. The law of diminishing returns holds that increments in the agents of production added to a parcel of property produce greater net income up to a certain point. At this point, the point of decreasing or diminishing returns, maximum value is achieved. Any additional expenditures will not produce a return commensurate with the additional

> The principles of balance, increasing and decreasing returns, contribution, surplus productivity, and conformity explain how the **integration of property components** affects property value.

---

2. The specific issues involved in the valuation of unique properties are addressed in Frank E. Harrison, *Appraising the Tough Ones: Creative Ways to Value Complex Residential Properties* (Chicago: Appraisal Institute, 1996).

balance: The principle that real property value is created and sustained when contrasting, opposing, or interacting elements are in a state of equilibrium.

law of decreasing returns: The premise that additional expenditures beyond a certain point (the point of decreasing returns) will not yield a return commensurate with the additional investment; also known as *law of diminishing returns*.

law of increasing returns: The premise that larger amounts of the agents of production produce greater net income up to a certain point (the point of decreasing returns).

investment. When the point of decreasing returns is reached, further increments in the agents of production will cause productivity to decline proportionally. This is also known as the *principle of diminishing marginal productivity.*

The fertilization of farmland provides a simple example. Applying fertilizer to a land parcel increases crop yield only up to a point. Beyond that point the additional fertilizer will produce no further increase in the marginal output of the acreage. The optimum amount of fertilization is achieved when the value of the increment in yield resulting from the last unit of fertilizer equals the additional expenditure on fertilizer. This is the point of balance.

As a further illustration, consider a developer who is deciding how many bedrooms to include in a single-family house being developed for sale on the residential market. The typical single-family house in this residential market has three bedrooms. It may be uneconomic to include a fourth bedroom if the cost to build exceeds the value added to the property.

The principle of balance also applies to the relationship between a property and its environment. A proper mix of various types and locations of land uses in an area creates and sustains value. A residence near other residences has much more market appeal than a residence next to a landfill.

The principle of balance and the principles of contribution, surplus productivity, and conformity are interdependent and crucial in highest and best use analyses and market value estimation. These concepts form the theoretical foundation for estimating all forms of depreciation in the cost approach, making adjustments in the sales comparison approach, and calculating expected earnings in the income capitalization approach.

Contribution

The principle of contribution states that the value of a particular component is measured in terms of its contribution to the value of the whole property or as the amount that its absence would detract from the value of the whole. The cost of an item does not necessarily equal its value. A swimming pool that costs $10,000 to install does not necessarily increase the value of a residential property by $10,000. Rather, the pool's dollar contribution to value is measured in terms of its benefit or utility in the market. The swimming pool's contribution to value may be

- Higher than its cost (if properties with swimming pools are in very high demand in the market).

- Equal to its cost.
- Lower than its cost, though still contributing positively to value. This is the most common situation, i.e., more than zero but less than its cost.
- No contribution to value. Adding a swimming pool could have no effect on the value of that property in that market at that time.
- Less than zero. The swimming pool may need to be removed at an additional cost for the property to reach its highest and best use.

> **contribution:** The concept that the value of a particular component is measured in terms of its contribution to the value of the whole property or as the amount that its absence would detract from the value of the whole.
>
> **surplus productivity:** The net income that remains after the costs of various agents of production have been paid.
>
> **conformity:** The appraisal principle that real property value is created and sustained when the characteristics of a property conform to the demands of its market.

The contribution of the existing improvements may not be in proper balance with the total property. Especially in transitional areas, a property's present use may underutilize the land. Nevertheless, an existing, less-than-optimal use, called an *interim use,* will continue until it is economically feasible for a developer to absorb the costs of converting the property, either by razing and replacing the existing improvements or by rehabilitating them.

Surplus Productivity

Surplus productivity is the net income to the land remaining after the costs of the other agents of production have been paid. The classical economists of the eighteenth and nineteenth centuries identified the surplus with land rent, which they understood to account for land value. Traditionally, the principle of surplus productivity has provided the basis for the residual concept of land returns and residual valuation techniques. (See Chapter 22.) The principles of surplus productivity and residual returns to the land are useful in establishing the highest and best use of land and in analyzing which option among alternative land use options will yield the highest value. Some twentieth-century economists argue that surplus productivity should be ascribed to a different agent of production, i.e., the entrepreneurial coordination required to combine the land, labor, and capital into a complete real estate product.

Conformity

Conformity holds that real property value is created and sustained when the characteristics of a property conform to the demands of its market. The styles and uses of the properties in a given area may conform for several reasons, including economic pressures and the shared preferences of owners for certain types of structures, amenities, and services. The imposition and enforcement of zoning ordinances and plans by local governments to regulate land use may also contribute to conformity. Standards of conformity set by the market are subject to change. Local building codes and private restrictions, which tend to establish conformity in basic property characteristics such as size, style, and

> **principle of progression:** In appraisal, the concept that the value of an inferior property is enhanced by its association with better properties of the same type.
>
> **principle of regression:** In appraisal, the concept that the value of a superior property is adversely affected by its association with an inferior property of the same type.
>
> **externalities:** The principle that economies outside a property have a positive effect on its value while diseconomies outside a property have a negative effect upon its value.

design, are often difficult to change and may hasten the pace of obsolescence.

Individual markets also set standards of conformity, especially in terms of price. According to the principle of progression, a lower-priced property will be worth more in a high-priced neighborhood than it would in a neighborhood of comparable properties. Under the principle of regression, a higher-priced property will be worth less in a low-priced neighborhood than it would in a neighborhood of comparable properties. Of course, there are exceptions to these principles. The seasonal cottages and luxurious vacation homes that line a popular recreational lake may exert no effect, either positive or negative, on the value of one another.

Externalities

The principle of externalities states that factors external to a property can have either a positive or negative effect on its value. Bridges and highways, police and fire protection, and a host of other essential structures and services are positive externalities that are provided most efficiently through common purchase by the government. Negative externalities result when inconveniences are imposed on property owners by the actions of others. For example, a firm that violates environmental law by dumping hazardous waste and manages to evade responsibility imposes the cleanup costs on others.

Because it is physically immobile, real estate is affected by external influences more strongly than most other economic goods, services, or commodites. *Externalities* may refer to the use or physical attributes of properties located near the subject property or to the economic conditions that affect the market in which the subject property competes. For example, an increase in the purchasing power of the households that constitute the trade area for a retail facility will likely have a positive effect on the sales (income-producing) potential of the property.

On a broad level, international economic conditions can influence real estate values through externalities such as the availability of foreign capital or the effect of increasing foreign trade on the growth of the national economy.

> Factors outside a property, or externalities, exert both positive and negative influences on the property's value.

The effects of foreign trade are particularly strong in states bordering Mexico and on the West Coast, which have economies subject to shifts in trade volume with Latin American and Pacific

Rim countries. Fallout from the economic crises in Asia and Eastern Europe in the late 1990s affected U.S. capital markets and the availability of financing for real estate.

National fiscal policy also plays a vital role in the economy and, consequently, in real estate markets. The Tax Reform Act of 1986 eliminated many of the tax advantages of investing in income-producing property. This change had a far-reaching effect on the value of investment-grade properties. Due in part to the tax advantages available prior to 1986, some real estate markets had been overbuilt. After the tax law was changed, the oversupply was recognized and values in these markets declined significantly.

During the recessionary period that followed the tax law changes, demand for loans decreased and interest rates declined. In the early 1990s, low interest rates stimulated a gradual economic recovery and sales of new and existing homes picked up. As business activity rebounded, the oversupply of office and industrial properties from the late 1980s was gradually absorbed. The government agency established in 1989 to dispose of the real estate assets held by failed savings and loan institutions, the Resolution Trust Corporation, eventually completed its mission and was dissolved. Throughout the unprecedented expansion of the stock market in the 1990s, the Federal Reserve slowly raised interest rates to resist inflationary pressures and help keep rates of return on U.S. securities attractive to foreign investors.

The economic slowdown of the late 1980s had varying effects in different areas of the country. The West Coast suffered the brunt of contractions and changes in the defense industry, while areas with more diversified economies like the Midwest did not experience as severe a recession. Throughout the 1990s, the growth of the information technology industry in various pockets across the country—the Pacific Northwest, Silicon Valley in Northern California, Boston, and Austin, Texas, among others—had profound impacts on real estate values in those areas. In the late 1990s, housing prices in San Francisco and the surrounding communities rose sharply with the influx of dot-com workers with great effective purchasing power.

At the community and neighborhood levels, property values are affected by local laws, local government policies and administration, property taxes, economic growth, and social attitudes. Different property value trends can be found in communities in the same region and among neighborhoods in the same community. Appraisers should be familiar with external events at all levels that can impact property values.

Forces That Influence Real Property Values

The value of real property reflects and is affected by the interaction of four basic forces that influence human activity:

1. Social trends
2. Economic circumstances

3. Governmental controls and regulations
4. Environmental conditions

The forces are interactive; they exert pressure on human activities and are, in turn, affected by these activities. The interaction of these forces influences the value of every parcel of real estate in the market.

An understanding of value-influencing forces is fundamental to the appraisal of real property. To develop an opinion of value, an appraiser investigates how the market views a particular property, and the scope of this investigation is not limited to static, current conditions. Rather, the appraiser analyzes trends in the forces that influence value to determine the direction, speed, duration, strength, and limits of these trends. (The observation and analysis of value influences are discussed in greater detail in Chapters 7, 8, and 11.)

> An appraiser must study the **interaction of the** social, economic, governmental, and environmental **forces that affect property value.**

Social Forces

The social forces studied by appraisers primarily relate to population characteristics. Because the demographic composition of the population reveals the potential demand for real estate, proper analysis and interpretation of demographic trends are required. Real property values are affected not only by population changes and characteristics but also by the entire spectrum of human activity. The total population, its composition by age and gender, and the rate of household formation and dissolution strongly influence real property values. Social forces are also reflected in attitudes toward education, law and order, and lifestyle options.

Economic Forces

To determine the influence of economic forces on value, appraisers analyze the fundamental relationships between current and anticipated supply and demand and the economic ability of the population to satisfy its wants, needs, and demands through its purchasing power. Many specific market characteristics are considered in the analysis of economic forces:

*   Employment
*   Wage levels
*   Industrial expansion
*   The economic base of the region and the community
*   Price levels
*   The cost and availability of mortgage credit
*   The stock of available vacant and improved properties
*   New development under construction or in the planning stage
*   Occupancy rates

- The rental and price patterns of existing properties
- Construction costs

Other economic trends and considerations may be studied as the appraiser's analysis focuses on successively smaller geographic areas.

Governmental Forces

Political and legal activities at all levels of government can have a great impact on property values. The legal climate at a particular time or in a particular place may overshadow the natural market forces of supply and demand. As mentioned previously, the government provides many necessary facilities and services that affect land use patterns. Therefore, appraisers must diligently identify and examine how the following factors could influence property values:

- Public services such as fire and police protection, utilities, refuse collection, and transportation networks
- Local zoning, building codes, and health codes, especially those that obstruct or support land use
- National, state, and local fiscal policies
- Special legislation that influences general property values:
  - Rent control laws
  - Statutory redemption laws
  - Restrictions on forms of ownership such as those imposed on condominiums and timeshare arrangements
  - Homestead exemption laws
  - Environmental legislation regulating new developments and wetlands as well as the control of hazardous or toxic materials
  - Legislation affecting the types of loans, loan terms, and investment powers of mortgage lending institutions

Environmental Forces

The natural and man-made environmental forces that may be analyzed for real estate appraisal purposes include the following:

- Climatic conditions such as snowfall, rainfall, temperature, and humidity
- Topography and soil
- Toxic contaminants such as asbestos, radon, and PCBs
- Natural barriers to future development such as rivers, mountains, lakes, and oceans
- Primary transportation systems, including federal and state highway systems, railroads, airports, and navigable waterways

location: The time-distance relationships, or linkages, between a property or neighborhood and all other possible origins and destinations of people going to or coming from the property or neighborhood.

- The nature and desirability of the immediate area surrounding a property

All of these factors are environmental, although market participants usually associate the term with the conservation of natural resources (e.g., wildlife, timberlands, wetlands) and the regulation of man-made pollution. (The treatment of hazardous substances in real estate appraisal is discussed in Chapter 9.)

The environmental forces that affect the value of a specific real property may be understood in relation to the property's location. Location considers time-distance relationships, or linkages, between a property or neighborhood and all possible origins and destinations of residents coming to or going from the property or neighborhood. Location has both an environmental and an economic character. Time and distance are measures of relative access, which may be considered in terms of site ingress/egress, the characteristics of the neighborhoods through which traffic to and from the site passes, and transportation costs to and from the site.

To analyze the value influence of location, the linkages between the property and important points or places outside the property are identified, and the distance and time required to cover those distances by the most

The proximity of industrial properties to residential areas provides the businesses located there with access to workers, but the market for residential properties may be penalized for its proximity to potentially hazardous substances.

commonly used types of transportation are measured. Depending on the area and the property type, the appraiser may investigate the property's access to the following:

- Public transportation
- Schools
- Stores
- Service establishments
- Parks
- Recreational and cultural facilities
- Places of worship
- Sources of employment
- Product markets
- Suppliers of production needs
- Processors of raw materials

FURTHER READING

Hoover, Edgar M. *The Location of Economic Activity.* New York: McGraw-Hill, 1963.

Noyes, C. Reinold. *The Institution of Property.* London: Longmans, Green and Company, 1936.

Mitchell, Phillip S. "The Evolving Appraisal Paradigm." *The Appraisal Journal* (April 1993).

Pearson, Thomas D. "Education for Professionalism: A Common Body of Knowledge for Appraisers, Part I: Background and Historical Trends." *The Appraisal Journal* (October 1988).

___. "Education for Professionalism: A Common Body of Knowledge for Appraisers, Part II: The Body of Knowledge." *The Appraisal Journal* (January 1989).

Perin, Constance. *Everything in Its Place: Social Order and Land Use in America.* Princeton, N.J.: Princeton University Press, 1977.

4 THE VALUATION PROCESS

The valuation process is a systematic procedure an appraiser follows to provide answers to a client's questions about real property value. It is a model that can be adapted to a wide variety of questions that relate to value.

The valuation process begins when the appraiser agrees to take an assignment and ends when the conclusions of the appraisal are reported to the client. Each property is unique, and opinions of many different types of value can be developed for a single property. The most common appraisal assignment is performed to render an opinion of market value. The valuation process contains all the steps appropriate to this type of assignment. The model also provides the framework for developing an opinion of other defined values.

The valuation process is accomplished through specific steps. The number of steps followed depends on the nature of the appraisal assignment and the available data. The model provides a pattern that can be used in any appraisal assignment to perform market research and data analysis, to apply appraisal techniques, and to integrate the results of these activities into an opinion of defined value. In addition to assisting appraisers in their work, models that apply the valuation process are recognized by the market of appraisal users and facilitate their understanding of appraisal conclusions.

Research begins after the appraisal problem has been defined and the scope of work required to solve the problem has been identified. The analysis of data relevant to the problem starts with an investigation of trends observed at the market level–international, national, regional, or neighborhood. This examination helps the appraiser understand the interrelationships among the principles, forces, and factors that affect real property value in the specific market area. Research also provides raw data from which the appraiser can extract quantitative information and other evidence of market trends. Such trends may include positive or negative percentage changes in property value over a number of years, the population movement into an area, and the number of employment opportunities available and their effect on the purchasing power of potential property users.

In assignments to develop an opinion of market value, the ultimate goal of the valuation process is a well-supported value conclusion that reflects all of the pertinent factors that influence the market value of

The valuation process is a systematic set of procedures an appraiser follows to provide answers to a client's questions about real property value.

the property being appraised. To achieve this goal, an appraiser studies a property from three different viewpoints, which are referred to as the *approaches to value*. The three approaches are described below.

1. In the cost approach, value is estimated as the current cost of reproducing or replacing the improvements (including an appropriate entrepreneurial incentive or profit) minus the loss in value from depreciation plus land or site value.
2. In the sales comparison approach, value is indicated by recent sales of comparable properties in the market.
3. In the income capitalization approach, value is indicated by a property's earning power, based on the capitalization of income.

Traditionally, specific appraisal techniques are applied within the three approaches to derive indications of real property value. One or more approaches to value may be used depending on their applicability to the particular appraisal assignment, the nature of the property, the needs of the client, or the available data.[1]

The three approaches are interrelated. Each requires the gathering and analysis of data that pertains to the property being appraised. Each approach is outlined briefly in this chapter and discussed in detail in subsequent sections of the textbook. From the approaches applied, the appraiser derives separate indications of value for the property being appraised. To complete the valuation process, the appraiser integrates the information drawn from market research, data analysis, and the application of the approaches to form a value conclusion. This conclusion may be presented as a single point estimate of value or, if the assignment permits, as a range within which the value may fall. An effective integration of all the elements in the process depends on the appraiser's skill, experience, and judgment.

The steps in the valuation process are depicted in Figure 4.1.

Definition of the Appraisal Problem

The first step in the valuation process is the development of a clear statement of the appraisal problem. This sets the limits of the appraisal and eliminates any ambiguity about the nature of the assignment. The definition of the problem should include the following:

*   Identification of the client and intended users of the appraisal
*   Intended use of the appraisal
*   Purpose of the appraisal (including the definition of value)

---

1. Other useful appraisal tools include inferential statistics, automated valuation models (AVMs), and econometric models. It should be noted, however, that AVMs and other computer applications are more useful when combined with the judgment and experience of a professional appraiser or analyst. A valuation model can generate an *estimate* of value, but only an appraiser following the valuation process can develop a qualified *opinion* of value.

Figure 4.1   The Valuation Process

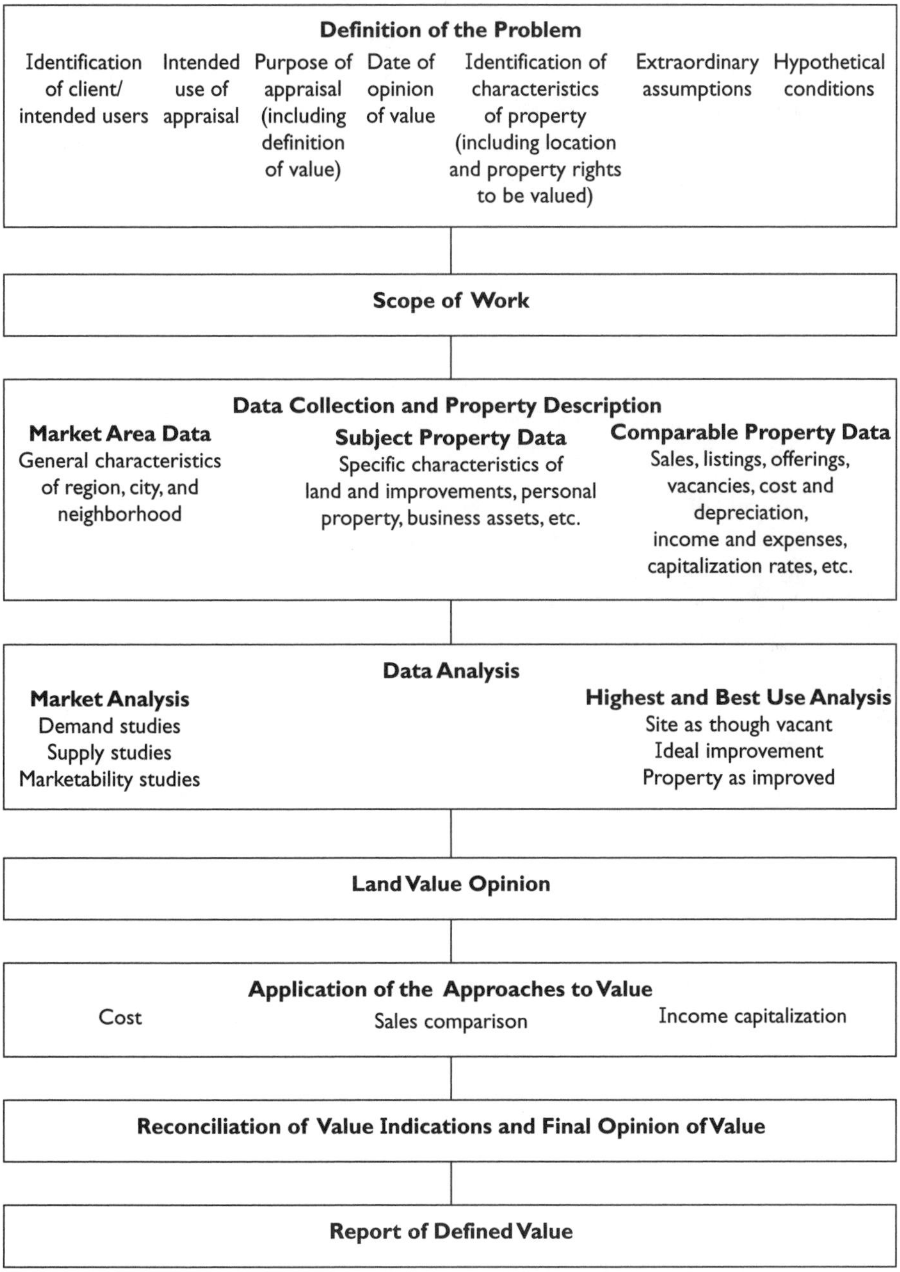

Definition of the Problem

| Identification of client/ intended users | Intended use of appraisal | Purpose of appraisal (including definition of value) | Date of opinion of value | Identification of characteristics of property (including location and property rights to be valued) | Extraordinary assumptions | Hypothetical conditions |

Scope of Work

Data Collection and Property Description

Market Area Data
General characteristics of region, city, and neighborhood

Subject Property Data
Specific characteristics of land and improvements, personal property, business assets, etc.

Comparable Property Data
Sales, listings, offerings, vacancies, cost and depreciation, income and expenses, capitalization rates, etc.

Data Analysis

Market Analysis
Demand studies
Supply studies
Marketability studies

Highest and Best Use Analysis
Site as though vacant
Ideal improvement
Property as improved

Land Value Opinion

Application of the Approaches to Value

Cost   Sales comparison   Income capitalization

Reconciliation of Value Indications and Final Opinion of Value

Report of Defined Value

Definition of the appraisal problem is the first **step in the valuation process.** The appraiser identifies the client and intended users of the appraisal, the intended use of the appraisal, the purpose of the appraisal (including the definition of value to be used), the date of the opinion of value, characteristics of the property (including its location and the property rights to be valued among other features), any extraordinary assumptions or hypothetical conditions, and, finally, the scope of work.

- Date of the opinion of value
- Identification of the characteristics of the property (including its location, the property rights to be valued, and other features)
- Extraordinary assumptions
- Hypothetical conditions

Before identifying the characteristics of the property and any extraordinary assumptions and hypothetical conditions that are relevant to the purpose of the assignment, the appraiser must clearly identify the client, intended use, purpose, and date of the appraisal. The process of defining the appraisal problem leads directly into the appraiser's decision about the scope of work necessary to fulfill the assignment.

Identification of the Client and Intended Users of the Appraisal

The valuation process begins before the client even engages the appraiser. In deciding whether or not to take an assignment, the appraiser must consider the client and any other professional obligations that the assignment will bring. The appraiser must clearly identify the client and, as far as possible and practical, any intended users of the appraisal. Even if the client wishes to remain anonymous, the appraiser must still identify the client in the work file for the assignment.[2]

Identifying the client and other intended users leads directly to identifying the intended use of the appraisal, which in turn is an integral part of determining the scope of work.

Intended Use of the Appraisal

The intended use of an appraisal is the manner in which the client will employ the information contained in the appraisal report. The client may specify the intended use of the appraisal when requesting it; if not, the appraiser may have to solicit this information, guiding the client to ensure a clear understanding of the question. Because an appraisal provides the basis for a decision regarding real property, the nature of the decision affects the character of the assignment and the appraisal report. An opinion of value may be needed to determine the following:

- Price at which to buy or sell
- Amount of a loan
- Basis for taxation

---

2.   See the Confidentiality section of the Ethics Rule of USPAP, the Statement on Appraisal Standards No. 5, and Advisory Opinion 10 for further discussion.

- Terms of a lease
- Value of real property assets in financial statements
- Basis for just compensation in eminent domain proceedings
- Other information useful in decision making involving real property

To avoid wasted effort, the appraiser and the client must reach a mutual understanding concerning the intended use of the appraisal report and its conclusions and who will own the final product.

Purpose of the Appraisal

The purpose of an appraisal is usually to develop an opinion of a certain type of value. Types of appraised value include the following:

- Market value
- Use value
- Going-concern value
- Investment value
- Assessed value

The Uniform Standards of Professional Appraisal Practice require that a written statement of the defined value to be developed must be included in every appraisal report. This statement establishes the precise question to be answered for the client, the appraiser, and all readers of the report. It explains the data selected for consideration and the methods employed to analyze the data and supports the logic and validity of the final opinion of value. The statement also specifies whether an opinion of market value is reported in terms of cash, terms equivalent to cash, or other precisely revealed terms.

It is the appraiser's responsibility to ensure that the purpose of the appraisal is consistent with and appropriate for its intended use.

Date of the Opinion of Value

The date of the opinion of value must be specified because the forces that influence real property value are constantly changing. Although conditions observed at the time of the appraisal may persist for a considerable time after that date, an opinion of value is considered valid only for the exact date specified. Market value is generally seen as a reflection of market participants' perceptions of future economic conditions. These perceptions are based on market evidence at a specific point in time. Value influences reflect

intended use of the appraisal: The manner in which a client will employ the information contained in an appraisal report.

definition of value: A written statement specifying the type of value to be estimated; must be included in every appraisal report.

date of the opinion of value: The date for which an opinion of value is valid. The sale of a property may be negotiated months or even years before the closing or final disposition of the property. In this case, an adjustment for changes in market conditions between the date the contract is signed and the effective date of value may be appropriate.

economic conditions at a particular time, and sudden changes in business and real estate markets can dramatically influence value. The date of the opinion of value should not be confused with the date on the letter of transmittal, which is usually a different date.

Most appraisals call for a current opinion of value, but in some cases a valuation as of a date in the past is required. Retrospective appraisals may be required for

- Inheritance tax—date of death
- Insurance claims—date of casualty
- Income tax—date of acquisition[3]
- Lawsuits—date of loss
- Other purposes

In condemnation proceedings, appraisers may render an opinion of property value as of the date of filing the declaration or petition to condemn, the date of trial, or another date stipulated by the parties involved or by the court. Historical market data is often available, so market value can be developed in retrospect. Sometimes appraisers must research historical trends to perform retrospective valuations.

Appraisals as of a future date, i.e., prospective appraisals, may be required to render an opinion of the likely value of property interests in proposed developments or the value at the end of a cash flow projection. In such cases care must be taken to avoid the implication that a future value opinion is market value. Of course, the anticipation of future benefits is involved whenever an appraiser estimates the present value of a projected income stream or reversion. Opinions of prospective value for proposed developments are frequently required as of the time the development is to be completed and when the development is projected to achieve stabilization. Appraisers may be employed to derive an opinion of prospective value that will be used by owners, buyers, investors, or lenders to make decisions relating to real estate.[4]

retrospective value opinion: An opinion of value as of a specified historic date. A retrospective value opinion is most frequently sought in connection with appraisals for estate tax, condemnation, inheritance tax, and similar purposes.

prospective value opinion: A forecast of the value expected at a specified future date. A prospective value opinion is most frequently sought in connection with real estate projects that are proposed, under construction, or under conversion to a new use, or those that have not achieved sellout or a stabilized level of long-term occupancy and income at the time the appraisal report is written.

---

3. The acquisition date of a property will determine which tax basis is applicable to the seller. The last major overhaul in the capital gains tax was made in the Tax Reform Act of 1986. However, the capital gains tax does change, and the appraiser should be aware of changes that impact the seller.

4. In USPAP, opinions of retrospective and prospective value are discussed in Statements on Appraisal Standards Nos. 3 and 4.

Identification of the Characteristics of the Property

The appraisal problem cannot be properly defined without certain information about the property in question. Essential items include

- Location and physical, legal, and economic attributes
- Real property interests to be valued (e.g., fee simple, fractional interest, physical segment, partial holding)
- Items included in the appraisal other than real property (e.g., personal property or trade fixtures)
- Restrictions on land use such as easements and leases.

The location of a property is identified by a street address or some other descriptive data. A complete legal description specifying the exact location and boundaries of the property is provided as well. Examples of property identification follow:

Reference:	The Kennedy Building, commercial offices
Street address:	2600 South Zephyr
	Denver, Colorado
Legal description:	Lots 7–10, inclusive, Block 3 of Sterns Addition,
	Fifth Filing, City and County of Denver, Colorado

A good source for the legal description is the owner's deed or mortgage.[5] Legal descriptions of real estate are usually derived from land surveys and preserved in public records in accordance with local or state law. Appraisers should be familiar with the specific system or systems used to describe land in various areas and be sure that the legal description is reasonable. (Legal descriptions are discussed in Chapter 9.)

The valuation of real property involves both the physical real estate and the rights that one or more individuals or legal entities may hold or contemplate holding in the ownership or use of the land and improvements. An appraiser may render an opinion of the value of a fee simple estate or of partial interests created by the severance or division of ownership rights. Special attention must be given to limitations on ownership rights, which include easements, encroachments, leases, and the disposition of air or subsurface rights. Financing must also be considered because both fee simple estates and partial interests can be mortgaged. The specific rights to be valued and the probable or actual financing involved must be ascertained at the start of the assignment because the complexity of these rights and terms will determine the procedures, skills, and time required to complete the assignment. (Ownership and interests in real property are covered in Chapter 5.)

---

5.   There are many different types of deeds that an appraiser may consult, e.g., warranty deed, administrator's deed, bargain and sale deed, executor's deed, grant deed, quit claim deed, and trust deed. However, the legal description in a deed is not always accurate. A title report, which relies on a plat of survey as the source of the legal description, may be the best source other than the original plat of survey itself.

Extraordinary Assumptions and Hypothetical Conditions

To describe the scope of work required in an assignment, the appraiser must first identify any extraordinary assumptions or hypothetical conditions affecting the appraisal. Extraordinary assumptions presume uncertain information to be factual. If found to be false these assumptions could alter the appraiser's opinions or conclusions. For example, consider an appraisal of a warehouse property that may be subject to environmental contamination. Even though the presence of contamination is suspected, it is possible for the appraisal to be based on the extraordinary assumption that the property is *not* contaminated. Hypothetical conditions are contrary to what exists, but the conditions are asserted by the appraiser for the purposes of analysis. For example, in the case of a manufacturing plant that is known to be subject to environmental contamination, it is possible for the appraisal to be based on the hypothetical condition that it is *not* contaminated. Whether or not it is appropriate to use such extraordinary assumptions or hypothetical conditions in an appraisal depends on the intended use and the nature of the appraisal problem.

General Assumptions and Limiting Conditions

The preliminary steps in the process of defining the appraisal problem—identification of the real estate and the property rights to be appraised, the date of the opinion of value, the intended use of the appraisal, and the definition of value—all serve to qualify the appraisal. Typically, some limiting conditions are also applicable. Statements of limiting conditions are included in the report to help protect both the appraiser and the client and to inform the client and other users of the report of limitations on the use of the appraisal. For example, an appraisal report may state that the valuation of subsurface oil, gas, or mineral rights is not part of the appraisal. Another general limiting condition might establish that the appraiser will not be expected to provide court or hearing testimony or to attend court proceedings unless arrangements are made a reasonable time in advance and compensation is agreed upon. (The courts may subpoena appraisers to testify despite a limiting condition to the contrary.) Other general limiting conditions might specify that no engineering survey was made or that, except as specifically stated, property data was taken from sources considered to be reliable. (For further examples, see the discussion of general assumptions and limiting conditions in Chapter 26.)

The use of extraordinary assumptions, hypothetical conditions, or general limiting conditions and assumptions may result in a circumstance in which an appraiser cannot render an unqualified opinion of value. Proper disclosure and explanations directly associated with citations of value estimates help avoid misunderstandings or abuses of appraisals.

Scope of Work

The scope of work is the amount and type of information researched and the analysis applied in an assignment. The appraiser is responsible for determining the appropriate scope of work in the appraisal assignment, given the client's intended use and the nature of the problem to be solved.[6]

> **scope of work:** The amount and type of information researched and the analysis applied in an appraisal assignment.

In the appraisal report, the scope must be clearly disclosed. It is often important for the appraiser to indicate what was *not* done in the appraisal as well as what was done. The appraiser may want to indicate the time spent and the area searched to gather the data, especially if only limited data was available. While it is possible to describe the scope of work in various sections of the appraisal report, it is best to include a separate section for this topic. If the appraisal was made using the Departure Rule of USPAP, the report should include the rationale for omitting any of the three traditional approaches to value from the analysis.

Planning the Appraisal

In addition to fulfilling certain formal requirements of the appraisal report, defining the scope of work helps the appraiser identify resources and data that will be needed in the assignment. This preliminary analysis helps the appraiser plan the subsequent steps in the valuation process. The work plan depends on the intended use of the appraisal, the scope of work, and the type of property being valued. For example, much more information will typically be required in the valuation of a large apartment building than in the valuation of a moderately priced single-family residence.

To complete an assignment quickly and efficiently, each step in the valuation process should be planned and scheduled. Time and personnel requirements will vary with the amount and complexity of the work. Some assignments may be completed in a few days. For more complex appraisal problems, weeks or months may be spent gathering, analyzing, and applying all pertinent data.

Some assignments can be performed by a single appraiser, while others require the assistance of other staff members or appraisal specialists. Sometimes the assistance of specialists in other fields is needed. For example, in valuing a hotel property, the appraiser's findings may be augmented by the professional opinion of a personal property appraiser. Recognizing when work can or must be delegated improves efficiency and enhances accuracy, but appraisers should also be aware of the responsibilities inherent in the use of reports prepared by others. (Such concerns are addressed in Guide Note 6 to the Appraisal Institute's Standards of Professional Appraisal Practice.) The appraiser bears the ultimate responsibility for the value opinion and must see

---

6. See also Advisory Opinion 22 in USPAP and Stephanie Coleman, "Scope of Work and Range of Services," *Valuation Insight & Perspectives, vol. 6, no. 1* (First Quarter 2001): 33–35 and Stephanie Coleman, "Scope of Work and Range of Services," *The Appraisal Journal* (April 2001): 211–218 for more discussion of how scope of work is determined in market value appraisal assignments.

the assignment as a whole as well as a collection of procedures and details. With a comprehensive view, the appraiser can recognize the type and volume of work to be done and schedule and delegate that work properly.

The appraiser's work plan usually includes an outline of the proposed appraisal report. The major parts of the report are delineated, and the data and procedures involved in each section are noted. Using this outline, data can be assembled intelligently and the appropriate amount of time can be allocated to each step in the valuation process.

Data Collection and Property Description

Following the preliminary analysis (i.e., the identification of the appraisal problem and determination of the scope of work), the appraiser gathers data on the market area, the subject property, and comparable properties in the market. The data needed by appraisers can be divided into general data and specific data.

General data includes information about trends in the social, economic, governmental, and environmental forces that affect property value in the defined market area. A *trend* is a momentum or tendency in a general direction brought about by a series of interrelated changes. Trends such as population shifts, declining office building occupancy rates and increased housing starts in a market area are identified by analyzing general data. General data can contribute significantly to an appraiser's understanding of the marketplace.

Specific data relates to the property being appraised and to comparable properties. This data includes legal, physical, locational, cost, and income and expense information about the properties and the details of comparable sales. Financial arrangements that could affect selling prices are also considered.

Data on comparable properties can be either general data that an appraiser has on file or specific data that must be gathered for a particular assignment. More often, comparable property data is specific supply and demand data that relates to the competitive position of property similar to the subject in its future market. Supply data includes inventories of existing and proposed competitive properties, vacancy rates, and absorption rates. Demand data may consist of population, income, employment, and survey data pertaining to potential property users. From this data an estimate of future demand for the present or prospective use or uses of the subject property is developed.

The amount and type of data collected for an appraisal depend on the approaches used to develop an opinion of value and on the defined scope of work. In a given valuation assignment, more than one approach to value is usually appropriate and necessary to arrive at a value indication. Depending on the problem or problems to be addressed, one approach

comparables: A shortened term for similar property sales, rentals, or operating expenses used for comparison in the valuation process; also called *comps.*

may be given greater emphasis in deriving the final opinion of value. In conducting a particular assignment, the appraiser's judgment and experience and the quantity and quality of data available for analysis may determine which approach or approaches are used.

The data collected should be meaningful and relevant. All pertinent value influences, facts, and conclusions about trends should be clearly indicated in the report and related specifically to the property being appraised. Because the data selected forms the basis for the appraiser's judgments, a thorough explanation of the significance of the data reported ensures that the reader will understand these judgments.

Data Analysis

Once the appropriate data on the market area, subject property, and site has been collected and reviewed for accuracy, the appraiser begins the process of data analysis, which has two components: market analysis and highest and best use analysis. Even the simplest valuation assignments must be based on a solid understanding of prevalent market conditions and the highest and best use of the real estate. The two forms of analysis are related. In fact, an appraiser's investigation into trends affecting the economic base of the market area leads directly into the determination of highest and best use.

Market Analysis

In the Uniform Standards of Professional Appraisal Practice, *market analysis* is defined as a study of market conditions for a specific type of property. A description of prevalent market conditions helps the reader of an appraisal report understand the motivations of participants in the market for the subject property. Broad market conditions provide the background for local and neighborhood market influences that have direct bearing on the value of the subject property.

Market analysis, which is discussed in detail in Chapter 11, serves two important functions. First, it provides a background against which local developments are considered. Second, a knowledge of the broad changes that affect supply and demand gives an appraiser an indication of how values change over time.

The data and conclusions generated through market analysis are essential components in other portions of the valuation process. Market analysis yields information needed for each of the three traditional approaches to value. In the cost approach, market analysis provides the basis for adjusting the cost of the subject property for depreciation, i.e., physical deterioration and functional and external

Analyses of market conditions and **highest and best use** are crucial to the valuation process.

market analysis: A study of market conditions for a specific type of property.

obsolescence. In the income capitalization approach, all the necessary income, expense, and rate data is evaluated in light of the market forces of supply and demand. In the sales comparison approach, the conclusions of market analysis are used to delineate the market and thereby identify comparable properties.

The extent of market analysis and the level of detail appropriate for a particular assignment depend on the appraisal problem under examination. When appraisers are doing business in a generally stable market on a daily basis, they should have all the necessary demographic and economic information to document market conditions on file. When the appraisal assignment is complex—e.g., an analysis of the feasibility of a subdivision development—a more detailed market analysis will be required. Regardless of the assignment's complexity, the logic of the market analysis should be communicated clearly to the reader in the appraisal report. The level of detail may depend on the report option used.

Highest and Best Use Analysis

Analysis of the highest and best use of the land as though vacant and of the property as improved is essential in the valuation process. Through highest and best use analysis, the appraiser interprets the market forces that affect the subject property and identifies the use or uses on which the final opinion of value is based. (Highest and best use analysis is discussed in detail in Chapter 12.)

Analyzing the highest and best use of the land as though vacant helps the appraiser identify comparable properties. Whenever possible, the property being appraised should be compared with similar properties that have been sold recently in the same market. Potentially comparable properties that do not have the same highest and best use are usually eliminated from further analysis. Estimating the land's highest and best use as though vacant is a necessary part of deriving an opinion of land value.

There are two reasons to analyze the highest and best use of the property as improved. The first is to help identify potentially comparable properties. Each improved property should have the same or a similar highest and best use as the improved subject property both as though vacant and as improved. The second reason to analyze the highest and best use of the property as improved is to decide which of the following options should be pursued:

- Maintain the improvements as is.
- Cure items of deferred maintenance and retain the improvements.
- Modify the improvements (e.g., renovate, modernize, or convert).

highest and best use of site as though vacant: Among all reasonable, alternative uses, the use that yields the highest present land value, after payments are made for labor, capital, and coordination. The use of a property based on the assumption that the parcel of land is vacant or can be made vacant by demolishing any improvements.

highest and best use of property as improved: The use that should be made of a property as it exists. An existing property should be renovated or retained as is so long as it continues to contribute to the total market value of the property, or until the return from a new improvement would more than offset the cost of demolishing the existing building and constructing a new one.

- Demolish the improvements.

Analysis of **highest and best use** includes consideration of both the land as though vacant and the property as improved. The conclusion is specified in terms of use, timing, and market participants.

In some situations, a property may be subject to restrictions (e.g., historic preservation) that prevent the improvements from being demolished and the property from being developed to its highest and best use.

The highest and best use conclusion should specify the optimal use (or uses), when the property will be put to this use or achieve stabilized occupancy, and who would be the most likely purchaser or user of the property (e.g., an owner-operator of the property or an equity or debt investor).

Land Value Opinion

Land valuation is directly related to highest and best use analysis. The relationship between highest and best use and land or site value[7] may indicate whether an existing use is the highest and best use of the land.

Land value can be a major component of total property value. Appraisers often develop an opinion of land value separately, even when valuing properties with extensive building improvements. Land value and building value may change at different rates because improvements are almost always subject to depreciation. For many appraisals, a separate opinion of land value is required.

Although a total property value estimate may be derived in the sales comparison or income capitalization approach without separating land and improvement values, it may be necessary to estimate land value separately to isolate the value the land contributes to the total property. In the cost approach, the value of the land must be estimated and stated separately.

Developing an opinion of land value can be considered a separate step in the valuation model or an essential technique for applying certain approaches to value, depending on the defined appraisal problem. An appraiser can use several techniques to obtain an indication of land value:

- Sales comparison
- Extraction
- Allocation
- Subdivision development
- Land residual
- Ground rent capitalization

Usually the most reliable way to estimate land value is by sales comparison. When few sales are available, however, or when the value indications

---

7. Appraisers distinguish between *land* (the earth's surface, both land and water, and anything that is attached to it, whether by the course of nature or by human hands) and *site* (land that is improved so that it is ready to be used for a specific purpose). The distinctions between the two terms are discussed more fully in Chapter 9.

Of the various techniques that can be applied to **estimate land value**, sales comparison is usually the most reliable.

produced through sales comparison need additional support, procedures like extraction or allocation may be applied. The other methods of land valuation, which all involve income capitalization techniques, are subject to more limitations and are used less often in everyday appraisal practice. The subdivision development technique is a specialized valuation method useful in specific land use situations.[8] The land residual technique is used most often in highest and best use analysis to test the feasibility of various uses than to estimate land value as part of one of the traditional approaches to value. Ground rent capitalization can be used when land rents and land capitalization rates are readily available—e.g., for appraisals in well-developed areas.

Application of the Approaches to Value

The valuation process is applied to develop a well-supported opinion of a defined value based on an analysis of pertinent general and specific data. Appraisers develop an opinion of property value with specific appraisal procedures that reflect three distinct methods of data analysis:

1. Cost
2. Sales comparison
3. Income capitalization

One or more of these approaches are used in all estimations of value; the approaches employed depend on the type of property, the intended use of the appraisal, the identified scope of work, and the quality and quantity of data available for analysis.

All three approaches are applicable to many appraisal problems, but one or more of the approaches may have greater significance in a given assignment. For example, the cost approach might not be applicable in valuing properties with older improvements that suffer substantial depreciation, which may be difficult to estimate. The sales comparison approach might not be applicable to specialized properties such as garbage disposal plants because comparable data may not be available. The income capitalization approach is not often used in the valuation of single-family homes. Income capitalization can be particularly unreliable in the market for commercial or industrial property where owner-occupants outbid investors. Appraisers should apply all the approaches that are applicable and for which there is data. The alternative value indications derived can either support or refute one another.

One of the three approaches—cost, sales comparison, and income capitalization—may be especially effective in a given situation. An appraiser often employs more than one approach.

---

8. The valuation of subdivisions is discussed more fully in Douglas D. Lovell and Robert S. Martin, *Subdivision Analysis* (Chicago: Appraisal Institute, 1993).

Cost Approach

The cost approach is based on the understanding that market participants relate value to cost. In the cost approach, the value of a property is derived by adding the estimated value of the land to the current cost of constructing a reproduction or replacement for the improvements and then subtracting the amount of depreciation (i.e., deterioration and obsolescence) in the structures from all causes. Entrepreneurial profit and/or incentive may be included in the value indication. This approach is particularly useful in valuing new or nearly new improvements and properties that are not frequently exchanged in the market. Cost approach techniques can also be employed to derive information needed in the sales comparison and income capitalization approaches to value, such as the costs to cure items of deferred maintenance.

The current costs to construct the improvements can be obtained from cost estimators, cost manuals, builders, and contractors. Depreciation is measured through market research and the application of specific procedures. Land value is estimated separately in the cost approach.

cost approach: A set of procedures through which a value indication is derived for the fee simple interest in a property by estimating the current cost to construct a reproduction of (or replacement for) the existing structure, including an entrepreneurial profit, deducting depreciation from the total cost, and adding the estimated land value. Adjustments may then be made to the indicated fee simple value of the subject property to reflect the value of the property interest being appraised.

sales comparison approach: A set of procedures in which a value indication is derived by comparing the property being appraised to similar properties that have been sold recently, applying appropriate units of comparison, and making adjustments to the sale prices of the comparables based on the elements of comparison. The sales comparison approach may be used to value improved properties, vacant land, or land being considered as though vacant; it is the most common and preferred method of land valuation when comparable sales data is available.

Sales Comparison Approach

The sales comparison approach is most useful when a number of similar properties have recently been sold or are currently for sale in the subject property's market. Using this approach, an appraiser produces a value indication by comparing the subject property with similar properties, called *comparable sales*. The sale prices of the properties that are judged to be most comparable tend to indicate a range in which the value indication for the subject property will fall.

The appraiser estimates the degree of similarity or difference between the subject property and the comparable sales by considering various elements of comparison:

• Real property rights conveyed
• Financing terms
• Conditions of sale
• Expenditures made immediately after purchase
• Market conditions

> **income capitalization approach:** A set of procedures through which an appraiser derives a value indication for an income-producing property by converting its anticipated benefits (cash flows and reversion) into property value. This conversion can be accomplished in two ways. One year's (stabilized) income expectancy can be capitalized at a market-derived capitalization rate or at a capitalization rate that reflects a specified income pattern, return on investment, and change in the value of the investment. Alternatively, the annual cash flows for the holding period and the reversion can be discounted at a specified yield rate.

- Location
- Physical characteristics
- Economic characteristics
- Use/zoning
- Non-realty components of value

Dollar or percentage adjustments are then applied to the (known) sale price of each comparable property to derive an indicated value for the subject property. Through this comparative procedure, the appraiser renders an opinion of the value that was defined in the problem identification as of a specific date.

Income multipliers and capitalization rates may also be extracted through analysis of comparable sales, though these factors are not regarded as elements of comparison in the sales comparison approach. Instead, they are usually applied in the income capitalization approach.

Income Capitalization Approach

In the income capitalization approach, the present value of the future benefits of property ownership is measured. A property's income and resale value upon reversion may be capitalized into a current, lump-sum value. There are two methods of income capitalization: direct capitalization and yield capitalization. In direct capitalization, the relationship between one year's income and value is reflected in either a capitalization rate or an income multiplier. In yield capitalization, the relationship between several years' stabilized income and a reversionary value at the end of a designated period is reflected in a yield rate. The most common application of yield capitalization is discounted cash flow analysis. Given the significant differences in how and when properties generate income, there are many variations in both direct and yield capitalization procedures, which is addressed in Chapter 20.

Like the sales comparison and cost approaches, the income capitalization approach requires extensive market research. Data collection and analysis for this approach are conducted against a background of supply and demand relationships, which provide information about trends and market anticipation.

The specific data that an appraiser investigates in the income capitalization approach might include the property's gross income expectancy, the expected reduction in gross income caused by vacancy and collection loss, the anticipated annual operating expenses, the pattern and duration of the property's income stream, and the anticipated reversionary value. After income and expenses are estimated, the income streams are capitalized by applying an appropriate rate or factor or converted into present value through discounting. In discounted cash flow analysis, the quantity, variability, timing, and duration of a set of periodic incomes and the quantity and timing of the reversion are specified and discounted to a present value at a specified yield rate. The rates used for capitalization or discounting are derived from acceptable rates of return for similar properties.

Final Reconciliation of Value Indications

The final analytical step in the valuation process is the reconciliation of the value indications derived into a single dollar figure or a range into which the value will most likely fall. The nature of reconciliation depends on the appraisal problem, the approaches that have been used, and the reliability of the value indications derived.

When all three approaches have been used, the appraiser examines the three separate indications and considers the relative dependability and applicability of each approach. In the reconciliation section of the report, the appraiser can explain variations among the indications produced by the different approaches and account for differences between the value conclusions and methods applied.

The final opinion of defined value, which is the goal of the valuation process, is usually reported as a single figure. However, it may be reported as a range of value or as a value in relation to some stated benchmark amount (i.e., more than or less than a given dollar amount).

> Value indications from different approaches are **reconciled** into a final opinion of value.

reconciliation of value indications: The last phase of a valuation assignment in which two or more value indications derived from market data are resolved into a final value opinion, which may be either a final range of value or a single point estimate.

report of defined value: The documented statement provided at the conclusion of an appraisal.

final opinion of value: The range of values or single dollar figure derived from the reconciliation of value indications and stated in the appraisal report.

range of value: The range, or confidence interval, in which the final market value opinion of a property may fall; usually stated as a variable amount between a high and low value limit.

Report of Defined Value

The assignment is not complete until the conclusion is stated in a report and presented to the client. The reported value is the appraiser's opinion and reflects the experience and judgment that has been applied to the study of the assembled data. The appraisal report is the tangible expression of the appraiser's work and the last step in the valuation process. The conclusions of an appraisal may be communicated to the client in writing or orally. Chapter 26 describes the requirements for the three types of appraisal reports defined by USPAP and the circumstances under which they are prepared and submitted.

> The **report of defined value**, which is the last step in the valuation process, summarizes the data analyzed, the methods applied, and the reasoning that led to the value conclusion.

FURTHER READING

Love, Terrence L. *The Guide to Appraisal Office Policies and Procedures*. Chicago: Appraisal Institute, 1991.

Schmutz, George L. *The Appraisal Process*. North Hollywood, Calif.: the author, 1941; New York: Prentice-Hall, Inc., 1949.

CHAPTER 5   REAL PROPERTY OWNERSHIP AND INTERESTS

Real property ownership involves not only the identification and valuation of a variety of different rights but also the analysis of the many limitations on those rights and the effect that the limitations have on value. Some limitations on ownership, such as eminent domain, are public while others such as deed restrictions are private. Holding a form of ownership in real property equates to having an interest in that real property. This chapter examines the types of real estate ownership, the types of property interests, and limitations on real property ownership and interests.

Real Property Ownership

Public and Private Ownership

One major distinction in real property ownership is the difference between private ownership and public ownership. Public ownership of real property takes many forms. Streets and roads, municipal utility systems, and other public facilities such as city halls, prisons, and public works facilities are usually owned by governmental bodies for the benefit of all citizens in a jurisdiction. School districts own land on which schools and sports facilities are maintained. Library districts create public libraries. Parks, recreation, and conservation districts acquire land for recreation, conservation, and preservation.

Most public ownership is created in response to public necessity or public demand. For example, in one community it might be necessary to acquire land for a commuter parking lot using the power of eminent domain. In another community, there might be sufficient demand by residents to acquire land for the development of soccer fields using money generated by real estate taxation. Rather than being concerned with the economic issues that are of importance to private owners of real property, a governmental entity often is more concerned with how publicly owned real property, which is usually not subject to real estate taxation, can be used in the best interests of the public.

Police power also regulates land use, and often its application can reflect the difference in a property viewed from the perspective of public versus private ownership. For example, a large municipal park might be an ideal location for industrial development, but the zoning imposed through the application of police power will ensure that the park continues to be used for recreational purposes. Also, government regulations will dictate how property acquired by a governmental entity through the process of escheat will best benefit the general public.

Although many appraisal assignments involve the valuation of publicly owned real property, most involve the valuation of private ownership interests. As discussed in this chapter, many forms of ownership can be applied to property. The appropriate form of ownership is usually selected based on the needs of the owner or owners. For example, a single-family residence might be owned by a husband and wife in joint tenancy with the right of survivorship. A more appropriate type of ownership for a chain of food stores, however, might be as a beneficial interest in a land trust or a limited liability corporation. Figure 5.1 illustrates the relationship of various types of real property ownership.

Standard 1 of the Uniform Standards of Professional Appraisal Practice (USPAP) requires the appraiser to identify the real property rights being appraised in every assignment. Therefore, an appraiser must thoroughly understand the form of ownership that exists for the property being appraised as well as the interests held by that ownership.

Figure 5.1   **Ownership Entities**

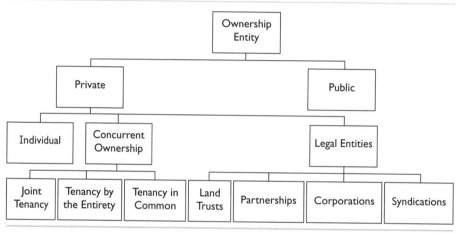

The Bundle of Rights

The most complete form of ownership is title in fee. Such ownership establishes an interest in real property known as *fee simple interest*—i.e., absolute ownership unencumbered by any other interest or estate, subject only to the limitations imposed by the governmental powers of taxation, eminent domain, police power, and escheat. Although fee simple interest represents the most complete form of ownership, often an appraiser will be asked to appraise the value of something less than the fee simple interest—i.e., a *partial interest* or a *fractional interest*.

The bundle of rights concept compares real property ownership to a bundle of sticks. Each stick in the bundle represents a separate right or interest inherent in the ownership. These individual rights can be separated from the bundle by sale, lease, mortgage, donation, or another means of transfer. The complete bundle of rights includes the following:

- The right to sell an interest
- The right to lease an interest and to occupy the property
- The right to mortgage an interest
- The right to give an interest away
- The right to do none or all of these things

fee simple: Absolute ownership unencumbered by any other interest or estate, subject only to the limitations imposed by the governmental powers of taxation, eminent domain, police power, and escheat.

partial interest: Divided or undivided rights in real estate that represent less than the whole.

Ownership of the fee simple interest is equivalent to ownership of the complete bundle of sticks, while one or more of the sticks (or a portion of individual sticks) can represent a partial interest in a specific property (see Figure 5.2). Each individual right in the bundle has some potential value; if any or all are removed from the fee simple interest, one or more partial interests are created and will have to be valued. Due to the nature of the real estate market, the sum of the values of the individual partial interests will usually not equal the value of the fee simple interest.

Problems arise in the valuation of undivided partial interests, a legal arrrangement in which no co-owner has the right to any specific part of the whole property. When multiple owners hold equal, undivided partial interests in a property, no party can exercise complete control, and the interest of each party is usually not worth as much as the corresponding fraction of the property's market value. For example, an undivided 50% interest in a property worth $100,000 would probably be worth something less than $50,000 because a 50% interest is not a controlling interest. However, if one tenant in common held an undivided 60% interest in a property and two other tenants in common held undivided 20% interests in the same property, the controlling interest would likely be worth more than $60,000, and the two minority interests would probably be worth something less than $20,000 each.

Figure 5.2   The Bundle of Rights

Minority interests have limited market appeal, so the appraiser must decide how to derive an appropriate value. Because any concurrent owner can bring

divided interest: An interest in part of a whole property, e.g., a lessee's interest.

undivided interest: Fractional interest without physical division into shares.

legal action to divide, or partition, the property, the cost of partition is one measure of value diminution. However, a sale in partition is a forced sale, which does not reflect free market action, and the price paid may or may not reflect market value. Valuations of co-ownerships are difficult and may be disputed.

Public Restrictions on Ownership

Private ownership of real property rights is guaranteed by the U. S. Constitution but is subject to certain restrictions, known as the *four powers of government*:

1. Taxation
2. Eminent domain
3. Police power
4. Escheat

Taxation is the right of government to raise revenue through assessments on goods, products, and rights. The U.S. Constitution effectively precludes the federal government from taxing real property directly; the right to tax property is reserved for state and local governments.

Eminent domain is the right of government to take private property for public use upon the payment of just compensation. This right can be exercised by a government agency or by an entity acting under governmental authority such as a housing authority, school district, park district, or right of way agency. *Condemnation* is the act or process of enforcing the right of eminent domain—i.e., the taking of private property for public use.

Police power is the right of government through which property is regulated to protect public safety, health, morals, and general welfare. Zoning ordinances, use restrictions, building codes, air and land traffic regulations, health codes, and environmental regulations are based on police power.

Escheat is the right of government that gives the state or a local government (e.g., township or county) titular ownership of a property when its owner dies without a will or any statutory heirs.

taxation: The right of government to raise revenue through assessments on valuable goods, products, and rights

eminent domain: The right of government to take private property for public use upon the payment of just compensation. The Fifth Amendment of the U.S. Constitution, also known as the *takings clause*, guarantees payment of just compensation upon appropriation of private property.

police power: The right of government through which property is regulated to protect public safety, health, morals, and general welfare.

escheat: The right of government that gives the state titular ownership of a property when its owner dies without a will or any ascertainable heirs.

Private Restrictions on Ownership

Private restrictions on property ownership can limit the use or development of a property and might limit the manner in which ownership can be conveyed. The purchaser of a property may be obligated to use the property subject to a private restriction such as an easement, right of way, or party-wall agreement. An appraiser usually must look into past actions of a property owner or developer to determine if private restrictions currently affect the property. Deed restrictions and subdivision covenants and restrictions are relatively easy to discover; they can be found in deeds recorded at the county courthouse or in information provided by a property owner. Restrictions such as easements and rights of way may be more difficult to uncover; they may only be found in title reports or through a diligent search of public records. Other restrictions such as an unrecorded agreement relative to water rights may be nearly impossible to discover.

> **easements:** An interest in real property that transfers use, but not ownership, of a portion of an owner's property. Access or right-of-way easements may be acquired by private parties or public utilities. Governments dedicate conservation, open space, and preservation easements.
>
> **right of way:** The right to pass over the land of another in some particular path; usually an easement over the land of another; a strip of land used in this way for railroad and highway purposes, for pipelines or pole lines, and for private or public passage.
>
> **party wall:** A common wall erected along the boundary between adjoining properties; the respective owners have a common right of use.

The complexity of real property ownership in the United States today suggests that a true fee simple interest seldom exists because nearly all properties are encumbered to some degree by easements, reservations, and/or private restrictions. Although most appraisers define the interest being appraised as a fee simple interest, such an interest can seldom, if ever, be appraised. To overcome this problem, many appraisers identify the interest appraised as "the fee simple interest in the appraised property, subject to zoning, easements, and restrictions of record as identified within the report." Once a partial interest is created by a lease or a mortgage, the fee simple interest becomes largely theoretical.

Concurrent Ownership of Real Property

Real estate can be owned by one or more entities. Individual ownership is legally known as *ownership in severalty*. However, individuals can hold ownership under certain legal entities, such as 100% ownership of the beneficial interest in a land trust or 100% ownership of the stock of a corporation that owns real estate. When the bundle of rights is owned as separate property interests, tenancy is created. With respect to ownership, *tenancy* can be defined as the holding of property by any form of title.

Concurrent ownership includes joint tenancy, tenancy by the entirety, and tenancy in common. *Joint tenancy* is joint ownership by two or more persons with the right of survivorship. Under this

> Various **tenancy arrangements** apply to property ownership by two or more persons.

> **tenancy:** The holding of property by any form of title.
>
> **ownership in severalty:** Ownership of real property vested in one person alone, rather than held jointly with another.
>
> **joint tenancy:** Joint ownership by two or more persons with the right of survivorship.
>
> **tenancy by the entirety:** An estate held by a husband and wife in which neither has a disposable interest in the property during the lifetime of the other, except through joint action.
>
> **tenancy in common:** An estate held by two or more persons, each of whom has an undivided interest.

arrangement, each party has an identical interest and right of possession. Upon the death of one joint tenant, ownership is automatically vested in the remaining joint tenant or tenants. *Tenancy by the entirety* is an estate held by a husband and wife in which neither has a disposable interest in the property during the lifetime of the other, except through joint action. It has the same survivorship provision as a joint tenancy, but tenancy by the entirety applies only to spouses. *Tenancy in common* is an estate held by two or more persons, each of whom has an undivided interest. In this estate the undivided interests may or may not be equally shared by the holders and there is no right of survivorship. One tenant in common may sell off an undivided interest without the approval or knowledge of the other tenant or tenants in common.

Legal Entity Ownership of Real Property

In addition to individual ownership, real property can be owned by a variety of different legal entities such as

- Land trusts
- Partnerships
- Corporations and companies
- Syndications

Like individuals, these entities can own a fee simple interest or partial interests in real property.

Land Trusts

Trusts are sometimes used as legal vehicles to create partial ownership interests in real property. In a land trust, one or more properties are conveyed by special deed to a trustee, which then owns the real property. Either the original owners or some other designated individual or persons become the owners of the beneficial interest in the trust. A trust agreement is established outlining the duties and functions of the trustee. A trustee is usually a separate, specialized company or an independent department of a bank.

> **land trust:** A legal vehicle for partial ownership interests in real property in which independently owned properties are conveyed to a trustee; may be used to effect a profitable assemblage or, in some cases, to facilitate the assigning of property as collateral for a loan.

A trustee can take no actions other than those specified and allowed in the trust agreement without written permission of the owner or owners of the beneficial interest. For example, in one trust agreement a trustee may be required to manage a property actively and collect rents. However, in another trust agreement regarding a different property, the same trustee will be prohibited from managing the property and collecting rents. One important legal aspect of a trust arrangement is that a judgment against a beneficiary is not a lien against the real estate.

The valuation of a fee simple interest in real property owned by a land trust is accomplished like any other appraisal assignment. If there are several beneficiaries in a land trust and the assignment is to value a beneficiary's partial interest, the appraiser must first develop an opinion of the market value of the total property. As with all minority interests, the appraiser must consider whether any particular beneficiary's partial interest should be discounted because it is a minority interest. The appraiser must also consider the effect on value that may result from the specific trust agreement provisions, which identify the rights and obligations of beneficiaries. These limitations may indicate that additional discounting or a significant downward adjustment is required.

Partnerships

A partnership is a business arrangement in which two or more persons jointly own a business and share in its profits and losses. Partnerships are used extensively in real estate acquisition because they pool individual funds for property ownership and operation. Two types of partnerships are prevalent in the ownership of real property: general partnerships and limited partnerships.

In a general partnership, all partners share in business gains and each is personally responsible for all liabilities of the partnership. The valuation of a property owned by a partnership is accomplished using traditional valuation techniques. However, to value any partner's partial interest, the appraiser must first develop an opinion of value of the partnership's total real property assets and then develop an opinion of value that reflects the partner's percentage of ownership. As with most minority interests, the value of a partner's percentage of ownership is usually not derived using simple mathematics. Factors considered in the valuation of such a minority interest include the terms of the partnership agreement, the partners' rights

partnership: A business arrangement in which two or more persons jointly own a business and share in its profits and losses.

general partnership: An ownership arrangement in which all partners share in investment gains and losses and each has personal and unlimited responsibility for all liabilities.

limited partnership: An ownership arrangement consisting of general and limited partners. General partners manage the business and assume full liability for partnership debt, while limited partners are passive and liable only to the extent of their own capital contributions.

state

and liabilities in sales and liquidations, the partners' ability or inability to control business operations, and, perhaps, the number of partners. One important aspect of a general partnership is that the agreement automatically terminates when a general partner dies.

Limited partnerships have both general partners and limited partners. All partners participate by pooling funds. However, unlike general partnerships in which all partners actively participate in the business of the partnership, in a limited partnership the partners can be either active or passive. General partners are active members of the partnership who manage the business and assume full liability for partnership obligations. Limited partners, on the other hand, are passive members of the partnership. They are not actively involved in the business of the partnership, and their liability is restricted to the amount of their capital contribution. Through a limited partnership, a group of investors can jointly acquire real property that they might be unable to acquire as individuals.

Stock Corporations

Like partnerships, stock corporations allow many investors to pool funds to purchase and own real property. However, unlike partnerships, the individual investors in a stock corporation do not hold an interest in the real property; rather, they own shares of stock, usually recognized as personal property. The owner of the real property is the legal entity, the corporation.

A stock corporation may be organized to hold title to a single asset, such as a parcel of real estate, or multiple assets, such as a portfolio of property investments. Ownership of the corporate entity is divided into partial interests by selling shares to an investment group. Any specific stock holding represents a percentage of total corporate ownership. For example, if a particular investor owns 250 shares out of 10,000 total shares issued by the corporation, that investor owns 2.5% of the corporation. This percentage is an ownership share in the corporation, *not* a percentage of any real property in the corporation.

Book value is commonly used to value shares in a stock corporation. The pro rata value of shares in a stock corporation is determined by applying the percentage of ownership represented by a block of stock to the book value of the corporation—i.e., the capital amount at which the property is shown in the account books of the corporation. Typically, shares of stock sell for less than pro rata value because they usually represent

stock corporation: A common legal entity in which investors provide organizational capital by subscribing to shares that represent ownership. In return they have a right to all proprietary benefits, subject to the prior claims of operating expenses and debt service on capital raised by selling bonds, debentures, and other money market instruments.

book value: The capital amount at which property is shown on the account books of a corporation. The net amount at which an asset is carried on the books or reported in financial statements; the asset's cost at acquisition, reduced by the amount of accumulated depreciation on the asset.

minority interests that do not have the ability to control the investment. Book value is usually calculated by subtracting depreciation from the original cost of the asset and adding improvements or additions. In valuing shares in a stock corporation formed for a real estate venture, additional discounts may be required to reflect illiquidity insofar as the market for shares is often limited by the type or quality of management and other factors.

Because stock market values often represent a discount from actual corporate net worth, the accounting profession and the Securities and Exchange Commission allow (and sometimes require) publicly owned real estate corporations to show both the book values and the current market values of assets on their annual financial statements. This practice, which is sometimes referred to as *current value accounting*, frequently reveals that present market values greatly exceed book values (i.e., cost less accumulated depreciation). Therefore, in a healthy market a corporation may have greater net worth than is indicated by book values; in a down market the reverse may be true. Publicly owned real estate corporations employ professional appraisers to render opinions of the current market values used in these reports.[1]

Limited Liability Companies

A limited liability company (LLC) incorporates features of both a corporation and a partnership. The owners of a limited liability company are members, rather than shareholders or partners. Unless otherwise specified, management is generally vested in the members in proportion to their contributions of capital. Members may separate their right to a share of the company profits from the right to participate in management or to vote on matters affecting the company. These separated rights can then be assigned to a transferee. To value a member's interest in a limited liability company, the appraiser must determine whether the member holds a complete interest in the company or a transferee interest in the profits. Over the past two decades, many states have adopted legislation authorizing the establishment of LLCs.

Syndications

Syndications are another means for selling interests or rights in real property. A syndication creates a private or public partnership to pool funds for the acquisition,

syndication: A private or public partnership that pools funds for the acquisition and development of real estate projects or other business ventures.

---

1. The International Valuation Standards Committee (IVSC) was formed in 1980 to establish worldwide standards for the valuation of fixed assets in financial statements. Under international accounting standards, fixed assets are divided into tangible assets, intangible assets, and financial assets. Many in the accounting and financial communities believe that evaluations of the current and historical performance of businesses should be made with reference to the current value of their assets. In the United States, historical costs are commonly used to report the value of fixed assets. See International Valuation Standards Committee, *International Valuation Standards 2000* (London: International Valuation Standards Committee, 2000) or http://www.ivsc.org for more information about international valuation standards.

development, holding, management, and/or disposition of real estate. Syndications are established when an individual or group purchases interests in real property for the purpose of transferring them to a limited partnership, which in turn sells the interests to investors.

At one time, syndications were popular because the investment value of syndicate shares usually included income tax shelter benefits. Such investments offered small income returns during the early years, when the value of the investment was perceived to lie largely in its income tax benefits (tax deductions and tax deferrals). However, the Tax Reform Act of 1986 significantly reduced the use of real estate investments as income shelters.[2]

Although syndications usually involve some sort of partnership, they differ from partnerships insofar as the rights of investors in a syndication are different than the rights of general or limited partners in a partnership. In theory syndication arrangements may be simple, but in practice they are often complex because syndications frequently purchase more than real estate, e.g., management services. Accordingly, the value of syndications depends not only on the property rights in the underlying real estate but also on the additional, or more limited, rights created by contracts and other non-realty considerations. Potential capital appreciation and eligibility for tax benefits also influence investors and may affect market value. These factors and conditions are difficult to isolate, so analysis of comparable sales may prove difficult. Appraisers must exercise great care in determining the exact nature of the rights or interests to be valued in any assignment involving syndications. The market values of syndication interests should not be presented as though they represent the assembled ownership of real property assets.

Special Forms of Ownership

In addition to concurrent ownership and ownership by legal entities, there are several special forms of ownership, including

- Condominium ownership
- Cooperative ownership
- Timesharing

Condominium Ownership

A condominium is a form of ownership of separate units or portions of multiunit buildings. While residential and retail properties were once the main types of property held in condominium ownership, most property types now exist in condominium ownership, including offices, industrial buildings, retail structures, and even garden plots and marina slips. A condominium unit is a separate ownership, and title is held by an individual owner. The unit may be separately leased, sold, or mortgaged. In a traditional condominium, the

---

2. Guide Note 1 to the Appraisal Institute's Standards of Professional Appraisal Practice addresses the valuation of real estate limited partnership interests.

owner holds title to an individual unit and an undivided partial interest in the common areas of the total condominium project—e.g., the land, the public portions of the building, the foundation, the outer walls, and the spaces provided for parking

> **condominium ownership:** A form of fee ownership of separate units or portions of multiunit buildings that provides for formal filing and recording of a divided interest in real property.

and recreation. Thus, the owner possesses a three-dimensional space within the outer walls, roof or ceiling, and floors and, along with other owners, has an undivided interest in common areas. In certain condominium projects, limited common elements also exist. In this arrangement, certain common elements—e.g., parking stalls, storage units, plots of surrounding land—are reserved for the use of some, but not all, of the condominium owners. The owners of units in a condominium project usually form an association to manage the project in accordance with adopted bylaws. The expenses of management and maintenance are divided proportionately among the owners, who pay a monthly fee.

To value individual condominium units, appraisers generally use the sales comparison approach. Recent sales of units of comparable size, location, and quality are the best indicators of value. The income capitalization approach can also be applicable if some condominium units are rented rather than occupied by the owners. For example, a leased office condominium unit could be valued by the income capitalization approach in its traditional application. The cost approach is usually not applicable in the apparaisial of any type of condominium unit, because it is difficult to estimate land value and the contributory value of common elements.

To value entire condominium projects, whether they are newly constructed buildings or conversions, appraisers typically use the sales comparison approach to establish individual unit prices and apply discounted cash flow analysis to value the whole project. Using the latter technique, the amount and timing of all capital outlays, expected monetary receipts, and returns are estimated, and these amounts are discounted at a rate consistent with competitive investment yields. The estimates of future sellout prices and the timing of sales are key elements in the valuation.

Although similar data may be used in both applications, the valuation of individual condominium units is distinct from the valuation of an entire condominium project. Appraisers do not value individual units and then sum the values to produce a value indication for the entire project. Likewise, individual units are not valued by appraising the entirety and then allocating the total value to individual units. Each assignment has separate and distinct considerations.

Cooperative Ownership

In certain areas cooperative ownership of apartments is popular. In a co-op, a stock corporation is organized, acquires title to an apartment building, prices the various apartments, and issues an authorized number of shares at a

cooperative ownership: A form of ownership in which each owner of stock in a cooperative apartment building or housing corporation receives a proprietary lease on a specific apartment and is obligated to pay a monthly maintenance charge that represents the proportionate share of operating expenses and debt service on the underlying mortgage, which is paid by the corporation. This proportionate share is based on the proportion of the total stock owned.

specified par value. Individual owners purchase shares of stock, with the price per unit determining the number of shares that an occupant must purchase. In cooperative ownership, each owner of stock receives a proprietary lease on a specific apartment and is obligated to make a monthly payment that represents the proportionate share of operating expenses and debt service on the underlying mortgage, which is paid by the corporation. The lease obligates the occupant to pay a monthly maintenance fee, which may be adjusted at times by the corporation's board of directors. The fee covers the expenses of management, operations, and maintenance of public areas. Because the shareholders can vote their shares in electing directors, they have some control over property conditions.

Recently, a method for financing cooperatives has emerged in some areas. In the past cooperative corporations arranged mortgages on entire apartment properties. Cooperative shareholders had to fund their purchases with 100% equity or borrow the money from commercial banks using short-term, personal notes. Now, however, a cooperative corporation can arrange a mortgage on the total property, and individual apartment shareholders can mortgage their stock for up to 75% of its value. These new mortgage arrangements have made cooperative apartment properties much more marketable.

If the market for cooperative apartments is active, appraisers can value individual units with the sales comparison approach. However, they must remember that prices are influenced by the amount and terms of the mortgage financing that the corporation has placed on the building. Often corporate bylaws impose limitations on the property's marketability, which can affect the validity of comparable sales data.

Timesharing

timesharing: Limited ownership interests in, or the rights of use and occupancy of, residential apartments or hotel rooms. There are two forms of timesharing: fee timeshares and non-fee timeshares. Fee timeshares may be based on timeshare ownership or interval ownership. There are three types of non-fee timeshares: a prepaid lease arrangement, a vacation license, and a club membership.

Timesharing involves the sale of either limited ownership interests in or rights to use and occupy residential apartments or hotel rooms. There are two forms of timesharing, and it is imperative that the appraiser distinguish between them when appraising timeshare projects or analyzing timeshare comparables. In the first form, *fee timesharing*, the purchaser of a fee timeshare receives a deed that conveys title to a unit for a specific part of a year, thereby limiting the ownership. The purchaser has the right to sell, lease, or bequeath the timeshare. The interest can be mortgaged and title can be recorded. The second form of timesharing, *non-fee timesharing*, does not convey a legal title in the property. Typically a purchaser receives only the right to use a timeshare unit and related premises.

There are subcategories for both types of timesharing. The two types of fee timesharing are timeshare ownership and interval ownership. In timeshare ownership a purchaser receives a deed to a particular unit as a tenant in common. Each purchaser agrees to use the unit only during the time period stipulated in the deed. In interval ownership the ownership period may only last for the duration of the project. At the end of the specified time period, the ownership reverts to the interval owners as tenants in common. They then have the option of selling the property and dividing the proceeds, or continuing as tenants in common and renewing the interval estate. Timeshare owners and interval owners pay operating expenses, including a proportionate share of taxes, insurance, and other costs and a fee for common area maintenance (CAM) and management. In many projects, 50 one-week intervals are created; the remaining two weeks of each year are reserved for maintenance and major repairs.

The three types of non-fee timesharing are known as *leasehold interest, vacation license,* and *club membership.*[3] The leasehold interest type of timesharing is essentially a prepaid lease arrangement. A vacation license involves the transfer of a license from the developer to the purchaser, giving the latter the right to use a given type of unit for specified time periods over the life of the vacation license contract. In the club membership form of ownership, timeshare patrons purchase membership for a specified number of years in a club that owns, leases, or operates the timeshare property. The purchaser receives the right to use a particular type of unit for a specified period during each year of membership.

Timeshare ownership is valued using the sales comparison approach. The appraiser begins by identifying the rights to be valued. The portion of the property allocated for use by the shareholder must be established, and any personal property included in the timeshare must be identified. In appraising existing timeshare properties, resales of comparables generally provide reliable indications of value. To value new timeshare projects, appraisers must consider the time required for sellout, seasonal variations, all direct and indirect costs required to create a timeshare project, and competition in the existing and projected market of timeshare properties.

Types of Property Interests

Regardless of the type of ownership, the owner of real property is said to have an interest in that property. An appraisal assignment can call for the valuation of the most complete interest in real property, the fee simple interest, or an

---

3.   Under the laws of some states, vacation licenses and club memberships are not considered interests in real estate, but personal property.

interest less than fee, i.e., a partial interest. Partial interests can be created in several ways:

- Economically
- Legally
- Physically
- Financially

Figure 5.3 illustrates alternatives an appraiser must consider when identifying the real property interest being appraised.

As mentioned earlier, a fee simple interest is only subject to the limitations imposed by the four powers of government. Although many appraisers state in their appraisals that the interest being valued is the fee simple interest, a true fee simple interest seldom exists as nearly all properties are encumbered by some form of easement, reservation, and/or private restriction. Often the valuation of a fee simple interest is hypothetical and is performed as the first step in the valuation of a partial interest. For example, in the valuation of a leased fee interest, the fee simple interest must also be valued to allow comparison between the two interests, which in turn will allow the appraiser to determine whether a leasehold interest is positive or negative.

Figure 5.3   **Interests Created by Real Property Ownership**

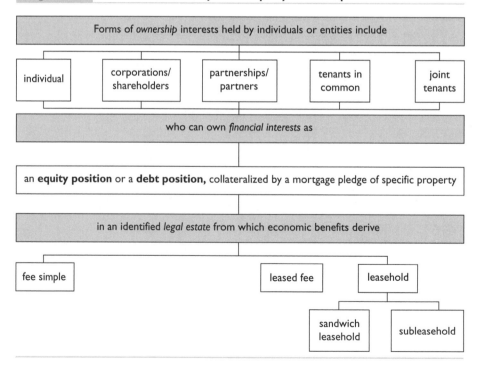

Since all partial and fractional interests are "cut out" of the fee simple interest, the appraiser must have an understanding of the fee simple interest in a property prior to appraising a fractional or partial interest.

Economic Interests

The most common type of economic interests is created when the fee simple interest is divided by a lease. In such a circumstance, the lessor and the lessee each obtain partial interests, which are stipulated in contract form and are subject to contract law. The divided interests resulting from a lease represent two distinct but related interests—the leased fee interest and the leasehold interest. Additional economic interests, including sub-leasehold (or sandwich) interests, can be created under special circumstances.

Leased Fee Interests

A leased fee interest is the lessor's, or landlord's, interest. A landlord holds specified rights that include the right of use and occupancy conveyed by lease to others. The rights of the lessor (the leased fee owner) and the lessee (leaseholder) are specified by contract terms contained within the lease. Although the specific details of leases vary, a leased fee generally provides the lessor with the following:

- Rent to be paid by the lessee under stipulated terms
- The right of repossession at the termination of the lease
- Default provisions
- The right of disposition, including the rights to sell, mortgage, or bequeath the property, subject to the lessee's rights, during the lease period

When a lease is legally delivered, the lessor must surrender possession of the property to the tenant for the lease period and abide by the lease provisions.

The lessor's interest in a property is considered a leased fee interest regardless of the duration of the lease, the specified rent, the parties to the lease, or any of the terms in the lease contract. A leased property, even one with rent that is consistent with market rent, is appraised as a leased fee interest, not as a fee simple interest. Even if the rent or the lease terms are not consistent with market terms, the leased fee interest must be given special consideration and is appraised as a leased fee interest.

The valuation of a leased fee interest is best accomplished using the income capitalization approach. Regardless of the

> Leases specify the **rights of the lessor** (e.g., to collect rent, to repossess the property upon lease expiration, to dispose of the property through sale or transfer) and the **rights of the lessee** (e.g., to use, occupy, improve, and sublease the property).

> **lessee:** One who has the right to use or occupy a property under a lease agreement; the leaseholder or tenant.
> **lessor:** One who holds property title and conveys the right to use and occupy the property under a lease agreement; the leased fee owner or landlord.

capitalization method selected, the value of the leased fee interest represents the owner's interest in the property. The benefits that accrue to an owner of a leased fee estate generally consist of income throughout the lease and the reversion at the end of the lease. The sales comparison approach can be used to value leased fee interests, but this analysis is only really meaningful when the sales being used as comparables are similar leased fee interests. If not, adjustments for real property rights conveyed must be considered. The cost approach is more suited to valuing a fee simple interest than a leased fee interest. If contract rent and terms are different than market rent and terms, the cost approach must also be adjusted to reflect the differences.

When an assignment involves the valuation of a leased fee interest, the appraiser often must also appraise the fee simple interest. If the rent and/or terms of the lease are favorable to the landlord (lessor), the value of the leased fee interest will usually be greater than the value of the fee simple interest, resulting in a negative leasehold interest. If the rent and/or terms of the lease are favorable to the tenant (or lessee), the value of the leased fee interest will usually be less than the value of the fee simple interest, resulting in a positive leasehold interest (see Figure 5.4). The negative or positive leasehold interests will cease if contract rent and/or terms equal market rent and/or terms any time during the lease or when the lease expires.

When analyzing a leased fee interest, it is essential that the appraiser analyze all of the economic benefits or disadvantages created by the lease. An appraiser should ask the following questions:

- What is the term of the lease?
- What is the likelihood that the tenant will be able to meet all of the rental payments on time?
- Are the various clauses and stipulations in the lease typical of the market, or do they create special advantages or disadvantages for either party?
- Is either the leased fee interest or the leasehold interest transferable, or does the lease prohibit transfers?
- Is the lease written in a manner that will accommodate reasonable change over time, or will it eventually become cumbersome to the parties?

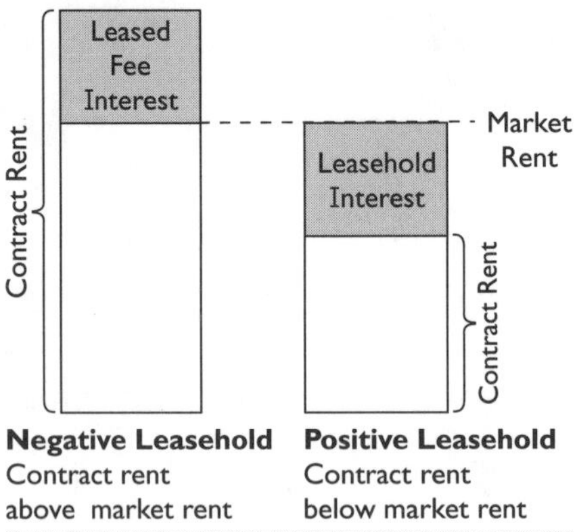

An appraiser cannot simply assume that each of the interests created by the lease has a market value. Many leases create no separate value for the tenant. For example, when the tenant cannot or will not pay the rent, the market value of the leased fee interest may be reduced to an

Figure 5.4   **Positive and Negative Leasehold Interests**

Negative Leasehold
Contract rent above market rent

Positive Leasehold
Contract rent below market rent

amount less than the market value of a comparable property that is unleased or a comparable property leased to a more reliable tenant at below-market terms.

Leasehold Interests

The leasehold estate is the lessee's, or tenant's, estate. When a lease is created, the tenant usually acquires the rights to possess the property for the lease period, to sublease the property (if this is allowed by the lease and desired by the tenant), and perhaps to improve the property under the restrictions specified in the lease. In return, the tenant is obligated to pay rent, surrender possession of the property at the termination of the lease, remove any improvements the lessee has modified or constructed (if specified), and abide by the lease provisions. The most important obligation of a tenant is to pay rent.

The relationship between contract and market rent greatly affects the value of a leasehold interest. A leasehold interest may have value if contract rent is less than market rent, creating a rental advantage for the tenant. This relationship, in turn, is likely to affect the value of the leased fee interest. The value of a leased fee interest encumbered with a fixed rent that is below market rates may be worth less than the unencumbered fee simple interest or the leased fee interest with rent at market levels. When contract rent exceeds market rent, the leasehold is said to have negative value. However, the contract advantage of the leased fee may not be marketable. Even in such circumstances, the tenant still has the right to occupy the premises and, despite the contractual disadvantage, may have other benefits that warrant continued occupancy. It is also possible that the contract disadvantage imperils the tenant's business and increases the risk of continued occupancy.

Leasehold interests are typically valued using the income capitalization approach. The income to the position is the difference between market rent and contract rent. The capitalization or discount rate selected usually depends on the relationship between contract rent and market rent, and frequently the appraiser's judgment is critical in the rate selection. Since the leasehold interest ceases to exist at the expiration of the lease, there is usually no reversion to the leasehold interest. The sales comparison approach is only meaningful in those relatively rare situations in which there are sales of

---

The market value of a **leased fee interest** depends on how contract rent compares to market rent. A **leasehold interest** may acquire value if the lease allows for subletting and the term is long enough so that market participants will pay something for the advantageous lease.

leased fee: An ownership interest held by a landlord with the rights of use and occupancy transferred by the lease to others. The rights of the lessor (the leased fee owner) and the leased fee are specified by contract terms contained within the lease.

leasehold: The interest held by the lessee (the tenant or renter) through a lease transferring the rights of use and occupancy for a stated term under certain conditions.

market rent: The rental income that a property would probably command in the open market; indicated by the current rents that are either paid or asked for comparable space as of the date of the appraisal.

contract rent: The actual rental income specified in a lease.

similar leasehold interests that the appraiser can analyze. The cost approach is rarely, if ever, applicable to the valuation of a leasehold interest.

Subleasehold or Sandwich Interests

Normally a tenant is free to sublease all or part of a property, but many leases require that the landlord's consent be obtained. A sublease is an agreement in which the tenant in an existing lease conveys to a third party the interest that the lessee enjoys (the right of use and occupancy of the property) for part or all of the remaining term of the lease. In a sublease, the original lessee is "sandwiched" between a lessor and a sublessee (see Figure 5.5). The original lessee's interest has value if the contract rent is less than the rent collected from the sublessee. Subleasing does not release the lessee from the obligations to the lessor defined in the lease agreement. A sublease may affect all the parties, including the owner of the leased fee interest, and such arrangements are common and increasingly upheld by the courts.

A lease contract may contain a provision that explicitly forbids subletting. Without either the right to sublet or a term that is long enough to be marketable, a leasehold position cannot be transferred and, therefore, has no market value. Furthermore, the value of the leased fee interest would likely be diminished in this case because a lessee who no longer has need of the leased premises and is not allowed to sublease the space is likely to default on the lease.

> **sandwich lease:** A lease in which an intermediate, or sandwich, leaseholder is the lessee of one party and the lessor of another. The owner of the sandwich lease is neither the fee owner nor the user of the property; he or she may be a leaseholder in a chain of leases, excluding the ultimate sublessee.
>
> **sublease:** An agreement in which the lessee in a prior lease conveys the right of use and occupancy of a property to another, the sublessee.

A tenant under a sublease may not have any of the rights of the leasehold interest under the original lease contract. It is also possible that the holder of the

---

Figure 5.5   Sandwich Position in a Sublease Transaction

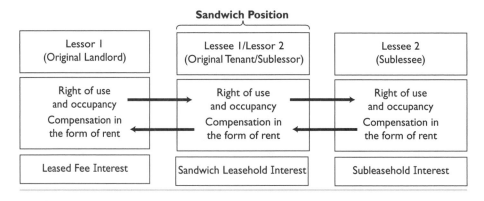

sandwich interest may offer various economic benefits that include allowing the new tenant to sublease the property. Thus, the contract between the original tenant and the subtenant may contain provisions that go beyond, but do not violate, the provisions of the original lease.

The discount rates used in valuing different lease interests will vary because the rates selected must reflect the risks involved. Generally, the leased fee interest entails less risk than the leasehold interest because the owner of the leased fee is entitled to a reversion whereas the owner of the leasehold is not. Also, the leased fee interest involves less risk because the rent is fixed and not subject to the volatility of the market. In turn, the lessee assumes less risk than the sublessee, whose position is exposed to greater risk. The subleasehold position is more risky because the subleasehold will only have value if it is rented to a subsequent subtenant for an amount that is more than the sublessee pays the original tenant.

Legal Interests

Virtually every property is subject to some kind of easement or other legal restrictions on use that creates a partial interest. Some are permanent easements, while others may only exist for a short period of time. Often appraisers have to either estimate the value of property subject to an easement or estimate the value of the easement itself. In certain ownership situations, a life estate may be created, which in turn creates several partial interests. Transferable development rights (TDRs) are another type of special partial interest created by legal circumstances.

Easements

An easement is an interest in real property that transfers use, but not ownership, of a portion of an owner's property. Easements usually permit a specific portion of a property to be used for identified purposes, such as access to an adjoining property or as the location of a certain underground utility. Although surface easements are the most common, subterranean and overhead easements are used for public utilities, subways, and bridges. Other easements may prohibit the owner of the underlying fee simple interest from certain uses of the property without giving the owner of the easement any possessory interest in the real estate, e.g., scenic easements and facade easements.

Clearly a property that enjoys the benefit of an easement gains additional rights, while a property that is subject to an easement is burdened. The easement attaches to the property benefitted and is referred to as an *easement appurtenant.* The property whose owner acquires an easement is known as the *dominant tenement;* the property that is subject to the easement is called the *servient*

> **easement appurtenant:** An easement that is attached to, benefits, and passes with the transfer of the dominant estate; runs with the land for the benefit of the dominant estate and continues to burden the servient estate, even if it is conveyed to new owners.

tenement. Easement rights can be transferred in perpetuity or for a limited time period. An easement can be created in several ways:

- By a contract between private parties
- By adverse possession in accordance with state law
- By governmental entities or public utilities through the exercise of eminent domain

Easements themselves are not usually valued. In most appraisal assignments involving easements, the value of the easement is reflected in how a property subject to an easement is affected by its presence or absence. For example, the value of a site ready for development but without the necessary easements to extend utilities to the site would be severely diminished in value by the lack of these easements. The value of an easement in and of itself is usually difficult to measure, primarily because easements are rarely sold. Paired data analysis can be used to estimate the impact on value of an easement, but only if adequate market data exists.

Under normal circumstances, a site without adequate access to allow for its development would have a value that reflects this problem. An easement that affords ingress and egress to this otherwise landlocked parcel would increase its value. Assume that market data supports a value of $10,000 for a site without sufficient access to allow its development. Now assume that if sufficient access could be acquired, the site would be worth $30,000. In this instance, the value of the property would be enhanced by $20,000 if an easement providing sufficient access could be acquired. The conclusion is reached by appraising the property twice—first before the access and then, after the access is obtained. Note that highest and best use, marketability, and other considerations must be analyzed as well.

A similar analysis can be made for a property that is diminished in value by an easement. A common example would be a property encumbered by a conservation easement. Prior to encumbrance with a conservation easement, the property has a value of $20,000 per acre, reflecting its development potential. Now assume that a conservation easement is placed on the property, removing all development rights and assuring that the property will be maintained in its natural state into perpetuity. After encumbrance with the conservation easement, the value of the property in the market may be reduced to $3,000 per acre. The diminution in value of the property is directly attributable to the conservation easement. A "before and after" appraisal methodol-

conservation easement: A restriction that limits the future use of a property to preservation, conservation, or wildlife habitat protection.

preservation easement: A restriction that prohibits certain physical changes in an historic property; usually based on the property's condition at the time the easement was acquired or immediately after proposed restoration of the property.

ogy is used to calculate the federal income tax deduction taken by a property owner who denotes a conservation or preservation easement.

Life Estates

A life estate is defined as the total rights of use, occupancy, and control of a specified property limited to the lifetime of a designated party. The designated party is generally known as the *life tenant* and is obligated to maintain the property in good condition and pay all applicable taxes during the term of the life estate. Two interests are created when a life estate is created, and both may need to be valued by an appraiser. The first interest is that of the life tenant; the second interest is that of the remainderman, who acquires the possessory interest in the property upon the death of the life tenant. Life estates can be created in several ways:

- By operations of law
- By wills
- By deeds of conveyance

For example, a fee owner may leave a will that gives land to his widow for her remaining lifetime and, at her death, the land is passed on to their children. Thus, the widow acquires a life estate and functions as a life tenant with the children becoming the remaindermen. A living fee owner may deed his property to a family member as remainderman and, by the terms of the conveyance, retain a life estate for himself. This practice might eliminate the expense of probating the will after the owner dies, but it may also call for the assessment of a gift tax.

If the life estate generates an income, the appraiser may estimate its probable duration from life expectancy statistics compiled in actuarial studies. Once the net operating income from the estate and its duration are established, an appropriate discount rate can be applied. If the life estate does not generate income, the appraiser may project its future value and then discount this value back to the current date. Because death is certain but its timing is indeterminable, discounting is generally accomplished by applying a safe rate. (The uncertainty of the timing may require the use of a range of years, which would call for a higher discount rate than the safe rate.) The discount rate selected also depends on the age and life expectancy of the person who holds the life estate.

Transferable Development Rights

Transferable development rights (TDRs), sometimes referred to as *severable use rights* (SURs), emerged in the real estate industry during the 1970s. A transferable development right is a development right that is separated from a landowner's bundle of rights and transferred, generally by sale, to another landowner in another

life tenant: One who owns an estate in real property for his or her own lifetime, the lifetime of another person, or an indefinite period limited by a lifetime.

remainderman: A person who is entitled to an estate after a prior estate or interest has expired.

> **transferable development rights (TDRs):** A development right that cannot be used by the landowner but can be sold to landowners in another location; generally used to preserve agricultural land; may also be used to preserve historic sites or buildings and open space or to protect scenic features.

location. Some TDRs preserve property uses for agricultural production, open space, or historic buildings. In this arrangement, a preservation district and a development district are identified. Landowners in the preservation district are assigned development rights, which they cannot use to develop their own land but can sell to landowners in the development district. These landowners can use the transferred rights to build at higher densities than zoning laws in the development district would normally permit.

Another situation in which development rights are transferred results from the constrained capacity of an existing utility. For example, consider a community that decides to impose a construction moratorium pending the expansion of its present sewage plant or the building of a new plant. Before the moratorium, a landowner was granted the right to hook up 100 projected single-family residences to the existing plant. A second landowner, however, did not obtain the right to link up his 50 proposed single-family residences to the sewage treatment plant and will have to wait for expansion of the plant's capacity. The second landowner risks financial loss if he cannot develop the land immediately, so he eagerly purchases the right to link up his 50 residential units to the plant from the first landowner.

Although such rights may vary from state to state, transferable development rights are generally an interest in real property only as long as they are attached to the land. When they are sold, they become personal property, becoming real property again when they are attached to another tract of land. Appraisers can value TDRs with ordinary sales comparison techniques if there are sufficient transactions to constitute a market. When market sales are lacking, the income capitalization approach may be applied. In such cases, the economic concept of contribution provides a foundation, and the value added to the property due to the acquisition of the TDR is adjusted for the administrative, legal, and other costs incurred. Some, though not all, of the property's net value increase can be attributed to the TDR; no one is likely to undertake such a complicated procedure without the prospect of a reasonable profit.

Physical Interests

Physical interests in real property can be achieved either horizontally or vertically. The most common methods of creating horizontal divisions of real property are through subdivision and assemblage. In subdivision, a large tract of land is broken down into smaller units, which are then marketed individually. In assemblage (or plottage), two or more parcels of real estate are combined into one parcel and a higher value is created for the assembled parcel than exists for the individual parcels. Consider two adjacent, half-acre industrial sites in an area where one-acre sites are most desirable. The value of the half-acre sites is $20,000 each, but when assembled the one-acre site has a value of $50,000. Conversely, when the market seeks smaller sites, the unit values of larger sites will likely be lower. Most appraisers are familiar with the valuation of horizontal interests, and traditional valuation techniques usually are applicable.

Vertical interests in real property may have to be considered separately by the appraiser in sales, leases, mortgages, and other realty transactions. The most common vertical interests in real property are subsurface rights and air rights. A subsurface right is the right to the use of and profits from the underground portion of a designated property. The term usually refers to the right to extract minerals from below the earth's surface and to construct tunnels for railroads, motor vehicles, and public utilities. Air rights are the property rights associated with the use, control, and regulation of air space over a parcel of real estate. Both of these fractional interests represent portions of a fee simple estate, and each embodies the idea of land as a three-dimensional entity.

The vertical division of real property is significant because engineering advances have dramatically affected land use and, therefore, highest and best use considerations. The development of steel-framed building construction, the passenger elevator, deep tunnel excavation techniques, and communications technology have all helped to shape the modern urban landscape. As the density of building in urban areas increases, fewer sites are available for new construction and land values escalate. This trend has produced a growing interest in developing air rights.

Air rights can be sold in fee, with the seller retaining one or more easements for a specialized use such as the operation of a railroad. They may also be subdivided, as when the owner of the fee simple interest sells or leases only the land and air that are to be occupied by a particular improvement. Air rights can be transferred in various ways as well. Often the air rights to one property are shifted to another within the same building zone under legal planning regulations. The transfer of air rights allows developers to adjust the density of land use without putting adverse pressure on owners, neighborhoods, or districts. This practice underscores the importance of local zoning authorities, which regulate building heights, building functions, setbacks, and other variables involved in the development of air rights.

subsurface rights
1. The rights to the use of and profits from the underground portion of a designated property; usually refers to the right to extract coal, minerals, oil, gas, or other hydrocarbon substances as designated in the grant; may include a right of way over designated portions of the surface.
2. The right to construct and maintain tunnels, subways, subcellars, pipelines, sewers, etc.

air rights: The right to undisturbed use and control of designated air space above a specific land area within stated elevations. Such rights may be acquired to construct a building above the land or building of another or to protect the light and air of an existing or proposed structure on an adjoining lot.

Financial Interests

The financial aspects of property interests have a major impact on real estate investment practices. The analysis of mortgage and equity components is of particular importance. Mortgage funds are secured debt positions, while equity investments are venture capital. Fee simple, leased fee, and leasehold interests can all be mortgaged, thereby subdividing these interests into mortgage and equity components. Other possible financial arrangements include senior and subordinated debt, sale-leaseback financing, and equity syndications. The influence of trends in capital markets on the valuation of real property is covered in Chapter 6.

FURTHER READING

American Association of State Highway Officials. *Acquisitions for Right of Way.* Washington, D.C., 1962.

Conroy, Kathleen. *Valuing the Timeshare Property.* Chicago: American Institute of Real Estate Appraisers, 1981.

Dombal, Robert W. *Appraising Condominiums: Suggested Data Analysis Techniques.* Chicago: American Institute of Real Estate Appraisers, 1981.

Gunn, Eleanor, and John Simpson. *Cooperative Apartment Appraisal.* Chicago: Appraisal Institute, 1997.

Keating, David Michael. *Appraising Partial Interests.* Chicago: Appraisal Institute, 1998.

Kratovil, Robert, and Raymond J. Werner. *Real Estate Law.* 10th ed. Englewood Cliffs, N.J.: Prentice-Hall, 1993.

Land Trust Alliance and National Trust for Historic Preservation. *Appraising Easements: Guidelines for Valuation of Land Conservation and Historic Preservation Easements.* 3d ed. Washington, D.C.: The Preservation Press, 1999.

Reynolds, Judith. *Historic Properties: Preservation and the Valuation Process.* 2d ed. Chicago: Appraisal Institute, 1996.

Sackman, Julius L., and Patrick J. Rohan. *Nichols' Law of Eminent Domain.* 3d rev. ed. Albany, N.Y.: Matthew Bender, 1973 (looseleaf service).

Schmutz, George L. *Condemnation Appraisal Handbook,* rev. and enl. by Edwin M. Rams. Englewood Cliffs, N.J.: Prentice-Hall, 1963.

Wolf, Peter. *Land in America: Its Value, Use, and Control.* New York: Pantheon, 1981.

CHAPTER 6
REAL ESTATE MARKETS, MONEY MARKETS, AND CAPITAL MARKETS

In valuing real property, the real estate appraiser must consider how real estate competes with other investment options for the available investment dollars. Each good and service has its own distinct market, but each must also compete with other products that the market at large may consider as trade-offs for that particular good or service. Market participants with desire and adequate purchasing power must make decisions such as

- Renting an apartment *or* buying a house
- Buying stocks and bonds *or* investing in a real estate partnership

Thus, the appraiser must understand the characteristics, advantages, weaknesses, and mechanisms of the competing investment markets that most influence real estate.

Although it is called a "market," the money market is not formally organized like the New York Stock Exchange. Rather, it is an over-the-counter operation that employs sophisticated communications and computer systems to provide traders with accurate, up-to-the-minute information on national and international transactions. Because the U.S. Federal Reserve regulates the money supply, it influences daily trading activity in the money market and the cost (i.e., interest rates) of money market funds. The money market, in turn, greatly affects the real estate industry because its short-term financing vehicles are needed to fund real estate construction and development. This is one of many ways in which the availability and cost of money regulates the volume and pace of activity in the real estate industry.

A capital market reflects the interaction of buyers and sellers trading long- or intermediate-term money instruments. Long- and intermediate-term instruments usually mature in more than one year and include

- Bonds or debentures
- Stocks
- Mortgages
- Deeds of trust

real estate market: The interaction of individuals who exchange real property rights for other assets such as money; a group of individuals or firms that are in contact with one another for the purpose of conducting real estate transactions.

money market: The interaction of buyers and sellers who trade short-term money instruments.

capital market: The interaction of buyers and sellers trading long- or intermediate-term money instruments.

Although stocks are capital market items, they are equity investments with no fixed maturities. The distinction between money markets and capital markets is not sharply defined because both involve trading in funds for varying terms and both are sources of capital for all economic activities, including real estate.

In money markets and capital markets, there are observable relationships between various instruments that stem from their differing interest rates, maturities, and investment risks. Normally an individual who invests in a long-term instrument is believed to assume greater risk than one who invests in a short-term instrument. Therefore, long-term instruments usually offer higher yields. This situation is graphically portrayed in what has come to be known as the *normal yield curve* (see Figure 6.1). The relationship is sometimes reversed. In periods of high inflation, investors are reluctant to take long-term positions. They fear that escalating interest rates will erode their capital, so they try to keep their money in short-term instruments. The Federal Reserve, however, wants to combat inflation, so it causes interest rates to rise. This action is intended to be temporary, lasting just long enough to dampen investors' inflationary expectations. Consequently, in inflationary times short-term yields may be greater than long-term yields, and the yield curve is said to be inverse.

For many years appraisers and others involved in real estate investment have debated the degree to which returns on real estate may be analogous with, or even directly parallel to, yields on other forms of investment, in particular real estate securities. The ongoing securitization of some forms of real estate investment has been accompanied by the evolution of a four-quadrant capital market (as illustrated in Figure 6.2). This

> The **two sources of capital** for real estate are the money market, trading in short-term money instruments, and the capital market, trading in long-term money instruments.

Figure 6.1   Normal Yield Curve

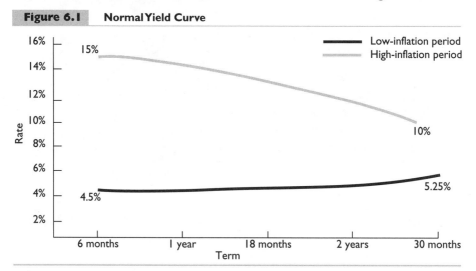

development has brought about a structural change in capital market financing for real estate. The pricing of publicly traded asset shares reflects continuous transactions in the securities market. The pricing of asset shares in the private market quadrants is readily linked to activity in the public markets.

There are both advantages and disadvantages associated with investor-driven pricing in contrast to real estate user-driven prices. Returns on certain real estate investments are becoming even more closely related to the returns on non-real estate investment alternatives. Real estate is an economic sector, however, not just another asset class. The value of real estate depends on performance, not simply investor behavior.

Relationship to Valuation Process

The various money market and capital market instruments and facilities described in this chapter should not be thought of as isolated elements. All are interrelated and exhibit sympathetic interest rate or yield movements. Certain rates—for example, those of federal funds and Treasury bills—are foundational. They are closely followed by traders and investors whose movements set rate levels and velocity throughout money markets.

In the real estate industry, development and construction sectors employ short- and medium-term funds, the cost of which largely influences a

| **Figure 6.2** | **The Four-Quadrant Investment Capital Market for Real Estate** |

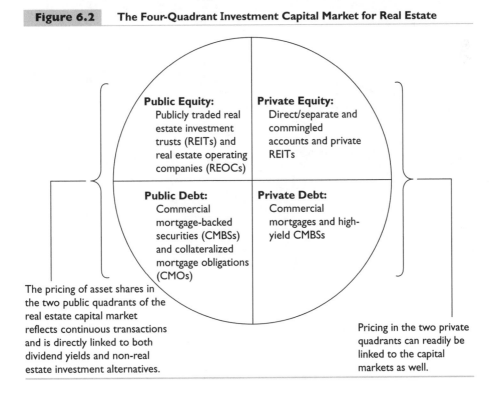

Public Equity:
Publicly traded real estate investment trusts (REITs) and real estate operating companies (REOCs)

Private Equity:
Direct/separate and commingled accounts and private REITs

Public Debt:
Commercial mortgage-backed securities (CMBSs) and collateralized mortgage obligations (CMOs)

Private Debt:
Commercial mortgages and high-yield CMBSs

The pricing of asset shares in the two public quadrants of the real estate capital market reflects continuous transactions and is directly linked to both dividend yields and non-real estate investment alternatives.

Pricing in the two private quadrants can readily be linked to the capital markets as well.

project's economic feasibility. Because this financing is priced on a variable-rate basis, with its cost tied to an index such as the commercial bank prime lending rate, cost estimating and project budgeting require interest rate forecasts covering the development period. Thus it is critical that a real estate appraiser be familiar with money markets and their activities.

Sales Comparison Approach

When mortgage financing is readily available at moderate cost, real estate markets function freely. They tend to slow to a halt when funds become scarce or unobtainable. Using high interest rates as an inflation antidote usually generates disintermediation in the thrift and life insurance industries.

RISK

Every real estate transaction contains an element of risk. A lender accepts the risk that a borrower may default on a loan. A landlord accepts the risk that tenants will not renew at the termination of a lease. Home buyers accept risks related to the quality and condition of unseen building elements and, on a larger level, the likelihood that property values in the neighborhood will go up or down in the future. Risk increases as the range of possible outcomes grows; the rate of return necessary to attract investment increases along with risk levels.

Various types of risk can affect an investment:

Market risk
Definition:	Risk that net operating income will be affected by changes in the market—e.g., shifts in demand and/or supply
Influenced by:	• Type of property
	• Location of property
	• Stage in cycle

Financial risk
Definition:	Risk related to the use of debt to finance an investment (e.g., default, prepayment, contractual financing terms that cannot respond to interest rate changes)
Influenced by:	• Amount of debt
	• Type of debt

Capital market risk
Definition:	Risk that market value will be affected by changes in capital markets—e.g., mortgage yield rates, equity yield rates, overall yield rates (due to the changes in mortgage or equity yield rates), or overall and terminal capitalization rates (due to changes in overall yield rates)
Influenced by:	• Changes in levels of interest rates
	• Changes in availability of capital (both mortgage and equity)
	• Rate of return for alternative investment opportunities

Inflation (purchasing power risk)
Definition:	Risk that unexpected inflation will cause cash flow from operations and reversion to lose purchasing power
Influenced by:	• Lease provisions that provide inflation protection

Scarce, expensive mortgage money causes market slowdowns. This prompts efforts to find alternative financial arrangements, or "creative financing," to maintain some sales volume.

In the residential real estate market, sellers are often compelled to take back purchase-money mortgages in amounts and at rates buyers can afford. If sales are structured around existing low-interest rate mortgages that are not due on sale, secondary mortgage financing must be sought from sellers or other financial sources. When large, high-quality commercial properties are involved, buyers capable of paying all cash can and do preempt the market. This crowds out buyers who require mortgage financing, which is scarce and expensive. For intermediate commercial grade and more modest properties, the investment

RISK *(continued)*

Liquidity (marketability) risk
Definition: Difficulty of converting a real estate investment into cash at market value in a reasonable time
Influenced by: • Inefficiency of real estate market

Environmental risk
Definition: Risk that the market value of a property will be affected by its physical environment
Influenced by: • Perceived health hazards
• Costs associated with dealing with potential environmental problems
• Acts of nature such as earthquakes and weather conditions

Legislative risk
Definition: Risk that legal factors will affect the market value of a property
Influenced by: • Tax law changes
• Environmental regulations
• Change in land use regulations (zoning)
• Ability to navigate permitting process

Management risk
Definition: Risk that the management cannot ensure that the property meets defined goals
Influenced by: • Competency of management
• Type of property (e.g., regional malls require more intensive management than warehouses)

Each of these types of risk can influence a property separately or in combinations. For example, a change in federal tax laws (legislative risk) may lead to changes in the required equity yield rate (capital market risk), or unexpected inflation (inflation risk) can cause mortgage interest rates to rise (capital market risk).

Comparable properties in the income capitalization approach should have the same degree of risk as the subject because risk is a consideration in the selection of overall capitalization and yield rates.

disintermediation: The transfer of money from low interest-bearing accounts to higher interest-bearing accounts.

market dries up and dies. Use of a high interest rate cure for inflation clearly diminishes the availability of comparables for use in the sales comparison approach.

In such situations, more than lower interest rates is needed to improve mortgage capital availability; there must be proper relationships between certain money rates. For example, if commercial bank certificate of deposit rates maintain a significant margin over U.S. Treasury bill rates, most savers will be persuaded to place their money in money market investment funds rather than in thrift institutions. None of this money will be available for mortgage loans.

Drastic money fluctuations and unpredictable interest rates are negative factors, retarding mortgage activity and slowing real estate investment activity. Under these conditions, lenders are constrained to keep very liquid, investing their available funds in high-quality, short-term debt instruments rather than in long-term, fixed-rate mortgages.

Income Capitalization Approach

The income capitalization approach is based on anticipation. Value may be expressed as the present worth of anticipated future benefits, and valuation involves a discounting of these benefits. One key element is the selection of an appropriate discount rate. One view is that the rate is basically a weighted average of the costs of the mortgage capital and equity funds used to create the investment. Credit stringency causes intense capital competition and high rates; more available credit loosens the market and tends to moderate rates. Changes of this sort clearly affect capitalization rates.

Although the capitalization rate may be a key valuation element, the forecast of investment benefits is of equal importance. An investor looks for income earnings over the term of the investment and hopes to realize reversionary profits upon its disposition. These benefits are clearly influenced by monetary conditions, particularly those related to inflation. The forecast of anticipated benefits should be based on the most complete information obtainable on real estate, capital, and money markets and employ logical and appropriate procedures.

Cost Approach

Money market and capital market activities are important in the cost approach because they affect land values, cost estimates, and depreciation.

Land Values

An owner of land for sale usually capitalizes ownership costs such as debt service and taxes. Inflationary interest rate escalations certainly cause mortgage debt service increases. Cities, towns, and counties incur higher capital borrowing costs in providing municipal services, and this brings about substantial increases in real estate tax burdens.

Cost Estimates

Proper cost estimates require interest rate forecasts covering the contemplated building period. Many real estate projects are so large that two to three years are required to complete construction and to achieve full occupancy and stabilized operation. To finance these operations, construction funds are acquired through building loan contracts with variable costs (interest rates) tied to an index such as the commercial bank prime lending rate.

Although certain loans include rate float ceiling and floor limitations, the more common arrangement provides for unlimited movement. Because building loan interest is the major "soft," or indirect, construction cost, its proper estimation calls for a long-term interest rate forecast. Because interest rates are volatile and affected by the Federal Reserve's monetary policies, the task is difficult but necessary. Hard construction costs, such as materials and labor, are also influenced by interest rate variations. Price escalations of this nature are called *cost-push inflation.*

Depreciation

Depreciation is often described as the difference between cost and value. During inflationary periods, when money costs escalate sharply, construction costs rise rapidly. As a result, the base building cost from which depreciation is subtracted shows substantial growth.

In income-producing properties, such as rental housing, income growth often lags behind operating expense increases, which erodes net earnings. At the same time, capitalization rates rise in response to interest rate escalations. This results in a reduction in investment values, and with rising replacement costs the measure of depreciation grows substantially. In other types of income-producing properties, such as shopping centers and office buildings, leases may call for rent escalations and overages that match and sometimes exceed the growth of operating expenses. In these cases, depreciation does not experience inflation-related growth.

Real Estate Markets

Buyers and sellers of different types of property interact in different areas for different reasons. Thus, real estate markets are divided into categories based on property types and their appeal to different market participants. The markets for various categories of real estate are further divided into submarkets, which correspond to the preferences of buyers and sellers. Differentiating real estate markets facilitates their study.

All real estate markets are influenced by the attitudes, motivations, and interactions of buyers and sellers of real property, which in turn are subject to many social, economic, governmental, and environmental influences. Real estate markets may be studied in terms of their geographic, competitive, and supply-and-demand characteristics, which relate to overall real estate market conditions.

The identification and interpretation of real estate markets are analytical processes. To answer questions about real estate markets and submarkets, appraisers analyze the utility and scarcity of property as well as the desires and effective purchasing power of those who seek to acquire property rights.

Characteristics of Real Estate Markets

The efficiency of a market is based on assumptions about the behavior of buyers and sellers as well as the characteristics of the products traded. Real estate markets differ significantly from the markets for other goods and services and have never been considered truly efficient markets (see Table 6.1).

In recent years, the securitization of real estate and increased access to property and transaction information, along with other changes in the larger economy, have made real estate markets more efficient than they once were. Efficiency in the real estate market has a direct bearing on rate of return requirements. Consequently, a purchaser who understands the inefficiencies of the real estate market can gain benefits in terms of rates of return, relatively stable income, inflation protection (usually), and other factors.

Real estate market analysis focuses on the motivations, attitudes, and interaction of market participants as they respond to the particular characteristics of real estate and to external influences that affect its value. This focus underscores the need for objective real estate appraisal in a free market economy and the responsibility of appraisers to the communities they serve. (Real estate market analysis is discussed in detail in Chapter 11.)

Real Estate Cycles

In the years following World War II (1946–1966), distinct patterns emerged in real estate and general business cycles. As business prospered, the demand for capital intensified, inflation accelerated, and an oversupply of goods and services was produced. Then Federal Reserve monetary policy and other economic controls would be used to slow the pace of the economy and a recession would ensue.

When Congress wanted to revive the economy, the industry invariably selected to provide economic stimulation was real estate, particularly home building.[1] Programs were developed to provide abundant, moderately priced mortgage money. These programs usually involved loan insurance or guarantees to induce capital managers to participate. Because there was a substantial demand for housing, the programs were well received and residential development expanded, increasing employment in all economic sectors. Manufacturers of hardware, supplies (e.g., heating, plumbing, and electrical), paints, furniture, equipment, and other goods saw business improve. The economy finally revived, then inflation started to accelerate, and the cycle was repeated.

---

1.   In developing countries and countries making the transition from a state-controlled economy to a market economy, promoting home ownership has been seen as a way of stabilizing the economy and establishing a middle class.

Table 6.1	Comparison of Efficient Markets and Real Estate Markets
Efficient Markets	**Real Estate Markets**
Goods and services are essentially homogeneous items that are readily substituted for one another.	No two parcels of real estate are physically identical.
The quality of goods and services tends to be fairly uniform, so prices are relatively low and stable.	Prices are not low.
A large number of market participants creates a competitive, free market, and none of these participants has a large enough share of the market to have a direct and measurable influence on price.	There are usually only a few buyers and sellers interested in a particular type of property at one time, in one price range, and in one location. An individual buyer or seller can influence price through exertion of control on supply and/or demand.
An efficient market is self-regulating. Open and free competition is subject to few restrictions.	Real estate markets are subject to regulation by many private and public entities.
Supply and demand are never far out of balance. The market returns to equilibrium quickly through the effects of competition.	In real estate markets, supply and demand are considered causal factors and price is the result of their interaction. Price changes usually are preceded by changes in market activity. Often supply or demand may shift suddenly in a period of no activity or increased activity.
Buyers and sellers are knowledgeable and fully informed about market conditions, the behavior of other market participants, past market activity, product quality, and product substitutability. Any information needed on bids, offers, and sales is readily available.	Buyers and sellers of real estate may not be well informed.
Buyers and sellers are brought together by an organized market mechanism, such as the New York Stock Exchange. Sellers can easily enter and exit the market in response to demand.	Buyers and sellers are not brought together formally.
Goods are readily consumed, quickly supplied, and easily transported from place to place.	Real estate is a durable product and, as an investment, it may be relatively unmarketable and illiquid.

When loan insurance and guarantee programs supplied inexpensive long-term capital, real estate prospered and the general economy expanded.

The larger economic cycle (see Figure 6.3) influences the real estate cycle, and so do demographic cycles and business cycles. As the economy expands, competition for capital intensifies, the costs of goods and services increase, and inflation escalates. The Fed then seeks to combat inflation by tightening money and credit until the economy slows down. The demand for funds subsides, interest rates decline, and economic conditions become stable enough for businesses to expand. When the frequency of the economic cycle

Figure 6.3 **Real Estate Cycles and Economic Cycles**

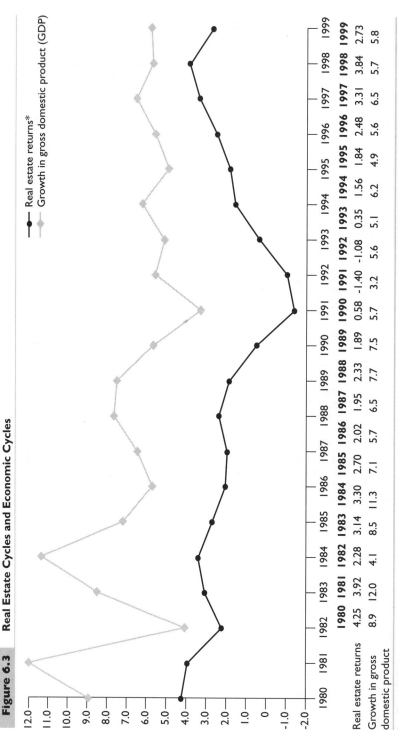

	1980	1981	1982	1983	1984	1985	1986	1987	1988	1989	1990	1991	1992	1993	1994	1995	1996	1997	1998	1999
Real estate returns	4.25	3.92	2.28	3.14	3.30	2.70	2.02	1.95	2.33	1.89	0.58	-1.40	-1.08	0.35	1.56	1.84	2.48	3.31	3.84	2.73
Growth in gross domestic product	8.9	12.0	4.1	8.5	11.3	7.1	5.7	6.5	7.7	7.5	5.7	3.2	5.6	5.1	6.2	4.9	5.6	6.5	5.7	5.8

* The NCREIF Property Index (NPI) tracks the performance of properties that are acquired on behalf of tax-exempt institutions in all-cash, unleveraged transactions and are held under a fiduciary or trusteeship arrangement. The formulas used to calculate the periodic rate of return over the holding period differ substantially from the methodology applied by appraisers to analyze period-to-period change in value.

Source: NCREIF average annual national NPI returns (http://www.ncreif.com/sub_ret_national.htm) and Bureau of Economic Advisors (http://www.bea.doc.gov/bea/dn/st1.txt)

accelerates and its range increases, business and money conditions change drastically and rapidly. This creates an unattractive economic environment for long-term investments.

The position of a real estate market in its cycle (see Figure 6.4) is determined by several factors:

- Supply
- Demand
- Vacancy
- Rents
- Capitalization rates
- Investor demand

The first four factors relate to the markets for real estate space, while the last two factors are functions of the financial markets. Trends in real estate markets can be measured by the interaction of several related market statistics:

- Vacancy rates
- Rental growth rates
- Capitalization rates
- Home price changes
- Changes in supply

If vacancy rates rise, rents will fall and capitalization rates will rise; if vacancy falls, then rents will rise and capitalization rates will fall. There is a lag in real estate markets while the market participants react to new information. Vacancy rates, which are one of the most readily available statistics, may

Figure 6.4   Real Estate Cycle

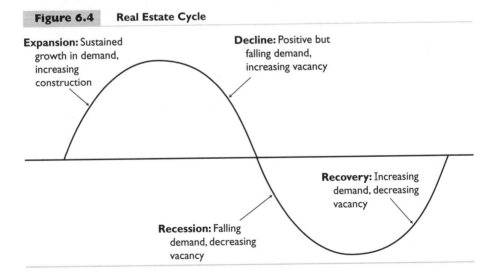

Expansion: Sustained growth in demand, increasing construction

Decline: Positive but falling demand, increasing vacancy

Recovery: Increasing demand, decreasing vacancy

Recession: Falling demand, decreasing vacancy

begin to fall, but rental rates will not change until the market has noticed the change in vacancy. Similarly, capitalization rates will not change until the trend in rental rates (and the potential gross income for a property) is evident.

In the 1990s, what became known as the "new economy" promised to eliminate, or at least smooth, the traditional business cycle of expansion, contraction, recession, and recovery. Applying information technology to inventory control was supposed to ensure that production never got too far ahead of sales, improving the efficiency of the operations of manufacturing companies. The economic downturn in the United States at the end of the 1990s proved some of these claims to be overly optimistic, but continued gains in productivity may be realized from greater use of information technology. The Internet is generally acknowledged as reducing transaction costs, promoting disintermediation, and, in real estate markets, helping eliminate the lag between the interrelated cycles of vacancy rates, rents, and capitalization rates.

Real estate appraisers need to know where a real estate market is in its cycle because certain types of assignments are more prevalent at different stages of the cycle:

- Foreclosures, bankruptcies, and tax appeal assignments are more common during a market contraction or recession.
- Appraisals for financing and traditional real estate transactions are more common during the upswing of a cycle, i.e., both the recovery and expansion phases.
- Many clients need appraisal consulting services when a market is expanding or contracting around its peak, the best time to sell an investment-grade property.

Likewise, real estate investors want to know when to hold or sell a property, when to write a long-term or short-term lease, when to hold down expenses, and when to invest in renovations and refurbishment. These questions and others require an opinion of the state of the real estate cycle.

Money Markets

money: The accepted common medium of exchange for goods and services in the marketplace.

The parties to a business transaction agree on the value of the good or service and this value is expressed in terms of *money*. The term *money* is difficult to define and various definitions are used by economists, but whether the money supply is defined in terms of currency, account balances, or both, its value is influenced by its availability. Although important relationships are well established, they are subject to variable exchange ratios for national currencies and the rapid movement of free-flowing funds.

Supply and demand relationships set the cost, or price, of money. When money becomes plentiful, the price declines; as it becomes scarce, the price

INFLATION

Inflation occurs when the general level of prices rises. The inflation rate is the rate of change in the price level as reflected in the Consumer Price Index (CPI). Other useful measures of inflation include the wholesale price index and the GDP implicit price deflator.

Inflation and appreciation have similar effects on future dollars but different effects on yield rates. Inflation tends to increase yield rates (and most rates of return) because investors require a higher nominal rate of return to offset the loss in purchasing power due to inflation. Appreciation will not affect the yield rate unless the risk associated with the property has changed.

In oversupplied markets, real estate may not always keep up with inflation. In an inflationary environment, the value of real estate may tend to increase with the value of other investments such as stocks and bonds. Rents under annual leases can be adjusted upward periodically, while the interest and dividends paid on longer-term securities are more fixed. In oversupplied commercial markets, rent spikes are sometimes used to allow market rents to catch up to levels that would have otherwise been achieved by annual inflationary increases in rents. Rent spikes are generally a function of demand.

The economic importance of inflation can be seen in the concept of "real" interest rates. Nominal interest rates, which are reported daily in the financial press, are said to be composites of the "real" cost of funds, or the real interest rate, and the premiums that investors demand to protect their currency value from being eroded by inflation. Thus, the nominal rate equals the real interest rate plus a premium for expected inflation. Economists suggest that the real interest rate has historically remained steady at 3% to 4%. Therefore, if the capital market were to show a nominal rate of 6% for 10-year U.S. Treasury notes, the real interest rate concept would indicate an inflation premium of 2%.

> 6% (nominal rate) − 4% (real interest rate) = 2% (inflation premium)*

> **inflation:** An erosion of the purchasing power of currency characterized by price escalation and an increase in the volume of money, i.e., the proliferation of monetary units and consequent decline in the value of each unit. Inflation tends to increase discount rates because investors require a higher nominal rate of return to offset the loss in value due to inflation. Investors often include an additional risk premium in the required rate of return on investments that do not respond well to unexpected inflation.

> **appreciation:** An increase in property value resulting from an excess of demand over supply.

An appraiser can account for the effects of inflation in capitalization by expressing future benefits in constant dollars, which are adjusted to reflect constant purchasing power. An appraiser can also express the yield rate as a real, uninflated rate of return on capital. In practice, however, appraisers usually project income and expenses in unadjusted, inflated dollars and express the discount rate as a nominal, or apparent, rate of return on capital that includes an allowance for inflation.

---

* In countries with low inflation like the United States, this formula is an adequate approximation. A more precise formula for computing the real interest rate would be

(1 + nominal rate) / (1 + inflation rate) = 1 + real interest rate

(1 + 0.06) / (1 + 0.02) = 1.03921, rounded to 1.04, or a real interest rate of 4%

> In the United States, the **money supply** is regulated by the credit policies of the Federal Reserve System, the fiscal policies of the Treasury Department, and supply and demand relationships.

rises. The price of money is expressed as an interest rate—i.e., the cost to borrow funds. Interest rates are particularly important in the real estate industry because most investments are created by combining debt and equity funds. When the demand for money is high and its supply is low, capital costs, or interest rates, increase. These higher interest rates, which are components of the capitalization and discount rates developed for valuation, affect real property values.

There is a difference between money and other commodities on the supply side of the pricing formula. The demand for money is a product of the operation of economic forces. The supply of money available for lending is a function of the level of savings, which reflects personal, corporate, and governmental accumulation, both domestic and foreign.

Economics determines the amount of savings, but the quantity of U.S. currency is subject to regulation by the Federal Reserve System (the Fed). The Fed has the power to regulate general interest rate levels, which strongly influence the discount rates and overall capitalization rates used in real estate valuation.[2] Housing affordability is greatly influenced by prevailing mortgage rates. For example, an increase of a single percentage point in the interest rate, from 7% to 8%, on a $150,000 interest-only mortgage would increase the monthly mortgage payment by $125, which may cause a significant number of households with a certain level of purchasing power to be priced out of the market for home ownership.

The bills and coins that constitute money are interchangeable (fungible) and can be used in all economic activities. Holders of capital will invest in whatever they believe will produce the optimum yield, considering the risk and maturity involved. Competition for capital involves all economic sectors.

Fiscal Policy

While the Fed determines monetary policy, the Department of the Treasury manages the government's financial activities by raising funds and paying bills. When income matches or exceeds spending, the federal budget is balanced. When the outflow of funds exceeds collections, a federal deficit results. Spending that is not covered by tax funds produces deficits, which are financed by the sale of public debt instruments such as government bonds, bills, and notes issued by the Treasury. When deficits are monetized by selling large amounts of debt, the Fed is tacitly expected, though not mandated, to cooperate by supplying the banking system with sufficient reserves to accommodate the debt sales program and still leave enough credit for the private sector.

---

2.   In foreign countries, various central banks perform the same functions as the Fed, and they generally have the same powers.

FEDERAL RESERVE SYSTEM AND CREDIT REGULATION

The Federal Reserve System is independent of the U.S. Congress and the president; this independence distinguishes it from central banks in most other countries, which are government entities. Although the Fed is independent, it functions within the general structure of the U.S. Government, operating in accordance with national economic policies.

The Federal Reserve regulates money and credit, which are the lifeblood of the real estate industry. Therefore, appraisers should be familiar with the Fed's day-to-day activities as they affect the supply of money and the level of interest rates. Because of the global nature of financial markets, the prevalence of instantaneous communications, and the securitization of realty interests, the monetary activities of the central bank can have an impact on real estate markets, just as they affect the markets for stocks and bonds.

The Fed uses three principal credit-regulation devices to accomplish the duties assigned to it by Congress:

1. Reserve requirements
2. The discount rate
3. The Federal Open Market Committee

In periods of economic crisis, the Fed supplies financial markets with necessary liquidity.

Reserve Requirements

Within statutory limits, the Federal Reserve Board can fix the amount of reserves that member banks must maintain. If the Fed wants to restrict the money supply, it increases deposit reserve obligations; if it wants to increase the supply, it lowers the obligations.

Federal Discount Rate

Banks in the Federal Reserve System can borrow from the Fed and obtain funds for their customers even in periods of great demand. To get these loans, member banks agree to pay the Federal Reserve interest at its established discount rate. The Fed can deny loan requests when it believes that borrowing is not in the best interests of the national or regional economy.

The borrowing privilege is a vehicle for expanding the monetary supply; curtailing that privilege limits or contracts credit. The federal discount rate helps determine the prime rate, the interest rate that a commercial bank charges for short-term loans to borrowers with high credit ratings. The federal discount rate is generally about two percentage points below the prime rate.

Federal Open Market Committee

The Federal Open Market Committee (FOMC) is probably the most extensively used and most potent of the Federal Reserve's credit-regulating devices. The FOMC buys and sells U.S. government securities in the open market, thereby exerting a powerful influence on the supply of money and the interest rate. In fact, through its daily operations, the FOMC maintains short-term money rates at selected target levels.

Fed Watchers

Financial market participants may be guided by the opinions of experts, called *Fed watchers*, who often correctly interpret and predict Fed policy by analyzing the committee's activities. Real estate investors and appraisers, whose success may also depend on interpreting and forecasting financial markets, may profit from the extensive information provided by Fed watchers.

Money Market Instruments

The prices of financial instruments, which are established in a free and active money market, determine their investment yields. These yields consist of the instruments' face, or stated, interest rates plus any price discounts earned or minus any price premiums paid. The price or cost of money is properly called an *interest rate* because when a borrowing instrument is created, it carries that day's market interest level for the risk rating and maturity involved.

Money markets, which deal in instruments with maturities of one year or less, are especially important to real estate development activities. Construction loans are short-term mortgages with variable interest rates that are tied to market indexes. For example, borrowing costs in the market might be two to four percentage points above the prime rate, which is the short-term loan rate that commercial banks offer to favored customers. When the demand for short-term money is intense and the supply is limited, market interest rates escalate and construction funds become expensive. The high real estate carrying costs that result can destroy economic feasibility and cause project failures and even bankruptcies.

The anticipated cost and availability of short-term funds are key considerations for developers, and their perceptions cause real estate activity to expand or contract. Appraisers must factor projected construction loan costs, which constitute a large portion of soft costs, into their cost approach valuations. This is particularly important when appraising projects that will require more than one year to complete.

In money markets, various instruments and arrangements are offered and sold by the federal government, banks, corporations, and local governments. Important instruments include

interest rate: The price of money; the level of market interest carried by a debt instrument from the day it is created over the duration of its life. The rate of return or yield rate on debt capital, usually expressed as the nominal annual percentage of the amount loaned or invested.

- Federal funds
- Treasury bills and Treasury notes
- Other government securities
- Repurchase and reverse repurchase agreements
- Certificates of deposit
- Commercial paper
- Bankers' acceptances
- Municipal notes
- Eurodollars

Short-term money market instruments include federal funds, Treasury bills and notes, repurchase and reverse repurchase agreements, certificates of deposit, commercial paper, bankers' acceptances, municipal notes, and Eurodollars.

These instruments are defined in Table 6.2.

Capital Markets

Traditional real estate investment practices involve the use of two types of capital—debt and equity—and a typical venture is structured with a substan-

Table 6.2	**Money Market Instruments**
Instrument	**Characteristics**
Federal funds	Funds available at a Federal Reserve Bank, including excess reserves of member banks and checks drawn to pay for purchases of government securities by the Federal Reserve Bank. Member banks may borrow these funds to meet Federal Reserve requirements.
Treasury bills or Treasury notes	Intermediate securities with maturities of one to ten years.
Other government securities	Securities created and sold by government-sponsored agencies such as the Federal National Mortgage Corporation, the Federal Farm Credit System, the Federal Home Loan Bank, the World Bank, and the Federal Land Bank.
Repurchase agreements and reverse repurchase agreements	Short-term financing arrangements made by securities dealers, banks, and the Federal Reserve System in which a person who needs funds for a short period uses a portfolio of money market investments as collateral and sells an interest in the portfolio with the obligation to repurchase it, with interest, at a specified future time. A reverse repurchase agreement refers to the obligation of the security dealer, bank, or Federal Reserve System to relinquish control over the portfolio upon fulfillment of the terms by the borrower; also called *repos.*
Certificates of deposit (CDs)	A financial instrument that represents a time deposit with a banking organization.
Commercial paper	A corporation's promissory notes used to borrow short-term funds for current operations; through trading, organizations with excess cash lend to those in need of money.
Bankers' acceptances	A bank's obligation or promise to pay; similar to commercial paper in that it is a marketable, short-term obligation.
Municipal notes	Short-term, federally tax-exempt obligations of local governments, e.g., villages, cities, counties, that are used to finance current operations until satisfactory long-term funds are obtained.
Eurodollars	Monies such as U.S. dollars deposited outside their countries of origin and used in foreign money markets, especially markets in Europe and the Far East.

tial mortgage amount and a smaller equity contribution. The most common capital market instruments are

Long- and intermediate-term **capital market instruments** include bonds, stocks, mortgages (including junior liens and home equity loans), and deeds of trust.

- Bonds
- Stocks
- Mortgages
- Deeds of trust

Appraisers must keep in mind that the conditions influencing the use of long-term, fixed-, or variable-rate instruments may change over time. Appraisers and market analysts must keep abreast of shifts in monetary policy that invariably produce market changes and interpret how they may influence the financing arrangements discussed below.

Bonds

A bond is a capital market instrument with a fixed interest rate issued for a term of one year or more. The bond market is closely related to real estate investment activities. Real estate is normally bought with a combination of equity capital and medium- to long-term debt funds, called *mortgage money*. Most real estate deals are structured with a substantial amount of mortgage money and a smaller amount of equity, or venture, funds. Institutions with long-term capital to invest usually survey bond markets, then examine mortgage opportunities, and finally make investment decisions to secure the best earnings for the risk involved by charging interest some number of basis points higher than the interest rate charged on a bond of the same maturity. The municipal bond yields observed in daily trading reflect investors' after-

YIELD LEVELS

Appraisers consult daily financial market reports to study money market activity for indications of changing monetary costs and values. These reports provide information on various debt and equity instruments and their yield rates. This information represents the market's discounting of economic futures, reflecting the state of the economy and possibly affecting real estate industry operations directly or indirectly. The sample report from the *New York Times* daily financial section shows the yield levels evidenced in the day's debenture trading. This information is also available from various online sources.

yield spread: The difference in yield between different investments, usually investments of different credit quality or risk.

Key Rates (Reported on 6/6/01)

	Yesterday	Previous Day	Year Ago
Prime rate	7.00	7.00	9.50
Discount rate	3.50	3.50	6.00
Federal funds†	4.00	4.03	6.46
3-mo. Treas. bills	3.54	3.59	5.73
6-mo. Treas. bills	3.47	3.52	5.94
10-yr. Treas. notes	5.27	5.32	6.11
30-yr. Treas. bonds	5.65	5.68	5.94
Telephone bonds	7.78	7.82	8.20
Municipal bonds‡	5.36	5.39	6.00

† Estimated daily average, source Telerate
‡ Municipal Bond Index, The Bond Buyer
Salomon Smith Barney; Telerate; The Bond Buyer

The yield levels of bonds are fixed by the contract between the buyer and seller of the bonds, but in real estate few of the elements needed to forecast yield and risk can be fixed in that manner. Comparing the yield spreads with some designated riskless rate that investors require for various assets in competitive markets indicates the levels of risk associated with a real estate investment. Given a range of yield rates, investors make judgments about the investment's uncertainties based on the characteristics of the property or the community in which it is located.

Yield levels are most sensitive to the following:

• Cost to construct, remodel, or acquire
• Loan ratio to cash costs
• Interest rate and rate of repayment of principal
• Real estate taxes
• Operating expenses
• Cost of land*

Several of these items are characteristics of real estate markets and others are characteristics of the financial markets.

* Stephen P. Jarchow, editor, *Graaskamp on Real Estate* (Washington, D.C.: Urban Land Institute, 1992), 253.

tax earnings requirements for a wide range of risk ratings. A popular proxy for these bonds is the Bond Buyers Index, which is published in the financial press. Some bonds are traded on organized exchanges such as the New York Stock Exchange, but many others are traded over the counter.

Stocks/REITs

A stock is an ownership share in a company or corporation. A stock corporation is a common legal entity in which investors provide organizational capital by buying shares that represent ownership and a right to all proprietary benefits. These shares are subject to the prior claims of operating expenses and debt service on the capital raised by selling bonds, debentures, and other money market instruments. Shareholder benefits consist of any cash or stock dividends declared, augmented by share price appreciation or diminished by price depreciation.

Real estate owners and developers did not look to stock markets as capital sources until real estate securitization began to grow in the early 1990s. Following the savings and loan crisis, many traditional real estate development companies restructured themselves as REITs, which can offer stock on the open market to raise capital for real estate acquisition and development and take advantage of the tax benefits REIT status allows. While the stock market establishes the value of REITs, the income performance of these assets tracks that of real estate markets. REIT prices tend to be less volatile than the Standards and Poor's 500, and the correlation between large cap stocks and REITs has been declining since 1990. Increasingly, analysts and money managers are pointing to REITs as major diversification tools.

Mortgages

A mortgage is a legal instrument for pledging a described property interest as collateral or security for the repayment of a loan under certain terms and conditions. Mortgage loans supply most of the capital employed in real estate

debt
1. One of two characteristic types of investment, the other being equity. The debt investor expects a priority claim on investment earnings and looks for security in the form of a lien on the assets involved. Debt investors participate in bonds or mortgages and receive fixed or variable interest on investments with repayment of the principal upon maturity.
2. Money borrowed, usually for a specified period of time, which may be secured or unsecured.

equity: The ownership claim on property. Total property value is obtainable by adding equity to the debt claim. Equity investors assume greater risk and their earnings are subordinate to operating expenses and debt service. They are compensated with dividends (cash flows) and possible appreciation in the value of their investments. Equity includes the residual claim to the assets, which is solely possessed by the owners.

bond: A debt instrument issued for a period of more than one year for the purpose of raising capital by borrowing. The federal government, states, cities, corporations, and many other types of institutions sell bonds. A bond is generally a promise to repay the principal along with interest on a specified date (maturity).

stock: The ownership shares of a company or corporation.

stock corporation: A common legal entity in which investors provide organizational capital by subscribing to shares that represent ownership and a right to all proprietary benefits, but are subject to the prior claims of operating expenses and debt service on capital raised by selling bonds, debentures, and other money market instruments.

mortgage: A pledge of a described property interest as collateral or security for the repayment of a loan under certain terms and conditions.

investments. A borrower gives a lender a lien on real estate as assurance that the loan will be repaid. If the borrower fails to make the debt service payments, the lender can foreclose the lien and acquire the real estate, thereby offsetting the loss.

The parties to a mortgage are usually free to contract in any fashion they desire, subject only to limitations of usury and public policy. Traditional mortgage loans are made for long terms of 20 to 30 years and carry fixed interest rates. A level-payment mortgage, which requires the same dollar amount of payment each period for the entire loan term, is the most popular contract. The payments are calculated to pay interest at a certain rate and to amortize the loan fully over its term so that less of each successive payment is required for interest and more is available for debt reduction. Other payment arrangements and schedules are also used, the most notable examples being variable-rate and balloon mortgages. (Other types of mortgages categorized by their repayment characteristics are shown in Table 6.3.)

A borrower may pledge a real property interest to more than one lender, thereby creating several liens; in such cases, the time sequence or order of the liens is important.

- The first loan contract executed and recorded is the **first mortgage,** which has priority over all subsequent transactions.

- **Second and third mortgages** are sometimes referred to as *junior liens.* Because they involve more lending risk than first mortgages, higher rates of interest are charged for second and third mortgages, which typically have shorter terms.

- **Home equity loans** are another common type of junior lien. Home equity loans generally run for terms of about five years, shorter than second or third mortgages, and, if the payments made cover only the interest on the loan, the principal is repaid in a lump sum at the end of the loan term. Many banks and thrift institutions deal in home equity loans on an enormous scale. Home owners use this type of financing for non-real estate purchases such as cars or appliances, which were formerly made by installment contracts. Home equity loans are popular because the interest paid on such loans may be deductible within certain limits. Home equity loans are also used to establish credit lines. In this arrangement, the borrower only pays interest on the amount borrowed.

junior lien: A lien placed on property after a previous lien has been made and recorded; a lien made subordinate to another by agreement; e.g., second and third mortgages; also called *second lien* or *third lien.*

Table 6.3	**Repayment Characteristics of Mortgages**

Type	**Repayment Characteristics**
Interest-only mortgage	Nonamortizing loan in which the lender receives interest only during the term of the loan and recovers the principal in a lump sum at the time of maturity.
Direct reduction mortgage	A mortgage repaid in periodic, usually equal, installments that include repayment of part of the principal and the interest due on the unpaid balance. Although the payments are level, the amount of principal and interest varies with each payment. In the most common type of direct reduction mortgage, the interest component decreases with each payment while the principal or amortization component increases.
Adjustable variable-rate mortgage	Mortgage with an interest rate that may move up or down following a specified schedule or in accordance with the movements of a standard or index to which the interest rate is tied.
Wraparound mortgage	A mortgage subordinate to, but inclusive of, any existing mortgage(s) on a property. Usually, a third-party lender refinances the property, assuming the existing mortgage and its debt service which are wrapped around a new, junior mortgage. A wraparound lender gives the borrower the difference between the outstanding balance on the existing mortgage(s) and the face amount of the new mortgage. Wraparound mortgages became widespread in periods of high mortgage rates and appreciating property values, but they have generally fallen into disuse with declining mortgage rates.
Participation mortgage	The lender receives a share of the income and sometimes the reversion from a property on which the lender has made a loan. Lenders may opt for this type of arrangement either as a hedge against inflation or as a means of increasing their total yield on the loan.
Shared appreciation mortgage	The borrower receives assistance in the form of capital when buying the real property in return for a portion of the property's future appreciation in value.
Convertible mortgage	The lender may choose to take an equity interest in the real estate in lieu of cash amortization payments by the borrower. In this way the mortgage interests of the lender may be converted into equity ownership at specified times during the life of the mortgage.
Graduated-payment mortgage	Designed to aid borrowers by matching mortgage payments to projected increases in income, this type of mortgage has periodic payments that start out low and gradually increase. Because the borrower's payments in the early years of the loan are not sufficient to pay the entire interest due or to amortize the mortgage, the borrower actually borrows the difference between the payments and the current interest due.
Zero-coupon mortgage	Debt secured by real estate with interest payments accruing rather than being paid by the borrower; in some circumstances, a rate of interest may be ascribed—e.g., for income taxation.
Reverse annuity mortgage (RAM)	A negative amortization mortgage that allows owners to use some or all of the equity they have accumulated in their property as retirement income while retaining ownership of the property. Typically, the loan increases as more money is borrowed and unpaid interest on the outstanding balance accumulates up to an agreed-upon amount, which is generally scheduled to coincide with the sale of the property.
Purchase-money mortgage (PMM)	A mortgage that is given by a purchaser to a seller in lieu of cash as partial payment for the purchase of real property; if the purchaser defaults on a payment, the seller may foreclose. A PMM is an alternative to an institutional loan and often resembles a junior lien.

Mortgages can also be categorized based on how they are protected against the risk of default. The three major categories are

1. Guaranteed—e.g., Veterans Administration (VA) home mortgages
2. Insured—e.g., Federal Housing Administration (FHA) mortgages
3. Conventional

FHA mortgages are the most common type of insured mortgages, but other government bodies and private insurance companies offer loan insurance as well. Conventional mortgages are neither insured nor guaranteed.

Although regulations vary from state to state, in most states institutional lenders are limited to a 75% to 80% conventional loan-to-value ratio. Private mortgage insurance (PMI) is used to facilitate conventional loans with higher loan-to-value ratios.

The effects of competition for capital are clearly evident in mortgage markets. In a volatile economic climate, some investors may resist long-term positions and fixed-rate instruments because they provide little protection against inflation. In response to erratic conditions during the late 1970s and early 1980s, balloon mortgages and contracts such as variable-rate mortgages, adjustable-rate mortgages, renegotiable rate mortgages, and rollover mortgages were created. These mortgage instruments provide for periodic adjustment of interest rates to keep yields competitive with those available in capital markets. Although these contracts may cover long periods, the payment requirements change at frequent intervals so borrowers may find it difficult to budget for fixed debt service. An owner managing a property subject to a variable-rate mortgage may, if the dynamics of the rental market permit, arrange leasing programs that permit rapid rental adjustments to offset increases in mortgage payments caused by money market fluctuations.

deed of trust: A legal instrument similar to a mortgage that, when executed and delivered, conveys or transfers property title to a trustee.

land contract: A contract in which a purchaser of real estate agrees to pay a small portion of the purchase price when the contract is signed as well as additional sums, at intervals and in amounts specified in the contract, until the total purchase price is paid and the seller delivers the deed; used primarily to protect the seller's interest in the unpaid balance because foreclosure can be exercised more quickly than it could be under a mortgage; also called *contract for deed* or *installment (sale) contract.*

Deeds of Trust/Land Contracts

A mortgage is a contract between a borrower (the mortgagor) and a lender (the mortgagee), but a deed of trust involves a third party. A deed of trust is defined as a legal instrument similar to a mortgage that, when executed and delivered, conveys or transfers property title to a trustee. In such an arrangement, a borrower conveys or transfers property to a trustee for the benefit of a lender. The borrower conveys title to the trustee but retains the right to use and occupy the property, which often eliminates the need for foreclosure proceedings against a defaulting debtor. In some states, deeds of trust are used in place of mortgage contracts.

Land contracts, frequently called *installment sale contracts* or *contracts for deed*, are instruments that provide for the future delivery of a property deed to a buyer after certain conditions are met. A seller finances the sale of a property by permitting the buyer to pay for it over a period of time, but the title is delivered only after all payments are made. In the event of default, the buyer normally forfeits all payments made and the seller may also elect to hold the buyer to the contract.

Rate Relationships

Observing daily trading activity over a period of time may reveal relationships among the earning rates of various instruments traded in money and capital markets (see Figures 6.5 and 6.6). For example, there may be a relatively constant spread of 50 basis points between the yields on three-month and six-month Treasury bills. However, market volatility can cause the spread between these yields to increase or decrease at times. Similarly, the spread between three-month and six-month commercial paper may widen to 70 basis points and remain steady at that level for several months. These observations are significant because they reveal how the length of an instrument's maturity influences its yield.

A key investment yield is reflected in the weekly auction of Treasury bills. Because these instruments represent top credit quality and short maturity, their yields establish a base from which market participants measure all short-term money costs, including some real estate construction loan rates. Money market and capital market rate relationships are created by prime investment considerations, which include borrowers' credit, loan maturity, monetary supply and demand conditions, and existing and anticipated inflation rates. All of these factors are important in rating the risk of various investments.

Understanding rate relationships can help appraisers correlate real estate investment risk with the risks associated with actively traded capital market instruments, providing support for market-derived discount and capitalization rates. The financial press contains a plethora of pricing and yield information to facilitate this process.

Sources of Capital for Real Estate

Equity and debt investors reveal their different aspirations through their market actions. The debt investor participates in bonds or mortgages, usually pursuing conservative paths in search of certain income and the repayment of principal. This type of investor expects a priority claim on investment earnings and often looks for security in the form of a lien on the assets involved. While a debt investor is relatively passive, an equity investor is active. An equity investor is more willing to assume risk, and the funds used for equity investment are known as *venture capital*.

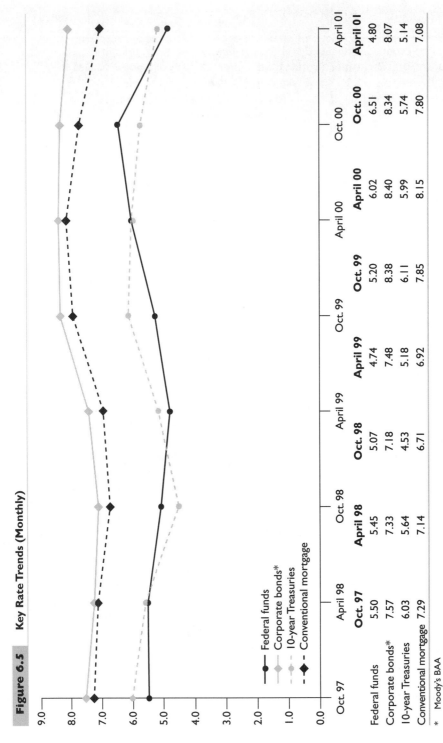

Figure 6.5   Key Rate Trends (Monthly)

	Oct. 97	April 98	Oct. 98	April 99	Oct. 99	April 00	Oct. 00	April 01
	Oct. 97	**April 98**	**Oct. 98**	**April 99**	**Oct. 99**	**April 00**	**Oct. 00**	**April 01**
Federal funds	5.50	5.45	5.07	4.74	5.20	6.02	6.51	4.80
Corporate bonds*	7.57	7.33	7.18	7.48	8.38	8.40	8.34	8.07
10-year Treasuries	6.03	5.64	4.53	5.18	6.11	5.99	5.74	5.14
Conventional mortgage	7.29	7.14	6.71	6.92	7.85	8.15	7.80	7.08

Federal funds
Corporate bonds*
10-year Treasuries
Conventional mortgage

*   Moody's BAA

Source: Federal Reserve Statistical Release, H.15 Selected Interest Rates (http://www.federalreserve.gov/releases/H15/data.htm)

Figure 6.6   **Key Rate Trends (Annual)**

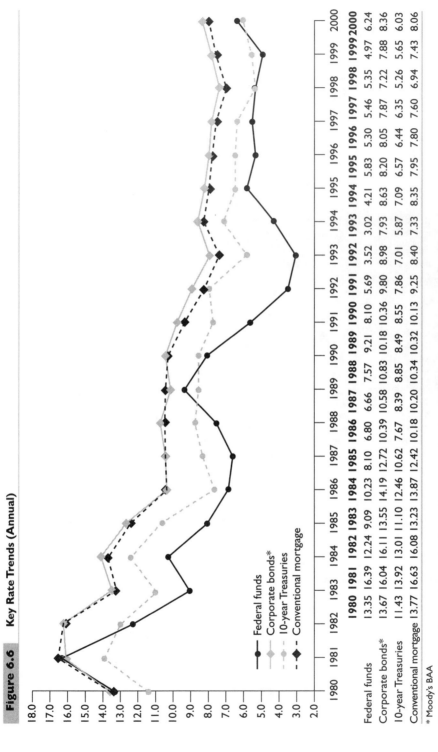

	1980	1981	1982	1983	1984	1985	1986	1987	1988	1989	1990	1991	1992	1993	1994	1995	1996	1997	1998	1999	2000
Federal funds	13.35	16.39	12.24	9.09	10.23	8.10	6.80	6.66	7.57	9.21	8.10	5.69	3.52	3.02	4.21	5.83	5.30	5.46	5.35	4.97	6.24
Corporate bonds*	13.67	16.04	16.11	13.55	14.19	12.72	10.39	10.58	10.83	10.18	10.36	9.80	8.98	7.93	8.63	8.20	8.05	7.87	7.22	7.88	8.36
10-year Treasuries	11.43	13.92	13.01	11.10	12.46	10.62	7.67	8.39	8.85	8.49	8.55	7.86	7.01	5.87	7.09	6.57	6.44	6.35	5.26	5.65	6.03
Conventional mortgage	13.77	16.63	16.08	13.23	13.87	12.42	10.18	10.20	10.34	10.32	10.13	9.25	8.40	7.33	8.35	7.95	7.80	7.60	6.94	7.43	8.06

* Moody's BAA

Source: Federal Reserve Statistical Release, H.15 Selected Interest Rates (http://www.federalreserve.gov/releases/H15/data.htm)

Home owners and other owner-occupants of single-family residential property are also equity investors and are major sources of capital. The investment criteria of home owners differ from those of investors in income-producing property. An owner-occupant trades the potential of receiving rental income for the enjoyment of the amenities provided by the property during the ownership period and the future financial benefit of the equity reversion when the house is eventually sold.

The **capitalization of real estate** is divided into debt investment and equity investment (or venture capital).

venture capital: A common term for funds used for equity investment.

dividends: The income earnings on an equity investment.

real estate investment trust (REIT): A corporation or trust that combines the capital of many investors to acquire or provide financing for all forms of real estate. A REIT serves much like a mutual fund for real estate. Its shares are freely traded, often on a major stock exchange. To qualify for the favorable tax treatment currently (as of 2001) accorded such trusts, 90% of the taxable income of a REIT must be distributed among its shareholders, who must number at least 100 investors; no fewer than five investors can own more than 50% of the value of the REIT. The Federal Securities and Exchange Commission stipulates that REITs with more than 300 investors have to make their financial statements public. (NAREIT)

REITs, partnerships, syndications, joint ventures, insurance companies, and international equity capital are **sources of equity investment.**

Equity

Equity investors realize that their earnings are subordinate to a project's operating expenses and debt service requirements. Equity income earnings are called *dividends;* one-year's worth of income to an equity investment is an *equity dividend.* But equity dividends are only one part of the total return that the investor anticipates. Investors may also expect the value of their original investment to increase, remain stable, or decrease, depending on the type of property and market conditions. The total return the investor anticipates is called the *equity yield.* An equity dividend represents the cash flow component of the equity yield.

Real Estate Investment Trusts

Real estate investment trusts (REITs) have been successful in pooling the funds of small investors to acquire real estate investment positions that could not be handled by these investors individually. Buying shares of REIT stock is not the same as direct investment in a given property. REITs offer shareholders freedom from personal liability, the benefit of expert management, and readily transferred shares. To qualify for a tax pass-through, a REIT must pay dividends of at least 90% of its taxable income.[3] With complicated income-measuring

3. The requirements for REITs to maintain their tax advantages are subject to change. The National Association of Real Estate Investment Trusts (NAREIT) provides up-to-date information on REIT regulations and trends through its Web site at http://www.nareit.org. See also Joseph L. Ferst and James R. MacCrate, "NAREIT and Tax Law Changes Will Foster Consistency in Accounting Practice and Disclosure Among REITs," *The Appraisal Journal* (January 2000): 14–19.

practices, these trusts attempt to pay out almost all their net income and, therefore, are substantially restricted in establishing reserves for possible losses. The liquidity of these securities is an attractive feature.

When analyzing comparable sales, appraisers should consider whether a REIT paid a premium to add the property to its portfolio. REITs tend to purchase properties with the following characteristics:

- Superior locations in superior markets
- Limited lease expiration exposure in any given year
- Improvements with minimal incurable obsolescence

Partnerships

A partnership is a common vehicle for pooling real estate equity funds. It is a business arrangement in which two or more persons jointly own a business and share in its profits and losses.

A general partnership is an ownership arrangement in which all partners share in investment gains and losses and each is fully responsible for all liabilities. A general partner has complete liability for the acts of the other partners and is responsible for debts incurred by them. This is one major disadvantage of this type of business arrangement. The most attractive feature of a general partnership in a real estate investment is the ability to pass the tax-shelter benefits of depreciation, interest, and real estate taxes through to partners.

A limited partnership is an ownership arrangement consisting of general and limited partners; general partners manage the business and assume full liability for partnership debt, while limited partners are passive and liable only to the extent of their own capital contributions. Limited partnerships are popular because they permit an uneven distribution of tax-shelter benefits. Although limited partners' financial liability is restricted to their capital contributions, they may receive tax benefits in excess of that amount.

Syndications

A syndication is a private or public partnership that pools funds for the acquisition and development of real estate projects or other business ventures. Private syndications are limited to small groups of investors and are relatively free from government regulation. Public syndications involve large groups of investors and generally operate in more than one state, so they are subject to Security Exchange Commission (SEC) registration regulations.

general partnership: An ownership arrangement in which all partners share in investment gains and losses and each has personal and unlimited responsibility for all liabilities.

limited partnership: An ownership arrangement consisting of general and limited partners. General partners manage the business and assume full liability for partnership debt, while limited partners are passive and liable only to the extent of their own capital contributions.

syndication: A private or public partnership that pools funds for the acquisition and development of real estate projects or other business ventures.

> **joint venture:** A combination of two or more entities that join to undertake a specific project.

Joint Ventures

A joint venture is a combination of two or more entities that join to undertake a specific project. Although a joint venture often takes the form of a general or limited partnership, it differs from a partnership in that it is intended to be temporary and project-specific. The parties may later embark on other ventures, but each venture is the subject of a separate contractual agreement.

A joint venture arrangement is frequently used in large real estate projects. One party, usually a financial institution, supplies most of the required capital and the other party provides construction or management expertise. Life insurance companies and pension trusts have joined with entrepreneurial building organizations in joint ventures to develop large offices, shopping malls, and other major real estate projects.

EQUITY INTERESTS

The equity in real property is the owner's interest after all claims and liens have been satisfied. An equity interest, like a mortgage loan, represents a financial interest in real property. Equity ownership in real property can be legally accomplished in many ways—e.g., as an individual owner, joint owner, partner, or shareholder in a corporation. The legal form of equity ownership does not affect property value in most appraisal assignments. However, an appraiser is sometimes called upon to render an opinion of the value of a specific legal form of equity interest.

For example, an appraiser may be asked to value a limited partner's equity interest in a partnership that was created solely to make the individual the legal owner of certain limited rights in the real property. Partial interests are often valued at less than their pro rata share of ownership, especially if the holder of the partial interest does not have any voice in the management or control of the asset. An assignment to value a limited partnership interest may be undertaken to appraise assets for estate tax purposes or for sale or purchase decisions.

Because the equity side of the real estate market dominates sales activity, appraisers must thoroughly understand the benefits that accrue to equity owners and know how equity yield is calculated.

Benefits of Equity Ownership

Equity owners look for two kinds of benefits:

1. Income, usually on an annual basis
2. Reversion at the end of the ownership period

Income is the annual cash flow; the reversion is the equity proceeds of resale after any outstanding mortgage balance and all selling expenses have been paid. Any refinancing benefits taken during the ownership period are usually viewed as a form of early reversion. In investment analysis assignments, the sum of all benefits received over the ownership period is analyzed in comparison to the equity invested to reveal the equity yield rate. In valuation assignments an equity yield rate is applied to the forecast benefits to produce a present value conclusion. If the market value of the equity interest is sought, the equity yield rate can be derived from the market.

Derivation of the Equity Yield Rate

For the investor the prime measures of investment performance are the equity yield rate and the first-year dividend, usually expressed as the equity capitalization rate (or equity dividend rate).* An

Pension Funds

Private and government-operated pension funds are a huge and rapidly growing source of investment capital. Usually the pension contributions of employers and employees are placed with a trustee, who is obliged to invest and reinvest the money prudently, accumulate funds, and pay designated plan benefits to retirees. The trustee may be a government body, a trust company, an insurance company, or an individual. In performing these duties, an individual trustee may employ the trust departments of commercial banks, insurance companies, and other financial institutions.[4]

EQUITY INTERESTS *(continued)*

investor may compare the expected equity yield on a real property investment with the yields on alternative investments with commensurate risk (e.g., stocks and bonds) and with a lender's yield on mortgages secured by similar real property. Usually the equity investor will seek a higher yield than the lender will because the lender has a more secure position. The lender can foreclose the mortgage and take title to the real property if the mortgage terms are not fulfilled.

To estimate equity yield rates, appraisers must research the market. This research can take many forms and may include one or more of the following analyses:

- Comparison with equity yield rates extracted from recent comparable sales; these equity yield rates are retrospective, however, and the appraiser's focus is more often prospective. (For an example, see the two-variable algebraic method of rate extraction described in Appendix C.)

- Verification of the prospective equity yields considered by market participants, particularly buyers, in recent or anticipated sales.

- Comparison with the equity yield rates achieved by alternative investments of comparable risk such as stocks and bonds.

- Review of published investor surveys, which can provide guidelines for appraisers.

Appropriate equity yield rates vary with property characteristics. To develop an equity yield rate from recent comparable sales, an appraiser analyzes the forecast benefits of equity ownership in relation to the equity capital invested. (This process is covered in Chapter 24.) Note that a distinction must be drawn between historical equity yield rates, which relate to the past, and currently required equity yield rates, which apply to anticipated future benefits.

* The *equity yield rate* (Y_E) must be distinguished from the *equity capitalization rate* (R_E). The equity yield rate is a rate of return on equity capital; the equity capitalization rate simply reflects the relationship between one year's equity income and equity capital (cash on cash). The equity capitalization rate may be more or less than the eventual equity yield on the capital invested, depending on future changes in equity income and equity value. The equity yield rate is a full measure of investment performance. Although the equity capitalization rate cannot be considered a full measure of performance, it is useful and important; in certain markets and at certain times, it is the preferred measure of investment performance.

---

4.   To protect American workers covered by pension and other benefit plans, Congress adopted the Employee Retirement Income Security Act (ERISA) in 1974. ERISA and its subsequent amendments establish a comprehensive legislative framework governing the investment, management, and administration of employee pension plans, profit-sharing plans, and welfare plans. ERISA also empowers government agencies to conduct audit programs in performing their duties. After more than two decades, the administrative structure and doctrine of ERISA continue to evolve as the courts and regulatory agencies make judgments concerning compliance by plan administrators and the claims due beneficiaries. See *Fiduciary Responsibilities for Plan Investments, Plan Administration, and Plan Audits,* (Washington, D.C.: Federal Publications, Inc., 1994), a–b, 1–17, 45–53, 57–76, 103–118.

Traditionally pension funds have been involved primarily in securities investments such as stocks and bonds. The development of pass-through securities by Ginnie Mae, however, has made it easier for pension funds to invest in mortgages, and they have made sizable investments. Pension trusts have also shown a willingness to invest in real estate equities by purchasing or participating in the real estate investments created by life insurance companies and commercial banks. Banks and life insurance companies acquire high-quality real estate equities, pool the investments in separate accounts, and supply the necessary portfolio management for a fee. Pension trusts commit funds to these accounts and share in all earnings, which consist of both income returns and sales profits. The real property holdings of a pension fund may be in a separate account or in a commingled fund with other investments.

Life Insurance Companies

Life insurance companies have always invested heavily in real estate. Their activities include both mortgage lending (debt) and property ownership (equity investment). Life insurance companies usually acquire real estate positions that are long-term and relate well to their regular business, in which policy premiums are collected over extended periods. Their investment officers regard equities as attractive earning situations that offer growth potential and reasonable protection against the capital erosion caused by inflation.

International Equity Capital

Although foreign investors represent only a very small fraction of total U.S. real estate investment, they supply needed equity capital to realty ventures in this country. Programs like the North American Free Trade Agreement (NAFTA) eliminate some of the obstacles to foreign investment. International capital comes from a variety of sources, such as foreign individuals, countries, financial institutions, and pension funds. The use of Eurodollars has a stabilizing effect on international exchange rates, which can have a negative effect on investment returns and impede foreign investment.

A foreign investor interested in buying U.S. property usually hires an American appraiser to value the property. A U.S. lender who is considering underwriting part of a real estate project in a foreign country also needs a meaningful appraisal report, and often retains an American appraiser to work on the assignment with a local appraisal firm. It is essential that the American appraiser understand the motivations of the foreign client and the behavior of foreign investors in general. For example, a favorable exchange rate or a special tax advantage may make investment in U.S. properties especially attractive. The investment horizon of foreign clients may be considerably longer than that of American investors. The appraiser should not ascribe the motives of typical U.S. buyers to foreign buyers whose perceptions may differ widely.[5]

---

5.   For further discussion of international valuation, see Chapter 27.

Saudi Arabian and Dutch investors were buying U.S. properties in the 1970s and Japanese investors were active in the 1980s. The favorable cost of capital in their native countries allowed these investors to make offers that did not make sense for U.S. investors. Despite the interest from foreign investors, not all U.S. properties qualified as potential acquisitions. Some appraisers valued properties according to the investment criteria of offshore capital even when the property in question was not appropriate for foreign investors. Real estate markets suffered as a result of faulty supply-demand relationships.

Debt

Because mortgage money is so important in real estate, investors, appraisers, and analysts must be familiar with the sources and costs of debt capital. Increased regulation in the wake of the savings and loan crisis has prompted many traditional providers of debt capital to restrict their lending activity in non-residential real estate. The focus of these institutions has been redirected to residential lending. Although commercial banks and life insurance companies are not precluded from originating loans for commercial real estate, increased reserve requirements make real estate a less attractive investment option.

Savings and Loan Associations

Like mutual savings banks, life insurance companies, credit unions, and other entities, savings and loan associations (S&Ls) are financial intermediaries. They receive savings deposits, lend them at interest, and distribute dividends to depositors after paying operating expenses and establishing appropriate reserves. When short-term interest rates are high, savers tend to withdraw funds and reinvest them in higher-yielding, short-term money market instruments and funds. Because savings and loan associations are financial intermediaries, high interest rates reduce the availability of mortgage funds and increase their cost.

> S&Ls, commercial banks, insurance companies, mutual savings and stock-holder-owned banks, junior mortgage originators, and the secondary mortgage market (CMOs, CMBSs) are **sources of debt investment**.

The failure of many S&Ls in the 1980s has had a profound effect on real estate appraisers. Today federal agencies are required to retain state-licensed or -certified appraisers to perform appraisals of properties for federally related transactions with values above a specified threshold or *de minimis*, which is fixed at $250,000 for residential properties.

> **savings and loan association:** A financial intermediary that receives savings deposits, lends money at interest, and distributes dividends to depositors after paying operating expenses and establishing appropriate reserves.
>
> **de minimis requirement:** A stipulation of Title XI of the Financial Institutions Reform, Recovery and Enforcement Act (FIRREA) of 1989 that federal agencies must retain state-certified appraisers to perform appraisals of properties with values above a specified dollar amount.

MORTGAGE INTERESTS

The purchase and ownership of real property often involves debt capital secured with the real estate as collateral. Mortgage investments have a great impact on real property value and equity yield rates. Because yield is a significant consideration in the lender's decision to invest in a mortgage interest in real estate, the lender's yield must be understood and often calculated. In the absence of points and any participation or accrual feature, the lender's yield is equivalent to the interest rate.

The monetary benefits that accrue to the lender are similar to the benefits received by the equity owner—i.e., periodic income from debt service and the reversion represented by the outstanding principal paid off prior to or at maturity. In some depressed markets, lenders may find that the property securing the loan has declined in value to the point that the loan balance exceeds the property's value. In this case there is no longer any equity interest in the property, and the value of the loan may often be calculated based on the actual cash flows to the property rather than the cash flows projected when the loan contract was obtained. To do otherwise would be to estimate the value of the mortgage interest as greater than the value of the property.

As explained previously, the lender's interest in a property is more secure than the equity interest because debt service is paid before any other claims on net operating income and the lender can foreclose if the borrower defaults on the loan. As an interest in real property becomes less senior—for example, the mortgage interest corresponding to a junior lien—the rate of return requirement to attract a purchaser rises. The combination of mortgage and equity interests divides a real property interest into tiers of risk:

- The first mortgage interest in the property is a low-risk investment.
- The second mortgage interest would require a higher rate of return to compensate for the increased risk.
- The equity interest would require an even higher rate of return because of its higher risk—and potentially higher profits.

These tiers of risk are often called *tranches* when referring to bonds or other securities.

Business loans of $1 million or less are exempt where the sale of, or income derived from, real estate is not the primary source of repayment. Mortgage loans that originate with federally regulated lenders or that are insured (e.g., by FHA or HUD) or guaranteed by federal agencies (e.g., the VA) qualify as federally related transactions

Commercial Banks

Commercial banks are privately owned institutions that offer a variety of financial services to businesses and individuals. In keeping with their role as short-term lenders, commercial banks have traditionally supplied construction and development loans. For short-term, interim financing, developers are usually required to obtain commitments from long-term, permanent lenders, whereby the lenders agree to "take out" the "end loan" with the developer once the project has been completed. Large commercial

commercial bank: A privately owned institution that offers businesses and individuals a variety of financial services; may be state- or federally chartered and is subject to government regulation; managed by boards of directors who are selected by stockholders.

banks have also become a principal source of takeout financing, i.e. long-term permanent mortgage loans and end loans, usually for commercial and industrial properties. In small communities, commercial banks are also expected to supply their customers with home loans.

Life Insurance Companies

The mortgage investments of life insurance companies cover the full range of realty types—e.g., residences, apartments, offices, shopping malls, hotels, and industrial properties. Because many companies have great financial resources, they have been important in mortgaging large, income-producing properties. Large companies prefer loans on offices and shopping malls.

Mutual Savings Banks and Stockholder-Owned Banks

Mutual savings banks are very similar to mutual savings and loan associations, promoting thrift and investing substantial amounts of savings in real estate mortgages. Generally they have broader investment powers than savings and loan associations do. Savings banks concentrate on mortgages, but they also invest in government bonds, corporate bonds, and, to a lesser degree, real estate and stock equity investments.

In the late 1980s and early 1990s, hundreds of mutual savings banks and savings and loan associations went public by converting to stock ownership. In the process, they raised vast amounts of new

> **mutual savings bank:** A financial institution owned by its depositors; a major source of home mortgage funds.

THE SAVINGS AND LOAN CRISIS

In the mid- and late 1980s, S&L institutions suffered enormous financial losses. Hundreds of S&Ls failed and had to be taken over by the government. The assets of these thrift institutions totaled hundreds of billions of dollars.

Until 1989 federal savings and loan associations were supervised by the Federal Home Loan Bank Board (FHLBB), which was created in 1932 to provide credit to thrift and home financing institutions and to alleviate liquidity problems in the savings and loan industry by assuring a constant flow of funds. The Financial Institutions Reform, Recovery and Enforcement Act of 1989 (FIRREA), the savings and loan bailout legislation, created the Office of Thrift Supervision (OTS) under the direction of the Treasury Department.

In addition to taking over the functions of the damaged FHLBB, the OTS had been authorized to examine and supervise all federal and state savings and loans (and all savings and loans holding companies) and to establish strict uniform accounting standards for thrift institutions similar to those established for commercial banks.

FIRREA also set up the Resolution Trust Corporation (RTC), which was charged with disposing of the assets of insolvent thrift institutions. This task involved handling hundreds of billions of dollars in deposits, performing and nonperforming mortgages, and real estate. As a result, the RTC quickly became the largest player in real estate markets. The collection of cash from liquidation of assets was substantial and helped reduce the national deficit. By 1994 the RTC had accomplished much of its mission and its position in the market was becoming less prominent; the agency closed at the end of 1995, a year earlier than originally anticipated. The assets of the now defunct Federal Savings and Loan Insurance Corporation (FSLIC) have been assumed by the Federal Deposit Insurance Corporation (FDIC).

junior mortgage originators: Private lenders such as real estate investment trusts (REITs), financing companies, and factoring organizations that provide secondary financing as a regular line of business; thrift institutions may also be included, but the funds used for such financing usually may not exceed 3% or 4% of their assets.

secondary mortgage market: A market created by government and private agencies for the purchase and sale of existing mortgages; provides greater liquidity for mortgages. Fannie Mae, Freddie Mac, and Ginnie Mae are the principal operators in the secondary mortgage market.

capital. As the net worth of these banks was augmented, their stock issues became very attractive to investors.

Junior Mortgage Originators

Junior mortgages can be used to raise substantial amounts of mortgage funds and to achieve various investment goals, such as creating additional leverage and facilitating sales of properties with first mortgages that cannot be refinanced. Junior mortgages involve greater risk than senior liens do and therefore command higher interest rates.

Legal regulations usually preclude banks, savings and loan associations, and life insurance companies from making large junior mortgage loans. Other private lenders such as REITs, financing companies, and factoring organizations provide secondary financing as a regular line of business. They offer expensive secondary financing in the form of junior mortgages or subordinated land sale-leasebacks, but they are not supervised to the same extent as banks and life insurance companies.

Secondary Mortgage Market

Government and private organizations stimulate home building through the secondary mortgage market. In this market, mortgagees sell packages of mortgages at prices consistent with existing money market rates. Selling mortgages frees up capital, creates liquidity, and permits mortgagees to lend when they might otherwise lack funds.

Although most secondary mortgage market activity is generated by Fannie Mae, Freddie Mac, and Ginnie Mae, the private sector has also played a role. Banks and insurance companies with mortgage-originating capability often sell loan portfolios, or mortgage participations, to private or institutional investors. Some REITs have purchased mortgages from institutions, thereby supplying the sellers with the liquidity needed to continue their lending programs.

The development and growth of private mortgage insurance programs have facilitated private secondary mortgage activity. In the residential market, private programs have successfully insured mortgage loan increments that exceed legal ratios. This has encouraged private secondary market operations that could not have occurred otherwise.

Securitization of Real Estate Investment Markets

Securities are investment instruments that convey partial ownerships (stocks) or establish debt obligations (bonds). By dividing a pool of properties into a series of ownerships through partnership, corporation, or trust entities, real estate

PRINCIPAL OPERATORS IN THE SECONDARY MORTGAGE MARKET

Activity in the secondary mortgage market is dominated by a handful of government and quasi-governmental agencies.

Fannie Mae

The Federal National Mortgage Association is a quasi-governmental agency that purchases mortgages from banks, trust companies, mortgage companies, savings and loan associations, and insurance companies to help distribute funds for home mortgages. Its important programs include

- Over-the-counter program in which Fannie Mae post the prices it will pay for the immediate delivery of mortgages
- Free market system commitment auction in which separate but simultaneous auctions are held for FHA, VA, and conventional mortgages

Freddie Mac

The Federal Home Loan Mortgage Corporation (FHLMC) is an agency that facilitates secondary residential mortgages sponsored by the Veterans Administration and the Federal Housing Administration as well as residential mortgages that are not government protected. Its important programs include

- Purchase programs in which Freddie Mac buys single-family and condominium mortgages from approved financial institutions
- Sales program in which Freddie Mac sells its mortgage inventories, acquiring funds from organizations that have excess capital

Ginnie Mae

The Government National Mortgage Association (GNMA) is a federally owned and financed corporation under the Department of Housing and Urban Development that subsidizes mortgages through its secondary mortgage market operations and issues mortgage-backed, federally insured securities. Its most important program is the mortgage-backed security program in which Ginnie Mae guarantees securities covered by pools of loans collected by mortgage originators

Farmer Mac

The Federal Agricultural Mortgage Corporation is a federally chartered but privately owned corporation that serves the same function for rural properties as Fannie Mae does for urban and suburban properties. Its most important programs are the secondary mortgage market programs for agricultural real estate and rural housing.

securities create opportunity and allow more investors to be involved. Because risk can be diffused through a greater number of smaller investments, securitization reduces the risk to the individual investor. Securitization usually ensures professional portfolio management as well as professional management of the assets that are securitized. Securitization also expands liquidity, which may not otherwise exist for the investments.

Securitization is rapidly spreading to real estate equity investments. The Resolution Trust Corporation (RTC)

securities: A class of investments represented by engraved, printed, or written documents that show ownership or creditorship in a corporation or other form of business organization; includes creditorship in public bodies, e.g., bonds, stocks, mortgages, notes, coupons, scrips, warrants, rights, options.

initiated the large-scale securitization of both mortgage and equity interests in the S&L cleanup. Wall Street has taken securitization much further, successfully handling large portfolios for commercial banks and insurance companies. Many observers believe that in real estate finance Wall Street has taken the place of traditional lenders.

The mechanism that the RTC used to liquidate the assets of insolvent S&Ls paved the way for large-scale securitization. This process involved the sale of pools of commercial mortgages, known as *commercial mortgage-backed securities* (CMBSs), through investment bankers to nontraditional mortgage investors. The RTC initially set up a guarantee fund to secure CMBSs, thereby facilitating the risk rating of these debt instruments. More recently, collateralization of CMBSs has taken other forms.

The recent emergence of collateralized mortgage obligations (CMOs) as a major investment banking instrument was prompted by Ginnie Mae guarantee arrangements. CMOs are bonds issued and sold in the capital markets. They are attractive to investors because the debt involved is usually collateralized by Ginnie Mae certificates covering pools of residential mortgages. This vehicle has been a huge source of liquidity for the mortgage industry and has monetized the mortgage element in real estate investment.

A variation in the CMO field is the real estate mortgage investment conduit (REMIC) option, which transforms the CMO from a pure debt (bond) vehicle into an equity-type investment. In a REMIC arrangement, the certificate represents a proportionate share of ownership in a pool of mortgages. The issuing organization, often an investment bank, avoids adding debt to its balance sheet by using the REMIC. The investor in a REMIC enjoys the benefit of a tax pass-through similar to that of a REIT, and thereby avoids the double taxation incurred by investors in corporations. CMOs of all types have brought enormous amounts of capital into the mortgage field.

The laws of some states once made little or no distinction between real estate and securities. In other states, however, the laws have tacitly acknowledged this distinction by recognizing the special attributes of real estate (e.g., immobility) that set it apart from stocks, bonds, and other investment vehicles. Until recently, regulations governing the securities industry also made this distinction. Just as questions have arisen about realty and

> The **securitization of real estate interests** through the trading of secondary mortgage market issues, CMOs, REITs, and CMBSs links real estate capitalization and discount rates to financial market activity.

> **real estate mortgage investment conduit (REMIC):** Equity instruments issued by an investment bank that are similar to collateralized mortgage obligations; in this arrangement, the certificate represents a proportionate share of ownership in a pool of mortgages. Investors in REMICs enjoy a tax pass-through similar to that of a REIT. Introduced as technical provisions of the Tax Reform Act of 1986, REMICs were created to facilitate broad participation in the mortgage-backed securities market.

non-realty components of property value, new attention has focused on the basic nature of real estate. As new investment vehicles proliferate, appraisers will want to know when to value the individual real estate and when to reflect any differences attributable to the ownership vehicle, within which the property is grouped with other properties.

Security vs. Real Estate

Although public market pricing has some advantages, investor-driven pricing does not necessarily reflect the value of the underlying real estate asset. There is wide variation among real estate securities, depending on the structure of the particular investment vehicle. For example, REITs are subject to stringent requirements as to the dividends paid to investors (expectations of higher or lower dividends can influence pricing) or to legal restrictions limiting the amount of property that can be sold in any given year. REITs can also employ investment leverage, which increases the potential return on the investment but can create difficulties for the investment in market downturns.

One of the newer real estate investment securities vehicles divides real estate interests into a series of layers called *tranches*. Property investments have long been divided into equity and mortgage layers, sometimes even into a series of mortgage layers. In the 1960s, L.W. Ellwood and others showed that the typical leased fee or fee simple estate was purchased with a combination of equity and mortgage funds and that analysis of the income and return requirements of each of these layers represented a valid approach to appraisal. The modern tranche goes well beyond this concept, but the mathematical processes used in investment analyses still apply. In 1998 the CMBS market came to a near halt as almost no one was willing to buy securities in the high-risk tranches, which was explained by most analysts as a "flight to quality" sparked by the Asian financial crisis.

Debt and Equity Relationships

In money markets and capital markets, when the risks associated with different investments are comparable, funds flow to the investment that offers the best prospective yield. Risks are related to rewards; if capital is to be attracted, competitive yields must be offered. The most persuasive indicators of competitive yield levels are found in money markets where billions of dollars of capital are traded daily, traders are sophisticated and well informed, and investments are often professionally rated for risk.

In an unstable economic climate, appraisers are well advised to search money markets and capital markets for data to support the conclusions they have developed from real estate market data. There are hundreds of thousands of transactions each day in financial markets and billions of dollars are involved. These transactions reflect the discounting of economic futures by well-informed investors and provide useful insights for investment analysts.

The largest equity market is the trading of common stocks. Transactions are reported daily, and share prices and current dividend rates are revealed.

Most major newspapers carry full details on stock market operations, and financial publications and online sources offer abundant information about corporate earnings and general conditions in commercial and industrial enterprises. This data provides the basis for risk rating the securities issued by businesses. In the field of debt investments (bonds and debentures), the rating task is often performed by professionals such as Standard & Poor's and Moody's; their opinions are widely published and respected by the financial community.[6] Other information is furnished by the securities analysts of major banking institutions, brokerage companies, and the investment banking industry. Their opinions are readily available to investors.

Analysts' reports and financial publications do not reveal prospective stock yields, but they do provide information from which investment indexes can be drawn. Because value is the present worth of future income and reversion combined, a key element of value is anticipated appreciation or depreciation. In the stock market, securities analysts are the best sources of the type of in-depth information on which the investment community bases its growth or depreciation forecasts. In this regard a securities analyst functions like a real estate appraiser, who arrives at an opinion of value by discounting market-supported income and reversion forecasts.

The second, larger component in real estate investment is the debt capital segment, or mortgage funds. Again, capital markets offer abundant information on investor yield requirements for a great variety of debt instruments with different maturities and risk ratings. In the bond and debenture markets, there are hundreds of thousands of daily transactions involving billions of dollars. Each transaction represents one investor's discounting of perceived future economic conditions. The entire volume of transactions presents an excellent picture of well-informed expectations of debt capital performance.

Investment Yields

There are differences in the investment yields produced by debt and equity instruments. With a debt instrument, the original lender is entitled to interest at a specified rate, either fixed or variable, and full payment of the loan amount at maturity. The arrangement may call for periodic payments of interest only and full repayment of the principal at maturity, as in the case of bonds, or it may require periodic payments that combine interest and debt reduction, as in most mortgage loans.

If the original lender sells the investment during its contractual term, a different yield will be realized. If financial market conditions are tight and interest rates are higher than when the loan was originated, the lender must

---

6. Standard and Poor's Corporation and Moody's Investor Services, Inc. publish a variety of data on the performance of stocks and bonds. Contact the Standard and Poor's Sales Office for a catalog of products at 1-800-221-5277, or visit the Standard and Poor's Web site at http://www.standardandpoors.com. Contact the Moody's Client Service Desk at 1-212-553-1653, or visit the Moody's Web site at http://www.moodys.com.

sell the position at a discount. If money is freer and rates are lower, the lender may be able to sell at a premium. The purchaser collects the amount of interest specified in the original contract, but the instrument's yield rate relates to a new investment basis. When the loan is repaid at maturity, the purchaser receives the full face amount, including any discount involved in the acquisition, minus any premium paid. The instrument's investment yield comprises the interest collected, plus any gain or minus any loss realized at loan maturity, and repayment.

It can be seen that the investment yield on a debt instrument is largely a contractual matter. Income earnings are defined in the instrument as a fixed or variable percentage of the debt's face amount and are paid at specified times over the term of the loan. The reversion is limited to the original face amount of debt, which may be more or less than the amount paid by the final holder of the instrument.

An equity investment has none of the contractual certainty or specificity of a debt position. The income or dividend earnings are simply the amount of a venture's income, if any, after operating expenses and debt service are paid. This cash flow can be positive or negative, depending on whether there is an excess or deficiency of income after all expenses. The reversion is simply the venture's market value at the end of the investment holding period—i.e., a future value. When entering into an investment, an investor considers the forecast dividend earnings and reversion in relation to the acquisition price; this relationship reflects the prospective equity yield. Upon termination of the investment, the dividends and reversion realized are related to the original amount of the investment to reflect the historic equity yield.

Leverage

The term *leverage* refers to how borrowed funds increase or decrease the equity return. The leverage an investor obtains by using borrowed funds to finance an investment is accompanied by risk. The

> **leverage:** The effect of borrowed funds, which may increase or decrease the return that would be realized on equity free and clear.

investor seeks compensation for this risk by requiring a higher equity yield rate. In analyzing cash flows, positive leverage is indicated when the overall capitalization rate is greater than the mortgage capitalization rate. The difference between the two rates directly benefits the equity owner, so the equity capitalization rate is higher than it would be if there were no mortgage. The same relationships hold for overall, equity, and mortgage yield rates. (See Table 6.4.)

The analysis of leverage is important because positive or negative leverage can affect the level of risk associated with a real property investment and the yield required to satisfy an investor willing to assume the risk. The use of leverage tends to magnify fluctuations in cash flow and enhanced variability translates into risk. If property performance falls below expecta-

Table 6.4   Types of Leverage

Using equity capitalization rates	Using equity yield rates
If $R_O > R_M$, then $R_E > R_O$: leverage is positive	If $Y_O > Y_M$, then $Y_E > Y_O$: leverage is positive
If $R_O = R_M$, then $R_E = R_O$: leverage is neutral	If $Y_O = Y_M$, then $Y_E = Y_O$: leverage is neutral
If $R_O < R_M$, then $R_E < R_O$: leverage is negative	If $Y_O < Y_M$, then $Y_E < Y_O$: leverage is negative

tions and periods of insufficient cash flow are protracted, the investor may become strapped for cash to service the debt on the property. If market conditions become illiquid, the investor may be unable to command a price for the property that allows for repayment of the debt.

FURTHER READING

Anderson, Joshua. "The ABCs of CMBS." *Valuation Insights & Perspectives*, vol. 4, no. 3 (Third Quarter 1999).

Clauretie, Terence M., and G. Stacy Sirmans. *Real Estate Finance: Theory and Practice*. 3d ed. Upper Saddler River, N.J.: Prentice Hall, 1999.

Dannis, Charles G. "Discover the Benefits of the NCREIF Property Index." *The Appraisal Journal* (October 1997).

Economic Report of the President. Washington, D.C.: Council of Economic Advisors, annual. Available online at http://w3.access.gpo.gov/eop/.

Fabozzi, Frank J., editor. *Handbook of Commercial Mortgage-Backed Securities*, 2d ed. New Hope, Penn.: Frank J. Fabozzi Associates, 1998.

____. *Trends in Commercial Mortgage-Backed Securities*. New Hope, Penn.: Frank J. Fabozzi Associates, 1998.

Kelly, Kevin. *New Rules for the New Economy: 10 Radical Strategies for a Connected World*. New York: Viking, 1998.

Oliner, Stephen, and Daniel E. Sichel. "The Resurgence of Growth in the Late 1990s: Is Information Technology the Story?" *Journal of Economic Perspectives*, vol. 14, no. 4 (Fall 2000).

Pratt, Shannon P. *Cost of Capital: Estimation and Applications*. New York: John Wiley & Sons, Inc., 1998.

Roulac, Stephen E. "Global Capital Flows: The New Market Dynamic." *Mortgage Banking*, vol. 60, no. 5 (February 2000), Commercial CREF Conference Special Issue.

Stocks Bonds Bills and Inflation Yearbook. Chicago: R.G. Ibbotson Associates, updated annually.

Winger, Alan R. "A Layman's Approach to Risk Analysis." *Real Estate Review*, vol. 25, no. 4 (Winter 1996).

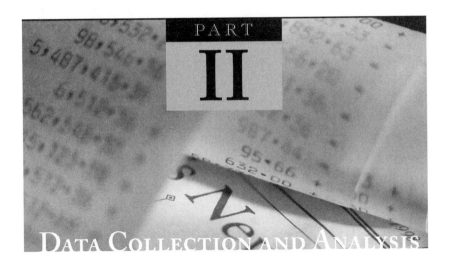

PART

II

DATA COLLECTION AND ANALYSIS

Part II examines the various basic forms of data collection and the types of analyses that lead up to the application of the three traditional approaches to value. **Chapter 7, Data Collection**, concentrates on the various types and sources of data real estate appraisers use. **Chapter 8, Market Areas, Neighborhoods, and Districts**, discusses how appraisers determine the geographic area in which a particular land use competes, which is an essential preliminary step for meaningful market analysis. **Chapter 9, Land or Site Analysis**, discusses the characteristics of land that an appraiser analyzes to determine its value. **Chapter 10, Improvement Analysis**, outlines the tasks of property inspection, building description, and analysis of architectural style and functional utility. **Chapter 11, Market Analysis**, discusses the techniques used by appraisers to forecast supply and demand within a market area and to extract other pertinent information from the available market data. **Chapter 12, Highest and Best Use Analysis**, covers one of the most important and difficult tasks in the valuation process, the determination of the highest and best use of the land as though vacant and the property as improved.

CHAPTER 7
DATA COLLECTION

In real estate appraisal, the quality and quantity of information available for analysis are as important as the methods and techniques used to process the data and complete the assignment. Therefore, the ability to distinguish between different kinds of data, to research reliable data sources, and to manage information is essential to appraisal practice.

Dealing with the requisite market, property, and transaction data in the valuation process involves three related processes:

1. Data collection
2. Data organization
3. Data analysis

Appraisers need patience, judgment, and research skills to direct the preliminary steps of data collection and analysis and to gather and manage information efficiently.

> **Data collection, organization, and analysis** are essential tasks in appraisal.

Identifying comparable properties and collecting other market data for use in the valuation process was once a time-consuming and expensive process. The growth of data vendors and the increasing accessibility of market data through electronic sources has shifted the historical emphasis of appraisal practice from data collection to analysis. Yet, collecting accurate, reliable data remains an essential task because the conclusions of appraisers' analyses are only as good as the data that supports them.

Uncovering all the necessary data remains a challenge for appraisers, even with technological innovations that facilitate the process. Data collection can be the same or very different from state to state. Many states have open property records available to appraisers, but many others are nondisclosure states where sales data can only be collected from the actual parties to the sale. Also, professional appraisal standards and government programs can require different levels of data collection and documentation. For example, the data required to complete the Uniform Residential Appraisal Report (URAR) or some other appraisal report form for a government-backed loan program may only meet the requirements of the Uniform Standards of Professional Appraisal Practice for a limited appraisal; for the appraisal to qualify as complete under USPAP guidelines, additional information may be needed.

Before beginning the process of data collection, the appraiser determines which types of data—general, specific, or competitive supply and demand data—will be useful in the different portions of the valuation process. Then, the appraiser communicates those choices to the client in the scope of work section of the appraisal report. In many cases an appraiser collects general data on the demographics of the market area and competitive supply and demand data on competitive properties to perform market analysis, while the highest and best use analysis requires specific data such as information on the physical character-istics of the subject property, zoning restrictions, and the income anticipated from alternative uses. The analysis undertaken in the application of the three approaches to value generally require both specific data for the subject property, such as cost data for the subject property improvements in the cost approach, and competitive supply and demand data, such as information on comparable sales transaction in the sales comparison approach.

Understanding the content and sources of general and specific appraisal data facilitates data analysis in valuation and appraisal consulting assignments. Before analyzing that data, however, an appraiser must organize all the specific data accumulated in the investigation. Market data grids like the cost survey worksheet used in the cost approach, the adjustment grid used in the sales comparison approach, and the reconstructed operating statement used in the income capitalization approach are carefully prepared spreadsheets that provide a tabular representation of market data organized into useful, measurable categories. If the information to be analyzed is complex, the appraiser may need to design several market data grids to isolate and study specific data.

Once the data has been collected and organized, it can be analyzed to solve the problem posed by the appraisal assignment. Market analysis and highest and best use analysis are the most obvious forms of data analysis, but each of the three approaches to value is a form of analysis that relies on market data as support for the value conclusions derived. The validity of each approach's conclusions and ultimately the final opinion of market value, depends largely on how well market data can support those conclusions.

In the appraisal report, the analysis must answer the reader's question, "So what?" The analysis should tie the economic and financial data to the real estate market in general and to the particular market in which the real estate being appraised is located. For example, if the appraiser's economic data shows that the rate of employment growth is decreasing, then how will this impact the market in general and specifically the type of property and the particular property being appraised?

Types of Data

In most appraisal analyses more than one type of data will need to be gathered and examined, including the following:

- General data
- Specific data
- Competitive supply and demand data

result, political instability in other countries can influence the demand for, and value of, real estate in the United States.

International economic trends can have significant effects on local economies and specific real estate markets. For example, the status of the Asian economy can affect the level of international trade, which in turn has a major impact on the economy of Pacific Rim port cities (and perhaps the demand for warehouse space). Increasingly, trends in international financing can influence local real estate markets as well. In the 1980s, using financing techniques unavailable to American investors, Japanese investors could pay inflated prices for prestigious properties in Hawaii and California, including most of the luxury hotel rooms in Hawaii. At the time, real estate appraisers in Hawaii had to provide two different values reflecting the influence of Japanese investment practices (often without the benefit of a pro forma, lease analysis, or market study) and traditional U.S. lending practices. The collapse of the Japanese economy, due in part to bad loans made by Japanese banks, eventually caused prices in the Hawaiian real estate market to plunge, with Japanese investors losing billions of dollars on their investments.

National and regional economic trends. The state of the national economy is basic to any real estate appraisal. Financial institutions must compete for funds to lend, not only with one another but also with money market mutual funds. Lending rates reflect this ongoing competition, and demand in the market adjusts itself accordingly.

Federal programs and tax policies can affect the value of real estate. The Tax Reform Act of 1986 eliminated many of the tax advantages of owning property by modifying the Accelerated Cost Recovery System, which often allowed a property to contribute more value as a tax shelter than as an operating business. Along with modification of Section 1031 of the Internal Revenue Code in 1984, the Tax Reform Act encouraged "like-kind" exchanges.[2] The 1031 exchange program allows a property owner to defer capital gains taxes if real property is exchanged for other real property, within certain limitations as defined in the code. The sale price of a comparable property involved in a 1031 exchange may have to be adjusted to reflect the tax savings of that transaction over a traditional sale.

The national economy also reflects the economic condition of the various geographic regions of the United States. The economic health of a region depends on the status of its economic activity, which in turn encompasses the economic activities in individual areas and communities within the region's geographic boundaries. Minor disruptions in the economic growth of one community may not appreciably affect the entire region if the regional and national economies are strong.

---

2.   See also Jack P. Friedman and Jack C. Harris, "Tax Reform Encourages 1031 Exchanges: What the Appraiser Should Know About Section 1031," *The Appraisal Journal* (January 1987): 79–93 and Joel Rosenfeld, "Section 1031—Tax-Deferred Exchanges: Real Estate's Best-Kept Secret for Tax Relief," *Real Estate Issues* (Winter 2000/2001): 12–16.

The extent to which an appraiser is concerned with the national or regional economy and the economy of the city or market area depends on the size and type of property being appraised. For example, a large regional shopping center that serves a trade area of 500,000 people and an automobile assembly plant that employs 5,000 workers are more sensitive to the general state of the economy than are medical-dental office buildings or retail service operations in suburban residential areas.

Local market considerations. To understand how national and even international economic trends influence property value, an appraiser studies how the region and community where the subject property is located may respond to these trends. The appraiser should examine the economic structure of the region and the community, the comparative advantages that each possesses, and the attitudes of local government and residents toward growth and change. For example, the increasing number of elderly households in the nation is less significant to property values in Minnesota than to values in Sunbelt states, which attract more retirees. A community with a no-growth policy may have substantially different local demographics and economic potential than one that does not discourage growth.

Regional economies influence local market conditions, but local markets do not necessarily parallel regional markets. Macroeconomic studies, which are concerned with broad areas such as cities and regions, are important to understanding real estate and real estate trends. These studies should not be confused with microeconomic studies, which appraisers perform to evaluate the factors influencing the market value of a particular real estate parcel. For example, regional trends may suggest an expected increase in population, but the local data available to the appraiser may indicate that the particular area will not benefit from this trend. While both studies are important, local trends are more likely to influence property values directly.

Trends affecting rural land. Appraisers of rural land should understand the links between the local rural economy, the regional economic base (agricultural, extractive, or recreational), and the national economy as well as the encroachment of suburban and urban land uses on rural land. The subject property should be analyzed in relation to comparable properties in the immediate agricultural, mining/drilling, or recreational district.

Climatic data can be important in analyzing many rural land uses. A drought in a grain-producing area or icy conditions in a citrus-growing region can have economic repercussions beyond disrupting local agricultural production. Tourism and recreational uses of rural land may be affected by the severe weather, and restaurants and hotels in the region may be forced to raise prices to keep up with the rising cost of food.[3]

---

3.   For further discussion of trends affecting rural property, see *The Appraisal of Rural Property,* 2d ed. (Denver: American Society of Farm Managers and Rural Appraisers and Chicago: Appraisal Institute, 2000).

Demographics

The population of a market and its geographic distribution are basic determinants of the need for real estate. Real estate improvements are provided in response to the demand generated by a population with effective purchasing power. A household—i.e., persons who occupy a group of rooms or a single room that constitutes one housing unit—imposes a basic demand for housing units. In analyzing a local housing market, a knowledge of trends in the formation of households and household characteristics is crucial. The age, size, income, and other characteristics of households must be considered to determine the demand for housing.

Two demographic categories generate demand for two different types of space:

1. *Households* generate demand for space designed to fulfill basic human needs such as housing, retail, and medical space.
2. *Employment* generates demand for space used in producing goods and services such as warehouse, industrial, office, and retail space.

Often households and employees generate demand for the same type of space, such as medical research and development space.

> **household:** A number of related or unrelated persons who live in one housing unit; all the persons occupying a group of rooms or a single room that constitutes one housing unit. A single person, a couple, or more than one family living in a single housing unit may make up a household.

The demand for commercial and industrial real estate is created by a population's demand for the goods and services to be produced or distributed at these sites. Appraisers must be aware of changes in the characteristics and distribution of the population that consumes goods and services as well as changes in the work force that produces them. A changing population coupled with technological advances can rapidly alter the demand for the services provided by property, which can affect property value. (See Chapter 11 for more discussion of economic base analysis and how appraisers use employment data in estimating supply and demand.)

Government Regulations

To develop an opinion of value properly, the appraiser should understand the government regulations and actions that affect the subject property. The comparable properties selected for analysis should be similar to the subject property in terms of zoning and other characteristics.

In response to social attitudes, the government establishes land use regulations and provides public services such as transportation systems and municipal utilities. Information on zoning, master plans, environmental impacts, transportation systems, local annexation policies, and other regulations reveals governmental and social attitudes toward real estate.

Trends in Building Activity

A property's value as of a specific date may rise or fall due to fluctuations in building activity. Housing starts and the construction of commercial and industrial properties fluctuate in response to business cycles, political events, and the cost and availability of financing. These fluctuations follow the long-term trend of new construction, which has been moving upward. Short-term fluctuations result in temporary misallocations of supply, which can depress rents and prices.

The standing stock of housing units at any point in time consists of all units, occupied or vacant. The stock is continually altered by the construction or conversion of units in response to developers' perceptions of the demand for new housing and by the need to replace existing units.

Six months to two years may pass between the time a developer decides to supply units and the time those units enter the market. During this period, changing conditions may reduce demand, and the units coming on the market may remain unrented and unsold, thus increasing vacancy rates. Developers may continue to produce additional units for some time, even in the face of rising vacancies. Once these excess units are produced, they remain on the market and can depress rents or prices until demand increases to remove the surplus. When the market tightens, the supply of units lags behind the increase in demand, resulting in abnormally low vacancy rates and upward pressure on rents and prices. Ultimately, supply materializes as developers respond to increased demand.

Fluctuations in the local supply of and demand for real estate (i.e., the life cycle of the market area, which is discussed in Chapter 8) are influenced by regional and national conditions. Therefore, an appraiser looks for regional and national trends that may indicate a positive or negative change in property values at the local level. Although all regions may not experience the same slump in construction, tight monetary policy affects the cost and availability of mortgage credit and exerts a moderating influence on supply, even in a rapidly growing region.

Commercial real estate is affected by business conditions and the cost and availability of financing. Because business firms pass their high financing costs on to consumers, residential construction may be restricted. If the demand for the goods and services produced or supplied by a business remains strong, the firm can raise prices and continue to expand even when credit is tight and interest rates are high.

Building Costs

The cost of replacing a building tends to follow the general price levels established over a long period, but these price levels vary from time to time and from place to place. Building costs generally decline or stabilize in periods of deflation and increase in periods of inflation. These costs are affected by material and labor costs, construction technology, architect and legal fees, financing costs, building codes, and public regulations such as zoning ordinances, environmental requirements, and subdivision regulations.

Construction costs can alter the quantity and character of demand and, therefore, the relative prices of property in real estate submarkets. The high cost of new buildings increases the demand for, and prices of, existing structures. When the cost of new structures increases, rehabilitation of existing buildings may become economically feasible. High building costs increase prices in single-family residential submarkets, which can increase the demand for rental units and their prices. The size and quality of the dwelling units demanded decrease when building costs increase more rapidly than purchasing power.

Cost services such as Marshall & Swift, R. S. Means, and others are the primary sources of information on building costs. Appraisers can also collect information on building costs from properties that have been developed in a market area. (Chapter 15 covers building cost estimates in more detail.)

Taxes

Real estate taxes are levied by both municipalities (cities, townships, or counties) and taxing districts (i.e., school, fire, water, local improvement district). The taxing body reviews the annual budget to determine the amount of money that needs to be raised. After revenues from other sources (such as sales or income taxes, state or federal revenue sharing, interest on investments) are deducted, the remaining funds must come from property taxes. Assessing officers estimate the value of each parcel of real estate in the jurisdiction periodically. Real estate taxes are based on the assessed value of real property, hence the term *ad valorem* ("according to value") taxes. The assessed value of property is normally based on, but not necessarily equivalent to, its market value.

The ratio of assessed value to market value is called the *common level ratio* or *assessment ratio*. If, for example, the tax rate is $60 per $1,000 of assessed value and the assessment ratio is 50%, then the annual real estate tax (or *effective tax rate*) equals 3% of market value:

> **ad valorem tax:** A real estate tax based on the assessed value of the property, which is not necessarily equivalent to its market value.

$$\frac{\$60}{\$1,000} \times 50\% = 3\%$$

If assessed value is not based on market value, the formula is modified to reflect the difference. An effective tax rate can also be calculated by dividing the total amount of taxes by the market value of the property. Effective tax rates can be used to compare the tax burden on properties.

In jurisdictions where ad valorem real estate tax assessments have an established or implied relationship to market value, appraisal services may be required to resolve tax appeals. In some communities, the trend in real estate taxes is an important consideration. In cities where public expenditures for schools and municipal services have increased, a heavy tax burden can cause real estate values to decline. Under these circumstances, new construction may be discouraged. There may be several tax districts in a metropolitan area, each with a different policy. Understanding the system of ad valorem taxation in an area facilitates the appraiser's analysis of how taxes affect value.

Different levels of sales taxes, personal property taxes, and taxes on earnings can also affect the relative desirability of properties. Although these taxes may be uniform within a state, properties in different states often compete with one another. To attract new residents and industries, a state may impose taxes that are lower than those of surrounding states. This may increase demand and enhance property values in the state relative to values in bordering states. For example, consider two adjacent states competing for the location of a commercial printing operation. The printing company owns machinery and equipment worth millions of dollars that may be taxed as personal property rather than real property, which is more often the case for industrial operations than for commercial operations. The state that does not have a personal property tax would be a more attractive location than the state that levies a personal property tax.

Financing

The cost of financing includes the interest rate and any points, discounts, equity participations, or other charges that the lender requires to increase the effective yield on the loan. Financing depends on the borrower's ability to qualify for a loan, which may be determined based on the loan-to-value ratio, the housing expense-to-income ratio allowed for loans on single-family homes, and the debt coverage and break-even ratios required for loans on income-producing properties. (These ratios are discussed in Chapter 22.) The cost and availability of financing typically have an inverse relationship; high interest rates and other costs usually are accompanied by a decrease in the demand for credit and a borrower's ability to qualify.

The cost and availability of credit for real estate financing influence both the quantity and quality of the real estate demanded and supplied. When interest rates are high or mortgage funds are limited, households that would have been in the home ownership market find that their incomes cannot support the required expenses. Purchases are delayed and smaller homes with fewer amenities are bought. The cost of land development financing and construction financing is reflected in the higher prices asked for new single-family homes, and higher prices reduce the quantity of homes demanded.

The rental market is affected by the demand pressure of households that continue to rent and by the high cost of supplying new units, which results in part from financing costs. Occupancy rates and rents rise. Businesses try to pass on their higher occupancy costs to customers by increasing the prices of their products or services. If they cannot fully recover the increased occupancy cost, the value of these properties will decline or the quantity of commercial and individual space supplied is reduced.

Specific Data

Specific data includes details about the property being appraised, comparable sales and rental properties, and relevant local market characteristics. In appraisals this

> **Specific data** comprises information on the subject property, comparable properties, and market transactions.

data is used to determine highest and best use and to make the specific comparisons and analyses required to develop an opinion of market value. The specific data about a subject property provided in land and building descriptions helps the appraiser select specific data pertaining to comparable sales, rentals, construction costs, and local market characteristics.

In analyzing general data, national, regional, and local trends in value are emphasized. In an analysis of specific data, the characteristics of the subject property and comparable properties are studied. At the conclusion of the general data analysis, the appraiser needs to clearly spell out what this data and analysis means or implies for the specific market and property being valued. It is the same process used in bringing comparable sales data together, analyzing it, and indicating what it implies in terms of an opinion of value for the subject property. From relevant comparable sales, an appraiser extracts specific sale prices, rental terms, income and expense figures, rates of return on investment, construction costs, estimates of the economic life of improvements, and rates of depreciation. These figures are used in calculations that lead to an indication of value for the subject property.

An appraiser needs specific data to apply each of the three approaches to value. The appraiser uses the data to derive adjustments for value-influencing property characteristics, to isolate meaningful units of comparison, to develop capitalization rates, and to measure depreciation. By extracting relevant data from the largest quantity of data available, an appraiser develops a sense of the market. This perception is an essential component of appraisal judgment, which is applied in the valuation process and in the final reconciliation of value indications.

Specific data is analyzed through comparison. In each approach to value, certain items of information must be extracted from market data to make comparisons. Specific data is studied to determine if these items are present or absent and if they can be used to make reliable comparisons with the subject property. Such specific data can include information about properties that have sold as well as properties that have not sold. If, for example, the subject property is an apartment building, the appraiser could use sales of other apartment buildings to support adjustments for changes in market condition, locational differences, or the contribution of various physical characteristics. Apartment buildings that have not sold can also be used to obtain information on rental rates and expenses.

The appraiser's analysis of the highest and best use of the land as though vacant and the property as improved determines what comparable specific data is collected and analyzed. The comparable properties must have the same highest and best use as the subject property. The nature and amount of research needed for a specific assignment depend on the property type, the purpose of the appraisal, and the complexity of the required analysis.

Competitive Supply and Demand Data

The valuation process requires that a property be appraised within the context of its market. Of particular significance to the analysis are the supply of competitive properties, the future demand for the property being appraised, and its highest and best use. After inspecting the subject property and

> Market data on **competitive supply and demand** allows the appraiser to estimate current and future demand for property.

gathering property-specific data, the appraiser inventories the supply of properties that constitute the major competition for the property in its defined market.

Competitive Supply Inventory

The supply inventory includes all competitive properties:

• Rental units
• Properties that have been sold
• Properties being offered for sale
• Properties that will come on the market

The subject property will have to be able to compete in a future market. Therefore, the appraiser's investigation must cover not only existing competition but also prospective projects that will compete with the subject.

Demand Study

Along with the supply inventory of major competitive properties, the appraiser analyzes the prospective demand for the subject property. The appraiser cannot assume the current use is necessarily the use for which the most demand will exist in the future. Even in the most stable markets, subtle shifts in the market appeal or utility of a category of properties can put some properties at a competitive disadvantage and benefit others. Even in volatile markets characterized by rapid changes due to factors such as accelerating growth, precipitous decline, or an upturn in proposed construction, appraisers need to quantify demand in some manner.

The specific techniques applied to study market demand can be highly sophisticated and may fall outside the scope of normal appraisal practice. In some cases the appraiser might use data compiled by special market research firms (proprietary data) to supplement the appraisal. All appraisers should, however, develop an understanding of market research techniques and acquire the skills needed to conduct basic demand studies. (For further discussion of market research and analysis techniques, see Chapter 11.)

Data Collection

The scope of work of an appraisal assignment includes consideration of the extent of the data collection process. If the assignment is simple, the appraiser may rely on general data on file and specific data about the subject and comparable properties. For a complex assignment, the data collection process may be one of the more difficult tasks.

Sources of General Data

The general data needed to appraise real property is available from a wide variety of sources. A substantial amount of information is compiled and disseminated by federal, state, and local agencies. Trade associations and private business enterprises may also provide data. Table 7.2 lists some common sources of general data.

> **Sources of general data** include federal government publications, state and local government offices, trade associations, and private research firms.

General data is an integral part of an appraiser's office files. Data obtained from various sources can be cataloged and cross-indexed. General data such as multiple listing information and census data can be accessed by computer. Many local and regional planning and development agencies computerize the following information by geographic area:

- Housing inventory and vacancies
- Demolitions and conversions
- Commercial construction
- Household incomes
- New land use by zoning classification
- Population and demographics
- Housing forecasts

In recent years many databases have been developed for online access to information. Large databases are also accessible to small computers through CD-ROM technology. Such databases cover a broad range of topics and offer many options to appraisers performing general or specialized research. The information available is virtually unlimited and includes topics such as

- Current and historical news
- Industry analyses and reports
- Corporate earnings and analyses
- Local, regional, and national Yellow Pages listings
- Publication indexes and articles

Recent developments in computer software and hardware have resulted in low-cost, high-performance databasing combinations for appraisers. Hundreds of individual programs are now used with desktop systems in appraisal offices. Some databases are contained in a single computer, while others are shared by

Table 7.2	**Commonly Used Sources of General Data**

Council of Economic Advisors

Publications	• *The Economic Report of the President* • *Economic Indicators* (monthly publication prepared for the Joint Economic Committee)

Information Available	Data and analysis of housing starts and financing
	Information on
	    • Total output, income, and spending
	    • Employment, unemployment, and wages
	    • Production and business activity
	    • Prices
	    • Money, credit, and security markets
	    • Federal finance
	    • International statistics

Where To Find It	http://w3.access.gpo.gov/eop http://www.access.gpo.gov/congress/eibrowse/broecind.html

Federal Reserve Board

Publications	• *The Federal Reserve Bulletin* • *Historical Chart Book*

Information Available	Information on
	    • Gross national product
	    • Gross domestic product
	    • National income
	    • Mortgage markets
	    • Interest rates
	    • Installment credit
	    • Sources of funds
	    • Business activity
	    • The labor force, employment, and industrial production
	    • Housing and construction
	    • International finance

Where To Find It	http://www.federalreserve.gov/publications.htm

National Vital Statistics System

Publications	• *Vital Statistics of the United States* • *National Vital Statistics Reports* (formerly the *Monthly Vital Statistics Report*)
Information Available	Statistics on birth and death rates
Where To Find It	http://www.cdc.gov/nchs/nvss.htm

U.S. Department of Commerce, Bureau of the Census

Publications	• *Census of Population* • *Census of Housing* • *Census of Manufacturers* • *Census of Agriculture* • *Annual Housing Survey* • *Statistical Abstract of the United States*
Information Available	• Current population • Population estimates • Population projections consumer income • Housing completions • Housing permits • Other housing statistics
Where To Find It	http://www.census.gov/prod/www/titles.html

Table 7.2	**Commonly Used Sources of General Data** *(continued)*

U.S. Department of Commerce, Bureau of Economic Analysis

Publication	• *Survey of Current Business*
Information Available	• Consumer Price Index • Wholesale price index • Data on mortgage debt • Value of new construction
Where To Find It	http://www.bea.doc.gov/bea/pubs.htm

U.S. Department of Housing and Urban Development

Publications	• *American Housing Survey* • *The State of the Cities* • *FHA Outlook*
Information Available	• Reports on FHA building starts, financing, and housing programs administered by the department • Also FHA vacancy surveys for selected metropolitan areas
Where To Find It	http://www.hud.gov

U.S. Department of Labor, Bureau of Labor Statistics

Publication	• *Monthly Labor Review*
Information Available	• Consumer Price Index • Wholesale prices • Monthly and annual employment and earnings figures
Where To Find It	http://stats.bls.gov/opub/mlr/mlrhome.htm

State and local departments of development, local and regional planning agencies, the state demographer, and regional or metropolitan transportation authorities

Publications	Often these agencies publish directories of manufacturers that list, by county, the names of firms, their products, and their employment figures as well as other reports.
Information Available	Information on • Population • Households • Employment • Master plans • Present and future utility • Transportation systems
Where To Find It	Use online search engines to search for relevant terms such as "economic development," formal names of various local agencies, or national associations of applicable agencies such as the National Association of Regional Councils (http://www.narc.org) and the Association of Metropolitan Planning Organizations (http://www.ampo.org). Appendix 3 of *Real Estate Damages: An Analysis of Detrimental Conditions* (Chicago: Appraisal Institute, 1999) lists contact information for many state agencies.

State bureaus of employment service or state bureaus of labor

Publications	Research reports on various topics, e.g., *Market Analysis of Key Workforce Trends* (published by the Ohio Bureau of Labor Market Information) and *Pennsylvania Labor Force* (published by the Pennsylvania Center for Workforce Information and Analysis)
Information Available	County data on • Employment • Unemployment • Wage rates
Where To Find It	Use online search engines to search for relevant terms such as "economic development" or formal names of state bureau of employment or labor. Appendix 3 of *Real Estate Damages: An Analysis of Detrimental Conditions* (Chicago: Appraisal Institute, 1999) lists contact information for many state agencies.

Table 7.2	**Commonly Used Sources of General Data** *(continued)*

Chambers of commerce

Publications	Publications related to local business and demographics, e.g., *The Economic Overview of Austin Texas* (published by the Greater Austin Chamber of Commerce) and *Washington Manufacturers Register* (published by the Greater Seattle Chamber of Commerce)
Information Available	Information, often obtained from secondary sources such as the census, on • Local population • Households • Employment • Industry
Where To Find It	Use online search engines to search for relevant terms such as "population statistics" or formal names of local chamber. Also, see: http://www.uschamber.com/Chambers/Chamber+Directory/default.htm

Real estate associations such as American Real Estate Society (ARES), American Society of Appraisers (ASA), American Society of Farm Managers and Rural Appraisers (ASFMRA), Appraisal Institute, Building Owners and Managers Association (BOMA), Counselors of Real Estate, International Association of Assessing Officers (IAAO), Mortgage Bankers Association of America (MBA), National Association of Realtors® and its affiliates, and Urban Land Institute (ULI)

Publications	Many publications with data useful to appraisers • *Journal of Real Estate Research* • *Valuation Insights & Perspectives* • *Real Estate Value Cycles* • *BOMA International/Cushman & Wakefield Market Intelligence Report* • *BOMA Experience Exchange Report* • *Real Estate Issues* • *Assessment Journal* • *Ratio Study Practices* • *The National Association of Realtors Commercial Real Estate Quarterly* • *National Real Estate Review: Market Conditions Report*
Information Available	Information on • National and regional economic indicators • Existing home sales for the nation as a whole and for individual regions • Office vacancy rates
Where To Find It	http://www.aresnet.org http://www.appraisers.org http://www.asfmra.com http://www.appraisalinstitute.org http://www.boma.org http://www.cre.org http://www.iaao.org http://www.mbaa.org http://nar.realtor.com http://www.uli.org

National Association of Homebuilders

Publications	• *Sales and Marketing Management Magazine* • *Survey of Buying Power*
Information Available	Information, by county and for selected cities, on • New housing starts • Prices • Construction costs • Financing • Households • Income distribution • Retail sales
Where To Find It	http://www.nahb.com

Table 7.2	**Commonly Used Sources of General Data** *(continued)*

Private sources such as banks, utility companies, university research centers, private advisory firms, multiple listing services, cost data services

Publications	• White papers and research reports
Information Available	Information on
	• Bank debt
	• Department store sales
	• Employment indicators
	• Land prices
	• Corporate business indicators
	• Mortgage money costs
	• Wage rates
	• Construction costs
	• Deeds
	• Mortgage recordings
	• The installation of utility meters
Where To Find It	Utilities
	• http://www.utilityconnection.com
	University research centers
	• http://www.ukans.edu/cwis/units/coms2/po/index.html
	• http://ideas.uqam.ca/EDIRC/index.html

several computers or terminals through local or telecommunication networks. Improvements in telecommunication programs and facilities, word processing, and electronic spreadsheets have facilitated appraisal analysis and report writing, as well as the use of database information.[4]

Sources of Specific Data

Like sources of general data, sources of specific data are diverse. In addition to the data obtained from public records and published sources, personal contact with developers, builders, brokers, financial and legal specialists, property managers, local planners, and other real estate professionals can provide useful information. Thus, practicing appraisers need communication skills as well as analytical techniques to research sales, improvement costs, and income and expense data thoroughly in the process of performing appraisal assignments.

> **Sources of specific data** are public records (e.g., deeds, recorded leases), newspapers (e.g., advertised sale prices and rentals), multiple listing services, cost-estimating manuals, and market participants such as brokers, lenders, contractors, owners, and tenants.

4. For further information on databases and electronic commerce, see Robert D. Butters, "Do You Own Your Data? Intellectual and Other Property Rights in Real Estate," *Valuation Insights & Perspectives*, vol. 4, no. 2 (Second Quarter 1999): 40–43; Bennie D. Waller, "Electronic Data Interchange and Electronic Commerce: The Future of Appraising," *The Appraisal Journal* (October 1999): 370–374; Bennie D. Waller, "A Survey of the Technology Astuteness of the Appraisal Industry," *The Appraisal Journal* (October 2000): 469–473; Gordon Jenkins and Ray Lancashire, *The Electronic Commerce Handbook: A Quick Read on How Electronic Commerce Can Keep You Competitive* (Etobicoke, Ontario, Canada: EDI Council of Canada, 1994); and Richard D. Wincott, "Addressing Electronic Commerce, Impact of Capital Markets in the Real Estate Industry, and Changes in Appraisal Licensing Regulations," *The Appraisal Journal* (July 1999): 313–314.

Public Records

The appraiser searches public records for a copy of the property deed of the subject or comparable properties as needed. In some jurisdictions, public property records can be searched electronically. The deed provides important information about the property and the sales transaction, including the full names of the parties involved and the transaction date. A legal description of the property, the property rights included in the transaction, and any outstanding liens on the title are indicated.

Occasionally the names of the parties may raise a concern that unusual motivations were involved in the sale. For example, a sale from John Smith to Mary Smith Jones may be a transfer from a father to a daughter; a sale from John Smith, William Jones, and Harold Long to the SJL Corporation may be a change of ownership in name only, not an arm's-length transaction arrived at by unrelated parties under no duress.

In some states the law requires that the consideration paid upon transfer of title be shown on the deed. However, this consideration does not always reflect the actual sale price. To reduce transfer taxes, some purchasers—e.g., buyers of motels or apartments—deduct the estimated value of personal property from the true consideration paid. Because these personal property values are sometimes inflated, the recorded consideration for the real property may be less than the actual consideration. In one case, the consideration indicated on the deed may be overstated to obtain a higher loan than is warranted; in another, the consideration may be understated to justify a low property tax assessment. Although some states require that the actual consideration be listed on the deed, other states—i.e., nondisclosure states—allow the consideration to be reported as "$10 and other valuable consideration."

The local tax assessor's records may include property cards for the subject property and comparables properties, with land and building sketches, area measurements, sale prices, and other information. In some locations, legal or private publishing services issue information about revenue stamps and other facts pertaining to current property transfers.

arm's-length transaction: A transaction between unrelated parties under no duress.

Published News

Most city newspapers feature real estate news, and many business trade publications cover real estate activity on a local, regional, or national basis. Although some of the news may be incomplete or inaccurate, an appraiser can use this secondary source to confirm details because the names of the negotiating brokers and the parties to transactions are usually published.

Market Participants

Other real estate professionals such as brokers, appraisers, managers, and bankers can often provide information about transactions and suggest valuable leads. Individual sources may be definitive, but if the information obtained from real estate professionals is third-party data, the appraiser should look for separate verification.

Listings and Offerings

Whenever possible, an appraiser should gather information about properties offered for sale. An appraiser can request that his or her name be added to the mailing lists of banks, brokers, and others who offer properties for sale. Classified ads of listed properties suggest the strength or weakness of the local market for a particular type of property and the sales activity in a particular area. Information on purchase offers may also be obtained from brokers or managers. Listings, which represent the owner's perception of the property's value, usually reflect the upper limit of value; offers, which represent the buyer's perspective, commonly set the lower limit of value.

Listings and offerings can be useful indicators of the values anticipated by sellers and buyers and reflect the likely turnover of competitive properties. Listings are usually set at a level that will excite market interest and therefore may be employed to test market activity. They are relevant market phenomena that the appraiser considers in analyzing competitive supply and demand. The appraiser may find that tabulating information about competitive properties in a market data grid facilitates comparing the market position of the subject property to that of the competition.

listing: A written contract in which an owner employs a broker to sell his or her real estate.

offering: A set of terms presented by the bidder, a prospective buyer or tenant, that are subject to negotiation. If the other party, a seller or landlord, accepts these terms, the offer will result in a contract.

Multiple listing services. In many communities the local Board of Realtors® publishes books and maintains electronic databases of listings, which are known as *multiple listing services* (MLS). These sources primarily contain data on residential properties listed for sale during the calendar year or fiscal quarter and cite their listing prices. They contain fairly complete information about these properties, including descriptions and brokers' names. However, details about a property's square footage, basement area, or exact age may be inaccurate or excluded. In certain areas, multiple listing books or access to electronic databases can be purchased. Multiple listing services sometimes publish the sale prices of properties that have been sold. Only a small percentage of commercial, industrial, or special-purpose properties are included in traditional MLS books, so appraisers must investigate other databases, often those of a commercial Board of Realtors®.

National property databases. Like traditional multiple listing services, shared data warehouses such as the Appraisal Institute Residential Database and Appraisal Institute Commercial Database provide property-specific information to analysts for a fee. The prime advantage of the databases sponsored by real estate organizations, as opposed to traditional MLS services and public databases maintained by local assessors offices, is the greater reliability of property data contributed by professional appraisers and the larger geographical scope of available data. Also, information on comparable leases and operating expenses, which are normally not available from data services, can be searched.

The potential for misuse of such pooled data is a concern. Any attempt to reduce the appraisal process to the perfunctory application of statistical and regression analyses is a disservice to both consumers and lenders. The increasing use of automated valuation models (AVMs)—computer applications that generate values using mathematical algorithms—by lenders who want to increase the speed of the appraisal process has been a troubling development for some appraisers who see AVMs as a threat to their businesses rather than a tool they can use to provide more accurate analyses to their clients more efficiently.[5] Also, the confidentiality of certain information in real property transactions is a continuously evolving issue. Both the Uniform Standards of Professional Appraisal Practice and federal legislation such as the Gramm-Leach-Bliley Act of 1999 set forth privacy regulations regarding confidential information. Certain shared databases allow for restricted access to certain fields within data records deemed confidential by the contributor of the data, and other databases only pool data that is not considered confidential.

Sources of Competitive Supply and Demand Data

A competitive supply inventory is compiled in several steps:

1. The appraiser first conducts a field inspection to inventory competitive properties in the subject market area and competitive market areas.
2. The appraiser then can interview owners, managers, and brokers of competitive properties in the area as well as developers and city planners. Field inspection and interviews are especially important because investors rely heavily on local competitive supply and demand analyses.
3. An examination of building permits (both issued and acted upon), plat maps, and surveys of competitive sites provides insight into prospective supply.
4. Data on available space as well as vacancy, absorption, and turnover rates in specific property markets can be obtained from electronic databases and reports prepared by real estate research firms.

Sources of competitive supply and demand data include field inspections, interviews with market participants, building permits and plat maps, proprietary data, and demographic and economic data compiled by the U.S. Census and Labor Bureaus.

Demand can be estimated using demographic data (population and vital

5. See also Mark R. Linne, M. Steven Kane, and George Dell, *A Guide to Appraisal Valuation Modeling* (Chicago: Appraisal Institute, 2000).

SAMPLING

Appraisers rarely have access to all available information for use in their analyses. Even when an appraiser has conducted extensive research, sample information frequently must be used. Therefore, the principles and implications of sampling should be understood.

Appraisers frequently must deal with incomplete information. Research involves the collection of both specific data and sample data for analytical purposes. The data used by appraisers is seldom a random sample. To establish a framework for selecting and drawing a random sampling, strict requirements must be met. More often, appraisers deal with *judgment samples*, i.e., sample data that is selected on the basis of personal judgment and is thought to constitute a representative group. While certain statistical tests used with random samples cannot be applied to judgment samples, in many circumstances judgment samples can produce superior results. For example, data selected from five shopping centers by an experienced analyst may be more comparable to the subject shopping center than a random sampling of data from a broader array of shopping centers.

The use of sample data has both strengths and weaknesses:

Strengths

- Samples are generally less expensive and more readily obtained than complete data. Selected samples are sometimes more indicative than a broader survey.
- Samples are easily tabulated, lend themselves to cross-referencing, and provide a foundation for statistical inference, including probability studies.
- Often samples may be the only source of data available.

Weaknesses

- Sampling must be conducted carefully and the data must be properly interpreted. If not, the results can be inaccurate and misleading, more expensive than they are worth, and less reliable than they appear.
- Sampling requires special training and understanding. Many people misunderstand or mistrust samples for a variety of reasons.

Whether or not the appraiser conducts formal sampling, the extent to which sample data has been used should be considered in the analytical process. The risks associated with identified sample data and the uncertainties associated with other potential data must be considered.

Data samples may be particularly important when other data is scarce or when the available data is less applicable due to market changes. Sampling may be the only way to obtain some types of data. Samples are particularly important in

- Quantifying market demand
- Defining market characteristics
- Identifying market attitudes, perceptions, and motivations
- Analyzing market behavior
- Interpreting market activities and intentions

statistics) and economic data (employment and income statistics) for the market area. The Census Bureau (Department of Commerce) and Bureau of Labor Statistics compile and publish statistical data, which is often also available in electronic form. Other private and public sources provide historical data and projections based on small area populations. Appraisers who rely on projections prepared by market research firms should have a clear understanding of the methodology used to make the projection, otherwise the data may represent little more than a blind data set. To test the reasonableness of small area projections, comparisons should be made between the demographic data and the supply data collected in the specified market. Supply data may include building permits and market sales or absorption rates kept by public agencies such as building inspection, city planning, and public works departments.

Personal observation is also useful in estimating local demand. For example, the planned closing of an army base should be considered in analyzing the future demand for adjacent commercial properties such as dry cleaners, motels, bars, and restaurants. An appraiser who has observed development near highway interchanges will be able to anticipate that a proposed freeway interchange will generate future demand for shops, service stations, and motels catering to the needs of motorists and tourists.

Geographic Information Systems and TIGER Data

The Topographically Integrated Geographic Encoding and Referencing (TIGER) system created by the U.S. Census Bureau in the 1980s is of special relevance to appraisals of sites being considered for development. TIGER files contain the geographic base information used to create maps based on the 2000 Census and are essential ingredients in a geographic information system (GIS). A GIS using TIGER/Line data allows an appraiser to analyze information on traffic analysis zones (TAZs), acreage available for development, zone densities, and other physical characteristics and geographical relationships in a market area. Other GIS databases contain information about local taxes (e.g., property assessments, school levies) and infrastructure (e.g., gas lines).[6]

Geographic information system technology facilitates the addition of geographic reference data to individual items in real estate databases. Personal computers and larger, networked computer workstations can draw on this information to map or model the spatial referents and represent the spatial relationships among the data points. Equally important, spreadsheets or tabular grids can be produced in written formats, which can help the user better understand these relationships.

Data from public sources at local, state, and national levels is available and, in most cases, less expensive than the cost of undertaking primary research. A combination of public data and other data available

Topographically Integrated Geographic Encoding and Referencing (TIGER) datafiles: Geographically referenced data files that are commercially available to GIS users.

geographic information system (GIS): A communications technology that combines spatial information from a national database compiled by the 1990 census with computer mapping and modeling capabilities.

6.   See also Gilbert H. Castle III, editor, *GIS in Real Estate: Integrating, Analyzing, and Presenting Locational Information* (Chicago: Appraisal Institute, 1998).

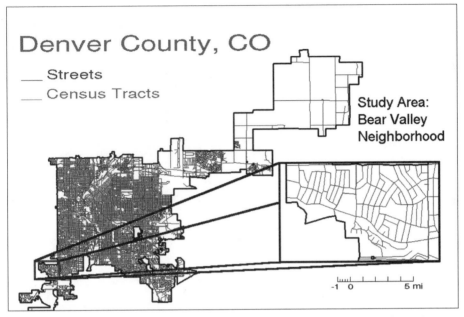

Geographic information systems facilitate the graphical presentation of geocoded data and the analysis of physical characteristics and geographic relationships in a market area

from proprietary sources allows an appraiser to assemble and map information and then analyze that information in ways previously regarded as technically infeasible or too costly. Initially, attention was largely focused on the mapping capabilities of GIS, but new technology is helping expand opportunities for data analysis and is promoting greater understanding of the results of such analysis.

GIS can integrate digital maps with point- or area-specific data to answer basic questions such as the following:

1. What is found in a specific location?
2. Where within a given area is a specific feature, activity, or event located?
3. What changes have occurred in an area over a given period of time?
4. What type of spatial patterns characterize a given area?
5. What impact will a specific change have on the area?

The data used to generate such maps is typically found in computer databases that include referents to a specific point on the earth's surface (i.e., latitude and longitude) and/or a specific area (e.g., city, zip code area, census tract).

Given sufficient information, the system can quickly pinpoint properties with specific characteristics. For example, the system can identify the locations of all parcels of vacant land in a given county that have the following characteristics:

- Contain 40 or more acres
- Meet specific soil suitability standards

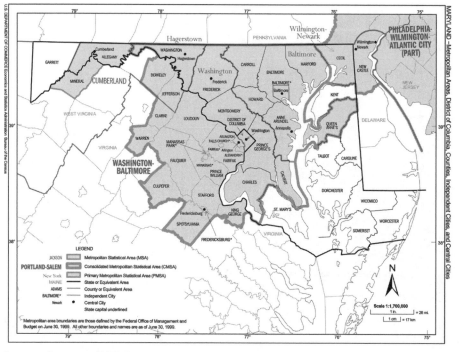

For more information on TIGER data and mapping, see http://tiger.census.gov.

- Are equipped with municipal water and sewer lines
- Are zoned for residential use
- Have an elementary school within a one-half mile radius and are adjacent to residential neighborhoods where median home value exceeds $150,000

The dramatic increase in the use of GIS equipment is the result of three factors:

1. The decline in the price of high-powered personal computers
2. Improvements in GIS software
3. Expansion of commercially available geocoded data

In addition to commercially available TIGER data, accurate digital base maps for most areas of the United States are also available at reasonable prices from the United States Geological Survey (USGS). (See Chapter 9 for more discussion of topography and land or site analysis.) Many local governments sell geocoded digital data on individual parcels that is compiled from assessment data and public record information. Data vendors will continue to expand the amount of commercially available data compatible with GIS.

ELECTRONIC DATA INTERCHANGE

Electronic data interchange (EDI) is the electronic exchange of information between entities using standard, machine-processable, structured data formats. Efforts by various mortgage originators, insurers, and secondary mortgage market agencies to set up a computer-to-computer information exchange led to the creation of EDI in 1994.*

Translation software for EDI enables computer users to electronically access a standardized database on residential properties created from EDI-formatted appraisals prepared on the Uniform Residential Appraisal Report (URAR) form. EDI was created to streamline the work of mortgage underwriters, reduce mortgage origination costs, and improve service to consumers.

As EDI technology reengineers the mortgage loan process, the lending industry has actively pursued the establishment of data standards for all mortgage market functions involving interaction among sellers, servicers, and investors in mortgages. Federal and secondary mortgage market agencies also have mandates to implement and standardize electronic information procurement.†

---

* Among the 27 firms and organizations that participated in the National Property Data Service Work Group and helped coordinate EDI were the Mortgage Bankers Association, Fannie Mae, Freddie Mac, and the Appraisal Institute. The Data Interchange Standards Association (DISA) is responsible for ensuring that EDI meets acceptable standards for electronic data transmission. The Accredited Standards Committee X12 of the American National Standards Association has approved the transaction sets used to format appraisal reports for EDI.

† W. Lee Minnerly, *Electronic Data Interchange (EDI) and the Appraisal Office* (Chicago: Appraisal Institute, 1995), 1–12.

Selecting Comparable Data and Establishing Comparability

Descriptions and classifications of the characteristics and components of comparable properties are assembled in land and improvement analyses. The appraiser selects data from these analyses and analyzes it in the sales comparison, cost, and income capitalization approaches. The data used for comparison in the three approaches should come from properties that are similar to the property being appraised. The selection of comparables is directed to some extent by the availability of data. Investigation of an active market usually reveals an adequate and representative number of transactions within a restricted area and time period.

An appraiser gathers broad information about a market from its pattern of sales. Important market characteristics can be revealed by significant factors such as the following:

- Number of sales
- Period of time covered by the sales
- Availability of property for sale
- Rate of absorption
- Rate of turnover—i.e., volume of sales and level of activity
- Characteristics and motivations of buyers and sellers
- Terms and conditions of sale
- Use of property before and after its sale

While analyzing data to establish comparability and select sales, an appraiser begins to form certain conclusions about the general market, the subject property, and the possible relationships between the data and the subject property. The appraiser ascertains the following:

- Market strengths and weaknesses
- The probable supply of, demand for, and marketability of properties similar to the property being appraised
- The variations and characteristics likely to have the greatest impact on the value of properties in the market

Thus, an appraiser analyzes data against a background of information about the particular area and the specific type of property.

The information needed to apply the cost and income capitalization approaches must often be obtained from market sources other than sales. This information may also be used to refine adjustments made in the sales comparison approach. In the investigation of general and market area data, an appraiser learns about trends in

- Construction costs
- Lease terms
- Typical expenses
- Vacancy rates

Examining trends in the market where the subject property is located provides additional specific data that can be used to derive value indications and successfully complete valuation assignments.

The geographic area from which comparable sales can be selected depends on the property type. In valuing certain types of retail property, only properties with main street frontage may be pertinent. For many large industrial properties and most investment properties, the entire community should be studied; for larger properties, the national market may be relevant. For a residential appraisal, adequate data can sometimes be found within a block of the subject property. Even in these cases, however, the appraiser should consider the broader market to place the subject property and the comparables in a general market context.

When comparable sales data is scarce in the subject property's immediate area, the appraiser may need to extend the data search to adjacent market areas and similar communities. The appraiser must establish the comparability of the alternative market before using the data from that market. When the selection of data is limited to an unacceptably narrow sample of current market activity, the appraiser may decide to use sales that are less current or to interview brokers, buyers, sellers, owners, and tenants of similar properties in the area to obtain evidence of potential market activity such as listing prices or offers to purchase. Listings and offers may be analyzed for comparability, but they are not generally adjusted.

In general, comparable properties fall into two categories:

1. The first and preferred category includes those that are comparable to and competitive with the property being appraised or have a demonstrable effect on prices or other relevant components of the market in question.
2. The second category includes those that are comparable to, but not competitive with, the subject.

With computer analysis, a large number of properties can be studied in the course of a single assignment, which may generate a deeper understanding of each property's contribution to, and influence on, a given market.

The appraiser should pay attention to several factors to judge if data is useful:

1. The degree of comparability
2. The quantity of information available
3. The authenticity and reliability of the data

The appraiser must not assume that all data pertinent to an assignment is completely reliable. Sales figures, costs, and other information subject to misrepresentation should be scrutinized for authenticity.

Appraisers seek data that will facilitate accurate comparisons, but every real estate parcel is unique. The comparability of properties varies, and the appraiser may find it necessary to place less confidence on a given comparable. Nevertheless, the appraiser may want to consider this comparable for its evidence of, and effect on, the marketplace.

Appraisers have a special responsibility to scrutinize the comparability of all data used in a valuation assignment. They must fully understand the concept of comparability and should avoid comparing properties with different highest and best uses, limiting their search for comparables, or selecting inappropriate factors for comparison.

Data Organization

Market data grids are the most common tool used to organize data. They can be as detailed as the analysis dictates. In a basic *data array grid*, the appraiser lists significant characteristics of the subject and comparable properties that have been isolated. This type of grid summarizes the data presented and allows the appraiser to identify those factors that may account for differences in value and those that probably do not. The data array grid only presents data; it is not used for comparing the properties. In an *adjustment grid* the sale properties are compared to the subject and specific adjustments are made to their prices.

The market data grid should include the total sale price of each comparable property and the date of each sale, which can be expressed in relation to the subject property's date of valuation—e.g., one

> Appraisers seek data that will facilitate **accurate comparisons,** but every real estate parcel is unique.

month ago, 16 months ago. The grid also includes information about the property rights conveyed, the financial arrangements of the sale, and any unusual motivations of the buyer or seller that may have resulted in a negotiating advantage, such as a desire to liquidate a property for inheritance tax or to acquire a particular property for expansion.

The market data grid can include characteristics of the subject and comparable properties, information on sales transactions, and pertinent market data from other sources. The appraiser may choose to use two or more market data grids, i.e., one grid for comparable sales data and other grids for information derived from other sources. Isolating specific data may indicate the type of information the appraiser will be able to derive from the collected data and identify variations among properties that may be significant to their value.

In examining the market data grid, the appraiser may find that certain data is not pertinent and will not be useful in applying the approaches to value. For example, if an appraiser who is valuing an industrial property finds that the subject and the comparables all occupy one-acre sites, site size will probably not account for differences in the properties' sale or unit prices. If the percentages of office space in the properties vary, however, the difference may have an effect on value.

Analysis of the data array grid may indicate that additional data is required and that the appraiser needs to create other grids to include more information or to isolate the data required for specific approaches. Appraisers should see data analysis as a process and the market data grid as a tool that facilitates this process and the derivation of valid indications of property value. Although many market data grids may be prepared in the development of an appraisal, not all grids are necessary for the appraisal report; only those that will help to explain the significance of the data to the client need to be included in the appraisal report. (Further discussion and examples of the use of adjustment grids for data analysis are provided in Chapter 18.)

market data grid: A tabular representation of market data organized into useful, measurable categories.

FURTHER READING

Byrne, Therese E. *A Guide to Real Estate Information Sources*, 1980.

Gilon, Paul, and C.A. Cardenas. "Appraisers and Cyberspace: the Internet." *The Appraisal Journal* (October 1995).

Minnerly, W. Lee. *Electronic Data Interchange (EDI) and the Appraisal Office*. Chicago: Appraisal Institute, 1996.

Nielson, Donald A. "World Wide Web Data Sources for the Appraiser: U.S. Census Changes for the Year 2000." *Valuation Insights & Perspectives*, vol. 5, no. 1 (First Quarter 2000).

Rayburn, William B., and Dennis S. Tosh. "Artificial Intelligence, the Future of Appraising." *The Appraisal Journal* (October 1995).

Simpson, John A. *Property Inspection: An Appraiser's Guide*. Chicago: Appraisal Institute, 1997.

United States Department of Commerce, Bureau of Census. *Statistical Abstract of the United States*, 1990. Washington, D.C.: U.S. Government Printing Office, 1990.

MARKET AREAS, NEIGHBORHOODS, AND DISTRICTS

Social, economic, governmental, and environmental forces influence property values in the vicinity of a subject property. As a result, they affect the value of the subject property. Therefore, to conduct a thorough analysis, the appraiser must delineate the boundaries of the area of influence. Although physical boundaries may be drawn, the most important boundaries are those that identify factors influencing property values.

The area of influence, commonly called a *neighborhood*, can be defined as a group of complementary land uses. A residential neighborhood, for example, may contain single-family homes and commercial properties that provide services for local residents. A *district*, on the other hand, has one predominant land use. Districts are commonly composed of apartments or commercial, industrial, or agricultural properties. In broader terms, appraisers analyze the *market area* within which a subject property competes for the attentions of buyers and sellers in the real estate market. A market area can encompass one or more neighborhoods and/or districts.

The term *market area* may be more useful than either *neighborhood* or *district* for several reasons:

- Using the umbrella term *market area* avoids the confusing and negative implications of the other terms.
- A market area can include neighborhoods, districts, and combinations of both.
- Understanding how real estate markets work is essential in almost every step of the valuation process. The term *market area*—more than the terms neighborhood and district— refers to an area where market participants live and work. The term also refers to areas on which appraisers focus when analyzing value influences.[1]

To identify a market area's boundaries, an appraiser examines a subject property's surroundings. The investigation begins with the subject property and

---

1. In the Uniform Standards of Professional Appraisal Practice, the word *neighborhood* has been replaced by *market area* in Standards Rule 1-3. In this edition of *The Appraisal of Real Estate, market area* will be used for specific references to the local market area as defined in an appraisal report as well as in the general manner the term has been traditionally used in market analysis. The term *neighborhood*, which is still used on the major residential appraisal report forms, will continue to be used for references to the concept of a specifically defined geographic area characterized by complementary land uses.

market area: The defined geographic area in which the subject property competes for the attentions of market participants; the term broadly defines an area containing diverse land uses.

neighborhood: A group of complementary land uses; a related grouping of inhabitants, buildings, or business enterprises.

district: A market area characterized by one predominant land use—e.g., apartment, commercial, industrial, agricultural.

In the analysis of the market area, an appraiser studies how **value influences** affect property.

Market areas are defined by a **combination of factors**—e.g., physical features, the demographic and socioeconomic characteristics of the residents or tenants, the condition of the improvements (age, upkeep, ownership and vacancy rates), and land use trends.

proceeds outward, identifying all relevant actual and potential influences on the property's value that can be attributed to the property's location. The appraiser extends the search far enough to encompass all of the influences the market indicates will affect a property's value. When no more factors that would impact the value of the subject and surrounding properties are found, the boundaries for analysis are set. The appraiser's conclusions regarding the market area's impact on a property's value are meaningful only if area boundaries have been properly drawn.

Analyzing the market area helps to provide a framework, or context, in which the opinion of property value is developed. The analysis identifies the area of influence and establishes potential limits within which the appraiser searches for data that can be used to apply the approaches to value. Market area analysis also helps the appraiser determine an area's stability and may indicate future land uses and value trends.[2]

Defining Geographical Boundaries

The boundaries of market areas, neighborhoods, and districts identify the areas that influence a subject property's value. These boundaries may coincide with observable changes in land use or demographic and socioeconomic characteristics. Physical features such as structure types, street patterns, terrain, vegetation, and lot sizes help to identify land use districts. Transportation arteries (highways, major streets, and railroads), bodies of water (rivers, lakes, and streams), and changing elevation (hills, mountains, cliffs, and valleys) can also be significant boundaries.[3]

---

2.   What has traditionally been called *neighborhood analysis* is referred to in this text as *market area analysis,* in part to distinguish that concept from *market analysis,* which is covered in Chapter 11. Market area analysis focuses on the identification of a market area's boundaries and the social, economic, governmental, and environmental influences that affect the value of real property within those boundaries. In conducting market analysis, the appraiser addresses the competitive supply and demand for the subject property more directly.

3.   In defining a district, variations in the relevant characteristics of properties may indicate that more limited boundaries should be established. For example, consider an urban area where many high-rise apartment buildings are constructed along a natural lakeshore and separated from other land uses by major transportation arteries. In this type of district, there may be great variations in apartment prices, sizes, views, parking availability, proximity to public transportation, and building ages. These variations suggest limited district boundaries that must be identified to reveal market and submarket characteristics.

To identify the boundaries of a market area, an appraiser

1. Examines the subject property. The process of defining a market area's boundaries must start with an analysis of the subject property.

2. Examines the area's physical characteristics. The appraiser should drive or walk around the area to develop a sense of place, noting the degree of similarity in land uses, structure types, architectural styles, and mainte-nance and upkeep. Using a map, the appraiser can identify points where these characteristics change and note any physical barriers—e.g., major streets, hills, rivers, railroad tracks—that coincide with these points.

3. Draws preliminary boundaries on a map. The appraiser draws lines on a map of the area to connect the points where physical characteristics change.

4. Determines how well the preliminary boundaries correspond to the demographic data. The market area boundaries are often overlaid on a map of geographical areas (e.g., zip codes, census tracts, block groups). The appraiser's observed market area and the areas for which data is available seldom match up perfectly. The information available for census tracts, zip code regions, and counties must be segmented to delineate pertinent submarkets.[4] Reliable data may also be available from local chambers of commerce, universities, and research organizations, often through online sources.

In unusual cases an appraiser might consider surveying area residents to identify relevant characteristics. Appraisers may also interview business people, brokers, and community representatives to establish how far they think the market area extends. Through experience, an appraiser learns to observe changes and recognize how market areas are perceived by their inhabitants.

Legal, political, and economic organizations collect data for standardized or statistically defined areas, such as cities, counties, tax districts, census tracts, or special enumeration districts. Although this data may be relevant, it rarely conforms to the market area boundaries identified for property valuation. If such secondary data is used to help identify market area boundaries, the appraiser should verify and supplement the data with primary research.

Change and Transition

In market area analysis, an appraiser recognizes the potential for change and tries to determine how an area may be changing. Appraisers usually consider trends in area growth and composition when analyzing change patterns.

---

4.   Every 10 years the Bureau of the Census of the U.S. Department of Commerce collects data on population and housing characteristics, employment, and earnings. For information on applying census and other data to the analysis of market areas, see Stephen F. Fanning, Terry V. Grissom, and Thomas D. Pearson, *Market Analysis for Valuation Appraisals* (Chicago: Appraisal Institute, 1994), Chapters 7 and 8.

principle of change: The result of the cause and effect relationship among the forces that influence real property value.

transition: Changes in land use in a market area, neighborhood, or district, e.g., agricultural to residential, residential to commercial.

Appraisers also investigate whether a market area is in a state of transition from one type of land use to another, which, although related to the principle of change, is a separate concept. Land in transition can be perceived as land that has acquired value chiefly as a result of economic forces outside of the property itself, unlike land that acquires value in the traditional manner, i.e., through the construction of new improvements on the land or the renovation of existing improvements.

Change and transition can occur at different rates and can affect different properties in the same market area. Change can be good or bad for the community, but transition is what causes positive or negative effects on value. Change can last for a short or long time, but transition is usually permanent. Most problems in determining highest and best use occur not in areas where change is occurring but rather in areas in transition because land in transition often has an interim use before it is ready for development.

The Life Cycle of a Market Area

Because market areas are perceived, organized, constructed, and used by people, each has a dynamic quality. Appraisers describe this quality as a market area's *life cycle*. The complementary land uses that make up neighborhoods and the homogeneous land uses within districts typically evolve through four stages:

1. Growth—a period during which the market area gains public favor and acceptance
2. Stability—a period of equilibrium without marked gains or losses
3. Decline—a period of diminishing demand
4. Revitalization—a period of renewal, redevelopment, modernization, and increasing demand

Transition often occurs in the revitalization stage, when a land use that is no longer financially feasible is discontinued in favor of a more productive use.

Although these stages can describe the life cycle of market areas in a general way, they should not be used as specific guides to market trends. No set number of years is assigned to any stage in the cycle. Many market areas remain stable for a long time, and decline is not necessarily imminent in all older areas. Unless decline is caused by a

Market areas often pass through a **four-stage life cycle** of growth, stability, decline, and revitalization. Some market areas may bypass stages in this cycle.

specific external influence—e.g., the construction of a new highway that changes traffic patterns—it may proceed at an imperceptible rate and can be interrupted by a change in use or a revival of demand. A market area has no set life expectancy and the life cycle is not an inexorable process. At any point in the cycle, a major change can interrupt the order of the stages. For example, a strong negative influence such as a major employer suddenly pulling out of a community or the closing of a military base can cause a market area that was growing to decline rather than stabilize.

After a period of decline, a market area may undergo a transition to other land uses or its life cycle may begin again due to revitalization. Revitalization often results from organized rebuilding or restoration undertaken to preserve the architecture of significant structures. It may also be caused by a natural resurgence of demand. The rebirth of an older, inner-city neighborhood, for example, may simply be due to changing preferences and lifestyles.

life cycle of a market area: The typical, but not necessarily universal, four-stage cycle that describes the life pattern of neighborhoods, districts, and other market areas; the stages include growth, stability, decline, and revitalization.

growth: A life cycle stage in which the market area gains public favor and acceptance.

stability: A life cycle stage in which the neighborhood experiences equilibrium without marked gains or losses.

decline: A stage of diminishing demand in a market area's life cycle.

revitalization: A life cycle stage characterized by renewal, redevelopment, modernization, and increasing demand.

GENTRIFICATION AND DISPLACEMENT

Gentrification is a phenomenon in which middle- and upper-income people purchase properties in a residential neighborhood to renovate or rehabilitate them. The residents displaced by this process are often lower-income individuals who moved into these older, urban neighborhoods when middle- and upper-income groups left because they found the neighborhoods unappealing and unattractive. Often two or more low-income households would occupy what was formerly a single-family residence. Such neighborhoods often became blighted.

Gentrification, which reverses the process of decline, appears to be the result of a large number of small families and single people who choose to live in urban areas. "Urban pioneers" will tolerate higher crime rates and poorer services in exchange for lower housing prices and the potential for great appreciation

gentrification: A neighborhood phenomenon in which middle- and upper-income persons purchase neighborhood properties and renovate or rehabilitate them.

in property value as the character of the once blighted neighborhood improves. Often, as demand and property values in a gentrifying area increase, the burden of increasing property taxes and increasing rents on longtime residents with lower incomes can become too great, leading to the displacement of those residents.

Displacement is often associated with the public housing projects built as part of urban renewal efforts in the 1950s and 1960s. As those failed high-rise developments are demolished to make way for scattered-site, mixed-income housing or some other use, residents must be relocated, although affordable housing is not always readily available. Displacement also occurs when homeowners, businesses, or farm operations are forced to vacate the properties they occupied as a result of governmental action, such as a taking through eminent domain. (For further discussion of eminent domain, see James D. Eaton, *Real Estate Valuation in Litigation,* 2d ed. (Chicago: Appraisal Institute, 1995).)

Evidence of Transition

Transition is often indicated by variations within the market area. New uses may indicate potential increases or decreases in property values. For example, a residential neighborhood in which some homes are well maintained and others are not may be undergoing either decline or revitalization. The introduction of different uses, such as rooming houses or offices, into a single-family residential neighborhood also indicates potential transition to a more intensive use.

Changes in one market area are usually influenced by changes in other, competing areas and in the larger region of influence. Growth of one market area may lead to the downfall of a competing market area. Suburban business centers may interfere with the success of a city's central business district. Newer residential areas may affect older areas. The added supply of new homes may cause residents to shift from old homes to new ones and place older homes on the market. This increase in supply may affect the market values of all homes in the area. If a market area's location makes it attractive for conversion to more intensive land uses, the existing improvements in that area may be remodeled or torn down to make way for redevelopment.

Analyzing Value Influences

Forces that influence value are important in market area analysis. Similar characteristics point to influences that have affected value trends in the past and may affect values in the future. A market area's character may be revealed by examining why occupants live or work in the area. Occupants are attracted to a location for its status, physical environment, services, affordability, and convenience.

Market area analysis focuses on the **four forces**—social, economic, governmental, and environmental—that influence value. Analysis of the four forces is performed by investigating specific factors pertaining to each.

Social Influences

In performing a market area analysis, an appraiser identifies relevant social characteristics and influences. To identify and describe these characteristics, the appraiser must know that the social or demographic characteristics that influence property values most in a community tend to overlap. Of course, price levels in the subject market in relation to prices in competing areas reflect the overall desirability of the subject market area.

In market area analysis, relevant demographic characteristics include the following:

* Population density, which is particularly important in central business districts and high-rise residential neighborhoods
* Skill levels or employment categories, which are particularly important in industrial or high-technology districts
* Age levels, which are particularly important in residential neighborhoods

- Household size
- Employment status, including types of unemployment (temporary, seasonal, or chronic)
- Extent of crime
- Extent of litter
- Quality and availability of educational, medical, social, recreational, cultural, and commercial services
- Presence of community organizations such as improvement associations, neighborhood block clubs, and crime watch groups

Although an appraiser can compile demographic information, it is difficult, if not impossible, to identify the social preferences of the individuals making up a given market and to measure how these preferences affect property value. Therefore, an appraiser should not rely much on social influences when arriving at a value conclusion. From an appraiser's viewpoint, the social characteristics of a residential neighborhood are significant only when they are considered by the buying public and can be objectively and accurately analyzed. Although race, religion, and national origin are social characteristics, they have no direct relationship to real estate values. Professional appraisers must perform unbiased neighborhood analyses.

Economic Influences

Economic considerations relate to the financial capacity of a market area's occupants and their ability to rent or own property, to maintain it in an attractive and desirable condition, and to renovate or rehabilitate it when needed.

The economic characteristics that an appraiser may consider include the following:

- Mean and median household income levels
- Per capita income
- Income distribution for households
- Extent of owner occupancy
- Property rent levels and trends
- Property value levels and trends
- Vacancy rates for various types of property
- Amount of development and construction

The physical characteristics of the area and of individual properties may indicate the relative financial strength of area occupants and how this strength is reflected in local development and upkeep. Ownership and rental data can also provide clues to the financial capability of residents. The income levels revealed by recent census information, newspaper surveys, and private studies may indicate the prices at which occupants can afford to rent or purchase property. Using vacancy statistics compiled by newspapers, the U.S. Postal Service, and other fact-finding agencies along with information about the number of properties for rent or sale found in classified newspaper ads, an appraiser can estimate the strength of demand and the extent of supply, as shown in Chapter 11.

The presence of vacant lots or acreage suitable for development in an area may indicate future development or a lack of demand. Current construction creates trends that affect the value of existing improvements. A careful study of these trends can help an appraiser predict the future desirability of an area. Block-by-block information helps identify the direction of growth. A trend may be a local phenomenon or it may affect the entire metropolitan area. A change in the economic base on which a community depends (e.g., the addition or loss of a major employer) is frequently reflected in the rate of population growth or decline. Ownership demand tends to remain strong and rental occupancy levels are high when the population is growing. Demand weakens and occupancy levels decrease when the population is declining.

To analyze the economic characteristics of a market area, an appraiser expands the analysis to include economic trends over a three- to five-year period. Then the appraiser decides which economic variables contribute most to value differences among locations and compares the economic characteristics of competing market areas.

Governmental Influences

Governmental considerations relate to the laws, regulations, and property taxes that affect properties in the market area and the administration and enforcement of these constraints, such as zoning laws, building codes, and housing and sanitary codes. The property tax burden associated with the benefits provided and the taxes charged for similar benefits in other areas are considered. The enforcement of applicable codes, regulations, and restrictions should be equitable and effective.

The governmental characteristics an appraiser considers in market area analysis include the following:

- Property tax burden relative to services provided, compared with other areas in the community
- Special assessments
- Zoning, building, and housing codes
- Quality of public services, such as fire and police protection, schools, and other governmental services
- Environmental regulations

The appraiser gathers data on these characteristics of the market area and compares them with the characteristics of other, competing areas.

Divergent tax rates may affect market value. Local taxes may favor or penalize certain property types. Therefore, an appraiser should examine the local structure of assessed values and tax rates to compare the tax burdens created by various forms of taxes and ascertain their apparent effect on the values of different types of real estate.

Local zoning ordinances regulate land use and the density of development. With varying degrees of success, communities regulate zoning to halt or slow growth. To encourage new development, they may expand capital improvement programs and construct sewage treatment facilities, fire stations, streets, and public recreational facilities. In the absence of zoning, the appraiser should determine if the private restrictions in place could protect long-term property values.[5]

Zoning may also be used to enforce a community's land use plan or comprehensive plan, which is usually based on economic growth projections and may be modified for political reasons. The appraiser should be aware of the assumptions on which the land use plan is based and of the potential for revision. The appraiser also must consider the date that the plan was adopted and the plan's projection term. Land use plans are typically projected 5 to 10 years into the future. The more recently the land use plan was adopted, the more meaningful it will be.

Environmental concerns have prompted increased regulation of land development at state and local levels. Zoning ordinances and building codes impose additional costs on developers. To preserve environmental quality, developers are required to consider the impact large developments will have on an area's ecology and on the larger environmental system. They may be required to improve public roads, construct sewage treatment facilities, preserve natural terrain, or take other actions to conform to the recommendations of local, regional, or state planning agencies. These regulations can significantly increase the time required to complete a development and hence increase its final cost. The value of subdivision land is influenced by environmental regulations, which can affect the amount of time required to develop and sell the sites.

The creation or modification of a transportation system is a government action. The government bases its action on an analysis of the direct and indirect impacts the system has on users and nonusers. An improvement in the transportation system can affect a site's accessibility and, thus, its value. Improved transportation routes often cause new areas to be developed, which affects the value of other sites that must compete with the increased supply. To a great extent, the suburbanization of an urban population results from improvements in highways, commuter railroads, and bus routes.

The movement of commercial and retail enterprises from downtown areas to the suburbs has changed real estate markets and placed new emphasis

---

5. Private restrictions on land use may be established by private owners through provisions in deeds or plat recordings. These restrictions may specify lot and building sizes in a subdivision, permitted architectural styles, and property uses. Condominium bylaws also restrict property use. The appraiser should make certain that private restrictions do not limit property uses inordinately.

on zoning systems, the administration of local government, and public expenditures. The highway system has opened certain regions to development and increased their comparative advantage by decreasing the cost of transporting products to markets.

A municipality's willingness to provide public services to outlying areas can affect the direction and amount of development. Conversely, sewer moratoriums have been used effectively to control local growth. This type of restriction can increase the value of existing developments if demand is pressing on a limited supply.

Environmental Influences

Environmental considerations consist of any natural or man-made features that are contained in or affect the market area and its location, including the following:

- Building size, type, density, and maintenance
- Topographical features (terrain and vegetation)
- Open space
- Nuisances and hazards emanating from nearby facilities such as shopping centers, factories, and schools—e.g., odors, noises, litter, vibrations, fog, smoke, and smog
- The adequacy of public utilities such as streetlights, sewers, and electricity
- The existence and upkeep of vacant lots
- General maintenance
- Street patterns, width, and maintenance
- The attractiveness and safety of routes into and out of the area
- Effective ages of properties
- Changes in property use and land use patterns
- Microclimate characteristics—e.g., high winds in a localized area, temperature and humidity differences between the area on the edge of a body of water and the surrounding area
- Environmental liabilities—e.g., threat of landslides or flooding
- Access to public transportation (and type of system, e.g., bus, rail), schools (and quality of schools), stores and service establishments, parks and recreational facilities, houses of worship, and workplaces

Topographical features can have positive or negative effects on property values in a given market area. The presence of a lake, river, bay, or hill in or near a market area may give it a scenic advantage. A hill may mean little in a mountainous area, but in a predominantly flat area, an elevated or wooded section can enhance property value. A river subject to severe flooding may cause the value of homes along its banks to decline due to the risk of such a hazard. Sometimes a river, lake, or park serves as a buffer between a residential district and commercial or industrial enterprises. Excessive traffic, odors, smoke, dust, or noise from commercial or manufacturing enterprises can make a residential neighborhood less desirable.

Gas, electricity, water, telephone service, cable television, and storm and sanitary sewers are essential to meeting the accepted standard of living in most municipal areas. A deficiency in any of these services tends to decrease property values in a market area. Access to fiber optic communications lines, though not yet an essential utility in most commercial districts, is an increasingly important amenity. The availability of utilities also affects the direction and timing of growth or development.

A market area's environmental characteristics cannot be judged on an absolute scale. Instead, they must be compared with the characteristics of competing areas. An appraiser asks:

> Do the terrain, vegetation, street patterns, density, property maintenance, public utilities, and other attributes of this market area make it more or less desirable than other areas?

Location may refer to the siting of a property and the effect of siting on accessibility—e.g., the ease of access to a corner lot compared to an interior lot. It can also refer to the time-distance relationships, or linkages, between a property or market area and all other possible origins and destinations of people going to or coming from the property or market area. Time and distance are measures of relative access. Usually all the properties in a well-defined market area have the same or similar locational relationships.

To analyze the impact of a market area's location, an appraiser must identify important linkages and measure their time-distances by the most commonly used types of transportation. The type of transportation usually depends on the preferences and needs of neighborhood occupants. It is not enough to note that transportation exists; the type of service provided and how it addresses the needs of local residents must be considered.

Linkages should be judged in terms of how well they serve the typical users of real estate in the market area. For example, in analyzing a single-family residential neighborhood, an appraiser considers where typical occupants need to go. If adequate facilities are not available for necessary linkages, the neighborhood will not be

Proximity to recreational facilities such as a golf course can influence the value of residential real estate.

> **location:** The time-distance relationships, or linkages, between a property or market area and all other possible origins and destinations of people going to or coming from the property or market area.
>
> **linkages:**
> 1. The time and distance relationship between a particular use and supporting facilities—e.g., between residences and schools, shopping, and employment.
> 2. The movement of people, goods, services, or communications to and from the subject site, measured by the time and cost involved.

regarded as favorably as competing neighborhoods that have better linkages. For single-family residential neighborhoods, linkages with schools, grocery stores, and employment centers are usually the most important. Linkages with recreational facilities, houses of worship, restaurants, and retail stores may be less important. For a neighboring industrial district, linkages to the available labor supply in those residential neighborhoods are as important as access to trade routes, both for receiving raw materials and distributing finished goods.

The distance to public transportation is considered in relation to the people who will use it. Access to public transportation is more important in a residential neighborhood with a high percentage of residents who cannot afford a car or choose not to drive than it is in a neighborhood where car ownership is predominant. A study of local transportation facilities must consider the territory through which users must pass. Most people would rather avoid poorly lighted streets and rundown areas. Generally, the closer a property is to good public transportation, the wider its market.

When current zoning does not restrict changes from the present land use or when a change in land use is evident, the appraiser may need to examine linkages in terms of both the current land use and the anticipated land use in the market area.

The market's idea of what makes market areas desirable can be studied by analyzing comparable sales. The dollar and percentage differences among the sale prices of similar properties in different locations can provide the basis for this analysis.

Characteristics of Real Estate Districts

The value influences that affect different types of districts—e.g., residential districts, commercial districts, industrial districts—are the same as those affecting larger, more diverse market areas, but the emphasis and relative importance of the factors change with the type of district being analyzed.

The availability of public utilities, including sanitary sewers and municipal or well water, is one important factor that affects land value in all districts. Prevailing levels of real estate and personal property taxes also influence the desirability of districts and may be reflected in real estate values. Of course, the four forces that influence all real estate value affect districts.

Single-Family Residential Districts

Home ownership has long symbolized economic prosperity, and the residents of an area dominated by owner-occupied single-family homes often take an active

CITY ORIGINS AND GROWTH PATTERNS

Appraisers of urban and suburban property recognize that growth and change in a community can affect neighborhoods, districts, and other market areas differently. An appraiser must understand the factors that contribute to urban and suburban growth patterns to analyze the market area where the subject property is located and to determine how the area affects the quantity, quality, and duration of the subject property's future income or the amenities that create value.

The structure of land uses in an urban community usually reflects the settlement's origin; this is known as the *siting factor*. Some U.S. cities were established at transportation centers such as seaports, river crossings, or the intersection of trade routes. Other cities were founded near power sources useful to manufacturing, and still others were located for defensive, commercial, or political reasons. As the national standard of living improved, climate and other natural advantages became siting factors responsible for the development of retirement areas, recreational resorts, and other specialized communities. From its initial site, a community grows outward in a pattern dictated by the nature and availability of developable land, the evolution of technology, and the government's ability and willingness to provide essential public services.*

> **siting factor:** The origin of settlement in a city, which generally influences subsequent land use and growth patterns.

Where land is scarce, communities often experience an increase in land use density. Development corridors channel new construction to usable land. New technology, building materials, and construction methods make it possible to construct high-rise buildings in cities without bedrock and those subject to earth tremors.

Transportation improvements and the proliferation of automobiles have also shaped modern cities. Improved transportation allows urban settlements to expand and serve larger markets. The pattern of city growth is influenced by the local transportation network. Growth usually radiates from the central business district along major transportation routes; major freeway systems can cause widespread migration from the city's core.

---

* Various conceptual models of urban growth are used to describe land use patterns. These "social ecology" models include the concentric zone theory, the sector (wedge) theory, the multiple nuclei theory, and the radial (axial) corridor theory. For a more complete discussion of urban growth patterns, see Stephen F. Fanning, Terry V. Grissom, and Thomas D. Pearson, *Market Analysis for Valuation Appraisals* (Chicago: Appraisal Institute, 1994), Chapter 5.

role in maintaining or enhancing the value of their properties. Through formal home owners' associations, which often enforce conditions, covenants, and restrictions in a development, or voluntary associations such as crime watch groups and neighborhood block clubs, property owners attempt to ensure conformity of land uses within a residential district and thus safeguard the character, appeal, and value of neighboring homes.

Community spirit, which is evidenced in activities such as block parties and street fairs, and activist efforts, such as lobbying against undesirable rezoning or development, can make a residential area more stable or even reverse a trend toward declining property values.

In built-up urban areas, single-family homes will usually be integrated into the complementary land uses that make up a residential neighborhood. In outlying suburban areas where developable green space is relatively cheap, single-family residential districts can cover large amounts of land. In some growing metropolitan areas, suburban sprawl has become as much of a social

Table 8.1	**Single-Family Residential Districts**
Defining characteristic	• Predominance of owner-occupied homes
Subdistricts	• Custom-built subdivisions
	• Attached housing, e.g., condominuims, townhouses
	• Senior housing
	• Rural housing
Value influences	• Access to workplaces
	• Transportation service
	• Access to shopping centers and cultural facilities
	• Quality of local schools
	• Reputation of area
	• Residential atmosphere and appearance and protection from unwanted commercial and industrial intrusion
	• Proximity to open space, parks, lakes, rivers, or other natural features
	• Supply of vacant land likely to be developed could make present accommodations more or less desirable
	• Private land use restrictions—e.g., conditions, covenants, and restrictions

problem as flight from central cities was in the 1960s and 1970s. Therefore, the influence of commuting time on the value of residential districts in distant suburbs should be considered.

Just as the availability of labor and consumer purchasing power is essential to the economic health of commercial and industrial districts, proximity to employment opportunities significantly influences property values in a residential district. As employers relocate from central cities to areas closer to their employees' homes, former bedroom communities can develop thriving commercial districts. These districts can rival the central business district of the larger metropolitan area and may serve as an economic base for surrounding residential areas. Long-term migratory patterns within a metropolitan area can be analyzed to forecast possible growth trends.

The topographical and climatic features of land in a residential district are generally analyzed as possible amenities or potential hazards. Access to a body of water can increase a home's value if the location provides a scenic view, but the same lake or stream may reduce value if flooding occurs frequently. Sometimes a river, lake, hill, park, or other natural feature may act as a buffer between a residential district and commercial or industrial areas and thereby reinforce the residential area's identity.

Multifamily Residential Districts

In large cities, multifamily residential districts usually cover an extensive area. In smaller cities such districts may be dispersed or limited in size. Units may

Table 8.2	Multifamily Residential Districts
Defining characteristics	• Generally a predominance of renter occupancy and higher density than single-family residential districts
Subdistricts	• Multistory/high-rise buildings
	• Garden apartments
	• Row houses
	• Townhouses
	• Cooperative apartments
Value influences	• Access to workplaces
	• Transportation service
	• Access to shopping centers, cultural facilities, and entertainment
	• Reputation of area
	• Residential atmosphere and appearance, and protection against unwanted commercial and industrial intrusion (Proximity to employment, however, may be highly desirable for multifamily districts, which often act as buffers for commercial and industrial districts.)
	• Proximity to open space, parks, lakes, rivers, or other natural features
	• Supply of vacant apartment sites that are likely to be developed and could make present accommodations more or less desirable
	• Parking for tenants and guests
	• Vacancy and tenant turnover rate

be rented, i.e., apartments, or privately owned as cooperatives and condominiums. Multifamily districts are subject to many of the same influences that single-family residential areas are, but the emphasis on certain influences differs in multifamily districts because of their higher density.

In some cities, statistics on the supply of apartments, vacancy rates, and rent levels are available. When statistics are not available, the appraiser will have to gather data through primary research.

Commercial Districts

A commercial district is a group of offices or stores. Included in this category are

• Highway commercial districts—i.e., enterprises along a local business street or freeway service road and developments adjacent to a traffic intersection

In developed urban areas apartment districts are often found near the workplaces of prospective residents, e.g., in or on the border of central business districts.

- Retail districts—e.g., regional and neighborhood shopping centers
- Downtown central business districts (CBDs)

To analyze a commercial district, an appraiser identifies its trade area—i.e., the area the businesses serve. Because a commercial district's economic health depends on the vibrancy of the surrounding trade area, property values in a commercial district are affected by the type and character of nearby land uses and other factors that influence the values of surrounding properties.

Office Districts

Office districts can contain combinations of buildings ranging from small structures to large, multistory buildings. The buildings in an office district may be owner-occupied structures or serve a variety of tenants. The offices may serve multinational corporations, local corporations, small service companies, and professionals.

Office districts include planned office parks and strip developments on or near major traffic arteries. Office parks, which are also known as *business parks,* often have industrial users among their tenants because the parks offer good locations, easy access, attractive surroundings, and utility without the congestion and high rents of the CBD. Office parks increasingly provide facilities for service industries as well, such as retailers, restaurants, computer stores, branch banks, day care centers, and others. Because office parks and industrial parks rely on surrounding areas to supply the labor force, those developments are often located near residential districts, and their park-like appearance may be an advantage in the eyes of nearby residents.

Retail Districts

More than any other type of real estate, retail properties rely on the local trade area for their economic base. The customers for all but the largest destination shopping centers are drawn from the surrounding areas. The common types of retail property can be classified by the sizes of the trade areas they serve.

central business district (CBD): The core, or downtown area, of a city where the major retail, financial, governmental, professional, recreational, and service activities of the community are concentrated.

trade area: The geographic area from which the steady, sustaining patronage for a shopping center is obtained; its extent is governed by many factors, e.g., the shopping center itself, its accessibility, the extent of physical barriers, the location of competing facilities, the limitations of driving time and distance.

- Regional shopping centers and super-regional centers can serve hundreds of thousands of people in many communities along major transportation routes.
- Community shopping centers serve a neighborhood or group of neighborhoods within a three- to five-mile radius

| **Table 8.3** | **Commercial Districts** |

Office

Defining characteristic	• Office uses with supporting retail services and other related services
Subdistricts	• Central business districts
	• Suburban office parks
	• Concentrations of office properties of a particular class, as defined by the market
Value influences	• Significant locational considerations such as the time-distance from potential labor force, access, highway medians, and traffic signals
	• Physical characteristics such as the visibility, attractiveness, quality of construction, and condition of properties
	• Direction of observable growth
	• Character and location of existing or anticipated competition
	• Availability of land for expansion
	• Pedestrian or vehicular traffic count

Retail

Defining characteristic	• Concentration of competing retail locations, often along a major street
Subdistricts	• Regional and super-regional shopping centers
	• Community shopping centers
	• Neighborhood and strip shopping centers
	• Specialty centers
Value influences	• Focus on quantity and quality of the purchasing power of the population likely to patronize a shopping area and any trends affecting purchasing power
	• Significant locational considerations such as the time-distance from potential customers, access, highway medians, and traffic signals
	• Physical characteristics such as the visibility, attractiveness, quality of construction, and condition of properties
	• Direction of observable growth
	• Character and location of existing or anticipated competition
	• Retailers' inventory, investments, leasehold improvements, and enterprise
	• Availability of land for expansion and customer parking
	• Pedestrian or vehicular traffic count
	• The 100% location or anchors and core groupings

- Neighborhood and strip shopping centers serve their immediate neighborhoods.

Specialty shopping centers, such as outlet malls, warehouse clubs, and power centers, serve a wide range of trade areas, depending on the tenant makeup and demographic and psychographic target markets.

Although the appraiser focuses on the sales potential of a given retail trade area, various other considerations can complicate the analysis of value influences. Like certain central business districts, some retail districts may contain a destination shopping attraction. Multiplex movie theater anchors in regional shopping centers in urban or suburban areas often serve as destinations for consumers from a wider trade area than a similar-sized shopping center would normally attract. On the other hand, the growth of online shopping and continued competition from catalog retailers may weaken the sales potential of existing shopping centers.[6]

When analyzing a group of local retail enterprises that are not located in a shopping center, an appraiser also examines the zoning policies that govern the supply of competing sites, the reasons for vacancies and business failures, and the level of rents compared with rent levels in new buildings.

Central Business Districts

A central business district (CBD) is traditionally the core, or downtown area, of a city where the major retail, financial, governmental, professional, recreational, and service activities of the community are concentrated. Over the past quarter of a century, CBDs have not experienced the same pattern of growth and development that other commercial districts have. The development of suburban commercial centers in edge cities and the corresponding decline of inner urban areas have undercut the predominance of CBDs. Even in smaller cities and exurban towns, the development of commercial districts

centered on a category-killer retailer outside the town center can have a negative impact on the economic viability of the area's traditional business core and the value of aging properties there.

Appraisers should be aware of this trend but should also recognize that some CBDs have brighter prospects than others, possibly as a result of economic development efforts or a concentration of companies in strong business sectors. The economic life cycle of CBDs is often scrutinized closely by analysts. Transpor-

Central business districts contain diverse land uses, such as housing, office, retail, and recreational properties.

---

6. For additional discussion of retail market research and trade area delineation, see Joseph Rabianski, "Elements of Retail Market Research," *Real Estate Review*, vol. 27, no. 4 (Winter 1998): 52-55.

Table 8.4	Shopping Centers

Neighborhood or Strip Shopping Center

Typical size	• 30,000 to 100,000 sq. ft.
Typical trade area	• Immediate neighborhood
	• Population of 2,500 to 40,000
	• Radius of 1.5 miles
	• Driving time of 5 to 10 minutes
Typical tenants	• Convenience goods—e.g., food, drugs, and sundries—and personal services—e.g., laundry, dry cleaning, shoe repair, and hair styling; often a supermarket as an anchor

Community Shopping Center

Typical size	• 100,000 to 300,000 sq. ft.
Typical trade area	• Population of 40,000 to 150,000
	• Radius of 3 to 5 miles
	• Driving time of 10 to 20 minutes
Typical tenants	• One junior department store, a variety store or discount department store, a supermarket, and specialty shops; may also offer professional and financial services and recreational facilities

Regional Shopping Center

Typical size	• 300,000 to 900,000 sq. ft. (one or more department stores of at least 100,000 sq. ft. each plus small tenant space)
Typical trade area	• May include several neighborhood centers
	• Minimum population of 150,000
	• Radius of 8 miles
	• Driving time of 20 minutes
Typical tenants	• Full department stores plus banks, service establishments, medical and business offices, and theaters, among general merchandise, apparel, furniture, home furnishings, service, and recreational facilities

Super-Regional Center

Typical size	• 500,000 to 1.5 million sq. ft. or more
Typical trade area	Trade areas are also extended by major transportation arteries and linkages, so the trade areas for some super-regional centers transcend state boundaries
	• Minimum population of 300,000
	• Radius of 12 miles or more
	• Driving time of 30 minutes or more
Typical tenants	• In addition to the types of tenants in a regional center, specialty shops, arcades, and restaurants

Sources: *Shopping Center Development Handbook* (Washington, D.C.: Urban Land Institute, 1988); *Dollars and Cents of Shopping Centers: 1990. A Study of Receipts and Expenses in Shopping Center Operations* (Washington, D.C.: Urban Land Institute, 1990); Patrick O'Connor, "Which Retail Properties Are Getting Market Share?" *The Appraisal Journal* (January 1999): 37–40.

tation facilities in most cities are oriented to the CBD. Through downtown development associations, many merchants have made efforts to revitalize CBDs with improved public transportation, larger parking areas, better access, and coordinated sales promotion programs.

The diverse enterprises located in CBDs usually reflect several types of land use, e.g., housing, retail stores, offices, financial institutions, and entertainment facilities. Housing is usually not considered an essential land use within a central business district, but it can help to revitalize or maintain an area's viability. Retail clothing stores may primarily serve office employees, and other retail establishments tend to locate where large numbers of people work, shop, and live. Financial institutions are often found in areas with other financial institutions. In major cities, entertainment and cultural facilities usually operate in or near CBDs to serve the greatest number of residents and out-of-town visitors. Different parts of the CBD attract different users, and the enterprises within a single general use category may be diverse. For example, office buildings in different parts of a CBD may house a wide variety of business and professional firms.

Appraisers should recognize that shifting functions within CBDs can lead to changes in land use and potential increases in real estate values. For example, the addition of entertainment uses to an area dominated by office uses may attract more restaurants, art galleries, and specialty shops to a downtown area. Over the past decade, some major CBDs have come to represent destinations. Many of them include prominent stores with well-known names and complementary entertainment or recreational facilities. Quite often, destination shopping is an outing that allows the entire family to participate in both shopping and entertainment activities.

To assess the viability of a CBD, an appraiser must consider the sales potential of various commercial products and services and determine whether establishments in the CBD can attract a share of the market. To evaluate the utility of a particular location within a CBD, the appraiser considers which use or mix of uses—e.g., office, hotel, retail, housing, or entertainment—is most appropriate.

Heavy industry districts are often established by ordinances limiting land uses and placing controls on air pollution, noise levels, and outdoor operations.

Industrial Districts

Industry is often the engine of economic growth in a community. Governmental and public-private economic development efforts are often targeted at manufacturing and other industrial concerns that may bring high-paying jobs to an area. In the 1980s and 1990s, major manufacturers sought to control inventory costs by implementing just-in-time production techniques, and the suppliers who serve those companies began to cluster around their headquarters.

Table 8.5	Characteristics of Industrial Districts
Defining characteristic	• Cluster of related industrial concerns, e.g., a manufacturer and its suppliers
Subdistricts	• Manufacturing facilities
	• Research & development facilities/science parks
	• Warehouse/distribution facilities
Value influences	• Nature of the district (distribution, manufacturing, R&D, etc.)
	• Availability of labor
	• Transportation facilities
	• Availability of raw materials
	• Distribution facilities
	• Political climate
	• Availability of utilities and energy
	• Effect of environmental controls

Industrial districts range from those that contain heavy industry, such as steel plants, foundries, and chemical companies, to those that contain assembly, distribution, and other "clean" operations. In most urban areas, heavy industry and light industry districts are established by zoning ordinances, which may limit uses and place controls on air pollution, noise levels, and outdoor operations. In older manufacturing or warehouse districts, obsolete, multistory, elevator buildings are typical and parking and expansion areas are limited. Newer manufacturing districts and industrial parks usually consist of one-story buildings with greater ceiling heights than were typical previously. Each industrial district has a value pattern that reflects the market's reaction to its location and the characteristics of its sites and improvements.

The environmental liabilities incurred by industrial properties are considerably more complex than those that affect other property types. Industrial properties may contain underground storage tanks for a broad range of chemicals. The presence of asbestos and PCBs may be more widespread. Long-term contamination tends to be more severe and cleanup costs can be high. (Environmental liabilities are discussed more fully in Chapter 9.)

Agricultural Districts

Agricultural districts can be as small as a portion of a township or as large as several counties. Most important value influences relate to individual properties rather than to entire agricultural districts because farms may be far apart. Nevertheless, an agricultural district's physical features are usually representative of the individual farms within it and contribute to their desirability.

The emphasis on the value influences in an agricultural district depends on what is produced there. Agricultural production areas are served by

Table 8.6	Characteristics of Agricultural Districts
Defining characteristic	• Undeveloped land used for production of foodstuffs, timber, oil, and other agricultural products
Subdistricts	• Grain farms
	• Orchards, groves, and nurseries
	• Grasslands
	• Dairies
	• Timberland and sod farms
	• Land used for oil and/or mineral extraction
Value influences	• Climate
	• Topography
	• Soil types
	• Crops grown
	• Animals raised
	• Typical land use
	• Average size of the farming operations in the district
	• Whether the farming operations are run by owners or tenants
	• Transportation
	• Availability of farm labor/immigration

highways that lead to marketing centers where farm products are sold. Like an urban neighborhood, the farm community depends on government services such as roads and schools and on the availability of electricity.

Infrastructure to support the particular land use dominant in a district is important in all districts, but it is particularly important in agricultural districts. The infrastructure for agriculture includes such land uses as

- Equipment sales and repair
- Outlets for seed, feed, fertilizer, herbicides, etc.
- Processors or intermediaries to buy farm products

For many years urban encroachment into agricultural districts and the erosion of the agricultural infrastructure has been a concern of property owners in rural areas because urban land uses generally do not complement agricultural uses. Governmental attempts to preserve agricultural land have had limited effectiveness because the causes of encroachment are so complex.

Environmental liabilities for agricultural properties may include cattle vats, turpentine stills, fertilizers, pesticides, and underground storage tanks.

Specialty Districts

Individual properties are sometimes appropriate for only an existing special-purpose use. Similarly, if some specialized activity is predominant in a market area, that area may qualify as a specialty district, such as the following:

- Medical district

- Research and development park
- High technology park
- Education district
- Historic district

The value influences at work in these specialty districts may be similar to those of areas where traditional land uses dominate (in particular, office districts), but the emphasis often changes depending on the activity that characterizes the specialty district.

Medical Districts

A district may be composed entirely of hospitals, health care facilities, and physicians' offices. A medical district may include one or more hospitals with related facilities such as parking lots and patient services buildings, a number of physicians' offices, and several pharmacies. Medical districts can be found in densely populated urban areas and in spacious, park-like settings, although the general trend of suburbanization may be causing medical uses to spread out.

The desirability and value of a property such as a doctors' office building depend on its age and proximity to hospitals and other medical offices. The quality of professional personnel and the availability of modern equipment are also important considerations.

Demographics are an additional concern. Medical buildings in or near residential neighborhoods with many seniors, the prime consumers of health care services, may have an advantage over medical buildings in other areas and those with poor access to public transportation.

Utilities are a particular concern in medical districts because power outages can have disastrous effects in hospitals. To increase reliability, most hospitals augment the electrical service available from the power grid with backup systems. Also, the disposal of medical waste and potentially infectious materials has become highly controversial. Many hospitals incinerate their waste, while others have it shipped offshore.

Research and Development Parks

Characterized by a mix of office and industrial uses, research and development parks (also known as *science parks*) may contain the research and development departments of large drug, chemical, or computer companies, or they may cater to firms specializing in research activities. Research firms are usually small and specialize in identifying and developing new products, which are sold to other firms. Occasionally a small research firm will create, develop, and market a new product with considerable success, but then the nature of the firm must shift from research to marketing.

Research and development parks are often sponsored and promoted by universities, which provide a convenient source of technical expertise and qualified employees. Universities may sponsor a park to sell excess land, provide employment for students and faculty, and raise an area's level of economic activity.

High Technology Parks

Firms engaged in high-tech activities often locate near one another or in parks where technical expertise may be available from a nearby university or research park. Electronics and computer firms have dominated high technology parks, but firms involved with space equipment, drugs, cosmetics, and aviation may also have offices in these areas.

Sometimes local governments and economic development corporations will create designated technology corridors in the hopes of attracting growing high technology companies. Real estate developments in technology incubator areas may benefit from favorable financing packages.

Education Districts

Local schools, colleges, and universities may constitute a district if they have several buildings or facilities and are considered an integral part of the surrounding residential neighborhood. Education districts may contribute economically as well as socially and culturally to the surrounding community.

Colleges and universities often attract students from far away who bring income to the community and thus contribute to its economic base. In some towns and smaller cities, universities and colleges may provide most of the economic base. An education district should be accessible to the surrounding residential neighborhood if student housing is needed; access to public transportation is more important to commuter institutions.

Historic Districts

Since 1931, when the first historic district zoning ordinance was passed in the United States, interest in preserving historically and architecturally significant properties has grown and given rise to a unique type of district.[7] The establishment of historic districts is one of the most widely applied and rapidly developing techniques for preserving cultural heritage. Overlay districts also can be used to preserve an area's architectural character.

historic district: An area designated to retain and preserve its historic quality. The 1966 Historic Preservation Act defined the involvement of the federal government in historic preservation. The authority to create local historic districts usually comes from state legislation authorizing municipalities or counties to establish historic districts under their general zoning powers.

Historic districts may be informally perceived by observers, or they may be formally designated by local, state, or federal agencies. Historic districts are federally certified only after stringent requirements have been met, including substantial

---

7. Russell V. Keune, ed., *The Historic Preservation Yearbook* (Bethesda, Md.: Adler & Adler, 1984), 461. See also Judith Reynolds, *Historic Properties: Preservation and the Valuation Process,* 2d ed. (Chicago: Appraisal Institute, 1997); Paul K. Asabere and Forrest E. Huffman, "Historic Designation and Residential Market Value," *The Appraisal Journal* (July 1994): 396–410; and Patrick Haughey and Victoria Basolo, "The Effect of Dual Local and National Register Historic District Designations on Single-Family Housing Prices in New Orleans," *The Appraisal Journal* (July 2000): 283-289.

compliance with the criteria of the National Register of Historic Places.[8] Once districts are federally certified, developers, investors, and renovation specialists can qualify for tax incentives such as the tax credits allowed under the Economic Recovery Tax Act of 1981 (which were subsequently reduced by the Tax Reform Act of 1986).

Historic districts may include residential, commercial, industrial, or other types of property alone or in

Historic districts may be formally designated by local, state, or federal agencies.

combination with one another. Appraisers must become thoroughly familiar with the criteria applicable to each district's designation status and how these criteria are, or may be, applied to properties within district boundaries. Preservation easements and historic façade easements can limit future uses of a property and thereby impact value, either negatively or positively.

FURTHUR READING

American Society of Farm Managers and Rural Appraisers and Appraisal Institute. *The Appraisal of Rural Property,* 2d ed. Denver and Chicago, 2000.

Garreau, Joel. *Edge City: Life on the New Frontier.* New York: Doubleday, 1991.

Girling, Cynthia L. and Kenneth I. Helphand. *Yard-Street-Park: The Design of Suburban Open Space.* New York: John Wiley & Sons, Inc., 1994.

Perin, Constance. *Everything in Its Place: Social Order and Land Use in America.* Princeton, N.J.: Princeton University Press, 1977.

Schwanke, Dean. *Mixed-Use Development Handbook.* Washington, D.C.: Urban Land Institute, 1987.

Urban Land Institute. *Dollars and Cents of Shopping Centers®: 2001.* Washington, D.C.: ULI, 2001. (Updated annually.)

---

8.   Keune, 328

LAND OR SITE ANALYSIS

Appraisal assignments may be undertaken to develop an opinion of the value of land only or the value of both land and improvements. In either case the appraiser must provide a detailed description and analysis of the land. Land can be raw or improved; raw land can be undeveloped or put to an agricultural use. Land may be located in rural, suburban, or urban areas and may have the potential to be developed for residential, commercial, industrial, agricultural, or special-purpose use.

This chapter focuses on the description and analysis of the land component of real property. Because appraisers typically deal with land that has been improved to some degree, the term *site* is used except when raw land is specified. The information needed to complete a full site description and analysis is noted and explained, and sources for obtaining this information are presented. Although this discussion relates primarily to the property being appraised, the same type of data is collected and examined in analyzing the comparable properties used in the appraisal.

A parcel of land can have various site improvements that enable the vacant parcel to support a specific purpose. Land can have both on-site and off-site improvements that make it suitable for its intended use or development. Off-site improvements may include water, drainage, and sewer systems, utility lines, and access to roads. On-site improvements may include landscaping, site grading, access driveways, drainage improvements, accessory buildings, and support facilities.

In valuing any type of property, the appraiser must describe and analyze the land. Land description consists of comprehensive factual data, information on land use restrictions, a legal description, other title and record data, and information on pertinent physical characteristics. Land analysis goes further. The analysis is a careful study of factual data in relation to the neighborhood characteristics that create, enhance, or detract from the utility and marketability of specific land or a given site as compared with other land with which it competes.

> **raw land:** Land on which no improvements have been made; land in its natural state before grading, construction, subdivision, or the installation of utilities.
>
> **site:** Land that is improved so that it is ready to be used for a specific purpose.
>
> **land (or site) analysis:** A careful study of factual data relating to the neighborhood characteristics that create, enhance, or detract from the utility and marketability of the land (or site) as compared with competing, comparable land.

A **land (or site) description** is a comprehensive listing of data, including a legal description, other title and record data, and information on the physical characteristics of the land.

One primary objective of land analysis is to gather data that will indicate the highest and best use of the land as though vacant (or the site as though vacant) so that land value for a specific use can be estimated. (See Chapter 12 for a complete discussion of highest and best use.) Whether a site or raw land is being valued, the appraiser must determine and evaluate its highest and best use. When the highest and best use of land is for agriculture, the appraiser usually analyzes and values the land by applying the sales comparison approach. If the land is to be developed for urban use, the appraiser may use a more sophisticated technique such as subdivision development analysis.

Legal Descriptions of Land

Land boundaries differentiate separate ownerships, and the land within one set of boundaries may be referred to as a *parcel, lot, plot,* or *tract.* These terms may be applied to all types of improved and unimproved land, and they are often used interchangeably by market participants. The appraiser, however, should use the terms consistently to avoid confusing the client in the appraisal report.

A parcel of land generally refers to a piece of land that may be identified by a common description and is held in one ownership. Every parcel of real estate is unique. To identify individual parcels, appraisers rely on legal descriptions, surveys, or other descriptive information typically provided by the client or found in public records. A legal description identifies a property in such a way that it cannot be confused with any other property; therefore, a legal description is usually included or referenced in an appraisal report.

legal description: A description of land that identifies the real estate according to a system established or approved by law; an exact description that enables the real estate to be located and identified.

In the United States the **three principal methods** used to describe real property are the metes and bounds system, the rectangular survey system, and the lot and block system.

In the United States three methods are commonly used to describe real property legally:

1. The metes and bounds system
2. The rectangular survey system
3. The lot and block system

An appraiser should be familiar with these forms of legal description and know which form or forms are accepted in the area where the appraisal is being conducted.

Metes and Bounds

The oldest known method of surveying land is the metes and bounds system, in which land is measured and identified by describing its boundaries. A metes and bounds description of a parcel of real property describes the property's boundaries in terms of precise reference points.

> **metes and bounds system:** A system for the legal description of land that refers to the parcel's boundaries, which are formed by the point of beginning (POB) and all intermediate points (bounds) and the courses or angular direction of each point (metes).

To follow a metes and bounds description, one starts at the point of beginning (POB), a primary survey reference point that is tied to a benchmark and/or adjoining surveys, and moves along past several intermediate reference points before finally returning to the POB. The return and joining is called *closing* and is necessary to ensure the survey's accuracy.

Surveyors in the field increasingly rely on modern "total stations" to collect data in digital form. The familiar surveyor's measuring instrument mounted on a tripod uses infrared technology and today is augmented by portable computer technology. The data is downloaded into the surveyor's office computer for plotting the property boundaries and computing the land area. Coordinate geometry software and Global Positioning System (GPS) technology allow for more accurate determinations of directions, distances, and areas. GPS technology is only limited by physical obstructions that prohibit receiving satellite transmissions, and its use in surveying will probably increase.

The metes and bounds system is the primary method for describing real property in 21 states. It is often used in other states as a corollary to the rectangular survey system, especially in describing unusual or odd-shaped parcels of land.

Rectangular Survey System

The rectangular survey system, which is also known as the *government survey system,* was established by the Land Ordinance of May 20, 1785. The rectangular survey system became the principal method of land description for most land north of the Ohio River and west of the Mississippi River.

The initial reference points for government surveys were established in the late eighteenth century. From each point specified, true east-west and north-south lines were drawn. The east-west lines are called *base lines* and the north-south lines are called *principal meridians.*

> **rectangular (government) survey system:** A land survey system used in Florida, Alabama, Mississippi, and all states north of the Ohio River or west of the Mississippi River except Texas; divides land into townships approximately six miles square, each normally containing 36 one-square-mile sections of 640 acres, except when adjusted for the curvature of the earth.
>
> **base line:** In the government survey system of land description, a line running due east and west through the initial point of a principal meridian from which township lines are established.
>
> **principal meridian:** In land surveying, major north-south lines established as general reference points. There are about 25 principal meridians in the 48 contiguous states of the United States.

In this system, each parcel of land is identified in terms of its relationship to a single base line and a single principal meridian.

Lot and Block System

The lot and block system was developed as an outgrowth of the rectangular survey system and can be used to simplify the locational descriptions of small parcels. The system was established when land developers subdivided land in the rectangular survey system and assigned lot numbers to individual sites within blocks. The maps of these subdivisions were then filed with the local government to establish a public record of their locations. Each block was identified precisely using a ground survey or established monuments.

> **lot and block system:** A system for the legal description of land that refers to parcels' lot and block numbers, which appear on recorded maps and plats of subdivided land; may also be used for assessment maps.

Applying the lot and block system to old, unsurveyed communities helped to identify each owner's site or parcel of land. Typically a surveyor located the boundaries of streets on the ground and drew maps outlining the blocks. Then lot lines were established by agreement among property owners. A precise, measured description was established for each lot and each was given a number or letter that could be referred to in routine transactions. This information was recorded in public records and was known as a *recorded plat of the defined area or subdivision.*

Title and Record Data

Before making an on-site inspection, an appraiser should obtain an appropriate description and other property data from the client or from published sources and public documents. Most jurisdictions have a public office or depository for deeds where transactions are documented and made public. The accessibility of public records, which is legally known as *constructive notice*, ensures that interested individuals are able to research and, if necessary, contest deed transfers.

Sometimes public records do not contain all relevant information about a particular property. Although official documents are dependable sources of information, they may be incomplete or not suited to the appraiser's purposes. Useful support data can be found in land registration systems, land data banks, and assessors' maps.

> **WHERE TO FIND**
> **Title and Record Data**
> Most county recorders' offices keep index books for land deeds and land mortgages from which the book and page number of a recorded deed may be found. In addition, official county plat books may be examined in the county auditor's office.

Ownership Information

If a partial interest in a property is to be appraised rather than the fee simple interest, the elements of title that are to be excluded should be indicated and carefully analyzed. An appraiser who is asked to develop an opinion of the value of a fractional ownership interest must understand the exact type of legal ownership to define the property rights to be appraised.

After defining the property rights being appraised, the appraiser must identify any excluded rights that may affect value. In addition USPAP requires appraisers to analyze and report any prior sales occurring within a specified number of years.[1] The appraiser should also investigate the ownership of surface and subsurface rights through a title report, an abstract of title, or other documentary evidence of the property rights to be appraised. Title data indicates easements and restrictions, which may limit the use of the property, as well as special rights such as air rights, water rights, mineral rights, obligations for lateral support, and easements for common walls. Typically the appraiser is not an expert in title information but must rely on legal opinions, title research reports, and title data provided by other professionals. Easements, rights of way, and private and public restrictions affect property value.

Easements may provide for overhead and underground electrical transmission lines, underground sewers or tunnels, flowage, aviation routes, roads, walkways, and open space. Some easements or rights of way acquired by utility companies or public agencies may not have been used for many years, and the appraiser's physical inspection of the property may not disclose any evidence of such use. In certain jurisdictions, easements that are not used for a finite period of time may be automatically terminated. Use of a property for access without the owner's written permission may give the user a prescriptive easement across the property. This type of easement usually must be used for several years without being contested or challenged by the property owner. Title insurance companies often overlook this easement unless it has been perfected in court. Nevertheless, the appraiser should search diligently for information pertaining to any limitations on ownership rights.

Restrictions cited in the deed may limit the type of building or business that may be conducted on the property. A typical example is a restriction that prohibits the sale of liquor or gasoline in a certain place. Often a title report will not specify the details of private restrictions; a copy of the deed or other conveyance must be obtained to identify the limitations imposed on the property. Appraisers often include a limiting condition in their appraisal reports regarding easement or private restrictions that have not been recorded in public records.

WHERE TO FIND

Ownership Information

A property's legal owner and type of ownership can be ascertained from the public records maintained by the county clerk and recorder. Local title or abstract companies may also provide useful information.

---

1. See Standards Rule 1-5 of the current edition of the Uniform Standards of Professional Appraisal Practice. Other standards such as the Uniform Appraisal Standard for Federal Land Acquisitions also apply in the federal jurisdiction.

Zoning and Land Use Information

Land use and development are usually regulated by city or county government, but they are often subject to regional, state, and federal controls as well. In analyzing zoning and building codes, an appraiser considers all current regulations and the likelihood of a change in the code. Usually a zone calls for a general use (such as residential, commercial, or industrial) and then specifies a type or density of use. Zoning and other land use regulations often control the following:

- Height and size of buildings
- Lot coverage (density) or floor area ratio (FAR)
- Required landscaping or open space
- Number of units allowed
- Parking requirements
- Sign requirements
- Building setbacks
- Plan lines for future street widenings
- Other factors of importance to the highest and best use of the site

Most zoning ordinances identify and define the uses to which a property may be put without reservation or recourse to legal intervention. This is also referred to as a *use by right*. They also describe the process for obtaining nonconforming use permits, variances, and zoning changes, if permitted. In areas subject to floods, earthquakes, and other natural hazards, special zoning and building regulations may impose restrictions on construction. In coastal and historic districts, zoning restrictions may govern building location and design.

Potential changes in government regulations must also be considered. If, for example, a building moratorium or cessation of land use applications is in effect for a stated period, a property's prospective highest and best use may have to be delayed. The appropriateness of current zoning and the reasonable probability of a zoning change must be considered. Highest and best use recommendations may rely on the probability of a zoning change. One of the criteria for the highest and best use conclusion is that the use must be legally permissible. If the highest and best use of a site is predicated on a zoning change, the appraiser must investigate the probability that such a change will occur. The appraiser may interview planning and zoning staff and study patterns of zoning change to assess the likelihood of a change. The appraiser can generally eliminate those uses that are clearly not

WHERE TO FIND

Zoning and Land Use Information
Although zoning ordinances and maps are public records that are available at zoning offices, an appraiser may need help from planning and zoning staff to understand the impact of zoning regulations. Often an appraiser must contact several agencies. Zoning and land use restrictions are not usually listed in the recorded title to a property, so confirmation from controlling agencies is necessary.

compatible with existing uses in the area as well as uses that have previously been denied. After reviewing available public and private land use information, the appraiser may also prepare a forecast of land development for the area. If the

> **assessed value:** The value of a property according to the tax rolls in ad valorem taxation. May be higher or lower than market value, or based on an assessment ratio that is a percentage of market value.

zoning of the subject site is not compatible with the probable forecast uses, the likelihood of a change in the zoning is especially high and speculative. The appraiser should recognize, however, that a zoning change is never 100% certain and should alert the client to that fact if it is relevant to the purpose of the appraisal.

Assessment and Tax Information

Real property taxes in all jurisdictions are based on ad valorem assessments. Taxation levels are significant in considering a property's potential uses. From the present assessment, the current tax rate, and a review of previous tax rates, the appraiser can form a conclusion about future trends in property taxation. Assessed values may not be good indicators of the market value

> **WHERE TO FIND**
>
> **Assessment and Tax Information**
> The records of the county assessor or tax collector can provide details concerning a property's assessed value and annual tax burden. Often, an appraiser obtains the property information from the local assessor before conducting a physical inspection of the property.

of individual properties because mass appraisals based on statistical methodology tend to equalize the application of taxes to achieve parity among assessment levels in a given district. Nevertheless, in some areas and for some property types, assessed value may approximate market value. The reliability of local assessments as indicators of market value varies from district to district.

Physical Characteristics of Land

In site description and analysis, an appraiser describes and interprets how the physical characteristics of the site influence value and how the physical improvements relate to the land and to neighboring properties. Important physical characteristics include

- Site size and shape
- Corner influence
- Plottage
- Excess land and surplus land
- Topography
- Utilities
- Site improvements
- Accessibility
- Environment

> The **physical characteristics of a site** relate to size, shape, plottage potential, corner influence, the presence of excess or surplus land, topography, available utilities, on-site and off-site improvements, location, and environment.

Size and Shape

A size and shape description states a site's dimensions (street frontage, width, and depth) and sets forth any advantages or disadvantages caused by these physical characteristics. The appraiser describes the site and analyzes how its size and shape affect property value. Special attention is given to any characteristics that are unusual for the neighborhood. The effects of the size and shape of a property vary with its probable use. For example, an odd-shaped parcel may be appropriate for a dwelling but unacceptable for certain types of commercial or industrial use. A triangular lot may not have the same utility as a rectangular lot due to its size and shape

Land size is measured and expressed in different units, depending on local custom and land use. Large tracts of land are usually measured in acres. Smaller sites are usually measured in square feet, although acreage may also be used. Dimensions are expressed in feet (and tenths of feet for easy calculation).

Frontage is the measured footage of a site that abuts a street, lake or river, railroad, or other feature recognized by the market. The frontage may or may not be the same as the width of the property because a property may be irregularly shaped or have frontage on more than one side.

Size differences can affect value and are considered in site analysis. Reducing sale prices to consistent units of comparison facilitates the analysis of comparable sites and can identify trends in market behavior. Generally, as size increases, unit prices decrease. Conversely, as size decreases, unit prices increase. The functional utility or desirability of a site often varies depending on the types of uses to be placed on the parcel. Different prospective uses have ideal size and depth characteristics that influence value and highest and best use. An appraiser should recognize this fact when appraising sites of unusual size or shape. Value tendencies can be observed by studying market sales of lots of various sizes and their ability to support specific uses or intensities of development. In residential appraisal, a large triangular lot may not have any greater value because only one dwelling unit may be built on it according to zoning and subdivision regulations. The large undeveloped remainder would be surplus land, which is discussed below.

Corner Influence

Properties with frontage on two or more streets may have a higher or lower unit value than neighboring properties with frontage on only one street. The advantage of easier access to corner sites may be diminished by a loss of privacy or a loss of utility due to setback requirements. An appraiser must determine whether the local market considers a corner location to be favorable or unfavorable. This determination can change depending on the use (or uses) anticipated for the site.

In the layout of building improvements and the subdivision of large plots, corner sites have more flexibility and higher visibility than interior properties. A store on a corner may have the advantage of direct access from both streets and prominent corner visibility and exposure. Corner exposure may provide advantageous ingress and egress for a drive-in business. For residential properties, corner locations may have negative implications; quiet, cul-de-sac sites in the interior of a subdivision may be more

> **frontage:** The measured footage of a site that abuts a street, stream, railroad, or other feature.
>
> **corner influence:** The effect on value produced by a property's location at or near the intersection of two streets; the increment of value or loss in value resulting from this location or proximity.

desirable and command higher prices. Residences on corner sites are exposed to more traffic noise and provide less security. Owners of corner sites may pay higher costs for front-footage sidewalks and assessments, and the side street setback may affect the permitted size of the building. Usually owners of residences on corner lots have to maintain a larger landscaped area that may in fact be public property.

Plottage

Sometimes highest and best use results from assembling two or more parcels of land under one ownership. If the combined parcels have a greater unit value than they did separately, plottage value is created. Plottage is an increment of value that results when two or more sites are combined to produce a larger site with greater utility. For example, there may be great demand for one-acre lots in an industrial park where most of the platted lots are of one-half acre. By itself, a half-acre lot has a value of $1.00 per square foot. When combined with an adjacent half-acre lot, however, the value may increase to $1.50 per square foot. The value difference may be offset by the premium a developer often has to pay to combine adjacent properties, or the reverse may occur if the lots are very large and assemblage yields a lower value per square foot in the marketplace due to economies of scale. Plottage value may also apply to an existing site of a special size or shape that has greater utility than more conventional, smaller lots. Neighboring land uses and values are analyzed to determine whether an appraised property has plottage value.

Plottage is significant in appraising agricultural land. Properties of less-than-optimum size have lower unit values because they cannot support the modern equipment needed to produce maximum profits. In an urban area, plottage of commercial office and retail sites and of residential apartment sites may increase the unit values of the lots assembled.

Although the assemblage of land into a size that permits a higher and better use may increase the land's unit value (dollars per square foot or acre), the reverse may also occur. Land that must be divided or

> **plottage:** The increment of value created when two or more sites are combined to produce greater utility.
>
> **assemblage:** The combining of two or more parcels, usually but not necessarily contiguous, into one ownership or use; the process that creates plottage value.

subdivided to achieve a higher and better use is commonly sold in bulk at a price less than the sum of the retail prices of its components. The lower unit price for the bulk sale reflects market allowances for risk, time, management, development and related costs, sales costs, profit, and other considerations associated with dividing and marketing the land.

Excess Land and Surplus Land

A given land use has an optimum parcel size, configurations, and land-to-building ratio. Any extra or remaining land not needed to support the specific use may have a different value than the land area needed to support the improvement. The portion of property that represents an optimal site for the existing improvements will reflect a typical land-to-building ratio. Land area needed to support the existing or ideal improvement can be identified and quantified by the appraiser. Any remaining site area is either excess land or surplus land.

   Excess land, in regard to an improved site, is land that is not needed to serve or support the existing improvement. In regard to a vacant site or a site considered as though vacant, excess land is not needed to accommodate the site's primary highest and best use. Such land may have its own highest and best use or may allow for future expansion of the existing or anticipated improvement. If the excess land is marketable or has value for a future use, its market value as vacant land is added to the estimated value of the economic entity.

   Surplus land is not needed to support the existing improvement and typically cannot be separated from the property and sold off. Surplus land does not have an independent highest and best use and may contribute a minimal value.

   As an example, consider a residential property comprising a single-family home and two standard-size lots in a fully developed subdivision. If the house was situated within the boundaries of a single lot and the normal land area for properties in the neighborhood is a single lot, then the second, vacant lot would most likely be considered excess land, which could be separated from the lot of the existing structure for future development to that parcel's highest and best use. If land values in the neighborhood is $1.00 per square foot, then the excess land in this situation would probably add the full $1.00 per square foot to the value of the subject property (i.e., the house and the two lots). If the typical land area for properties in

excess land: In regard to an improved site, the land not needed to serve or support the existing improvement. In regard to a vacant site or a site considered as though vacant, the land not needed to accommodate the site's primary highest and best use. Such land may be separated from the larger site and have its own highest and best use, or it may allow for future expansion of the existing or anticipated improvement.

surplus land: Land not necessary to support the highest and best use of the existing improvement but, because of physical limitations, building placement, or neighborhood norms, cannot be sold off separately. Such land may or may not contribute positively to value and may or may not accommodate future expansion of an existing or anticipated improvement.

the neighborhood were a double lot, regardless of building placement, then the same property would have neither excess land nor surplus land.

Now consider an industrial park where land-to-building ratios for warehouse properties range from 2.8-to-1 to 3.5-to-1 and land value is $2.00 per square foot. The subject property is a 20,000-sq.-ft. warehouse on a 100,000-sq.-ft. site, which results in a land-to-building ratio of 5-to-1, well above the market area norm. If the additional land not needed to support the highest and best use of the existing property were in the back portion of the site, lacking access to the street, that land would probably be considered surplus land because it could not be separated from the site and does not have an independent highest and best use. In this situation, the surplus land would probably still contribute positively to the value of the subject property (because the existing improvements could still be expanded onto the surplus land), but it would also most likely be worth much less than the $2.00 per square foot price commanded by vacant land elsewhere in the industrial park. If an adjacent property owner could expand onto the unused portion of the site of the subject property, that land could then be considered excess land because it could be separated from the existing property and used by the other property owner. In this case, the value of the excess land could be comparable to that of vacant land elsewhere in the industrial park or it may even command a premium if the owner of the adjacent property needs the land to complete an assemblage.

Topography

Topographical studies provide information about land's contour, grading, natural drainage, soil conditions, view, and general physical usefulness. Sites may differ in value due to these physical characteristics. Steep slopes often impede building construction. Natural drainage can be advantageous or, if a site is downstream from other properties or is a natural drainage basin for the area, it may have severely limited use. Adequate drainage systems can offset the topographic and drainage problems that would otherwise inhibit the development of such a site. Upland land area or land with good drainage can typically support more intensive uses.

In describing topography, an appraiser must employ the terminology used in the area. What is described as a steep hill in one part of the country may be considered a moderate slope in another. In some instances, descriptions of a property's topography may be taken from published sources such as topographic maps (see Figure 9.1).

> **Topographical characteristics,** surface soil and subsoil quality, grade, drainage, and the bearing capacity of the soil determine the suitability of a land parcel for an agricultural use or a proposed improvement.

Geodetic Survey Program

Topographic maps prepared under the direction of the U.S. Geological Survey, which are referred to as *quadrangles* or *quads,* provide information that is useful in land descriptions. (See Figure 9.2.) Base lines, principal meridians,

Figure 9.1   Topographic Map

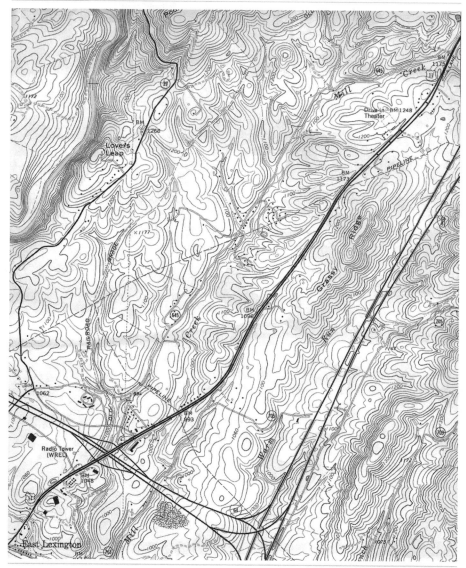

and township lines are shown along with topographic and man-made features. The topographic features commonly depicted on these maps include land elevations (represented by contour lines at specified intervals), rivers, lakes, intermittent streams and other bodies of water, poorly drained areas, and forest. The man-made features identified include improved and unimproved roads, highways, bridges, power transmission lines, levees, railroads, airports, churches, schools, and other buildings. Quandrangle maps also show National Forest and Bureau of Land Management (BLM) boundaries.

Soil Analysis

Surface soil and subsoil conditions are important for both improved properties and agricultural land. A soil's suitability for building or for accommodating a septic system is important for all types of improved property, and it is a major consideration when the construction of large, heavy buildings is being contemplated. The need for special pilings or floating foundations has a major impact on the adaptability of a site for a particular use. Soil conditions affect the cost of development and, therefore, the property value.

Agronomists and soil scientists measure the agricultural qualities of soil and capacity of soil for specific agricultural uses. Engineers trained in soil mechanics test for soil consistency and load-bearing capacity. Subsoil conditions are frequently known to local builders, developers, and others, but if there is any doubt about the soil's bearing capacity, the client should be informed of the need for soil studies. All doubts must be resolved before the land's highest and best use can be successfully analyzed, or a description of any special assumptions must be included in the appraisal report.

Floodplain and Wetlands Analysis

The appraiser should check floodplain maps prepared by local governments and review any available surveys or topographical data provided by the client. Proximity to any flood zones may be determined by studying maps published by the Federal Emergency Management Agency (FEMA). Each map panel is identified by a FEMA number and shows properties within the 100-year

---

WHERE TO FIND

Topographic Maps
Indexes of U.S. Geological Survey quadrangles for states east of the Mississippi River are available from:

U.S. Geological Survey
Eastern Distribution Branch
1200 S. Eads Street
Arlington, VA 22202

To obtain quadrangles for states west of the Mississippi, contact:

U.S. Geological Survey
Western Distribution Branch
Box 25286
Federal Center
Denver, CO 80225

For more information, see: http://mapping.usgs.gov/mac/findmaps.html

geodetic survey program: The United States Coast and Geodetic Survey System; a network of benchmarks located throughout the United States and identified by latitude and longitude; initially established to identify tracts of land owned by the federal government, but gradually extended across the nation.

Figure 9.2   U.S. Department of the Interior Geological Survey

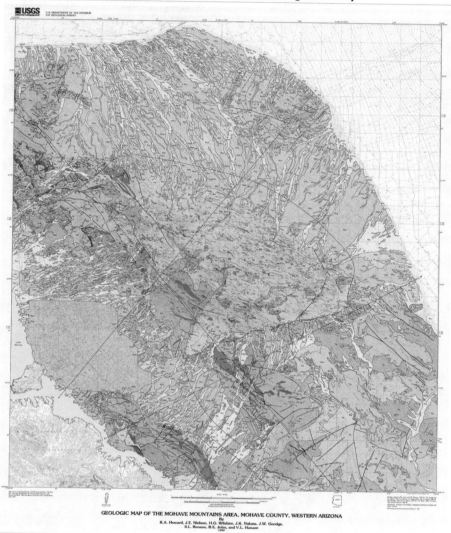

GEOLOGIC MAP OF THE MOHAVE MOUNTAINS AREA, MOHAVE COUNTY, WESTERN ARIZONA
By
K.A. Howard, J.E. Nielson, H.G. Wilshire, J.K. Nakata, J.W. Goodge,
S.L. Reneau, B.E. Johns, and V.L. Hansen
1999

Figure 9.3   **Floodplain Map**

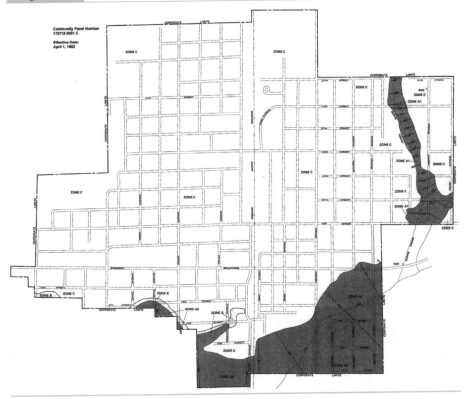

floodplain, floodways, or other districts (see Figure 9.3). These maps also provide base data for Flood Insurance Rate Maps (FIRMs).

The definition of what constitutes a wetland varies. Most laws describe wetlands in terms of three possible characteristics:

1. Soils
2. Hydrology
3. Vegetation

WHERE TO FIND

Floodplain Maps

To obtain FEMA floodplain maps, contact:

Federal Emergency Management Agency
Map Service Center
P.O. Box 1038
Jessup, MD 20794-1038
Tel: (800) 358-9616
Fax: (800) 358-9620

For more information, see:
http://www.fema.gov/library

Section 404 of the Clean Water Act, the major federal environmental legislation regulating activities in wetlands, defines a wetland as land that is inundated or saturated by surface or groundwater at a frequency and duration sufficient to support, and under normal circumstances does support, a prevalence of vegetation typically adapted for life in saturated soil conditions.

Federal Emergency Management Agency (FEMA): A federal agency established by the Flood Disaster Protection Act to provide directives on where to build and where not to build in coastal and floodplain areas.

floodplain: The flat surfaces along the courses of rivers, streams, and other bodies of water that are subject to overflow and flooding.

wetlands: Areas that are frequently inundated or saturated by surface or ground water and support vegetation typically adapted for life in saturated soil conditions; generally include swamps, marshes, bogs, and similar areas, but classification may differ in various jurisdictions. Section 404 of the Clean Water Act defines wetlands as "those areas that are inundated or saturated by surface or ground water at a frequency and duration sufficient to support, and that under normal circumstances do support, a prevalence of vegetation typically adapted for life in saturated soil conditions."

Swamps, bogs, fens, marshes, and estuaries are subject to varying degrees of influence from local, state, and federal governments. In 2001 the U.S. Supreme Court curtailed the power of the U.S. Army Corps of Engineers (and, by extension, other federal authorities such as the U.S. Environmental Protection Agency) to claim jurisdiction over certain wetlands using the Clean Water Act.[2] The court ruled that the act does not give the federal government jurisdiction over inland bodies of water that do not flow to the sea, such as landlocked ponds, wetlands, or mud flats, only navigable waterways or marshes that drain into navigable waters. To value wetlands, appraisers must understand the unique features of the land, the evolving laws protecting these areas, the niche market for such properties, and the proper application of the approaches to value.

Utilities

An appraiser investigates all the utilities and services available to a site. Off-site utilities may be publicly or privately operated, or there may be a need for on-site utility systems such as septic tanks and private water wells. The major utilities to be considered are

- Sanitary sewers
- Domestic water (i.e., potable water, for human consumption)
- Types of raw water for commercial, industrial, and agricultural uses
- Natural gas
- Electricity
- Storm drainage
- Telephone service
- Cable television

Although market area analysis describes in general the utility systems that are available in an area, a site analysis should provide a detailed description of the utilities that are available to the appraised site. The location and capacity of the utilities should be determined and any unusually high connection fees should be noted. Atypically high or low service costs should also be

2.   *Solid Waste Agency of Northern Cook County v. U.S. Army Corps of Engineers,* 531 U.S. 1 (2001).

Figure 9.4 Wetlands Map

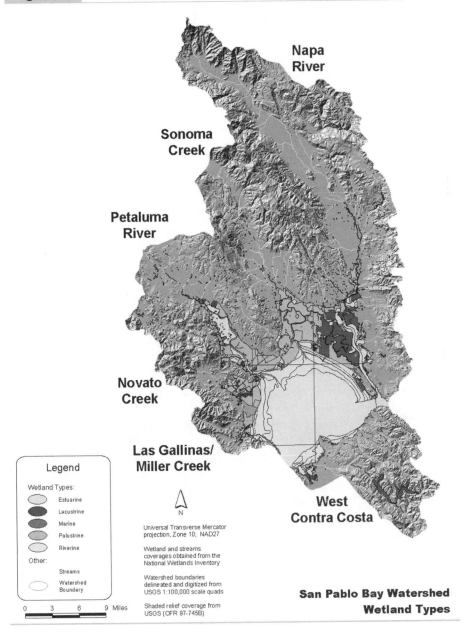

Napa
River

Sonoma
Creek

Petaluma
River

Novato
Creek

Las Gallinas/
Miller Creek

West
Contra Costa

Legend

Wetland Types:
Estuarine
Lacustrine
Marine
Palustrine
Riverine

Other:
Streams
Watershed
Boundary

0   3   6   9 Miles

N

Universal Transverse Mercator
projection, Zone 10; NAD27

Wetland and streams
coverages obtained from the
National Wetlands Inventory

Watershed boundaries
delineated and digitized from
USGS 1:100,000 scale quads

Shaded relief coverage from
USGS (OFR 97-745B)

**San Pablo Bay Watershed
Wetland Types**

WHERE TO FIND

Data on Utilities
Accurate information on public utilities
can be obtained from
• Local utility companies or agencies
• Local public works departments
• Providers of on-site water and sewage
  disposal systems

The **cost of installing utilities** is
considered in the highest and best use
conclusion and may be reflected directly
or indirectly in the analysis, depending on
the selection of comparables sales used in
the valuation.

identified and analyzed. It is not sufficient simply to establish which utilities are available. Any limitations resulting from a lack of utilities are important in highest and best use analysis, and all available, alternative sources of utility service should be investigated.

The rates for utility service and the burden of any bonded indebtedness or other special utility costs should also be considered. Of particular concern to residential, commercial, and industrial users are

• Quality and quantity of water and its cost

• Costs and dependability of energy sources

• Adequacy of sewer facilities

• Any special utility costs or surcharges that might apply to certain businesses

• Impact of special improvement districts (SIDs) on tax rate and repayment methods (special assessment, etc.)

Site Improvements

In a site description an appraiser describes off-site, as well as on-site, improvements that make the site ready for its intended use or development. Then the appraiser analyzes how the site improvements affect value. On-site improvements include grading, landscaping, fences, curbs, gutters, paving, drainage and irrigation systems, walks, and other improvements to the land. Off-site improvements include access roads, utility hookups, remote water retention ponds, and sewer and drainage lines. The value of off-site improvements is typically considered with site value.

The location of existing buildings on a site must also be described and analyzed. Many appraisers make approximate plot plan drawings that show the placement of major buildings in relation to lot lines, access points, and parking or driveway areas. Land-to-building ratios and overall site configuration are usually quite important to a site's appeal and ability to support specific uses. The space allotted for parking influences a site's value for business and commercial use, so the parking space-to-building ratio in a commercial and industrial property must be analyzed. Zoning codes or planned unit developments (PUDs) will specify the minimum number of spaces required.

The appraiser considers any on-site improvements that add to or detract from a property's optimal use or highest and best use. For example, a lot zoned for multifamily use may be improved with an 18-unit apartment building that is too valuable to demolish. If the site as vacant could accommodate a 24-unit building but the location of the present structure blocks the ability to add additional units, the appraiser may conclude that the site is underimproved and not developed to its highest and best use.

Accessibility

Site analysis focuses on the time-distance relationships between the site and common origins and destinations. An appraiser describes and analyzes all forms of access to and from the property and the neighborhood. In most cases, adequate parking area and the location and condition of streets, alleys, connector roads, freeways, and highways are important to land use. Industrial properties are influenced by rail and freeway access and the proximity of docking facilities. Industrial, commercial, and residential areas are all affected by the location of airports, freeways, public transportation, and railroad service.

Traffic volume may be either advantageous or disadvantageous to a site, depending on other conditions that affect its highest and best use. High-volume local traffic in commercial areas is usually an asset; heavy through traffic may hurt retail stores, except those that serve regional travelers. Heavy traffic within residential areas is usually detrimental for single-family neighborhoods, but high-traffic streets to access a subdivision or development are advantageous.

The noise, dust, and fumes that emanate from a heavily traveled artery or freeway are not desirable for most low-density, residential lots. On the other hand, the advertising value of locations on major arteries can benefit offices and shopping centers, unless congestion restricts the free flow of traffic. The visibility of a commercial property from the street is an advertising asset; this asset is most valuable when the driving customer can easily exit the flow of traffic and enter the property.

Median strips, turning restrictions, one-way streets, and access restrictions can limit the potential uses of a parcel. In site analysis the appraiser should test the probable uses of the site in relation to the flow of traffic. Planned changes in access should be verified with the appropriate authority and considered in the appraisal.

WHERE TO FIND

Traffic Volume Data
The volume of traffic passing a property is determined by a traffic count, which can usually be obtained from local or state road departments. Traffic counts indicate average daily traffic, peak hours, and direction. Observing the speed and turning movements of actual vehicles helps an appraiser judge how traffic affects a property's highest and best use.

Environment

Appraisers also analyze land use in light of environmental conditions. Environmental considerations include factors such as

- Local climate
- Availability of adequate and satisfactory water supply
- Pattern of drainage

- Quality of air
- Presence of wildlife/endangered species habitats
- Location of earthquake faults and known slide or avalanche zones
- Proximity to streams, wetlands, rivers, lakes, or oceans

Air and water pollution are by-products of increased population and urbanization. Public concern over pollution has prompted political action and legislation to protect the environment. In areas subject to extreme air pollution, regulations may exclude certain industries and limit the volume of traffic; such restrictions impact land use in these jurisdictions. Pollution rights have also become a salable commodity.[3] In locations near natural water sources, industrial uses may be prohibited while recreational uses are promoted. Environmental and climatic advantages and constraints must be analyzed to determine the proper land use for a site. Future land uses must be compatible with the local environment.

A site in a specific location may be influenced by its exposure to sun, wind, or other environmental factors. A very windy location can be disastrous to a resort but beneficial to a fossil-fuel power plant. The sunny side of the street is not always the most desirable for retail shops. In hot climates, the shady side of the street often gets more pedestrian traffic and greater sales, thus producing higher rents and higher land values. Ski resorts almost always have slopes facing north for snow retention, and buildings facing south are desirable.

Analysis of a site's environment focuses on the interrelationships between the appraised site and neighboring properties. The effects of any hazards or nuisances caused by neighboring properties must be considered. Of particular importance are safety concerns—e.g., the safety of employees and customers, of occupants and visitors, or of children going to and from school.

A site's value is also influenced by nearby amenities and developments on adjoining sites such as parks, fine buildings, and compatible commercial buildings. The types of structures surrounding the property being appraised and the activities of those who use them can greatly influence site value.

Environmental Liabilities

In recent years the federal government has issued many environmental laws and regulations; state and local governments have added even more. This vast network of regulations defines the natural and man-made conditions that constitute environmental liabilities affecting property values. Natural areas to be protected include wetlands, aquifer replenishment areas, and habitats for endangered or threatened species. Man-made liabilities may be indicated by

---

3. The Clean Air Act of 1990 regulated the tonnage of acid-rain emissions that smokestack industries may release in proportion to plant size. Industries that do not use their full legal allowance can transfer or sell their pollution rights to other industries. Since 1993 pollution rights have been sold on both the Chicago Board of Trade and in the off-exchange pollution-rights market.

the presence of leaking underground storage tanks (LUSTs), asbestos, PCBs, or other hazardous materials. The existence of one or more environmental conditions can reduce the value of a property or even create a negative value.

The typical appraiser may not have the knowledge or experience needed to detect the presence of hazardous substances or to measure their quantities. Like buyers and sellers in the open market, the appraiser must often rely on the advice of others. Appraisers are not expected or required to be experts in the detection or measurement of hazardous substances. The role and responsibility of the appraiser in detecting, measuring, and considering environmental substances affecting a property are addressed in Advisory Opinion 9 of USPAP and Guide Note 8 of the Appraisal Institute's Guide Notes to the Standards of Professional Appraisal Practice (see Figure 9.5).

The Property Observation Checklist (Figure 9.6), developed and adopted by the Appraisal Institute in 1995, is consistent with Advisory Opinion 9 and Guide Note 8. The checklist provides appraisers conducting property inspections with a uniform, easy-to-use guideline for recording observations about the presence of possible environmental factors. To the extent possible, voluntary use of the checklist limits the appraiser's liability. (Note: the checklist was not developed for single-family residential or agricultural properties.)

Even if there is no reason to believe that the property being appraised is affected by hazardous substances, appraisers are advised to include a standard disclaimer or statement of limiting conditions concerning hazardous substances

---

Figure 9.5   **Consideration of Hazardous Substances in the Appraisal Process**

Advisory Opinion 9, which was adopted December 8, 1992, addresses the following areas of concern:

• An appraiser who is requested to complete a checklist as part of a process to detect contamination should only respond to those questions that can be answered competently by the appraiser within the limits of his or her particular expertise.

• An appraiser may reasonably rely on the findings and opinions of qualified specialists in environmental remediation and compliance cost estimation.

• An appraiser may appraise an interest in real estate that is or is believed to be contaminated based on the hypothesis that the real estate is free of contamination when 1) the resulting appraisal is not misleading, 2) the client has been advised of the limitation, and 3) the Ethics Rule of USPAP is satisfied.

• The value of an interest in impacted or contaminated real estate may not be measurable by simply deducting the remediation or compliance cost estimate from the estimated value as if unaffected.

Guide Note 8 was adopted January 1, 1991, and amended January 25, 1994. This guide note takes its direction from the Competency Rule of USPAP, which requires appraisers to either

• have the knowledge and experience necessary to complete a specific appraisal assignment competently

or

• disclose their lack of knowledge or experience to the client, take all steps necessary or appropriate to complete the assignment competently, and describe in the report their lack of knowledge or experience and the steps taken to competently complete the assignment

Figure 9.6   **Property Observation Checklist Form**

**APPRAISAL
INSTITUTE®**

PROPERTY OBSERVATION CHECKLIST

SCOPE OF ANALYSIS

The Property Observation Checklist is prepared by the appraiser in conjuction with his/her inspection of the subject property in the normal course of an appraisal assignment. In completing the checklist, only visual observations are recorded. The intent of the checklist is to help identify possible environmental factors that could be observable by a non-environmental professional. The appraiser did not search title, interview the current or prior owners, or do any research beyond that normally associated with the appraisal process, unless otherwise stated.

The user of this checklist is reminded that all responses to the questions are provided by an appraiser who is not an environmental professional and is not specifically trained or qualified to identify potential environmental problems; therefore, it should be used only to assist the appraiser's client in determining whether an environmental professional is required. The checklist was not developed for use with single-family residential or agricultural properties.

The appraiser is not liable for the lack of detection or identification of possible environmental factors. The appraisal report and/or the Property Observation Checklist must not be considered under any circumstances to be an environmental site assessment of the property as would be performed by an environmental professional.

GENERAL INSTRUCTIONS

The appraiser should distinguish, as appropriate, between the physical presence of possible environmental factors and the economic effect such factors may have in the marketplace or on the value estimate. In completing the checklist, the appraiser should attach reports, photographs, interview records, notes, public records, etc., as documentation for specific observations. The instructions for each section of the checklist specify the kinds of documentation required.

If, for any reason, this checklist is prepared as a stand-alone document, it must be accompanied by an appropriate statement of assumptions and limiting conditions, as well as the appraiser's signed certification.

TERMINOLOGY AND APPRAISAL STANDARDS

The following checklist terms appear in *The Dictionary of Real Estate Appraisal*, Third Edition (Chicago: Appraisal Institute, 1993) and are specifically referenced in the Property Observation Checklist: *adjoining properties; environmental professional; environmental site assessment;* and *pits, ponds, or lagoons.* Please refer to *The Dictionary of Real Estate Appraisal*, Third Edition, for discussions of these terms.

Please refer to Guide Note 8, "The Consideration of Hazardous Substances in the Appraisal Process," *Guide Notes to the Standards of Professional Appraisal Practice* (Chicago: Appraisal Institute, current edition); Advisory Opinion G-9, "Responsibility of Appraisers Concerning Toxic or Hazardous Substances Contamination," in Addenda to *Uniform Standards of Professional Appraisal Practice* (Washington, D.C.: The Appraisal Foundation, current edition); and other appropriate statements in the professional standards documents for additional information.

© 2001 by the Appraisal Institute. All rights reserved. Appraisal Institute members and affiliates may reproduce this document, providing this copyright is included. All others must obtain permission.

http://www.appraisalinstitute.org/download/

Figure 9.6   Property Observation Checklist Form *(continued)*

SECTION 1	Extent of Appraiser's Inspection of the Property

Describe the appraiser's on-site inspection of the subject property and, as applicable, the adjoining properties:

_____

_____

_____

_____

SECTION 2	Possible Environmental Factors Observed by the Appraiser

Indicate below if any of the following possible environmental factors were observed during the appraiser's visual inspection(s) of the subject property and, as applicable, the adjoining properties. A written description of possible environmental factors should be provided for all questions where "Yes" is checked.

1. Did the appraiser observe an indication of current or past industrial/manufacturing use on the subject property or adjoining properties?

   ○ Yes   ○ No   **If observed, describe below:**

   _____

   _____

2. Did the appraiser observe any containers, storage drums, or disposal devices not labeled or identified as to contents or use on the subject property?

   ○ Yes   ○ No   **If observed, describe below:**

   _____

   _____

3. Did the appraiser observe any stained soil or distressed vegetation on the subject property?

   ○ Yes   ○ No   **If observed, describe below:**

   _____

   _____

4. Did the appraiser observe any pits, ponds, or lagoons on the subject property?

   ○ Yes   ○ No   **If observed, describe below:**

   _____

   _____

5. Did the appraiser observe any evidence of above-ground or underground storage tanks (e.g., tanks, vent pipes, etc.) on the subject property?

   ○ Yes   ○ No   **If observed, describe below:**

   _____

   _____

© 2001 by the Appraisal Institute. All rights reserved. Appraisal Institute members and affiliates may reproduce this document, providing this copyright is included. All others must obtain permission.

http://www.appraisalinstitute.org/download/

Figure 9.6 **Property Observation Checklist Form** *(continued)*

6. Did the appraiser observe any flooring, drains, or walls associated with the subject property that are stained or that emit unusual odors?

   ○ Yes ○ No **If observed, describe below:**

7. Did the appraiser observe any water being discharged on or from the subject property?

   ○ Yes ○ No **If observed, describe below:**

8. Did the appraiser observe any indication of dumping, burying, or burning on the subject property?

   ○ Yes ○ No **If observed, describe below:**

9. Did the appraiser observe any chipped, blistered, or peeled paint on the subject property?

   ○ Yes ○ No **If observed, describe below:**

10. Did the appraiser observe any sprayed-on insulation, pipe wrapping, duct wrapping, etc., on the subject property?

    ○ Yes ○ No **If observed, describe below:**

11. Did the appraiser observe any transmission towers (electrical, microwave, etc.) on the subject property or adjoining properties?

    ○ Yes ○ No **If observed, describe below:**

12. Did the appraiser observe any coastal areas, rivers, streams, springs, lakes, swamps, marshes, or watercourses on the subject property or adjoining properties?

    ○ Yes ○ No **If observed, describe below:**

13. Did the appraiser observe any other factors that might indicate the need for investigation(s) by an environmental professional?

    ○ Yes ○ No **If observed, describe below:**

© 2001 by the Appraisal Institute. All rights reserved. Appraisal Institute members and affiliates may reproduce this document, providing this copyright is included. All others must obtain permission.

http://www.appraisalinstitute.org/download/

Figure 9.6   **Property Observation Checklist Form** *(continued)*

| **SECTION 3** | Possible Environmental Factors Reported by Others |

Indicate below if in completing this assignment the appraiser was informed—verbally or in writing—of any information concerning possible environmental factors reported by others. "Others" may include the client, the property owner, the property owner's agent, or any other person conveying such information. Documentation should be provided for all instances where "Yes" is checked. If the information was presented verbally, then a written description of the source and circumstance of the communication should be attached to this checklist and/or the appraisal report. Copies of printed reports provided to the appraiser should be attached to this checklist and/or the appraisal report.

14. Has the appraiser been informed about federal- or state-maintained records indicating that environmentally sensitive sites are located on the subject property or adjoining properties?

  ○ Yes   ○ No   **If yes, provide documentation.**

15. Has the appraiser been informed about past or current violations (e.g., liens, government notifications, etc.) of environmental laws concerning the subject property?

  ○ Yes   ○ No   **If yes, provide documentation.**

16. Has the appraiser been informed about past or current environmental lawsuits or administrative proceedings concerning the subject property?

  ○ Yes   ○ No   **If yes, provide documentation.**

17. Has the appraiser been informed about past or current tests for lead-based paint or other lead hazards on the subject property?

  ○ Yes   ○ No   **If yes, provide documentation.**

18. Has the appraiser been informed about past or current tests for asbestos-containing materials on the subject property?

  ○ Yes   ○ No   **If yes, provide documentation.**

19. Has the appraiser been informed about past or current tests for radon on the subject property?

  ○ Yes   ○ No   **If yes, provide documentation.**

20. Has the appraiser been informed about past or current tests for soil or groundwater contamination on the subject property?

  ○ Yes   ○ No   **If yes, provide documentation.**

21. Has the appraiser been informed about other professional environmental site assessment(s) of the subject property?

  ○ Yes   ○ No   **If yes, provide documentation.**

Signature

Name

Date Checklist Signed

State Certification or State License #   State

© 2001 by the Appraisal Institute. All rights reserved. Appraisal Institute members and affiliates may reproduce this document, providing this copyright is included. All others must obtain permission.

http://www.appraisalinstitute.org/download/

Advisory Opinion 9 of USPAP and Guide Note 8 of the Appraisal Institute's Guide Notes to the Standards of Professional Appraisal Practice address the **responsibility of appraisers** in detecting environmental problems. The Property Observation Checklist published by the Appraisal Institute may be used to inspect a property and to record observations about possible environmental factors.

in their appraisal reports. Such a statement clarifies the normal limits of the appraisal, discloses the appraiser's lack of expertise with regard to hazardous substances, and disclaims responsibility for matters beyond the appraiser's experience. (An example of such a disclaimer is provided in Chapter 26.) The determination of due diligence remains at issue, even when a disclaimer is used.

Environmental Site Assessments and Environmental Property Assessments

Because of the existence of environmental liability laws and the significant effect that environmental contamination may have on a given property, appraisers and property owners or purchasers should make reasonable inquiries to determine whether there is a likelihood that a particular property may be affected by either apparent or latent environmental conditions. Today this is as common as testing for termites, hidden structural problems, and other factors that may influence value. Most appraisers and property owners are not trained and qualified to make technical assessments, but reasonable examination and inquiry can produce evidence of conditions that are already known to the market.

In most parts of the country, lenders commonly require a specific environmental study before a loan for an income-producing property is processed. While formal studies are less common for single-family residential properties, lenders and secondary markets officials may require studies in Superfund areas and other areas known to have possible environmental contamination to ensure that the condition does not adversely affect the property for which a loan is proposed (see Figure 9.7).

Most environmental site assessments (ESAs) or environmental property assessments (EPRAs) required for real estate transactions are conducted by environmental consultants who are trained to investigate a broad range of environmental issues.

An environmental assessment cannot guarantee that a property is totally free of hazardous substances. An investigation does provide limited legal protection for the innocent purchaser, however, and a reasonable margin of assurance that contamination from hydrocarbons, asbestos, PCBs, or other hazardous substances is unlikely. To guarantee that a property is completely free of contaminants, every building component would have to be examined for asbestos and every cubic foot of soil and groundwater to the earth's core would have to be tested. The science of various environmental conditions and the laws relating to liabilities continue to change as

Environmental site assessments (ESAs) and environmental property assessments (EPRAs) are often required for approval of a sale or loan. The extent of an **environmental assessment** may correspond to one of three phases.

Figure 9.7   Environmental Site Assessments

Many real estate transactions require:

Phase I
- Site visit (interview occupants of the subject and neighboring properties and look for signs of contamination such as stained ground, defoliation, noxious odors, areas of inconsistent surface height or depth, uneven pavement, or the presence of drums or other debris)
- Examination of aerial photographs
- Study of records kept by local, state, and federal environmental agencies
- Review of pertinent regulatory legislation

If a Phase I environmental assessment uncovers evidence of possible contamination or past or present violations of environmental regulations, then:

Phase II
- Invasive sampling of the soil

If contaminants are present, then:

Phase III
- Further invasive sampling of soil to establish the horizontal and vertical extent of soil and groundwater contamination
- Usually a plan for remediation or mitigation is developed, including a timetable and the estimated costs associated with the environmental cleanup.

See Robert V. Colangelo and Ronald D. Miller, *Environmental Site Assessments and Their Impact on Property Value: The Appraiser's Role* (Chicago: Appraisal Institute, 1995), 218–219 and the workbook for the *Environmental Risk and the Real Estate Appraisal Process* seminar (Chicago: Appraisal Institute, 1994), 78–80.

Note: The American Society for Testing and Materials (ASTM) has developed specific standards for such assessments:
- Standard Practice for Environmental Site Assessments: Phase I Environmental Site Assessment Process (Practice 3 1527-93)
- Standard Practice for Environmental Site Assessments: Transaction Screen Process (Practice 1528-93)

knowledge of and experience with these conditions increase.

Special Characteristics of Rural, Agricultural, or Resource Land

Rural or agricultural resource lands have specific characteristics that appraisers should investigate to describe these properties adequately.

- *Soil.* Precise soil surveys that indicate the soils found on properties, appropriate crops, and expected production are often available (see Figure 9.8). These surveys are useful in comparing agricultural properties.
- *Water rights, drainage, and irrigation.* The legal right to water is as important to the value of a property as the physical source of the water. Although

environmental property assessment (EPRA): A procedure commonly conducted at commercial and industrial sites to identify potential environmental problems prior to the transfer of the property. EPRAs are performed in phases. A Phase I audit focuses on evidence of potential contamination; a Phase II audit confirms the presence of contamination; and a Phase III audit describes its extent. Also called *environmental survey* or *transactional audit.*

environmental site assessment (ESA): The process by which a person or entity seeks to determine if a particular parcel of real property (including improvements) is subject to recognized environmental conditions. … An environmental site assessment is both different from and less rigorous than an environmental audit. (American Society for Testing and Materials)

Environmentally Impacted Properties

A stigma is an externality that negatively impacts the value of a property or properties in proximity to it. A good way to view stigma in the valuation process is in the application of the cost approach. To calculate the impaired value, one begins with the unimpaired value and deducts the cost to remediate the site and the impact of stigma. The same phenomenon is witnessed in the analysis of a sale of contaminated property. The property sells to a knowledgeable buyer at an impaired price. This price generally consists of two elements:

- First, the buyer's estimate of the of the cost to remediate
- Second, a discount due to uncertainty (stigma)

Totaling the two yields the unimpaired value.

Two sets of risks are associated with environmentally impacted properties. The first set of risks are real or scientifically quantifiable risks, such as the cost to cure or manage the problem. The second set consists of perceived risks (stigma), which vary depending on the following:

- The characteristics of the contamination—i.e., whether it can be concealed, how much it disrupts everyday activities, and what degree of peril is associated with it
- The extent of media exposure
- The nature of the liability (to an individual or entity)

Because an environmental stigma is likely to evoke a reaction from both buyers and lenders, it can result in the effective cessation of mortgage lending for an entire area. Different types of hazardous and toxic materials have different stigmatic effects. Few problems are associated with contained asbestos insulation in buildings, but suspected leakage of a contaminant (i.e., a plume) into the groundwater can stigmatize property greatly even if the contaminant is absent from the ground under the property being appraised.

The appraisal of real property impacted by environmental contamination and any accompanying stigma is an area of ongoing investigation and appraisal scholarship subject to an ever-changing legal environment. Appraisers must be mindful of their liability when performing assignments involving properties subject to environmental contamination and possible stigma, and they must also recognize the special expertise required in such situations. Currently a diverse array of techniques are being used to value contaminated properties, and the evolution of a standardized approach to the challenges presented by such assignments is unlikely.

Further Reading: Bill Mundy, "Stigma and Value," *The Appraisal Journal* (January 1992); William N. Kinnard, Jr., and Elaine M. Worzala, "How North American Appraisers Value Contaminated Property and Associated Stigma," *The Appraisal Journal* (July 1999); Richard Roddewig, "Stigma, Environmental Risk, and Property Value: 10 Critical Inquiries," *The Appraisal Journal* (October 1996); and Richard Roddewig, "Classifying the Level of Risk and Stigma Affecting Contaminated Property," *The Appraisal Journal* (January 1999).

water rights vary greatly throughout the United States, state law, as administered by the state department of natural resources or another government agency, have the greatest influence on access to water. Evidence of water rights may be in the form of a contract with the Water and Power Resources Service (formerly the U.S. Bureau of Reclamation) or a public utility water distributor. Water rights may also be given by an individual state certificate or decree, by shares of stock in an irrigation company, or by location in an organized irrigation district. The long-term dependability and cost of adequate drainage and water supplies should be analyzed. (Evaluating on-site drainage and irrigation may require special expertise.) For an appraisal of irrigated properties, it is always necessary to know whether the water rights are appurtenant to the land or transferable separately from the land. If water rights do not transfer with the land, the property's value may decline significantly and its highest and best use may be changed.

- *Climate.* General climatic conditions and growing seasons can affect crop production and, therefore, land value.

- *Potential crops.* The crops grown on a property are related not only to climate, soil, and irrigation, but also to the availability of labor, transportation, and access to the markets that make, transport, and sell the products produced from crops.

- *Environmental controls.* Cropping patterns are influenced by regulations on herbicides, insecticides, fertilizers, air and water pollution, and wildlife protection. Underground storage tanks, asbestos in farm buildings, and cattle vats are common environmental liabilities.

- *Mineral rights.* The presence of precious metals, oil and gas, sand and gravel, quarry red rock such as building stone, clay deposits, or gemstones on a plot of land can affect its value; as with water rights, the legal right to extract all minerals contained in or below the surface of a property is

Figure 9.8   Soil Map

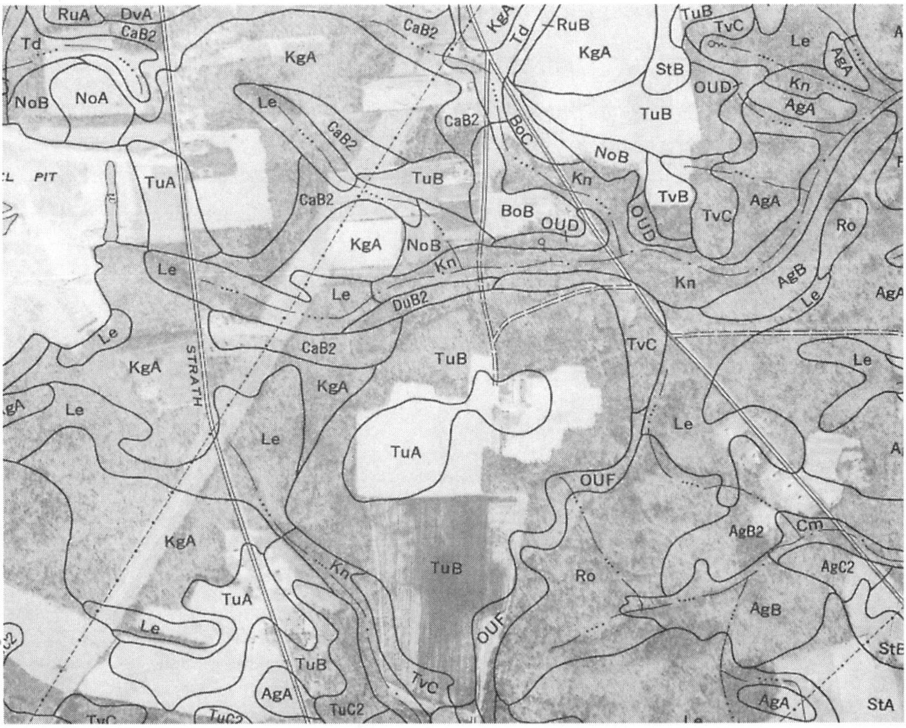

WHERE TO FIND

Soils Data
Soils surveys conducted by the U.S. Department of Agriculture, along with state agricultural experiment stations and other federal and state agencies, are used to create soil maps for farmers and ranchers.

For more information, see:
http://www.statlab.iastate.edu/soils/nssc/geography.html

as important as ownership of the land itself. Mineral rights may be granted with surface rights or without surface entry because the *mineral estate* is the dominant tenant in most states. Various lease and ownership relationships may be in effect and should be investigated.

- *Unapparent environmental hazards.* Although the environmental liabilities associated with industrial plants are well known, many of the same liabilities may be present in other properties. One cannot assume that green rural properties that appear clean are actually free of environmental liabilities. In the 1940s and 1950s, farmers commonly used cattle vats—i.e., trenches filled with fuel oil through which cattle were led to rid them of mites and small insects. The fuel oil was often treated with DDT and other pesticides. When this practice fell into disuse, the trenches were simply filled in. Farms often have aging underground storage tanks that held gasoline used to fuel farm vehicles. Farmland may also be contaminated by the accumulation of fertilizers and pesticides. Old railroad beds can constitute an environmental hazard because railroad ties were commonly soaked in creosote-filled trenches dug on site when tracks were laid. Timberlands are not free of contaminants either. Old turpentine stills are often found in areas where forests were once harvested.

- *Other considerations.* The location of wildlife habitats, the distances from populated areas, and the potential for recreational land uses are among the many other considerations to be analyzed in appraising agricultural land. Special tax provisions, such as reduced taxes on agricultural or resource properties, should also be studied.[4]

---

4.   For a thorough discussion of the methods used to describe and analyze the significant characteristics of land used for agricultural production, see American Society of Farm Managers and Appraisal Institute, *The Appraisal of Rural Property,* 2d ed. (Denver and Chicago, 2000).

FURTHER READING

American Society of Farm Managers and Rural Appraisers and Appraisal Institute. *The Appraisal of Rural Property,* 2d ed. Chicago and Denver, 2000.

Andrews, Richard N. L. *Land in America.* Lexington, Mass.: D. C. Heath, 1979.

Bible, Douglas S., and Chengo Hsieh. "Determinants of Vacant Land Values and Implications for Appraisers." *The Appraisal Journal* (July 1999).

Boykin, James H. *Land Valuation: Adjustment Procedures and Assignments.* Chicago: Appraisal Institute, 2001.

Colangelo, Robert V., and Ronald D. Miller. *Environmental Site Assessments and Their Impact on Property Value.* Chicago: Appraisal Institute, 1995.

Keating, David M. *The Valuation of Wetlands.* Chicago: Appraisal Institute, 1995.

Owens, Robert W. "Appraising Floodplain Properties." *The Appraisal Journal* (April 1991).

Rinehart, James R. "Estimating the Effect of a View on Undeveloped Property Values." *The Appraisal Journal* (January 1999).

Rubenstein, Harvey M. *A Guide to Site Planning and Landscape Construction.* New York: John Wiley & Sons, Inc., 1996.

Uniform Appraisal Standards for Federal Land Acquisitions. Washington, D.C.: Interagency Land Acquisition Conference, 2000.

Witherspoon, Robert E., Jon P. Abbett, and Robert M. Gladstone. *Mixed-Use Developments: New Ways of Land Use.* Washington, D.C.: Urban Land Institute, 1976.

10 IMPROVEMENT ANALYSIS

An important part of every appraisal is the description of the type, quality, and condition of the building or buildings on the site and the analysis of the structure's design. The process of improvement analysis encompasses three interrelated tasks:

1. Property inspection
2. Building description
3. Analysis of architectural style and functional utility

In the valuation process, the appraiser gathers much of the information needed to adequately describe and analyze the improvements in the firsthand inspection of the property. Improper or inadequate inspection of the physical characteristics and features of the subject and comparable properties can create difficulties for an appraiser in later phases of the appraisal. For example, an overlooked structural problem could render the conclusions of the three approaches to value meaningless.

Accurate building descriptions are essential to all valuation assignments. In the description and analysis of the site and improvements, the appraiser should address all pertinent concerns, expand on any problem areas, and interpret the significance of the data to lay a foundation for the discussion of highest and best use. The appraiser needs a thorough understanding of the physical characteristics of the subject property to identify and select suitable comparables. A thorough building description helps the appraiser identify the extent and quality of building improvements, calculate their cost, and determine most forms of depreciation. Therefore, the quality of building descriptions directly affects the opinion of value produced by applying the three approaches to value.

Architectural style and functional utility are interrelated, and their combined effect on property value must be analyzed by appraisers. *Architectural style* is the character of a building's form and ornamentation.

property inspection: The act or process of inspecting firsthand the typical improvements and building components of the properties involved in an appraisal assignment, either the subject property or comparable properties. Property inspection is the most visible step in the process of improvement analysis.

building description: The analysis of a building's design, layout, construction details, size, condition, current use, and alternative uses that provides the basis for comparing the subject property's improvements and the improvements typically accepted in the subject property's market.

architectural style: The character of a building's form and ornamentation

functional utility: The ability of a property or building to be useful and to perform the function for which it is intended according to current market tastes and standards; the efficiency of a building's use in terms of architectural style, design and layout, traffic patterns, and the size and type of rooms.

Functional utility is the ability of a property or building to be useful and to perform the function for which it is intended, according to current market tastes and standards. Functional utility also relates to the efficiency of a building's use in terms of architectural style, design and layout, traffic patterns, and the size and type of rooms. Both architectural style and functional utility influence human lives by providing or withholding beauty, comfort, security, convenience, light, and air. They may also ensure reasonable maintenance expenditures, preserve valuable traditions, and indicate the need for change.

Considerations of style and functional utility are integral to an appraisal. They are noted along with other physical characteristics during property inspection. Using comparable data an appraiser can analyze how style and function influence a property's market value. Style and functional utility are examined in terms of

1. The use for which a particular property was designed
2. Its actual or contemplated use
3. Its most productive use

These three uses may or may not be the same.

The ultimate goals of improvement analysis are

- Proper identification of the important building components for the appraisal analysis
- Sound judgment of quality and condition of improvements and components
- Convincing support for conclusions in the highest and best use analysis and application of the approaches to value

This chapter focuses on the structural elements and features that an appraiser will rate in the quality and condition survey, which is the groundwork for the analyses that follow improvement analysis in the valuation process.

Property Inspection

Sometimes consumers equate *appraisal* with *property inspection*, but the latter procedure is just one of the many tasks performed in an appraisal analysis. Professional property inspectors are specialized contractors with expertise in uncovering defects in the structure and materials of various types of properties. Appraisers must be familiar with the property inspection process, but the aim of an appraiser in the field is not to comprehensively research the subject property; rather, an appraiser observes the components and characteristics of the subject property that will influence value in the marketplace.

The importance of property inspection should not be underestimated. Much of the primary data an appraiser collects comes from the property inspection process. Comparison of the subject and comparables is crucial for the sales comparison and income capitalization approaches, and estimating building costs in the cost approach is impossible without an accurate inventory of the building components in the subject. In addition, comparison of the quality and condition of building components can be essential in making adjustments.

Many appraisers learn how to inspect a property through on-the-job training. Formal training has increased as property inspection has come under more scrutiny—from both state licensing agencies and clients demanding better service.[1] The property inspection can be one of the longest periods of face-to-face interaction between the appraiser and the client, so fundamental mistakes in the performance of the property inspection and in interactions with the client can be embarrassing or even costly, damaging the relationship between appraiser and client and jeopardizing any future business between them. Failure to disclose defects in a property (because those defects were missed in the property inspection) or to verify information gathered through other means are flaws of an appraisal report that can result in litigation against an appraiser.

Sometimes an appraiser will not have the expertise to judge the quality and condition of specialized equipment or atypical building materials and may have to rely on the judgment of other professionals.[2] For a complex property, such as a manufacturing plant containing sophisticated equipment and mechanical systems, blueprints provided by the developer/owner can be helpful.

Building Description

> A **building description includes** specific information about the size, design or layout, structural components, construction materials, equipment, and mechanical systems of a building.

In the valuation process, an appraiser describes the design, layout, and construction details of the subject improvements, which include structural components, materials, and mechanical systems of each building under investigation. The appraiser also determines building size and the condition of each element described. The building description provides the basis for comparing the subject property's improvements with improvements that are considered typically in the subject property's market and with the ideal improvements as determined in highest and best use analysis.

---

1. See John A. Simpson, *Property Inspection: An Appraiser's Guide* (Chicago: Appraisal Institute, 1997).

2. The Competency Rule of the Uniform Standards of Professional Appraisal Practice can apply to certain complex property inspection situations. Advisory Opinion 5 of USPAP provides direction on assistance in the preparation of an appraisal, and Advisory Opinion 2 discusses what constitutes a minimum inspection of the subject property.

To analyze the quality and condition of improvements, appraisers need a general understanding of the building construction process and the operation of essential building systems.[3] The typical construction materials and techniques used in a region can change over time for a variety of reasons:

- New building technologies evolve.
- The prices of materials fluctuate significantly.
- Rising or falling energy prices make a particular building material more desirable.
- The dictates of fashion affect the demand for a certain building material or feature.

With experience and through the observation of market trends, appraisers will gain insight into how building components are perceived and valued in a particular market.

Elements of a Building Description

An appraiser prepares a building description by considering a variety of specific information in sequence. Primary concerns include

1. The type of use represented by the existing building
2. The codes and regulations affecting this use
3. Building size, plan, and construction
4. Details of the building's exterior and interior and its equipment and mechanical systems (both those included in the original construction and subsequent improvements)

An appraiser must view a building objectively and analytically, paying careful attention to all components that ultimately contribute to the determination of the building's highest and best use as improved and any alternative uses to be considered in the assignment. The sheer number of components listed in a comprehensive building description should not be misinterpreted in the application of the approaches to value. The market's reaction to the presence or absence of structural components in a property is a more important consideration than the simple fact that those components exist.

> A **building description addresses** the current use, the zoning codes that govern that use, the plan and construction of the structure, relevant building codes, and the size of the building.

Use Classification

Land uses can be divided into any number of types, depending on market norms and personal preferences. Traditionally, most appraisers have divided land uses into five major groups:

---

3. For an up-to-date and easy-to-read guide to construction materials and techniques, see Francis D.K. Ching and Cassandra Adams, *Building Construction Illustrated*, 3d ed. (New York: John Wiley & Sons, Inc., 2000).

1. Residential
2. Commercial
3. Industrial
4. Agricultural
5. Special-purpose

Each of these groups can be broken down into increasingly specific sub-groups.

Systems of use classification may vary from market to market. For example, in some markets hotels and motels are considered a major property classification, whereas in other markets they are considered a subset of commercial properties. Appraisers should be familiar with the types of property defined by the market they are working in and employ a system of use classification that their clients will understand.

Zoning regulations establish the permitted uses of property. Existing and potential property uses must be checked against zoning regulations to determine if they are conforming or nonconforming uses. When the present use does not conform to current zoning regulations, the appraiser should consider how this fact might affect property value.

Building Codes

In addition to any use restrictions imposed by zoning, the planning and construction of buildings are restricted by various laws, codes, and regulations enacted at all levels of government to protect the health, safety, and welfare of the public. Many states have codes that control the kinds of buildings that are constructed within their borders. Federal regulations are established to ensure occupational health and safety, environmental protection, pollution control, and consumer protection. Municipal building codes establish requirements for the construction and occupancy of buildings, and the codes contain specifications for building materials, methods of construction, and mechanical systems. These codes also establish standards of performance and address considerations such as structural strength, fire resistance, and adequate light and ventilation.

Size

Determining the size of a building may seem like the easiest step in preparing a building description, but it can be a formidable task for an appraiser who is not prepared for the inherent difficulties. The methods and techniques used to calculate building size vary regionally, differ among property types, and may reflect biases that significantly affect opinions of value. The appraiser must know the measurement techniques used in the area where the building is located as well as those used to describe properties elsewhere. Failure to apply measurement techniques and report building dimensions consistently within an assignment can impair the quality of the appraisal report.

An appraiser uses the system of measurement commonly employed in the area and includes a description of the system in the appraisal report.

> **Systems for measuring** residential and non-residential properties vary. Gross building area is measured for all property types. Gross living area and gross leasable area are other common measurements.

Gross building area is always calculated. Measurements taken from plans should be checked against actual building measurements because alterations and additions are often made after plans are prepared. The areas of attached porches, freestanding garages, and other minor buildings are always calculated separately.

Standards for measuring residential property have been developed by several federal agencies, including the FHA, the VA, Fannie Mae, and Freddie Mac (see Table 10.1). Because there is a close relationship between these agencies and the mortgage market industry, these standards have been used in millions of appraisals.

Office buildings present special problems for appraisers because they are measured differently in different regions. The Building Owners and Managers Association International (BOMA) has established a method for measuring office building floor area. This widely used method is described in BOMA's publication *Standard Method for Measuring Floor Area in Office Buildings*, which is updated periodically. The description of an office building should include measurements of

- Gross building area
- Finished building area
- Leasable building area

Table 10.1	Building Measurement Standards
Gross living area (GLA)	
Definition	Total area of finished, above-grade residential space; calculated by measuring the outside perimeter of the structure and includes only finished, habitable, above-grade living space. (Finished basements and attic areas are not generally included in total gross living area. Local practices, however, may differ.)
Use	Used by federal agencies to measure single-family properties.
Gross building area (GBA)	
Definition	Total floor area of a building, excluding unenclosed areas, measured from the exterior of the walls; includes both the superstructure floor area and the substructure or basement area.
Use	Used by federal agencies to measure multifamily properties; also the standard of measurement for industrial buildings.
Gross leasable area (GLA)	
Definition	Total floor area designed for the occupancy and exclusive use of tenants, including basements and mezzanines; measured from the center of joint partitioning to the outside wall surfaces.
Use	Commonly used to measure shopping centers.

Note that the acronym GLA can stand for two different area measurements. Residential appraisers use GLA for gross living area; non-residential appraisers use it to refer to gross leasable area.

Some methods of office measurement allocate a pro rata portion of the restrooms, elevator lobbies, and corridors to each tenant; one variation also includes a pro rata portion of the ground floor main lobby in each tenant's leased area. Office building management may measure single-tenant and multitenant floors in the same building in different ways. Because these measurements vary with occupancy, the appraiser must apply a consistent method in calculating the floor-by-floor rentable area of a building.

The appraiser should not accept a statement about the size of a subject or comparable property without knowing the basis for the calculation. Unverified size information can cause the resulting opinion of value to be erroneous or misleading.

Format

A complete building description includes information about the details and condition of a building's exterior, interior, and mechanical systems. Although there is no

> A **building description includes** a description of the exterior, the interior, and the equipment and mechanical systems.

prescribed method for describing all buildings, the outline in Figure 10.1 may be used to establish a format for building descriptions.

Other formats can be useful in different circumstances, depending on the type of property concerned and the nature of the appraisal assignment. The level of detail required in the building description varies according to the assignment's scope of work.

Exterior Description

An exterior description provides information on the following:

- Substructure—foundation
- Framing
- Insulation
- Ventilation
- Exterior walls and doors
- Roofs and drains
- Chimneys

Substructure

Substructure usually refers to a building's entire foundational structure, which is below grade and includes such foundation supports as footings, slabs, piles, columns, piers, and beams. To evaluate the quality and condition of footings (and other items of concealed construction throughout a building), which are visible only when a building is under construction, an appraiser must look for evidence of structural problems. Footings that are improperly designed and constructed often cause settling and wall cracks.

Figure 10.1   **Elements of a Building Description**

A. Substructure
    1. Footings
    2. Slabs
    3. Piles
    4. Columns
    5. Piers
    6. Beams
    7. Foundation walls
B. Exterior description
    1. Framing
    2. Insulation
    3. Ventilation
    4. Exterior walls
    5. Exterior doors
    6. Windows, storm windows, and screens
    7. Facade
    8. Roof and drain system
    9. Chimneys, stacks, and vents
    10. Special features
C. Interior description
    1. Interior walls, partitions, and doors
    2. Division of space
        a. Storage areas
        b. Stairs, ramps, elevators, escalators, and hoists
    3. Interior supports
        a. Beams, columns, and trusses
        b. Flooring system (subflooring)
        c. Ceilings
    4. Painting, decorating, and finishing
        a. Basements
        b. Floor coverings
        c. Walls, partitions, and ceilings
        d. Molding and baseboards
        e. Fireplaces
    5. Protection against decay and insect damage
    6. Miscellaneous and special features
D. Equipment and mechanical systems
    1. Plumbing system
        a. Piping
        b. Fixtures
        c. Hot water system
    2. Heating, ventilation, and air-conditioning systems
        a. Heating systems
            (1) Warm or hot air
            (2) Hot water
            (3) Steam
            (4) Electric
        b. Air-conditioning and ventilation systems
    3. Electrical systems
    4. Miscellaneous equipment
        a. Fire protection
        b. Elevators, escalators, and speed ramps
        c. Signals, alarms, and call systems
        d. Loading facilities
        e. Attached equipment (process-related)

Substructure: A building's entire foundational structure, which is below grade and provides a support base or footings on which the superstructure rests.

Footings

Type	Perimetric base
Materials	Concrete
Characteristics/Use	Most common type of footing; a concrete base rests on undisturbed earth below the frost line and distributes the load of the walls over the subgrade.

Type	Plain footing
Materials	Concrete
Characteristics/Use	Unreinforced and designed to carry light loads.

Type	Reinforced footing
Materials	Concrete and steel
Characteristics/Use	Contain steel to increase their strength.

Type	Column
Materials	Concrete
Characteristics/Use	Long, relatively slender pillars.

Type	Spread footing
Materials	Concrete
Characteristics/Use	Frequently used where the soil has poor load-bearing capacity.

Foundations

Type	Slab-on-ground
Materials	Poured concrete
	Concrete or cinder block walls on concrete footings
	Cut stone or stone and brick (in older buildings)
Characteristics/Use	Most common type of foundation.

Type	Mat and raft (floating foundation)
Materials	Concrete slab heavily reinforced with steel
Characteristics/Use	Used over soils that have poor load-bearing capacity. Steel reinforcing makes the entire foundation function as a unit.

Piles

Type	Columnar units
Materials	Concrete
	Metal
	Wood
Characteristics/Use	Piles serve as substitutes for footings, transmitting loads through soil with poor load-bearing capacity to lower levels where the soil's load bearing capacity is adequate.

Columns, piers, and beams

Materials	Concrete
	Steel
Characteristics/Use	Foundation supports that can be used separately or in combination.

Superstructure

Superstructure usually refers to the portion of the building above grade. In multipurpose buildings, however, components such as parking garages that are above grade but not used for habitable space are often considered part of the substructure.

Framing. The structural frame is the load-bearing skeleton of a building to which the exterior and interior walls are attached. The structural frames of most houses in the United States are made of wood. Many commercial and industrial buildings have steel or concrete frames.

A wood framing system that is defective can cause walls to crack, exterior walls to bulge, windows to stick, and doors to open or close improperly. Steel framing is usually less expensive than precast or reinforced concrete, and it is easier and faster to erect. Steel framing has one major disadvantage, however. Unless it is encased in heat-resistant, fireproof material such as plaster or concrete, the steel will buckle and bend in a fire, pulling adjacent structural members out of position and greatly increasing fire damage to the building. Reinforced and precast concrete framing is the most expensive and difficult to construct, but it is highly resistant to fire damage.

Superstructure: The portion of a building that is above grade.	
Framing	
Type	Platform
Materials	Wood
Characteristics/Use	Vertical framing members (studs) are cut to the ceiling height of one floor, horizontal plates are laid on top, then more studs are cut for the next floor.
Type	Post-and-beam
Materials	Wood
Characteristics/Use	Heavier and larger framing members support widely spaced beams. Fewer interior load-bearing walls.
Type	Precast concrete
Characteristics/Use	Prefabricated walls and floors are "tilted up" at the construction site.
Type	Steel framing
Characteristics/Use	For functional, single-story industrial plants with increasing large bays between columns. Usually less expensive than precast or reinforced concrete and easier and faster to erect.
Type	Solid masonry exterior walls with steel beam or reinforced concrete interior framing (newer buildings) or interior framing of wood beams and posts (older buildings)

Insulation. Insulation not only helps economize on fuel and ensure the comfort of occupants in both warm and cold climates, but it also reduces noise transmission and impedes the spread of fire. The ability of an insulation material to resist the flow of heat is measured in R values. R value is derived by measuring the British thermal units (Btus) that are transmitted in one hour through one layer of the insulation. The higher the R value, the better the insulation. There is no universal standard for the amount of insulation required in a structure because the amount varies with the climate and the type of building. For example, overceiling or underroof insulation with an R value of 13 might be satisfactory in a mild climate if there is gas or oil heat and no air-conditioning. In cold or hot climates and in structures with electric heat or air-conditioning, insulation with an R value of 24 might be necessary. There has been a growing trend to superinsulate structures using insulation with much higher R values.

Ventilation. All buildings need ventilation to reduce heat in closed-off areas such as attics and spaces behind walls. Ventilation also prevents the condensation of water, which collects in unventilated spaces and causes building materials to rot and decay. When condensation seeps into insulation it reduces its R rating. Ventilation can be accomplished with holes that range from one inch to several feet in diameter; these holes should be covered with screening to keep out vermin. Also, ventilation can be increased by using fans.

Superstructure: The portion of a building that is above grade.	
Insulation	
Type	Loose-fill
Materials	Mineral wool (rock, slag, or glass wool) or cellulosic fiber (recycled newsprint, wood chips, or other organic fibers)
Characteristics/Use	Poured or blown by a machine into a building's structural cavities.
Type	Flexible
Characteristics/Use	Generally used where it is not practical to install loose-fill insulation or where the foil or kraft paper facing is needed as a vapor barrier.
Type	Rigid
Characteristics/Use	Structural wall insulation
	Fiberboard
	Structural deck insulation
	Rigid board insulation
Type	Reflective
Materials	Foil
Characteristics/Use	Used to reflect heat transferred by radiation.
Type	Foamed-in-place
Materials	Polyurethane

Exterior walls and doors. Exterior walls are either load-bearing or nonload-bearing. When the quality of the exterior walls is below the standard for buildings in the same market, the property may suffer a loss in value. The presence or absence of energy-conserving material such as weatherstripping around doors should also be noted. Door shoes, weatherproof thresholds, and sweeps will prevent air from leaking through cracks at the bottom of a door.

Windows, storm windows, and screens. In describing a building, the appraiser notes the type of window, its material or manufacture, and any energy-saving features. Because windows are a major source of heat and cooling loss, their design and installation is important. In commercial and industrial

ASBESTOS IN BUILDINGS

Asbestos is a nonflammable, natural mineral material that separates into fibers. Asbestos-containing materials (ACMs) were widely used in structures built between 1945 and 1970 as thermal and acoustical insulation or for fireproofing and soundproofing. Other ACMs were used in siding and roofing shingles. Airborne asbestos fibers pose a threat to human health when they are distributed in the air. The potential of any ACM to release fibers depends on its degree of friability—i.e., how easily it is crumbled or pulverized. Dry, sprayed-on thermal insulation over structural steel is highly friable. Densely packed, nonfibrous ACMs such as vinyl asbestos floor covering and pipe insulation are not considered friable under normal conditions. Nevertheless, these materials will become friable if they are broken, sawed, or drilled.

Encapsulation or enclosure of asbestos is effective as a short-term solution. The Environmental Protection Agency (EPA) has guidelines for the removal of asbestos when a building is being demolished or renovated, but these regulations have been difficult to enforce.

The EPA regulates asbestos under the authority provided by the Clean Air Act and the Toxic Substances Control Act. The National Emissions Standards for Hazardous Air Pollutants (NESHAP), which were drawn up as part of the Clean Air Act, apply to asbestos emissions in manufacturing, waste disposal, building demolition, and renovation. The Asbestos Hazard Emergency Response Act (AHERA), which was amended to the Toxic Substances Control Act in 1986, empowered the EPA to regulate asbestos in public schools and to enact regulations for asbestos removal.

One market's reaction to the effect asbestos has on the value of income-producing properties may differ from the reaction of other markets. There is little evidence, however, that investors are willing to sell properties at sharp discounts because of the problem.

For more information on federal regulations concerning asbestos, see Chapter 2 of Warren G. Miller (primary author), *Managing Environmental Mandates for Multifamily Housing: 1997/A Compendium of Federal Laws and Regulations* (Washington, D.C.: Urban Land Institute, National Apartment Association, and National Multi Housing Council, 1996), 9–38 and updates to that publication available at http://www.uli.org. See also the Environmental Protection Agency's Web site at http://www.epa.gov/asbestos/index.htm. For additional discussion of the influence of asbestos on real estate value, see Jeffrey D. Fisher, George H. Tse, and K.S. Maurice, "Effects of Asbestos on Commercial Real Estate: A Survey of MAI Appraisers," *The Appraisal Journal* (October 1993): 587–599; Robert Simons, "How Clean is Clean?" *The Appraisal Journal* (July 1994): 424–438; and Daniel F. Ryan, "A Lender's View of Hazardous Substances… And Appraiser Responsibility," *Real Estate Appraiser & Analyst* (Fall 1989): 10–12.

buildings, windows of double or triple glazing are generally installed, and occasionally casement windows may be used.

Facade. Many houses, stores, office buildings, and industrial buildings have a facade, or front, that differs from the design and construction of the rest of the building. Special facades may cost extra and thus affect the property's value.

Roof and drainage system. A roof is designed and constructed to support its own weight and the pressure of snow, ice, wind, and rain. The roof covering prevents moisture from entering the structure. The water that falls on a roof must be directed to the ground or into a drainage system. Even so-called "flat" roofs may be slightly pitched to direct water to drains and gutters.

Most roofs need to be replaced several times during a building's life, so a roof's condition and age are investigated to determine its remaining useful life.

Superstructure: The portion of a building that is above grade.

Exterior Walls

Type	Load-bearing
Materials	Solid masonry (cement block, brick, or a combination)
	Poured concrete
	Prestressed concrete
	Steel beams covered with siding material
	Wood framing
Characteristics/Use	May be strengthened with masonry pilasters attached to the exterior of the wall.
Type	Nonload-bearing
Materials	Porcelain enamel
	Steel
	Aluminum
	Precast aggregate concrete
	Glass
	Corrugated iron, tilt-up precast concrete asbestos board, fiberglass and metal sandwich panels for industrial buildings
Characteristics/Use	Commonly used in larger buildings; attached to the framing system.

Exterior Doors

Type	Standard
Materials	Wood
	Metal
	Glass
Characteristics/Use	Exterior doors are usually solid. Hollow exterior doors are a sign of poor-quality construction.
Type	Large truck doors (commercial and industrial buildings)
Materials	Steel
Types/Components	Special-purpose doors with automatic door openers
Materials	Wood
	Metal
	Glass

Chimneys, stacks, and vents. Exhaust systems range from simple metal vents and flues to complex masonry fireplaces, industrial chimneys, and ventilation systems. The efficiency of any fuel-burning heating system depends on its chimney, stack, or vent. Chimneys and stacks with cracked bricks, loose mortar joints, or other leaks may be serious fire and health hazards.

Superstructure: The portion of a building that is above grade.

Windows

Types	Single- and double-hung
	Casement
	Horizontal sliding
	Clerestory
	Fixed
	Awning
	Center pivot
	Jalousie
Materials	Glass with wood framing (usually for houses) or aluminum or steel framing (often in residential, commercial, and industrial buildings)
Characteristics/Use	Windows should be tightly sealed, with caulking at the joints and between the wall and the window. The use of insulated glass, multiple glazing, and storm sashes helps keep cold air out and heat in.
	In most parts of the country, screens are needed for all windows that open. Most screens have aluminum frames, and in residences screens are often combined with storm windows.

Facade

Types	Multifamily
	Retail
	Industrial, office, etc.
Materials	Masonry veneer or contrasting siding
	Glass or other decorative material
	More elaborate facade than exterior of walls
Characteristics/Use	In modern industry and commerce, public image is important. An attractive store, warehouse, industrial plant, or office building has both advertising and public relations value to the occupant. Ornamentation, identifying signs, lighting, and landscaping all contribute to a building's aesthetics.

Roof

Types	Flat
	Lean-to (saltbox)
	Gable
	Gambrel
	Hip
	Mansard
	Monitor
	Sawtooth
Materials	Wood trusses, joists or horizontal beams, joists and rafters, or posts and beams in residential construction.
	Steel or wood trusses, glued wood beams, or steel or concrete frame with wood joists or purlins or with steel bar joists in commercial and industrial construction.
Characteristics/Use	Flat roofs are used extensively in industrial and commercial buildings but are less common in residences. Lean-to roofs, often called shed roofs, are used on saltbox houses, and gambrel roofs are popular for barns and Cape Ann and Dutch Colonial houses. Monitor and sawtooth roofs are sometimes used in industrial construction.

Superstructure: The portion of a building that is above grade.

Drain System

Components	Gutters and downspouts
Materials	Galvanized steel
	Aluminum
	Copper
Characteristics/Use	Channel water from roofs to prevent damage and protect the appearance of walls when roof overhangs are not provided.
Components	Gutters or eave troughs
Materials	Galvanized steel
	Aluminum
	Copper
Characteristics/Use	Catch rainwater at the edge of the roof and carry it to downspouts or leaders.
Components	Downspouts or leaders
Materials	Galvanized steel
	Aluminum
	Copper
Characteristics/Use	Vertical pipes that carry the water to the ground or into sewers, dry wells, drain tiles, or splash pans.
Components	Roof drains (in large buildings)
Materials	Galvanized steel
	Aluminum
	Copper
Characteristics/Use	Connected to storm drains by pipes in the building.

Roof Covering

Materials	Asphalt shingles (prevalent in residential construction)
	Wood, asbestos, fiberglass, or cement shingles or shakes
	Metal
	Clay tile
	Slate
	Built-up layers of felt or composition material covered with tar and then gravel or another surfacing material (most common on flat roofs of commercial and industrial buildings)
	Single-membrane roof assembly
Characteristics/Use	Joints in roofs are created where two different roof slopes meet or where the roof meets adjoining walls or projections such as chimneys, pipes, and ventilation ducts. All joints must be flashed. Flashing is usually accomplished by nailing strips of galvanized metal, aluminum, or tin across or under the point, applying a waterproofing compound or cement, and securing the roofing material over the edges to hold it permanently in place.

Roof sheathing

Materials	Plywood
	Steel roof deck
	Lightweight precast concrete slabs
	Reinforced concrete slabs
	Insulated sheathing in large sheets

Superstructure: The portion of a building that is above grade.	
Chimneys, stacks, and vents	
Materials	Brick
	Metal
Characteristics/Use	Should be structurally safe, durable, and smoketight; should also be able to withstand the action of flue gases

Special features. Special features that must be carefully described and considered in the valuation process might include

- Artwork that is attached to the real estate and is not personal property
- Ornamentation
- Exterior elevators
- Solar and wind equipment
- Unique window installation
- Special masonry work and exterior materials
- Items required for the commercial or industrial use of buildings

Unique building features can present a valuation problem. The appraiser must decide if the items increase the property's market value or are valuable only to the current user. In the latter case the items may add use value but little or no market value. If such items are expensive to remove they may not appeal to a prospective buyer and the property could therefore lose value.

Interior Description

An interior description provides information about

- Interior walls, partitions, and doors (including how the space is divided)
- Internal supports
- Stairways
- Painting, decorating, and finishing (including floor and ceiling coverings)
- Protection against decay and pests

Interior Walls, Partitions, and Doors

Like exterior walls, interior walls and partitions can be either load-bearing or nonload-bearing. In general, having fewer load-bearing interior walls allows for greater flexibility in the division of space within the structure.

Interior Supports

A building description includes consideration of the building's internal supports, which include

- Beams, columns, and trusses
- The flooring system
- Ceilings

DIVISION OF SPACE

A building description provides a complete list of the number of rooms in the structure and their uses. Room sizes may also be stated. The number of bedrooms and bathrooms in a residential property usually influences the market for the property and its value. The number of units in an apartment building and the types and sizes of the rooms within the units significantly influence the property's income-producing potential. Similarly, the amount of office space in an industrial property and the partitioning of office suites may affect property value.

In certain parts of the United States, many types of buildings have basements. In these areas buildings without basements may have substantially less value than similar buildings with basements. If basements are not common in the area a basement may add little or no value to a building.

Storage Areas

Home owners often complain about a lack of adequate storage space, especially in kitchens. Ample cabinets, closets, and other storage areas are important, particularly in homes without basements. Storage is particularly important in multifamily residential buildings. The value of apartment and condominium projects is often enhanced by the availability of storage space. Frequently, mini-storage facilities are located near apartment complexes because apartment units often have inadequate storage space. Storage problems can also exist in commercial and industrial buildings.

Interior Description

Walls

Type	Residential buildings
Materials	Wood studs covered with drywall materials (gypsum board, wood panels, ceramic tile, plywood, hardboard)
	Plaster (less popular now)
	Masonry (in masonry houses)
Characteristics/Use	Interior walls can be painted, papered, or decorated in other ways.
Type	Commercial Buildings
Materials	Wire partitions
	Glass
	Wood
	Plywood
	Hardboard
	Metals
	Tile
	Concrete
	Solid masonry walls for fire protection
Characteristics/Use	Interior walls can be painted, papered, or decorated in other ways.

Partitions

Materials	Various materials
Characteristics/Use	Generally nonload-bearing and movable.

Interior Description

Doors

Types	Simple hollow-core doors in most residential construction
	Solid-core doors in older buildings and office buildings
	Complex, self-closing, fire-resistant doors in commercial and industrial buildings
	Specialty, self-opening and -closing doors in offices and commercial buildings
	Special-purpose doors (e.g., doors to bank vaults)
Characteristics/Use	Hanging a door is complicated and often done improperly. Most poorly hung doors close improperly or fail to touch an edge of the frame when closed.

Interior Supports

Types	Beams
	Columns
	Trusses
Materials	Wood, masonry, concrete, or steel
Characteristics/Use	Designed to support heavy loads. Cracked or sagging beams may be an early indication of more serious problems in the future.
Type	Flooring system
Materials	Generally wood or concrete
Characteristics/Use	Serves as a base for floor covering.
Type	Ceiling
Materials	Same material as interior walls (e.g., gypsum), tile, or underside of upper floor
Characteristics/Use	Ceilings that are too high or low for the property's current highest and best use as improved may be considered items of functional obsolescence and decrease the property's value.

Stairs and Ramps

Type	Residential buildings
Characteristics	Provides for safe ascent and descent, with adequate headroom and space for moving furniture and equipment. Railings should be installed on the sides of all interior stairways, including stairways in attics and basements, where they are often omitted.
Type	Public buildings
Characteristics	Codes often regulate where stairs are located, how they are designed and constructed, and how they are enclosed for fire protection. Public buildings may also have to be barrier-free to provide access for handicapped people as mandated by the Americans with Disabilities Act of 1990 (ADA), which may require that ramps be installed both inside and outside the structure.

Beams, columns, and trusses. Beams and columns are used in many residential, commercial, and industrial buildings with basements or crawl spaces that are too wide for the first-floor joists or subfloor systems and cannot be supported by the foundation walls alone. As interior support systems, traditional joist construction is being replaced by both roof and floor truss systems.

AMERICANS WITH DISABILITIES ACT IN IMPROVEMENT ANALYSIS

An appraiser cannot assume that improvements comply with the requirements of the Americans with Disabilities Act (ADA) of 1990. Enforcement of the requirements can be triggered by a change in use or a title transfer. Owners of older properties may have to add ramps, elevators, or other special equipment to comply with ADA regulations, which can impact value greatly.

Along with related legislation such as the Fair Housing Amendments Act of 1988 and the Uniform Federal Accessibility Standards, ADA extends protection under civil rights laws to people with disabilities. Among other provisions directed toward employment opportunities, the legislation guarantees access to places of public accommodation to persons with disabilities. Specifically, Title III of the act, which deals with "places of public accommodations" and "commercial facilities," is of particular importance to appraisers; government publications regarding ADA are available online at http://www.usdoj.gov/crt/ada/publicat.htm and the ADA information line is 800-514-0301 (voice) or 800-514-0383 (TDD).

A real estate appraiser is not required to become an expert in the field of ADA requirements, but the Competency Rule of the Uniform Standards of Professional Appraisal Practice requires appraisers to have the knowledge and experience necessary to complete a specific assignment competently or to disclose the lack of knowledge and experience to the client, take all steps necessary to complete the assignment competently, and in the report describe their lack of knowledge or experience and the steps taken to competently complete the assignment. Further guidance on ADA-related matters is provided in Guide Note 9: The Consideration of the Americans with Disabilities Act in the Appraisal Process, in the Guide Notes to the Standards of Professional Appraisal Practice of the Appraisal Institute.

For an overview of specific requirements of ADA in building design, see Randall Bell, "Appendix 2: Americans with Disabilities Act (ADA) Overview," *Real Estate Damages: An Analysis of Detrimental Conditions* (Chicago: Appraisal Institute, 1999), 268–272. For further discussion of ADA considerations in the valuation process, see Richard W. Hoyt and Robert J. Aalberts, "Appraisers and the Americans with Disabilities Act," *The Appraisal Journal* (July 1995): 298–309 and Robert J. Aalberts and Terrence M. Clauretie, "Commercial Real Estate and the Americans with Disabilities Act: Implications for Appraisers," *The Appraisal Journal* (July 1992): 53–58.

Flooring system. Subflooring provides safe support for floor loads without excessive deflection and an adequate base for the support and attachment of finish floor material. Bridging stiffens the joists and prevents them from deflecting.

Ceilings. In some structures, the underside of the upper story is an adequate ceiling. Appraisers must measure and consider ceiling height.

Stairs, Ramps, Elevators, Escalators, and Hoists

Designing and constructing even the simplest staircase is complicated. Local building codes dictate the minimum and maximum tread and rise of stairs, which should be consistent within a building. The Americans with Disabilities Act of 1990 (ADA) established accessibility guidelines, and public buildings that do not meet those regulations may suffer a value penalty based on the cost of necessary changes.

In multistory buildings, appraisers must evaluate how efficiently the elevators and escalators in a building move people and freight. The elevators and escalators in many multistory buildings are inadequate and fall short of current market standards. Curing these deficiencies is often expensive or impossible.

Special elevators and hoists are often considered part of a building, although they may be studied under the equipment category.

Painting, Decorating, and Finishing

Most buildings are decorated many times during their useful lives. An appraiser reports the condition of the painting and decorating in a structure and notes when they will need to be redone. The attractiveness of painting and decorating is subjective. Many new owners and tenants will redecorate to suit their personal tastes. Unusual decorations and colors may have limited appeal and, therefore, may detract from a building's value. The quality of decoration is sometimes an important consideration in valuing a restaurant, store, or other commercial building.

Some considerations of interior finishes and decorating include the following:

- If finished basements are used for purposes other than storage and these uses are accepted and typical in the area, they can add significantly to the property's value.
- The types and finishes of various wall and ceiling components should be differentiated.
- A wide variety of flooring is available, and some flooring materials are selected primarily for their low cost and durability. An appraiser should consider whether floor coverings can endure wear and tear and how they conform to a building's design and decoration.
- Unique, restored molding can add value to older houses, but use of moldings is decreasing.
- Most fireplaces in homes and commercial buildings such as restaurants, inns, and specialty stores do not provide the building's primary source of heat; in fact, because of their design, many have little heating power. Because fireplaces are difficult to construct, many are badly made and function poorly. One common problem is downdraft, whereby smoke is blown into the building by the wind outside. This can happen if the chimney does not extend at least two feet above any part of the roof within 10 feet of the chimney.

Protection Against Decay and Insect Damage

All wood is susceptible to decay and insect damage. When wood is consistently exposed to moisture and water, destructive organisms propagate on or beneath its surface. Insects damage wood more rapidly and visibly than decay does. Although several species of insects destroy wood, termites are by far the most destructive to both damp and dry wood. They colonize in moist soil or in dry wood and create infestations that are extremely difficult to eradicate.

Builders employ various techniques to protect against decay and insect damage:

- Sloping the ground away from foundations for good drainage and putting vapor barriers on the interior sides of exposed walls

Interior Painting, Decorating, and Finishing

Basement finishes

Types	Unfinished used for storage
	Finished (in residences and some commercial buildings) used for storage and other purposes
Characteristics	Dampness, which is often a problem in basements, may be caused by poor foundation wall construction, excess groundwater that is not properly drained by ground tiles, poorly fitted windows or hatches, poor venting of equipment, or poorly constructed or operating roof drains that allow water to enter. Signs that may indicate a wet basement include a powdery white mineral deposit a few inches off the floor, stains near the bottom of walls and columns or equipment that rests close to the floor, and the smell of mildew.

Flooring and floor coverings

Components	Sand, compressed dirt, bituminous paving, brick, stone gravel, concrete, and similar products
Characteristics	Suitable for many industrial buildings, warehouses, garages, and basements. In many commercial and industrial buildings, floors must be especially thick or reinforced to support heavy equipment.
Components	Terrazzo flooring
Characteristics	Made of colored marble chips that are mixed into cement and ground smooth; used for high traffic areas such as the lobbies of public buildings.
Components	Wood in various forms
Characteristics	Continues to be a popular material for floors. Planks and blocks are used for industrial floors, and many commercial buildings use wood floors to conform with the design and overall decoration. Wood planks and hardwood strips are found in many residences, although other types of flooring have become more popular.
Components	Resilient, ceramic, and quarry tiles
Characteristics	Used in all types of buildings.
Components	Resilient flooring
Characteristics	Usually a combination of vinyl and asphalt; produced as sheet goods.
Components	Carpeting
Characteristics	Once considered a luxury in residences, offices, stores, and commercial buildings, but today is widely used in all types of buildings.

Interior wall coverings and ceilings

Types	Walls and partitions
Characteristics	May be painted, papered, or paneled. Supplemental finishings include ceramic tile and wainscot paneling.
Types	Ceilings
Characteristics	Can be drywall, plaster, or suspended panel (drop ceilings).
Types	Partitioning
Characteristics	Can be wood or metal.

- Using polyethylene as a soil cover in crawl spaces
- Flashing gutters, downspouts, and splash blocks to carry water away from foundation walls
- Using poured concrete foundation walls, concrete caps over unit masonry foundations, wood treatments, soil treatments, or metal termite shields

Building with dry, naturally durable woods and conducting regular maintenance inspections can also help prevent insect infestation and damage.

Miscellaneous and Special Features

In valuing industrial and commercial properties, an appraiser may find it helpful to distinguish between two categories of equipment:

- Equipment and mechanical systems that provide for human comfort—e.g., plumbing, heating, air-conditioning, and lighting
- Fixed building equipment that is process-related—e.g., air hoses, process piping, craneways, bus ducts, heavy electrical lines, and freezer equipment[4]

Because different users of structures and related improvements frequently adapt them for their own particular needs, some elements may not be suited for other users and therefore will not contribute to market value. Limited-market properties may require additional research because there is less data to support the estimate of utility and market acceptance of extra or unusual elements of the improvements.

Some properties with specialized functions and design features that may require additional research include

- Steel mills
- Oil refineries
- Chemical plants
- Concrete factories
- Mines
- Commercial establishments with unique design features (e.g., drive-in restaurants) or special facilities (e.g., the cooling room in a furrier's shop)
- Amusement parks
- Sports complexes
- Wharves and docks
- Transportation terminals
- Television and radio transmission towers, studios, and theaters

---

4.   For discussion of the distinction between fixtures, personal property, and real estate, see Tables 1.1 and 1.2 in Chapter 1.

Equipment and Mechanical Systems

Most buildings cannot perform the functions for which they were designed and constructed unless their equipment and mechanical systems are in working order. Major equipment and mechanical systems include

> **Equipment and mechanical systems** provide for human comfort; industrial buildings also contain process-related equipment.

- The plumbing system
- The heating, ventilation, and air-conditioning (HVAC) system
- The electrical system

Plumbing System

Plumbing is an integral part of most buildings. It consists of supply, waste, and vent piping (which is usually covered or hidden except in industrial buildings) and fixtures and fittings (which are visible). Laundries, laundromats, and certain industrial buildings have elaborate plumbing systems.

Piping. Much of the cost of a plumbing system may be due to piping. The quality of the materials used, the way the pipes were installed, and how easily they can be serviced are significant considerations in estimating how long the pipes will last and how much they will cost to maintain. In many areas and building types a high-quality piping system will last as long as the building.

Fixtures and fittings. The appraiser must decide which building fixtures are part of the real estate and which are personal property. The design of bathroom fixtures can change substantially over time, and old fixtures may become obsolete during a building's economic life. An appraiser should report the need for modernization, but old fixtures of good quality, such as porcelain pedestal basins and footed tubs, are often rehabilitated.

Hot water system. All homes and many commercial and industrial buildings need an adequate supply of hot water. Buildings with inadequate hot water systems suffer from functional obsolescence. The size of the hot water storage tank needed is determined by the number of occupants and their water-using habits and by the recovery rate of the tank. The size and recovery rate of a storage tank may be limited to what the market will pay for. Commercial and industrial buildings often require much more hot water than homes.

Heating Systems

Most heating systems use warm or hot air, hot water, steam, or electricity and are powered by fuel oil, natural gas, electricity, or coal. The heating capacity required relates to the cubic content, exposure, design, and insulation level of the structure to be heated and appropriate standards for the local market area. The appraiser cannot assume that a building's

---

Plumbing System

Piping

Types	Supply pipes
	Waste pipes
	Vent pipes
Materials	Copper, cast iron, or plastic
Characteristics/Use	Galvanized steel, lead, or brass pipes in older buildings may need to be replaced.

Bathroom fixtures

Types	Lavatories (or washbasins)
	Bathtubs
	Showers
	Toilets (or water closets)
	Bidets
	Urinals
Materials	Cast iron covered with acid-resistant vitreous enamel or porcelain (fiberglass or other materials are also used in lower-quality fixtures)

Types	Sinks (or double sinks)
Materials	Monel metal, stainless steel, enameled steel, or cast iron covered with acid-resistant enamel

---

Kitchen fixtures

Types	Sinks (or double sinks)
	Garbage disposals
	Dishwashers
Materials	Monel metal, stainless steel, enameled steel, or cast iron covered with acid-resistant enamel

---

Other fixtures

Types	Instant hot water units
	Laundry tubs
	Wet bars
	Swimming pools or saunas
	Janitor sinks
	Drinking fountains
	Handwashing and eyewashing fountains

Fittings

Types	Faucets
	Spigots
	Drains
	Shower heads
	Spray tubes
	Floor drains in industrial buildings
Characteristics/Use	The water in an area may be hard—i.e., it contains minerals that react unfavorably with soap and make it difficult to rinse from clothing, hair and skin. Often hard water cannot be used until it is treated, either with simple equipment or with automatic, complex, multistage systems.

Hot water system

Types	Self-standing heater (in residential buildings)
	Large cast iron or steel boiler and storage tanks (in commercial and industrial buildings)
Characteristics/Use	Generally powered by electricity, gas, or oil.

HVAC System	
Heating system	*Heating is rated in British thermal units (Btus).*
Types	Warm or hot air
Characteristics/Use	Air heated in a furnace and circulated by a pressure blower or relying on the force of gravity. May include thermostats, filters, humidifiers, air cleaners and air purification devices.
Types	Hot water (or hydronic systems)
Characteristics/Use	Hot water pumped by a circulator through pipes to radiators and cold water is returned to the boiler to be reheated. In radiant heating systems, hot water is pumped through narrow pipes embedded in floors, walls, and ceilings rather than through radiators.
Types	Steam
Characteristics/Use	Produced by a boiler, distributed through a one-pipe gravity system (identical to the piping used in hot water systems), and transferred through radiators. More complex and expensive two-pipe systems are found in larger, high-quality structures. In many states, licenses are required for certain classes of steam boilers; appraisers must be familiar with local boiler license laws and ascertain whether boilers have current, valid licenses.
Types	Electric
Characteristics/Use	Includes heat pumps, wall heaters, baseboard units, duct heating units, heating units installed in air-conditioning ducts, and radiant heat produced by electric heating elements embedded in floors, walls, and ceilings. The automatic regulation of a heating system helps it operate efficiently. A multiple-zone system with separate thermostats is more efficient than a single zone system with one thermostat. Complex systems provide an individual temperature control for each room. The efficiency of certain systems can be increased by putting a thermostat on the outside of the building. This helps building operators anticipate how much heat the system will need to produce.

heating system contributes maximum value to a property. A heating system installed at the time of construction may not be acceptable to potential buyers today. New technology continues to reduce energy consumption for large heating systems. Many industrial users who once depended on gas alone now install more efficient oil or electric systems to provide heat when the gas supply is curtailed. Electric heat has become so expensive in some areas that buildings using it sell for substantially less than similar properties using other types of fuel. Cogeneration, the simultaneous production of electrical energy and low-grade heat from the same fuel, is also being used in some parts of the country.

Buyers are sensitive to energy costs. In some markets, apartments in which the owner supplies heat and hot water will sell for less than similar properties in which tenants pay for utilities. Buildings that have high ceilings, many openings, and poor insulation may be at a disadvantage in the market.

cogeneration: The simultaneous production of electrical energy and low-grade heat from the same fuel.

Heating Fuels

The type of fuel used in a building's heating system should be explained in the building description. Depending on the area and the type of building, one type of fuel may be more desirable than another. Nevertheless, many building heating systems do not use the most economical fuel. For any specific use, different fuels have different advantages and disadvantages, which are subject to change.

Type	Characteristics
Fuel oil	In spite of its high cost, fuel oil is a popular energy source that is easy to transport and store. On-site, 275-gallon tanks are used in millions of houses, and tanks that hold thousands of gallons of fuel oil are buried on industrial and commercial sites.
Natural gas	Natural gas is a convenient type of fuel because it is continuously delivered by pipelines; no storage tank is needed. In many parts of the United States, natural gas is the most economical fuel. Liquid petroleum gas, such as butane and propane, is used in many rural areas. It requires on-site storage tanks and is usually more expensive, but in other respects it is similar to natural gas.
Electricity	Like oil, gas, or coal, electricity can be used to produce heat in a furnace or to heat water in a boiler. In most areas electrical heating costs are high, but good insulation and control can eliminate waste.
Coal	In the past coal was the most popular fuel for heating; it is still used in electrical generating plants and to generate power for some industrial and commercial uses. Coal is also used in residences for stoves and fireplaces, but the burning of certain types of coal creates environmental pollution.

Air-Conditioning and Ventilation Systems

The most common type of air-conditioning system consists of an electrically powered compressor that compresses a coolant from gas into liquid outside the area being cooled. The heat released in this process is either blown away or carried away by water. Air-conditioners range from small, portable units to units that provide many tons of cooling capacity.

Commercial and industrial air-conditioning and ventilation systems are more complex. Some simply bring in fresh air from the outside and distribute it throughout the building; others merely remove foul air. Still others combine these two functions, but do not have any cooling or heating capacity. More complex systems wash, filter, and add or remove humidity from the air. The most complex systems perform all of these functions and also heat and cool air through a complex system of ducts and fans. In larger systems that use less electricity, water cools the pipes in which the gas has been compressed. The water is then conserved in towers that cool it for reuse.

Electrical Systems

In an electrical system, power is distributed from the electrical service station through branch circuits, which are wires located throughout the building, to electrical outlets. Each branch circuit starts at a distribution box, where it is

Air-conditioning and ventilation system

Types	Electrically powered compressor and Freon as coolant
	Gas-powered compressor and ammonia as coolant
	Combination with water-cooled pipes in which gas is compressed
Characteristics/Use	Standards depend on climate. Capacity is rates in tons of refrigeration. In some buildings the central air-conditioning equipment uses the same ducts as the hot air heating system. This is not always possible, however, because the air-conditioning may require ducts of a different size. Furthermore, heating registers should be placed low on the walls, while air-conditioning registers should be higher up or in the ceiling.

Electrical system

Components	Rigid or flexible conduit
	BX or armored cable
Characteristics/Use	Most electrical wire is copper. A typical residential electrical system is a single-phase, three-wire system that provides a minimum of 100 amperes of electricity. Ampere services of 150, 200, 300, and 400 are needed when electric heating and air-conditioning are used. Most of these services can provide up to 220 volts by connecting three wires to the outlet.
Components	Power wiring
Characteristics/Use	Used in commercial and industrial buildings to operate utility systems, appliances, and machinery. The electrical power is generally carried at higher voltages (e.g., 240, 480, 600 volts or more) and higher amperages (e.g., 400, 800, 1,200 amperes or more). Power wiring is usually three-phase or three-phase-four-wire, which allows both lighting and three-phase power loads to be delivered by the same supply. It is carried in conduit or by means of plug-in bus ducts. Overhead bus ducts are frequently found in manufacturing plants where flexible service is needed.
Components	Switches and lighting fixtures
Characteristics/Use	Because lighting fixtures are stylized and styles change, they are often obsolete before they wear out. Fluorescent lighting, which may be suspended, surface-mounted, or recessed, is used extensively in commercial and industrial buildings. Often continuous rows are used in large spaces. Incandescent fixtures may be used for smaller rooms, accents, or special purposes. Sodium, mercury vapor, halogen, and halide lights are often installed in industrial buildings.
Components	Outside, yard, and parking lot lighting
Characteristics/Use	Usually downlighting of some kind; often mercury vapor, halogen, or halide lights.
Components	Floor outlets or floor duct systems
Characteristics/Use	Used extensively in commercial and office buildings; provide convenient electrical outlets for office machines and telephone outlets at desks using a minimum number of cords.
Components	Low-voltage switching systems
Characteristics/Use	In some houses and commercial buildings; allow many outlets and lights to be controlled from one place.

separated from the main service by a protection device such as a fuse or circuit breaker.

In commercial and industrial buildings, the wiring between the distribution boxes and the outlets is usually a rigid or flexible conduit. In most houses BX or armored cable is used. Plastic-coated wire is used in certain areas, and the old knob-and-tube wiring is still used in rural areas and older buildings, although it is considered obsolete.

Large-capacity power wiring may contribute to the value of an industrial improvement. However, if the wiring is an uncommon type and adds to a building's operating costs or will be expensive to remove, it may result in functional obsolescence. Similarly, any building with insufficient electrical service or wiring suffers from functional obsolescence.

Miscellaneous Equipment

In the building description, the appraiser must also consider miscellaneous equipment, such as

- Fire protection
- Elevators, escalators, and speed ramps
- Signals, alarms, and call systems
- Loading facilities
- Attached equipment

Miscellaneous Equipment	
Fire protection	
Components	Fire escapes
	Standpipes and hose cabinets
	Alarm services
	Automatic sprinklers
Characteristics/Use	A wet sprinkler system must have adequate water pressure to ensure that the pipes are always filled. A dry system has pressurized air in the pipes. When a sprinkler head opens, the pressure is relieved and water enters. Dry systems are used on loading docks, in unheated buildings where there is a danger of water freezing, and in areas where there is no city water (usually because a well cannot supply sufficient pressure to operate a wet system).
Elevators	
Type	Passenger
Characteristics/Use	Generally electric. Most modern elevators are high-speed and completely automatic.
Type	Freight
Characteristics/Use	Electric or hydraulic. Hydraulic elevators are suitable for low-speed, low-rise operations.
Escalators and speed ramps	
Type	Passenger
Characteristics/Use	Used to move large numbers of people up and down or along horizontal or gradual slopes; must be adequate to accommodate those who use the building.

Miscellaneous Equipment	
Signals, alarms, and call systems	
Components	Smoke detectors
Characteristics/Use	Required by law in many areas.
Components	Security alarm systems
Characteristics/Use	Available for residential, commercial, and industrial use to warn occupants of forced entry, fire, or both.
Components	Clocks, pneumatic tube systems, mail chutes, and incinerators
Components	Telephone wiring
Characteristics/Use	In small buildings the telephone company supplies the wiring and equipment; larger buildings may have extensive systems of built-in cabinets, conduits, and floor ducts for telephone service. The telephone service in a building may be suitable for the current occupant but unsuitable for a potential buyer.
Loading facilities	
Type	Open loading docks
Characteristics/Use	May be important in commercial and industrial buildings. Off-street loading docks are usually required by zoning ordinances. Many older buildings have loading doors only or substandard loading facilities. The floor of an efficient, one-story industrial building may be built above grade at freight car or truck-bed level.
Type	Covered loading docks
Characteristics/Use	In some buildings, docks are enclosed for trucks and freight cars, and leveling devices are provided to assist in loading or unloading. A properly designed industrial building has space in front of truck docks so that vehicles can maneuver.
Attached equipment	
Components	Air hoses
	Process piping
	Industrial wiring for heavy electrical capacity
	Bus ducts
	Freezer equipment
Characteristics/Use	Often considered in terms of use value.

Analysis of Architectural Style and Functional Utility

A building may have functional utility but lack architectural style, such as a multipurpose precast concrete warehouse near an interstate interchange, or it may have admirable style but little utility, such as a cavernous 1920s-vintage movie palace in a declining urban neighborhood. Form and function work together to create successful architecture. Functional utility is not necessarily exemplified by minimal space or form; people's need for comfort and pleasure must also be considered in the design of offices, stores, hospitals, and houses. An appraiser must recognize and rank market preferences regarding style and functional utility and then relate these preferences to market value.

Good design meets the following criteria:

• Functions well—fitness of intended use
• Looks good—appeals to aesthetic sense

In architecture, **style and functional utility** are necessarily interrelated because form and function work with design and construction to create a successful product.

- Feels good—carries meaning; recreates feeling from another time or place
- Balance—sense of correct proportion; compatibility
- Affordable—consistent with market expectations for price range

Social and economic issues have the greatest impact on residential design. Governmental issues have a larger impact on non-residential design through zoning and building codes. Environmental issues affect the site more than the improvements, although topography and other factors may impact the placement of the improvements on the site.

Architectural Style

Architecture is the art and science of building design and construction. Architectural style affects the market value of property, so an understanding of its nature is important to appraisers. Two basic types of styles are distinguished in American architecture: formal architecture and vernacular architecture. Figures 10.2 and 10.3 illustrate formal and vernacular architectural styles.

Formal architecture refers to the art and science of designing and building structures that meet the aesthetic and functional criteria of those trained in architectural history. Formal architectural styles are identified by common attributes of expression and are frequently named in reference to a geographic region, cultural group, or time period—e.g., the Italianate, Second Empire, and Prairie School styles.[5]

architecture: The art and science of building design and construction.

formal architecture: Architecture identified by its conformity to aesthetic and functional criteria recognized by persons trained in architectural history.

vernacular architecture: Architecture designed and built by individuals according to custom and for its adaptive response to the environment and contemporary lifestyles, without reference to the aesthetic and functional criteria of architectural history.

American architecture is characterized by both **formal and vernacular styles.**

To a degree, the distinction between formal and vernacular architecture is analogous to the difference between fine art and folk art. Vernacular architecture identifies structures designed and built without reference to the aesthetic and functional criteria of architectural history, often buildings with an emphasis on function over form. Vernacular architecture reflects custom and responds to the environment and contemporary lifestyles. Vernacular styles share common attributes and may be technologically simple or

5. Literature on American architectural history is abundant. For a description of architectural styles in a real estate appraisal context, see Judith Reynolds, *Historic Properties: Preservation and the Valuation Process*, 2d ed. (Chicago: Appraisal Institute, 1996) and Carole Rifkind, *A Field Guide to American Architecture*, rev. ed. (New York: Dutton, 1998). Additional sources are cited in the bibliography of this chapter.

Figure 10.2 **Formal Architecture**

Figure 10.3 **Vernacular Architecture**

sophisticated. These styles are usually unnamed because they are not formally studied by architectural historians. The traditional barn, the mass-produced homes constructed in modern subdivisions, and multitenant industrial park buildings are examples of vernacular styles.

Architectural style is influenced by market standards and tastes, which are influenced both by the desire to preserve tradition and by the desire for change, variety, and efficiency. The market's desire for change provides the impetus for developing new elements of architectural design. Changes in architectural trends are caused by the market's reaction to current styles. When a style becomes too extreme, a shift to elements of past styles frequently occurs. A reactive shift, then, provides contrast to the preceding, dominant architectural style. Such changes also produce avant-garde or experimental building styles, which are tested in the market and ultimately accepted or discarded.

Changes in architecture can also be generated by external forces. For example, in the 1970s rising energy costs prompted new developments in the heating, ventilation, and air-conditioning systems used in office buildings. These developments include the trend toward stand-alone HVAC systems and the use of new exterior materials that conserve energy.

Architectural styles are modified over periods that are loosely related to the economic life cycles of buildings. Newly constructed buildings usually contrast in style with buildings of the previous period. Newly constructed buildings of all architectural styles enjoy broad market appeal, whether they are professionally designed or not. When a

Market preferences are influenced both by the desire to maintain tradition and by an expectancy of innovation.

building is no longer new, however, it is compared with other buildings in terms of the quality and usefulness of its architectural style. Form and structure, the most basic components of architectural style, limit and define a building's potential uses (and changes in use). These factors become more influential as time passes.

Functional Utility

To be functional an item must work and be useful. The definition of functional utility, however, is subject to changing expectations and standards. Optimal functional utility implies that the design and engineering of a building are considered to best meet perceived needs at a given time.

Functional inutility is an impairment of the functional capacity of a property or building according to market tastes and standards. It qualifies as functional obsolescence when ongoing change, caused by technological advances and economic and aesthetic trends, renders building layouts and features obsolete. (The concept of functional obsolescence is discussed in detail in Chapter 16.) Functional inutility must be judged in light of market standards of acceptability, specifically the standards of buyers who make up the market for a particular type of building within a particular period of time. Certain design elements of "smart office buildings," such as extra cooling capability, more flexible cabling systems, and additional power to run more sophisticated computer systems, may have been superadequate when they were originally constructed, but changing market desires have made some of those items standard.

Standards of functional utility vary with the type and use of property. Specific considerations for different types of property are discussed in the remainder of this chapter. Some general standards of functional utility considered by appraisers include

functional utility: The ability of a property or building to be useful and to perform the function for which it is intended according to current market tastes and standards; the efficiency of a building's use in terms of architectural style, design and layout, traffic patterns, and the size and type of rooms.

functional inutility: Impairment of the functional capacity of a property or building according to market tastes and standards; equivalent to functional obsolescence because ongoing change renders layouts and features obsolete.

- Compatibility
- Suitability or appropriateness
- Comfort
- Efficiency
- Safety
- Security
- Accessibility
- Ease and cost of maintenance
- Market standards
- Attractiveness
- Economic productivity

Design and Functional Utility by Property Type

Marketability is the ultimate test of functional utility. Generally, a building is functional if it successfully serves the purpose for which it was designed or adapted. Specific design considerations that affect the functional utility of residential, commercial, industrial, agricultural, and special-purpose buildings are discussed below.

Residential

Trends in single-family and apartment design change, and building components such as porches, balconies, fireplaces, dining rooms, large kitchens, entry halls, and family rooms may be included or excluded. Housing standards vary widely for different income levels and in different regions. Historic houses are often less functional, but they may be in great demand due to their preservationist appeal. To evaluate the functional utility of residential buildings, appraisers should analyze standard market expectations. The functional utility of a single-family or multifamily dwelling results primarily from its layout, accommodation of specific activities, adequacy, and ease and cost of maintenance.[6]

In general, more people have better housing today than they had in past years. Many amenities are now considered necessities and their inclusion is taken for granted. Even in periods of high construction and financing costs when average houses are smaller, the tendency is to retain extra bathrooms, labor-saving devices, and fireplaces.

In apartment buildings, amenities tend to be more important than space; apartment buyers and sellers often prefer a fireplace or an extra bathroom to an additional 200 square feet of area. Smaller kitchens and bathrooms tend to be more acceptable to the market for apartments than the market for houses. A dining area that is a part of the living room or kitchen is generally acceptable. Family rooms and living rooms may be spacious to offset the smallness of other rooms, and closet space must be plentiful.

> **Functional inutility** is judged in relation to market standards.
>
> **Functional utility** depends on several interactive factors, i.e., design or layout, ease and cost of maintenance, amenity or comfort level, safety and security, market standards for the property, the compatibility of the building and its use and environment, and property marketability.
>
> **Standards** for functional utility vary according to property type, i.e., residential (single-family, multifamily), commercial (office, retail, and hotel), industrial (manufacturing, research and development, warehouse), farm, special-purpose, and mixed-use.

---

6. For further discussion of single-family home design and functional utility, see Henry S. Harrison, *Houses—The Illustrated Guide to Construction, Design & Systems*, 3d ed. (Chicago: Real Estate Education Company, a division of Dearborn Financial, 1998) and Appraisal Institute, Appraising Residential Properties, 3d ed. (Chicago: Appraisal Institute, 1999). For discussion of apartment analysis, see Arlen C. Mills and Anthony Reynolds, *The Valuation of Apartment Properties* (Chicago: Appraisal Institute, 1999) and Daniel J. O'Connell, *The Appraisal of Apartment Buildings* (New York: John Wiley & Sons, Inc., 1990).

Emerging Trends in Residential Design

Remodeling	Becoming as common as new construction.
Great room	Importance to the functions of the residence increasing.
Floors	Wood or wood-look floors gaining popularity.
Tile counters	Tile is a typical material; Corean countertops may be an overimprovement in all but the highest-priced residences.
Windows	Often retrofitted with vinyl coverings on frames for ease of maintenance.
Recessed ceiling lights	High ceilings are currently popular despite the energy costs, and recessed lighting increases the feeling of space.
Electrical, plumbing, and heating systems	Often replaced with more efficient systems in resale homes.
Cabinet finishes	Subject to the whims of fashion.
Doors	Heavy, solid-core doors are replacing standard, hollow-core doors.

Source: Kathy Price-Robinson, "Remodeling Trends," *Valuation Insights & Perspectives* (First Quarter 2001): 5-7.

The layout of a residential property relates to traffic patterns--i.e., where kitchens and bathrooms should be located for convenience and how private and non-private areas should be separated (see Table 10.2.) A layout has functional inutility if it causes awkward traffic patterns. For example, inutility may result if people have to cross the living room to get to a bedroom, if the dining area is not adjacent to the kitchen, or if groceries have to be brought through the living room to the kitchen.

Standards of adequacy vary. For the most part, the market will not accept a one-bathroom house, although one-bedroom apartments and condominium units remain popular. New kitchens and baths are larger, better equipped, and more expensively finished than the small, utilitarian kitchens and baths of the recent past. Dishwashers, garbage disposals, and wall ovens are usually standard in new construction and their absence may create a value penalty. Ceramic tile in baths and more elegant fixtures are becoming commonplace. The master bedroom frequently has its own compartmentalized bath with a spa tub and a separate dressing area. Closets are abundant in new apartments and houses. Some examples of functional obsolescence in residential property are listed in Table 10.3.

Commercial

Commercial buildings are used for offices, stores, hotels, banks, restaurants, and service outlets. Frequently, two or more commercial uses are combined in a single building, e.g., a high-rise office building with ground-level retail or a hotel with a retail arcade off the lobby. The structural and design features of commercial buildings are constantly changing. Developers want the most competitive building possible, within the cost constraints imposed by economic pressures, so they incorporate technological changes to meet the demand for innovation whenever possible.

The efficiency of commercial construction today is much greater than it was in the past. Greater utility can be observed both in the portion of the

---

Table 10.2   Residential Layout Considerations

Poor floor plans are easily recognized by those who make up the market for houses, but standards often vary with current trends in a region and neighborhood. The location of various rooms in relation to the site can increase or diminish a dwelling's privacy and comfort.

Single-Family Homes
- Bedrooms and living rooms are increasingly found in the rear of residences, often accessible to the garden or backyard. Formerly it was considered desirable for the living room and largest bedroom to be at the front of the house, oriented to the street.
- Kitchens, which were once relegated to the rear, are now just as likely to be on one side of a hall in the middle or at the front of a residence.
- Full bathrooms, which include facilities for bathing, are most convenient, accessible, and private when they are near the bedrooms; they should be accessed directly or through a hall, not through a bedroom. Powder rooms should be located off a hall and near, but not too near, the living room or dining room.

Multifamily Units
- Two-story duplexes with vertical access from within the unit, rather than from public space, have strong market appeal.
- Multiunit housing is also built in stacked configurations with access on more than one level to minimize stair climbing.
- Low-rise, multifamily housing projects can be designed in a great many ways.
- Elevator apartment buildings tend to have more standardized, predictable floor plans to make the best use of space within a simple rectangular configuration.
- Structures designed for other uses are now being converted to apartments. Silos, breweries, warehouses, and schools have been successfully converted into multiunit projects.

Table 10.3   Examples of Functional Obsolescence in Residential Property

- Interior and exterior finishes that require extensive maintenance can make a structure less competitive.
- In most markets a house that wastes fuel and electricity suffers major functional obsolescence. Energy-conserving features are particularly important in multifamily dwellings and often make the difference between a profitable operation and an unprofitable one.
- The mix of units in an apartment project should meet market demands. An improper unit mix may indicate functional inutility.

---

total area enclosed by the structure, which produces direct income in the form of rent, and in the structural facilitation that has evolved out of new materials and construction methods. No single method of commercial building construction predominates. Methods vie with one another, and one may surpass others in a given area at a particular time.

Important considerations of functional utility in commercial properties include

- Column spacing
- Bay depth
- Live-load floor capacity

- Ceiling height
- Module width
- Elevator speed, capacity, number, and safety
- Level of finish
- Energy efficiency
- Parking

Functional utility in shopping centers. Trends in shopping centers change so rapidly that many structures become functionally obsolete before they deteriorate physically. Because retail space is relatively easy to renovate, many centers are streamlined and modernized when they lose their market appeal. Enclosed malls developed in the 1980s have been adapted to other uses or have been leveled and redeveloped as big-box power centers for value-oriented shoppers or lifestyle-oriented centers for high-end consumers. Many modern community shopping centers are designed with the power center concept, incorporating a larger number of smaller anchors and a higher ratio of anchor space to minimize risk.[7]

Visibility and access are the primary considerations in the analysis of retail improvements. Other building amenities that can contribute to the functional utility of shopping centers include

- Attractive public areas
- Well-kept grounds
- Adequate, well-located restroom facilities
- Suitable traffic patterns for shoppers
- Adequate column spacing
- Sufficient number of escalators
- Durable and easily maintained surface and finish elements
- Areas for shoppers and workers to rest
- Strong lighting and attractive, coordinated signs

Functional utility in office buildings. Modern office buildings are often able to fulfill their primary function—accommodating the activities of office workers—longer than any other property type, with the possible exception of residential property. Although trends in office construction move more slowly than in retail and hotel design, flexibility of office space is increasingly important to an office building's viability. Older office buildings that cannot be retrofitted to contemporary standards for wiring, HVAC capacity, and other essential systems will suffer in competition with more functional office space.

---

7.   For a discussion of the spatial analysis of a shopping center, see M. Gordon Brown, "Design and Value: Spatial Form and the Economic Failure of a Mall," *Journal of Real Estate Research*, vol. 17, no. 1/2 (1999): 189–225.

Emerging Trends in Shopping Center Design

Individuality	In contrast to the trend of branding a product to promote consumer loyalty, shopping center developers are emphasizing regional differences in architectural style to avoid homogeneity. Strong brand names within a shopping center are still desirable, but the shopping center itself should not be seen as a carbon copy of another property in a chain.
Entertainment retailing	Entertainment functions—movie theaters, restaurants, themed retailers—are becoming increasingly common in "destination" shopping centers. Research has yet to demonstrate conclusively that the presence of movie theaters increases overall sales within a shopping center, but properties that lack entertainment options may be at a competitive disadvantage in the investment market.
Themed districts within shopping center	In the past, the tenant mix was often adjusted so that a competitors would be in different areas of a shopping center. To foster convenience, comfort, and control for consumers with limited time, shopping center owners are starting to cluster related retailers—e.g., wings of a mall focusing on fashion boutiques, sports-oriented retailers, and family-oriented stores. The effectiveness of the tenant mix of a shopping center remains a good indicator of the competency of leasing and management.

Office tenants are more likely to pay higher rents for space in an attractively designed building or for a prestigious address, but tenants are unlikely to renew their leases if the office space is unable to adapt to their changing needs. Even if a developer plans to rent full floors of a new office building, there may come a time when the owner must subdivide floors and rent space to smaller tenants.

Functional considerations for office buildings include

- Appropriate density (low-, medium-, or high-rise structure) for market area
- Building shape and size
- Flexible and efficient use of space (larger floorplates are desirable)
- Expansion capabilities, including potential vertical expansion
- HVAC, plumbing, electrical, security, and communications systems
- Floor-to-floor heights
- Facade and interior and exterior signage
- Attractive streetscape and landscaping
- Access to lobbies and public space
- Vertical transportation
- Amenities, e.g., retail and restaurants, fitness centers, day care facilities

---

Emerging Trends in Office Building Design

Office-hotel concept	As an alternative to negotiating 10- to 20-year office leases, some office building owners are experimenting with providing short-term or temporary space and services as needed by tenants.
Panel systems	Panel systems for separating workspaces are replacing traditional methods of dividing space in offices for several reasons: 1. Cost—the cost of technology needed for the average office worker is rising. 2. Flexibility—more diverse work teams need adaptable meeting space. 3. Private office spaces can be arranged with new panel systems.
Data and power infrastructure	Raised floors and carpet tile allow greater access to data and power cabling as well as denser bundling. (Carpet tile helps muffle the hollow sound of raised floors.) Sufficient space for telecommunications closets is important for long-term flexibility.
Indoor air quality	The Environmental Protection Agency has ranked indoor air pollution among the top five environmental risks to public health. Poor indoor air quality can be reduced using proper ventilation and air exchange rates.

Access to retail and support services is an important amenity in suburban office parks because, unlike in urban office districts with a concentration of diverse uses, such services may not be within easy driving distance.

Functional utility in hotels. Hotels range from tiny inns with fewer than a dozen rooms to huge convention hotels with more than a thousand rooms.[8] All hotels and motels were once measured against standard, current designs. This tendency continues for medium-priced hotels and the various extended-stay and limited-service categories, but in appraising older facilities and luxury hotels, variation in architectural styles and interior finish must be considered.

The physical configuration of a hotel or motel is determined by the type of patrons it serves. A motel must be oriented to the needs of drivers who wish to spend a minimum amount of time on the premises. A resort hotel, on the other hand, must provide a variety of entertainment facilities for its guests.

The amount of hotel space devoted to guest rooms varies. A hotel that is a major meeting and entertainment center has a much lower proportion of guest rooms to public areas than an extended-stay hotel. Many extended-stay hotels consist entirely of suites with small equipped kitchens, living rooms, and separate bedrooms. These hotels usually have small lobbies and restaurants. Because few hotels contain lodging facilities alone, appraisers must often consider multiple, mixed uses when analyzing the functional utility of the improvements.

---

8.   For a thorough discussion of hotels, see Stephen Rushmore, MAI, *Hotels and Motels: A Guide to Market Analysis, Investment Analysis, and Valuations* (Chicago: Appraisal Institute, 1992) and Stephen Rushmore, Dana Michael Ciraldo, and John Tarras, *Hotel Investments Handbook* (Boston: Warren, Gorham & Lamont, 1997).

Emerging Trends in Hotel Design

Needs of the business traveler	Access to communications technology (jacks for modems and fax machines either in guest rooms or in a business center) is increasingly important to business travelers. At a minimum, hotels catering to business centers should have a health club in addition to a business center.
Product types	All-suite, extended-stay, and hard budget hotels are the newest lodging concepts. The hard budget category avoids "amenity creep"—i.e., renovation that is beyond typical maintenance and upkeep and that over time has turned limited-service hotels into mid-priced hotels.

Industrial

The most flexible design for industrial buildings, and the one with the greatest appeal on the open market, is a one-story, square or nearly square structure that complies with all local building codes.[9] Even for the simplest industrial buildings, though, the factors in Table 10.4 must be considered.

The combination of old and new industrial space may create substantial functional obsolescence if the new construction contributes less than its cost to the value of the whole. The layout of industrial space should allow operations to be carried out with maximum efficiency. Typically, receiving functions are performed on one side of the building, shipping functions on the other, and processing or storage functions in the middle.

Some industrial buildings include special features such as sprinkler systems, scales, loading dock levelers, cranes and craneways, refrigeration areas, conveyor systems, process piping (for compressed air, water, and gas), power wiring, and employee lockers and lunchrooms. These features may be standard equipment for certain industrial operations but not standard for the local real estate market.

Functional utility in manufacturing plants. Buildings used for industries that involve bulky or volatile materials and products have specialized equipment and building designs, so they have few potential users. The facilities for some industries such as food processing or manufacturing computer chips must maintain prescribed levels of cleanliness; for example, the "clean rooms" needed for silicon wafer production may not contribute as much value as they cost to construct if used for alternative industrial uses. Buildings used for light manufacturing and processing have fewer limitations and greater appeal in the market.

Functional utility in warehouse and distribution facilities. Storage and distribution facilities range from simple cubicles, known as *mini-warehouses*, to huge

---

9. See also Douglas McKnight, "A Practical Guide to Evaluating the Functional Utility of Warehouses," *The Appraisal Journal* (January 1999): 29–36 and Donald Sonneman, "Challenges in Appraising 'Simple' Warehouse Properties," *The Appraisal Journal* (April 2001): 174–181.

Table 10.4	Functional Utility of Industrial Properties
Surplus land*	In new construction surplus land on the site is frequently allocated for future expansion.
Clear span	Anywhere from 21 to 35 feet; many smaller warehouses can be operated with a clear span of 15 to 20 feet, but higher ceilings may be standard in the market.
Percentage of office space	Varies widely depending on specific operation. If potential alternate uses of an existing property do not require as much finished office space, the excess may be an overimprovement.
Loading facilities	Multiple load facilities can reduce delays in incoming deliveries and outgoing orders. Overhead doors are less efficient loading facilities than loading docks, dock-high floors, and truck wells.
Floor thickness and loading capacity	Typically, 5 to 8 inches of reinforced concrete. Live-load capacity—the ability to support moving or movable objects in the building at a certain weight—is a minimum 125 pounds per square foot for light warehouse and manufacturing buildings and 250 pounds per square foot for heavy warehouses.
Power service	Manufacturing plants generally require more electrical service than warehouses.
Land-to-building ratio or floor area ratio	Typically, 2.5 to 3.5 land-to-building area; many older facilities have ratios from 1.3 to 2.5. The land-to-building ratio must allow plenty of space for parking, truck maneuvering, yard storage, and expansion. Floor area ratio (FAR) is also known as building-to-land ratio.
Size relative to typical building size	Big-box warehouses can be significantly larger than competitive buildings in the market. The cost of reconfiguring a large industrial building for multitenant use is a measure of functional inutility.
Slope of access to the site	Steep inclines can reduce loading efficiency.

*   See the discussion of excess land and surplus land in Chapter 9.

regional warehouses with more than a million square feet. For optimal functional utility, warehouses should have adequate access, open areas, ceiling height, floor load capacity (often 300 pounds or more for heavy-duty industrial storage buildings), humidity and temperature controls, shipping and receiving facilities, fire protection, and protection from the elements.

The primary consideration in warehouse location is good access. Just-in-time inventory practices require a distribution facility to be accessible to a greater variety of vehicles and cargo containers making more frequent and often smaller pickups and deliveries. As a result, docks and dock areas must be designed with greater flexibility. Trucking is the most common means of transporting goods, but certain warehouse operations also need access to rail, water, and air transportation. If electric trucks are used, a battery-charging area should be included.

Emerging Trends in Industrial Building Design

Automation	Industrial operations are less labor-intensive and more equipment-intensive than they once were, and the buildings that house those operations can devote more space to machinery and systems than to break rooms, locker rooms, etc. For example, telecom hotels, Internet switching centers, and data centers often consist of bare storage space for computer equipment and are rarely visited by the people who own the equipment. Also, automated inventory operations increase efficiency, particularly when dealing with small electronic components or other products that are difficult to distinguish by the naked eye.
Just-in-time manufacturing and inventory practices	Manufacturers do not want to be burdened with the cost of storing large quantities of the products they produce, so their suppliers—and the warehouse operators who serve them—focus less on the long-term storage of inventory and more on the movement of inventory.

Forklifts, conveyor belts, and automatically guided vehicle conveyor systems are used to move materials inside warehouses. Pallets, or portable platforms, are used for moving and storing materials in most distribution operations. Therefore, ceiling heights in warehouses should accommodate the stacking of an ideal number of pallets. Newly constructed high-cube warehouses may be more efficient than older buildings with larger footprints and fewer automated systems for moving materials. Because wide spans provide maximum flexibility, a square structure generally is the most cost-effective.

Sprinkler systems are needed in warehouses where flammable goods are stored. The nature of the stored material determines whether the system should be wet or dry, using water or chemicals.

Buildings on Agricultural Properties

As the small, family farm has given way to fewer, larger farms, the contribution of farm buildings to the total value of farm real estate has been steadily decreasing. The number of farm buildings per acre of farmland has also decreased. Farms are increasingly operated by large, specialized business concerns, and the equipment and management needed to run agricultural operations have become increasingly specialized.[10]

Farm buildings must accommodate the type of machinery and equipment currently used in farming (see Table 10.5). To be useful, each farm building must contribute to the operating efficiency of the entire farm. Each building's usefulness relates to the type and size of the farm. Functional inutility can result from having too many farm buildings when fewer would be more efficient.

---

10. For additional information on improvements to rural land, see American Society of Farm Managers and Rural Appraisers and Appraisal Institute, *The Appraisal of Rural Property,* 2d ed. (Denver and Chicago, 2000).

Table 10.5	**Characteristics of Improvements on Agricultural Land**
Type of Building	**Characteristics**
Barns	• Some barns have traditionally been multifunctional, providing animal shelter, grain storage, and a threshing floor. Other structures, such as tobacco barns and modern farm buildings, serve a single, specialized purpose.
	• The traditional American barn is 60 feet long and 30 feet wide, with two gable ends, a loft, and double doors.
	• Most barns are built of wood, but some are made of stone, logs, or brick.
	• Old barns are suitable for modern, general-purpose farming if they are sufficiently adaptable. Virtually all newer barns have pre-engineered pole construction, which is less expensive and can accommodate more farming activities than older, multistory barns can.
Silos	• Silos have become more prevalent and larger. The use of baled, rather than loose, hay and the increased use of ensilage have lessened the need for barn storage.
Animal shelters	• Should be dry and clean, provide protection from the wind and sun, and be adaptable to equipment storage.
Machine sheds	• Needed to house tractors, combines, discs, plows, harrows, cultivators, pickers, trucks, and other equipment.
Shop	• Most farms have an area for maintenance of mechanical equipment; often the shop is a pole barn with concrete floors that has been modified. In winter, this may be the most important building on the property.
	• Usually heated, cooled, and insulated.
Dairy production facilities	• Pipeline milking machines and overhead feed bins dictate the requirements for milking parlors and loafing sheds where livestock are sheltered.

Special-Purpose Buildings

Although most buildings can be converted to other uses, the conversion of special-purpose buildings generally involves extra expense and design expertise. Special-purpose structures include

- Houses of worship
- Theaters
- Sports arenas

The functional utility of a special-purpose building depends on whether or not there is continued demand for the use for which the building was designed. When there is demand, functional utility depends on whether or not the building conforms to competitive standards. For example, there is a continued demand for movie theaters, but their design has changed due to high maintenance and utility costs. Ornate movie theaters have been replaced with simple, unembellished structures containing a larger number of smaller screens.[11]

---

11. See also Arthur E. Gimmy and Mary G. Gates, *The Business of Show Business: The Valuation of Movie Theaters* (Chicago: Appraisal Institute, 2000).

EVALUATING FUNCTIONAL UTILITY IN SPECIAL-PURPOSE BUILDINGS

To investigate the functional utility and value of building components designed specifically to serve the use of a special-purpose property, the appraiser can employ several strategies:

• Review appraisal literature pertaining to properties in a similar product category

• Search for market data on similar—i.e., not directly comparable—or related facilities

• Interview the current or recent occupant and other operators in that particular field

• Interview brokers or other appraisers specializing in that product or with experience in that segment of the market

• Interview the project architects and engineers

• Review building plans with a cost estimator or architects/engineers experienced in that product type

• Review taxation case studies for pertinent precedents

The appraiser should also analyze the Competency Rule of the Uniform Standards of Professional Appraisal Practice in assignments regarding a special-purpose property.

Source: David Paul Rothermich, "Special-Design Properties: Identifying the 'Market' in Market Value," *The Appraisal Journal* (October 1998): 410–415.

The design and materials used in houses of worship are simpler today to keep maintenance and utility costs down. The functional utility of these structures, like sports and concert arenas, is primarily related to seating capacity. The structure's support facilities, general attractiveness, and appeal must also be considered.[12]

The adaptive-use movement has generated public interest in the conversion of special-purpose buildings to preserve architecturally significant structures that have outlived their function. Railroad stations, schools, firehouses, and grist mills are popular structures for conversion. The functional utility of these buildings relates to how much they deviate from building codes and how the cost of rehabilitation compares with the potential economic return. A typical item of functional inutility in adaptive-use projects is an insufficient number of staircases to meet building codes. By contrast, a high ceiling in a specialty property does not indicate functional inutility if it is considered a desirable architectural feature. Compliance with the Americans with Disabilities Act is an additional consideration in evaluating the adaptive use of older buildings.

Mixed-Use Buildings

Many buildings successfully combine two or more revenue-producing uses:

• Research and development facilities often combine office, laboratory, and industrial space within a single structure.

• Office buildings often contain ground-level retail space and restaurants.

• Hotels can be combined with retail, office, or residential uses.

In mixed-use buildings each type of use reflects a number of design criteria, which must be analyzed separately. The structure must also be

---

12. For more information on houses of worship, see Martin H. Aaron and John H. Wright, Jr., *The Appraisal of Religious Facilities* (Chicago: Appraisal Institute, 1997).

mixed-use development (MUD): An
income-producing property that
comprises multiple significant uses
within a single site such as retail, office,
residential, or lodging facilities. (R.S.
Means)

considered as a whole to determine how
successfully it combines uses. The uses
combined should be compatible, but
minor incompatibilities can be alleviated
with separate entrances, elevators, and
equipment. In a mixed-use building
without separate entrances and elevators,
the residential units on upper floors and the office units below would both
suffer. Only in a rather large building can the extra expense of separate
features be justified. A hotel located in an office building should have its own
entrance and elevators. Security and privacy should characterize a building's
residential area, while a professional, prestigious image is desirable for the
office portion of the structure.

Mixed-use developments (MUDs) are characterized by the physical and
functional integration of their components. They are often sprawling structures built around centrally located shopping galleries or hotel courtyards.
Walkways, plazas, escalators, and elevators provide an interconnecting
pedestrian thoroughfare with easy access to parking facilities located underground, at street level, or aboveground. Because mixed-use developments
bring together diverse participants, they require extensive, extraordinarily
coherent planning.[13]

Quality and Condition Survey

The building description and analysis of architectural style and functional utility
culminate in the quality and condition survey. A structure can have a functional
layout and an attractive design but be built with inferior materials and poor
workmanship. These deficiencies increase maintenance and utility costs and
adversely affect the property's marketability. Conversely, a building can be built
too well or at a cost that cannot be justified by its utility. Most purchasers will not
pay for these excess costs and only part of the original investment can be recaptured by the original owner through reduced maintenance expenses.

Practical or reasonable economy of construction results in an improvement that will produce rental income or value commensurate with its cost.
Maintenance and operating expenses for an economically constructed
building may be slightly higher than minimum expenses, but it is usually
better to pay those expenses than to invest in a building of superior construction that will have higher taxes. To achieve the desired level of construction
quality and cost, building materials and construction methods must be chosen
and used properly. An appropriate combination of elements results in a
building that is adequate for its intended purpose.

The character, quality, and appearance of building construction are
reflected in each of the three approaches to value. The quality and condition

---

13.   For a comprehensive analysis of mixed-use developments, see Dean Schwanke, *Mixed-Use
      Development Handbook* (Washington, D.C.: Urban Land Institute, 1987).

of building components greatly influence the cost estimate, the depreciation estimate, the ability of the property to produce rental income, and the property's comparability with other properties. Analysis of the quality of construction and the methods and materials used complements the appraiser's analysis of the building's structural design and architecture.

When a contractor takes quality shortcuts and fails to meet the advertised or contracted quality level of new construction, property owners and lenders can find themselves embroiled in litigation with aggrieved occupants. Because of the growing complexity of building design and construction, the quality of building components and construction is often best judged by a consulting engineer. The engineer can monitor the construction process to ensure that the work conforms to approved drawings and that the workmanship is satisfactory. An experienced appraiser may be able to relate evidence of construction problems—sagging floors, leaks, drafts, etc.—gathered in the property inspection to materials of poor quality or shoddy workmanship.

In the condition component of a quality and condition survey, the appraiser generally distinguishes among three types of building components:

1. Items in need of immediate repair on the date of the appraisal (i.e., deferred maintenance items)

2. Items that may be repaired or replaced at a later time (i.e., short-lived items)

3. Items that are expected to last the full economic life of the building (i.e., long-lived items)

Examples of each type of building component are shown in Table 10.6.

Items in Need of Immediate Repair

Although a building may be in excellent condition, the appraiser usually finds some items in need of repair on the date of the appraisal. Repairing these items will normally add as much or more value to the property than the cost of their repair. When the cost approach to value is applied, these are considered items of curable physical deterioration.

> In the **condition component** of a quality and condition survey, the appraiser distinguishes among items in need of immediate repair (deferred maintenance items), short-lived items that can be replaced at a later date, and long-lived items expected to last for the remaining economic life of the building.

The appraiser's repair list should include items that constitute a fire or safety hazard. Many clients request that these items be listed separately in the report. Sometimes the appraiser is asked to estimate the cost of each repair, which is called the cost to cure. (Techniques for estimating the *cost to cure* are discussed in Chapter 16.)

Short-lived Items

During the building inspection, an appraiser usually encounters other items that show signs of wear and tear but would not be economical to repair or

Table 10.6	**Sample Items Considered in the Quality and Condition Survey**

Deferred Maintenance Items
- Touch-up exterior paint on buildings and the removal of graffiti
- Minor carpentry repairs on stairs, molding, trim, floors, and porches
- Redecorating interior rooms
- Fixing leaky or noisy plumbing
- Loosening stuck doors and windows
- Repairing torn screens and broken windows
- Rehanging loose or damaged gutters and leaders
- Replacing missing shingles, tiles, and slates and repairing leaky roofs
- Fixing cracked sidewalks, driveways, and parking areas
- Doing minor electrical repairs
- Replacing rotten floor boards
- Exterminating vermin
- Fixing cracked or loose tiles in bathrooms and kitchens
- Repairing septic systems
- Eliminating safety hazards such as windows that have been nailed shut
- Eliminating fire hazards such as paint-soaked rags in a storage area

Short-lived Items
- Interior paint and wallpaper
- Exterior paint
- Floor finishes
- Shades, screens, and blinds (often considered personal property)
- Waterproofing and weatherstripping
- Gutters and leaders
- Roof covering and flashing
- Water heater
- Furnace
- Air-conditioning equipment
- Carpeting
- Kitchen appliances (considered short-lived items only if built-in)
- Sump pump
- Water softener system (often rented, not owned)
- Washers and dryers (often considered personal property)
- Ventilating fans

Long-lived Items
- Hot and cold water pipes
- Plumbing fixtures (may also be considered functional components)
- Electric service connection (may also be considered functional components)
- Electric wiring
- Electric fixtures
- Ducts and radiators

replace on the date of the appraisal. The economic life of a building is the period over which the improvements contribute to property value. Many building components have to be repaired at some time during the economic life of the building. If the remaining life of the component is shorter than the remaining economic life of the structure as a whole, the component

> **short-lived items:** A building component with an expected remaining economic life that is shorter than the remaining economic life of the entire structure.
>
> **long-lived items:** Building components with an expected remaining economic life that is the same as the remaining economic life of the entire structure.

is identified as a short-lived item. (Age-life concepts such as economic life and remaining economic life are discussed in more detail in Chapter 16.)

The appraiser must decide if an item needs immediate repair or replacement or whether this work can be done later. If the repair or replacement will add less to the value of the property than it will cost, the maintenance should usually be delayed. For example, a building with a sound, 10-year-old roof may hold up well for at least another five years. Although the roof has suffered some deterioration, replacing it probably would not add more value to the property than the cost of a new roof.

The appraiser should consider whether repairing an item is necessary to preserve other components. For example, sometimes the roof cover must be replaced or the economic life of the other components will be reduced. The appraiser should note whether the condition of the short-lived item is better or worse than the overall condition of the building.

Long-lived Items

The final step in a quality and condition survey is to describe the condition of those items that are not expected to require repair or replacement during the economic life of the building, assuming they are not subject to abnormal wear and tear or accidental damage. A building component with an expected economic life that is the same as the remaining economic life of the structure is called a long-lived item. Repair may not be required because the component has been built to last and has been well maintained. All the long-lived components of a building are rarely in the same condition; the items that are not in the same condition as the rest of the building are the important ones in the appraisal analysis.

Some defective long-lived items are not considered in need of repair because the cost of their replacement or repair is greater than the amount these items contribute to the value of the property. A serious crack in a foundation wall, for example, would probably be considered incurable physical deterioration. Incurable depreciation that results from problems in the original design of a structure is considered incurable functional obsolescence.

Further Reading

Brand, Stewart. *How Buildings Learn: What Happens After They're Built.* New York: Viking Penguin, 1994.

Ching, Francis D. K., and Cassandra Adams. *Building Construction Illustrated,* 3d ed. New York: John Wiley & Sons, Inc., 2001.

Duffy, Francis, and Kenneth Powell. *The New Office.* London: Conran Octopus Books, 1997.

Harris, Cyril M. *Dictionary of Architecture and Construction.* New York: McGraw-Hill, 1975.

Harrison, Henry S. *Houses—The Illustrated Guide to Construction, Design & Systems,* 3d ed. Chicago: Real Estate Education Company, a division of Dearborn Financial, 1998.

Keune, Russell V., ed. *The Historic Preservation Yearbook.* Bethesda, Md.: Adler and Adler, 1984.

Love, Terrence L. "New Light Construction Technologies for Residential and Small Commercial Buildings." *The Appraisal Journal* (January 1997).

McKnight, Douglas. "A Practical Guide to Evaluating the Functional Utility of Warehouses." *The Appraisal Journal* (January 1999).

Myers, John. "Fundamentals of Production that Influence Industrial Facility Designs." *The Appraisal Journal* (April 1994).

PKF Consulting and Urban Land Institute. *Hotel Development.* Washington, D.C.: Urban Land Institute, 1996.

R.S. Means, Inc. *Means Illustrated Construction Dictionary,* 3d. ed. Kingston, Mass.: R.S. Means, Inc., 2000.

Sharkawy, M. Atef., and Joseph Rabianski. "How Design Elements Create and Enhance Real Estate Value." *Real Estate Review* (Summer 1995).

Simmons, H. Leslie, Harold B. Olin, John L. Schmidt, and Walter H. Lewis. *Construction Principles, Materials and Methods,* 7th ed. New York: John Wiley & Sons, Inc., 2001.

Reynolds, Judith. *Historic Properties: Preservation and the Valuation Process,* 2d ed. Chicago: Appraisal Institute, 1996.

Ruegg, Rosalie T., and Harold E. Marshall. *Building Economics: Theory and Practice.* New York: Van Nostrand Reinhold, 1990.

Simpson, John A. *Property Inspection: An Appraiser's Guide.* Chicago: Appraisal Institute, 1997.

White, John Robert, ed. *The Office Building: From Concept to Investment Reality.* Chicago: Appraisal Institute, Counselors of Real Estate, and Society of Industrial and Office Realtors Educational Fund, 1993.

11 MARKET ANALYSIS

The term *market analysis* is used broadly in economics but has more specific meaning within the appraisal discipline. For appraisers, market analysis is the identification and study of the market for a particular economic good or service. Appraisers generally consider market analysis at two levels:

- First, from a broad market viewpoint, without a specific property as the focus of the study
- Second, from the perspective of the market in which a given property competes

Although there is a logical continuum from the general to the specific, market analysis applied to a specific property is of particular importance in the valuation process and should not be confused with general market analysis or related studies.

In the valuation process, an appraiser talks to many market participants while gathering data. Key sources are those involved, or likely to be involved, in the transaction for the appraised property or for other properties that can be used reliably for supporting comparisons; other sources may provide only general information about the local economy. When this investigation helps the appraiser distinguish the most relevant market participants from the market at large, the appraiser is involved in market analysis for valuation.

In the appraisal of a specific property, market analysis must show how the interaction of supply and demand affects the property's value. Through the investigation of sales transactions, offerings, listings, and the behavior of market participants, an appraiser can ascertain supply and demand relationships, investigate the reasoning behind the prices paid and the prices accepted, and ascertain market attitudes toward current trends and anticipated changes. If current market conditions do not indicate adequate demand for a proposed development, market analysis may identify the point in time when adequate demand for the project will likely emerge. Thus, market analysis helps an appraiser forecast the timing of a proposed improvement and the amount of demand anticipated in a particular period of time.

> **market analysis**
> 1. The identification and study of the market for a particular economic good or service.
> 2. A study of real estate market conditions for a specific type of property. (USPAP, 2001 ed.)

> **Market analysis investigates** the relationship between the demand for and competitive supply of real estate in a defined market.

Market analysis also provides a basis for determining the highest and best use of a property. An existing or proposed improvement under a specified use may be put to the test of maximum productivity only after it has been demonstrated that an appropriate level of market support exists for that use. In-depth market analyses go much further in specifying the character of that support. Such studies may determine key marketing strategies for an existing or proposed property, address the design characteristics of a proposed development, or provide estimates of the share of the market the property is likely to capture and its probable absorption rate.

To measure the market support for a specified property use, the analyst must identify the relationship between demand and competitive supply in the subject real estate market—both now and in the future. This relationship indicates the degree of equilibrium or disequilibrium that characterizes the present market and the conditions likely to characterize the market over the forecast period.

The market value of a property is largely determined by its competitive position in its market. Familiarity with the characteristics and attributes of the subject property will enhance the appraiser's ability to identify competitive properties (supply) and to understand the comparative advantages and disadvantages that the subject offers potential buyers or renters (demand). With an understanding of economic conditions, their effect on real estate markets, and the momentum of these markets, an appraiser can better appreciate the externalities affecting the property. In its broadest sense, therefore, market analysis provides vital information needed to apply the three approaches to value, as shown in Table 11.1.

Table 11.1	Market Analysis in the Approaches to Value
Approach	**Uses of Market Analysis**
Cost	Market analysis provides an appraiser with information about current building costs and market conditions. This information helps the appraiser estimate the profit an entrepreneur will expect (or, for an owner-built property, the intangibles associated with owner occupancy) and any economic advantage or obsolescence the property may have suffered since its construction.
Sales comparison	Market analysis helps the appraiser identify competitive properties and determine their exact degree of comparability with the subject. With a thorough understanding of current market conditions gained through market analysis, the appraiser can adjust the sale prices of comparable properties for changes in market conditions that may have occurred since the sales occurred.
Income capitalization	In the market analysis process, an appraiser also collects data on vacancy and absorption rates, market rents, current and anticipated rates of return, and the competitive position of the subject property in its specific market. In the income capitalization approach, this information is used to determine the anticipated lease-up or sell-out rate for the subject, the share of the market that the subject is likely to capture, the future income stream it is likely to enjoy, and an appropriate discount rate or capitalization rate to apply to the income stream projection or annualized income expectancy.

Fundamental Concepts

Market Definition and Delineation

At the outset of the market analysis process, the appraiser must clearly identify the real estate product and the real estate market in which the subject competes. These two tasks may be considered complementary. Analyzing the characteristics and attributes of the real estate product helps the appraiser identify competitive properties that constitute the applicable market. Defining the real estate market for the subject property clearly enhances the appraiser's understanding of how externalities affect the subject. Through market analysis the appraiser breaks down a specific real estate market into consumer submarkets or market segments and disaggregates the real estate product from other types of properties.

To understand market analysis, it is useful to reexamine the definition of a real estate market. A real estate market is a group of individuals or firms that are in contact with one another for the purpose of conducting real estate transactions. Possible market participants include the following:

- Buyers
- Sellers
- Renters
- Lessors
- Lessees
- Mortgagors
- Mortgagees
- Developers
- Builders
- Managers
- Owners
- Investors
- Brokers

Each market participant does not have to be in contact with every other participant; a person or firm is part of the market if that person or firm is in contact with another subset of market participants.

The actions of market participants are prompted by their expectations about the uses of a property and the benefits that property will offer its users. Market segmentation, therefore, differentiates the most probable users of a property from the general population by their consumer characteristics. The activity of individual

---

Specific real estate markets can be identified by property type, property features, market area, substitute properties, and complementary properties.

submarket: A division of a total market that reflects the preferences of a particular set of buyers and sellers.

market segmentation: The process by which submarkets within a larger market are identified and analyzed.

disaggregation: The differentiation of a subject property from other properties based on their differing product characteristics.

Real estate market definition, segmentation, and disaggregation are **fundamental procedures** in market analysis.

market participants in a real estate market focuses on a real estate product and the service it provides. Product disaggregation, therefore, differentiates the subject property and competitive properties from other types of properties on the basis of their attributes or characteristics.

A market segment is delineated by identifying the market participants likely to be involved in transactions focused on the subject real estate and the type of real estate product and service it provides. Product disaggregation includes both the subject property and competitive and complementary properties. Thus, market analysis combines market segmentation and product disaggregation. The characteristics of a subject property and its market area that are investigated by an appraiser in the process of delineating the market are illustrated in Figure 11.1.

Demand

Demand reflects the needs, material desires, purchasing power, and preferences of consumers. Demand analysis focuses on identifying the potential users of a subject property—i.e., the buyers, renters, or clientele it will attract. For each particular type of property, demand analysis focuses on the end product or service that the real estate provides. Thus, a demand analysis for retail space would attempt to determine the demand for retail services generated by potential customers in the market area. A demand analysis for office space would attempt to identify businesses in the area that occupy office space and their space or staffing needs.

Figure 11.1 **Market Delineation Process**

To identify a specific real estate market, an appraiser investigates the following factors:
1. Property type (e.g., single-family residence, retail shopping center, office building).
2. Property features such as occupancy, customer base, quality of construction, and design and amenities.
   a. Occupancy—single-tenant or multitenant (residential, apartment, office, retail).
   b. Customer base—the most probable users. Data on population, employment, income, and activity patterns is analyzed. For residential markets, data is broken down according to the profile of the likely property owner or tenant; for commercial markets, data is segmented according to the likely users of the space. For retail markets, the clientele that the prospective tenants will draw represents the customer base; for office markets, the customer base reflects the space needs of prospective companies leasing office units.
   c. Quality of construction (class of building).
   d. Design and amenity features.
3. Market area—defined geographically or locationally. A market area may be local, regional, national, or international in scope. It may be urban or suburban; it may correspond to a district or neighborhood of a city. Retail and residential market areas are often delineated by specific time-distance relationships.
4. Available substitute properties—i.e., equally desirable properties competing with the subject in its market area, which may be local, regional, national, or international.
5. Complementary properties—i.e., other properties or property types that are complementary to the subject. The users of the subject property need to have access to complementary properties, which are also referred to as *support facilities*.

Demand analyses for residential and retail markets specifically investigate the households in the subject's market area. (A household is defined as a number of related or unrelated people who live in one housing unit; thus, a single individual may constitute a household.) In addition to the number of households in the market area, these analyses focus on the disposable income or effective purchasing power of these households and the ages, gender, preferences, and behavioral patterns of household members.

The demand for housing and most retail space is projected on the basis of growth rates in population, income, and employment levels.[1] The four key points discussed below can be especially useful in understanding demand projections for a particular land use.

Important factors in demand analysis for: A Residential Market

- Population of the market area—size and number of households, rate of increase or decrease in household formation, composition, and age distribution.
- Income (household and per capita).
- Employment types and unemployment rate.
- Percentage of owners and renters.
- Financial considerations such as savings levels and lending requirements (e.g., interest rates on mortgages, points charged, loan-to-value ratios).
- Land use patterns and directions of city growth and development.
- Factors affecting the physical appeal of the neighborhood, e.g., geography and geology (climate, topography, drainage, bedrock, and natural or man-made barriers).
- Local tax structure and administration, assessed values, taxes, and special assessments.
- Availability of support facilities and community services (cultural institutions, educational facilities, health and medical facilities, fire and police protection).

Important factors in demand analysis for: A Retail Market

- Population of trade area(s)—size and number of households, rate of increase or decrease in household formation, composition and age distribution of households.
- Per capita and household income (mean and median).
- Percentage of household income spent on retail purchases and percentage of disposable income (effective purchasing power) spent on various retail categories.
- Rate of sales retention in the trade area.
- Required volume of sales for a retail facility to operate profitably and existing sales volume per square foot.
- Retail vacancy rate in the market.
- Percentage of retail purchases captured from outside the trade area.
- Land use patterns and directions of city growth and development.
- Accessibility (transportation facilities and highway systems) and cost of transportation.
- Factors that affect the appeal of the retail center (image, quality of goods, and tenant reputation).

---

1. See Chapter 7 for a discussion of the sources of the data used to estimate the demand for and competitive supply of a specific property type or use.

First, the rate of household formation varies significantly with income and age (cohort) groups in the existing population; this rate is even more sensitive to migration. Estimating the number of households in an area by dividing the total population by the average household size may result in considerable error. The rate of household formation is much higher for people between the ages of 25 and 34 and those between 35 and 54 than for people between the ages of 15 and 24. However, precise data may be difficult to obtain.

Second, household size is not a constant. Over the past 30 years, average household size has declined significantly. Between 1970 and 1998, household size in the United States fell from 3.14 to 2.62.[2]

Important factors in demand analysis for: An Office Market

* Area employers who use office space; current and estimated future staffing needs.
* Average square foot areas of office space required by an office worker. Requirements vary according to the category of work, the rank of the office worker, and the location of the office in the suburbs or the central business district.
* Vacancy rate for the specific class of office building.
* Move-up demand for Class A and Class B buildings or fall-out demand for Class B and Class C buildings.
* Land use patterns and directions of city growth and development.
* Accessibility (transportation facilities and highway systems) and cost of transportation.
* Factors that affect the appeal of the office building (quality of construction, management, and tenancy) and the availability of support facilities (shops, restaurants, recreational centers).

Important factors in demand analysis for: An Industrial Market

* Presence of raw materials.
* Exchange capability (currency values and trade barriers).
* Area employers who use industrial space; current and estimated availability of skilled and unskilled labor.
* Land use patterns and directions of city growth and development.
* Accessibility (transportation facilities and highway systems) and cost of transportation.
* Employment in manufacturing, wholesale, retail, transportation, communications, or public utilities.
* U.S. and regional economic growth that affects local demand.
* Overall employment growth.
* Retail sales (applicable in market analysis for retail storage and wholesale distribution properties).
* Cargo flows by transport type (e.g., truck, rail, water, air) and product type (e.g., high or low bulk).

Demand in industrial property markets is generally more limited than the demand in residential or commercial markets.

---

2.   U.S. Department of Commerce, Bureau of the Census, *Current Population Reports*, Series P-20, No. 515 (March 1998). Note that the rate of decline was sharper in the 1970s and held fairly constant throughout the mid-1990s.

Third, while average or median income is generally projected in current dollars, real income in the United States calculated in constant dollars did not grow between 1973 and 1984, increased very modestly between 1985 and 1989, declined between 1989 and 1993, and has again increased since 1993.[3] Income projections based on current dollars will thus reflect future, inflated dollars.

Finally, population projections for small areas are published by public agencies and market research firms, but such projections can be misleading. Therefore, the appraiser should also consult projections for the overall metropolitan area. The availability of land and the adequacy of the infrastructure in the subject area will help determine how much of the overall growth projected will go to that area.

Competitive Supply

Supply refers to the production and availability of the real estate product. To analyze supply, the appraiser must compile an inventory of properties that compete with the subject. Competitive properties include the stock of existing units, units under construction that will enter the market, and projects in planning. Care must be exercised in developing and analyzing data on proposed or announced projects because some may not ultimately be constructed. The appraiser must also determine the number of units lost to demolition and the number added or removed through conversion. Data may be gathered in various ways:

*   Field inspection
*   Review of building permits (issued and acted upon), plat maps, and surveys of competitive sites
*   Interviews with developers and city planners

Factors Studied in the Analysis of the Supply of Competing Properties
*   Quantity and quality of available competition (standing stock)
*   Volume of new construction (competitive and complementary)—projects in planning and under construction
*   Availability and price of vacant land
*   Costs of construction and development
*   Currently offered properties (existing and newly built)
*   Owner occupancy versus tenant occupancy
*   Causes and number of vacancies
*   Conversions to alternative uses
*   Special economic conditions and circumstances
*   Availability of construction loans and financing
*   Impact of building codes, zoning ordinances, and other regulations on construction volume and cost

---

3. U.S. Department of Commerce, Bureau of the Census, *The Statistical Abstract of the United States: 1999,* 119th ed. (Washington, D.C.: U.S. Government Printing Office, 1999), 474, Table 742; and U.S. Department of Commerce, Bureau of the Census, *Current Population Reports,* Consumer Income Series P-60, No. 200 (March 2000): Table H-5.

market equilibrium

1. The theoretical balance toward which the supply of and demand for real estate move over the long run—a balance that is seldom achieved.
2. The balance created at any given point by the interaction of market participants, i.e., sellers representing the supply of properties and buyers representing the demand for properties.

market disequilibrium: A general characteristic of real estate markets over the short term in which the supply and demand for real estate are out of balance.

active (seller's) market: An active market in which the sellers of available properties can obtain higher prices than those obtainable in the immediately preceding period; a market in which a few available properties are demanded at prevailing prices by many users and potential users.

depressed (buyer's) market: A depressed market in which buyers have the advantage; exists when market prices are relatively low due to an oversupply of property.

Market Equilibrium

Over the short term, the supply of real estate is relatively fixed and prices are responsive to demand. If demand is unusually high, prices and rents will start to rise before new construction can begin. The completion of a building may lag considerably behind the shift in demand. Thus, disequilibrium generally characterizes markets over the short term.

Theoretically, the supply of and demand for real estate move toward equilibrium over the long term. However, this point is seldom achieved. In some markets, such as those characterized by a very specialized economy, supply responds slowly to changing demand conditions. Even when an excess in the quantity of goods offered for sale becomes apparent, projects currently under construction generally have to be completed. More stock will continue to be added to the existing surplus, causing greater disequilibrium. A decline in demand may also occur while new real estate units are being constructed, further exacerbating the oversupply.

Trends in Market Activity

Analysts and market participants describe the activity of real estate markets in a variety of ways. An active market is a market characterized by growing demand, a corresponding lag in supply, and an increase in prices. An active market is also referred to as a *seller's market* because the sellers of available properties can obtain higher prices. A depressed market is a market in which a drop in demand is accompanied by a relative oversupply and a decline in prices. A depressed market is also referred to as a *buyer's market* because buyers have the advantage.

Other terms applied to markets are subject to interpretation. For example, markets are sometimes characterized as *strong* or *weak*. Strong markets may reflect either high demand and increasing price levels or a large volume of transactions. Weak, or *soft*, markets may be identified by low demand and declining price levels. Other loosely defined terms include *broad* and *narrow* markets, *loose* and *tight* markets, and *balanced* and *unbalanced* markets.[4]

4. For further discussion of categorizing real estate markets, see Neil Carn, Joseph Rabianski, Ronald Racster, and Maury Seldin, *Real Estate Market Analysis* (Englewood Cliffs, N.J.: Prentice-Hall, 1988), 76–77 and 81–82.

All markets cannot be described with simple characterizations. Sometimes supply and demand do not act as expected. Supply may fail to respond to increasing demand because the rate of demolition exceeds the rate of new construction. In this case, prices will continue to rise. Or supply may outpace rising demand

> **strong market:** A market that reflects either high demand and increasing price levels or a large volume of transactions.
>
> **weak market:** A market characterized by low demand and declining price levels; also called a *soft market.*

because of a glut of existing properties on the market, and prices will decline.

As shown in Chapter 6, the activity of the real estate market is cyclical. Like the business cycle, the real estate cycle is characterized by successive periods of expansion, decline, recession, and recovery. The real estate cycle is not, however, synchronized with the business cycle. Real estate activity responds to both long-term and short-term stimuli. The long-term cycle is a function of changes in the characteristics of existing employment, population, income, and shifts in consumer preferences. The short-term cycle is largely a function of the availability of credit.

Levels of Market Analysis

The principles of market analysis seem simple, but the techniques and procedures applied by market analysts can be extremely sophisticated. Market studies can be developed into elaborate analyses. The levels of market analysis that can be performed reflect a spectrum of increasingly complicated methodologies.[5]

Estimates of demand are formulated differently depending on the level of analysis. In some cases, demand may simply be inferred from current market conditions, or rates of change may be used to develop projections. Because of shortcomings in this simple approach, caution is advised. To perform an in-depth analysis of forecast (fundamental) demand, the analyst must gather and segment extensive data and apply sound judgment to make projections. The analyst refines the forecast demand estimate by considering the perceptions of market participants and assessing the likelihood that current trends will continue.

Inferred Analysis and Fundamental Analysis

An appraiser can use current and historical market conditions to *infer* future supply and demand conditions. In addition, to forecast subject-specific supply, demand, absorption, and capture over a property's holding period, the appraiser can augment the analysis of

> **inferred demand:** Investment analysis that studies the functioning of the market as a discrete mechanism unaffected by external conditions.
>
> **fundamental analysis:** Investment analysis that investigates both basic and economic factors and conditions affecting specific sectors and industries.

---

5. For a comprehensive discussion of the various levels of market analysis, see Stephen F. Fanning, Terry V. Grissom, and Thomas D. Pearson, *Market Analysis for Valuation Appraisals* (Chicago: Appraisal Institute, 1994).

Table 11.2	Types and Levels of Analysis

Levels of Analysis*

Inferred Analysis		Fundamental Analysis	
A →	**B**	**C** →	**D**
Inferred subject attributes		Quantified subject attributes	
Inferred locational determinants of use and marketability by macroanalysis		Quantitative and graphic analysis of location determinants of use and marketability by macro- and microanalysis	
Inferred demand from general economic base analysis conducted by others		Demand derived by original economic base analysis	
Inferred demand by selected comparables		Forecast demand by subject-specific market segment and demographic data	
Inferred supply by selected comparables		Quantified supply by inventorying existing and forecasting planned competition	
Inferred equilibrium/highest and best use and capture conclusions		Quantified equilibrium • Highest and best use—concept plan • Timing—quantified capture forecast	
Emphasis is on: • Instinctive knowledge • Historical data • Judgment		Emphasis is on: • Quantifiable data • Forecast • Judgment	

* As defined in Stephen F. Fanning, Terry V. Grissom, and Thomas D. Pearson, *Market Analysis for Valuation Appraisal* (Chicago: Appraisal Institute, 1994), 19–32.

current and historical market conditions with *fundamental analysis*. (Table 11.2 summarizes the distinctions between inferred and fundamental analysis.)

Inferred analysis, which is sometimes called *trend analysis,* is descriptive and emphasizes historical data rather than future projections. The focus can be general, with selected comparable properties representing the larger market, or more specific and include area-wide market data and subject-specific conclusions.

Fundamental analysis is a more detailed study of market conditions, focusing on the specific submarket of the subject property and providing strong reasoning and quantifiable evidence for projections of future development. This level of analysis is based on the premise that real estate value is tied to the services the property provides and that a study of the market for those services will reveal influences on the value of the real estate.

Types of Analysis

In addition to different levels of analysis, the discipline of market analysis comprises several related types of analysis. For a given appraisal assignment, the appraiser must determine which of the following variations of market analysis is most appropriate for the appraisal problem:

•   Economic base analysis
•   Market studies and marketability studies

- Investment analysis
- Feasibility analysis

The types of market analysis differ more in scope than in procedure. All forms of market analysis investigate local economic activity and factors influencing the supply and demand of a particular type of property or in a specific market area—though not always focusing on a specific property. Also, the conclusions of these analyses all lead the appraiser into the highest and best use analysis required in the valuation process.

Economic Base Analysis

As defined in Chapter 7, the economic base of a community is the economic activity that allows local businesses to generate income from markets outside the community's borders. Thus, economic base analysis is a survey of the industries and businesses that generate employment and income in a community as well as of functions of employment such as the rate of population growth and levels of income.

Employment figures serve as a proxy for income in economic base analysis. *Basic* employment industries provide the economic foundation for a community by producing goods and services that can be exported to bring money into the local economy. Although some segments of the service sector can be considered basic economic activities, most service industries are *nonbasic* because the service provided and the income generated remain within the community's borders. Growth in basic employment can reflect changes in population, household income, or other economic factors influencing land use and real estate value.

Often the structure of a community's business sector can be discussed using the North American Industry Classification System (NAICS) developed and used by the Bureau of the Census.[6] Government publications such as the *Census of Retail Trade* use NAICS codes in describing the composition of trade in a metropolitan statistical area.

Surveys and other data-gathering techniques employed in economic base analysis generate primary data that can be used in other types of market analysis.

> **economic base analysis:** A survey of the industries and businesses that generate employment and income in a community as well as the rate of population growth and levels of income, both of which are functions of employment. Economic base analysis is used to forecast the level and composition of future economic activity. Specifically, the relationship between basic employment (which brings income into a community) and nonbasic employment (which provides services for workers in the basic employment sector) is studied to predict population, income, or other variables that affect real estate values or land utilization.

---

6. In 1997, the Standard Industrial Classification system (SIC) was replaced by the North American Industry Classification System (NAICS). See Carole A. Ambler and James E. Kristoff, "Introducing the North American Industry Classification System," *Government Information Quarterly*, vol. 15, no. 3 (1998): 263–273.

Market Studies and Marketability Studies

A macroeconomic market study provides a broad picture of supply and demand conditions for a specific property type (e.g., residential units, retail space, office space, industrial plant, agricultural operation) or for a specific area. In a market study, the appraiser does not focus on a specific property, though, so for most valuation assignments a more detailed marketability study is necessary.

In a marketability study, the appraiser investigates how a particular property will be absorbed, sold, or leased under current or anticipated market conditions; a market study or analysis of the general class of property should be included. In contrast to market studies, a marketability study is property-specific. It should identify the characteristics of the subject's market and quantify their effect on the value of the property.

A marketability study is founded on analysis of four factors of value—utility, scarcity, desire, and effective purchasing power. The interaction of these four factors will determine the marketability of a property. Utility and scarcity are supply-side factors, while desire and effective purchasing power are demand-side factors.

The development of a property usually entails both a construction (conversion or renovation) phase and a marketing phase. The marketability study must describe the demand and supply situation under current market conditions (for the estimate of "as is" value) as well as the demand and supply situation over the planned construction period (for the value upon completion) and the marketing period (for the estimate of value upon stabilization). In other words, a marketability study for a property must focus on each point on the development timeline for which a value is to be estimated. The demand and supply analysis must investigate market conditions, both current and future, to determine the absorption rate and other factors that will affect value during the marketing period.

A marketability study must answer the following questions:
- Who will the end users be—i.e., buyers or tenants?
- What are the characteristics of the expected end users? (age, family size, space needs, and preferences as to facilities and amenities)
- Does the utility of the improvements, whether proposed or existing, satisfy the requirements of the intended market?
- What is the demand for the proposed property that is to be marketed?
    - How many end users would want the property? (desire)
    - How many potential users can afford it? (effective purchasing power)
    - What share of demand is the property likely to capture? (capture rate)
- What is the supply of competitive properties that will be marketed?
    - How many competitive units currently exist?
    - How many competitive units are under construction?
    - How many competitive units are planned?
- What is the estimated absorption rate for the proposed property to be marketed?
- Are there alternative uses for the property that would provide a higher return on the investment?
    - What are the relative risks associated with the alternative uses?

An appraiser must be careful not to misinterpret data or use historical data as an absolute prediction of the future. For example, the absorption rate experienced by competitive projects is sometimes incorrectly assumed to indicate the absorption rate for the subject when it is actually an indication of demand. Consider an appraiser who is analyzing a proposed residential subdivision and finds three competitive subdivisions in the subject's market area. Over the past year, these subdivisions have had average sales rates of three lots per month, five lots per month, and seven lots per month. Simply using the average sales rate for the three competitive subdivisions, five lots per month, as the estimated absorption rate for the subject would most likely be incorrect. The total lot sales for the three competitive subdivisions can, however, be used as an indication of the total historic demand for similarly developed residential lots in the subject's market area—i.e., 15 lots per month is the implied demand for this type of real estate product. The appraiser should study additional market factors, including growth patterns and the development of new competitive subdivisions, to support the estimate of total demand over the subject's marketing period.

> **market study:** A macroeconomic analysis that examines the general market conditions of supply, demand, and pricing or the demographics of demand for a specific area or property type. A market study may also include analyses of construction and absorption trends.
>
> **marketability study:** A microeconomic study that examines the marketability of a given property or class of properties, usually focusing on the market segments in which the property is likely to generate demand. Marketability studies are useful in determining a specific highest and best use, testing development proposals, and projecting an appropriate tenant mix.

The subject's marketing period can be determined by analyzing the supply of competitive residential subdivision lots in the market area, including the subject and all other proposed and existing subdivisions. Consider the following situation:

- The appraiser expects the three existing subdivisions mentioned above to continue to sell off lots during the subject's marketing period.
- Another proposed subdivision will be added to the competition in the subject's market during this period.
- Total demand is 15 lots per month.

Then, the average absorption rate for the five subdivisions will be three lots per month. The appraiser can then determine whether the subject's absorption rate will be the same as, higher than, or lower than the average rate. The reasoning for the rate chosen should be explained in the appraiser's conclusion.

If a marketability study prepared by another party is being used in the valuation, the appraiser must recognize that this study represents secondary data. The appraiser should carefully review the study to determine its validity and whether it can be used.

opportunity cost: The cost of options foregone or opportunities not chosen.

investment analysis: A study that reflects the relationship between acquisition price and anticipated future benefits of a real estate investment.

feasibility analysis: A study of the cost-benefit relationship of an economic endeavor.

Investment Analysis

Investment analysis helps appraisers determine whether a specific property meets the risk and return requirements of an investor. By comparing the prospective rates of return offered by alternative investment opportunities, the appraiser can estimate the required rate of return for the property being appraised. Measures of return and risk are related to standards of market performance and opportunity cost.

An investor who selects one investment forgoes the opportunity to invest in other investments. An investor will select the investment that best meets specific investment objectives. Some investors look for the highest rate of return at the lowest risk, while others seek the assurance of long-term growth at a more conservative rate of return. In addition to the illiquidity the investor endures over the term of the investment, there is a potential for opportunity cost if alternative investments at comparable levels of risk outperform the investment chosen.

Interviews with investors regarding their expectations about yield, inflation, and market growth may provide support for estimated property yield rates. Actual investor projections for properties recently acquired lend further credence to estimates of property yield.

TIMING CONSIDERATIONS IN MARKET ANALYSIS

The determination of economic feasibility requires a market value estimate of the property as it currently exists (its "as is" value) and a value estimate at a prospective time—i.e., upon completion of some phase of construction, achievement of a stabilized condition, or both. Stabilized condition (or *stabilization*) indicates that the property has reached the level of utility for which it was designed or planned. For rental projects, this means stabilized occupancy and income; for projects in which units are to be sold to multiple end users, it means sellout. For a subdivision in which the lots have been improved for sale to end users, who intend to build homes for their own use or for sale to other users, stabilization occurs when all the improved subdivision lots are sold. For a residential subdivision in which homes have been developed by a builder for sale to multiple end users, it means sellout of all the subdivision homes. In addition to stabilized occupancy and income, *stabilized operation* can be a consideration for properties housing an ongoing business enterprise. For example, a restaurant may fully occupy a new retail building and be paying the market rent for that space, but the operation of that new business may not stabilize until local consumers have had a chance to compare the restaurant with its competition.

It is essential to recognize that the values of a property as is, upon completion of construction, and upon stabilization are not concurrent; they occur at different times on the development timeline. An appraiser who fails to remember this may lose sight of predictable changes in market conditions and make erroneous assumptions in feasibility analysis and value estimation.

stabilization: The point in a property's life when it has reached a level of utility commensurate with supply and demand.

Feasibility Analysis

Economic feasibility analysis is defined as an analysis undertaken to investigate whether a project will fulfill the objectives of the investor. The profitability of a specific real estate project is thus analyzed in terms of the criteria of a specific market or investor. Alternatively, the term may be defined as an investment's ability to produce sufficient revenue to pay all expenses and charges and to provide a reasonable return on and recapture of the money invested.[7] Economic feasibility is indicated when the market value or gross sellout of a project upon achievement of a stabilized condition equals or exceeds all costs of production. Market value applies to a planned rental property; gross sellout applies to a project that will be developed as multiple units to be sold to multiple users.

Analyzing the feasibility of proposed uses requires appraisers to forecast future market conditions and the timing of events such as the sellout of new homes in a subdivision. Inadequate analysis of development projects, large or small, can contribute to a project's failure. Table 11.3 lists several reasons commonly cited for the poor feasibility studies.

Feasibility and Highest and Best Use

Highest and best use and feasibility analysis are interrelated, but feasibility analyses may involve data and considerations that are not directly related to highest and best use determinations. Such analyses may be more detailed than highest and best use analyses, have a different focus, or require additional research. Generally, the feasibility of developing real estate under a variety of alternative uses is studied. (See Table 11.4.) The use that maximizes value represents the highest and best use.

Traditionally highest and best use analysis has been associated with land residual analysis, which is derived from classical economics. In a classic land residual analysis, land value is attributed to the income that remains after improvement costs are compensated. Highest and best use of the land as though vacant indicates only how the land should be used if it were vacant. Although highest and best use analysis is primarily a tool for land valuation, it is also used by appraisers to measure a building's value contribution on the assumption that property value minus land value under highest and best use equals improvement value. While buildings can be modified and changed, the essential characteristics of sites cannot. The income to any particular site depends on the use decision. From this vantage point, land value is the driving force, and property values in a specific market are a function of the income to the land.

---

7. *The Dictionary of Real Estate Appraisal*, 3d ed. (Chicago: Appraisal Institute, 1993). The terms *feasibility analysis, economic feasibility analysis,* and *financial feasibility analysis* are often used interchangeably. See also Stephen Fanning, Terry Grissom, and Thomas Pearson, *Market Analysis for Valuation Appraisals* (Chicago: Appraisal Institute, 1994), 190, fn. 1.

Table 11.3	**10 Principal Reasons for Inadequate Feasibility Studies**

1. Faulty or inadequate instructions to the market analyst
2. Failure to show a range of probable results
3. Overstatement of growth projections
4. Over-allocation of real estate market to the project
5. Insufficient use of microeconomics
6. Inflated land values
7. Failure to retain consultant on a continuing basis
8. Plan too large in relation to the market area
9. Overly rigid land use plan
10. Poor sequencing and underestimation of infrastructure costs

Source: John Robert White, *Real Estate Valuing, Counseling, Forecasting: Selected Writings of John Robert White* (Chicago: American Institute of Real Estate Appraisers, 1984), 214–220.

Six-Step Process

Most market analysis assignments can be performed using a six-step process, which is illustrated in Table 11.5. For proposed properties, a seventh step can be added for financial feasibility analysis of alternative uses and threshold testing, often using the breakeven point of the investment as the threshold.

Market analysis assignments can be elaborate undertakings, particularly if a large amount of primary research is required. The following examples outline the procedures and thought processes an appraiser will apply in using the six-step process to analyze the markets for an appraised property of each of the major types of real estate. In the valuation process, an investigation of the economic overview of the market for the properties normally precedes the procedures that make up market analysis.

Housing Demand

Proposed Single-family Subdivision

Real estate developers often want to know how many homes they can build in a subdivision, what prices they could expect to receive for those properties, and the timing of sales over an anticipated holding period. A typical market analysis for a new single-family subdivision involves the following considerations in the six-step process:

Step 1. *Property productivity analysis.* As in any market analysis, the first step is a preliminary analysis of the legal, physical, and locational attributes of the subject units and units in competitive subdivisions. Important characteristics of a new subdivision include

- Infrastructure
- Zoning
- Deed restrictions
- Linkages to major employers and amenities

Table 11.4   **Comparison of Real Estate Analyses**

Goal/Purpose

General market analysis	Identify demand for appropriate potential uses
Feasibility analysis	Determine values of appropriate potential uses (based on data collected during market analysis—e.g., residual land value, rate of return, capitalized value of overall property)
Highest and best use analysis	Of the appropriate potential uses, determine the use that yields the maximum value

Processes/Steps

General market analysis	Perform supply and demand analysis for appropriate potential uses
Feasibility analysis	Calculate *NOI*/cash flows of appropriate potential uses and select appropriate cap rate/discount rate to form an opinion of property values
Highest and best use analysis	Specify terms of use, timing, and market participants (e.g., user of the property, equity investor, debt investor) and compare values of appropriate potential uses

Results (Data Generated)

General market analysis	Forecasts of absorption rates and probable rents for appropriate potential uses
Feasibility analysis	Property value of appropriate potential uses based on respective data
Highest and best use analysis	Highest and best use of property

- Public planning for growth
- Population trends

Step 2. *Market delineation.* To analyze the characteristics of likely buyers of the specified housing units, the analyst develops a consumer profile describing income levels, household size, age, and preferences. The market area of potential buyers may be defined in terms of

- Time-distance relationships—the commuting time to employment centers and support facilities
- Social or political boundaries—school districts, voting precincts
- Man-made or natural boundaries—major thoroughfares, physical barriers
- The location of competitive housing

Step 3. *Forecast demand.* Demand for single-family homes is generally analyzed using demographic data. Once the market area is defined, the analyst can compile various figures for that area:

- The current and projected population within the defined market area.

Table 11.5		Six-Step Market Analysis Process
Step 1	Property productivity analysis	First, the appraiser or analyst identifies which features of the subject property shape productive capabilities and potential uses of the property. Those attributes can be physical, legal, or locational, and they will be the basis for the selection of comparable properties.
Step 2	Market delineation	Given the potential uses of the subject property, the appraiser identifies a market for the defined use (or more than one market if the property has alternative uses).
Step 3	Demand analysis and forecast	Economic base analysis is the basis of the analysis of existing and anticipated market demand. An appraiser studies population and employment data to analyze and forecast demand. The scope of work required by the assignment (as well as time and budgetary constraints) will dictate to what extent demand-side variables must be investigated.
Step 4	Competitive supply analysis and forecast	Marginal demand is established through analysis of existing and anticipated supply of the property type under investigation.
Step 5	Supply and demand study	The analyst investigates the interaction of supply and demand to determine if marginal demand exists and then makes predictions as to when the market will move out of equilibrium.
Step 6	Capture estimation	By comparing the productive attributes of the subject property to those of competitive properties, the analyst can judge the market share the subject is likely to capture given market conditions, demand, and competitive supply.

- The current and projected number of households, keeping in mind that household size varies with the age of the head of the household.
- The number of current and projected households headed by owners and those headed by renters. (There may be an overlapping category of renters who can afford to buy.)

With that population information, the analyst can break down the number of owner-headed households according to their income levels to determine the percentage of households that are or will be able to meet the mortgage payments required by local lending practices and interest rates and other housing costs such as expenses for maintenance, insurance, and taxes. Adjusting the number of owner-headed households that can or will be able to afford the housing by the vacancy rate in the market yields measures of the existing and anticipated demand for the subject property.

Step 4. *Competitive supply analysis.* An inventory of competitive supply includes identifying the number of

- Existing competitive properties within the subject's identified market area
- Properties under construction in that area
- Planned properties in the area for which building permits have been obtained
- Proposed properties in the area

The total number of competitive properties in the defined market area for the projection period can be refined by checking the total number of building permits issued against those actually put to use in recent years. In addition to quantitative measures of current and anticipated supply, this step in the analysis process includes comparison of the subject and its competition for specific amenities and attributes that give housing units a competitive advantage or disadvantage.

Step 5. *Equilibrium or residual analysis.* Existing and potential demand can be compared with current and anticipated competitive supply to determine whether demand for additional units or square footage of housing (marginal demand) exists or when it may develop.

Step 6. *Forecast subject capture.* The final step of the market analysis process for a proposed subdivision is to analyze the competitive rating to forecast the likely capture rate for the subject. The analyst makes qualitative judgments regarding the relative appeal of the subject property in the marketplace that must be reconciled with the quantitative evidence of marginal demand.

The goal of the market analysis for a proposed subdivision is often more than just a forecast of subject capture. The client often also wants to know if the project is economically feasible and what prices the market will bear for the product. In the optional seventh step of the market analysis process, the analyst tests the feasibility of various market scenarios. The breakeven point, where expected construction costs and the client's desired profit margin match the anticipated sale price, often serves as a starting point for testing pricing alternatives. The analyst can also test exceptionally optimistic or pessimistic market forecasts, providing best- and worst-case scenarios.

Existing Apartment Complex

To retain its value over time, an existing apartment complex needs to be able to compete effectively in the marketplace. The subject property's vacancy rate is one indicator of the relative health of a property, but market analysis for such a property involves additional considerations.

Step 1. *Property productivity analysis.* As for most property types, the first step in market analysis for an apartment building involves a preliminary analysis of the legal, physical, and locational attributes of the subject property and similar buildings in competitive apartment districts. Important characteristics of an existing apartment complex include

- Design and appearance of the property
- Number, size, and mix of units
- Site improvements and amenities (in units and for complex as a whole)
- Parking
- Zoning (particularly the possibility of a zoning change for potential condominium conversion)
- Infrastructure
- Public planning for growth
- Natural features and land use trends
- Linkages to major employers and amenities

Step 2. *Market delineation.* The market area of potential renters is similar to that of potential home buyers. The boundaries of the market area for an existing apartment are based on

- Time-distance relationships—the commuting time to employment centers and support facilities
- Social or political boundaries—school districts, voting precincts
- Man-made or natural boundaries—major thoroughfares, physical barriers
- The location of competitive housing

In addition, the analyst investigates the tenant profile (occupational profile, income level, and other demographic information) of the subject property and the market area in this step of the market analysis process.

Step 3. *Forecast demand.* The demand for an existing apartment complex is forecast using both inferred and fundamental methods. The inferred (trend) analysis of the subject's market area includes investigation of

- General growth trends
- Residential construction trends
- Historical absorption figures
- Real rental rates

Relevant information gathered in the fundamental analysis of apartment demand includes

- The current and projected population within the defined market area
- The current and projected number of households (dividing population figures by average household size)
- The number of current and projected households headed by owners and those headed by renters
- The number of households that are or will be able to meet the monthly rent on units in the subject property

An adjustment for frictional vacancy in the market may need to be made for proposed construction, but for existing projects the analysis usually focuses on the ability of the subject property to capture actual occupancy so an adjustment is not necessary. Additional adjustments may be needed for move-up demand, which is generated by the upward mobility of lower-income households, and latent (or pent-up) demand, which is often a result of underbuilding or high financing costs that restrict new construction.

Step 4. *Competitive supply analysis.* The competitive supply of apartments in a market area takes into account

- Existing competitive properties
- Properties under construction
- Planned properties for which building permits have been obtained
- Proposed properties

To complete the analysis of competitive supply, the location, age, and amenities of the subject are compared to those of the competitive properties.

Step 5. *Equilibrium or residual analysis.* A net excess or shortage of apartment units in the market can be determined by comparing the results of the analyses in Steps 3 and 4.

Step 6. *Forecast subject capture.* The inferred analysis of the market area is revisited along with additional fundamental analysis to generate a subject capture rate. The subject's current occupancy can be compared to the estimated number of occupied units in the market, or a pro rata share can be calculated by dividing the total number of units in the subject with the total number in the market. In addition, competitive ratings for the subject property and competitive properties can be compared. If more than one form of fundamental analysis is used to calculate a capture rate, the separate conclusions should be reconciled.

Retail Space Demand

To forecast the demand for an existing or proposed community shopping center at a specific site over a given period (say, five or ten years), an appraiser follows these steps:

Step 1. *Property productivity analysis.* Analysis of the legal, physical, and locational attributes of the subject retail center and competitive centers in or near its trade area focuses on current industry standards. Retail properties can become outdated quickly as industry norms change. Particular attention is given to the following attributes of the subject site and improvements:

- Land-to-building area ratio
- Building area
- Parking
- Frontage, visibility, and signage
- Topography
- Utilities
- Landscaping
- Design and building layout
- Amenity features
- Store size
- Store depth
- Tenant mix and marketing

Locational factors are also important for retail properties. The locational attributes that should be investigated include

- Land uses and linkages with the surrounding community
- Site location in relationship to patterns of urban growth
- Proximity to competitive supply

Step 2. *Market delineation.* Effective analytical tools for defining the primary and secondary trade areas of a shopping center have been objects of study for many years. The most commonly used techniques include

- Trade area circles, in which preliminary trade area boundaries are adjusted for the specific geographic, demographic, and economic characteristics of the community
- Gravitational models, a variation of trade area circles that takes into account the effects of competition[8]

---

8. See William Reilly, *Methods for the Study of Retail Relationships* (Austin: University of Texas, 1959).

- Customer spotting, a more detailed form of trade area circles in which actual customer addresses are surveyed to determine distances and linkages

Step 3. *Forecast demand.* Inferred analysis of retail demand may include study of the following:

- Economic base and city growth trends
- Citywide retail center occupancy
- Competitive center occupancy

Fundamental demand for retail space requires further scrutiny of market data, including

- Overall population of the trade area
- Number of households
- Average household income
- Percentage of average household income spent on retail purchases
- Percentage of retail purchases typically made at shopping centers similar to the subject
- Percentage of purchases made at the shopping center allocated to primary and secondary trade areas
- Volume of sales per square foot of retail area required to support the subject
- Normal vacancy rate in the market

The estimates of inferred and fundamental demand can be reconciled with a ratio analysis of the trade area in which the current amount of occupied retail square footage per capita is compared to the future population forecast. The conclusions of these analyses may be further adjusted to account for retail income from outside the trade area and leakage of retail income to other areas.

Step 4. *Competitive supply analysis.* As for other property types, an inventory of competitive retail space covers

- Existing competitive properties
- Properties under construction
- Planned properties for which building permits have been obtained
- Proposed properties

To complete the analysis, the supply of competitive space is rated according to

- Size
- Access and location

- Quality of merchandise
- Reputation
- Rental rates
- Vacancy
- Tenant mix

The analysis of competitive supply should yield estimates of the square footage of specific competition, the market rent the subject can expect to generate in the current market, and a comparative ranking of the subject.

Step 5. *Equilibrium or residual analysis.* The difference between supportable leasable space and the amount of existing and anticipated retail space will be the estimate of additional space needed. Sales per square foot in individual retail stores may also indicate the performance level of an existing shopping center, the center's share of the market, and whether there is opportunity for expansion. This data may be used to check the reasonableness of the estimate of additional space demanded. If there is a current surplus of retail space, the forecast of market conditions may identify when in the future the available retail space will be absorbed and demand for additional retail space will begin to come on line.

Step 6. *Forecast subject capture.* Because retail concepts can changes so quickly, subject capture is especially difficult to forecast for retail properties. In addition to inferred analysis of historical capture rates of the subject and competitive properties, several fundamental methods can be used to support an estimate of subject capture:

- Quantitative ratings of the subject and its competition
- The size-of-the-center technique, in which the drawing power of a shopping center is related to its size relative to competing properties
- Ratio analysis, which is applied like the size-of-the-center technique but segments demand to the subject property only

Office Space Demand

To forecast the demand for existing or additional office space in a particular node or district over a given period, an appraiser analyzes the relationship between supply and demand in the overall market area and the district's actual and potential share of the existing and projected demand. The time when a proposed building will reach stabilized occupancy can be forecast in this way. Demand for office space in the overall market area is estimated with the following steps:

Step 1. *Property productivity analysis.* Tenancy and class are primary identifiers of an office building's competitive status. Physical items of comparison include

- Building design and construction materials
- Signage
- Exterior lighting
- Street layout
- Utilities
- Parking
- Lot and building lines
- Landscaping and grading
- Office space layout
- Tenant finish
- Floor sizes
- Stairways, corridors, and elevators
- Electrical system
- Heating, ventilation, and air-conditioning
- Amenities
- Security
- Building management and tenant mix

> **node:** A cluster of properties with the same or complementary uses, generally a nucleus of office buildings and retail stores. Downtown central business districts (CBDs), the primary sites of office building nodes, usually house financial institutions, corporate headquarters, and government offices. Other office building nodes include uptown areas, which develop along the axis between the CBD and the suburbs; office parks, which accommodate the needs of research and development and manufacturing industries; and shopping centers, which provide office space for tenants serving residents of the trade area.

Locational considerations for office buildings are often analyzed both in terms of the subject's location within a cluster of office buildings and that node's location relative to other nodes in the competitive market area.

Step 2. *Market delineation.* Unlike residential and retail trade areas, which are defined by the consumers they serve, an office market is tied more to the reputation of the businesses housed in the office than by convenience of the location. The market area for an office building is generally diffused over a broad metropolitan area, with law firms and financial institutions often seeking space in prestigious, centrally located buildings, while businesses providing other types of services may prefer suburban offices with ample parking facilities and reasonable rents.

Step 3. *Forecast demand.* To estimate office demand, the analyst must investigate various types of information:

- Size of the workforce occupying office space, segmented by occupational category[9]
- Size of the workforce occupying office space in the subject's class
- Requisite space per worker[10]
- Normal vacancy rate

Projections may be made in annual, biannual, or multiyear increments. If a 10-year forecast is being developed and steady growth is anticipated, the demand for the first period is subtracted from the demand for the last period and the difference is divided by the number of periods in the forecast to yield an annual demand estimate.

Step 4. *Competitive supply analysis.* In addition to competitive space under construction or in planning, the competitive supply of office space in a market may also be affected by demolitions, renovations, and the adaptation of space now under other uses. Information on proposed office properties may be difficult to obtain, especially reliable information on the timing of new construction and its completion. Important characteristics of competing properties include

- Size (gross building area or rental area)
- Age
- Vacancy level
- Access
- Parking

---

9. One way to calculate the number of office space occupants in economic and occupational sectors involves establishing the ratio between the number of office workers and the number of total workers in each sector. In a sector such as finance, insurance, and real estate (FIRE), a high percentage (more than two-thirds) of all office workers occupy space in freestanding office buildings—i.e., buildings entirely occupied by office workers. The number of FIRE office workers in freestanding buildings may be estimated by multiplying the total number of workers by this percentage. In sectors such as manufacturing, however, a very low percentage of office workers occupy space in freestanding office buildings. Using these ratios, the number of office workers in each sector can be determined and the aggregate of office workers in all sectors can be calculated. See Ian Alexander, *Office Location and Public Policy* (New York: Chancer Press, 1979).

10. The average space required for an office worker ranges from 125 to 150 square feet. Very general estimates of average area requirements are published by the Building Owners and Managers Association (BOMA). Because the square foot area required per employee varies widely with community size and the type of employment in the community, market analysts should compare BOMA estimates with area-per-worker data developed as part of the competitive supply analysis. Estimates obtained from other national and local sources may also vary.

- Tenant quality
- Building management
- Building quality and condition
- Amenities
- Support facilities

Step 5. *Equilibrium or residual analysis.* The comparison of existing and projected demand for office space with the total supply of current and anticipated competitive office space should consider potential move-up or fall-out demand for Class A and Class B buildings—i.e., some tenants move up from Class B to Class A space in a down market with declining rents, while others fall out from Class A to Class B space in an active market where rents are increasing. In an in-depth analysis, an appraiser also considers space subject to pre-leasing and space that will become vacant when current tenant leases expire. If demand for space is anticipated to grow at a steady rate, the total supply that is available for occupancy may be divided by projected annual demand to determine the absorption period. At the end of the absorption period, additional space will be required. This point in time represents a "window" for development.

> **move-up demand:** In markets characterized by declining rents, office building tenants who "move up" from Class B to Class A space or from Class C to Class B space.
>
> **fall-out demand:** In markets characterized by increasing rents, office building tenants who "fall out" of the market for Class A space to Class B space or from Class B to Class C space.

Step 6. *Forecast subject capture.* To determine a particular node or district's share of the overall market projection, development patterns in the district must be analyzed. Central business districts are characterized by the greatest density of development, while suburban office complexes attract tenants with lower rents and easier access, for both employees and customers. Not all suburbs share equally in the market for office space. Development patterns in areas that closely resemble the subject district should be compared. Key demographic features such as total population and educational and income levels are believed to be closely correlated with the ability of a suburban area to support an office building.

The appraiser can develop a ratio by dividing the amount of existing office space in the district by the amount of office space in the overall market area. Such a ratio only reflects the district's "fair share" of the market, however, and may not provide an accurate forecast. Market preferences must also be considered in determining the ratio.

To forecast when a proposed building will reach stabilized occupancy, the appraiser can estimate the construction period and an absorption rate based on pre-leasing and the historic performance of competitive buildings. Historic performance is interpreted and used to forecast expectations, but it must be considered in its proper context. Performance may have been especially high during periods of rapid growth and unusually low during periods of stagnation. Detailed data on occupancy may describe not only nodal and district patterns, but also absorption rates for different building types (e.g., low-, mid-, and high-rise) or different building classes (e.g., Class A, Class B, Class C) and different occupants (e.g., anchor tenants or non-anchor tenants, corporate management, research and development departments, professional services).

Hotel Demand

The source of demand for hotel rooms depends largely on the nature of the subject property—i.e., whether it is a commercial establishment, a convention hotel, or a leisure or resort property. A proposed hotel near an established suburban office park would probably target business travelers, and the future absorption of office space in that submarket may be a good indicator of demand growth in the commercial sector. A large resort hotel in an undeveloped coastal area would draw from a much different demographic, and the market analysis process would differ as well, if only in the sources of data used by the analyst.

Step 1. *Property productivity analysis.* In general, the following attributes of a hotel's site and improvements are important factors in determining the property's competitive ability:

- Size
- Room rate structure
- Overall decor and physical appearance
- Quality of management
- Chain affiliation
- Quality and character of the market area
- Facilities and amenities offered
- Revenue per available room (RevPAR), which is a common unit of comparison used in the lodging industry to compare the income of competing facilities

The importance of these factors may depend on the type of lodging being analyzed. Access and visibility will be more important factors in the competitive ability of a highway-oriented property, but amenities will be more important for a resort hotel.

The location of a hotel often indicates the likely clientele.

- Airport hotels and highway-oriented hotels cater to transient guests.
- Center city hotels draw both tourists and business travelers.
- Hotels in suburban locations often rely on adjacent commercial or industrial businesses.
- Convention center hotels or resort properties are themselves the destination rather than any nearby land use.

Step 2. *Market delineation.* Defining the market area for a hotel can be difficult because this type of property does not necessarily rely on households in nearby communities to generate demand. Instead, linkages to sources of visitations in the area can be more significant than the characteristics of the surrounding neighborhood. Hotel development often occurs in clusters, and the emergence of a new cluster nearby can have an impact on the competitiveness of existing properties.

Step 3. *Forecast demand.* The inferred analysis of demand for hotel rooms may include study of

- Travel and tourism data
- Hotel employment data and convention center activity
- Office space absorption and employment statistics—particularly regarding wholesale and retail trade; financial, insurance, and real estate (FIRE); and services
- Occupancy rates at competitive lodging facilities in the subject's class and market area

Fundamental analysis of the demand for hotel rooms is based on historical occupancy and room rate data. Interviews with demand generators such as major employers or officials at chambers of commerce or visitor information centers may yield information that supports an estimate of hotel demand calculated from occupancy figures. Data useful in quantifying hotel demand includes

- Number of nights per stay
- Number of people per room
- Periods of use during the year
- Prices paid for rooms
- Food, beverage, entertainment, and telephone usage
- Methods of travel

Seasonal fluctuations in demand must be taken into account for leisure-oriented properties.

Step 4. *Competitive supply analysis.* Information on existing hotel properties and developments under construction is generally available, but the difficulties in obtaining hotel financing and the influence of foreign investors complicate the analysis of proposed hotels. Even if market evidence supports demand for a proposed property, new development may be hindered by external factors such as fluctuations in the economies of foreign countries whose citizens invest in U.S. hotel properties. The analysis of all the hotels in the market area concludes with a comparison of the relative competitiveness of all existing and planned properties.

Step 5. *Equilibrium or residual analysis.* The current and anticipated demand for hotel rooms, measured in total room nights per year, can be compared with the existing and planned supply of available rooms. There may be a lag between when demand is evident and when supply can be added to the marketplace to accommodate that demand.

Step 6. *Forecast subject capture.* The ratio of room nights that any hotel in a market area can be expected to capture can be derived from the fair share allotted to the property adjusted for competitive penetration factors. The allocation of the total number of room nights demanded between competitive properties can be refined by considering customer preferences such as

- Room price
- Travel distance
- Quality of facilities
- Amenities
- Management
- Image

Hotels with particularly high market penetration in one segment will generally have lower penetration rates in other segments.

Industrial Properties
Market analysis for industrial properties is complicated by three factors:

- The market areas for these properties are more widely scattered.
- Demand is more limited.
- Supply is highly differentiated according to the operation of the enterprise.

The market for industrial real estate reflects the unique characteristics of the property type. High-priced industrial machinery is generally custom-built, and, except for the flex space in multitenant research and development (R&D) facilities, industrial plants are typically custom-designed to the needs of the particular production line. The owners and users of industrial real estate have necessarily made a long-term commitment. Many older industrial firms are precluded from ever moving due to the difficulty and expense of relocation, although newer industrial facilities are less specialized, providing more flexibility in the marketplace in anticipation of growing tenants moving to larger facilities or tenants leaving for other reasons.

Plants are often built with custom financing, which is the result of lengthy negotiation. Transactions may vary considerably even for highly similar properties, particularly when a business is sold along with the real estate. In the latter situation, transactional information may be confidential, so market data will not be readily available.

Market analysis is generally much easier for multitenant warehouses and distribution centers than for facilities housing more specialized industrial operations.

Step 1. *Property productivity analysis.* Location and access to transportation are primary determinants of a distribution facility's competitive ability. All industrial properties need access to an adequate supply of skilled labor, to meet both the current demand and any anticipated growth in the industrial sector. If warehouse tenants provide parts or raw materials for manufacturing operations in the immediate area, proximity to those businesses is essential, whereas access to major trade routes is more important to large distribution centers that serve a wider market area, such as a regional distribution hub for a major retailer. Manufacturing plants that produce potentially hazardous waste materials need to be located near or have affordable access to disposal sites. Physical elements of comparison include

- Size (and land-to-building ratio or floor area ratio)
- Ceiling height
- Loading capacity
- Climate control
- Percentage of office space
- Automated operations (including the use of robotics and other evolving technologies)
- Utilities
- Security
- Building management and tenant mix
- Environmental regulations

Step 2. *Market delineation.* Established trade routes can define the boundaries of the competitive market for multitenant industrial space. Because warehouses and distribution centers must be close to major highways or railroad lines, industrial development will tend to cluster around those features, especially major freeway interchanges in centrally located states, where a large percentage of the region's or even the country's population can be within a day's drive.

Step 3.   *Forecast demand.* Demand analysis for industrial space is similar to the procedure for analyzing office space, but the analysis of industrial demand must take into account the functional limits on the use of industrial property and the different physical characteristics of warehouses and distribution centers. Less emphasis is placed on general population change. Export activity may be a better indicator of industrial demand in a market area than population growth because the businesses that occupy warehouse space generally serve a wider clientele than the local community. The analyst investigates the following:

- Employment in manufacturing, wholesale, retail, transportation, communications, or public utilities
- Cost of available labor force in relation to alternative locations
- Patterns and directions of industrial growth and development, which often cluster along major highways and around intersections
- Presence of raw materials
- Exchange capability

For retail storage and wholesale distribution properties, the level of retail sales in a market may serve as an indicator of demand for that type of industrial space.

Step 4.   *Competitive supply analysis.* Because industrial operations are such a fundamental part of a community's economic base, information on the competitive supply of warehouse space and vacancy levels is often compiled in research reports. Competing properties can be compared in terms of

- Size, particularly in relation to other industrial buildings
- Age
- Vacancy level
- Access
- Building management and tenant quality
- Building quality and condition

Building size and tenant quality are particularly important. Large, single-tenant distribution facilities do not compete with smaller, multitenant warehouses, and a building housing several closely related industrial tenants may not be competitive with buildings with more diverse tenant mixes.

Step 5.   *Equilibrium or residual analysis.* Industrial real estate markets can react to increasing demand with more agility than the markets for other types of properties can because raw storage space is easier to construct than most other sorts of buildings with more intensive finishes. When comparing the existing and project demand for industrial space with the total supply of current and anticipated industrial space and historical absorption trends, an analyst should keep in mind an industrial real estate market's potential for change at short notice.

Step 6.   *Forecast subject capture.* As long as the forecast period is not extended too far into the future, the share of marginal demand that a warehouse or distribution center can expect to capture can be estimated with about as much certainty as the capture rate for office space. Historical absorption rates may help support an estimate of the general length of cyclical shifts in demand and supply for industrial space of the subject's type.

Agricultural Properties

Like industrial properties, agricultural properties often have large market areas, with limited demand and highly segmented supply based on the agricultural product at a given operation. Forecasting demand for agricultural land is even more difficult, however. To conduct market analysis for agricultural properties, appraisers must examine factors as diverse as national and regional economic trends, ecological and environmental considerations, and the character of the subject agricultural district. Land prices are affected by both short-term commodity prices and long-term federal policy involving farm subsidies and the leasing of adjacent public lands for grazing range or timber stands. The condition of the regional economy generally exerts an influence on land prices also. For example, a boom or slump in an energy or extractive industry that represents a region's economic base (e.g., Texas or Colorado) may generally enhance or depress property values.

Rural appraisers must consult statistical data on soil productivity and crop yields as well as analyses of the effects of erosion on future soil productivity and forecasts of artesian (aquifer) reserves and water available for irrigation. The appraiser should be aware of current and future environmental legislation and any momentum toward land or wildlife conservation.

Finally, the appraiser must be familiar with the characteristics of the immediate agricultural district and the specific types of agriculture and complementary land uses found in the area (e.g., fodder production for a livestock ranch or dairy farm). Other essential information includes local assessment rates, the principal type of ownership (e.g., family farm or agribusiness), and the level of recent sales activity or foreclosures.

Further Reading

General Surveys

American Institute of Real Estate Appraisers. *Real Estate Market Analysis and Appraisal. Research Series Report 3.* Chicago, 1988.

Appraisal Institute. *Real Estate Market Analysis: Supply and Demand Factors.* Chicago, 1993.

Carn, Neil, Joseph Rabianski, Maury Seldin, and Ron Racster. *Real Estate Market Analysis: Applications and Techniques.* Englewood Cliffs, N.J.: Prentice-Hall, 1988.

Clapp, John M. *Handbook for Real Estate Market Analysis.* Englewood Cliffs, N.J.: Prentice-Hall, 1987.

Epley, Donald R., and Joseph Rabianski. *Principles of Real Estate Decisions.* Englewood Cliffs, N.J.: Prentice-Hall, Inc., 1986.

Fanning, Stephen F., Terry V. Grissom, and Thomas D. Pearson. *Market Analysis for Valuation Appraisals.* Chicago: Appraisal Institute, 1994.

Graaskamp, James A. *A Guide to Feasibility Analysis.* Chicago: Society of Real Estate Appraisers, 1970.

Malizia, Emil E. "Clarifying the Structure and Advancing the Practice of Real Estate Market Analysis." *The Appraisal Journal* (January 1995).

Myers, Dowell, and Phillip S. Mitchell. "Identifying a Well-Founded Market Analysis." *The Appraisal Journal* (October 1993).

Seldin, Maury, and James H. Boykin. *Real Estate Analyses.* Homewood, Ill.: American Society of Real Estate Counselors and Dow Jones-Irwin, 1990.

Vandell, Kerry D. "Market Analysis: Can We Do Better?" *The Appraisal Journal* (July 1988).

Wincott, D. Richard. "Market Analysis in the Appraisal Process." *The Appraisal Journal* (January 1995).

Economic Base Analysis, Location Theory, and Census Data

Haggett, Peter. *Locational Analysis in Human Geography.* New York: St. Martin's, 1965.

Hoover, Edgar M. *The Location of Economic Activity.* New York: McGraw-Hill, 1963.

Perin, Constance. *Everything in Its Place: Social Order and Land Use in America.* Princeton, N.J.: Princeton University Press, 1977.

United States Department of Commerce, Bureau of Census. *Statistical Abstract of the United States, 2000.* Washington, D.C.: U.S. Government Printing Office, 2000.

Specific Property Types

Gimmy, Arthur E., Joseph S. Rabianski, Stephen Rushmore, James D. Vernor, and Marvin L. Wolverton. "Market Analysis Applied: Snapshots of Four Property Types." *Valuation Insights & Perspectives,* vol. 1, no. 4 (Fall 1996).

Hughes, William T., Jr. "Determinants of Demand for Industrial Property." *The Appraisal Journal* (April 1994).

Kimball, J.R. "Office Space Demand Analysis." *The Appraisal Journal* (October 1987).

Kimball, J.R., and Barbara S. Bloomberg. "The Demographics of Subdivision Analysis." *The Appraisal Journal* (October 1986).

Mills, Arlen, and Anthony Reynolds. "Apartment Property Market Analysis." *The Real Estate Appraiser & Analyst,* vol. 57, no. 3 (December 1991).

Myers, Dowell. "Housing Market Research: A Time for a Change." *Urban Land* (October 1988).

Rabianski, Joseph S., and Roy T. Black. "Why Analysts Often Make Wrong Estimates About the Demand for Industrial Space." *Real Estate Review,* vol. 27, no. 1 (Spring 1997).

Rushmore, Stephen. *Hotels and Motels: A Guide to Market Analysis, Investment Analysis, and Valuations.* Chicago: Appraisal Institute, 1992. (Note: A second edition of this text is tentatively scheduled for publication in late 2001.)

FURTHER READING *(continued)*

Vernor, James D., and Joseph Rabianski. *Shopping Center Appraisal and Analysis.* Chicago: Appraisal Institute, 1992.

Witherspoon, Robert E., Jon P. Abbett, and Robert M. Gladstone. *Mixed-Use Developments: New Ways of Land Use.* Washington, D.C.: Urban Land Institute, 1976.

12 HIGHEST AND BEST USE ANALYSIS

Market forces create market value, so the analysis of market forces that have a bearing on the determination of highest and best use is crucial to the valuation process. When the purpose of an appraisal is to develop an opinion of market value, highest and best use analysis identifies the most profitable, competitive use to which the property can be put.

The highest and best use of a specific parcel of land is not determined through subjective analysis by the property owner, the developer, or the appraiser; rather, highest and best use is shaped by the competitive forces within the market where the property is located. Therefore, the analysis and interpretation of highest and best use is an economic study and a financial analysis focused on the subject property.

In all valuation assignments, opinions of value are based on use. The highest and best use of a property to be appraised provides the foundation for a thorough investigation of the competitive position of the property in the minds of market participants. Consequently, highest and best use can be described as the foundation on which market value rests.

Fundamentals of Highest and Best Use

Highest and best use may be defined as follows:

> The reasonably probable and legal use of vacant land or an improved property that is physically possible, appropriately supported, and financially feasible and that results in the highest value

Fundamentally, the concept of highest and best use applies to land alone because the value of the improvements is considered to be the value they contribute to the land. Land is said to *have* value, while improvements *contribute to* the value of the property as a whole. The theoretical emphasis of highest and best use analysis is on the potential uses of the land as though vacant. In practice, though, the contribution of value of the existing improvements and any possible alteration of those improvements must be recognized, so the highest and best use of the property as improved is equally important in developing an opinion of market value of the property. In many appraisal assignments

Highest and best use is the reasonably probable and legal use of vacant land or an improved property that is physically possible, legally permissible, appropriately supported, financially feasible, and that results in the highest value.

> A **distinction** is made between the highest and best use of the land or site as though vacant and the highest and best use of the property as improved.

of improved properties, there may be little if any question of possible change in the property's use at the date of valuation because the market is significantly built-up and properties are being sold on the basis of their continued use.

In the development of an appraisal, the appraiser must distinguish between highest and best use of the land as though vacant and highest and best use of the property as improved. The appraisal report should clearly identify, explain, and justify the purpose and conclusion for each type of use and, if a separate conclusion of highest and best use of land as though vacant was not made, explain and justify why it was omitted.

To clarify the distinction between the highest and best use of 1) the land or a site as though vacant and 2) property as improved, consider a single-family residential property located in an area zoned for commercial use. If there is market demand for a commercial use, the maximum productivity of the land as though vacant will most likely be based on a commercial use. In this case, the single-family improvements may contribute little if any to the value of the property as a whole. If, however, the market value for residential use is greater than the market value for the permitted commercial use less demolition costs, then the highest and best use of the property as improved will be for continued residential use.

In the analysis of highest and best use of land as though vacant, the appraiser seeks the answers to several questions. First:

Should the land be developed or left vacant?

If the answer to this question is that the land should be developed, a second question is:

What kind of improvement should be built?

The third question the appraiser asks relates to the highest and best use of the property as improved, which is a distinct concept developed by valuation theorists and practitioners to answer an important question that the original concept does not address. This question is:

Should the existing improvements on the property be maintained in their current state or should they be altered in some manner to make them more valuable?

Appraisal theory holds that as long as the value of a property as improved is greater than the value of the land as though vacant, the highest and best use is the use of the property as improved. In practice, however, a property owner who is redeveloping a parcel of land may remove an improvement even when the value of the property as improved exceeds the value of the vacant land. Investors are not likely to pay large sums for the underlying land simply to hold onto the property until the value of the remaining improvement has decreased to zero. The costs of demolition and any remaining improvement value are worked into the test of financial feasibility for redevelopment of the land.

> **highest and best use of land as though vacant:** Among all reasonable, alternative uses, the use that yields the highest present land value after payments are made for labor, capital, and entrepreneurial coordination.
>
> **highest and best use of property as improved:** The use of a property, as improved, that will maximize its value.

The timing of a specified use is an important consideration in highest and best use analysis. In many instances, a property's highest and best use may change in the foreseeable future. For example, the highest and best use of a farm in the path of urban growth could be for interim use as a farm, with a future highest and best use as a residential subdivision. (The concept of interim use, which is a special situation in highest and best use analysis, is discussed in more detail later in this chapter.) If the land is ripe for development at the time of the appraisal, there is no interim use. If the land has no subdivision potential, its highest and best use would be for continued agricultural use. In such situations, the immediate development of the land or conversion of the improved property to its future highest and best use is usually not financially feasible.

The intensity of a use is another important consideration. The present use of a site may not be its highest and best use. The land may be suitable for a much higher, or more intense, use. For instance, the highest and best use of a parcel of land as though vacant may be for a 10-story office building, while the office building that currently occupies the site has only three floors.

Testing Criteria in Highest and Best Use Analysis

In addition to being reasonably probable, the highest and best use of both the land as though vacant and the property as improved must meet four implicit criteria. That is, the highest and best use must be

1. Physically possible
2. Legally permissible
3. Financially feasible
4. Maximally productive

These criteria are often considered sequentially.[1] The tests of physical possibility and legal permissibility must be applied before the remaining tests of financial feasibility and maximum productivity. A use may be financially feasible, but this is irrelevant if it is legally prohibited or physically impossible.

---

1. Although the criteria are considered sequentially, it does not matter whether legal permissibility or physical possibility is addressed first, provided both are considered prior to the test of financial feasibility. Many appraisers view the analysis of highest and best use as a process of elimination, starting from the widest range of possible uses. The test of legal permissibility is sometimes applied first because it eliminates some alternative uses and does not require a costly engineering study. It should be noted that the four criteria are interactive and may be considered in concert.

> The highest and best use of a property is concluded after the **four criteria** have been applied and various **alternative uses** have been eliminated. The remaining use that fulfills all four criteria is the highest and best use.

The initial analysis of the market and land use regulations usually limits the number of property uses to a few logical choices. For example, market analysis may suggest that there is demand for a large office building in a community. If the subject site is surrounded by modern, single-family residential developments, however, a large, multistory office building would probably not be a logical use, even if it were legally permitted. Similarly, a housing development for the elderly might be a permissible use for a site, but, if most residents of the area are under 40 years old, this use may be illogical and might not meet the criterion of financial feasibility. Consideration of whether a use is reasonably probable should continue throughout the analysis of highest and best use as more is learned about the potential use of the property. Reasonable probability is both a tentative starting point and a conclusion for the use or uses that are ultimately deemed probable.

Appraisers must exercise caution in performing the market analysis that results in the determination of highest and best use. Although a given site may be particularly well-suited for a specific use, there may be a number of other sites that are equally or more appropriate. Therefore, the appraiser must test the highest and best use conclusion to ensure that existing and potential competition from other sites has been fully recognized.

An appraiser must also consider the competition among various uses for a specific site. For example, competition for available sites along a commercial strip development may be intense. Developers of community retail uses, garden office uses, and fast food franchises may bid against one another for these sites. The highest and best use and the value of the sites will reflect this competition. In turn, the competing commercial uses will price their goods and services to accommodate the competitive prices dictated by the market.

The same observation may be applied to central business districts (CBDs). The market may define the highest and best use of land in the CBD simply as high-rise development, which often includes a mix of uses such as office, retail, hotel, and residential apartment or condominium use. At times the highest and best use conclusion for a CBD site does not indicate a specific highest and best use but rather a class of uses that is supported by market area trends and reflects a consistent density of development. Although the appraiser considers specific uses in determining highest and best use, the appraiser's analysis of these uses is often general, based on commonly accepted operating expense ratios and other data inputs. Often the appraiser stops short of detailed feasibility analysis, which may involve extensive consultation with planners, architects, engineers, and cost estimators.

Highest and Best Use of Land as though Vacant

The value of land is generally determined as though vacant.[2] When land is already vacant, the reasoning is obvious—an appraiser values the land as it exists. When land is not vacant, however, its contribution to the value of the property as improved depends on how it can be put to use. Therefore, the highest and best use of land as though vacant must be considered in relation to its existing use and all potential uses. In general, the conclusion of highest and best use of land as though vacant is required except in circumstances where improved properties have structures with significant remaining economic lives and little or no indication of market demand for a change in use.

The possibility of removing existing improvements underlies the concept of highest and best use of land as though vacant, even when improvements are present. Any building can be demolished; the fact that most buildings in a given area are not does not negate the possibility. Land values are not penalized so long as the existing buildings have economic value. If the buildings no longer have value, demolition is appropriate. For example, consider a valuable commercial site in an excellent location that is currently improved with a service station that is free of any negative environmental features.[3] A purchaser who wants to build a high-rise office building on the site may pay a price for the property that includes no value, or even negative value, for the existing improvements. The potential use, not the existing use, usually governs the price that will be paid for land if that use is economically feasible.

> **Highest and best use of the land or site as though vacant** may be the existing use, a projected development, a subdivision, or an assemblage; alternatively, it may involve holding the land as an investment.

---

2. Standards Rule 1-3(b) directs an appraiser to "develop an opinion of the highest and best use of the real estate." The comment to this rule explains, "An appraiser must analyze the relevant legal, physical, and economic factors to the extent necessary to support the appraiser's highest and best use conclusion(s). The appraiser must recognize that land is appraised as though vacant and available for development to its highest and best use, and that the appraisal of improvements is based on their actual contribution to the site."

    For an improved property, the valuation of the land as though vacant is a necessary procedure within the appraisal process, but it is one that is performed under a hypothetical condition, i.e., that the subject site is vacant. In essence, the fundamental concept of highest and best use applies to land alone. By considering land alone, the appraiser can then determine the contributory value, if any, of any improvements. Seen in this light, the highest and best use of property as improved is a special case that requires market evidence to support the assumption that the property can be appraised with land and improvements combined.

3. When the highest and best use of the land as though vacant is different from that of the property as currently improved, demolition may be considered as one alternative. At this time the costs of demolition are addressed as well as the costs of curing any environmental problems—e.g., the removal of underground storage tanks, the abatement of asbestos, the replacement of transformers containing PCBs.

Historic district zoning controls and historic easements (deed restrictions) have made demolition permits difficult, if not impossible, to obtain in some areas. Furthermore, special tax incentives for older buildings can substantially enhance their value and alter the highest and best use of the property in certain cases.

In some cases an appraiser may conclude that the highest and best use of a parcel is to hold the land for investment purposes—i.e., to remain vacant or to be employed in some interim use until development is justified by market demand. This frequently occurs when there is external obsolescence present in the market—e.g., when real estate markets are temporarily oversupplied, extremely high financing costs impair development, a major plant in the area closes or a major environmental disaster occurs during early phases of redevelopment projects, or other, similar situations. For many parcels of land, achieving the highest and best use requires some change in zoning or an improvement in roads or other infrastructure needed to accommodate the new use. The highest and best use of land as though vacant may call for its subdivision into smaller parcels of land or its assemblage with other land.

The Ideal Improvement

If a building improvement is determined to be the highest and best use of the vacant land, the appraiser must determine and describe the type and characteristics of the ideal improvement to be constructed. The appraiser compares any existing improvements on the site with the ideal improvement and the differences are analyzed to determine the depreciation suffered by the existing improvements. The ideal improvement should meet the following criteria:

- Takes maximum advantage of the site's potential given market demand
- Conforms to current market standards and the character of the market area
- Contains the most suitably priced components

If a new improvement is considered to be the highest and best use of the land as though vacant, it presumably will have no physical deterioration or functional obsolescence—i.e., it would be neither an underimprovement nor an overimprovement. Thus, any difference in value between the existing improvement and the ideal improvement would be attributable to these forms of depreciation. The appraiser must still consider external obsolescence, which may affect both the existing improvement and the ideal improvement.

The conclusion of highest and best use for a parcel of land should be as specific as the marketplace suggests. General categories such as "an office building," "a commercial building," or "a single-family residence" may be adequate in some situations, but in others the particular use demanded by market participants must be specified, such as "a suburban office building with 10 or more floors" or "a three-bedroom single-family residence with at least 2,500-sq.-ft."

> The **conclusion** of the highest and best use analysis of a site as though vacant should be as specific as the market suggests.

Test of Legal Permissibility of Land as though Vacant

In all instances the appraiser must determine which uses are legally permissible. Private restrictions, zoning, building codes, historic district controls, and environmental regulations must be investigated because they may preclude many potential uses. Frequently the appraiser must consider whether there is a reasonable probability that the zoning could be changed in order for the highest and best use of the property to be realized.

The test of legal permissibility helps the appraiser determine which uses are permitted by current zoning, which uses could be permitted if a zoning change were granted, and which uses are restricted by private restrictions on the site. Private restrictions, deed restrictions, and long-term leases relate to the covenants under which some properties are acquired. These restrictions may prohibit certain uses or specify building setbacks, heights, and types of

PROBABILITY OF A ZONING CHANGE

In investigating the reasonable probability of a zoning change, the appraiser must consider trends in the market area and the history of zoning requests in the area as well as documents such as a community's comprehensive or master plan. Uses that are not compatible with the existing land uses in the area (such as a gas station in the middle of an exclusive single-family residential subdivision) and uses for which zoning changes have been requested but denied in the past (such as an industrial use where several industrial zoning changes have been turned down in the past two years) can usually be eliminated from consideration as potential highest and best uses. On the other hand, a zoning change from residential to commercial may be reasonable if other properties in the market area have received a similar zoning change recently or if a community's comprehensive plan designates the property for a use other than its current use. For example, consider a site zoned single-family residential in a transitional neighborhood where the zoning on several similar sites has been changed recently to commercial. Also, the city's comprehensive plan designates the property as a future commercial corridor. Both of these factors may support an appraiser's conclusion that there is a reasonable probability of rezoning the subject site for commercial use.

Additional evidence of the possibility of new zoning includes land assemblage, removal of structures, and new construction in an area. This evidence may be supported by zoning change applications, zoning hearings, actions by municipalities, and interviews with planning and zoning officials. Even if there is no current market evidence of a zoning change, documented interviews with officials and discussion of zoning practices and histories can be helpful in evaluating the possibility of a zoning change.

In preparing a land development forecast for an area, the appraiser must fully disclose all pertinent factors relating to a possible zoning change, including the time and expense involved and the risk that the change will not be granted. The appraiser should consider the time and expense of obtaining a zoning change in estimating the land value of the property. Consider a site that would be worth $125,000 if the zoning were changed to commercial. The appraiser realizes that the cost of obtaining a zoning change will be $10,000 and that it would take about six months to achieve the zoning change. Thus the appraiser should make a $10,000 downward adjustment to account for the cost of obtaining the zoning change and consider whether any discounting is necessary to reflect the six months it will take to achieve the zoning change.

The probability of a zoning change may not be 100% certain, and the challenge is to determine whether market participants will pay a premium in anticipation of a potential zoning change and to document the conclusion. Many sales never close because they are subject to rezoning that could not be obtained.

materials. If deed restrictions conflict with zoning laws or building codes, the more restrictive guidelines usually prevail. A long-term lease may affect the highest and best use because lease provisions may limit use over the remaining term of the lease. For example, if a property is subject to a land lease that has 12 years to run, it may not be economically feasible for the tenant to construct and move to a new building with a longer remaining economic life. In such a case, the appraisal report should state that the determination of highest and best use as leased is influenced by the lease's impact on future utility over the remaining lease term.

Successful application of the legal permissibility test to a site as though vacant relies on analysis of zoning laws. If there are no private restrictions, the uses allowed by the zoning laws prevail. However, if the zoning is not appropriate for the subject site, or if a more appropriate highest and best use could be obtained with a zoning change, then the possibility of a change in zoning should be considered.

In addition to analyzing zoning and private restrictions, testing the legal permissibility of a land use also requires the appraisers to investigate, other applicable codes and ordinances, including building codes, historical district ordinances, and environmental regulations. All of these codes and ordinances can have an impact on the way a site is developed and can limit how a site can be developed.

Building codes can prevent land from being developed to what would otherwise be its highest and best use by imposing burdensome restrictions that increase the cost of construction. For example, the additional cost of a water retention pond with excess capacity that is required by local ordinance could impact the size of a proposed community shopping center. Less restrictive codes typically result in lower development costs, which attract developers; more restrictive codes tend to discourage development. In some areas, more restrictive building codes are used to slow new construction and limit growth. Historical ordinances, such as historic facade easements, and overlay districts may be so restrictive that they preclude development.

Concerns over the long-range effects of certain land uses sometimes result in increased environmental regulation and stricter development controls. Appraisers must be familiar with environmental regulations pertaining to clean air, clean water, and wetlands, and they should be sensitive to the public's reaction to proposed development projects. When resistance from local residents and the general public (known as NIMBY, i.e., "not in my back yard") occurs, it can pressure city officials to stop or limit certain real estate developments or change the density or character of a specific plan.

As with zoning ordinances, if there are any limitations inherent in other applicable codes, ordinances, and regulations, the appraiser should investigate whether there is a reasonable probability of a change relative to the subject property.

POSSIBILITY OF ASSEMBLAGE

Certain parcels can achieve their highest and best use only as a part of an assemblage. In such a case, the appraiser must either determine the feasibility and probability of assembly or make the highest and best use determination and other appraisal decisions on the assumption that such an assembly would be made. For example, a large petrochemical plant may be constructed on a site that has been created by assembling several smaller tracts. The individual tracts may not have had the potential for such a large-scale industrial use separately and, therefore, may have had much lower unit values for alternative uses.

If the appraiser concludes that the highest and best use can be achieved through an assemblage, the costs and timing of achieving the assemblage must be taken into consideration. In the example of the petrochemical plant, assembling the site might take more than two years. Although the assemblage would allow the smaller parcels to accommodate the plant, the time delay may be too long for the developer of the petrochemical plant. The appraiser must also recognize that frequently a higher-than-market price might have to be paid to assemble a tract of land, particularly for properties acquired near the end of the assemblage period. These costs must be reflected in the resulting land value estimate and in the appraiser's conclusions as to the reasonable probability of assemblage.

Test of Physical Possibility of Land as though Vacant

The test of physical possibility addresses the physical characteristics associated with the site that might affect its highest and best use. The size, shape, terrain, and accessibility of land and the risk of natural disasters such as floods or earthquakes affect the uses to which land can be put. The utility of a parcel may also depend on its frontage and depth. Irregularly shaped parcels can cost more to develop and, after development, may have less utility than regularly shaped parcels of the same size.

Ease of access enhances the utility of a site. The capacity and availability of public utilities are also important considerations. If a sewer main located in front of a property cannot be tapped because of a lack of capacity at the sewage disposal plant, the property's use might be limited. When topography or subsoil conditions make development difficult or costly, the land's utility may be adversely affected. If the cost of grading or constructing a foundation on the subject site is higher than is typical for sites in the area competing for the same use, the subject site may be economically infeasible for the highest and best use that would otherwise be indicated.

Test of Financial Feasibility of Land as though Vacant

In determining which uses are legally permissible and physically possible, an appraiser eliminates some uses from consideration. Only those uses that meet the first two criteria are analyzed further. As long as a potential use has value commensurate with its cost and conforms to the first two tests, the use is financially feasible.

If the physically possible and legally permissible uses are income-producing, the analysis of financial feasibility will often focus on which potential uses are likely to produce an income (or return) equal to or greater than the amount needed to satisfy operating expenses, financial obligations,

> To test **financial feasibility and maximum productivity,** the respective values under alternative uses are developed by analyzing data such as land value, the rate of return and risk associated with the use, and capitalized overall property value.

and capital amortization of the investment. To determine the financial feasibility, the appraiser estimates the future gross income that can be expected from each use. Vacancy and collection losses and operating expenses are then subtracted from each gross income to obtain the likely net operating income (*NOI*) from each use. A rate of return on the invested capital can then be calculated for each use. If the net revenue capable of being generated from a use is sufficient to satisfy the required market rate of return on the investment, the use is said to be financially feasible.

If the uses are not income-producing, the analysis will determine which are likely to create a value or result in a profit equal to or greater than the amount needed to develop and market the property under those uses. Analyses of supply and demand and of location are needed to identify those uses that are financially feasible and, ultimately, the use that is maximally productive. To determine the financial feasibility of a use that will not generate income, the appraiser compares the value benefits that accrue from the use against the expenses involved. If the value benefits exceed the costs, the use is considered feasible. If the value benefits fall below the costs or exceed costs by only a marginal amount, the use may not be financially feasible.

Successful application of the financial feasibility test to land as though vacant relies on interpretation of relevant and credible market evidence collected and analyzed in the market area and in the subject property's competitive market. Risk is an important consideration and must be weighed along with other feasibility factors. Any external obsolescence related to a specific use should be incorporated into the test of financial feasibility.

Test of Maximum Productivity of Land as though Vacant

The test of maximum productivity is applied to the uses that have passed the first three tests. Additional analysis of the market forces of supply and demand may aid in the process of elimination. The test addresses not only the value created under the maximally productive use but also the costs to achieve the value, if any, such as demolition and removal of structures, environmental remediations costs, and zoning changes. Of the financially feasible uses, the highest and best use is the use that produces the highest residual land value consistent with the market's acceptance of risk and with the rate of return warranted by the market for that use. To determine the highest and best use of land as though vacant, rates of return that reflect the associated risks are often used to capitalize income from different uses into their respective values. The use that produces the highest residual land value is the highest and best use.

The residual land value (R_L) can be found by estimating the value of the proposed use (land and improvements) and subtracting the cost of the labor, capital, and entrepreneurial coordination expended to create the improvements. Alternatively, the land value can be estimated by capitalizing the residual

> **residual:** The quantity left over; in appraising, a term used to describe the result of an appraisal procedure in which known components of value are accounted for, thus solving for the quantity that is left over, such as land residual or building residual.

income to the land. The land income that is capitalized into value is the residual income remaining after operating expenses and the return attributable to the improvements have been deducted from the income to the total property.[4] In testing alternate uses with the land residual technique, any differences in the residual income attributable to the land are magnified by the process of capitalization, so the appraiser should take special care in considering the assumptions of highest and best use. While not usually a persuasive indication of land value on its own, the land residual technique is useful in highest and best use analysis because the relative residual land values of alternate uses can be compared to determine the use that yields the highest value. (The land residual technique and other types of residual techniques are discussed further in Chapter 22.)

The potential highest and best use of the land is usually a long-term land use that is expected to remain on the site for the normal life of the improvements. Normal life expectancy depends on building type, quality of construction, and other factors. The stream of benefits (income and amenities) produced by the buildings reflects a carefully considered, and usually very specific, land use program.

Highest and Best Use of Property as Improved

Highest and best use of a property as improved pertains to the use that should be made of an improved property in light of the existing improvements and the ideal improvement described at the conclusion of the analysis of highest and best use as though vacant. The highest and best use of a property as improved may be continuation of the existing use. In such a case, the appraiser need not analyze expenditures or rates of return for alternative uses except to test or support the conclusion of highest and best use. However, the highest and best use of a property as improved may involve renovation or rehabilitation, expansion, adaptation or conversion to another use, partial or total

> The **highest and best use of a property as improved** may be continuation of the existing use, renovation or rehabilitation, expansion, adaptation or conversion to another use, partial or total demolition, or some combination of these alternatives.

---

4.   According to traditional economic theory, income attributable to the three other agents of production (labor, capital, and entrepreneurial coordination) is paid, and then the remaining income—i.e., the *residual*—is attributable to the land.

demolition, or some combination of these alternatives. If no capital expenditures are required to effect the necessary changes to the existing improvements, estimated returns can be compared directly. If capital expenditures are required, however, rates of return for each potential use must be calculated, considering the total investment in the property and all capital expenditures. These rates of return can then be compared with rates of return for other similar types of investments to determine whether the potential uses are financially feasible. Alternatively, the appraiser may compare all costs of acquisition and capital improvements with other competing properties in the same market.

In analyzing the highest and best use of owner-occupied properties, appraisers must consider any rehabilitation or modernization that is consistent with market preferences. For example, the highest and best use of a luxury residence should reflect all rehabilitation that would be required for maximum enjoyment of the property. The rehabilitation program should ensure the maximum profit upon future sale of the property in order to be deemed economically feasible. For a leased property, rehabilitation should focus on maximizing profit (rental income) or value to the owner-landlord.

Test of Legal Permissibility of Property as Improved

In the analysis of the highest and best use of the property as improved, the test of legal permissibility addresses whether the subject property conforms with existing legal requirements and how that compliance or noncompliance affects the property's value. The appraiser reviews many of the same public and private restrictions that were examined in testing the legal permissibility of the land as though vacant. However, for the highest and best use of the property as improved, the analysis shifts from a survey of potential uses to an evaluation of the existing improvements.

Often, although not always, the results of this test are implicit—i.e., the existing use is legally permissible because it conforms with all of the codes, ordinances, and restrictions reviewed by the appraiser. In this situation, the appraiser may conclude that the existing use is legally permissible and that no alternative uses are legally permissible, and then proceed with the test of physical possibility. In other instances, an appraiser may determine that the existing improvements are nonconforming—i.e., do not conform to some aspect of the codes, ordinances, and private restrictions that affect that property. For nonconforming properties or properties with improvements that differ significantly from the ideal improvement, the appraiser must determine whether the codes, ordinances, or private restrictions allow modification of the improvements that would bring them into conformity. This may involve the same type of analysis of a reasonable probability of change as is conducted in the application of this test to the highest and best use of the land as though vacant. Again, the appraiser should report any evidence supporting a reasonable probability that a change could be made to bring the improvements into conformity with a particular code, ordinance, or restriction. Such evidence could include trends in the market area, historical changes to codes or ordinances in the area, and a community's master plan. The appraiser should incorporate the costs of obtaining the changes and the time necessary to achieve the changes into the value estimate of the subject property as improved.

The appraiser also should investigate how rigorously the city or private organization (such as a homeowner's association) enforces its codes, ordinances, and restrictions and the impact of enforcement on value. For example, an existing single-family residence on land zoned for commercial use obviously does not conform to zoning restrictions. However, if the community is not enforcing its codes and ordinances with respect to such a residential use and the property is not a recognized legally nonconforming use, the appraiser might conclude that the nonconforming use has no negative impact on the value of the property. (Legally nonconforming uses, which are a special situation in highest and best use analysis, are discussed later in this chapter.)

Test of Physical Possibility of Property as Improved

Testing the physical possibility of highest and best use as improved addresses the physical and functional problems associated with physical characteristics such as size, location, design, and condition and how these factors affect the highest and best use of the improved property. The test usually reveals the major items of physical and functional depreciation and whether or not they are curable.

An existing improvement that is substantially larger than the ideal improvement might represent an overimprovement in a particular market, while an existing improvement that is substantially smaller than the ideal improvement might represent an underimprovement. Depreciation may be present in both situations, but, depending on the specific facts associated with the property and its market, one may be curable whereas the other is incurable.

The location of an improvement can have a substantial impact on the highest and best use of the property as improved. For example, consider a building that requires substantial rehabilitation to achieve its highest and best use. If the property shares party walls on both sides, its location could effectively prohibit rehabilitation. Likewise, the interior and exterior design of a building may or may not be adaptable to change, making any related depreciation either curable or incurable. Also, the physical condition of the existing improvements will have a significant effect on the value of the property as well as its highest and best use. The appraiser should be able to separate physical deterioration into the deferred maintenance, incurable short-lived, and incurable long-lived categories.

Almost all the factors analyzed in testing the physical possibility of the property as improved have some form of cost associated with them, particularly if some form of physical change is necessary to achieve the highest and best use. The costs (including a provision for profit) of curing physical deterioration or functional obsolescence, redesigning a building, or converting the existing improvements into an alternative use must be analyzed in light of the value created in the market; the effect of the changes on value is more important than simply how much the costs will be. If the changes will not be profitable, the expenditures would not be made—a point that the appraiser would be wise to incorporate into the highest and best use analysis.

As in the application of the test of legal permissibility, the results of the test of physical possibility are often implicit—i.e., the existing use is obviously physically possible, and no significant physical modifications need to be considered because of the condition, functional utility, and maintenance associated with the improvement. In these situations, the appraiser would conclude that continuation of the existing use meets the physical possibility test and proceed on to the test of financial feasibility.

Test of Financial Feasibility of Property as Improved

The test of financial feasibility of the property as improved addresses the market demand for the subject property in its current state. If the existing use creates a positive return on the investment, that use is financially feasible.

The test of financial feasibility relies on the conclusions of the three approaches to value as well as the land value estimate. If the value of the propery as improved exceeds the value of the land as though vacant, the appraiser could reasonably conclude that continuation of the existing use is financially feasible. However, certain actions such as curing deferred mainte-nance or rewriting a below-market lease may still increase the value of the property and should be considered. These factors are usually addressed in the test of maximum productivity.

Test of Maximum Productivity of Property as Improved

Often the appraiser concludes that continuation of the existing use is legally permissible, physically possible, and financially feasible. However, in any of the first three tests, the appraiser may have determined that some actions should be taken, and corresponding costs should be incurred, to make the subject property more valuable. These factors are considered in the test of maximum productivity.

In one of the first three tests of the highest and best use of the property as improved, the appraiser may have concluded that the property owner should fix deferred maintenance or a curable functional problem. In this case, as part of the test of maximum productivity the appraiser compares the costs of curing the deferred maintenance or the functional problem to the resulting value. If the changes to the property result in a higher value or if they preserve the existing value, then those expenditures would contribute to the maximally productive use and that should be stated in the highest and best use conclusion. Other factors that may have to be analyzed in a similar manner include conversion costs, rehabilitation or remodeling costs, and, in the extreme, demolition and removal costs.

Successful completion of the test of maximum productivity should allow the appraiser to specify exactly what expenditures, if any, would allow the subject property to achieve its highest and best use. These expenditures should be reflected in the conclusion of the highest and best use of the property as improved as well as in the application of each approach to value.

Reporting Highest and Best Use Conclusions

All appraisal reports should contain statements that describe the appraiser's analyses and conclusions pertaining to the highest and best use of the land as though vacant or of the property as improved. Both must be addressed in market value assignments that include a separate site valuation. As a general rule, the highest and best use statement should summarize the discussion that precedes it and follow the sequence of the four tests. A logically structured review of the four tests forms the foundation for the opinion of value. Certain conditions of an appraisal assignment may alter the information that should appear in the appraisal report regarding highest and best use, as illustrated in Table 12.1.

Highest and best use analysis often incorporates techniques and data from the application of all three approaches to value. Table 12.2 illustrates where in the appraisal report supporting documentation is found for the reported conclusions of each test of highest and best use. In many appraisal assignments, the final tests of financial feasibility and maximum productivity require information that is obtained from the application and development of the approaches. Therefore, even though the discussion of highest and best use traditionally precedes the approaches to value in narrative appraisal reports, the conclusion of highest and best use often can be finalized only after a preliminary analysis of alternative land uses has been performed. The conclusions reported in the highest and best use section of a report should be consistent with conclusions in the other parts of the report.

Special Situations in Highest and Best Use Analysis

In identifying and testing highest and best use, special considerations are required to address the following situations:

- Single uses
- Legally nonconforming uses
- Interim uses (including land held for investment purposes)
- Uses that are not the highest and best uses
- Multiple uses
- Special-purpose uses

Table 12.1   Highest and Best Use Statements in Appraisal Reports

If ...

The goal of the analysis is to identify the highest and best use among two or more potential uses **or** the highest and best use conclusion is the primary objective of a consulting assignment.

Then the report should include...

The results of "testing" alternatives (e.g., income and rent calculations for income-producing properties and/or the different value opinions derived for each alternative use) and the reasoning employed.

If...

The highest and best use of an improved property is different from its existing use.

Then the report should include...

Justification for this conclusion in a market value appraisal report.

If...

A separate estimate of land value **is** presented in the appraisal.

Then the report should include...

Discussion of the highest and best use of the land as though vacant as well as the highest and best use of the property as improved.*

If...

A separate estimate of land value **is not** presented, **and** continued use of the property as improved is an appropriate limiting condition of the appraisal.

Then the report should include...

Discussion of only the highest and best use of the property as improved, although discussion of the highest and best use of the land as though vacant is usually included anyway, even when it is not required. In such cases—which are generally use value situations—the existing improvements may not represent the highest and best use of the land, but they are expected to continue in use and thus add value to the land. If an opinion of market value is needed, such a limiting condition is probably not appropriate. The rationale for applying such a limiting condition needs to be thought through carefully.

If ...

The highest and best use of the land as though vacant and highest and best use of the property as improved are different.

Then the report should include...

Identification of each highest and best use separately with the statement that the highest and best use of the land as though vacant was determined under the theoretical presumption that the land is vacant and available for development and the statement that the highest and best use of the property as improved was determined based on the continued economic viability of the property in its current state.

If ...

The land is already improved to the highest and best use.

Then the report should include...

Separate statements on highest and best use and a statement that the determination is the same for both the land as though vacant and the property as improved or a statement that the land is improved to its highest and best use. The identification of the highest and best use of the land as though vacant and of the property as improved can be combined, but better appraisal reporting entails distinct statements of each. There are different reasons for analyzing both and separate thought processes for each analysis.

---

*   Standards Rules 1-3(b) and 1-4(b)(i) of USPAP, which are specific guidelines rather than binding requirements, advise appraisers in developing a real property appraisal to "recognize that land is appraised as though vacant and available for development to its highest and best use, and that the appraisal of improvements is based on their actual contribution to the site;" and to "develop an opinion of site value by an appropriate appraisal method or technique."

Table 12.2	**Location of Supporting Documentation**	
	———————— Section of Appraisal Report ————————	
Test	**Site as Though Vacant**	**Property as Improved**
Legal permissibility	• Zoning and other restrictions	• Zoning and other restrictions
Physical possibility	• Market area data • Site data	• Improvement data
Financial feasibility (Demand and supply) (Value and profit/return)	• Region • City • Neighborhood • Subject's market area	• Region • City • Neighborhood • Subject's market area
Maximum productivity	• Land valuation	• Cost approach • Sales comparison approach • Income capitalization approach

Single Uses

The highest and best uses of land as though vacant and property as improved are often consistent with surrounding uses. For example, a single-family residential use is usually not appropriate in an industrial district. However, a property's

> Single uses, interim uses, legally noncon-forming uses, uses that are not the highest and best use, multiple uses, and special-purpose uses all require **special consideration.**

highest and best use may be unusual or even unique. For example, market demand may be adequate to support one large, multistory office building in a community, but it may not support more than one. A special-purpose property such as a museum may be unique and highly beneficial to its site, but it might not be supported by surrounding land uses or comparable properties. Land value should be based on the highest and best use of the property, regardless of its most likely use as suggested by surrounding land uses and comparable properties. However, regardless of what improvement is on a site, the highest and best use of the land as though vacant should be the one that meets all four tests. Therefore, the ideal improvement might be significantly different than the existing improvements, and the highest and best use of the land as though vacant of a single-use property might be to develop it differently than it is currently developed.

If an existing single-use property is being appraised, some level of market analysis should be performed to determine whether the single use should be continued or discontinued. If the analysis reveals that the single use should be discontinued, the appraiser should then ask what, if anything, should be done with the improvement? If the improvement does not contribute to value and the assignment involves an opinion of market value, then the highest and best use would probably be something other than maintaining the existing use. (An entirely different conclusion relative to highest and best use as improved would result if use value were being determined rather than market value.) For a proposed single-use property, the market should be carefully analyzed to determine whether another single use of the same type already exists.

Legally Nonconforming Uses

A legally nonconforming use is a use that was lawfully established and maintained but no longer conforms to the land use regulations of the zone in which it is located. Some legal nonconformities can be created by governmental action such as a partial taking in an eminent domain proceeding. Consider a gas station property with 20,000 square feet of land, which is the minimum amount of land area required by zoning for gas station use. If the city acquired 1,000 square feet of the land for an intersection improvement, the site would then contain 19,000 square feet and would no longer conform to the zoning requirements for site size. Other legally nonconforming use situations can be created when codes and ordinances are changed. For example, a single-family residence on a 7,500-sq.-ft. site in the core residential district of a community zoned R-1 requires at least 7,500 square feet of land area. If the city adopts a new zoning ordinance in which the minimum site size for a lot zoned R-1 is increased to 10,000 square feet, the existing property will no longer conform. In both instances the nonconforming use situations are considered *legal* nonconformances because they were caused by an action of a governmental body. Most zoning ordinances have special sections that deal with nonconforming use situation; appraisers must be familiar with these sections when appraising legally nonconforming uses.

> **legally nonconforming use:** A use that was lawfully established and maintained, but no longer conforms to the use regulations of the current zoning in the zone where it is located; also known as a *grandfathered use.*

Zoning changes may create underimproved or overimproved properties. A single-family residence located in an area that is subsequently zoned for commercial use may be an underimproved property. In this case, the residence will most likely be removed so that the site can be improved to its highest and best use, or the house will be considered an interim use until conversion to commercial use is financially feasible. A legally nonconforming property can become overimproved when zoning changes reduce the permitted intensity of property use. For example, the site of an older apartment building with eight units in a fully built-up neighborhood might be downzoned to a less intense use. That is if the vacant site were developed now, the new zoning restrictions would only allow six units to be built. Nonconforming uses may also result from changes in the permitted density of development and changes in development standards that affect features such as landscaping, parking, setbacks, and access.

Zoning ordinances vary with the jurisdiction. They usually permit a preexisting, or grandfathered, use to continue but prohibit expansion or major alterations that support the nonconforming use. Some jurisdictions specify a time period for phasing out legally nonconforming uses. When a nonconforming use is discontinued, it usually cannot be reestablished. In most jurisdictions, a nonconforming use must be eliminated if the property suffers major damage or if the property is abandoned for a statutory period of time. In some instances, a nonconforming use can be rebuilt to the same intesnity of use that it had prior to its destruction, provided it has no more impact on the market area than it did before.

> **downzoning:** A public action in which the local government reduces the allowable density for subsequent development, e.g., fewer housing units, fewer stores, or changes the allowable use from a more intensive use to a less intensive use, e.g., multifamily to single-family.

When valuing land with a legally nonconforming use, an appraiser must recognize that the current use may be producing more income, and thus have more value, than the property could produce with a conforming use.[5] The legally nonconforming use may also produce more income and have a higher value than comparable properties that conform to the zoning. Therefore, when the value of the legally nonconforming use of the property is developed by comparing similar, competitive properties to the subject in the sales comparison approach, the appraiser should consider the higher intensity of use allowed for the subject property and also consider the risks and limitations associated with the nonconformity. In the case of the eight-unit apartment building in an area downzoned to six-unit developments, for example, the appraiser will have to determine whether sales of properties with six units are appropriate comparables, in applying the sales comparison approach.

Legally nonconforming uses that correspond to the highest and best use of the property as improved are often easy to recognize. Sometimes, however, it is not clear whether an existing nonconforming use is the site's highest and best use. The question can only be answered by careful analysis of the income and/or selling price produced by the nonconforming use and the incomes and/or selling prices that would be produced by alternative uses if the property were brought into conformity with existing regulations.

Interim Uses

The use to which a site or improved property is put until it is ready for its future highest and best use is called an *interim use*. Thus, interim use is a

---

5. In most nonconforming use situations, the opinion of market value reflects the nonconforming use. Land value, however, is based on the legally permissible use, assuming that the land is vacant. Some practitioners believe the difference between the final opinion of market value of a nonconforming use and the land value reflects the contribution of the existing improvements and possibly a bonus for the nonconformance. In this scenario, the appraiser separates the value of the nonconforming improvements and the bonus created by the nonconforming use. Alternatively, some practitioners believe that the value added in a downzoning should not be attributed solely to the improvement but should be allocated between the improvement and the land. This is commonly accomplished by applying a ratio to the overall property value that reflects typical ratios of the contributions of land and improvements to value in similar market properties not affected by downzoning.

interim use: The temporary use to which a site or improved property is put until it is ready to be put to its future highest and best use.

current highest and best use that is likely to change in a relatively short time—say, five to seven years. Farms, parking lots, golf courses, old buildings, and temporary buildings may be interim uses. Mining and quarry operations may be considered special cases of interim uses that usually continue until depletion of the resource. Mobile home parks were once considered an ideal interim highest and best use; more recently, mobile home park owners have found it difficult and expensive to accomplish a change in use.

The appraiser must identify the interim uses of the property being appraised and all comparable properties. Differences in the interim uses of comparable properties must be taken into account even though their future highest and best uses are identical. Differences in the prices paid may be due to different return requirements and different anticipated demolition costs.

An interim use may or may not contribute to the value of the land or the improved property. If an old building or other use cannot produce gross revenues that exceed reasonable operating expenses, it does not contribute to property value. If the net return of the improvements is less than the amount that could be earned by the vacant land, the buildings do not have contributory value (although in some markets, property owners may prefer to retain a single-family dwelling on commercial land in transition rather than leave the land vacant). Indeed, the value of an improved property may be less than the value of the land as though vacant when demolition costs are considered. The value of the land is based entirely on its potential highest and best use.

The principle of consistent use, which holds that land cannot be valued based on one use while improvements are valued based on another, must be considered when properties are devoted to temporary, interim uses. The use value of a site under an interim use may differ substantially from the market value of the same site as though vacant and available for development under its long-term highest and best use. Many outmoded improvements clearly do not resemble the ideal improvement, but they do create increments of value over the value of the vacant land. These improvements may appear to violate the principle of consistent use, but in fact the market simply acknowledges that, during the transition to a new use, the value contributed by old improvements to an improved property make the land and the existing improvements worth more than the vacant land.

Land that is held primarily for future sale, with or without an interim use, may be regarded as a speculative investment.[6] The purchaser or owner may believe that the value of the land will increase, but there is a risk that the

---

6. In general usage, the term *speculative investment* can carry pejorative implications of high risk or uncertainty. In the language of real estate appraisal, *speculation* is defined as the purchase or sale of property motivated by the expectation of realizing a profit from a rise or fall in its price.

expected appreciation will not occur while the investor holds the land. Nevertheless, the current value of the land is a function of its future highest and best use, so the appraiser should discuss its potential highest and best use. The appraiser may not be able to predict the exact future highest and best use, but the general type of future use (e.g., as a shopping center or industrial park) is often known or anticipated by the zoning, surrounding land-use patterns, or a comprehensive city plan. Because there may be several types of potential highest and best use (e.g., single-family or multifamily residential developments), appraisers usually cannot identify a specific future highest and best use; they can, however, discuss logical alternative uses and anticipated income and expense levels.

Use That Is Not the Highest and Best Use

According to the concept of consistent use, an improvement must be valued based on a use that is consistent with the property's highest and best use. However, many existing buildings and other improvements are inconsistent with the ideal improvement for their sites and are developed differently than they would be if the land were vacant. Nevertheless, the highest and best use may be in the same category as the existing use. For example, the highest and best use of a site improved with a 10-year-old apartment building may be for a new, more functional apartment building. Similarly, the highest and best use of a residential site improved with a 20-year-old house may be for a new, more modern single-family residence.

For certain sites the general category of highest and best use may have changed—e.g., from apartment to industrial use or from single-family residential to commercial use. If the improvements on these sites existed prior to the change in the market area, they suffer from external obsolescence and are likely to have less value than similar improvements on more appropriate sites. It would be incorrect to value such an improvement as if it were located on an appropriate site.

Multiple Uses

Highest and best use often includes more than one use for a parcel of land or an improved property. A large tract of land might be suitable for a planned unit

> **multiple use:** A combination of compatible land uses in an area or in a single building.

development with a shopping center in front, condominium units around a golf course, and single-family residential sites on the remainder of the land. Business parks often have sites for retail stores in front and warehouse or light manufacturing structures in the rear.

One parcel of land may serve many functions. Timberland or pastureland may also be used for hunting, recreation, and mineral exploration. Land that serves as a right of way for power lines can double as open space or a park. Public streets with railroad siding are also considered multiple-use land.

A single building can have multiple uses as well. A hotel may include a restaurant, a bar, and retail shops in addition to its guest rooms. A multistory building may contain offices, apartments, and retail stores. A "single-family," owner-occupied home may have an apartment upstairs.

If the highest and best use of a property is for more than one use on the same parcel or in the same building, the appraiser must estimate the contributory value of each use. If, for example, the market value of a timber tract that can be leased for hunting is compared on a unit basis with the value of another timber tract that cannot, the difference should be the value of the hunting rights; in the opinion of market value, the appraiser would have to account for both the value of the hunting rights and the value of the timber operation on the site. In oil-producing areas, appraisers are often asked to segregate the value of mineral rights from the value of other land uses; properties with mineral rights value can be compared with properties that do not have such rights. In multiple-use assignments, the sum of the values of the separate uses may be less than, equal to, or greater than the value of the total property.

Special-Purpose Uses

Because special-purpose properties are appropriate for only one use or for a very limited number of uses, appraisers may encounter practical problems in specifying highest and best use. The highest and best use of a special-purpose property as improved is probably the continuation of its current use if that use remains viable. For example, the highest and best use of a plant currently used for heavy manufacturing is probably continued use for heavy manufacturing, and the highest and best use of a grain elevator is probably continued use as a grain elevator. If the current use of a special-purpose property is physically, functionally, or economically obsolete and no alternative uses are feasible, the highest and best use of the land may be realized by demolishing the structure and selling the remains for their scrap or salvage value.

Sometimes a special-purpose property must be analyzed and appraised on the basis of two highest and best uses—i.e., continuation of the existing, special-purpose use and conversion to an alternative use. In such a situation, the highest and best use conclusion depends largely on how the market is defined. For example, a house of worship may first be analyzed based on its highest and best use as a place of worship. In this analysis, the contributory value of the improvements would be supported by cost, sales, or income data. If market demand exists, the members of a congregation may be willing to purchase the subject property at a value that reflects its present use as a house of worship. If the market demand for such buildings is low or nonexistent, however, the appraiser may also project a highest and best use as conversion to commercial office space or some other appropriate alternative use. The estimated value of the improvements for conversion to the alternative use would probably be derived from a detailed cost study or from sales data on houses of worship converted to commercial uses. The market value (and the potential users) of the property converted to a commercial use would probably differ from its market value (and potential users) as a house of worship. Thus, the highest and best use of a special-purpose property, such as a house of worship, depends on the amount of market demand for such space.

FURTHER READING

Finch, J. Howard. "Highest and Best Use and the Special-Purpose Property." *The Appraisal Journal* (April 1996).

Galleshaw, Mark. "Evaluating Interim Uses." *The Appraisal Journal* (January 1994).

Graaskamp, James A. *A Guide to Feasibility Analysis.* Chicago: Society of Real Estate Appraisers, 1970.

Greer, Gaylon E. *The Real Estate Investment Decision.* Lexington, Mass.: D. C. Heath, 1979.

Harrison, Frank E. *Appraising the Tough Ones: Creative Ways to Value Complex Residential Properties.* Chicago: Appraisal Institute, 1996.

Lennhoff, David C. "Highest and Best User." *The Appraisal Journal* (July 1995).

Love, Terrence L., Sr. "The Appraiser's Role in Zoning Litigation." *The Appraisal Journal* (July 1998).

North, Lincoln W. *The Concept of Highest and Best Use.* Winnipeg, Manitoba: Appraisal Institute of Canada, 1981.

Seldin, Maury, and James H. Boykin. *Real Estate Analyses.* Homewood, Ill.: American Society of Real Estate Counselors and Dow Jones-Irwin, 1990.

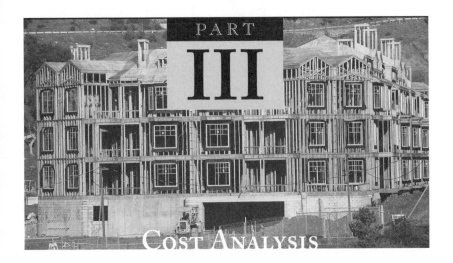

PART

III

COST ANALYSIS

Part III is concerned with the cost approach, which encompasses the valuation of land and the development of an indication of value for the improvements along with an estimate of any depreciation those improvements may suffer. **Chapter 13, Land or Site Valuation,** explores the various techniques used to develop a reliable opinion of land value, either as an end in itself or as part of the valuation of a property as a whole. **Chapter 14, The Cost Approach,** explains how the cost of developing land and improvements serves as a measure of value and the appraisal principles that support this approach to value. In addition, the chapter outlines the procedure for estimating cost, paying special attention to the differences between reproduction and replacement cost. In **Chapter 15, Building Cost Estimates,** the various methods of estimating building costs are explained and illustrated using a warehouse property as an example. Also discussed are techniques for estimating the reward an entrepreneur receives for coordinating the development of a property and incurring the risk associated with the project. **Chapter 16, Depreciation Estimates,** explains the difficult task of determining how physical deterioration and functional and external obsolescence affect the estimated cost of improvements.

13   Land or Site Valuation

Land has value because it provides potential utility as the site of a structure, recreational facility, agricultural tract, or right of way for transportation routes. If land has utility for a specific use and there is demand for that use, the land has value to a particular category of users. Beyond the basic utility of land, however, there are many principles and factors that must be considered in land valuation. Although it is sometimes considered the simplest of appraisal tasks, the valuation of land requires analysis of a complex variety of factors and in practice can be the most difficult of appraisal procedures.

Relation to Appraisal Principles

Value Concepts and Principles

Anticipation, change, supply and demand, substitution, and balance are appraisal principles that influence land value. Anticipation means that value is created by the expectation of benefits to be derived in the future. If buyers anticipate that raw land in a certain location will be in demand for office use within the next five years, they may be motivated to acquire land for future development even though the development of office space is not presently tenable. The competition among the buyers who make up the market for such sites creates a price level for the land that may have little to do with its current use. In such circumstances, the highest and best use of the sites could be an interim use while the land is held for future office development.

The supply of land is relatively stable. Although vast changes have occurred in the earth's surface over the ages and slight modifications in the supply and quality of land may occur over a lifetime, these natural events rarely affect the land that appraisers are concerned with. There are, however, a few notable exceptions to the permanence of land, such as the accretion or erosion of land along a shoreline, the pollution of land with harmful wastes, the exhaustion of agricultural land through improper farming methods, and the transformation of arable land into desert due to ecological imbalances. Earthquakes may change the surface of the earth and faults beneath the surface can create vast sinkholes, and old underground mines can cause subsidence. Fortunately, these occurrences are rare.

Land value is substantially affected by the interplay of supply and demand, but it is the economic use of a parcel of land that determines its value in a particular market. For example, the price that a developer can afford to pay for a warehouse site is determined by the net income that the warehouse will earn and the cost of constructing it. Intense competition for choice lots or for the last remaining lots in a particular location can cause prospective owners or owner-occupants to pay more for a particular parcel of land than is indicated by the broad spectrum of market activity and the highest and best use of the land. No object, including real property, can have value unless scarcity is coupled with utility.

The principle of substitution, which holds that a buyer will not pay more for one parcel of land than for an equivalent parcel, applies to land values. Substitution indicates that the greatest demand will be generated for the lowest-priced land with similar utility. The principle of balance is also applicable to land values. When the various elements of a particular economic mix or a specific environment are in a state of equilibrium, land value is sustained; when the balance is upset, values change. If, for example, a district has too much industrially zoned land, the value of industrial land will probably fall or remain the same over a period of time.

Property Rights and Public Controls

The appraisal of land focuses on valuing the physical component and the accompanying property rights. These rights may include the right to

- Develope the land within certain limits
- Lease the land to others
- Farm the land
- Mine the land
- Alter the land's topography
- Subdividing the land
- Assemble the lot with other lots
- Hold the land for future use
- Construct or alter building improvements

Whenever possible, an appraiser should consult title reports, public records, or available survey information to identify easements, rights of way, and private or public restrictions that affect the subject property.

In an effort to encourage planned growth and compatibility among different land uses, governments regulate how land can be used. Most municipalities and counties have some form of zoning regulations that specify how a parcel of land can be developed. In addition to zoning, many jurisdictions now have master plans or comprehensive plans that specify long-term development goals. Frequently, developers must have amenities such as open space, streets, and off-site public improvements in place or dedicated before a proposed development receives approval from the appropriate public agency. Usually developers will proceed with development only after they have submitted detailed development plans and obtained building department approval. In many areas, citizen groups will protest a development they do not like, and their objections frequently influence the type of development that is finally approved.

Through the power of eminent domain, the government can acquire land from the private sector to be used for public projects and augment the supply of public land. This is accomplished through urban renewal programs that return the land to the private sector in the form of publicly financed redevelopment projects. In some rural jurisdictions, land use is influenced by government-sponsored transferable development rights (TDRs), which compensate farmers for retaining land in agricultural use and shift the benefit of those development rights to other locations. Lower ad valorem taxes on agricultural land also affect rural land use; this form of tax subsidy tends to extend the duration of agricultural uses.

A relatively recent trend in the United States has been the acquisition of land for open space or conservation easements that are held in perpetuity by qualified agencies. These permanent encumbrances limit or prohibit the development potential of land. The use of land subject to perpetual open space or conservation easements is usually restricted, as specified in the deed of easement. These deeds are vested in preservation or conservation trusts. Another way to preserve open space is through donation of specified easement rights to a qualified recipient such as a land trust.

Water, mineral, and air rights can be important in the appraiser's consideration of property rights.[1] Water rights cover the flow of water, usually for stated times and in stated quantities, for irrigation and hydroelectric power generation. Water rights also can take the form of riparian rights which, under common law, grant a landowner the ownership of waters that share a border with his or her land. In certain areas of the country, these rights are critical to real estate valuation. The valuation of mineral rights requires specialized research, but appraisers should be aware if mineral rights are excluded from land ownership. Mineral rights cover the underground portion of the land and usually refer to the right to extract underground minerals or to use underground caverns or reefs for storage. Real estate developments established on air rights, usually over railways, can be found in older urban areas, particularly where density is high and less land is available for new construction.

Physical Characteristics and Site Improvements

The physical characteristics of land, the utilities available, and site improvements affect land use and value. The physical characteristics of a parcel of land that an appraiser must consider include size, shape, frontage, topography, location, view, and topographical characteristics such as contour, grade, and drainage. The availability of water, sewers, electricity, natural gas, and telephone service also influences the use and development potential of a parcel of land. (See Chapter 9.)

---

1.   See also Appendix G of American Society of Farm Managers and Rural Appraisers and
     Appraisal Institute, *The Appraisal of Rural Property*, 2d ed. (Denver and Chicago, 2000).

off-site improvements: Improvements such as streets, sidewalks, curbing, traffic signals, and water and sewer mains; typically considered with site value.

on-site improvements: Improvements such as grading, landscaping, paving, and utility hookups; subject to physical deterioration and functional obsolescence; are always required for development of a structure on a site.

A parcel of land becomes a site when it is improved and ready to be used for a specific purpose. A site may have both on-site and off-site improvements that make it suitable for its intended use or for new construction. Off-site improvements are typically considered with land value and are included in the market value for the site; only rarely are they valued with other property improvements. Like buildings and other structures, on-site improvements are subject to physical deterioration and functional obsolescence.

Highest and Best Use

Land value must always be considered in terms of highest and best use. Even if the land has improvements, the land value is based on its highest and best use as though vacant and available for development to its most economic use. Consideration of the land as though vacant is a commonly accepted procedure that facilitates the orderly analysis and solution of appraisal problems that require land to be valued separately. The comparability of competitive sites is based on the highest and best use of potential comparable sites on the date of sale. Regardless of how physically similar a potential comparable sale is to the subject site, if the comparable site does not have the same highest and best use as though vacant as the subject, the transaction does not qualify as a comparable sale and should be dismissed from further consideration in the analysis of the subject property.

Highest and best use is also affected by how much the existing improvements contribute to property value. Land value may be equal to, or even greater than, total property value, even when substantial improvements are located on the site. The contribution of the improvements is estimated by subtracting the market value of the land from the market value of the total property. When improvements do not contribute to the overall property value, demolition is usually appropriate. Exceptions to this are found when an improvement has a historic designation and demolition is prohibited. The cost of converting the property into vacant land may be a penalty and deducted from the value of the land. However, to achieve the highest and best use of the land with another use, the cost to raze the improvements is added to the land value to reflect the value of the land as though vacant. In some cases the cost of converting the property into vacant land is a penalty to be deducted from the value of the land.

In some circumstances the appraisal of a property may require that the land be considered in terms of a use other than its highest and best use. In an appraisal to develop an opinion of the use value or legal, nonconforming use value of an improved site, an appraiser may need to value the land according to its specified use or the existing improvements, not its highest and best use. In this case the appraiser should value the land both in terms of its highest and best use and its conditional use.

Applicability and Limitations

The land value analysis in an appraisal report can appear as a separate stand-alone section or as a subsection of the cost approach. Typically land value analysis is a separate section when the property being appraised is vacant land or an agricultural property with minimal improvements. In the model of the valuation process described in Chapter 4, land value is a separate analysis, performed before the application of the three approaches to value. This placement emphasizes the importance of land value in developing the highest and best use analysis and in assignments conducted primarily to derive a valuation of underlying land in its present use as the primary appraisal problem. Occasionally a property is appraised without a separate land value conclusion such as in the valuation of a condominium interest.

The sales comparison approach is usually the preferred methodology for developing a land value conclusion. When this approach is used, most of the techniques described in Chapter 17, with respect to selecting market sales and the adjustment process, can be applied to land valuation. When sales of similar parcels of land are not plentiful enough for the application of sales comparison, alternative techniques such as extraction, allocation, and various income capitalization techniques may be used. The income capitalization techniques can be divided into direct capitalization techniques (e.g., land residual and ground rent capitalization) and yield capitalization techniques (e.g., discounted cash flow analysis/subdivision development analysis). All these land valuation

An appraiser begins the **valuation of a parcel of land** by identifying the real estate and property rights to be valued, any encumbrances on those property rights (e.g., easements, rights of way, use restrictions in deeds or zoning ordinances), the land's physical characteristics, and the available utilities and site improvements. Comparable data on similar parcels is collected and the highest and best use of the subject site is analyzed.

sales comparison approach: A set of procedures in which a value indication is derived by comparing the property being appraised to similar properties that have been sold recently, applying appropriate units of comparison, and making adjustments to the sale prices of the comparables based on the elements of comparison. The sales comparison approach may be used to value improved properties, vacant land, or land being considered as though vacant; it is the most common and preferred method of land valuation when an adequate supply of comparable sales are available.

extraction: A method of estimating land value in which the depreciated cost of the improvements on the improved property is estimated and deducted from the total sale price to arrive at an estimated sale price for the land; most effective when the improvements contribute little to the total sale price of the property.

allocation: A method of estimating land value in which sales of improved properties are analyzed to establish a typical ratio of land value to total property value and this ratio is applied to the property being appraised or the comparable sale being analyzed.

Table 13.1	Applicability and Limitations of Land Valuation Techniques

Sales Comparison

Procedure	Sales of similar, vacant parcels are analyzed, compared, and adjusted to provide a value indication for the land being appraised.
Applicability	Sales comparison is the most common technique for valuing land, and it is the preferred method when comparable sales are available.
Limitations	A lack of sales and the comparability of the available data may weaken the support for the value estimate.

Extraction

Procedure	An estimate of the depreciated cost of the improvements is deducted from the total sale price of the property to arrive at the land value.
Applicability	This technique is applicable when
	• The building's contribution to total property value is generally small and relatively easy to identify. (The technique is frequently used in rural areas.)
Limitations	The appraiser must be able to determine the value contribution of the improvements, estimated at their depreciated cost.

Allocation

Procedure	A ratio of land value to property value is extracted from comparable sales and applied to the sale price of the subject property to arrive at the land value.
Applicability	This technique is applicable when
	• The number of vacant land sales is inadequate.
	• A check for reasonableness is needed rather than a formal opinion of land value.
Limitations	The allocation method does not produce conclusive value indications and is rarely used as the primary land valuation technique. Also, land-to-property value ratios can be difficult to support.

Income Capitalization Techniques

Direct Capitalization: Land Residual Technique

Procedure	The net operating income attributable to the land is capitalized at a market-derived land capitalization rate to provide an estimate of value.
Applicability	This technique is *only* applicable in testing the feasibility of alternative uses of a particular site in highest and best use analysis or when land sales are not available.
Limitations	The technique is generally recognized by the courts as too speculative to yield a reliable indication of land value.* The following conditions must be met:
	1. Building value is known or can be accurately estimated.
	2. Net operating income to the property is known or can be estimated.
	3. Both building and land capitalization rates are available from the market.

Direct Capitalization: Ground Rent Capitalization

Procedure	A market-derived capitalization rate is applied to the ground rent of the subject.
Applicability	This method is useful when
	• Comparable rents, rates, and factors can be developed from an analysis of sales of leased land.
Limitations	An adjustment to the value indication for property rights may be necessary when current rent under the existing contract does not match market rent.

Table 13.1	**Applicability and Limitations of Land Valuation Techniques** *(continued)*
Yield Capitalization: Discounted Cash Flow Analysis—Subdivision Development Analysis	
Procedure	Direct and indirect costs and entrepreneurial profit are deducted from an estimate of the anticipated gross sales price of the finished lots, and the net sales proceeds are discounted to present value at a market-derived rate over the development and absorption period.
Applicability	This technique is applicable when • Vacant land that has the potential for development as a subdivision represents the likely highest and best use of the land.
Limitations	Discounted cash flow analysis requires significant amounts of data on development sales and costs for the developed lots.

Note: Certain states do not recognize subdivision development analysis as a valid valuation technique for litigation valuation or other purposes.

* J. D. Eaton, *Real Estate Valuation in Litigation*, 2d ed. (Chicago: Appraisal Institute, 1995), 106.

procedures, which are summarized in Table 13.1, are derived from the three traditional approaches to value.

Sales Comparison

The sales comparison approach may be used to value land that is actually vacant or land that is being considered as though vacant for appraisal purposes. Sales comparison is the most common technique for valuing land and it is the preferred method when comparable sales are available. To apply this method, data on sales of similar parcels of land is collected, analyzed, compared, and adjusted to provide a value indication for the land being appraised. In the comparison process, the similarity or dissimilarity of the parcels is considered.

> **Sales comparison** is the most commonly used and preferred method of valuing land. Data on sales of similar parcels of land is collected, analyzed, compared, and adjusted to reflect the similarity or dissimilarity of those parcels to the site of the subject property.

The appraiser must perform several tasks in developing an opinion of land value:

• Gather data on actual sales as well as listings, offers, and options.
• Identify the similarities and differences in the data.
• Identify the highest and best use of each potential comparable sale.
• Identify units of comparison that explain market behavior.
• Adjust the sale prices of the comparables to account for the dissimilar characteristics of the land being appraised.
• Form a conclusion as to the market value of the subject land.

The goal of the sales comparison approach is to select the most comparable market sales and then adjust for differences that cannot be eliminated within the selection process. Elements of comparison include property rights, financing terms, conditions of sale (motivation), expenditures immediately after purchase, market conditions (sale date), location, physical characteristics, available utilities, and zoning. The physical characteristics of a parcel of land include its size, shape, frontage, topography, location, and view. (For a detailed discussion of elements of comparison, see Chapter 18.) Unit prices may be expressed as price per square foot, front foot, acre, lot, dwelling unit, or other unit used in the market.

If sale prices have been changing rapidly over the past several years and an adequate amount of sales data is available, the sales selected for comparison should take place as close to the effective appraisal date as possible. When current data on local sales is not available, the appraiser may need to expand the search to another market area, which usually calls for an adjustment for location, or extend the search back in time in the same market area, which usually calls for an adjustment for market conditions. The decision to use sales from another market area or older sales should be based on which adjustment has more support, the location adjustment or the market conditions adjustment.

Among generally similar sales, size is often a less important element of comparison than date and location. Most types of land use have an optimal site size; if the site is too large, the value of the excess land tends to decline at an accelerating rate. Because sales of different sizes may have different unit prices, appraisers ordinarily give more weight to comparables that are approximately the same size as the subject property.

Zoning is often the most basic criterion in selecting comparables. Sites zoned the same as the subject property generally have the same or a similar highest and best use and are the most appropriate comparables. If sufficient sales in the same zoning category are not available, data from similar zoning categories can be used and adjustments may be necessary. As a general rule, the greater the difference between the subject and the comparables, the more potential there is for distortion and error in sales comparison.

In addition to recorded sales and signed contracts, appraisers should consider offers to sell and offers to purchase. Offers provide less reliable data than signed contracts and completed sales. Usually the final sale price is lower than the initial offer to sell but higher than the initial offer to buy. Negotiations can take place in several stages.

Data on land sales is available from sources such as electronically transmitted and printed data services, newspapers, and deed and assessment records. Interviews with the parties involved in transactions—i.e., the buyers, sellers, lawyers, and brokers—can provide more direct information and may reveal adjustments that should be made for conditions of sales

adjustments: Mathematical changes made to basic data to facilitate comparison or understanding. When dollar adjustments are used, individual differences between comparables and the subject property are expressed in terms of positive or negative dollar amounts; when percentage adjustments are made, individual differences are reflected in positive or negative percentage differentials.

and/or sales concessions. After comparable data is collected and categorized and the comparable properties are examined and described, sales data can be assembled in an organized, logical manner. Sales are commonly arranged in a market data grid that has separate rows (or columns) for important property characteristics. Appropriately developed adjustments for significant differences between the subject property and the comparable properties may be made to the sale or unit prices of the comparables using a variety of techniques. (Techniques for making adjustments in sales comparison analysis are discussed in Chapter 18.[2])

Generally, separate adjustments are made to the comparable sale prices for each element of comparison. The magnitude of each adjustment is indicated by the data and the judgment of the appraisers. Land parcels of different sizes sell at different unit prices because the optimal size of a parcel depends on its use. Unit prices also vary with the date of sale and location. If the data selected is not sufficient to indicate the magnitude of the adjustments required, the appraiser should gather and analyze additional comparable data.

A sale price adjustment may be simply an acknowledgment of a property's superiority or inferiority; alternatively, it may be a precise dollar amount or percentage developed from market evidence. Adjustments can also be totaled and factored into the comparable sale prices as part of the initial data gathering process. Typically, adjustments are made in a particular order—i.e., adjustments for property rights, financing, and sale and market conditions are made before adjustments for location and physical characteristics. All adjustments should be presented in the appraisal report in a logical and understandable manner.

Alternative Techniques

Vacant parcels of land in densely developed urban locations may be so rare that their values cannot be estimated reliably by direct comparison. Similarly, sales of vacant parcels of land in remote areas may occur so seldom that sufficient comparable data is not available. In such cases land value can be estimated by extraction, allocation, or one of the income capitalization techniques.

Extraction

Extraction is a technique in which land value is extracted from the sale price of an improved property by deducting the value contribution of the improvements, estimated at their depreciated cost. The

> To apply the **extraction method,** an estimate of the depreciated cost of the improvement(s)—i.e., contributory improvement value—is deducted from the total sale price of the property to arrive at the land value. Extraction is used to estimate the land value of improved properties in rural areas and properties in which the improvements contribute little to total property value.

2. See also James H. Boykin, *Land Valuation Adjustment Procedures and Assignments* (Chicago: Appraisal Institute, 2001).

remaining value represents the value of the land. Improved sales in rural areas are frequently analyzed in this way because the building and site improvements have a minimal contributory value in comparison to the underlying land value. The improvement contribution is typically small and relatively easy to identify.

For example, assume an appraiser is estimating the value of the land under an aging, deteriorated automobile service garage that was recently sold for $575,000. No vacant lots have been sold in the market area recently. The appraiser estimates the cost of the improvement at $200,000 and total depreciation at 80%, indicating that the depreciated cost of the improvement is $40,000. Deducting $40,000 from the $575,000 sale price, the appraiser obtains a residual land value indication of $535,000 by the extraction technique.

Allocation

The allocation method is based on the principle of balance and the related concept of contribution. Both affirm that there is a normal or typical ratio of land value to property value for specific categories of real estate in specific locations. Meaningful support for an allocation ratio may be derived from a variety of sources:

- Mass appraisals prepared by assessors
- Observed patterns over time in an area
- Consultation with developers who sell improved properties and can allocate sale prices between the land and the improvements based on their costs

The **allocation method** is based on typical ratios of land value to improvement value for specific categories of real estate in specific locations. Allocation is useful when transactional data on comparable sites in the immediate area is not available. The typical land value can be inferred by the price range of improved properties in the immediate area if an appropriate allocation ratio can be established in the community for a specific property type.

The allocation method does not produce conclusive value indications, but it can be used to establish land value when the number of vacant land sales is inadequate.

For example, the appraiser could use allocation to value the site for a new single-family home in a large, newly developed subdivision where few sales of vacant land have occurred but data from several recent sales of improved properties is available. The sale prices of new homes in the development range from $275,000 to $315,000, and land values range from 15% to 20% of sale prices. Based on these figures, land values may range from $41,250 to $63,000.

Because of the relatively large number of sales needed to support the analysis, allocation is rarely used as the primary method of land valuation. Its most common application is in subdivision lot sales analysis, where the appraiser can assume a fairly uniform ratio of lot value to total property value. The technique is not used often for commercial properties because of the wide ranges of parcel size and intensity of use, particularly in industrial properties. Parcels with excess land are also difficult to value using allocation.

Income Capitalization Procedures

The various income capitalization procedures used to estimate land values rely on information that is often difficult for an appraiser to obtain (e.g., reliable land and building capitalization rates for the land residual technique), so these techniques are generally not used as primary valuation techniques except in special situations such as subdivision development analysis.

Direct Capitalization: Land Residual Technique

Historically, the land residual technique was used to estimate land value when sales data on similar parcels of vacant land was not available. Techniques like extraction and allocation have superseded the land residual technique in land valuation because the other techniques rely on fewer variables subject to an appraiser's judgment and expertise and thus are more persuasive. In current practice, the land residual technique is used almost exclusively in highest and best use analysis to test the productivity of alternate uses of the land as though vacant (see Chapter 12).

The land residual technique requires more data than any other valuation technique. The following conditions must be met:

1. Building value is known or can be accurately estimated. (Chapter 15 discusses procedures for estimating building costs.)
2. Net operating income to the property is known or can be estimated. (Chapter 21 discusses the development of income and expense estimates.)
3. Both building and land capitalization rates can be extracted from the market. (Chapter 22 discusses the extraction of land and building capitalization rates.)

Small variations in any of these variables can result in a dramatic change in land value.

To apply the land residual technique, an appraiser first determines what actual or hypothetical improvements represent the highest and best use of the land as though vacant. Then the net operating income (*NOI*) of the property is estimated from market rents and operating expenses as of the date of the appraisal. Next, the appraiser calculates how much of the income is attributable to the building and subtracts this amount from the total net operating income. The remainder is the residual income to the land, which is capitalized at a market-derived land capitalization rate to provide an estimate of land value.

> **land residual technique:** A method of estimating land value in which the net operating income attributable to the land is isolated and capitalized to produce an indication of the land's contribution to the total property.

Direct Capitalization: Ground Rent Capitalization

Ground rent is the amount paid for the right to use and occupy the land according to the terms of the ground lease. It can be used in estimating the value of the landowner's interest in the land, i.e., the leased fee interest. Market-derived capitalization rates are used to convert ground rent into market value.

The ground rent capitalization procedure is useful when an analysis of comparable sales of leased land indicates a range of rents and capitalization rates. If the current rent corresponds to market rent, the value indication obtained will be equivalent to the market value of the fee simple interest in the land. If the ground rent paid under the terms of the existing contract does not correspond to market rent, the value estimate given the current ground rent must be adjusted for the difference in property rights (i.e., the leased fee interest versus the fee simple interest) to obtain an indication of the market value of the fee simple interest.

> Market-derived **capitalization rates** are used to convert ground rent into an indication of land value.

> **ground rent capitalization:** A method of estimating land value that is applicable when the ground rent corresponds to the owner's interest in the land, the leased fee interest; applied by capitalizing ground rent at a market-derived rate. This method is useful when comparable rents, rates, and factors can be developed from an analysis of sales of leased land.

Ground leases can have different terms and escalation clauses, so the appraiser should consider all the benefits to the lessor during the term of the lease and any option periods and determine when the reversion of the property will take place.

If information on sales of comparable sites subject to land leases is unavailable, the appraiser can investigate sales of comparable plots of land that are not leased. Analysis of these transactions may yield an estimate of the rate of return an investor expects from comparable sites—i.e., a market-derived capitalization rate that can be applied to the ground rent of the subject property.

Yield Capitalization: Discounted Cash Flow Analysis (Subdivision Development Analysis)

Discounted cash flow analysis is used to value vacant land that has the potential for development as a subdivision when that use represents the likely highest and best use of the land at the time of the appraisal.[3] Valuing lots in a subdivision is a common assignment for real estate appraisers, but subdivision development analysis is a complex procedure. When used on its own without an abundance of reliable market data, it can be the least accurate raw land valuation technique. The technique is most useful for reporting the bulk sale value of a proposed subdivi-

---

3. For further discussion, see Douglas D. Lovell and Robert S. Martin, *Subdivision Analysis* (Chicago: Appraisal Institute, 1993).

sion, and the value indication is most persuasive when the sales comparison method provides additional support. To use discounted cash flow analysis to estimate raw land value, the appraiser must thoroughly understand the land development process and all the factors influencing the subject property's market area.

> **subdivision development analysis:** A method of estimating land value when subdivision and development are the highest and best use of the parcel of land being appraised. Direct and indirect costs and entrepreneurial profit are deducted from an estimate of the anticipated gross sales price of the finished lots and, the resultant net sales proceeds are then discounted to present value at a market-derived rate over the development and absorption period to indicate the value of the raw land.

The development of any project extends over a construction stage and a marketing stage. Data on development sales and costs for the developed lots must be available. The developer usually provides the necessary information, including the subdivision plat; the costs of development; a feasibility, marketability, and/or absorption study; and a schedule of prices. When the developer supplies this information, the appraiser has a responsibility to compare that information with other data in the market to determine whether it is appropriate or not.

Subdivision development analysis may involve tracts of residential, commercial, or industrial land (or mixes of land uses) that are large enough to be subdivided into smaller lots or parcels and sold to builders or end users. A planned subdivision can create a higher, better, and more intense use of the property when zoning, available utilities, access, and other influential elements are favorably combined.

To estimate raw land value with subdivision development analysis an appraiser is required to

- Accurately determine the highest and best use of the land
- Create or affirm a supportable subdivision development plan
- Determine the timing and cost for approval and development (including mitigation needs and costs of obtaining development entitlements)
- Forecast a realistic pricing schedule over time
- Forecast accurately the lot absorption rate and price mix (including properly supported projections of community or market growth over the absorption period)
- Estimate accurately the staging or phasing of land development and related expenses
- Forecast marketing and related holding expenses over the absorption period
- Estimate the annual real estate taxes
- Include overhead and an entrepreneurial profit allowance in the discount rate and/or line item allocation for entrepreneurial profit
- Estimate the appropriate discount rate consistent with the selection of the line item allocation for entrepreneurial profit

In simplified form, an appraiser begins the analysis of a subdivision development by determining the number and size of the lots that can be created from the appraised land physically, legally, and economically. The proposed lots must conform to jurisdictional and zoning requirements with regard to size, frontage, topography, soil quality, and off-site improvements—e.g., water facilities, drainage, sewage, streets, curbs, and gutters. The lots must also meet the demands of the market in which the property is located. Without surveys and engineering studies, an appraiser cannot know exactly how many lots can be created from a particular parcel of land. However, a reasonable estimate of the number of potential lots can often be deduced from zoning information, subdivision ordinances, or, preferably, the number of lots or typical unit density reflected in similar subdivisions. Allowances must also be made for the land needed for streets, green space, water retention facilities, and any common areas.

A preliminary development plan for the hypothetical subdivision of the vacant land being appraised will specify much of the data the appraiser needs:

- Number and size of the lots
- Construction work to be accomplished
- Hard and soft construction costs
- Probable time required to subdivide the land and construct the on-site and off-site infrastructure
- Expenses to be incurred during the marketing period

The appraiser then undertakes a preliminary marketability analysis to assess the supply and demand situation and the probable absorption rate and marketing period needed for the market to absorb the proposed lots. Accurate forecasts of product demand and competitive supply can reduce development risk and are critical to the analysis because the raw land value can vary widely depending on the rate at which lots are absorbed over time.[4] The appraiser estimates the projected retail prices of the lots by applying the sales comparison approach. In some models the appraiser may also estimate the amount of profit a typical developer would require to develop the land or, alternatively, to both develop and market the lots.

> **Subdivision development analysis is applied** when subdivision and development represent the highest and best use of the land and when sales data on finished lots is available. The number and size of the finished lots, their likely sale prices, the length of the development and marketing periods, and the absorption rate are estimated. Gross income and expenses are projected when they are expected to occur. The resulting net sales proceeds are then discounted back to arrive at an indication of land value.

The next step in subdivision development analysis requires the appraiser to project the income and expenses associated with selling the lots over the absorption period. Depending on the project size

4.   Robert W. Owens, "Subdivision Development: Bridging Theory and Practice," *The Appraisal Journal* (July 1998): 274–281.

and sales velocity, annual, semiannual, or quarterly periods are used. The projection periods begin with the property as is and continue until sellout is completed or stabilized occupancy is achieved. For a raw land value conclusion, the net cash flows for each period are discounted back to time zero to arrive at the present value of the net cash flows. (Discounting is discussed in Chapter 23.) The discount rate applied, which is derived from and supported by the market, should reflect the risk involved and appropriate entrepreneurial profit.

The following example illustrates how discounted cash flow analysis is applied in subdivision analysis to estimate raw land value. A 20-acre tract of vacant land is being considered for development as a residential subdivision with 48 lots. It will take six months to plat the subdivision and construct all the infrastructure. After construction is completed, the developer anticipates a two-year marketing period to be conducted in four semiannual phases. The market supports an average retail sale price of $40,000 per lot in the first semiannual marketing period. Average lot prices will increase $2,000 in each succeeding six-month period. Expenses are projected as follows:

- Marketing costs equal to 7% of the retail sale prices.
- Legal and closing costs equal to 2% of the retail sale prices.
- Real estate taxes of $1,300 during the first six-month construction phase for the land as undeveloped and $400 per year for each developed lot in inventory thereafter (calculated for the average number of lots in inventory in each period).
- Average annual project overhead and maintenance of $200 per lot for the average number of lots in inventory during each period (calculated for 48 lots during the first period due to higher overhead costs during construction).
- An annual developer's fee of $40,000 for coordination and supervision.
- Entrepreneurial profit equal to 15% of the gross sale price. (Note that the discount rate is selected in conjunction with the appropriate line item allocation for entrepreneurial profit.)
- Off-site development costs in the first six months of $5,000 per lot, or a total of $240,000 to cover the cost of extending infrastructure such as roads, sidewalks, and utilities to the site.
- On-site construction costs, including all soft costs, of $10,500 per lot, or a total cost of $504,000 (spread over Periods 1, 2, and 4).

The DCF analysis anticipates that sale prices will increase and expenses will reflect the pattern shown in the 30-month projection. A 12% discount rate (or 6% over each six-month period) is based on market conditions and the selection of an appropriate line item profit allocation. The DCF analysis shown in Table 13.2 results in a value conclusion of $470,000 for the parcel of vacant land.

Table 13.2 **DCF Analysis (Subdivision Development Analysis)**

	1	2	3	4	5	Total
Beginning inventory of lots	0	48	36	24	12	
Number of developed lots	48	0	0	0	0	
Number of lots sold	0	12	12	12	12	48
Ending inventory of lots	48	36	24	12	0	0
Cumulative no. of lots sold	0	12	24	36	48	48
Average price per lot	$40,000	$40,000	$42,000	$44,000	$46,000	
Gross lot sales income	0	$480,000	$504,000	$528,000	$552,000	$2,064,000
On-site expenses						
Marketing costs	0	$33,600	$35,280	$36,960	$38,640	$144,480
Legal/closing costs	0	9,600	10,080	10,560	11,040	41,280
Real estate taxes	1,300	8,400	6,000	3,600	1,200	20,500
Overhead/ maintenance	4,800	4,200	3,000	1,800	600	14,400
Coordination/ supervision	20,000	20,000	20,000	20,000	20,000	100,000
Total	$26,100	$75,800	$74,360	$72,920	$71,480	$320,660
Entrepreneurial profit	0	72,000	75,600	79,200	82,800	309,600
Off-site development costs	240,000	0	0	0	0	240,000
On-site development costs	384,000	95,000	0	25,000	0	504,000
Net cash flow	($650,100)	$237,200	$354,040	$350,880	$397,720	$689,740
Present value	($613,302)	$211,107	$297,259	$277,930	$297,200	$470,194
Indication of land value	$470,194					
	$470,000	(rounded)				

The use of subdivision development analysis to value vacant land is most applicable when sales data on vacant tracts of land is inadequate but market data is available on the probable sale prices of developed lots and the demand for such lots. This application of DCF analysis is also useful as a method for checking the reasonableness of value indications derived from other methods applied to estimate the value of vacant land with development potential. Comparing the value indication derived from DCF analysis with a value indication derived from sales comparison allows an appraiser to test the feasibility of a proposed project and solve for the appropriate discount rate and associated line item profit allocation. If the value indication from the DCF analysis is less than the value indication from the sales comparison approach, the appraiser may judge the proposed project to be infeasible.

FURTHER READING

American Society of Farm Managers and Rural Appraisers and Appraisal Institute. *The Appraisal of Rural Property,* 2d ed. Denver and Chicago, 2000.

Bible, Douglas S., and Chengo Hsieh. "Determinants of Vacant Land Values and Implications for Appraisers." *The Appraisal Journal* (July 1999).

Boykin, James H. "Impropriety of Using Dissimilar-size Comparable Land Sales." *The Appraisal Journal* (July 1996).

____. *Land Valuation: Adjustment Procedures and Assignments.* Chicago: Appraisal Institute, 2001.

Entreken, Henry C., Jr. "Analysis of Land Value Under Differing Land Use Restrictions." *The Appraisal Journal* (October 1994).

Lovell, Douglas D., and Robert S. Martin. *Subdivision Analysis.* Chicago: Appraisal Institute, 1993.

Miller, Steven E. "Land Value in a Collapsing Market." *The Appraisal Journal* (January 1994).

14 | THE COST APPROACH

Like the sales comparison and income capitalization approaches, the cost approach to value is based on comparison. In the cost approach, the appraiser compares the cost to develop a new property or a substitute property with the same utility as the subject property. The estimate of development cost is adjusted for differences in the age, condition, and utility of the subject property to generate a value indication by the cost approach. The cost approach reflects market thinking because market participants relate value to cost. Buyers tend to judge the value of an existing structure not only by considering the prices and rents of similar buildings but also by comparing the cost to create a new building with optimal physical condition and functional utility. Moreover, buyers adjust the prices they are willing to pay by estimating the costs to bring an existing structure up to the physical condition and functional utility they desire.

In applying the cost approach, an appraiser estimates the market's perception of the difference between the property improvements being appraised and a newly constructed building with optimal utility. Generally, the cost approach supports two methods for estimating cost and three methods of estimating depreciation. In its classic form, the cost approach produces an opinion of value of the fee simple interest in the real estate at stabilized occupancy, so the total cost must include any costs needed to achieve typical stabilized occupancy. Also, if the purpose of the appraisal is to estimate the value of an interest other than fee simple, an adjustment may be required. For example, a property rights adjustment could be made as a lump-sum adjustment at the end of the cost approach or in the final reconciliation of the approaches to value.

In applying the cost approach, an appraiser must distinguish between two cost bases, which should be used consistently throughout. Typically one of the following cost bases is applied:

> **cost approach:** A set of procedures through which a value indication is derived for the fee simple interest in a property by estimating the current cost to construct a reproduction of, or replacement for, the existing structure plus any profit or incentive; deducting depreciation from the total cost; and adding the estimated land value. Other adjustments may then be made to the indicated fee simple value of the subject property to reflect the value of the property interest being appraised.

> In the **cost approach**, a property is valued based on a comparison with the cost to build a new or substitute property. The cost estimate is adjusted for the depreciation evident in the existing property.

- Reproduction cost
- Replacement cost

The market and physical condition of the appraised property usually suggest whether an exact replica of the subject property (reproduction cost) or a substitute property with similar utility (replacement cost) would be a more suitable comparison.

The appraiser estimates the cost to construct the existing structure and site improvements (including direct costs, indirect costs, and an appropriate entrepreneurial profit or incentive) using one of three traditional techniques:

1. Comparative-unit method
2. Unit-in-place method
3. Quantity survey method

The appraiser then deducts all depreciation in the property improvements from the cost of the new structure as of the effective appraisal date. The amount of depreciation present is determined using one or more of the three fundamental methods:

1. Market extraction method
2. Age-life method
3. Breakdown method

When the value of the land is added to the cost of the improvements less depreciation, the result is an indication of the value of the fee simple interest in the real estate component of the property, assuming stabilization.

This chapter provides an outline of the cost approach and explains the fundamental appraisal concepts that support this approach to value. Chapters 15 and 16 discuss the specifics of cost and depreciation estimates—i.e., the essential techniques applied to render a convincing opinion of value using the cost approach.

Relation to Appraisal Principles
Substitution

The principle of substitution is basic to the cost approach. This principle affirms that a prudent buyer would pay no more for a property than the cost to acquire a similar site and construct improvements of equivalent desirability and utility without undue delay. Older properties can be substituted for the property being appraised, and their value is also measured relative to the value of a new, optimal property. In short, the cost of property improvements on the effective date of the appraisal plus the accompanying land value provides a measure against which prices for similar improved properties may be judged.

Figure 14.1   Classic Cost Approach Analysis

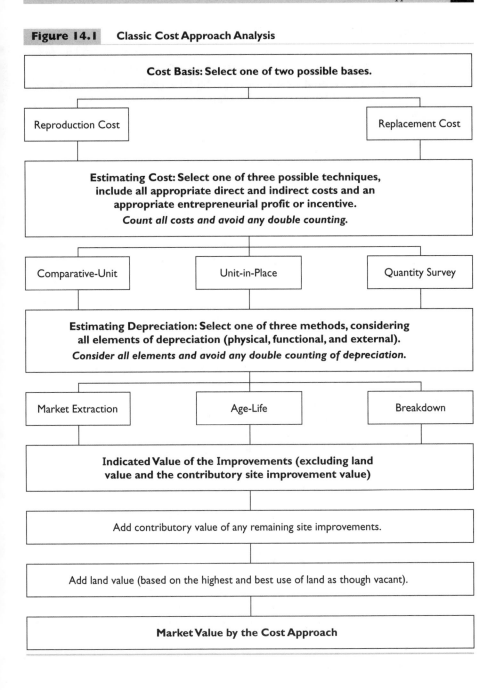

Cost Basis: Select one of two possible bases.

Reproduction Cost

Replacement Cost

Estimating Cost: Select one of three possible techniques, include all appropriate direct and indirect costs and an appropriate entrepreneurial profit or incentive.
Count all costs and avoid any double counting.

Comparative-Unit

Unit-in-Place

Quantity Survey

Estimating Depreciation: Select one of three methods, considering all elements of depreciation (physical, functional, and external).
Consider all elements and avoid any double counting of depreciation.

Market Extraction

Age-Life

Breakdown

Indicated Value of the Improvements (excluding land value and the contributory site improvement value)

Add contributory value of any remaining site improvements.

Add land value (based on the highest and best use of land as though vacant).

Market Value by the Cost Approach

Supply and Demand

Shifts in supply and demand cause prices to increase or decrease. Thus, one property may have different values over time. If costs do not shift in proportion to price changes, the construction of buildings will be more or less profitable and the value of existing buildings will increase or decrease commensurately.

Contribution

The principle of contribution holds that the agents of production and the various property components must be in proper proportion if optimum value is to be achieved or sustained. An improper economic balance may result in an underimprovement or an overimprovement. An underimprovement is created by too little investment in the improvements relative to the value of the site; an overimprovement is created by too much investment. An overimprovement may be a larger building than is needed or a building of typical size with superadequate components.

In the cost approach, the effect on value of a superadequacy or deficiency is addressed in the estimation of depreciation. Any excess or deficiency in the proportionate contributions of the site and the improvements may result in a loss in value relative to their cost. An imbalance in the various components of the improvements may also produce a loss in value. The imbalance can be recognized by comparing the existing improvements with the ideal improvement.

Externalities

The thesis of the cost approach is that the cost of new improvements plus an appropriate entrepreneurial profit or incentive minus depreciation plus the value of the land equals market value. That is:

$$
\begin{array}{l}
\text{Cost} \\
+ \text{ Entrepreneurial Profit or Incentive} \\
- \text{ Depreciation} \\
\underline{+ \text{ Land Value}} \\
\text{Market Value}
\end{array}
$$

The construction cost and market value of a property may be affected differently by externalities. An externality such as inflation may sometimes increase material and labor costs while not affecting market values. On the other hand, completion of a sewer line may increase the value of a property but have no impact on its cost. Gains or losses in value caused by externalities may accrue to both land and buildings. Rising construction costs often can significantly affect the market value of new construction and, in turn, the market value of older, substitute properties.

In the cost approach a loss in building value due to external causes is attributed to external obsolescence, one of the three major types of depreciation. If, for example, an industrial plant that depends on trucks to transport its product is located a great distance from a recently completed highway, the property may suffer from external obsolescence. External conditions can also cause a newly constructed building to be worth more or less than its cost. If properties of a certain type are scarce or it is difficult to construct new competitive properties, the value of a newly constructed building may be higher than its cost. On the other hand, an economic recession might create an oversupply of a particular type of property, which would cause the value of a new property to be less than its cost. Externalities may have an especially strong effect on older properties. Externalities can be temporary and may work in positive and negative directions over the life of a building improvement.

Highest and Best Use

In the first series of tests of highest and best use, land is first valued as though vacant and available to be developed to its highest and best use; the ultimate conclusions of highest and best use analysis are based on the highest and best use of the property as improved. Thus, a parcel of land may have one highest and best use as though vacant, and the existing combination of the site and improvements may have a different highest and best use as improved. Existing improvements have a value equal to the amount they contribute to the site, or they may penalize value, often by an amount equal to the cost to remove them from the site.

If the existing improvements do not develop the site to its highest and best use, the improvements are worth less than their cost. A new building that is poorly designed is worth less than its cost because of the functional obsolescence in its design, which is discussed in more detail later in this chapter. Thus, the improvements that constitute the highest and best use add the greatest value to the site.

Stabilization

The value of a property indicated by the cost approach assumes stabilized occupancy and income, a concept similar to, but distinct from, the balance of the agents of production and property components within the subject property. An appraiser considers the holding costs accrued during the leasing phase of the development of a property among the other indirect costs applicable to that property. The tenant finish costs are also a necessary cost to achieve stabilized occupancy and they must be added as either a direct cost or an indirect cost. Also, a property in a market that is out of balance may be fully occupied and yet may not have reached stabilized income if the effective rental rates for the subject are higher or lower than market rents, which would require an adjustment to the indication of value by the cost approach.

Applicability and Limitations

In any market, the value of a building can be related to its cost. The cost approach is particularly important when a lack of market activity limits the usefulness of the sales comparison approach and when the properties to be appraised—e.g., single-family residences—are not amenable to valuation by the income capitalization approach. Because cost and market value are usually more closely related when properties are new, the cost approach is important in estimating the market value of new or relatively new construction. The approach is especially persuasive when land value is well supported and the improvements are new or suffer only minor depreciation and, therefore, approximate the highest and best use of the land as though vacant. The cost approach can also be applied to older properties given adequate data to measure depreciation.

The cost approach is also used to develop an opinion of market value (or use value, if the appraisal assignment allows for the development of a value other than market value) of proposed construction, special-purpose or specialty properties, and other properties that are not frequently exchanged in the market. Buyers of these properties often measure the price they will pay for an existing building against the cost to build minus depreciation or the cost to purchase an existing structure and make any necessary modifications. If comparable sales are not available, they cannot be analyzed to develop an opinion of the market value of such properties. Therefore, current market indications of depreciated cost or the costs to acquire and refurbish an existing building are the best reflections of market thinking and, thus, of market value (or use value).

When the physical characteristics of comparable properties differ significantly, the relative values of these characteristics can sometimes be identified more precisely with the cost approach than with sales comparison. Because the cost approach starts with the cost to construct a replica or a substitute property with optimal physical and functional utility, it can help an appraiser determine accurate adjustments for physical differences in comparable sale properties. If, for example, an appraiser must make an adjustment for inadequate elevators in a comparable property, the cost to cure the deficiency can be used as a basis for this adjustment. The cost approach provides the appraiser with data to use both in estimating depreciation and in deriving an adjustment to apply in the sales comparison approach.

The cost approach is especially useful when building additions or renovations are being considered. The approach can be used to estimate whether the cost of an improvement, including profit, will be recovered through an increased income stream or in the anticipated sale price; its use can help identify and prevent the construction of overimprovements.

Because the cost approach requires that land and improvements be valued separately, it is also useful in appraisals for

> The cost approach is **most applicable** in valuing new or proposed construction when the improvements represent the highest and best use of the land and land value is well supported.
>
> Depending on the **purpose of the appraisal assignment**, the cost approach can be used to develop an opinion of the market value or use value of special-purpose properties and properties that are not frequently exchanged in the market.

insurance purposes, when noninsurable items must be segregated from insurable items. In appraisals for accounting purposes, the cost approach is applied to estimate depreciation for income taxes. In cases where land value tends to make up a considerable portion of overall property value (such as agricultural properties or high-exposure commercial outparcels), the cost approach can take on greater significance because it is the only approach requiring a separate conclusion of land value.

Finally, an estimate of probable building and development costs is an essential component of feasibility studies, which test the investment assumptions on which land use plans are based. A proposed property is considered financially feasible when market value exceeds total building and development costs plus a reasonable, market-supported entrepreneurial incentive (i.e., the anticipated profit necessary for an entrepreneur to proceed with the project).

The fundamental thesis of the cost approach is that the market value of new construction may be represented by the sum of the land value and the cost of the improvements, each at its highest and best use. The cost approach is commonly thought to set an upper limit of value. The sum of land value and building costs sets a maximum only within the cost approach because of the interaction of mathematical factors within the approach—i.e., the only other variable in the cost approach, besides land value and cost of construction, is depreciation, which has always been treated as a deduction from total cost. Market evidence may reveal a value that is higher than the value indicated by the cost approach, but the cost approach has no internal mechanism to deal with the addition. (Some appraisers do include a market premium in the cost approach when it is indicated, applying the same rationale to the positive adjustment as they do to a negative adjustment.) When a higher value occurs, it is usually measurable only through one or more of the other approaches and is explained in reconciliation.

When improvements are considerably older or do not represent the highest and best use of the land as though vacant, the physical deterioration, functional obsolescence, and external obsolescence of the structure are more difficult to estimate. Furthermore, relevant comparable data may be lacking or the data available may be too diverse to indicate an appropriate estimate of entrepreneurial profit (i.e., the profit actually earned from a completed project).

One of the weaknesses of the cost approach from an investment perspective is the assumption that newly constructed improvements are immediately available on the date of the appraisal. An investor looking at options for an immediate purchase may consider the months or years required to develop and construct a new property to be an undue and unacceptable delay.

Appraisers must remember that the cost approach results in an indication of the value of the fee simple interest in a property. To value real estate held in leased

> The **difficulty of estimating depreciation** in older properties may diminish the reliability of the cost approach in that context.

fee or property subject to other partial interests, appraisers must make adjustments to reflect the specific real property rights being appraised.

Procedure

After gathering all relevant information and analyzing data on the market area, site, and improvements, an appraiser follows a series of steps to derive a value indication by the cost approach. The appraiser will

1. Estimate the value of the land as though vacant and available to be developed to its highest and best use.
2. Determine which cost basis is most applicable to the assignment: reproduction cost or replacement cost.
3. Estimate the direct (hard) and indirect (soft) costs of the improvements as of the effective appraisal date.
4. Estimate an appropriate entrepreneurial profit or incentive from analysis of the market.
5. Add estimated direct costs, indirect costs, and entrepreneurial profit or incentive to arrive at the total cost of the improvements.
6. Estimate the amount of depreciation in the structure and, if necessary, allocate it among the three major categories:
   - Physical deterioration
   - Functional obsolescence
   - External obsolescence
7. Deduct estimated depreciation from the total cost of the improvements to derive an estimate of their depreciated cost.
8. Estimate the contributory value of any site improvements that have not already been considered. (Site improvements are often appraised at their contributory value—i.e., directly on a depreciated-cost basis—but may be included in the overall cost calculated in Step 2.)
9. Add land value to the total depreciated cost of all the improvements to arrive at the indicated value of the property.
10. Adjust the indicated value of the property for any personal property (e.g., furniture, fixtures, and equipment) or any intangible asset value that may be included in the cost estimate. If necessary, this value, which reflects the value of the fee simple interest, may be adjusted for the property interest being appraised to arrive at the indicated value of the specified interest in the property.

Land Value

In the cost approach, the estimated market value of the land is added to the depreciated cost of the improvements. The value of the land depends on its potential highest and best use. Land value can be estimated using various techniques, which are discussed in Chapter 13. Appraisers must remember that the land value estimates produced with these techniques reflect the value of the fee simple interest. If another interest is being appraised, an appropriate adjustment to the indicated value by the cost approach may be necessary.

Reproduction Cost versus Replacement Cost

The cost to construct an improvement on the effective appraisal date may be developed as the estimated reproduction cost or replacement cost of the improvement. The theoretical base (and classic starting point) for the cost approach is reproduction cost, but replacement cost is commonly used because it may be easier to obtain and can reduce the complexity of depreciation analysis. An important distinction must be made between the terms:

- *Reproduction cost* is the estimated cost to construct, as of the effective appraisal date, an exact duplicate or replica of the building being appraised, insofar as possible using the same materials, construction standards, design, layout, and quality of workmanship and embodying all the deficiencies, superadequacies, and obsolescence of the subject building.

- *Replacement cost* is the estimated cost to construct, as of the effective appraisal date, a building with utility equivalent to the building being appraised, using contemporary materials, standards, design, and layout. When this cost basis is used some existing obsolescence in the property is assumed to be cured.

The decision to use reproduction cost or replacement cost is often dictated by the age of the structure, its uniqueness, and any difference between its intended use at the time of construction and its current highest and best use. In theory, the use of reproduction cost or replacement cost should yield the same indication of value, but in practice both cost estimates and depreciation estimates will be different. If reproduction cost or replacement cost is used inconsistently, double counting of items of depreciation and other errors can be introduced. The cost basis selected for a particular appraisal must be clearly identified in the report to avoid misunderstanding and must be consistently applied throughout the cost approach to avoid errors in calculating an estimate of value.

The use of replacement cost can eliminate the need to measure many, but not all, forms of functional obsolescence. Replacement structures usually cost less than identical structures (i.e., reproductions) because they are constructed with materials and techniques that are more readily available and less expensive in the current market and because correcting deficiencies may result in lower costs. Thus a replacement cost figure is usually lower

> Cost may be estimated on **two different bases**—replacement cost or reproduction cost. Specific types of obsolescence would be precluded by a replacement cost estimate.

replacement cost: The estimated cost to construct, at current prices as of the effective appraisal date, a building with utility equivalent to the building being appraised, using modern materials and current standards, design, and layout.

reproduction cost: The estimated cost to construct, at current prices as of the effective date of the appraisal, an exact duplicate or replica of the building being appraised, using the same materials, construction standards, design, layout, and quality of workmanship and embodying all the deficiencies, superadequacies, and obsolescence of the subject building.

and may provide a better indication of the existing structure's contribution to value. A replacement structure typically does not suffer functional obsolescence resulting from superadequacies. However, if functional problems persist in the hypothetical replacement structure, an amount must be deducted from the replacement cost. Estimating replacement cost generally simplifies the procedure for measuring depreciation in components of superadequate construction. Common examples of functional obsolescence include the absence of a desirable feature such as air-conditioning or excessively thick foundations in an existing improvement. Such obsolescence would be corrected in a replacement building.

Estimating reproduction cost may be complicated because the improvements may include materials that are now unavailable and construction standards may have changed. Nevertheless, reproduction cost usually provides a basis for measuring depreciation from all causes when such measurement is necessary.

Cost Estimates

To develop cost estimates for the total building, appraisers must consider direct (hard) and indirect (soft) costs. Both types of cost are essential to a reliable cost estimate. (The traditional data sources and appraisal techniques used to estimate building costs are discussed in Chapter 15.)

Direct construction costs include the costs of material and labor as well as the contractor's profit required to construct the improvement on the effective appraisal date. The overhead and profit of the general contractor and various subcontractors are part of the usual construction contract and, therefore, represent direct costs that should always be included in the cost estimate. In more complex projects, where multiple contractors, construction staging, or other complications are involved, a management fee may be required. Indirect costs are expenditures or allowances that are necessary for construction but are not typically part of the construction contract. Because the entrepreneur provides the inspiration, drive, and coordination necessary to the overall project, the cost approach should include an appropriate entrepreneurial profit or incentive, which will be discussed later in this chapter.

Because the quality of materials and labor greatly influences costs, the appraiser should be familiar with the costs of the materials used in the subject property. A building can cost substantially more than is typical if items such as walls and windows are overinsulated or thicker slabs are used to accommo-

Table 14.1   **Direct Costs and Indirect Costs**

Direct Costs	Indirect Costs
• Building permits	• Architectural and engineering fees for plans, plan checks, surveys to establish building lines and grades, and environmental studies
• Materials, products, and equipment	
• Labor used in construction	
• Equipment used in construction	• Appraisal, consulting, accounting, and legal fees
• Security during construction	
• Contractor's shack and temporary fencing	• The cost of carrying the investment in land and contract payments during construction*
• Material storage facilities	
• Power line installation and utility costs	
• Contractor's profit and overhead, including job supervision; coordination and management (when appropriate); worker's compensation; and fire, liability, and unemployment insurance	• All-risk insurance expense and ad valorem taxes during construction
	• The cost of carrying the investment in the property after construction is complete but before stabilization is achieved
• Performance bonds	• Supplemental capital investment in tenant improvements and leasing commissions
	• Marketing costs, sales commissions, and any applicable holding costs to achieve stabilized occupancy in a normal market
	• Administrative expenses of the developer

* If the property is financed, the points, fees or service charges, and interest on construction loans are indirect costs.

date greater floor loads. Many newer structures contain elements that may not be found in older buildings with which they compete. At one time the market may have considered features such as Internet connectivity, networking and telecommunications capabilities, and adequate, reliable power in "smart" office buildings to be high-tech overimprovements. Such features may not have contributed as much value as they cost then, but as demand for these building materials and features continues to increase so does their contribution to value.

The competitive situation in the local market can also affect cost estimates. Actual contractor bids based on the same set of specifications can vary substantially. A contractor who is working at capacity is inclined to make a high bid, while one who needs the work is likely to submit a lower figure. The items cited in the right-hand column of Table 14.1 reflect typical indirect costs incurred in a balanced market; in markets that are out of balance, higher costs may result from a prolonged absorption period—e.g., additional marketing or carrying costs, tenant improvements, leasing commissions, and administrative expenses. The increase in costs can contribute to external obsolescence.

Some indirect costs, such as architectural fees and property taxes, are generally related to the size and cost of the project; these are often estimated as a percentage of direct costs. Other costs, such as leasing and sales commis-

direct costs: Expenditures for the labor and materials used in the construction of improvements; also called *hard costs*.

indirect costs: Expenditures or allowances for items other than labor and materials that are necessary for construction but are not typically part of the construction contract. Indirect costs may include administrative costs; professional fees; financing costs and the interest paid on construction loans; taxes and the builder's or developer's all-risk insurance during construction; and marketing, sales, and lease-up costs incurred to achieve occupancy or sale. These costs can vary by property type. Also called *soft costs*.

sions, are related to the type of property or market practice. Still others, such as appraisal fees and environmental studies, are a function of the time required to accomplish the task. The indirect costs of carrying an investment during and after construction are a combination of all of the above. Although total indirect costs are sometimes estimated as a percentage of direct costs, more detailed studies of these costs are recommended.

Entrepreneurial Profit and Entrepreneurial Incentive

When the direct and indirect costs of developing a property are used to provide an indication of value, the appraiser must also include an economic reward sufficient to induce an entrepreneur to incur the risk associated with a building project. For a completed project at stabilization, the difference between the sum of direct and indirect costs and the market value of the property is the entrepreneurial profit (or loss) realized:

Market Value
− Total Cost of Development
Entrepreneurial Profit (or Loss)

In other words, to solve for profit the appraiser may compare market value and the value indicated by the cost approach without profit. Whether or not a profit is actually realized depends on how well the entrepreneur has analyzed the market demand for the property, selected the site, and constructed the improvements. In the case of income-producing properties, the profit realized will also depend on the entrepreneur's ability to obtain the proper tenant mix and negotiate leases.

entrepreneurial profit: A market-derived figure that represents the amount an entrepreneur receives for his or her contribution to a project and risk; the difference between the total cost of a property (cost of development) and its market value (property value after completion), which represents the entrepreneur's compensation for the risk and expertise associated with development.

entrepreneurial incentive: A market-derived figure that represents the amount an entrepreneur expects to receive for his or her contribution to a project and risk.

The term *entrepreneurial incentive* represents the amount an entrepreneur expects to receive as compensation for providing coordination and expertise and assuming the risks associated with the development of a project. *Entrepreneurial profit* is the difference between total cost of development and marketing and the market value of a property after completion and achievement of stabilized occupancy and/or income.[1] In essence, incentive is anticipated while profit is earned.

Estimating Entrepreneurial Profit and Entrepreneurial Incentive

As market-derived figures, estimates of entrepreneurial profit and entrepreneurial incentive are only as reliable and precise as the available market data warrants. Nevertheless, most market areas have a typical or appropriate range of profit that can be determined through market research, and the estimate of profit is a necessary component of total cost. The range of profit will vary for different types of structures and with the nature or scale for a given project. For example, the entrepreneurial incentive for a proposed development may be higher where creative concepts, greater risk, or unique opportunities are found to have market acceptance. Less risky, more standard competitive projects may merit a lower measure of profit.

Also, the amount of profit earned can relate to the stage of development and to the different levels of risk and expertise that may be required at different stages. The entrepreneur can start earning a reward from the start of the project. This reward can increase as the land is acquired, plans are drawn up, permits are approved, financing is secured, contracts are doled out, construction is completed, and the units are sold off or leased. It is difficult to estimate exactly how much would be earned at each phase of the project.

> The **estimation of entrepreneurial profit** is problematic, but the estimate is a necessary component of total cost.

Some appraisers observe that in owner-built, owner-occupied properties, entrepreneurial profit often represents an intangible. Entrepreneurial profit is realized only when the property is first sold, even if the sale takes place years after the property was built. Over time, entrepreneurial profit becomes obscured by the appreciation in property value.

Some practitioners point out that the value associated with the amenities of a property may be such that the sale price of the property could significantly exceed the sum of the costs of the land, building, and marketing (e.g., in a seller's market where sale prices are inflated). These appraisers contend that it would be a mistake to attribute the entire difference between the sale price and the total development costs to entrepreneurial profit. Thus, to ensure the reasonableness of the estimate of entrepreneurial profit, an appraiser should carefully examine the source of additional property value over and above the cost of development and the effects of supply and demand for properties of that sort in the subject market area.

---

1. Historically, *entrepreneurial profit* has been the more common term in general usage and serves as a broader term in the discussion of the cost approach. In this text, the term *entrepreneurial incentive*, which is a more recent addition to the appraisal lexicon, is used specifically in reference to a situation that calls for a forecast of the reward an entrepreneur expects to receive at the completion of a real estate development.

The way in which comparable properties have been developed affects the availability of data. Appraisers are sometimes able to calculate entrepreneurial profit from actual cost comparables for speculatively built properties such as condominiums and multifamily developments. In the value estimate of a speculatively built property, entrepreneurial profit represents a return to the entrepreneur for the skills employed and the risks incurred, although this return may differ from the anticipated return. In large-scale developments, however, the issue is complicated because the entrepreneurial profit may not reflect the proportionate contributions of the improved site and the improvement to the overall property value. Developers of tract subdivisions, for example, often realize most of their profit on the value of the houses built on the finished lots, not necessarily the value of the lots.

Data on entrepreneurial profit for custom-built properties may not be available if the property owner who contracted the actual builders was acting as the developer. The prices of upscale, custom-built properties often reflect the attractiveness of these amenity-laden properties as well as the high costs of the materials used. Thus, the breakdown of costs for custom-built properties may not be comparable to the breakdown for speculatively built properties, which further complicates the task of estimating a rate of entrepreneurial profit. Theoretically, however, the value of custom-built properties should also reflect an entrepreneurial profit.

The appraiser must also scrutinize the cost data on which the value estimate is based to determine whether or not an allowance for entrepreneurial profit has already been made. If this is not done, the entrepreneurial profit could be included twice. Data derived from sales of comparable sites often includes a profit for the land developer. Cost-estimating services quote direct costs (e.g., contractor's profit) and indirect costs (e.g., sales costs), but they may or may not

CONTRIBUTIONS OF THE ENTREPRENEUR, DEVELOPER, AND CONTRACTOR

In analyzing the components of reward and compensation received (or anticipated) by an entrepreneur, the appraiser may choose to further distinguish between the concepts of project profit, entrepreneurial profit, developer's profit, and contractor's profit:

- *Project profit* is the total amount of reward for entrepreneurial coordination and risk.
- *Entrepreneurial profit* refers to the portion of project profit attributable to the efforts of the entrepreneur, distinct from the efforts of the developer, if one is present. In projects in which the entrepreneur and the developer are one and the same, the entrepreneurial profit is equivalent to total project profit.
- *Developer's profit* represents compensation for the time, energy, and expertise of an individual other than the original entrepreneur—usually, in large projects, the person responsible for managing the overall development process.
- *Contractor's profit* (including subcontractors' fees) is essentially a portion of the project's overhead and is not usually reflected in the entrepreneurial reward.

The measure of project profit used in cost approach calculations usually includes both a developer's profit and an entrepreneurial profit. The profit a contractor receives is often already reflected in the fee a contractor charges and would therefore be included in the direct costs.

provide estimates of entrepreneurial profit. Because different sources of data reflect costs in different ways, the appraiser should identify where the entrepreneurial profit is considered in the estimate—i.e., whether it is an item already included in the sum of total cost and land value or a stand-alone item added to the sum of total cost and land value.

Depreciation

Depreciation[2] is the difference between the contributory value of an improvement and its cost at the time of appraisal:

> Reproduction or Replacement Cost of Improvement
> − Contributory Value of Improvement
> ───────────────────────────────────
> Depreciation

By estimating the depreciation incurred by an improvement and deducting this estimate from the improvement's reproduction or replacement cost, an appraiser can conclude the depreciated cost of the improvement. This depreciated cost approximates the improvement's contribution to the property's market value as illustrated in Figure 14.2. (Techniques for estimating depreciation are discussed in Chapter 16.)

Depreciation in an improvement can result from three major causes operating separately or in combination:

- Physical deterioration—wear and tear from regular use and the impact of the elements.

- Functional obsolescence—a flaw in the structure, materials, or design that diminishes the function, utility, and value of the improvement.

- External obsolescence—a temporary or permanent impairment of the utility or salability of an improvement or property due to negative influences outside the property. (External obsolescence may result from adverse market conditions. Because of its fixed location, real estate is subject to external influences that usually cannot be controlled by the property owner, landlord, or tenant.)

Figure 14.2   Depreciation's Portion of Cost

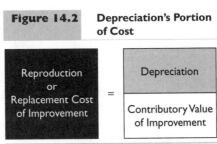

Depreciation is the difference between the market value of an improvement and its reproduction or replacement cost at the time of appraisal. The depreciated cost of the improvement can be considered an indication of the improvement's contribution to the property's market value.

---

2.   Many of the terms appraisers use are also used by accountants, economists, and other real estate professionals. The term *accrued depreciation,* which appeared in previous editions of *The Appraisal of Real Estate,* was originally borrowed from accounting practice. In accounting the term refers to the total depreciation taken on an asset from the time of purchase to the present, which is normally deducted from an asset's account value to derive net book value. While *accrued depreciation* has long been used in an appraisal context, the more concise term *depreciation* is equally suitable and has been used throughout this edition.

depreciation: In appraising, a loss in property value from any cause; the difference between the reproduction or replacement cost of an improvement on the effective date of the appraisal and the market value of the improvement on the same date.

deterioration: Impairment of condition; a cause of depreciation that reflects the loss in value due to wear and tear, disintegration, use in service, and the action of the elements.

obsolescence: One cause of depreciation; an impairment of desirability and usefulness caused by new inventions, changes in design, improved processes for production, or external factors that make a property less desirable and valuable for a continued use; may be either functional or external.

The sum of all these components is total depreciation. The market recognizes the occurrence of depreciation; the appraiser merely interprets how the market perceives the effect of depreciation.

Theoretically, depreciation can begin in the design phase or the moment construction is started, even in a functional building that represents the highest and best use of a site. Improvements are rarely built under ideal circumstances and their construction takes considerable time. During the construction process, physical deterioration can be temporarily halted or even corrected, but physical deterioration tends to persist throughout the life of the improvements. Moreover, as time goes on and a building's features become dated in comparison to new buildings, functional obsolescence sets in. Consider, for example, an industrial building that was built in the early 1970s. The structure's 12-ft. ceilings, which were the market standard then, might be considered totally inadequate now that greater clear heights are the norm. New buildings can have functional obsolescence even before they are constructed, which is usually attributable to poor design.

In the cost approach, the depreciation attributable to all causes is extracted from the market, or calculated when market extraction is not possible, and deducted from the cost to arrive at the depreciated cost:

Total Cost
− Total Depreciation Applicable
———————————————
Depreciated Cost

The depreciated cost of the site improvements and the value of the land are added together to provide an indication of the market value of the property:

Depreciated Cost
+ Land Value
———————————————
Market Value

Depreciation is a penalty only insofar as the market recognizes it as causing a loss in value. For some older buildings, the value loss due to apparent depreciation may be offset by a temporary scarcity relative to demand or by an improvement's historical or architectural significance. In these situations, an appraiser should exercise caution not to penalize a property unduly in the cost approach.

As mentioned earlier, an appraiser's use of reproduction cost rather than replacement cost to derive a current cost estimate will affect the estimation of depreciation. Some forms of functional obsolescence are eliminated when replacement cost is used, but other forms remain unaffected. Consider an industrial building with a poor layout and a 28-ft. story height in a market where 24-ft. story heights are the norm. A replacement cost estimate would be based on a building with a 24-ft. story height, while a reproduction cost estimate would be based on a building with a 28-ft. story height. By using replacement cost instead of reproduction cost, the appraiser eliminates the superadequacy attributable to the story height but not the deficiency caused by the poor layout. Moreover, any additional costs of ownership caused by the superadequacy would not be eliminated in the replacement cost estimate. An appraiser using replacement cost would have to consider any excess operating costs associated with the superadequate construction.

> In the cost approach, the depreciation attributable to all causes is calculated and deducted from total cost to arrive at depreciated cost. Then, an estimate of the value of the land is added to depreciated cost to provide an indication of the **market value** of the property.

DEPRECIATION IN APPRAISING AND ACCOUNTING

The term *depreciation* is used in both accounting and appraisal so it is important to distinguish between the two usages. *Book depreciation* is an accounting term that refers to the amount of capital recapture written off for an asset on the owner's books. The term is typically used in income tax calculations to identify the amount allowed as accruals for the retirement or replacement of an asset under the federal tax laws. Book depreciation may also be estimated using a depreciation schedule set by the Internal Revenue Service. Book depreciation is not market-derived, but depreciation estimates developed by appraisers are. The two concepts are distinct and should not be confused.

FURTHER READING

Akerson, Charles B. *The Appraiser's Workbook.* 2d ed. Chicago: Appraisal Institute, 1996.

Coggin, Dana T. "Let's Not Abandon the Cost Approach." *The Appraisal Journal* (January 1994).

Dannis, Charles G. "Pulling Back the Curtain on Tradition." *The Appraisal Journal* (January 1993).

Iwan, Gregory A. "The Cost Approach: Inflexible or Infeasible?" *The Appraisal Journal* (January 1993).

Marchitelli, Richard. "Rethinking the Cost Approach." *The Appraisal Journal* (July 1992).

Mason, James J. "Under the Microscope: The Cost Approach." *The Appraisal Journal* (January 1993).

Oetzel, Terrell R. "Some Thoughts on the Cost Approach." *The Appraisal Journal* (January 1993).

Ramsett, David E. "The Cost Approach: An Alternative View." *The Appraisal Journal* (April 1998).

15 | Building Cost Estimates

To apply the cost approach to value, an appraiser must prepare an estimate of the cost of the improvements as of the effective date of appraisal. Such an estimate can be prepared by an appraiser who understands construction plans, specifications, materials, and techniques and can access a variety of data sources or computer programs available for this purpose. Alternatively, the work can be done with the assistance of expert cost estimators. In either case, the appraiser is responsible for the result. Existing improvements should be carefully reviewed and described by all individuals who are delegated to estimate costs.

Proposed improvements may be valued based on plans and specifications provided the appraiser discloses that the improvements have not yet been built and that their completion as specified is a hypothetical condition of the appraisal. Residential appraisers are commonly asked to provide an opinion of prospective value under the hypothetical condition that a property will be completed as planned. Nonresidential appraisers are also asked to value property that has not yet been completed, and sometimes two prospective values are called for: the value at the time of completion and the value at the time stabilized occupancy and income are achieved. These values are based both on a hypothetical condition (because the improvements do not exist on the date of value) and on the extraordinary assumptions that as of those future dates the improvement will be complete as proposed (for the value upon completion) and the property will be stabilized (for the value upon reaching stabilization).

Cost Data Sources

Construction contracts for buildings similar to the building being appraised provide a primary source of comparable cost data. Some appraisers maintain comprehensive files of current cost data, including current costs for completed houses, apartments, hotels, office buildings, retail buildings, and industrial buildings. These costs can provide a basis for calculating the cost to construct an existing or proposed building. Contract-reporting services may indicate building areas or a general building description, the low bids, and the contract award. The appraiser can then obtain any missing information, such as the breakdown of office and warehouse space in an industrial property, and classify the building type for filing purposes. When cost comparable files are carefully developed and managed, they can supply authentic square-foot costs on buildings of all types for use in appraisal assignments.

Cost data may be obtained from construction contracts, building contractors, and published or computer-assisted cost-estimating services.

In the absence of construction contract data, local building contractors and professional cost estimators can be reliable data sources. In an active market, cost information can also be obtained by interviewing local property owners who have recently added building or land improvements similar to those found on the subject property. If work contracts and accounting records of recently improved properties are available, they can provide significant details.

Cost-Estimating Services

Many cost-estimating services publish data for estimating the current cost of improvements. These services including the following:

*   Marshall and Swift Publication Company (http://www.marshallswift.com/index.html)
*   Boeckh Publications, a division of Thompson Publishing Corporation (http://www.boeckh.com)
*   F. W. Dodge Corporation (http://www.fwdodge.com)
*   R. S. Means Company, Inc. (http://www.rsmeans.com)

Published cost manuals usually include direct unit costs and some indirect costs. (Appraisers should be aware that published cost estimates may or may not include indirect costs such as loan interest during construction.) An appraiser must research the market to determine which costs are most applicable to the appraisal assignment. National cost services list the costs of many site improvements separately, rather than as part of building costs. This data includes the costs of roads, storm drains, rough grading, soil compaction, utilities, and jurisdictional utility hookup fees and assessments. Demolition costs are usually not provided by published cost services. More often they are obtained from actual costs or from demolition contractors. Also, entrepreneurial profit is usually not included in cost service data. The appraiser usually estimates such costs separately and includes them in the estimate of total cost.

Although buildings can be measured in several ways, appraisers should measure buildings according to local custom. To use cost service data effectively, an appraiser must understand the measurement technique used by the service. Several cost-estimating services publish manuals or maintain electronic databases that break down costs into square foot increments. Unit costs for building types usually start with a building of a certain size (i.e., a base area), which serves as a benchmark. Then additions or deductions are made to account for the actual number of square feet and building components in the subject property. Data provided by cost-estimating services can be used to confirm estimates developed from local cost data.

Cost Index Trending

Cost manuals and electronic databases are updated periodically by including cost index tables that reflect changes in the cost of construction over a period of years.

> **Cost index trending** may be used to convert historical data into a current cost estimate.

Cost indexes convert a known cost as of a past date into a current cost estimate. Sometimes cost index tables can be used to adjust costs for different geographic areas. Cost index trending is also useful for estimating the current cost of one-of-a-kind items when standard costs are not available. However, there are practical limitations in applying this procedure because, as the time span increases, the reliability of the current cost indication tends to decrease.

As an example of cost index trending, assume the contract cost for constructing a building in January 1994 was $1,000,000. The index for January 1994 is 285.1 and the current index is 327.3. To trend the historical cost into a current cost, the current cost index is divided by the historical cost index and the result is multiplied by the historical cost. In this case the current cost is calculated as follows:

$$327.3 \div 285.1 = 1.148$$
$$1.148 \times \$1,000,000 = \$1,148,000$$

Problems can arise when cost index data is used to estimate current cost. The accuracy of the figures cannot always be ascertained, especially when it is not clear which components are included in the data (i.e., only direct costs or direct costs and some indirect costs). Furthermore, historical costs may not be typical for the time period, and the construction methods used at the time of the historical cost may differ from those used on the effective appraisal date. Although cost index trending may be helpful in confirming a current cost estimate, it is not a reliable substitute for the cost-estimating methods described in the following section.

Cost-Estimating Methods

The three traditional cost-estimating methods are

1. The comparative-unit method
2. The unit-in-place method
3. The quantity survey method

The quantity survey method produces a cost estimate based on a detailed inventory of the labor, materials, and equipment used in the subject improvements. The comparative-unit and the unit-in-place methods provide less detail, but they are the primary bases for the cost estimates used in most appraisals.

> Building costs may be estimated using one of **three methods:** the comparative-unit method, the unit-in-place method, or the quantity survey method.

ESTIMATING ENTREPRENEURIAL INCENTIVE

Regardless of the general cost-estimating method applied, estimates of entrepreneurial profit should be derived through market analysis and interviews with developers to determine the expectations of entrepreneurial reward required as motivation to undertake a particular development. The actual entrepreneurial profit earned is a record of results and can differ from the anticipated profit (i.e., the incentive) that originally motivated the entrepreneur to proceed. The typical level of anticipation or incentive should be used in the cost estimate.

Depending on market practice, entrepreneurial profit may be estimated in different ways:

- As a percentage of direct costs
- As a percentage of direct and indirect costs
- As a percentage of direct and indirect costs plus land value
- As a percentage of the value of the completed project

When interviewing local developers about an appropriate level of entrepreneurial incentive for a project, the appraiser must use the same base cost (only direct costs, only direct costs and indirect costs, etc.) as the market in any calculations of a lump-sum figure for entrepreneurial incentive. Presumably, the amount of entrepreneurial profit would be the same regardless of how it is calculated—e.g., as 22%, 20%, 15%, or 13% of the appropriate base cost selected, as shown below.

In the following example, the appraiser investigated the dollar amount of certain costs and ratios (or relative percentages) of entrepreneurial incentive attributable to the same set of costs and then calculated entrepreneurial incentive:

Base Cost	% Applied	Entrepreneurial Incentive
Direct costs	22.0% × $545,000	= $120,000 (rounded)
Direct costs + indirect costs	20.0% × ($545,000 + $55,000)	= $120,000
Direct costs + indirect costs + land value	15.0% × ($545,000 + $55,000 + $200,000)	= $120,000
Completed project	13.0% × ($545,000 + $55,000 + $200,000 + $120,000)	= $120,000 (rounded)

Note that in the calculation of entrepreneurial incentive as a percentage of the value of the completed project (direct costs + indirect costs + land value + entrepreneurial incentive), a figure for the variable being solved for (i.e., entrepreneurial incentive) appears in the equation. The final calculation of entrepreneurial incentive as a percentage of the value of the completed project would actually be expressed as follows:

$$[(\$545,000 + \$55,000 + \$200,000) \times 0.13]/(1 - 0.13) = \$120,000 \text{ (rounded)}$$

$$\text{entrepreneurial incentive} = \frac{[(\text{direct costs} + \text{indirect costs} + \text{land value}) \times (\text{market-derived percentage of value of the completed project})]}{[1 - (\text{market-derived percentage of value of the completed project})]}$$

In depressed markets the appraiser should focus on whether diminished entrepreneurial incentive or entrepreneurial loss represents a form of external obsolescence. Considering entrepreneurial coordination as a component of cost in a depressed market helps establish a basis for estimating the level of rent required to induce new construction, which may in turn provide some insight into problems of absorption and stabilized occupancy. Estimating an appropriate amount of entrepreneurial incentive remains a challenge for appraisers because expectations of profit vary with different market conditions and property types. Consistent relationships between profit and other costs are difficult to establish.

Comparative-Unit Method

The comparative-unit method is used to derive a cost estimate in terms of dollars per unit of area. The method employs the known costs of similar structures adjusted for market conditions and physical differences. Indirect costs may be included in the unit cost or computed separately. If the comparable properties and the subject property are in different markets, the appraiser may need to make an adjustment for location.

> **comparative-unit method:** A method used to derive a cost estimate in terms of dollars per unit of area or volume based on known costs of similar structures that are adjusted for time and physical differences; usually applied to total building area.

Unit costs vary with size; all else being equal, unit costs decrease as buildings increase in area. This reflects the fact that plumbing, heating units, elevators, doors, windows, and similar building components do not usually cost proportionately more in a larger building than in a smaller one.

The comparative-unit method is relatively uncomplicated, practical, and widely used. Unit cost figures are usually expressed in terms of gross building dimensions converted to square feet. Total cost is estimated by comparing the subject building with similar, recently constructed buildings for which contract prices are available. The trend in costs between the date of the contract (or construction) and the effective appraisal date must be factored into the comparison.

In the absence of contract prices, an indication of the total cost of a building can be extracted from sales of similar, newly constructed buildings as long as the following tests are met:

1. The improvements reflect the highest and best use of the site.
2. The property has reached stabilization.
3. Supply and demand are in balance.
4. Site value can be reasonably ascertained.

The value of the site is subtracted from the sale price of each comparable property, and the residual indicates the cost of the improvements.

Most appraisers using the comparative-unit method apply unit cost figures developed using data from a recognized cost service. Unit costs for the benchmark buildings found in cost-estimating manuals usually start with a base building of a specified size. Adjustments or refinements are then made to the base cost for any differences between the subject building and the benchmark building. If the subject building is larger than the benchmark building, the unit cost is usually lower; if the subject building is smaller, its unit cost will probably be higher.

Because few buildings are identical in terms of size, design, and quality of construction, the benchmark building is often different from the subject building. Different roof designs, interior design characteristics, and irregular perimeters and building shapes can affect comparative-unit costs substantially. Figure 15.1 illustrates this situation. Most cost services include adjustment criteria to alter or adjust the base cost to the specific criteria of the subject structure. However, all elements may not be addressed by the cost service and a more "building-specific" cost analysis developed by the unit-in-place method may be needed.

To develop a reliable estimate with the comparative-unit method, an appraiser calculates the unit cost from similar improvements or adjusts the unit cost figure to reflect variations in size, shape, finish, and other characteristics. The unit cost applied should also reflect any changes in cost levels between the date of the benchmark unit cost and the effective appraisal date.

Figure 15.1   Unit Costs of Buildings with Different Shapes

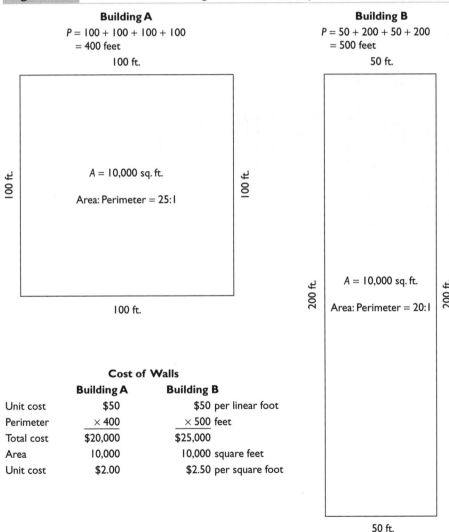

Cost of Walls		
	Building A	**Building B**
Unit cost	$50	$50 per linear foot
Perimeter	× 400	× 500 feet
Total cost	$20,000	$25,000
Area	10,000	10,000 square feet
Unit cost	$2.00	$2.50 per square foot

The ratio between the costs of mechanical equipment and the basic building shell has increased consistently through the years. Equipment tends to increase unit building costs and depreciate more rapidly than other building components.

To use area cost estimates, an appraiser assembles, analyzes, and catalogs data on actual building costs. These costs should be divided into general construction categories, and separate figures should be used to account for special finishes or equipment. The overall area unit cost can then be broken down into its components, which may help the appraiser adjust a known cost for the presence or absence of items in later comparisons.

The apparent simplicity of the comparative-unit method can be misleading. To develop dependable unit cost figures, an appraiser must exercise judgment and carefully compare the subject building with similar or standard structures for which actual costs are known. Errors can result if an appraiser selects a unit cost that is not comparable to the building being appraised. When it is correctly applied, however, the method produces reasonably accurate estimates of cost.

The warehouse shown in Figure 15.2 will be used to illustrate the comparative-unit method (and later the unit-in-place, or segregated-cost, method and the quantity survey method).

Table 15.1 shows how comparative-unit costs from a published cost manual can be applied to the warehouse building. Calculations such as those shown can be used to confirm a cost indication obtained from construction contracts for similar properties in the same market as the property being appraised on or about the effective appraisal date. Published data can be used independently when no local cost data is available.

In Table 15.1 an adjustment for the warehouse's sprinkler system was made using a square-foot unit cost. In other cases similar adjustments may be appropriate for observed physical differences in the amount of office area, construction features, or specific equipment.

Cost manuals rarely include all indirect costs or an allowance for entrepreneurial profit, so adjustments must often be made to obtain an indication of the total cost. In Table 15.1 adjustments are made for:

1. Indirect costs not included in the base price quoted in the cost manual
2. Indirect costs after construction needed to achieve typical stabilized occupancy[1]
3. Entrepreneurial profit calculated as a percentage of total direct and indirect costs

---

1. The cost to achieve stabilized occupancy may be nominal for a single-tenant building or a typical owner-occupied building. However, large multitenant warehouse, office, or apartment properties can have substantial lease-up costs, promotional expenses, or other costs (or loss in income) that must be considered.

Figure 15.2   **Plan of a Warehouse**

Basic Construction
Exterior walls, block and brick facade; structural steel columns, steel roof deck with rigid insulation; single-ply membrane roofing with ballast. Structure has full fire sprinkler system. Other details are typical.

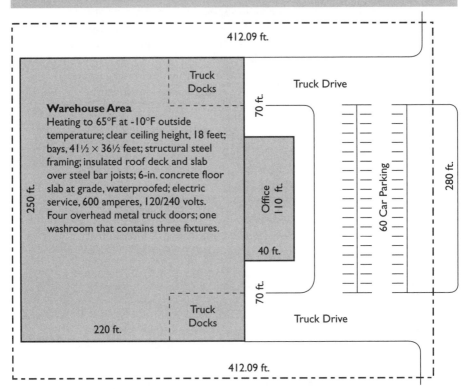

Office Area
Heated, with air-conditioning equipment rated at 15 tons; ceiling height, 9 feet; flooring, asphalt tile over concrete slab; illumination, 60 foot-candle intensity, fluorescent lighting; ceiling, acoustical tile; partitions, stud and gypsum board; two washrooms that contain six fixtures.

The estimate of the value of the site and site improvements was derived through sales comparison.

Table 15.1 indicates the cost of the warehouse building plus the site value, but the result shown is more likely to represent the value of a close substitute than a duplicate structure. Cost services use typical buildings for their base cost, so an appraiser can apply the comparative-unit method, develop reliable adjustment amounts and factors, and produce a reasonable property value estimate.

Table 15.1	Warehouse Property—Comparative-Unit Method
Base cost per sq. ft.	$27.22
Add for sprinkler system per sq. ft.	1.14
Subtotal	$28.36
Adjustment for ceiling height variations	× 1.086
Subtotal	$30.80
Adjustment for area/perimeter	× 0.895
Subtotal	$27.57
Current cost multiplier	× 1.120
Subtotal	$30.88
Local cost multiplier	× 0.980
Total cost per sq. ft.	$30.26
Indirect costs not included in cost manual*	× 1.050
Subtotal	$31.77
Indirect costs from completion to stabilized occupancy*	× 1.070
Subtotal	$33.99
Entrepreneurial profit at 10.0% of total direct and indirect costs	
$33.99 × 0.10	+ 3.39
Subtotal	$37.38
Total cost for warehouse building:	
59,400 sq. ft. @ $37.38/sq. ft.	= $2,220,372
	$2,220,000 (rounded)
Site value and site improvements per sq. ft. of building	
59,400 sq. ft. @ $10.94/sq. ft.	= 650,000 (rounded)
Total value indicated by the cost approach	= $2,870,000

Source: *Marshall Valuation Service*

* Note: Contractor's overhead and profit and some other indirect costs are included in these base costs and adjustments. The source of published cost data should be studied for a complete understanding of what is included in quoted costs.

For purposes of simplicity, a percentage was applied to account for indirect costs.

Construction contracts normally include other improvements to the land such as auxiliary buildings, driveways, water retention basins, underground drainage facilities, rail sidings, fences, and landscaping. The possible combinations and varied value contributions of these improvements can cause a wide divergence in unit cost if the total contract is related to the size of the major improvement only. Therefore, when actual contract costs from the local market are used in the comparative-unit method, it is imperative that the costs of these other improvements be excluded from the determination of the base price so that these costs are not counted twice—first implicitly in the base unit cost and then again explicitly as an adjustment based on actual costs.

Unit-in-Place Method

In the unit-in-place (or segregated-cost) method, individual unit costs for various building components are applied to the various subcomponents in the

unit-in-place method: A cost-estimating method in which total building cost is estimated by adding together the unit costs for the various building components as installed; also called the *segregated-cost method.*

structure or to linear, area, volume, or other appropriate measures of these components. Using this method the appraiser computes a unit cost based on the actual quantity of materials used plus the labor of assembly required for each square foot of area. For example, the cost can be applied based on the square feet of floor area or linear feet of wall of a certain height. The same procedure is applied for other structural components.

Unit-in-place cost estimates are made using specific cost data for standardized structural components as installed, such as the following:

Structural Component	Unit
Excavation	Dollars per cubic yard
Foundation	Dollars per linear foot of foundation or cubic yard of concrete
Floor construction	Dollars per square foot
Interior partitions	Dollars per linear foot
Roofing	Dollars per square (i.e., 100 square feet of roof area)

The unit-in-place concept is not limited to cubic, linear, or area units. The measure on which the cost is based may be the measure employed in a particular trade, such as the cost per ton of air-conditioning. The unit-in-place concept may also be applied to the cost of complete, installed components such as the cost of a roof truss that is fabricated off site, delivered, and erected.

All unit costs are totaled to provide the estimated direct cost of the entire improvement. Unit-in-place cost estimates may be based on an appraiser's compiled data, but they are usually obtained from a cost-estimating service that provides updated monthly figures. Contractor's overhead and profit may be included in the unit cost figures provided by some cost services, or they may be computed separately. The appraiser must know exactly what is included in any unit price quoted. Indirect costs are usually computed separately. The objective is to count all appropriate costs and to avoid any double counting.

The following example shows how the cost of a brick veneer wall would be calculated on a unit-in-place basis. Costs such as these vary with market conditions and location; the figures shown are used only for purposes of illustration.

Description	Cost	Unit
4-in. face brick, installed: common bond, ½-in. struck joints, mortar, scaffolding, and cleaning included	$460.00	per 1,000
Dimension lumber, erected: 2-in.-x-4-in. wood stud framing, 16 inches on center	$360.00	per 1,000 bd. ft.
Sheathing, installed: impregnated 4 ft. × 8 ft., ½-in.	$0.42	per sq. ft.
Insulation, installed: 2½-in., foil backing on one side	$0.22	per sq. ft.
Gypsum board: ½-in. with finished joints	$0.30	per sq. ft.
Paint: primer and one coat flat	$0.25	per sq. ft.

From this data the cost per square foot of wall can be estimated as follows:

Description	Cost	Unit
Bricks	$3.45	per 7½*
Wood stud framing	$0.24	per ⅔ bd. ft.*
Sheathing	$0.42	per sq. ft.
Insulation	$0.22	per sq. ft.
½-in. gypsum board	$0.30	per sq. ft.
Paint	+ $0.25	per sq. ft.
Total for finished wall	$4.88	per sq. ft.

* To calculate a total unit cost, the unit cost of certain construction elements must be converted to the unit measure of the total cost. In this example, each square foot of wall requires 7½ bricks and ⅔ board feet of wood stud framing.

After calculating the unit cost of $4.88 per square foot, the appraiser can estimate the total cost of a veneer wall that meets these standards without detailing the quantities of material and labor. In practice, a cost analyst would refine the procedure by adjusting for waste and for extra framing for windows and doors, which require wall openings, lintels, and facing corners.

The unit costs for all components can be calculated in a similar fashion and, once these are established, the appraiser can estimate the cost of an entire building. When fully developed, the unit-in-place method provides a substitute for a complete quantity survey and produces an accurate cost estimate with considerably less effort. Table 15.2 illustrates how the unit-in-place method can be used to estimate the reproduction cost of the warehouse shown in Figure 15.2.

In Table 15.2 adjustments are made for the following:

1. Indirect costs not included in the cost manual's base price
2. Indirect costs after construction needed to achieve typical stabilized occupancy
3. Entrepreneurial profit calculated as a percentage of total direct and indirect costs

Note the difference in total adjustments for indirect costs in Tables 15.1 and 15.2. As the cost of the property is broken down into more precise increments in the unit-in-place method, a smaller portion of the total indirect costs is included in the base price quoted in the cost manual for each building component. The single figure of cost per square foot that is used in the comparative-unit method accounts for more of the total indirect costs than the individual cost figures for excavation, site, foundation, framing, and so on. Therefore, the adjustment for "indirect costs not included in cost manual" in the comparative-unit method is smaller than the adjustment for "indirect costs not included in cost manual" in the unit-in-place method.

In the unit-in-place method, the value of site improvements may be estimated separately on a depreciated-cost basis and added to the depreciated cost of the improvements. More typically, the value of site improvements,

Table 15.2   **Warehouse Property—Unit-in-Place Method**

Excavation	59,400 cu. ft.	@	$0.24	per cu. ft. =	$14,256
Site	115,385 sq. ft.	@	$0.17	per sq. ft. =	19,615
Foundation	59,400 sq. ft.	@	$1.79	per sq. ft. =	106,326
Framing	59,400 sq. ft.	@	$4.82	per sq. ft. =	286,308
Floor (concrete)	59,400 sq. ft.	@	$3.12	per sq. ft. =	185,328
Floor (asphalt tile)	4,400 sq. ft.	@	$1.02	per sq. ft. =	4,488
Ceiling (acoustical tile)	4,400 sq. ft.	@	$4.35	per sq. ft. =	19,140
Plumbing (three rooms)					
Fixtures	9 fixtures	@	$2,525	per fixture =	22,725
Drains	6 units	@	$380	per unit =	2,280
Sprinkler system	59,400 sq. ft.	@	$1.48	per sq. ft. =	87,912
HVAC	55,000 sq. ft.	@	$0.84	per sq. ft. =	46,200
	4,400 sq. ft.	@	$4.20	per sq. ft. =	18,480
Electrical and lighting	59,400 sq. ft.	@	$1.70	per sq. ft. =	100,980
Exterior wall					
Concrete block	15,180 sq. ft.	@	$12.09	per sq. ft. =	183,526
Brick facade	5,060 sq. ft.	@	$13.80	per sq. ft. =	69,828
Partitions					
Walls	8,650 sq. ft.	@	$3.70	per sq. ft. =	32,005
Doors	10 sq. ft.	@	$103	per sq. ft. =	1,030
Overhead doors (10 ft. × 12 ft. × 4)	480 sq. ft.	@	$18.25	per sq. ft. =	8,760
Roof joists and deck	59,400 sq. ft.	@	$6.86	per sq. ft. =	407,484
Roof cover and insulation	59,400 sq. ft.	@	$2.18	per sq. ft. =	129,492
Miscellaneous specified items					30,000
Subtotal					$1,776,163
Current cost multiplier (different base from Table 15.1)					× 1.030
Subtotal					$1,829,448
Local cost multiplier					× 0.980
Total cost (from manual—$30.18 per sq. ft.)					$1,792,859
Indirect costs not included in cost manual*					× 1.100
Subtotal					$1,972,145
Indirect costs from completion to date of stabilized occupancy*					× 1.050
Subtotal					$2,070,752
Entrepreneurial profit at 10.0% of total direct and indirect costs					
$2,070,752 × 0.10				=	207,075
Total cost ($38.35 per sq. ft.)					$2,277,827
				(rounded)	$2,278,000
Plus site value and site improvements					650,000
Total project value					$2,928,000

Source: *Marshall Valuation Service*

*   Note: Contractor's overhead and profit and some indirect costs are included in the base costs; architect's fees and other indirect costs are not. The source of published cost data should be studied for a complete understanding of what is included in the quoted costs.

For purposes of simplicity, a percentage was applied to account for indirect costs.

estimated either on a depreciated-cost basis or extracted from market data, may be added as a contributory amount to total property value.

Quantity Survey Method

The most comprehensive and accurate method of cost estimating is the quantity survey method, which will more often be applied by a contractor or professional cost estimator than an appraiser. A quantity survey reflects the quantity and quality of all materials used in the construction of an

> **quantity survey method:** A cost-estimating method in which the quantity and quality of all materials used and all categories of labor required are estimated and unit cost figures are applied to arrive at a total cost estimate for labor and materials.

improvement and all categories of labor required. Unit costs are applied to these figures to arrive at a total cost estimate for materials and labor; then the contractor adds a margin for contingencies, overhead, and profit.

Depending on the size of the project and the resources of the contractor, the quantity survey and cost calculations may be prepared by a single cost estimator or by a number of subcontractors whose bids are compiled by a general contractor and submitted as the final cost estimate. In either case, the analysis details the quantity, quality, and cost of all materials furnished by the general contractor or subcontractor and the appropriate cost allowances.

A general contractor's cost breakdown for the warehouse shown in Figure 15.2 is summarized in Table 15.3. This is only a summary; the specific quantities and costs are not indicated.

Contractor bids do not usually include indirect costs or entrepreneurial profit. The analysis illustrated in Table 15.3 reflects indirect costs and the calculation of entrepreneurial profit as a percentage of total direct and indirect costs. In the examples presented, indirect costs are considered in various stages of the cost-estimating procedure. A breakdown of the costs that make up these estimates is preferred to the percentage adjustment, and the appraiser should provide a breakdown to support the percentages applied. Note that when the direct costs of the individual elements of construction are broken down into discrete amounts, as shown in Table 15.3, less of the indirect costs are accounted for in those cost figures than in the figures for other cost-estimating methods and thus the percentage adjustment for total indirect costs is higher.

Although site improvements such as parking facilities, landscaping, and signage are commonly included in a general contractor's bid, they are not detailed in Table 15.3. They should be included in a cost estimate of all improvements. In a cost estimate of an existing building, a separate itemization of site improvements facilitates the consideration of depreciation. Because the quantity survey method usually produces a cost estimate of a duplicate building, Table 15.3 indicates the reproduction cost of the warehouse building as of the effective appraisal date.

In recent years the percentage of a construction contract that is subcontracted out has increased. Subcontractors have become more efficient in their

Table 15.3	Warehouse Property—Contractor's Breakdown
General conditions of contract	$7,854
Excavating and grading	24,781
Concrete	182,053
Carpentry	25,473
Masonry	194,231
Structural steel	280,343
Joist, deck, and deck slab	329,827
Roofing	57,494
Insulation	32,378
Sash	5,256
Glazing	11,329
Painting	7,611
Acoustical material	5,803
Flooring	3,335
Electric	75,334
HVAC	67,560
Piping	6,458
Plumbing and sprinkler system	77,461
Subtotal	$1,394,581
Contingencies @ 5.0%	69,729
Contractor's overhead and profit @ 12.0%	167,350
Total proposed contract costs ($27.46 per sq. ft.)	$1,631,660
	(rounded) $1,631,700
Indirect costs before, during, and after construction*	× 1.27
Subtotal	$2,072,259
Entrepreneurial profit ($2,072,259 × 0.10)	+ 207,226
Total reproduction cost	$2,279,485
Plus site value and site improvements	+ 650,000
Total project value	$2,929,485
	(rounded) $2,929,000

* For purposes of simplicity, a percentage was applied to account for indirect costs.

specializations. Subcontractor unit-in-place costs compare favorably with the cost of work done by employees of the general contractor, and the general contractor can operate with reduced overhead. To produce a quantity survey estimate, each contractor and subcontractor must provide a breakdown of materials, labor, overhead, and profit. The contractor's profit may depend on the volume of work that the contractor has lined up.

Although the quantity survey method produces a complete cost analysis of the improvements being appraised, it is time-consuming, costly, and frequently requires the services of an experienced cost estimator. For these reasons this method is seldom used in routine appraisal assignments.

FURTHER READING

Akerson, Charles B. *The Appraiser's Workbook*. 2d ed. Chicago: Appraisal Institute, 1996.

Ruegg, Rosalie T., and Harold E. Marshall. *Building Economics: Theory and Practice*. New York: Van Nostrand Reinhold, 1990.

Building Cost Manuals

Boeckh Building Valuation Manual. Milwaukee: Thompson Publishing Corp. [http://www.boeckh.com], 1979. 3 vols.

Vol. 1—Residential and Agricultural; Vol. 2—Commercial; Vol. 3—Industrial and Institutional. Uses 1979 cost database and includes a wide variety of building models. Built up from unit-in-place costs converted to cost per square foot of floor or ground area. *Boeckh Building Cost Modifier* is published bimonthly for updating with current modifiers.

Building Construction Cost Data. Duxbury, Mass.: Robert Snow Means Co. [http://www.rsmeans.com], annual.

Lists average unit prices on many building construction items for use in engineering estimates. Components arranged according to uniform system adopted by the American Institute of Architects, Associated General Contractors, and Construction Specifications Institute.

Dodge Building Cost Calculator & Valuation Guide. New York: McGraw-Hill Information Systems Co. [http://www.fwdodge.com] looseleaf service, quarterly supplements.

Lists building costs for common types and sizes of buildings. Local cost modifiers and historical local cost index tables included. Formerly *Dow Building Cost Calculator*.

Marshall Valuation Service. Los Angeles: Marshall and Swift Publication Co. [http://www.marshallswift.com] looseleaf service, monthly supplements.

Cost data for determining replacement costs of buildings and other improvements in the United States and Canada. Includes current cost multipliers and local modifiers.

Residential Cost Handbook. Los Angeles: Marshall and Swift Publication Co. [http://www.marshallswift.com] looseleaf service, quarterly supplements.

Presents square-foot method and segregated-cost method. Local modifiers and cost-trend modifiers included.

16 DEPRECIATION ESTIMATES

Several methods may be used to estimate depreciation. Each is acceptable and should result in roughly the same value as long as the appraiser applies the method consistently and logically. The method used should reflect the reaction of an informed and prudent buyer to the condition and quality of the property and the market in which the property is found. The primary goals of depreciation analysis are to identify all forms of depreciation recognized by the market, to treat all these forms of depreciation, and to charge only once for each form of depreciation (i.e., to avoid double counting items of depreciation). The various methods of estimating depreciation may be used in combination to solve specific problems or each may be applied separately to test the reasonableness of the estimates derived from other methods.

The three principal methods for estimating depreciation are

- The market extraction method
- The age-life method
- The breakdown method

Market extraction and age-life calculations are the primary methods used by most appraisers to estimate the total depreciation in a property. The breakdown method is a more comprehensive method that identifies specific elements of depreciation and treats each element separately. It enumerates the components of total depreciation—i.e., physical deterioration, functional obsolescence, and external obsolescence.

> The three methods used to **estimate depreciation** are the market extraction, age-life, and breakdown methods.

The market extraction and age-life methods tend to deal with the whole property and are easier to understand and apply. The elements of depreciation are implicit, not explicit. Both are limited in that they assume lump-sum depreciation from all causes can be expressed in an overall estimate, do not always distinguish between short-lived and long-lived items, and rely on general forecasts of effective age and remaining economic life. The age-life method is further limited in that it typically reflects a straight-line pattern of depreciation.

Regardless of the method applied, the appraiser must ensure that the final estimate of depreciation reflects the loss in value from all causes and that no form of depreciation has been considered more than once. Double charges for depreciation may produce inappropriately low value indications in the cost approach. Also, the analysis of depreciation must be internally consistent, using either reproduction cost or replacement cost as the cost basis throughout. As explained in Chapter 14, replacement cost eliminates the need to consider certain forms of obsolescence; switching between reproduction and replacement cost within the analysis of depreciation greatly increases the chances of double counting items of depreciation.

Age and Life Relationships

All three methods of estimating depreciation consider age-life relationships either directly or indirectly. The overall concept of depreciation as used in appraisal is based on age and life relationships, which relate to the entire improvement and also to its various components. Depreciation occurs over the life of an improvement or a component; in theory an improvement or component loses all of its value over its life. For example, assume that the typical life expectancy of a freestanding retail store in a given market is 40 years. Theoretically, when the building is 40 years old, it will have reached the end of its life expectancy and will have lost all of its value to depreciation, with no contributory value remaining to add to the value of the vacant site. The life expectancy of a water heater installed in the building will be much shorter than 40 years, and some components may have to be replaced several times over the building's 40-year life. In the development of depreciation estimates, age-life relationships are primarily used to estimate the total depreciation of the improvement and the physical deterioration of the improvement's components.

Age-life relationships used to develop an estimate of total depreciation in the market extraction and age-life methods include economic life, effective age, and remaining economic life; age-life relationships used to estimate deterioration in individual physical components in the breakdown method include useful life, actual age, and remaining useful life.

In estimating the total depreciation of an improvement, the age-life concepts most important to the market extraction and age-life methods are

- Economic life
- Effective age
- Remaining economic life

The concepts of economic life, effective age, and remaining economic life expectancy consider all elements of depreciation in one overall calculation. Therefore, the effective age estimate considers not only physical wear and tear but also any loss in value for functional and external considerations. This type of analysis is characteristic of the market extraction and age-life depreciation methods. However, the age-life method can be modified to reflect the presence of any known items of curable physical depreciation or incurable deterioration in short-lived building components.

When estimating physical deterioration in the breakdown method, the most important age-life concepts are

- Useful life
- Actual age
- Remaining useful life

The use of these terms in the breakdown method relates to the separation of physical depreciation from functional and external obsolescence. Economic life considers all three components of depreciation in one age-life estimate, whereas useful life considers only the depreciation of the physical components of a property. A building's useful life would probably be longer than the economic life of the same building. In spite of that difference, the application of useful life in the breakdown method and economic life in the market extraction and age-life methods should yield the same approximate estimate of total depreciation.

Actual Age and Effective Age

Actual age, which is sometimes called *historical age* or *chronological age,* is the number of years that have elapsed since building construction was completed. Actual age serves two purposes in depreciation analysis. First, it is the initial element analyzed in the estimation of effective age. Second, in the application of the breakdown method, it is fundamental to the age-life analysis needed to estimate physical deterioration in the long-lived and short-lived components of an improvement.

Effective age is the age indicated by the condition and utility of a structure and is based on an appraiser's judgment and interpretation of market perceptions. Even in the same market, similar buildings do not necessarily depreciate at the same rate. The maintenance standards of owners or occupants can influence the pace of building depreciation. If one building is better maintained than other buildings in its market area, the effective age of that building may be less than its actual age. If a building is poorly maintained, its effective age may be greater than its actual age. If a building has received typical maintenance, its effective age and actual age may be the same.

As an example, consider a 23-year-old strip retail center that has been redecorated on the inside but has not been modernized. The original roof and HVAC components are still in place. The building would probably have an estimated effective age of 23 years. The small amount of work done in redecorating is usually not sufficient to reduce the effective age. Now assume that, in addition to the redecorating, the roof and furnace have been replaced in the 23-year-old building. In this case the building would probably have an estimated effective age of less than 23 years. If the same 23-year-old building were in poor condition, had not been redecorated, had a defective HVAC system, and had below-average occupancy because of poor maintenance, it would probably have an estimated effective age greater than 23 years.

Economic Life and Useful Life

An improvement's economic life begins when it is built and ends when the improvement no longer contributes any value to the property (i.e., to the underlying site at its highest and best use). This period is usually shorter than the improvement's physical life expectancy, which is the total period the improvement can be expected to exist physically. At the end of a building's economic life, there are several options available to the property owner:

- Renovation
- Rehabilitation
- Remodeling
- Demolition and replacement with a suitable new structure

Both economic life and useful life consider that market forces operate in such a way that buildings are either renovated, rehabilitated, remodeled, or torn down long before they physically wear out.

All aspects of a property and its market, including the quality and condition of the construction, the functional utility of the improvements, and market and locational externalities, must be considered in the estimation of a property's economic life. The condition and functional utility of an improvement as well as market and locational factors must also be taken into account in estimating an improvement's effective age. Although the economic life of an improvement is difficult to predict, it is shaped by a number of factors, including

- Physical considerations—i.e., the rate at which the physical components of an improvement wear out, given the quality of construction, the use of the property, maintenance standards, and the region's climate.
- Functional considerations—i.e., the rate at which construction technology, tastes in architecture, energy efficiency, and building design change. These factors can render an improvement functionally obsolete, regardless of its age and/or condition.
- External considerations—i.e., short-term and long-term influences such as the stage of a neighborhood's life cycle, the availability and affordability of financing, and supply and demand factors.

economic life: The period over which improvements to real property contribute to property value; the term relates to the market extraction and age-life methods of estimating depreciation.

Many physical, functional, and external considerations may not have any effect on the value of an improvement as recognized by the market on the date of the opinion of value, but they will likely have a profound effect at some future time—say, in 20, 50, or even 100 years. Although, it is difficult to forecast economic life expectancy, market study and analysis of historical trends and neighborhood life cycles may provide important information.

To estimate an improvement's economic life, an appraiser studies the typical economic life expectancy of recently sold improvements similar to the subject in the market area. To calculate total economic life expectancy as of the date of sale, an appraiser takes the reciprocal of the average annual depreciation rate. For example, consider a residential subdivision where recent sales indicate an average annual rate of depreciation of 2% for properties that are very comparable to the subject property (i.e., all built in the same phase of the subdivision's development and sold near the time of the sale of the subject). Calculating the reciprocal of 2% (1/0.02) results in a total economic life expectancy for the subject property of 50 years as of the date of the opinion of value. This does not mean that the total economic life expectancy of the subject has always been and will always be 50 years. Rather, at the time the property was sold, its average annual rate of depreciation indicated a total economic life expectancy of 50 years.

Renovation and modernization can effectivly extend a building's life expectancy by "resetting the clock." For example, consider a building with a 40-year economic life expectancy. If at the 10-year mark the property was substantially modernized, bringing the physical components up to current market standards for new construction, then the effective age of the property would be reset to zero and the remaining economic life expectancy (before the renovation) of 30 years would be reset to the original 40 years—or to some other figure, depending on the extent of modification to the property. Many historic properties have an economic life equal to or greater than the physical life of the building materials because of continued renovation and restoration.

Useful life, as used in age-life calculations in the breakdown method, is the period of time over which the components of the improvement may reasonably be expected to perform the functions for which they were designed. Although the physical life expectancy of some components, such as structural elements made of concrete and steel, may be hundreds of years, the useful life recognizes economic influences acting on the improvements containing these components. Accordingly, if a 40-year-old industrial building is being demolished so that its site can be redeveloped, it is probable that all components of the building will be demolished, regardless of their remaining physical utility.

The useful life of short-lived physical components (HVAC components, roof covering, interior decorating, floor finishes, etc.) is shorter than the improvement's economic life expectancy. Long-lived components (usually the structural components of a building, such as foundations, framing, and underground piping) have a useful life at least as long as the improvement's economic life expectancy. Distinguishing between long-lived and short-lived components is important

useful life: The period of time over which a structure may reasonably be expected to perform the function for which it was designed.

when breakdown techniques are applied and gives the appraisar flexibility in estimating component depreciation that is not available with the market extraction and age-life methods.

Remaining Economic Life and Remaining Useful Life

Remaining economic life is the estimated period over which existing improvements are expected to continue to contribute to property value. The concept is applied in the market extraction and age-life methods. Usually improvements can be regarded as investments designed to contribute to value over a long period of time. Some depreciation occurs between the date when the improvements begin to contribute to value and the date of the opinion of value; wear and tear can take their toll even during construction, which is usually a long process. The remaining economic life extends from the date of the opinion of value to the end of the improvement's economic life. An improvement's remaining economic life is always less than or equal to its total economic life, but never more than its total economic life as long as the highest and best use of the property does not change. In the breakdown method, remaining useful life is the estimated period from the actual age of a component to the end of its total useful life expectancy. The remaining useful life of any long-lived component is equal to or, typically, greater than its remaining economic life.

The total economic life of similar structures minus the effective age of the improvement will approximate the remaining economic life of the subject property improvements. As an example, consider a 15-year-old property. The appraiser searches the market area and finds three sales involving properties that are very comparable in size, layout, and other physical characteristics:

- Sale 1, an 8-year-old building, has an annual depreciation rate of 1.21% and a total economic life expectancy of 83 years. Its remaining economic life expectancy is therefore 75 years (83 − 8 = 75).
- In contrast, Sale 2, a 19-year-old building, has an annual depreciation rate of 1.51% and a total economic life expectancy of 66 years. Its remaining economic life expectancy is 47 years (66 − 19 = 47).
- Sale 3, a 14-year-old building, has an annual depreciation rate of 1.39% and a total economic life expectancy of 72 years (1/1.39%). Its remaining economic life expectancy is 58 years (72 − 14 = 58).

A pattern can be observed here. As a building ages and the average annual depreciation rate increases, the total economic life expectancy decreases. Reconciliation should be based on the improvement that is most similar in age to the subject property. The improvement closest to the subject property in age is Sale 3. In light of this similar sale and the pattern indicated by the market data, the appraiser could reasonably reconcile the total economic life expectancy for the subject property at 70 years. Using the age-life method, which will be discussed in detail later in this chapter, the total depreciation would equal 21.43% (15/70) of the property's cost.

Market Extraction Method

The market extraction method relies on the availability of comparable sales from which depreciation can be extracted. It makes direct comparisons with market sales and is easy to understand and explain, but, in considering all elements in one calculation, market extraction can be an oversimplification of the complex interplay of physical, functional, and external causes of depreciation. The technique is primarily used to extract total depreciation, to establish total economic life expectancy, and to estimate external obsolescence. The market extraction method includes the following steps:

1. Find and verify sales of similarly improved properties that appear to have incurred a comparable amount of depreciation as the subject property. Although it is desirable, it is not essential that the comparables be current sales. Similarly, the comparables do not have to be from the subject's market; they can be from a market that is comparable (i.e., with similar tastes, preferences, and external influences) but not necessarily competitive.

2. Make appropriate adjustments to the comparable sales for certain factors, including property rights conveyed, financing, and conditions of sale. If an appraiser can quantify curable depreciation for either items of deferred maintenance or functional obsolescence, this estimate should be applied to the sale price as an adjustment. (Depreciation extracted in this way will exclude curable items.) A market conditions adjustment is not made because the appraiser is estimating depreciation at the time of the sale. Adjustments for other physical, functional, or external impairments are not made either because these factors are the source of the depreciation in the comparable sale.

3. Subtract the value of the land at the time of sale from the sale price of each comparable property to obtain the depreciated cost of the improvements.

4. Estimate the cost of the improvements for each comparable at the time of sale. The cost estimates should have the same basis—i.e., reproduction cost or replacement cost. Typically replacement cost is used and the cost estimate should include all improvements.

5. Subtract the depreciated cost of each improvement from the cost of the improvement to arrive at total depreciation in dollars. If no adjustments have been made in Step 2 to the sale prices for curable items, this extracted depreciation will include all forms of depreciation, both curable and incurable, from all three causes. If adjustments have been made to the sale prices for curable items, the extracted depreciation will not include curable items; it will represent a lump-sum depreciation estimate for incurable items from all causes.

6. Convert the dollar estimates of depreciation into percentages by dividing each estimate of total depreciation by the cost. If the ages of the sales are relatively similar to the age of the subject property, the percentages of

total depreciation can be reconciled into a rate appropriate to the subject property. This rate is applied to the subject's cost to derive an estimate of the subject's total depreciation.

If there are differences between the sales (e.g., in age, location, degree of maintenance), further calculations can be performed to offer additional support for the estimate of total depreciation. The appraiser first annualizes the percentages of total depreciation by dividing each percentage by the actual age of the property or, if there is a significant difference between the actual age and the effective age, by the effective age estimate. Whether actual or effective age is used, the same age basis should be applied consistently to all sales. Because accurate estimates of effective age are difficult to derive, the most consistent range of annual depreciation rates is developed using the actual ages of the comparables. Then the appraiser compares the range of annual percentage rates with the calculated annual depreciation rate for the subject improvements to see if the latter figure is reasonable.

Consider the sales in Example 1. All are of fee simple interests and the ages, function, and external influences of the sale properties are similar to the subject property.

Example 1				Step in
	Sale 1	Sale 2	Sale 3	Procedure
Sale price	$215,000	$165,000	$365,000	1, 2
Less value of land	− 60,000	− 40,000	− 127,750	3
Depreciated cost of improvements	$155,000	$125,000	$237,250	3
Cost of improvements	$230,000	$195,000	$375,000	4
Less depreciated cost of improvements	− 155,000	− 125,000	− 237,250	5
Lump-sum dollar depreciation	$75,000	$70,000	$137,750	5
Lump-sum percentage depreciation	32.61%	35.90%	36.73%	6

In this case the range of lump-sum percentage depreciation estimates is so narrow that it is not necessary to annualize them. The cost of the subject improvements is $240,000 (more than the price of Sale 1 but much less than the price of Sale 3), so the percentage of depreciation can be reconciled to 33% of cost. The total lump-sum dollar depreciation estimate comes to $80,000 ($240,000 × 0.33).

The comparable sales in Example 2 have a wider range of ages. Assume again that all the sales are of a fee simple interest and that no major functional or external obsolescence is evident.

Example 2	Sale 1	Sale 2	Sale 3	Step in Procedure
Sale price	$998,000	$605,000	$791,000	1, 2
Less value of land	− 140,000	− 100,000	− 125,000	3
Depreciated cost of improvements	$858,000	$505,000	$666,000	3
Cost of improvements	$950,000	$627,000	$934,000	4
Less depreciated cost of improvements	− 858,000	− 505,000	− 666,000	5
Lump-sum dollar depreciation	$92,000	$122,000	$268,000	5
Lump-sum percentage depreciation	9.68%	19.46%	28.69%	6
Age of comparable property	8	14	19	
Average annual depreciation rate	1.21%	1.39%	1.51%	

In Example 2 the range of lump-sum percentage depreciation estimates is so wide that they are difficult to reconcile. Assuming that the subject improvements are 15 years old, which is closest to the actual age of Sale 2, a reasonable estimate of total depreciation for the subject improvements would be 21%. This rate can be applied to the subject's cost. To check the lump-sum figure, the appraiser could calculate average annual depreciation rates for the subject and comparables. The average annual depreciation rate for the subject improvements of 1.40% (21%/15) falls within the range of 1.21% to 1.51% for the comparables and supports the estimate of 21% total depreciation for a 15-year-old property.

Applicability and Limitations

When sales data is plentiful, the market extraction method provides a reliable and convincing estimate of depreciation. However, the comparable properties should have similar physical, functional, and external characteristics as the subject, and they should have incurred similar amounts and types of depreciation.

When the comparable properties differ in design, quality, or construction, it is difficult to ascertain whether differences in value are attributable to these differences or to a difference in depreciation. The market extraction method is also difficult to apply when the type or extent of depreciation varies greatly among the comparable properties. If the sales analyzed were affected by special financing or unusual motivation, the problem is further complicated.

The usefulness of the method depends heavily on the accuracy of the site value estimates and the cost estimates for the comparable properties. If the sales are located in market areas that are not comparable to the subject's, the method may not be appropriate. Market extraction considers all types of depreciation in a lump sum and does not break down the estimate into the various components of depreciation.

Age-Life Method

The effective age and economic life expectancy of a structure are the primary concepts used by an appraiser in measuring depreciation using age-life relationships. In the age-life method, total depreciation is estimated by calculating the ratio of the effective age of the property to its economic life expectancy and applying this ratio to the property's total cost. The formula is

$$\frac{\text{effective age}}{\text{total economic life}} \times \text{total cost} = \text{depreciation}$$

Although it is not always as accurate as other techniques, the age-life method is the simplest way to estimate depreciation. The method is applied in the following steps:

1. Conduct research to identify the anticipated total economic life of similar structures in the market area and estimate the effective age of the subject building. The data used in the market extraction method would also be applicable in the age-life method.

2. Divide the estimated effective age of the subject by the anticipated total economic life of similar structures. The resulting ratio is then applied to the subject's cost to estimate total lump-sum depreciation.

3. Subtract the lump-sum estimate of depreciation from the cost of the subject improvement to arrive at the improvement's contribution to property value.

As an example, market research (Step 1) yields the following information about the subject and comparable properties:

Total cost	$668,175
Land value	$180,000
Estimated effective age	18 years
Total economic life expectancy of comparables	50 years

The total percentage of depreciation is determined by dividing the estimated effective age of 18 years by the total economic life expectancy of 50 years (Step 2). Thus, the age-life formula indicates total depreciation of 36%. When this rate is applied to the cost of $668,175, the total depreciation indicated is $240,543 (Step 3). The cost approach is applied as follows:

Total cost	$668,175
Less total depreciation	− 240,543
Depreciated cost	$427,632
Plus land value	+ 180,000
Indicated value by the cost approach	$607,632

Applicability and Limitations

The age-life method is simple, easy to apply, and easy to understand. It allows an appraiser to determine total depreciation, which can subsequently be allocated among its various causes using breakdown procedures. Although this method is usually the simplest way to estimate depreciation, it does have certain limitations.

First, because the percentage of depreciation is represented by the ratio of effective age to total economic life, this method assumes that every building depreciates on a straight-line basis over the course of its economic life. The straight-line pattern of depreciation is only an approximation, although it is usually a sufficiently accurate one.

Second, the age-life method, like the market extraction method, does not divide depreciation into its various components. In market areas where comparable properties incur different types and different amounts of depreciation than the subject property, the age-life method may be difficult to justify.

Finally, the age-life method, again like the market extraction method, does not recognize the difference between short-lived and long-lived items of physical deterioration. Because a single figure is assumed to reflect all the depreciation in the structure as a whole, varying amounts of deterioration in short-lived items are not directly indicated in the age-life method. For example, a structure as a whole may be estimated to be 20% depreciated except for the roof, which, unlike other roofs in the neighborhood, is estimated to be 90% depreciated. In this situation, the breakdown method would allow an appraiser to make a more refined analysis.

Variations of the Age-Life Method

In some situations, the impact of certain items of depreciation on value is known or can be easily and accurately estimated and an appraiser can deduct those items from total cost before applying the age-life ratio. Such variations combine techniques from the market extraction and breakdown methods as well as the traditional age-life method.

In the most common variation of the age-life method, the cost to cure the curable items of depreciation (both physical and functional) is known. Deducting curable items of depreciation from the cost of improvements before the age-life ratio is applied mirrors what typical purchasers consider when deciding on whether to invest in a property. This procedure is most meaningful when the subject property has curable depreciation not typically found in the market data at the time of appraisal. When the curable items are dealt with first, the appraiser may have to consider using a shorter effective age and/or a longer economic life expectancy in calculating the age-life ratio.

For example, consider a 20-year-old property with a total cost of $892,000. The interior needs to be completely refurbished at a documented cost of $82,500. Sales of similar buildings that were sold after being refurbished were used to extract a total economic life expectancy of 50 years. In deriving a total economic life expectancy for each comparable building, the appraiser used an effective age that was 25% lower than the building's actual age because investors in the market feel that the effective age of a building will be lower than its actual age once the interior has been refurbished. This avoids any double counting of depreciation. After the completion of the refurbishment, the subject's effective age is assumed to be 15 years—i.e., 25% lower than its actual age of 20 years. Dividing 15 years by the market-extracted total economic life expectancy of 50 years indicates total depreciation (excluding the interior) of 30%. This ratio is applied to the subject's cost less the cost of interior refurbishment ($892,000 – $82,500, or $809,500) to derive a depreciation estimate of $242,850. Assuming a land value estimate of $100,000, the cost approach can be applied as follows:

Total cost	$892,000
Less cost to refurbish interior	– 82,500
Remaining cost	$809,500
Less depreciation	
(Remaining cost × age-life ratio: $809,500 × 30%)	– 242,850
Depreciated cost	$566,650
Plus land value	+ 100,000
Indicated value by cost approach	$666,650

In situations where external obsolescence is present, another variation of the age-life method can be applied. If external obsolescence is affecting the subject property and there are sales of properties in the subject market that have incurred the same external obsolescence, the appraiser should use the total economic life extracted from these sales in the age-life ratio. However, if external obsolescence is affecting the subject property and there are no sales in the subject market similarly affected, the appraiser should estimate depreciation exclusive of external obsolescence using a market-extracted economic life expectancy in the age-life ratio and then estimate external obsolescence using techniques from the breakdown method. The estimated depreciation from the age-life method and the estimated external obsolescence from the breakdown method would be added together to arrive at an estimate of total depreciation.

As an example, consider a property in a district where there is an over-supply of competitive properties. This glut of competitive space has resulted in a 10% reduction in rents, which the appraiser equates with a 10% loss in building value. Land value is affected as well, though not as severely as building value, and the effect is reflected in the current estimate of the land value. Until the oversupply is corrected through the natural interaction of supply and demand, the building and land will continue to be affected. The cost of the 10-year-old building improvement is $696,000, and the land value is estimated at $255,000. The market extraction method, applied to comparables in the subject's market a year earlier when there was no oversupply, indicated a total economic life expectancy of 50 years. Using the age-life method, depreciation is thus estimated at 20% (10/50).

The physical and functional depreciation estimated for the subject improvements by the age-life method is $139,200 ($696,000 × 0.20) and the additional external obsolescence for the building is estimated to be $69,600 ($696,000 × 0.10). Total depreciation, therefore, is allocated as follows:

Depreciation attributable to all causes except external obsolescence	$139,200
Depreciation attributable to the external obsolescence	+ 69,600
Total depreciation	$208,800

Note that the external obsolescence is caused by an oversupply in the market, and it is unlikely that such a situation will be permanent. As supply and demand again approach equilibrium, the oversupply will probably disappear.

The modified age-life techniques work best when relatively few adjustments need to be made to the age-life method of estimating total depreciation. Usually, relatively nominal adjustments are made for curable physical items or for a functional or external influence. If more than one atypical element exists in a property, it may be advisable to convert to the more detailed breakdown method.

Breakdown Method

The breakdown method is the most comprehensive and detailed way to measure depreciation. When used in conjunction with the market extraction and age-life methods, the breakdown method disaggregates a total depreciation estimate into its component parts—physical deterioration, functional

Figure 16.1   Components of Depreciation

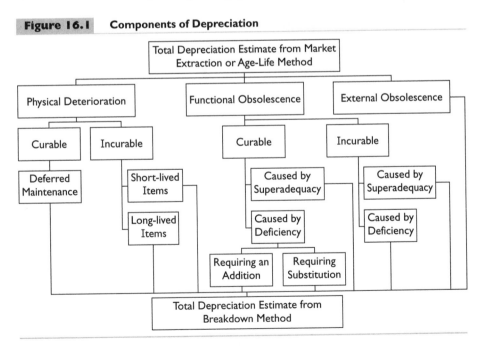

obsolescence, and external obsolescence—which can, in turn, be broken down into more precise components as illustrated in Figure 16.1.

The primary techniques used to calculate the different types of depreciation include the following:

- Estimation of *cost to cure*, which is a measure used for curable physical deterioration and curable functional obsolescence

- Application of an *age-life ratio* to measure curable physical deterioration and incurable physical deterioration for both short-lived and long-lived components

- Application of the *functional obsolescence procedure* to estimate all types of functional obsolescence

- Analysis of *market data* (paired sales or other techniques), which may be used to estimate incurable functional obsolescence caused by a deficiency as well as external obsolescence

- *Capitalization of income loss,*[1] which may also be used to estimate incurable functional obsolescence caused by a deficiency as well as external obsolescence

The breakdown method can be applied to allocate an estimate of total depreciation among its various components or to develop a conclusion for total depreciation by adding together estimates of each item of depreciation (see Table 16.1).

Applicability and Limitations

Generally, full application of the breakdown method requires too much time and expense to serve as a practical appraisal technique in all situations. It is primarily used when the appraisal assignment requires that each form of depreciation be accounted for in the appraisal report. In addition to allocating lump-sum estimates of total depreciation among their various components, the breakdown method is used when the market extraction and age-life methods cannot be applied. This usually occurs when the multiple elements of depreciation that exist in the subject property are not accurately reflected in available sales data and a closer analysis of these elements of depreciation is required. Other situations may require the breakdown method when the age-life method is too simplistic to account for the varied forms of depreciation present.

When using the breakdown method, several cautions and considerations should be kept in mind. First, if the sum of all items of physical deterioration estimated using the breakdown method is equivalent to the total depreciation derived from the market extraction or age-life methods, then no functional or external obsolescence is present. Second, if the sum of all items of physical

---

1. In previous editions of *The Appraisal of Real Estate*, the term *rent loss* had been used to denote the loss of income from rent. The term *income loss*, which is used in this edition, denotes lost rent as well as other income that may be lost to depreciation.

Table 16.1	**Procedures for Applying the Breakdown Method**
Purpose	To allocate a known estimate of total depreciation developed with the market extraction or age-life methods among its various components
Procedure	1. Estimate total depreciation using the market extraction or age-life method.
	2. Calculate all items of *physical deterioration*, add them up, and subtract the total from the lump-sum depreciation estimate. The residual amount, if any, represents depreciation attributable to functional and external obsolescence.
	3. Calculate all items of *functional obsolescence*, add them up, and subtract that total from the total amount of obsolescence.
	4. Any residual represents the depreciation attributable to *external obsolescence*.
Purpose	To develop an estimate of total depreciation one item at a time
Procedure	1. Calculate all items of *physical deterioration*, using the appropriate techniques, and then add up all estimates to arrive at total physical deterioration.
	2. Calculate all items of *functional obsolescence*, again using appropriate techniques, and add these estimates together to arrive at total functional obsolescence.
	3. Calculate *external obsolescence*. When external obsolescence cannot be allocated from a lump-sum estimate, it is calculated either through analysis of paired data or by capitalization of income loss. The estimate of external obsolescence may have to be allocated between the site and the improvements, depending on how it is derived.
	4. Calculate *damage* or deferred maintenance, if present, on a cost-to-cure basis.
	5. Add together all physical deterioration, functional obsolescence, external obsolescence, and cost to cure physical damage to arrive at an estimate of *total depreciation*.

deterioration and functional obsolescence estimated with breakdown techniques is equivalent to the total depreciation derived from the market extraction or age-life methods, then no external obsolescence is present. Finally, if the sum of the items of depreciation estimated by the breakdown method substantially differs from the total depreciation derived from the market extraction method or age-life method all the methods applied should be reviewed as a test of reasonableness. There are several reasons why there might be a difference in the results obtained from the breakdown method and the market extraction method or age-life method.

• The total depreciation derived from the market extraction method or age-life method may have been estimated incorrectly or does not reflect the characteristics of the depreciation in the subject property.

• The subject property may suffer from an element of depreciation that is indicated in the breakdown method but not in the market extraction method or age-life method possibly due to dissimilarities in the comparable data.

• One or more of the breakdown techniques may have been applied incorrectly.

- Certain applications of the breakdown method may have resulted in double counting some element of depreciation.

Physical Deterioration

In the breakdown method, all physical building components fall into one of three categories:

1. Deferred maintenance
2. Short-lived components
3. Long-lived components

Deferred maintenance is curable whereas short-lived and long-lived items of physical deterioration are incurable. Elements of total depreciation that are not physical deterioration must be some form of obsolescence (either functional or external).

Curable Physical Deterioration—Deferred Maintenance

Curable physical deterioration, also known as *deferred maintenance,* applies to items in need of immediate repair on the effective date of the appraisal. Some examples include broken windows, a broken or inoperable HVAC system, carpet needing immediate replacement, a hole in an interior partition, or a cracked lavatory. For most properties, deferred maintenance involves relatively minor items that are 100% physically deteriorated (i.e., broken). The item must be replaced or repaired for the building to continue to function as it should. By definition, most repairs must be performed for the building to continue to function, so they are usually curable items.

There are two major tests of the curability of a physically deteriorated item:

- First, if spending the money to "cure" the item will result in a value increment equal to or greater than the expenditure, the item is normally considered curable.
- Second, if spending the money to cure the item will not result in a value increment equal to or greater than the expenditure *but will allow other existing items to maintain their value,* then the item is normally considered curable.

Deferred maintenance is measured as the cost to cure the item or to restore it to a new or reasonably new condition. The cost to cure may exceed the item's cost when it is installed new. Cost to cure is analogous to an age-life procedure because the age of a curable item equals (or exceeds) its total useful life expectancy, resulting in 100% deterioration. All deferred maintenance items are completely deteriorated, and therefore they may all be treated together in the breakdown method.

> Components of **physical deterioration** include items of deferred maintenance, short-lived items, and long-lived items.

For example, assume that during the inspection of an office the appraiser notes that the exterior walls need to be scraped, primed, and painted. A painting contractor quotes a price of $5,000 to do the work; however, according to the appraiser's cost manual, the job performed at the present time should only cost $3,500. In this instance the correct measure of cost to cure is $5,000. If the painting were done during the original construction, the walls would not have had to be scraped; the contractor could have just primed and painted them. The extra cost is the difference between the cost to cure and the total cost. The higher amount should be used by the appraiser as the cost to cure and the appropriate measure of curable physical deterioration for this building component.

Incurable Physical Deterioration—Short-Lived Items

Once any curable physical deterioration is estimated, the remaining physical deterioration is allocated to either long-lived or short-lived building components. Short-lived items are those that are not ready to be replaced on the date of the opinion of value but will probably have to be replaced in the foreseeable (i.e., "short-term") future. Examples include the roof covering, interior floor finish, furnaces, and water heaters. A short-lived item is not 100% physically deteriorated, so it does not yet need to be cured. However, the appraiser draws the same conclusions that market participants do—i.e., that the items will be 100% deteriorated before the end of the building's total useful life expectancy and will have to be replaced. When those items reach the point of 100% physical deterioration, they become curable items. The same tests of curability that are applied to items of deferred maintenance are applied to short-lived items. Unlike items of deferred maintenance, which have lasted beyond their useful life expectancy and need to be replaced immediately, the short-lived items have generally not reached the end of their total useful life expectancy and are not completely deteriorated, but they are substantially depreciated in comparison with the overall structure.

The deterioration in short-lived items is measured by estimating a separate age-life ratio and applying it to the cost to replace each short-lived item on the date of value. As with items of deferred maintenance, the cost to cure may exceed total cost. Because all short-lived items ultimately will become deferred maintenance items and because deferred maintenance items are measured by the cost to cure, the proper place to begin analysis of the short-lived components is with the estimation of the cost to cure each item. Because each short-lived item usually has a different age and a different total useful life expectancy, a separate age-life ratio or schedule must be calculated for each item.

As an example, consider a 20-year-old boiler in an apartment building. According to a boiler contractor, the total useful life expectancy of a boiler such as this is 25 years. On the date of the opinion of value, the boiler is operative and there is no need to replace it. However, a prudent purchaser or owner would anticipate that the boiler will have to be replaced within a few years. If the boiler were to be replaced on the date of the opinion of value, the cost would be $30,000. The age-life ratio is used to estimate a depreciation rate of 80% (20/25 = 0.80). When this ratio is applied to the cost to replace the boiler ($30,000), the deterioration indicated is $24,000 ($30,000 × 0.80). The boiler would not be considered a short-lived item if its remaining useful life were equal to or greater than the remaining economic life of the overall property.

Incurable Physical Deterioration—Long-Lived Items

Long-lived items include all items that were not treated as items of deferred maintenance or as short-lived items. Long-lived items are assumed to have the same age and life expectancy and, therefore, they are all treated together. Examples of long-lived items include wall studs, underground piping, foundation walls, and insulation. A long-lived item is not 100% physically deteriorated; therefore, it does not need to be cured. In addition, such an item is not normally replaced except under extraordinary circumstances–e.g., if a foundation wall is damaged. The same tests of curability that are applied to the other physical components are applied to the long-lived items. The deterioration of long-lived items is measured by estimating an age-life ratio and applying it to all components of cost that have not already been treated for physical deterioration.

As an example, consider a small industrial building with a total cost of $700,000. It is 35 years old and has a total useful life expectancy of 100 years. The cost to cure the curable items (deferred maintenance) is $10,000. Short-lived building components include the boiler, roof cover, and floor covering. The cost to replace the boiler is $40,000, the cost to replace the roof covering is $60,000, and the cost to replace the floor finish is $20,000. There are no other short-lived items. The age-life ratio is calculated to be 35% (35-year actual age divided by 100-year useful life = 0.35). Physical deterioration in the long-lived items is estimated by deducting the cost to cure the curable items and the sum of the costs to replace the short-lived items from the cost of the structure ($700,000 − $10,000 − [$40,000 + $60,000 + $20,000] = $570,000). The age-life ratio is applied to the untreated costs (0.35 × $570,000) and the resulting amount of deterioration attributable to the long-lived items is $199,500.

Estimating All Forms of Physical Deterioration Using the Age-Life Procedure

Figure 16.2 illustrates an age-life procedure that can be used to estimate all forms of physical deterioration, both curable and incurable. In addition to showing the correct way to estimate all items of physical deterioration, the diagram was designed to ensure that no items of physical deterioration are treated more than once. This age-life procedure works whether the breakdown method is being used to allocate

The **age-life procedure** is a useful model for ensuring that all forms of physical deterioration are correctly estimated and dealt with only once.

Figure 16.2   Age-Life Procedure for Estimating All Items of Physical Deterioration

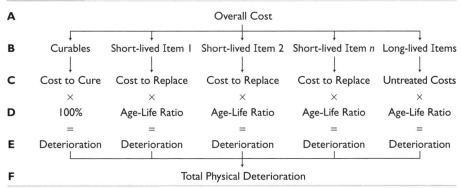

a known total depreciation amount among its components or to develop an estimate of total depreciation.

The procedure has four steps. First, the total cost is allocated among the curable items, the incurable short-lived items, and the incurable long-lived items. Second, an age-life ratio is calculated for each allocated cost item. Third, the appropriate age-life ratio is applied to the estimated cost of each item. Finally, the individual items of physical deterioration are added together to develop an estimate of total physical deterioration.

Reading across the top row of the diagram, Row A, the appraiser enters the overall cost of the improvement. Note the arrows leading from Row A to Row B. Row B is used to separate the various building components into curables, short-lived components, and long-lived components. The first column on the left is for the curable items, which are grouped together because they are all 100% physically deteriorated. The last column on the right is for the long-lived items, which are also grouped together because they all have incurred the same amount of physical deterioration. In the center of the diagram, there are separate columns for each short-lived item because each typically has a different age and a different total useful life. The number of interior columns depends on the number of short-lived items observed by the appraiser.

Row C is used to allocate the improvement's overall cost on Row A among the individual items. The sum of the cost to cure all curable items is entered in the left column. The cost to replace each of the short-lived items is entered in the appropriate column in the central portion of the diagram. The cost to cure the curable items and the individual costs to replace all short-lived items on Row C are added up and the total is deducted from the cost on Row A. The result is entered in the column on the right, which represents the remaining costs attributable to the long-lived items. All of the items on Row C, when added together, should equal the overall cost on Row A. By allocating costs before estimating the deterioration in any item, the appraiser is assured that all items will be treated for physical deterioration and none will be treated more than once.

The appraiser enters the age-life ratio of each item on Row D. All curable items are completely deteriorated, so 100% should be entered in the left-hand column of Row D. A separate age-life ratio is calculated for each short-lived item, using the actual age and useful life expectancy of the specific item. Total useful life for short-lived items may be obtained from the actual age of a component at the time of its replacement, analysis of manufacturer warranties, and information from property managers, contractors, and suppliers—i.e., building equipment stores and lumber yards.

Also, an age-life ratio is calculated based on the actual age of the long-lived items, which is usually equivalent to the chronological age of the building, and the total useful life expectancy of the long-lived items, which is usually extracted from the market. The age-life ratio calculated for long-lived items is entered in the right-hand column of Row D. The appraiser should recognize that the total useful life expectancy of long-lived items tends to be longer than economic life. Moreover, regardless of how long physical components may last (e.g., concrete might last indefinitely), an economic factor must also be considered, which is why the term *useful life* is used rather than *physical life*. Economic reasons will prevail when a building reaches the end of its economic life and is torn down. Total useful life for long-lived components can be estimated using neighborhood data, information from structural engineers, analysis of demolition permits, or direct market extraction. If a building is torn down and the site is redeveloped with a use similar to the use of the building that was torn down, the age of the building at the time it was torn down may be indicative of the building's useful life.

Physical deterioration estimates are calculated on Row E. The age-life ratio in each column on Row D is applied to the corresponding cost on Row C. The result is the physical deterioration for each item. The deterioration estimates on Row E should be less than the costs on Row C for all columns except the first, where the deterioration estimate on Row E should equal the cost on Row C. The total physical deterioration for the subject property is calculated by adding up all of the items on Row E and recording the sum on Row F.

DAMAGE/VANDALISM

Damage or vandalism requires special treatment in the estimation of depreciation. The measure of damage is the cost to cure. Damage or vandalism must be treated separately from other forms of physical deterioration because it is not considered in the estimate of cost. By curing damage or vandalism, the life of the damaged component is neither renewed nor prolonged; it simply is restored to its condition prior to the damage.

As an example, consider a brick wall that has been spray painted with graffiti. The cost of sandblasting the wall to remove the graffiti is $5,000. Nowhere in the overall cost is there a provision for the removal of graffiti. The measure of damage in this instance would be $5,000, the full cost to cure.

Typically, the cost to cure damage is added to the curable physical deterioration and included among the items of physical deterioration in the breakdown method. However, the $5,000 cost to cure is not subtracted from cost when calculating long-lived physical deterioration.

Figure 16.3   **Age-Life Estimation of Physical Deterioration**

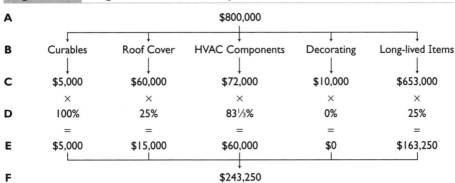

A			$800,000		
B	Curables	Roof Cover	HVAC Components	Decorating	Long-lived Items
C	$5,000	$60,000	$72,000	$10,000	$653,000
	×	×	×	×	×
D	100%	25%	83⅓%	0%	25%
	=	=	=	=	=
E	$5,000	$15,000	$60,000	$0	$163,250
F			$243,250		

As an example of these calculations, consider a 25-year-old industrial building in average condition. Its overall cost is $800,000 (see Figure 16.3). On the date of inspection, the appraiser found one overhead door damaged beyond repair, which will cost $5,000 to replace. The roof was replaced five years ago and has a 20-year guarantee; the cost to replace it is $60,000. The original HVAC components should last another five years, which indicates they are 83⅓% deteriorated (25/30). The cost to replace the HVAC components is $72,000. The offices were just completely redecorated at a cost of $10,000. The appraiser estimates that they will not have to be redecorated for another five years. Based on an analysis of demolition permits, the appraiser concludes that the total useful life expectancy of the long-lived items is 100 years.

In this example, the total physical deterioration is the sum of the individual deterioration calculations, $5,000 + $15,000 + $60,000 + $163,250, or $243,250.

Functional Obsolescence

Functional obsolescence is caused by a flaw in the structure, materials, or design of the improvement when compared with the highest and best use and most cost-effective functional design requirements at the time of appraisal. A building that was functionally adequate at the time of construction can become inadequate or less appealing as design standards, mechanical systems, and construction materials change over time. Functional obsolescence is attributable to defects within the property, while external obsolescence is caused by external factors. Functional obsolescence, which may be curable or incurable, can be caused by a deficiency, which means that some aspect of the subject property is below standard in respect to market norms. It can also be caused by a superadequacy, which means that some aspect of the subject property exceeds market norms.

There are five types of functional obsolescence:

- Curable functional obsolescence caused by a deficiency requiring an addition (installation) of a new item

- Curable functional obsolescence caused by a deficiency requiring the substitution (replacement) of an existing item (i.e., "curing a defect")
- Curable functional obsolescence caused by a superadequacy that is economically feasible to cure
- Incurable functional obsolescence caused by a deficiency
- Incurable functional obsolescence caused by a superadequacy

Table 16.2		Types of Functional Obsolescence
Type		**Characteristics/Measure**
Curable*	Deficiency requiring an addition	The subject suffers functional obsolescence because it lacks something that other properties in the market have. Since the item is not present, the property cannot be penalized for any deterioration the item may have incurred. However, because it usually costs more to add an item to an existing property, the excess cost to cure is the appropriate measure of functional obsolescence.
	Deficiency requiring substitution or modernization	A curable deficiency requiring substitution or modernization is caused by something that is present in the subject property but is either substandard compared to other properties on the market or is defective and thereby prevents some other component or system in the property from working properly. The measure is the excess cost to cure plus the depreciated cost of the existing item.
	Superadequacy	A superadequacy is a type of functional obsolescence caused by something in the subject property that exceeds market requirements but does not contribute to value an amount equal to its cost. The superadequacy may have a cost to carry (i.e., higher operating costs) that must be considered. A superadequacy is only curable if it can be removed and value is added (or costs reduced) to the property—including any salvage value—from its removal.
Incurable	Deficiency	The subject suffers functional obsolescence from some lack that is not economically feasible to correct.
	Superadequacy	An item of incurable functional obsolescence caused by a superadequacy is a property component that exceeds market requirements. It represents a cost without any corresponding increment in value or a cost that the increment in value does not meet. Note that in most applications of the cost approach, the need to estimate the functional obsolescence attributable to an incurable superadequacy is eliminated by using replacement cost instead of reproduction cost; superadequacies are not replicated in a replacement cost estimate. Nevertheless, whether replacement or reproduction cost is used, any extraordinary expense of ownership associated with the superadequacy must be quantified and deducted as a penalty from the value of the property. Essentially, the property must suffer the loss or added costs of ownership over time because the component is incurable. Also, over time the cost of ownership can increase, making the component curable.

* Functional obsolescence is considered curable when it is economically feasible to do so.

Characteristics of the different types of functional obsolescence are illustrated in Table 16.2. Elements of total depreciation not identified as physical deterioration or as functional obsolescence must be external obsolescence.

Like the curability of physical deterioration, there are two major tests of curability for functional obsolescence caused by a deficiency or superadequacy:

- If spending the money to cure the item will result in a value increment equal to or greater than the expenditure, the item is normally considered curable.

> **Functional obsolescence** may be caused by a deficiency or a superadequacy; some forms are curable and others are incurable.

- If spending the money to cure the item will not result in a value increment equal to or greater than the expenditure but will allow existing items to maintain their value, the item is again considered curable.

If the cost to cure the item will not result in a value increment greater than the loss in value caused by the item or building component, then the item is considered incurable.

Functional obsolescence can be corrected in two ways:

- The functional obsolescence is cured by the property owner when this is economically feasible (and sometimes when it is not economically feasible).

or

- Market norms change, eliminating the cause of the functional obsolescence.

Problem-Solving for Functional Obsolescence

A simple process can be used to identify and select the appropriate treatment for a functional problem. The first step is to identify the functional problem (see Figure 16.4). In many cases this is readily apparent from the property inspection and information from the highest and best use analysis or other analyses in the valuation process. Once the functional problem has been identified, the next step is to determine which building components are causing the problem and identify possible corrective measures (and associated costs to cure).

Figure 16.4	**Solving a Functional Problem**

1. Identify the functional problem.
2. Identify the component(s) in the facility or lack of component(s) associated with the problem.
3. Identify possible corrective measure(s) and the related cost to cure.
4. Select the most appropriate corrective measure.
5. Quantify the loss caused by the functional problem, which results in added value if the problem is corrected.
6. Determine if the item is curable or incurable. (If the value added is greater than the cost to cure, the functional problem is curable.)
7. Apply the functional obsolescence procedure.

In many cases there will be only one cost-to-cure program to fix or improve a functional problem. Often, especially for superadequate components, there may be no economically feasible or practical method to cure the problem. In this case the component is incurable and the property must endure the loss in value. If there are multiple cost-to-cure scenarios to cure a particular problem, the appraiser should select the most appropriate or cost-effective measure.

The cost to cure must consider the cost to tear out or replace the existing component, plus the cost of the correct replacement component, plus any other costs above and beyond the total cost if the component was included in the initial construction, less any salvage value. Essentially, the final measure is total cost to cure offset by any salvage value:

> Cost to tear out or remove existing component
> + Cost of correct replacement component
> + Any costs above and beyond total cost if included in initial construction
> − Salvage value (if any)
> Cost to cure

The next step is to quantify the loss caused by the functional problem associated with the building component. The value loss could be caused by a loss in income, an increase in expenses or operating costs, or a combination of both. By definition, the loss cured will be the added value once the cure is accomplished.

Now the cost to cure is compared with the quantified loss. If the added value (once the cure is accomplished) is greater than the cost to cure, then the functional problem is curable. Otherwise, the functional problem is incurable. The next step is to solve for the dollar amount of depreciation using the functional obsolescence procedure.

Using the Functional Obsolescence Procedure

Figure 16.5 diagrams a procedure that can be used to calculate all forms of functional obsolescence caused by a deficiency or a superadequacy, whether the obsolescence is curable or incurable. Use of this model ensures that all components of functional obsolescence will be treated in a consistent manner, that none of the items will be treated more than once, and that no double charges will be made for items that have already been depreciated (i.e., charged under physical deterioration), which is particularly important for superadequacies.

First, the cost of the existing item is identified. If the item is a form of functional obsolescence caused by a deficiency requiring an addition, there will be no cost for the item and zero will be entered on this line. Also, when replacement cost, rather than reproduction cost, is used for the cost basis, there typically will be no cost allotted for any superadequate items. As stated earlier in the text, all forms of

> The **functional obsolescence procedure** ensures that all items of functional obsolescence will be treated consistently, that none will be considered more than once, and that double depreciation charges will not be made.

Figure 16.5	**Procedure for Estimating All Forms of Functional Obsolescence**	
Step 1.	Cost of existing item	$xxx,xxx
Step 2.	Less depreciation previously charged	− xxx,xxx
	plus	
Step 3.	Cost to cure (all costs)	+ xxx,xxx
	or	*or*
	Value of the loss	+ xxx,xxx
Step 4.	Less cost if installed new	− xxx,xxx
Step 5.	Equals depreciation for functional obsolescence	$xxx,xxx

functional obsolescence present in the subject property would also be present in a reproduction of that property, whereas a replacement structure would not exhibit certain forms of obsolescence present in the original improvement.

In the second step, any depreciation that has already been charged for the item is deducted. In nearly all instances, this depreciation will be physical deterioration. As in the first step, if the item does not already exist in the building, no depreciation will have been charged and zero will be entered on this line. The net effect of the first two steps is to completely remove the total cost of the item (i.e., physical depreciation already taken plus remaining cost not depreciated in the first two steps).

Regardless of the type of functional obsolescence, the appraiser must evaluate an alternative cost to cure to determine whether the item is curable or not. If the functional obsolescence is curable, the third step is to add up all the costs associated with curing the item. This includes the cost of purchasing and installing a new item, the cost of removing the old item, and any net salvage value. If the functional obsolescence is incurable, the third step is to add the value of the loss attributable to the obsolescence. This value can be obtained by capitalizing an income loss (using an income multiplier or a capitalization rate) or through analysis of market data such as paired sales.

The fourth step is to enter a deduction for the cost of the item as though installed new on the date of the value opinion, if appropriate. When the third step involves a curable item, the combination of the third and fourth steps essentially yields the excess cost to cure. As the final step, the appraiser adds up all of the entries to derive the total functional obsolescence attributable to each factor. The model described here works for all types of functional obsolescence. The following examples demonstrate how the procedure is used to estimate different types of functional obsolescence.

Curable Functional Obsolescence Caused by a Deficiency Requiring an Addition

Consider a small office building without air-conditioning in a market where that feature is standard. Because of retrofit requirements, it is more costly to install the air-conditioning now than it would have been as a part of the original construction. The current cost of installing the air-conditioning is $12,000; if the work had been done as a part of new construction, the cost would have been only

$10,000. Installing air-conditioning would allow the property owner to raise rents, and effective gross income would increase an estimated $2,000 per year. The current effective gross income multiplier (*EGIM*) is 7.0. The functional obsolescence is curable because the value increase ($2,000 × 7.0 = $14,000) is greater than the cost to cure ($12,000).

1.	Cost of existing item	$0
2.	Less depreciation previously charged	− 0
	plus	
3.	Cost to cure (all costs)	+ 12,000
	or	
	Value of loss	—
4.	Less cost if installed new	− 10,000
5.	Equals depreciation for functional obsolescence	$2,000

Note that because the air-conditioning is not present in the existing improvement, no cost is shown as total cost and no deterioration was charged (Steps 1 and 2). The cost to install the air-conditioning as a part of new construction on the date of the opinion of value is $10,000 (Step 4), but the actual cost to retrofit and install the air-conditioning is $12,000 (Step 3). The curable functional obsolescence is the excess cost to cure, or $2,000 (Step 5).

Incurable Functional Obsolescence Caused by a Deficiency

Now suppose that installing an air-conditioning system in the office is not economically feasible—e.g., the current cost of the necessary renovations (say, $20,000) is greater than the value gained by adding the item ($14,000). For each building component in the functional depreciation area, two elements must be identified:

- The cost to cure
- The amount of loss caused by the component or lack of the component

When the loss is cured, the amount of the loss essentially becomes the value added. In this case, the cost to cure is $20,000. If the item is cured, the value added (or reduction in loss) is only $14,000, which means the item is incurable. The depreciation charged is the amount of the loss, over and above the cost if installed new. In the previous example, the item was curable and the measure of depreciation was the excess cost to cure.

1.	Cost of existing item	$0
2.	Less depreciation previously charged	− 0
	plus	
3.	Cost to cure (all costs)	—
	or	
	Value of loss	+ 14,000
4.	Less cost if installed new	− 10,000
5.	Equals depreciation for functional obsolescence	$4,000

Costs to cure and losses sustained by a component can and do change over time. Items identified as incurable at one point in time can become curable and vice versa over the life of the property.

Again, because the air-conditioning is not present in the existing improvement, no deterioration was charged. The value of the loss is equivalent to the lost income attributable to the deficiency. The effect of this loss is partially offset by the $10,000 that would have been expended to install air-conditioning as part of new construction. The incurable functional obsolescence is $4,000.

Curable Functional Obsolescence Caused by a Deficiency Requiring Substitution or Modernization

Now suppose that the office building has an outdated air-conditioning system that does not meet market standards and needs to be retrofitted. The reproduction cost of the existing air-conditioning system is $8,000, and the item is 25% physically deteriorated ($8,000 × 0.25 = $2,000). The cost to remove the existing air-conditioning is $4,500, the salvage value of that equipment is $3,000, and the current cost of installing an appropriate air-conditioning system is $12,000 ($10,000 to install the correct component and $2,000 to retrofit the space). The property can still be expected to increase effective gross income by $2,000 per year (with an *EGIM* of 7.0) if an appropriate air-conditioning system is installed, so the extra income generated ($14,000) would exceed the cost to cure ($4,500 − $3,000 + $12,000 = $13,500) and the item is therefore curable. If the correct air-conditioning system had been installed as part of new construction, the cost would have been $10,000.

1.	Cost of existing item	$8,000
2.	Less depreciation previously charged	− 2,000
	plus	
3.	Cost to cure (all costs)	+ 13,500
	or	
	Value of loss	—
4.	Less cost if installed new	− 10,000
5.	Equals depreciation for functional obsolescence	$9,500

In this case, application of the formula essentially removes the existing component from cost (the $8,000 cost of the existing equipment less physical depreciation already charged of $2,000) in the first two steps and penalizes cost by the excess cost to cure of $3,500 ($13,500 − $10,000) in the third and fourth steps.

Suppose that the existing equipment had no salvage value. The cost to cure the deficiency ($4,500 for removal of existing equipment plus $12,000 for installation of the new system, or $16,500) would exceed the value gained by replacing the air-conditioning system ($14,000), and the item of functional obsolescence would be incurable. Incurable functional obsolescence caused by the deficiency (i.e., the inadequacy of the existing air-conditioning system) would be $10,000.

1.	Cost of existing item	$8,000
2.	Less depreciation previously charged	− 2,000
	plus	
3.	Cost to cure (all costs)	—
	or	
	Value of loss	+ 14,000
4.	Less cost if installed new	− 10,000
5.	Equals depreciation for functional obsolescence	$10,000

Curable Functional Obsolescence Caused by a Superadequacy

Consider a warehouse built for an owner-occupant with an HVAC system providing excess cooling capacity for the storage of perishable goods. When the property goes on the rental market, the HVAC system will be superadequate in relation to most typical warehouse uses. The current reproduction cost of the existing HVAC system is $40,000, and the component is 30% depreciated. Removing the superadequate item would cost $5,000, the salvage value is $8,000, and installing an HVAC system with typical capacity for the market would cost $22,000 for a total cost to cure of $19,000 ($5,000 − $8,000 + $22,000). If a lower-capacity HVAC system had been installed as part of new construction, the item would have only cost $16,000. The lower-capacity HVAC would save the property owner $200 a month in electricity and maintenance expenses. Capitalized at an annual rate of 12% (a building capitalization rate derived from analysis of comparable sales), the value of the cost savings would be $20,000, which exceeds the cost to cure. The item is therefore curable.

1.	Reproduction cost of existing item	$40,000
2.	Less depreciation previously charged	− 12,000
	plus	
3.	Cost to cure (all costs)	+ 19,000
	or	
	Value of loss	—
4.	Less cost if installed new	− 16,000
5.	Equals depreciation from functional obsolescence	$31,000

If replacement cost of the appropriate HVAC system is used as the cost basis rather than reproduction cost, the superadequate item would not be included in the substitute property, so there would be no charge for the existing item, nor for the item as installed new. The measure of depreciation due to curable functional obsolescence caused by a superadequacy would be the cost to cure (i.e., the cost to remove the superadequate item less salvage value plus the cost to install the appropriate item).

1.	Replacement cost of existing item	$0
2.	Less depreciation previously charged plus	− 0
3.	Cost to cure (all costs)	+ 19,000
	or	
	Value of loss	—
4.	Less cost if installed new	− 0
5.	Equals depreciation from functional obsolescence	$19,000

Note that the depreciation estimate when replacement cost is used as the cost basis ($19,000) is less than the depreciation estimate when reproduction cost is used ($31,000). As stated in earlier chapters, the corresponding estimates of total cost using replacement cost would probably be lower than the estimate provided by reproduction cost figures. Therefore, less depreciation would be subtracted from the replacement cost estimate than from the reproduction cost estimate to arrive at the same figure (or similar amounts) for both cost bases.

Incurable Functional Obsolescence Caused by a Superadequacy

A superadequacy is often difficult to cure. Consider an industrial building with 24-ft. ceiling heights where the market norm is 18-ft. ceilings. The cost of a building with 24-ft. ceilings is $1.2 million whereas the cost of a building with 18-ft. ceilings is $1.0 million. The subject building costs $5,000 more per year to heat and cool than comparable properties in the subject's market. The extra $200,000 spent in the original construction on the extra six feet of ceiling height adds no value to the property and there is no reasonable cost to cure, so the superadequacy is incurable.

In this market, the higher ceiling would not be installed in a substitute property. Therefore, in the calculation of functional obsolescence, the amount entered as cost if installed new is zero. Note also that if replacement cost is used, the $200,000 cost of the superadequacy will be eliminated and the measure of functional obsolescence would be only the capitalized additional costs of ownership. The extra ceiling height costs the subject property $5,000 more per year than the costs incurred by competitive buildings, and analysis of income and expense data for comparable buildings yields a building capitalization rate of 12.5% in this market. The incurable functional obsolescence is estimated to be $40,000 ($5,000/0.125). Because the item is

> When **estimating functional obsoles-cence caused by a superadequacy**, the appraiser must remember whether the cost basis in the calculations is reproduc-tion cost or replacement cost. A super-adequacy in an existing improvement would not be installed in a replacement structure, so the cost of that item would not be included in the estimation of functional obsolescence when replace-ment cost figures are used.

superadequate, it does not belong in the structure and there is no correct replace-ment component, so there is no entry in Step 4. The replacement cost calculation is as follows:

1.	Replacement cost of existing item	$0
2.	Less depreciation previously charged	– 0
	plus	
3.	Cost to cure (all costs)	—
	or	
	Value of the loss	+ 40,000
4.	Less cost if installed new	– 0
5.	Equals depreciation from functional obsolescence	$40,000

If reproduction cost is used, the additional $200,000 cost of the superadequacy will not be eliminated. The incurable functional obsolescence would be measured as the cost of the superadequate item less the physical deterioration already charged plus the capitalized additional costs of ownership. Assuming that a 10% charge has already been levied for incurable physical deterioration due to the extra ceiling height, the incurable functional obsolescence would be the cost of the superadequate item ($200,000 for the extra six feet of ceiling height) less the physical deterioration already charged ($20,000) plus the added costs of ownership ($40,000). The resulting depreciation estimate is $220,000.

1.	Reproduction cost of existing item	$200,000
2.	Less depreciation previously charged	− 20,000
	plus	
3.	Cost to cure (all costs)	—
	or	
	Value of the loss	+ 40,000
4.	Less cost if installed new	− 0
5.	Equals depreciation from functional obsolescence	$220,000

External Obsolescence

External obsolescence is a loss in value caused by factors outside a property. It is often incurable. External obsolescence can be either temporary (e.g., an oversupplied market) or permanent (e.g., proximity to an environmental disaster). External factors frequently affect both the land and building components of a property's value. The current land value considers the effect of external factors. External obsolescence usually carries a marketwide effect and influences a whole class of properties, rather than just a single property. External obsolescence may affect only the subject property when its cause is location–e.g., proximity to negative environmental factors or the absence of zoning and land use controls.

> **External obsolescence may be caused by** economic or locational factors. It may be temporary or permanent, but it is not usually considered curable on the part of the owner, landlord, or tenant.

When market data is studied to develop an estimate of external obsolescence, it is important to isolate the effect of the obsolescence on land value from the effect on the value of the improvements. In some situations, external obsolescence may be attributed entirely to the land; in other situations, it may be attributed entirely to the improvements. Often external obsolescence can be allocated between land and improvements. This is critical if external obsolescence is already reflected in the estimate of land value. A building- to-property-value ratio derived through market area analysis may be used to determine the loss in value to be allocated to the building.

The three primary methods of measuring external obsolescence are

- Allocation of market-extracted depreciation
- Analysis of market data
- Capitalization of an income loss

External Obsolescence Estimated by Allocation of Market-Extracted Depreciation

When a lump-sum figure of total depreciation is estimated through market extraction, that amount can be allocated between the three major types of depreciation to generate an estimate of external obsolescence. As an example, consider an industrial property with a reproduction cost of $1 million in a market where similarly depreciated buildings have sold for $800,000. Total physical deterioration is calculated at $80,000, and total functional obsolescence is calculated at $10,000. The remaining portion of total depreciation, $110,000, can be allocated to external obsolescence.

Total cost		$1,000,000
Sale price (excluding land value)		− 800,000
Depreciation from all sources		$200,000
Allocation		
Physical deterioration		
Curable	$10,000	
Incurable	+ 70,000	
Total physical deterioration	$80,000	
Functional obsolescence		
Curable	$2,500	
Incurable	+ 7,500	
Total functional obsolescence	$10,000	
Total physical deterioration and functional obsolescence		− 90,000
Allocation to external obsolescence		$110,000

External Obsolescence Estimated by Market Data Analysis

Using paired data analysis, consider a subject property that is a 12-unit apartment building located downwind of a relatively new asphalt batching plant. Sale A is a vacant lot adjacent to the subject that is zoned for a 12-unit apartment building and was just sold for $36,000 ($3,000 per unit). Sale B is a vacant site on the other side of town that is also zoned for a 12-unit apartment building and was recently sold for $48,000 ($4,000 per unit). Sale C is a 9-unit apartment building in the subject's neighborhood that was recently sold for $459,000 ($51,000 per unit). Sale D is a 10-unit apartment building on the other side of town that was sold for $540,000 ($54,000 per unit). Using Sales C and D, the external obsolescence attributable to the property as a whole is estimated at $3,000 per unit. The subject property would thus incur $36,000 in external obsolescence (12 units × $3,000). Sales A and B indicate that $12,000 of this external obsolescence ($1,000 per unit) is recognized in the land value; the remaining $24,000, therefore, is attributable to the building.

External Obsolescence Estimated by Capitalization of Income Loss

When a property produces income, the income loss caused by the external obsolescence can be capitalized into an estimate of the loss in total property value. This procedure is applied in two steps. First, the

> **External obsolescence may be estimated** by allocation of market-extracted depreciation, market data analysis, or capitalization of income loss.

market is analyzed to quantify the income loss. Next, the income loss is capitalized to obtain the value loss affecting the property as a whole. If the income loss is anticipated to be permanent, it can be capitalized by applying either a gross income multiplier to a gross income loss or an overall capitalization rate to a net income loss. If the income loss is not anticipated to be permanent, it can be estimated using discounted cash flow analysis.

For example, consider a 4,000-sq.-ft. retail establishment in an oversupplied market. In a normal market, net operating income would be $8.00 per square foot. However, since the oversupply began, net operating income has fallen to $6.25 per square foot. The oversupply, which is unique to the subject's market, was caused by overbuilding. The overall capitalization rate indicated by the market is 10%. Since the oversupply is anticipated to continue indefinitely, the external obsolescence can be calculated by direct capitalization. The total income loss of $7,000 ([$8.00 − $6.25 = $1.75] × 4,000 square feet) is capitalized by the overall capitalization rate of 10%. The resulting external obsolescence of $70,000 would probably be attributed entirely to the improvements (if land value is not impacted).

If the oversupply were anticipated to continue for a relatively short period of time, the external obsolescence could be calculated by discounted cash flow analysis. Assume that the $7,000 income loss will only last three years and that the appropriate discount rate is 13%. The external obsolescence could be calculated as the present value of $7,000 per year for three years, discounted at 13% (*PV* of $1 per period at 13% for three years = 2.361153), or $16,528. As in the previous example in which direct capitalization was used, it is likely that the entire amount of external obsolescence would be attributable to the improvement.

FURTHER READING

Akerson, Charles B. *The Appraiser's Workbook.* 2d ed. Chicago: Appraisal Institute, 1996.

Cappello, Steve. "Incurable What?! Incurable Functional Obsolescence." *Assessment Journal* (July/ August 1995).

Derbes, Max J., Jr. "Accrued Depreciation Redefined and Reordered." *The Appraisal Journal* (April 1998).

Ellsworth, Richard K. "Estimating Depreciation for Infrequently Transacted Assets." *The Appraisal Journal* (January 2000).

Laronge, Joseph A. "Solving the Functional Obsolescence Calculation Question?" *The Appraisal Journal* (July 2000).

Laronge, Joseph A., and Kerry Dean Vandell. "Solving the Functional Obsolescence Calculation Question? Part II." *The Appraisal Journal* (April 2001).

Ramsett, David E. "The Cost Approach: An Alternative View." *The Appraisal Journal* (April 1998).

Williams, Thomas P. "Categorizing External Obsolescence." *The Appraisal Journal* (April 1996).

Wolverton, Marvin L. "Empirical Analysis of the Breakdown Method of Estimating Physical Depreciation." *The Appraisal Journal* (April 1998).

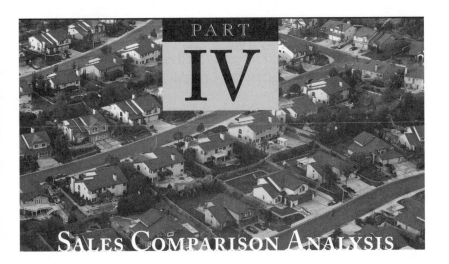

PART

IV

SALES COMPARISON ANALYSIS

Part IV focuses on the sales comparison approach, which is often considered the easiest approach to understand but can be one of the most difficult to support convincingly, especially when market data is hard to find. **Chapter 17, The Sales Comparison Approach,** covers the fundamental theories underlying the approach, while **Chapter 18, Adjustment and Analytical Techniques in the Sales Comparison Approach,** outlines the techniques used to analyze and make adjustments to comparable sales. **Chapter 19, Applications of the Sales Comparison Approach,** illustrates the calculation of quantitative adjustments for the various elements of comparison and the application of qualitative analysis.

CHAPTER 17

THE SALES COMPARISON APPROACH

In the sales comparison approach, the appraiser develops an opinion of value by analyzing similar properties and comparing these properties with the subject property. The comparative techniques of analysis applied in the sales comparison approach are fundamental to the valuation process. Estimates of market rent, expenses, land value, cost, depreciation, and other value parameters may be derived in the other approaches to value using similar comparative techniques. Similarly, conclusions derived in the other approaches are often analyzed in the sales comparison approach to estimate the adjustments to be made to the sale prices of comparable properties.

In the sales comparison approach, an opinion of market value is developed by comparing properties similar to the subject property that have recently sold, are listed for sale, or are under contract (i.e., for which purchase offers and a deposit have been recently submitted). A major premise of the sales comparison approach is that the market value of a property is related to the prices of comparable, competitive properties.

Comparative analysis of properties and transactions focuses on similarities and differences that affect value, which may include variations in the following:

- Property rights appraised
- The motivations of buyers and sellers
- Financing terms
- Market conditions at the time of sale
- Size
- Location
- Physical features
- Economic characteristics, if the properties produce income

Elements of comparison are tested against market evidence to estimate which elements are sensitive to change and how they affect value.

This chapter focuses on the theory and concepts underlying the sales comparison approach. Chapters 18 and 19

> **sales comparison approach:** A set of procedures in which a value indication is derived by comparing the property being appraised to similar properties that have been sold recently, applying appropriate units of comparison, and making adjustments to the sale prices of the comparables based on the elements of comparison. The sales comparison approach may be used to value improved properties, vacant land, or land being considered as though vacant.

further the discussion with a deeper examination of the techniques employed by appraisers to analyze and adjust comparable sales.

Relationship to Appraisal Principles

The concepts of anticipation and change, which underlie the principles of supply and demand, substitution, balance, and externalities, are basic to the sales comparison approach. Guided by these principles, an appraiser attempts to consider all issues relevant to the valuation problem in a manner that is consistent and reflects local market conditions.

Supply and Demand

Property prices result from negotiations between buyers and sellers, and they are influenced by the activities of lenders. Buyers constitute market demand, and the properties offered for sale make up the supply. This assumes a market with many buyers and sellers acting in their own interests. To estimate demand, appraisers consider the number of potential users of a particular type of property, their purchasing power, and their tastes and preferences. To analyze supply, appraisers focus on existing unsold or vacant properties as well as properties that are being constructed, converted, or planned. Shifts in any of these factors may cause the prices of the subject property and comparable properties to vary. Sales activity is also influenced by lenders, as most real estate purchases are financed. If interest rates drop, market activity will tend to accelerate and prices will tend to rise. If interest rates rise, market activity will tend to slow down and prices will tend to fall. If loan money becomes scarce, either due to high interest rates or restrictive underwriting standards, market activity can be severely reduced.

Substitution

The principle of substitution holds that the value of a property tends to be set by the price that would be paid to acquire a substitute property of similar utility and desirability within a reasonable amount of time. This principle implies that the reliability of the sales comparison approach is diminished if substitute properties are not available in the market.

Balance

The forces of supply and demand tend toward equilibrium, or balance, in the market, but absolute equilibrium is almost never attained. Due to shifts in population, purchasing power, and consumer tastes and preferences, demand varies greatly over time. The construction of new buildings, conversion to other uses, and the demolition of old buildings cause supply to vary as well.

Another aspect of this principle holds that the relationship between land and improvements and the relationship between a property and its environment must both be in balance for a property to reflect its optimum market value. If, for example, a property has too much land in relation to its improvements or too many expensive amenities for its location, an imbalance in the property is created. Appraisers must watch for imbalances in the market and within specific properties because they can cause the market to ascribe different prices to otherwise comparable properties.

Externalities

Positive and negative external forces affect all types of property. Periods of economic development and economic depression influence property values. An appraiser analyzes the market area of the subject property to identify all significant external influences. To a great extent, the adjustments made for location reflect these external forces. Two competitive properties with identical physical characteristics may have quite different market values if one of the properties has less attractive surroundings. The condition and lighting of streets, the convenience of transportation facilities, the adequacy of police protection, the enforcement of municipal regulations, and the proximity to shopping and restaurant facilities vary with location.

Applicability and Limitations

The sales comparison approach is applicable to all types of real property interests when there are sufficient recent, reliable transactions to indicate value patterns or trends in the market. For property types that are bought and sold regularly, the sales comparison approach often provides a supportable indication of market value. When data is available, this is the most straight-forward and simple way to explain and support a value opinion.

When the market is weak and few market transactions are available, the applicability of the sales comparison approach may be limited. For example, the sales comparison approach is usually not applied to special-purpose properties because few similar properties may be sold in a given market, even one that is geographically broad. To value special-purpose properties, the cost approach may be more appropriate and reliable. Nevertheless, sales and offers for properties in the same general category may be analyzed to establish broad limits for the value of the property being appraised, which may help support the findings of the other value approaches applied.

The sales comparison approach usually provides the primary indication of market value in appraisals of properties that are not usually purchased for their income-producing characteristics. These types of properties are amenable to sales comparison because similar properties are commonly bought and sold in the same market. Typically, the sales comparison approach provides the best indication of value for owner-occupied commercial and industrial properties.

Buyers of income-producing properties usually concentrate on a property's

> The sales comparison approach is **applicable** when sufficient data on recent market transactions is available. Essential information on income-producing properties derived through sales comparison is used in the income capitalization and cost approaches.

economic characteristics. Thoroughly analyzing comparable sales of large, complex, income-producing properties is difficult because information on the economic factors influencing the decisions of buyers is not readily available from public records or interviews with buyers and sellers. For example, an appraiser may not have sufficient knowledge of the existing leases applicable to a neighborhood shopping center that is potentially comparable to the subject. Property encumbered by a lease is a sale of rights other than fee simple rights and requires knowledge of the terms of all leases and an understanding of the tenant(s) occupying the premises. Some transactions include sales of other physical assets or business interests. In each instance, if the sale is to be useful for comparison purposes, it must be dissected into its various components. Even when the components of value can be allocated, it must be understood that because of the complexity of the mix of factors involved, the sale may be less reliable as an indicator of the subject's real property value.

Changing market conditions may reduce the validity or applicability of older sales that do not reflect the change. Trends from changing market conditions can be useful, but appraisers must be careful not to project trends without current market support of some form. Historical sales may be valuable to retrospective valuations and may assist in time series analysis; however, changes in market conditions make their use less reliable for current valuations with long-term adjustments for market conditions. Legal changes constitute a broad array of possibilities including tax laws, zoning, moratoriums, buildings codes, and others. The appraiser must look for a series of possible changes that may be imposed upon the market, thus changing the applicability of historical data. Likewise, some sales may reflect anticipations of such changes and may reflect market attitudes in advance of the actual change. Financing is also important to market sales behavior. Appraisers must seek and understand information concerning financing applicable to the particular property type and market at large as a part of the analysis processes.

A single sale may or may not be indicative of the market at large. Regardless of the number of sales analyzed, the appraiser must sufficiently understand each sale used for comparison to supportably draw comparison conclusions. A limitation of the approach is that the apparent value reflected by a sale price may not even reflect the market value of the property sold; it is only possible to determine that relationship after the sale, its property, and its market are researched and understood. In contrast, many sales that cannot be effectively used for direct comparison are at least part of the market at large and can be used for bracketing, understanding general market activity, or other analytical purposes. Thus, market data is classified and weighted for its importance, relevance, and reliability.

To ensure the reliability of value conclusions derived by applying the sales comparison approach, the appraiser must verify the market data obtained and fully understand the behavioral characteristics of the buyers and sellers involved in property transactions. Caution should be exercised when sales data is provided by someone who is not a party to the transaction. Incorrect conclusions may result if the appraiser relies on such data without considering the motivation of the parties to the transactions. Sometimes brokers will be able to provide more reliable information than the buyer or seller. Similarly, errors can result if anticipated income and expense schedules are inaccurate or if potential changes in use are not considered.

It is imperative that the appraiser identify and analyze the strengths and weaknesses of the quantity and quality of the data compiled and the extent of the comparative analyses undertaken in the sales comparison approach. All relevant facts and opinions must be considered in the analysis and reported in the amount of detail required by the type of appraisal report. The reliability of the data, the analyses performed, and the final conclusion of value should be presented in both the sales comparison approach and, where appropriate, the final opinion of value.

The sales comparison approach is a significant and essential part of the valuation process, even when its reliability is limited. Although appraisers cannot always properly identify and quantify how the factors affecting property value are different, they can still use the sales comparison approach to determine a probable range of value in support of a value indication derived using one of the other approaches. Furthermore, the comparison process often provides data needed to apply the other approaches—e.g., overall capitalization rates for the income capitalization approach or depreciation estimates for the cost approach.

Income multipliers, capitalization rates, and yield rates are applied in the income capitalization approach to value, but it is appropriate to extract such rates and factors from comparable properties in sales comparison analysis. Comparable prices are not adjusted on the basis of differences in net operating income per unit because rents and sale prices tend to move in relative tandem. However, the appraiser should consider why the income from units varies among the sale properties. Sensitivity and trend analyses may be performed to gain an understanding of this variance.

For example, an appraiser may analyze sales of income-producing properties to derive potential and effective gross income multipliers, overall and equity capitalization rates, and even total property yield rates. These factors are not adjusted quantitatively. Instead, the appraiser considers their ranges and the similarities and differences between the subject and comparable sale properties that cause the multipliers and rates to vary. The appraiser then selects the rate from within the bracket that is most appropriate to the property being appraised for use in the income capitalization approach.

A **systematic procedure** for applying the sales comparison approach includes the following steps: 1) researching transactional data, 2) verifying the data as accurate and representative of arm's-length transactions, 3) selecting relevant units of comparison, 4) determining how the comparables differ from the subject and adjusting their prices for differences in various elements of comparison, and 5) reconciling multiple value indications into a single value or range of values.

Procedure

To apply the sales comparison approach, an appraiser follows a systematic procedure:

1. Research the competitive market for information on sales transactions, listings, and offers to purchase or sell involving properties that are similar to the subject property in terms of characteristics such as property type, date of sale, size, physical condition, location, and land use constraints. The goal is to find a set of comparable sales as similar as possible to the subject property.

2. Verify the information by confirming that the data obtained is factually accurate and that the transactions reflect arm's-length market considerations. Verification may elicit additional information about the market.

3. Select relevant units of comparison (e.g., price per acre, price per square foot, price per front foot) and develop a comparative analysis for each unit. The goal here is to define and identify a unit of comparison that explains market behavior.

4. Look for differences between the comparable sale properties and the subject property using the elements of comparison. Then adjust the price of each sale property to reflect how it differs from the subject property or eliminate that property as a comparable. This step typically involves using the most comparable sale properties and then adjusting for any remaining differences.

5. Reconcile the various value indications produced from the analysis of comparables into a single value indication or a range of values.

Researching Transactional Data

In the first step of the sales comparison approach, an appraiser gathers data on sales, contracts, offers, refusals, options, and listings of properties considered competitive with, and comparable to, the subject property. Data from completed transactions is considered the most reliable value indicator. First, the appraiser thoroughly researches the prices, real property rights conveyed, financing terms, motivations of buyers and sellers, dates of the property transactions, and any expenditures made immediately after the purchase. Then details on each property's location, physical and functional condition, economic characteristics, use, and non-realty components of value must be considered. Because conclusions must be market-derived, the appraiser will rely heavily on interviews, personal contacts, and proprietary research.

Most appraisers maintain data files with the details of market transactions and add information as new transactions occur. Potential sources of sales data are many and varied. Primary sources include

- Courthouse records
- Government sales tax records
- Commercially available data from electronic reporting, multiple listing, and subscription services
- Real estate periodicals
- Interviews with the parties to transactions, their employees, attorneys, appraisers, counselors, brokers, property managers, and lenders.

> To apply the sales comparison approach, the appraiser first **gathers data** from sales, contracts, offers, refusals, and listings of competitive properties. Sources of this information include public records, multiple listing services, subscription services, real estate brokers, real estate periodicals, and interviews with the parties involved in market transactions.

Assessment data should generally not be used to develop an opinion of market value. Budgetary and time constraints on the public agencies responsible for collecting and maintaining assessment data can cast doubt on the accuracy of that data.

The geographic limits of the appraiser's search for sales data depend on the nature and type of real estate being valued and available sales information. Certain types of properties have regional, national, and even international markets. Market boundaries are defined by the area potential buyers would consider for alternative properties and the character of the property being appraised. If similar properties are commonly bought and sold in the same market area as the subject property, the search will probably be relatively confined. However, appraisers must sometimes extend the area of their searches to other, similar market areas. For example, little comparable data may be found for the first property to be renovated in an area of deteriorated buildings or for the only property of a given type in a market area. In situations of those sorts, the appraiser must establish the comparability of the other areas and the competitiveness of the properties with the subject. To estimate the values of regional shopping malls, large office buildings, resort hotels, large multiuse complexes, and large industrial properties, for example, appraisers may gather data from a wide geographic area within which the competitive properties are located.

Verifying Transactional Data

Appraisers should verify information to ensure its accuracy and to gain insight into the motivation behind each transaction. The buyer's view of what was being purchased at the time of sale is very important. Sales that are not arm's-length market transactions (in accordance with the definition of *market value* used in the appraisal) should be identified and used with caution. To verify sales data an appraiser confirms statements of fact with the principals to the transaction, if possible, or with the brokers, closing agents, or lenders involved. Owners and tenants of neighbor-

> **arm's-length transaction:** A transaction between unrelated parties under no duress.

ing properties may also provide helpful information. Sometimes income and expense data for income-producing properties is unobtainable. If data on a particular sale is unavailable, assigning rents and expenses "based on market parameters" may be improper, especially for properties with existing leases.

Selecting Units of Comparison

After sales data has been gathered and verified, systematic analysis begins. Because like units must be compared, each sale price should be stated in terms of appropriate units of comparison. The units of comparison selected depend

Table 17.1	**Typical Units of Comparison**

Property Type	Typical Units of Comparison
Single-family residential property	Total property price
	Price per square foot of gross living area
Apartment properties	Price per apartment unit (price per room or price per square foot of gross building area)
Warehouses	Price per square foot of gross building area
	Price per cubic foot of gross building volume
Factories	Price per square foot of gross building area
	Price per machine unit
Office properties	Price per square foot of gross building area
	Price per square foot of net rentable area
	Price per square foot of usable area
Hotels and motels	Price per guest room
Restaurants, theaters, and auditoriums	Price per seat
Hospitals	Price per square foot of gross building area
	Price per bed
Golf courses	Price per round (annual number of rounds played)
	Price per membership
	Price per hole
	Price per acre
Tennis and racquetball facilities	Price per playing court
Mobile home parks	Price per parking pad
Marinas	Price per slip
Automobile repair facilities	Price per bay
	Price per square foot of gross building area
Agricultural properties	Price per acre
	Price per animal unit (for pastureland)
	Price per board foot (for timberland)
Vacant land	Price per front foot
	Price per square foot
	Price per acre

on the appraisal problem and nature of the property, as illustrated in Table 17.1.

> **units of comparison:** The components into which a property may be divided for purposes of comparison, e.g., price per square foot, front foot, cubic foot, room, bed, seat, apartment unit.

Units of comparison are used to facilitate comparison of the subject and comparable properties. Converting sale prices to size-related unit prices usually eliminates the need to make adjustments for size differences. Differences in size are considered in reconciliation, and the unit (or units) of comparison selected can have a significant bearing on the reconciliation of value indications in this approach. It may sometimes be necessary to adjust for differences in economies of scale. Even if all other property characteristics appear similar, a sale property that is substantially larger or smaller than the subject property may not be a particularly meaningful comparable because the per unit price of the larger property may be lowered by economies of scale. As much as possible, appraisers should try to select comparables in the same size range as the subject so that economies of scale do not enter into the process.

Analyzing and Adjusting Comparable Sales

Ideally, if all comparable properties are identical to the subject property, no adjustments would be required. However, this is rarely the case, especially for nonresidential properties. In this step of the analysis the appraiser adjusts for any differences.

After sales information has been collected and confirmed, it can be organized in a variety of ways. One convenient and commonly used method is to arrange the data on a market data grid. Each important difference between the comparable properties and the subject property that could affect property value is considered an element of comparison. Each element is assigned a row on the grid, and total property prices or unit prices of the comparables are adjusted to reflect the value of these differences. The process is a way for appraisers to model typical buyer actions and to analyze sales data to quantify the impact of certain characteristics on value. (A sample market data grid and the procedures used to make adjustments on such a grid are presented in the next chapter.)

A sale price reflects many different factors that affect a property's value in varying degrees. Qualitative and quantitative techniques are employed to estimate the relative significance of these factors. Appraisers employ mathematical applications to derive quantitative adjustments. When sufficient data to support a quantitative adjustment is not available, appraisers investigate qualitative relationships through direct comparison of market data and analysis of market trends.

Adjustments can be made either to total property prices or to appropriate units of comparison. Often adjustments for property rights conveyed, financing, conditions of sale (motivation), date of sale (market conditions), and expenditures made immediately after purchase are made to the total sale price. The adjusted

> **elements of comparison:** The characteristics or attributes of properties and transactions that help explain the variance of prices paid for real estate; include real property rights conveyed, financing terms, conditions of sale, market conditions, expenditures made immediately after purchase, location, physical characteristics, and other characteristics such as economic characteristics, use, and non-realty components of value.

price is then converted into a unit price and adjusted for other elements of comparison such as location and physical characteristics.

Elements of Comparison

Elements of comparison are the characteristics of properties and transactions that help explain the variance of prices paid for real estate. The appraiser determines the elements of comparison for a given appraisal through market research and supports those conclusions with market data. When properly identified, the elements of comparison describe the factors that are associated with prices paid for competing properties.

There are 10 basic elements of comparison that should be considered in sales comparison analysis:

1. Real property rights conveyed
2. Financing terms
3. Conditions of sale
4. Expenditures made immediately after purchase
5. Market conditions (time)
6. Location
7. Physical characteristics—e.g., size, construction quality, condition
8. Economic characteristics—e.g., expense ratios, lease provisions, management, tenant mix
9. Use (zoning)
10. Non-realty components of value

In most cases these elements of comparison cover all the significant factors to be considered, but on occasion additional elements may be relevant. Other possible elements of comparison include governmental restrictions such as conservation or preservation easements and water and riparian rights, access to the property, and off-site improvements required for the development of a vacant site. Often a basic element of comparison is broken down into subcategories that specifically address the property factor being analyzed. For example, physical characteristics may be broken down into subcategories for age, condition, size, and so on. (Adjustment techniques applicable to each of the 10 standard elements of comparison are discussed in Chapter 18 and illustrated with examples in Chapter 19.)

Sales adjustment processes require a sufficient number of sales from which to extract the adjustments. Often there may not be enough sales to provide a basis for all adjustment calculations. The appraiser should recognize and explain in the appraisal report that a lack of supporting data may either reduce the validity of the adjustments made or eliminate the possibility of applying any direct sales adjustment process. When these conditions exist, the appraiser distinguishes any adjustments that are made as explanatory or judgment factors from those that are drawn from market data. In such situations appraisers commonly look to a broader array of market sales for bracketing and indirect market support.

Larger databases may allow for more detailed study and greater understanding of the value influence of differences between properties such as zoning or location, but a sheer volume of data is not an implicit indication of quality or reliability of an appraiser's conclusions. The larger the data set, the more responsibility the appraiser has to understand and properly apply the various forms of statistical analysis that may be appropriate for appraisal analysis. However, statistical results such as averages should not be misinterpreted as, or substituted for, a full understanding of market behavior.

Identification and Measurement of Adjustments

Comparative analysis includes the consideration of both quantitative and qualitative factors. Quantitative adjustments are developed as either dollar or percentage amounts. Factors that cannot be quantified are dealt with in qualitative analysis. Various techniques used in quantitative adjustments and qualitative analyses are shown in Table 17.2 and are discussed more fully in the following chapter.

Quantitative adjustment techniques include paired data analysis, grouped data analysis, secondary data analysis, statistical analysis, graphic analysis, trend analysis, cost analysis, direct comparisons, and capitalization of income differences. **Qualitative analysis** includes relative comparison analysis, ranking analysis, and personal interviews. Both quantitative and qualitative techniques are employed in comparative analysis.

Table 17.2	Techniques Used in Quantitative and Qualitative Analysis

Quantitative Analysis
- Paired data analysis (sales and resales of the same or similar properties)
- Grouped data analysis
- Secondary data analysis
- Statistical analysis
- Graphic analysis
- Trend analysis
- Cost analysis (cost-to-cure, depreciated cost)
- Direct comparisons
- Capitalization of income differences

Qualitative Analysis
- Relative comparison analysis
- Ranking analysis
- Personal interviews

Reconciling Value Indications in the Sales Comparison Approach

Reconciliation is the last phase of any valuation analysis in which two or more value indications have been derived from market data. In reconciliation, the appraiser summarizes and re-examines the data and analyses that resulted in each of the value indications. These value indications are then resolved into a range of value or a single value indication, known as a *point estimate*. It is important that the appraiser consider the strengths and weaknesses of each value indication derived, examining the reliability and appropriateness of the market data compiled and the analytical techniques applied. It is also good practice to re-examine the major elements of comparison for which no adjustments were made and to explain why these elements did not require any adjustments or how they were accounted for in the reconciliation. The appraisal report should clearly communicate how the appraiser arrived at the value conclusion.

In the sales comparison approach, reconciliation may involve two levels of analysis. The first level of analysis pertains to the derivation of a value indication from the adjusted prices of two or more comparables expressed in terms of a single unit of comparison. A second level of analysis is required when the appraiser derives two or more value indications expressed in different units of comparison. For example, value indications expressed in price per square foot and price per dwelling unit must be reconciled into a value range or a single value indication for the sales comparison approach.

Reconciliation is also required when value indications are derived using two or more approaches to value. At this point in the valuation process, reconciliation results in the opinion of value identified in the definition of the appraisal problem. Reconciliation of the final opinion of value is discussed in Chapter 25.

FURTHER READING

Akerson, Charles B. *The Appraiser's Workbook.* 2d ed. Chicago: Appraisal Institute, 1996.

Boronico, Jess S., and Donald M. Moliver. "Appraisal Reliability and the Sales Comparison Approach." *The Appraisal Journal* (October 1997).

Crookham, James. "Sales Comparison Approach: Revisited." *The Appraisal Journal* (April 1995).

CHAPTER 18

ADJUSTMENT AND ANALYTICAL TECHNIQUES IN THE SALES COMPARISON APPROACH

Comparative analysis is the general term used to identify the process in which quantitative and/or qualitative techniques are applied to derive a value indication in the sales comparison approach. The two types of techniques may be used separately or in combination.

The adjustments derived in comparative analysis and applied to the sale prices of the comparables may be expressed as percentages, as dollar amounts, or in descriptive terms that clearly convey the magnitude of the difference between the comparable and the subject in terms of each element of comparison. The process involves the following general steps:

1. Identify the elements of comparison that affect the value of the type of property being appraised.
2. Compare the attributes of each comparable with those of the subject property and then measure the difference in each element of comparison between the comparable and the subject. The goal is to justify and support the reasonableness of the adjustment.
3. Derive a net adjustment for each comparable and apply it to the sale price or unit price of the comparable to arrive at a range of adjusted sale or unit prices for the subject property.
4. Reconcile the range of adjusted sale or unit prices to the subject property, using qualitative analysis if appropriate.

When quantitative adjustments are being applied, the appraiser considers the array of value indications obtained in the third step to be the range of probable value indications for the subject property. The appraiser then determines the most probable position of the subject within this range of indications and reaches a final opinion of value. In this way the comparables most similar to the subject are given the greatest weight.

Applying qualitative analysis, the appraiser will normally divide the adjusted comparables into two groups: those that are qualitatively superior to the subject and those that are qualitatively inferior. The adjusted prices of these two groups will bracket the value of the subject by indicating a probable range of values. By considering those comparables most similar

comparative analysis: The process by which a value indication is derived in the sales comparison approach. Comparative analysis may employ quantitative or qualitative techniques, either separately or in combination.

bracketing: A process in which an appraiser determines a probable range of values for a property by applying qualitative techniques of comparative analysis to a group of comparable sales. The array of comparables may be divided into two groups—those superior to the subject and those inferior to the subject. The adjusted sale prices reflected by these two groups limit the probable range of values for the subject and identify a bracket in which the final value opinion will fall. The most comparable sales will typically fall near the middle of the range.

Quantitative and qualitative methodologies are often combined in practice. Generally quantitative adjustments are made before qualitative analysis is undertaken.

to the subject, some higher and some lower in value, the appraiser can conclude a single value indication for the subject property. If all the comparables are rated superior or all are rated inferior to the subject, it is more difficult to determine a reliable range of value and reach a single value indication using qualitative analysis.

An appraiser may use both quantitative adjustments and qualitative analysis in comparative analysis, but not concurrently. Generally, quantitative adjustments are made before qualitative analysis is performed. Care must be used to ensure that mathematical adjustments reflect the reactions of market participants. When reporting the analytical process, the appraiser must ensure that the reader of the appraisal report will not be confused. Appraisal reports that include qualitative analysis often require more extensive discussion of the reasoning that the appraiser applied, particularly if qualitative analysis is applied alone.

Elements of Comparison

The first step in any comparative analysis is to identify which elements of comparison affect property values in the subject market. Each of the basic elements of comparison must be analyzed to determine whether an adjustment is required. If sufficient information is available, a quantitative adjustment can be made. If there is insufficient support for a quantitative adjustment, the element is addressed using qualitative analysis.

Adjustments for differences are made to the price of each comparable property to make that property equivalent to the subject in market appeal on the effective date of the opinion of value. Adjustments for differences in elements of comparison may be made to the total property price, to a common unit price, or to a mix of both, but the unit prices used must be applied consistently to the comparable properties. The magnitude of the adjustment made for each element of comparison depends on how much that characteristic of the comparable property differs from the subject property. Appraisers should consider all appropriate elements of comparison and avoid adjusting for the same difference more than once.

Real Property Rights Conveyed

When real property rights are sold, they may be the sole subject of the contract or the contract may include other rights, less than all of the real property rights, or even another property or properties. Before the price of a comparable sale property can be used in sales comparison analysis, the appraiser must first ensure that the sale price of the comparable property applies to property rights that are similar to those being appraised. To do so may require one or more adjustments to the price before specific differences in the physical real estate can be compared.

For example, the rights conveyed by a quitclaim deed for real property may or may not include the total fee simple bundle of rights. Thus, the appraiser must determine that the buyer and seller considered the transaction to be equivalent to a fee simple transaction or must seek other supporting evidence before using the transaction. It is possible that the transaction cannot be used for direct comparison purposes at all because there is no available adjustment for the difference in rights.

Some contracts call for the sale of real property rights but add deed restrictions or other forms of limitations on the purchaser and/or future users of the property. Such title or use limitations may also reduce the transaction to use as a general market indicator but render the transaction unusable for direct market comparison because the rights are less than fee simple.

Income-producing real estate is often subject to an existing lease or leases that encumber the title. By definition, a property that is subject to one or more leases is no longer a fee simple estate. Thus, if the sale of a leased property is to be used as a comparable sale in the valuation of the fee simple estate for another property, the sale can only be used if reasonable and supportable market adjustments for the difference in rights can be made.

Appraisers must exercise caution in analysis of any transaction that involves more or less than fee simple property rights and in making comparisons with an appraised property. For example, the price of the comparable property must be divided among the various properties conveyed. These may include other real estate, personal property, contract rights, promises to perform or not to perform certain acts, special financing, business interests, or other things of value. Once the sale price is pared down to real property rights, these must be distinguished as either fee simple or less than fee simple rights and the appraiser must determine whether the sale property's reduced rights eliminate it from consideration as a comparable or whether there are supportable market grounds for adjustments.

Financing Terms

The transaction price of one property may differ from that of an identical property due to different financing arrangements. For example, the purchaser of a comparable property may have assumed an existing mortgage at a favorable interest rate. In another case a developer or seller may have arranged a buydown, paying cash to the lender so that a mortgage with a below-market interest rate could be offered. In both cases the buyers probably paid higher prices for the properties to obtain below-market financing. Conversely, interest rates at above-market levels often result in lower sale prices.

Other non-market financing arrangements include installment sale contracts, in which the buyer pays periodic installments to the seller and obtains legal title only after the contract is fulfilled, and wraparound loans, which are superimposed on existing mortgages to preserve their lower interest rates. These loans offer below-market or blended interest rates to borrowers (buyers). Below-market rates are sometimes extended to individuals who have substantial bank accounts and are therefore especially creditworthy. The appraiser needs to investigate if these arrangements will affect the sale price of the property.

A financing adjustment may or may not include an adjustment for conditions of sale. A conditions of sale adjustment recognizes that some sale transactions occur under undue duress, involving parties who are at a disadvantage. When favorable financing is a function of the seller's need to sell the property quickly, the appraiser should make an adjustment combining the effects of differences in both financing and conditions of sale. For example, beneficial financing may be offered to expedite the marketing time on a parcel of distressed real estate. In such a situation, the purchaser would refuse to pay a premium for beneficial financing. It is also likely that the seller would be offering the property at a discount. Appraisers should recognize that in some situations financing and conditions of sale are interdependent, and they should be careful not to "double count" the influence of these factors when making quantitative adjustments.

In cash equivalency analysis an appraiser investigates the sale prices of comparable properties that appear to have been sold with non-market financing to determine whether adjustments are warranted to reflect typical market terms at the time of sale. First, sales with non-market financing are compared to other sales transacted with market financing to determine whether an adjustment for cash equivalency can be made. Market evidence is always the best indicator of such an adjustment.

Financing adjustments derived from precise, mathematical calculations for analyzing cash equivalency must be rigorously tested against market evidence. Strict mathematical calculations may not, therefore, reflect market behavior. Market evidence must support whatever adjustment is made. If the cash discount indicated by the calculations is not recognized by buyers and sellers, the adjustment is not justified.

The typical definition of *market value* recognizes cash equivalent terms provided the calculation of these terms reflects the market. Conditions of sale may reveal other, non-economic interests on the part of buyers or sellers. Confirmation of the intent of buyers and sellers is one way to verify a cash equivalency adjustment. Caution must continually be exercised in applying cash equivalency calculations. The final adjustment must always be derived from the market.

Cash equivalency calculations vary depending on the kind of financing arrangement that requires adjustment. Appraisers may calculate adjustments for atypical financing by analyzing sales and resales of the same property (e.g., a sale is negotiated at a price subject to the buyer securing new market financing and, while still under contract, the deal is negotiated at a different face value with the seller providing terms) or paired data sets or by discounting the cash flows (e.g., payments and balloons) created by the mortgage contract at market interest rates. If discounting is used, the appraiser should not assume that the buyer will hold the property for the life of the mortgage. Market evidence often indicates otherwise. A mortgage is often discounted for a shorter term, but the balloon payment must still be included.

Appraisers must make sure that cash equivalency adjustments reflect market perceptions. It is necessary for the appraiser to talk with the buyers and sellers to determine if the financing terms affect value. In selecting an appropriate adjustment for use in cash equivalency analysis, the appraiser should give greater emphasis to the market-derived adjustment than to one derived by calculation.

Conditions of Sale

Adjustments for conditions of sale usually reflect the motivations of the buyer and the seller. In many situations the conditions of sale significantly affect transaction prices; these are not considered arm's-length transactions. For example, a developer may pay more than market value for lots needed in a site assemblage because of the plottage value expected to result from the greater utility of the larger site. A sale may be transacted at a below-market price if the seller needs cash in a hurry. A financial, business, or family relationship between the parties to a sale may also affect the price of property. Interlocking corporate entities may record a sale at a non-market price to serve their business interests. One member of a family may sell a property to another at a reduced price, or a buyer may pay a higher price for a property because it was built by his ancestors.

When non-market conditions of sale are detected in a transaction, the sale can be used as a comparable but only with great care. The circumstances of the sale must be thoroughly researched before an adjustment is made, and the conditions must be adequately disclosed in the appraisal. Any adjustment must be well supported with data. If the adjustment cannot be supported, the sale probably should be discarded.

Although conditions of sale are often perceived as applying only to sales that are not arm's-length transactions, some arm's-length sales may reflect atypical motivations or sale conditions due to unusual tax considerations, lack of exposure on the open market, or the complexity of eminent domain proceedings. If the sales used in the sales comparison approach reflect unusual situations, an appropriate adjustment (well supported by the market evidence) must be made for motivation or conditions of sale. Again, the circumstances of the sale must be explained in the appraisal report.

Expenditures Made Immediately After Purchase

A knowledgeable buyer considers expenditures that will have to be made upon purchase of a property because these costs affect the price the buyer agrees to pay. Such expenditures may include

- Costs to cure deferred maintenance
- Costs to demolish and remove any portion of the improvements
- Costs to petition for a zoning change
- Costs to remediate environmental contamination

These costs are often quantified in price negotiations and can be discovered through verification of transaction data. The relevant figure is not the actual cost that was incurred but the cost that was anticipated by the buyer and seller.

Market Conditions

Comparable sales that occurred under market conditions different from those applicable to the subject on the effective date of value require adjustment for any differences that affect their values. An adjustment for market conditions is made if general property values have appreciated or depreciated since the transaction dates due to inflation or deflation or a change in investors' perceptions of the market over time.

Although the adjustment for market conditions is often referred to as a "time" adjustment, time is not the cause of the adjustment. Market conditions that shift over time create the need for an adjustment, not time itself. In other words, appreciation or depreciation of property values in the market is the cause of the adjustment and time is the measure of the adjustment. If market conditions have not changed, no adjustment is required even though considerable time may have elapsed.

Changes in market conditions may result from changes in income tax laws, building moratoriums, and fluctuations in supply and demand. Sometimes several economic factors work in concert to cause a change in market conditions. A recession tends to deflate all real estate prices, but specific property types or submarkets may be affected differently. A decline in demand may affect only one category of real estate. If the demand for a specific type of property falls during a period of inflation, sales transacted during that period may not provide a reliable indication of the value of a similar property in a different period unless appropriate adjustments are made. Sales of other types of real estate that took place during the same period may better reflect the market conditions for the specific property being appraised. In a depressed economy, recent sales are often difficult to find. Older sales, occurring prior to the onset of the depressed economy, should be used with great caution because they may not reflect the problems associated with the depressed economy. In some instances when current sales do not exist, upward or downward shifts in rent and rent terms may help the appraiser ascertain the direction of market activity.

Appraisers must also recognize that the sale of a property may be negotiated months or even years before its final disposition. The buyer and the seller agree as of the contract date, but the agreement does not become effective until the closing date (and there are often changes in the agreement during the interim). An adjustment for changes in market conditions between the date the contract is signed and the effective date of value may be appropriate. Sometimes appraisers may also be called on to develop an opinion of retrospective or prospective value, which requires consideration of changes in market conditions. (For guidance on the estimation of retrospective and prospective values, see Statements Nos. 3 and 4 of the Uniform Standards of Professional Appraisal Practice.)

An adjustment for changes in market conditions is usually measured as a percentage of previous prices. While change is continuous, it typically occurs in discrete intervals. If the physical and economic characteristics of a property remain unchanged, analyzing two or more sales of the same property over a period of time will indicate the percentage of price change. An appraiser should always attempt to examine several sets of sales to arrive at an appropriate adjustment. An adjustment supported by just one set of sales may be unreliable.

Sales and resales of the same properties often provide a good indication of the change in market conditions over time. If data on resales is unavailable, however, sales of similar properties in the same market can be used. In either case, the sale transactions must be examined very carefully. Analysis of sale and resale data from the same property may indicate that non-market conditions were involved in one or both transactions.

Simple linear regression analysis and scatter diagrams may also be used to extract an annual rate of change in market conditions. The reliability of such analyses is affected by the number of market transactions studied. Unit prices can be graphed over time to indicate the trend in the market. Similarly, rents can be plotted on scatter diagrams to show differences over time.

Location

An adjustment for location within a market area may be required when the locational characteristics of a comparable property are different from those of the subject property. Excessive locational differences may disqualify a property from use as a comparable. Locational differences are usually handled with quantitative adjustments.

Most comparable properties in the same market area have similar locational characteristics, but variations may exist within that area of analysis. Consider, for example, the difference between a property with a pleasant view of a park and one located two blocks away with a less attractive view. Adjustments for location may also be needed to reflect the difference in demand for various office suites within a single building, the retail advantage of a corner location, the privacy of the end unit in a residential condominium project, or the value contribution of an ocean view.

A property's location is analyzed in relation to the location of other properties. Although no location is inherently desirable or undesirable, an appraiser can conclude that the market recognizes that one location is better than, similar to, or worse than another. To evaluate the desirability of one location relative to other locations, appraisers must analyze sales of physically similar properties situated in different locations. Although the sale prices of properties in two different areas may be similar, properties in one area may be sold more rapidly than properties in the other.

Physical Characteristics

If the physical characteristics of a comparable property and the subject property differ in many ways, each of these differences may require comparison and adjustment. Physical differences include differences in building size, quality of construction, architectural style, building materials, age, condition, functional utility, site size, attractiveness, and amenities. On-site environmental conditions may also be considered.

The value added or lost by the presence or absence of an item in a comparable property may not equal the cost of installing or removing the item. Buyers may be unwilling to pay a higher sale price that includes the extra cost of adding an amenity. Conversely, the addition of an amenity sometimes adds more value to a property than its cost, or there may be no adjustment to value for the existence of or the lack of an item.

Economic Characteristics

Economic characteristics include all the attributes of a property that directly affect its income. This element of comparison is usually applied to income-producing properties. Characteristics that affect a property's income include operating expenses, quality of management, tenant mix, rent concessions, lease terms, lease expiration dates, renewal options, and lease provisions such as expense recovery clauses. Investigation of these characteristics is critical to proper analysis of the comparables and development of a final opinion of value.

Appraisers must take care not to attribute differences in real property rights conveyed or changes in market conditions to different economic characteristics. Caution must also be exercised in regard to units of comparison such as net operating income per unit. *NOIs* per unit reflect a mix of interactive economic attributes, many of which should only be analyzed in the income capitalization approach. Sales comparison analysis must not be presented simply as a variation of the income capitalization approach, applying the same techniques to reach an identical value indication.

Use/Zoning

Any difference in the current use or the highest and best use of a potential comparable sale and the subject property must be addressed. The appraiser must recognize the difference and determine if the sale is an appropriate comparable and, if so, whether an adjustment is required. In most cases the buyer or buyer's agent must confirm the ultimate use for which the comparable was purchased.

For example, an apartment complex purchased for conversion to condominiums may reflect a sale price above the market level for apartment properties. This property would not be an appropriate comparable for the "as is" valuation of an apartment complex for which no change in use is intended or one for which the highest and best use remains apartment use.

In the valuation of vacant land, zoning is one of the primary determinants of the highest and best use of the property because it serves as the test of legal permissibility. Thus, zoning or the reasonable probability of a zoning change is typically a primary criterion in the selection of market data. When comparable properties with the same zoning as the subject are lacking or scarce, parcels with slightly different zoning but a highest and best use similar to that of the subject may be used as comparables. These comparables may have to be adjusted for differences in utility if the market indicates that this is appropriate; on the other hand, a difference in the uses permitted under two zoning classifications does not necessarily require an adjustment if the parcels have the same use.

Sometimes, dissimilarities in sale prices reduced to compatible units—e.g., price of land per square foot of permissible building area—can be attributed to the different zoning classification requirements. For example, because of differences in parking requirements or landscaping requirements, site development costs for two parcels under different zoning classifications may differ even if the parcels have the same highest and best use. These dissimilarities must be considered.

> **zoning:** The public regulation of the character and extent of real estate use through police power; accomplished by establishing districts or areas with uniform restrictions relating to improvements; structural height, area, and bulk; density of population; and other aspects of the use and development of private property.

Non-realty Components of Value

Non-realty components of value include personalty, business concerns, and other items that do not constitute real property but are included in either the sale price of the comparable or the ownership interest in the subject property. These components should be analyzed separately from the realty. In most cases the economic lives, associated investment risks, rate of return criteria, and collateral security for such non-realty components differ from those of the realty.

Furniture, fixtures, and equipment in a hotel or restaurant are typical examples of personalty. In appraisals of properties in which the business operation is essential to the use of the realty, the value of the non-realty component must be analyzed. If the value of the non-realty component cannot be separated from the value of the property as a whole, the appraiser should make clear that the value indication using the sales comparison approach reflects both the value of the real estate and the value of the business operation. Properties such as hotels and timeshare condominiums, which have high expense ratios attributable to the business operation, may include a significant business enterprise value component.

Quantitative Adjustments

Several techniques are available to quantify adjustments to the sale prices of comparable properties:

- Data analysis techniques (including paired data analysis, grouped data analysis, and secondary data analysis)
- Statistical analysis
- Graphic analysis
- Trend analysis
- Cost analysis (cost-to-cure, depreciated cost)
- Capitalization of rent differences

Data Analysis Techniques

Paired data analysis is based on the premise that when two properties are in all other respects equivalent, a single difference can be measured to indicate the difference in price between them. A related technique, *grouped data analysis*, involves grouping data by an independent variable such as date of sale and calculating equivalent typical values. The grouped sales are studied in pairs to identify the dependent variable (e.g., the property's price per acre).[1]

Secondary data analysis is a method for supporting adjustments derived by other methods. This technique makes use of data that does not directly pertain to the subject or comparable properties. This secondary data describes the general real estate market and is usually collected by a research firm or government agency.

Paired Data Analysis

Although paired data analysis is a theoretically sound method, it is sometimes impractical because only a narrow sampling of sufficiently similar properties may be available. This is particularly true for many commercial and industrial properties and properties that do not sell frequently in the market. This makes it difficult to quantify the adjustments attributable to all the variables present. An adjustment derived from a single pair of sales is not necessarily indicative, just as a single sale does not necessarily reflect market value.

When sufficient data is available, the method can be helpful and persuasive, but when judgments are substituted for market-derived adjustments, the process can be misleading. Even when limited data is available, however, the appraiser should not discard the technique. Rather, the appraiser should

---

1. Paired data and grouped data analysis are variants of sensitivity analysis, which is a method used to isolate the effect of individual variables on value. Often associated with risk analysis, sensitivity analysis studies the impact of variables on different measures of return.

estimate the amount of adjustment indicated by the data and use other analytical procedures or secondary data to test the reasonableness of the adjustment derived.

Special care must be taken when analyzing pairs of adjusted values because the difference measured may not represent the actual difference attributable to the distinguishing characteristic. The difference may include other aspects of the property, not just the one characteristic being studied. *Primary pairings* (i.e., pairs of sales that are identical except for the single element being measured) should be analyzed first. For example, data on a sale and resale of the same property may be compared to derive a market conditions adjustment. Pairings of adjusted sales (i.e., *secondary pairings*) should only be used as an analytical tool when primary pairings are unavailable. When more than one element of comparison is involved, additional pairs can be studied to isolate and abstract the differing elements.[2]

paired data analysis: A quantitative technique used to identify and measure adjustments to the sale prices or rents of comparable properties; to apply this technique, sales or rental data on nearly identical properties are analyzed to isolate a single characteristic's effect on value or rent.

statistical analysis: Quantitative techniques used to identify and measure adjustments to the sale prices of comparable properties; techniques include statistical inference and linear and multiple regression analysis.

Statistical Analysis

Statistical methods can sometimes be applied to calculate adjustments to comparable sales. To apply any statistical analysis, the appraiser must be familiar with (and properly apply) fundamental statistical concepts as well as the particular methodology selected.[3] In applying statistical analysis, the appraiser must be careful not to develop a result that is mathematically precise yet meaningless or inappropriate for the particular appraisal.

As an example, an appraiser may develop size adjustments for various sizes of land but not have a size adjustment for a parcel that is sufficiently comparable to the subject property to warrant the use of the adjustment. By creating a simple linear regression model, the appraiser may develop a series of adjustment

---

2. Comparable properties that contain different unit or inventory mixes should be adjusted for this difference before pairing analysis is conducted. Examples of properties with different unit or inventory mixes include apartment buildings with one-, two-, and three-bedroom units and agricultural lands with different types of soil. A unit or inventory mix adjustment is required to ensure that the comparables and subject are commensurate. The appraiser may be able to extract this adjustment by investigating the value relationships among the different classes of properties within the same property type.

3. Full discussion of the statistical methods applicable to the sales comparison approach is beyond the scope of this text. Appendix B provides a review of basic statistical techniques. For more information on applying statistical analysis to appraisals, see Mark R. Linne, M. Steven Kane, and George Dell, *A Guide to Appraisal Valuation Modeling* (Chicago: Appraisal Institute, 2000). Also, *The Appraisal Journal, Assessment Journal, The Journal of Real Estate Research, Real Estate Economics,* and other scholarly journals have published many articles on advanced statistical applications.

factors for differing tract sizes and use the results as a means of inferring the size adjustment for properties within the range of the data. If there is a reasonable pattern, it can be applied to a group of sales with differing land sizes to test its likely accuracy, although the process might also demonstrate that the adjustments compared are incorrect. The results of this process may be closer to qualitative analysis than a direct quantitative adjustment, but market support for the adjustment can be produced in this way.

Appraisers should recognize the differences between statistical processes in the collection and description of data and should be able to distinguish between descriptive and inferential statistics. Without an understanding of the issues, any use of statistical calculations is dangerous or ill-advised. For example, some appraisers extract adjustments for direct sales comparison processes directly from multiple regression analyses, without recognizing that regression studies do not develop indications of causation but rather of associations between and among independent variables and a dependent (or predicted) variable such as sale price. It is entirely improper to mix a value of a single regression coefficient that is developed for a given statistical model with other market adjustments developed from paired sales analysis or other market data comparison techniques.[4]

Graphic Analysis

Graphic analysis is a variant of statistical analysis in which the appraiser arrives at a conclusion by visually interpreting a graphic display of data and applying statistical curve fit analysis. A simple graphic display of grouped data may illustrate how the market reacts to variations in the elements of comparison or may reveal submarket trends. In curve fit analysis, different formulas may be employed to determine the best fit for the market data being analyzed. The most reliable equation for the best fit curve can be plotted, or the most appropriate equation of those commonly used to solve for an adjustment can be identified.

graphic analysis: Quantitative techniques used to identify and measure adjustments to the sale prices of comparable properties; a variant of statistical analysis in which an appraiser interprets graphically displayed data visually or through curve fit analysis.

trend analysis: A quantitative technique used to identify and measure adjustments to the sale prices of comparable properties; useful when sales data on highly comparable properties is lacking, but a broad database on properties with less similar characteristics is available. Market sensitivity is investigated by testing various factors that influence sale prices.

Trend Analysis

Trend analysis is applicable when a large amount of market data is available. It is especially useful when there is a limited number of closely comparable sales but a broad database of properties with less similar characteristics. The various

---

4. The difficulty in applying regression analysis to real estate appraisal is discussed in Gene Dilmore, "Appraising with Regression Analysis: A Pop Quiz," *The Appraisal Journal* (October 1997): 403–404.

elements influencing a sale price can be tested to determine their market sensitivity. Once the appraiser has determined which elements show market sensitivity, patterns for their adjustment can be analyzed.

Cost Analysis

In cost analysis, adjustments are based on cost indicators such as depreciated building cost, cost to cure, or permit fees. The appraiser should make certain that the adjustments derived are reasonable and reflect market expectations because cost and value are not necessarily synonymous.

Capitalization of Rent Differences

Capitalization of rent differences can be used to derive an adjustment when the income loss incurred by a comparable reflects a specific deficiency in the comparable, e.g., lack of an elevator in a low-rise office building or inadequate parking facilities for a convenience store.

Types of Adjustments

The adjustments derived with quantitative techniques can be applied to a comparable property as either percentage or dollar amounts. The manner in which the adjustment is derived from the market determines how it is expressed. Percentages are usually converted into dollar amounts that may be added to or subtracted from the price of the comparable on a market data grid.

> Quantitative adjustments may be applied to comparable sales prices as **percentage or dollar amounts**.

Adjustments can be applied in several ways depending on how the relationship between the properties (i.e., subject and comparable, comparable and subject, or comparable and comparable) is expressed or perceived by the market. This relationship is expressed as an equation that is solved to determine the amount of adjustment to be made for the differences between the properties.

An appraiser uses logical calculations to make adjustments, but the mathematics should not control the appraiser's judgment. Using computer and software technology, an appraiser can effectively apply mathematical techniques like multiple regression analysis that were once prohibitively time-consuming. These techniques can be used to narrow the range of value, but an opinion of market value is not determined by calculations. Appraisal has a creative aspect in that appraisers use their judgment to analyze and interpret quantitative data. Quantification helps the appraiser analyze market evidence and identify how various factors affect property value. Qualitative analysis can be used to identify a bracket in which the final opinion of value should fall and weight the value indicators based on market evidence. Preparing an organized grid that includes all quantitative elements and another grid containing all relevant qualitative elements can help ensure that all elements of comparison are considered. If market evidence is inconclusive, then the use of grids may be misleading. In this case the appraiser should clearly indicate the limitations of the grids.

Percentage Adjustments

Adjustments for differences between a comparable property and a subject property are frequently expressed in percentages. Percentage adjustments are often used to reflect differences in market conditions and location.

For example, the data may indicate that market conditions have resulted in a 5% increase in overall property prices during the past year or that prices for a particular category of property have recently increased 0.5% per month. Similarly, an appraiser may analyze market data and conclude that properties in one location are sold for prices approximately 10% higher than the prices of similar properties in another location. These percentages are usually converted into dollar amounts, which are then added to or subtracted from the price of the comparable. The percentages may also be directly applied to the sale price or unit price of the comparable. Of course, if the comparable is equivalent to the subject for all practical purposes, no adjustment is necessary.

The relationship between the subject property and the comparable property should be stated in a manner that corresponds to the way it is perceived by market participants.

percentage adjustments: Adjustments for differences between the subject and comparable properties expressed in percentages; percentage adjustments are often used to reflect changes in market conditions and differences in location.

dollar adjustments: Adjustments for differences between the subject and the comparable properties expressed in dollars; often used to reflect differences in financing terms or physical characteristics.

Dollar Adjustments

Adjustments can also be computed in dollars. For example, an appraiser may conclude that the favorable financing terms involved in the sale of a comparable property resulted in the buyer paying a $100,000 premium. In analyzing major investment properties, an appraiser can frequently use discounting to derive a dollar adjustment for financing terms. Adjustments for many physical characteristics may also be estimated in dollar amounts, which are added to or subtracted from the sale price of the comparable.

Sequence of Adjustments

The sequence in which adjustments are applied to the comparables is determined by the market data and the appraiser's analysis of that data. The sequence presented in Table 18.1 is provided for purposes of illustration. This sequence is often applicable when percentage adjustments are calculated and added, either in conjunction with other percentage adjustments or in combination with dollar adjustments. However, this is not the only order in which quantitative adjustments may be made. Adjustments may be applied in other sequences if the market and the appraiser's analysis of the data so indicate.

Using the adjustment sequence, the appraiser applies successive adjustments to the prices of comparable properties.

Once the percentage adjustments are extracted from market data, a dollar adjustment for each element of comparison is typically calculated and applied to the sale price of the comparable in the market data grid. For example, if the change in market conditions from the date of the comparable sale to the date of value is estimated at 5% per year, a lump-sum dollar adjustment based on that 5% is applied to the price of the comparable.

> **sequence of adjustments:** The order in which quantitative adjustments are applied to the sale prices of comparable properties. The sequence of adjustments is determined by the market and through analysis of the data.
>
> **adjusted sale price:** The figure produced when the transaction price of a comparable sale is adjusted for elements of comparison. When the appropriate sequence of adjustments is followed, several intermediate adjusted sale prices are calculated and used as the basis for subsequent adjustments.

Once adjustments for property rights conveyed, financing terms, conditions of sale, expenditures immediately after purchase, and market conditions are made, the adjusted sale price is typically converted into a relevant unit price for further comparative analysis. Most property types, except single-family

Table 18.1   Sequence of Adjustments

Element of Comparison	Market-Derived Adjustment	Adjustment Applied to Price
Sale price		$100,000
Adjustment for property rights conveyed	+ 5%	+ 5,000
Adjusted price		$105,000
Adjustment for financing terms	– 2%	– 2,100
Adjusted price		$102,900
Adjustment for conditions of sale*	+ 5%	+ 5,145
Adjusted price		$108,045
Adjustment for expenditures immediately after purchase	– $0	– $0
Adjustment for market conditions	+ 5%	+ 5,402
Adjusted price		$113,447
Unit price (for 50,000-sq.-ft. building)		$2.269 per sq. ft.†
Adjustment for		
Location	+ 3%	+ 0.0681
Physical characteristics	– 5%	– 0.1135
Economic characteristics	– 5%	– 0.1135
Use	+ 2%	+ 0.0454
Non-realty components	+ 3%	+ 0.0681
Indication of unit price of the subject		$2.224 per sq. ft.†
Value of subject (2.2236 × 50,000)		$111,180

* The conditions of sale adjustment may be combined with the financing adjustment depending on how it is extracted from the market.

† Rounded to four significant digits.

residences, are adjusted on a unit price basis. Subsequent adjustments for location, physical characteristics, economic characteristics, use, and non-realty components are typically applied to a unit price.

> To assist in the analysis of comparable sales, appraisers make use of **data array and adjustment grids**.

Market Data Grids

The sample market data grid shown in Table 18.2 reflects the initial elements of comparison in a typical sequence; blank lines are provided for other elements of comparison. If the comparable sales are similar to the subject in regard to an element of comparison, no adjustment is required for that element. The sample grid includes separate lines for each comparison and adjustment to ensure that adjustments are made in a consistent manner.

The section labeled "For reconciliation purposes" is provided to help the appraiser analyze the comparability of each sale, which indicates the relative reliability of the separate value indications derived. Each final adjusted sale price is a possible value indication for the subject property. Together the adjusted prices of the comparables may constitute a range of values within which the value of the subject property will likely fall. Each adjusted sale price can be analyzed to show the total, or absolute, adjustment made to the sale price of the comparable and the percentage of the sale price that is

Table 18.2	Sample Market Data Grid: Comparison and Adjustment of Market Data				
Element	**Subject**	**Sale 1**	**Sale 2**	**Sale 3**	**Sale 4**
Sale price	unknown	_____	_____	_____	_____
Real property rights conveyed adjustment	_____	_____	_____	_____	_____
Adjusted price*	_____	_____	_____	_____	_____
Financing adjustment	_____	_____	_____	_____	_____
Conditions of sale adjustment	_____	_____	_____	_____	_____
Adjusted price†	_____	_____	_____	_____	_____
Market conditions adjustment	_____	_____	_____	_____	_____
Adjusted price‡	_____	_____	_____	_____	_____
_____	_____	_____	_____	_____	_____
_____	_____	_____	_____	_____	_____
_____	_____	_____	_____	_____	_____
Final adjusted sale price	_____	_____	_____	_____	_____
Total net adjustment	_____	_____	_____	_____	_____
Total net adjustment as % of sale price	_____	_____	_____	_____	_____
Total gross adjustment	_____	_____	_____	_____	_____
Total gross adjustment as % of sale price	_____	_____	_____	_____	_____

*   Sale price adjusted for property rights conveyed.

†   Sale price further adjusted for financing and conditions of sale.

‡   Sale price further adjusted for market conditions.

reflected by this total adjustment. With these value estimates, the appraiser can rank the comparability of the sales to the subject and select an appropriate opinion of value, assuming the value conclusion is to be reported as a point estimate. The sale that requires the least significant or lowest total adjustment (i.e., the absolute adjustment based on the sum of the adjustments regardless of sign) is often the most comparable and generally should be given the most weight in reconciling the value indications from the sales comparison approach. In reconciling the value indications derived in the sales comparison approach, the appraiser must also consider the reliability of the data and methods used to make adjustments.

Qualitative Analysis

After an appraiser has applied quantitative adjustments to the comparables or when quantitative adjustments cannot be made, several forms of qualitative analysis can be applied:

- Relative comparison analysis
- Ranking analysis
- Personal interviews

Relative Comparison Analysis

Relative comparison analysis is the study of the relationships indicated by market data without recourse to quantification. Many appraisers use this technique because it reflects the imperfect nature of real estate markets. To apply the technique the appraiser analyzes comparable sales to determine whether the comparables' characteristics are inferior, superior, or similar to those of the subject property. Unlike quantitative analysis, the adjustments considered in relative comparison analysis are not expressed as dollar or percentage amounts. A detailed example of relative comparison analysis is presented in the next chapter.

relative comparison analysis: A qualitative technique for analyzing comparable sales; used to determine whether the characteristics of a comparable property are inferior, superior, or similar to those of the subject property. Relative comparison analysis is similar to paired data analysis, but quantitative adjustments are not derived.

ranking analysis: A qualitative technique for analyzing comparable sales; a variant of relative comparison analysis in which comparable sales are ranked in descending or ascending order of desirability and each is analyzed to determine its position relative to the subject.

Ranking Analysis

Ranking analysis is a variant of relative comparison analysis. In ranking analysis the comparable sales are ranked in descending or ascending order. Then the appraiser analyzes each sale to determine the relative position of the subject in the array. An example of such an array is provided in the next chapter. Ranking analysis may also be used to array or sort the comparable data for differences in specific elements of comparison, e.g., size, corner or interior lot, frontage. Specific value trends can thereby be established.

In qualitative analysis comparables are identified as either superior or inferior overall to the subject to bracket the probable value range of the subject property.

Personal Interviews

Personal interviews can reveal the opinions of knowledgeable individuals participating in the subject's market. This information is preferably regarded as secondary data. It should not be used as the sole criterion for estimating adjustments or reconciling value ranges if an alternative method that relies on primary data can be applied.

Reconciliation

When reconciling value indications within the sales comparison approach, the appraiser asks whether each comparable property or each method used is a valid and reliable indicator of the value of the subject property:

- Is the comparable property similar in terms of physical characteristics and location?
- Was it developed, rented, or sold in the same market as the subject property?
- Are the characteristics of the transaction similar to those expected for the subject property?
- Would a potential buyer of the subject property consider the comparable as a reasonable alternative to the subject?

In some cases the appraiser may also ask:

- Are the expenses of the comparables appropriate indicators of the expenses of the appraised property?
- Are the estimates of depreciation in the appraised improvements justified by the comparison of comparable costs and comparable sales?
- Is one method preferred over another given the data available for each analysis?

Evaluating Adjustments

If one or two comparable properties require fewer total adjustments than the other comparables, an appraiser may attribute greater accuracy and give more weight to the value indications obtained from these comparables, particularly if the magnitude of the adjustments is approximately the same. Although the number of adjustments made to the comparable properties may be similar, the gross dollar amount of the total adjustments might vary considerably. For example, an appraiser may analyze five comparable properties that each requires several adjustments. However, the gross dollar amount of adjust-ments for one comparable property may total 15% of the sale price, while the gross dollar adjustment for each of the other four properties may be less than 5% of the sale price. If the sales are similar otherwise, less accuracy will probably be attributed to the comparable property that required larger adjustments.

Usually the magnitude of net adjustments is a less reliable indicator of accuracy. The net adjustment is calculated by totaling the positive and negative adjustments and subtracting the smaller amount from the larger amount. A net adjustment figure may be misleading because one cannot assume that any inaccuracies in the positive and negative adjustments will cancel each other out. For example, if a comparable property is 20% superior to the subject in some characteristics and 20% inferior in others, the net adjustment is zero but the gross adjustment is 40%. Another comparable may require several adjustments, all positive or all negative, resulting in a net adjustment of 6%. This property may well be a more accurate indicator of the subject's value than the comparable with the 0% net adjustment with large positive and negative adjustments. Several adjustments that are all positive or all negative may be more correct and produce a smaller total gross adjustment than a combination of positive and negative adjustments.

Even when they are supported by comparable data, the adjustment process and the values indicated reflect human judgment. Small inaccuracies can be compounded when several adjustments are added or multiplied. For this reason, the precise arithmetic conclusion derived from adjusted data should support, rather than control, the appraiser's judgment.

Units of Comparison and Real Property Interests

Two related points should be stressed in any discussion of the reconciliation process. In arriving at a final value indication in the sales comparison ap-proach, the appraiser must ensure that the value concluded is consistent with the purpose of the appraisal and the value indications derived from the other approaches to value. This is especially important in regard to the date of the opinion of prospective value. For example, an appraiser may seek an opinion of the market value of an income-producing property at two different points in the future—e.g., upon project completion and upon stabilized occupancy. The only market data available, however, may pertain to comparable proper-ties at or near stabilized occupancy. Typically, this data is appropriate only for an analysis of the market value of the subject property at the point of stabi-lized occupancy. Thus, the appraiser has to reconcile the prospective value indication based on this data with value indications derived from the other approaches for the corresponding date of stabilized occupancy. This data should not be used to derive a value indication for the date of completion unless other, truly comparable sales can be identified with similar occupancy characteristics and leaseup potential.

As part of reconciliation, the appraiser checks to ensure that value indications are expressed in the same units of comparison and reflect estimates of the same property interests as of the same date.

The appraiser must also consider any differences in the property rights appraised between the comparables and the subject property because the comparable sales may include the transfer of a leased fee estate. If the data is not properly analyzed in the sales comparison approach, the value indication concluded for the leased fee estate in the subject property upon the achievement of stabilized occupancy might be lower than the value for the fee simple estate. This value indication would not be compatible with the corresponding value indications derived from the cost and income approaches for the fee simple estate in the subject property unless adjustments have been made. Failure to recognize that the value indications may apply to different property rights would likely result in an incorrect value conclusion.

FURTHER READING

Akerson, Charles B. *The Appraiser's Workbook.* 2d ed. Chicago: Appraisal Institute, 1996.

Ramsland, Maxwell O., Jr. "Market-Supported Adjustments Using Multiple Regression Analysis." *The Appraisal Journal* (April 1998).

19 | APPLICATIONS OF THE SALES COMPARISON APPROACH

The basic theory and procedures of the sales comparison approach were described and a number of specific techniques were introduced in Chapters 17 and 18. The most commonly used techniques of sales comparison are illustrated in this chapter. Quantitative and qualitative techniques may both be employed in the application of the sales comparison approach. If adjustments can be derived by quantitative techniques, they are generally applied first. Differences in specific elements of comparison that elude precise mathematical adjustment are subsequently considered in qualitative analysis. The two methodologies are complementary and are often used in combination.

Other techniques can also be used to identify and estimate adjustments. The appraiser should consider all applicable techniques to determine which ones are most appropriate to the appraisal. Generally, the more complex the property being appraised, the greater the number of techniques that may be applied to its valuation.

Quantitative Adjustment Techniques

Real Property Rights Conveyed

In comparing properties that are encumbered by long-term leases or are essentially fully leased with quality tenants, it must be recognized that these leased properties may have significantly less risk than a competitive property that has shorter-term tenants at market rental rates. In expanding markets the reverse may be true. The ability to obtain higher rentals and the ready availability of tenants may favor the shorter-term lease strategy. Further, there is an obvious difference between the market position of a fully leased building and one that has no leases at all. Thus, the appraiser must clearly identify what is being appraised, the effect of any existing leases, and the differences that may exist because of the lease situations of properties used as potential comparables.

Consider the appraisal of the fee simple interest in land improved with an office building. A comparable property was fully leased at the time of sale, the leases were long-term, and the credit ratings of the tenants were good. To compare this leased fee estate to the subject fee simple estate, the appraiser must determine if the contract rent of the comparable was above, below, or equal to market rent. If the market rent for office space is $25 per square foot and the average contract rent for the comparable sale property was $24 per square foot, then the difference between market and contract rent is $1 per square foot.

The comparable sale property in question is improved with a 100,000-sq.-ft. office building. The market indicates that 10% is an appropriate overall capitalization rate, the vacancy rate for the market in which the subject property is located is 5%, and 4% of effective gross income is a reasonable management expense.[1] The effective difference between the market rent of $25 per square foot and the contract rent of $24 per square foot is estimated by deducting the vacancy allowance (5%) and management expenses (4%) from the actual difference between these rents ($1). This amount is then multiplied by the total area of the sale property to derive the annual rent loss for the remaining term of the lease.

$$\$1.00 - 0.05 \text{ (5\% vacancy)} = \$0.95$$
$$\$0.95 - 0.004 \text{ (4\% management, rounded)} = \$0.91$$
$$\$0.91 \times 100,000 \text{ sq. ft.} = \$91,000/\text{year}$$

or

$$\$1.00 \times 0.95 \text{ (100\% − 5\%)} \times 0.96 \text{ (100\% − 4\%)} = \$0.91 \text{ (rounded)}$$
$$\$0.91 \times 100,000 \text{ sq. ft.} = \$91,000/\text{year}$$

Other expenses are not considered because the leases are net leases and expenses do not constitute percentage charges against income.

The annual rent loss is then discounted over the remaining term of the lease. In the above example, the lease has 10 more years to run and market evidence supports a discount rate of 15%. Discounting the $91,000 annual loss in income over 10 years at 15% indicates an upward adjustment of $457,000 (rounded). The present value of the $91,000 annual loss for 10 years at 15% is calculated below.

$$5.018769^* \times \$91,000 = \$456,708, \text{ or } \$456,700$$

* PV of $1 per period factor, 10 years @ 15%. Present value calculations are discussed in Chapters 23 and 24.

The calculation is based on the expectation that the $1.00 difference between market rent and contract rent remains constant over the entire 10 years.

Calculating an adjustment for differences in real property rights is also necessary when just the leasehold interest is to be conveyed. Although it is usually not recommended that the sale of a leasehold interest be compared to a fee simple interest, the limited availability of sales of directly comparable interests sometimes makes this necessary. For example, consider an office building that is owned and sold separately from its site, which is subject to a 99-year ground lease. The 100,000-sq.-ft. building, which is leased at market rent, sold for $7,500,000, or $75.00 per square foot. To develop an indication of the

1. The appraiser should ensure that the operating expenses of the properties are comparable. Generally the higher the rent the tenant pays, the more services the landlord provides, and often the property will have higher vacancy.

value of the fee simple estate in the total property, the value indication for the leased fee estate (the land) must be added to that of the leasehold estate (the building).

One way to calculate a value indication for the leased fee estate (land only) is to capitalize the rent that accrues to the land. Assume that the annual ground rent is $200,000, which is consistent with current market rents, and that market evidence supports a land capitalization rate (R_L) of 8%. The calculation is

Income to the land (I_L) divided by R_L	= $200,000/0.08
Value of the leased fee interest	= $2,500,000

Typically, the capitalization rate for the land will be lower than the rate for the building because the building incurs physical deterioration. In this case, an upward adjustment of $2,500,000 for property rights conveyed would be shown in the sales comparison grid.

Financing Terms/Cash Equivalency

When paired data analysis is used to derive a cash equivalency adjustment, the calculations for discounting and adjusting for atypical conditions of sale are often combined. In other words, the adjustments for financing and conditions of sale can be represented by a single figure.

For example, consider a house that sells for $125,000 with a down payment of $25,000 and a seller-financed $100,000 mortgage at 8% interest. The mortgage is amortized over 25 years with a balloon payment due in 8 years. To determine the appropriate discount rate, the appraiser checks the market for sales financed by similar mortgage arrangements and finds that an $80,000, 8% note has been sold for $65,000. The discount rate for this note is calculated as follows:

$$(\$80,000 - \$65,000)/\$80,000 = 0.1875 \text{ or } 18.75\%$$

This discount rate may be applied to the $100,000 loan to arrive at an indicated cash equivalent value of the mortgage.

$100,000 − ($100,000 × 0.1875)	$81,250
Plus down payment	$25,000
Sale price adjusted for financing	$106,250

Calculating a cash equivalency adjustment by discounting cash flows can be accomplished in different ways. When a seller finances a mortgage at a below-market interest rate, the appraiser can estimate the present value of the mortgage by applying a present value factor to the monthly mortgage payment at the market interest rate for the stated term of the mortgage. For example, an appraiser might find a comparable sale of a single-family residence that was sold for $110,000 with a down payment of $25,000 and a seller-financed mortgage of $85,000 for a 20-year term at 10% interest. Homes in the market area are typically held for full, 20-year terms and the market-derived rate is 13%. The cash equivalency adjustment is calculated in the table below.

Mortgage: $85,000, 20 years, 10%
Monthly Payment: $820.27
Present value of $820.27 per month for 20 years @ market rate of 13%
     85.355132* × $820.27 = $70,014

PV of mortgage, rounded	$70,000
Plus down payment	+ 25,000
Sale price adjusted for financing	$95,000

* PV of $1 per period factor, 20 years @ 13%, compounded monthly

---

Another way to calculate the present value of the mortgage is to divide the monthly factor (monthly constant) at the contract interest rate by the monthly payment factor at the market interest rate and multiply the mortgage by the result. In this case, 0.00965/0.011715 × $85,000 = $70,017. (Implicit in this method is the expectation that the difference between the market interest rate and the contract interest rate will remain constant for the entire 20 years.)

Discounting cash flows to calculate a cash equivalency adjustment may also take into account the expectation of a balloon payment. The following example incorporates the same mortgage terms set forth in the previous example, except the mortgagor (borrower) holds the mortgage for only seven years. (The average mortgage life for loans of different types of properties can be ascertained from sales data on loans that were paid off or refinanced rather then assumed by a buyer.) In the following example, the present value of the mortgage is computed as the sum of two components:

1. The present value of the mortgage payments at the market interest rate for the expected life of the mortgage
2. The present value of the future mortgage balance at the market interest rate

One way to obtain the latter is to first calculate the value in seven years of the remaining 13 years of monthly payments at the contract rate and then to calculate the present value of that lump sum:

Monthly payment: $820.27
Present value of $820.27 per month for 7 years @ 13%
     54.969328* × $820.27 = $45,090, rounded to $45,000
Value of remaining mortgage payments in 7 years
     PV of $820.27 per month for 13 years @ 10%
     87.119542† × $820.27 = $71,462
PV of mortgage balance
     0.425061‡ × $71,462 = $30,376, rounded to   +   30,000
PV of mortgage $75,000
Plus down payment   +   25,000
Sale price adjusted for financing $100,000

* PV of $1 per period factor, 84 months @ 13% (monthly frequency)
† PV of $1 per period factor, 156 months @ 10% (monthly frequency)
‡ PV of $1 factor, 7 years @ 13% (annual frequency)
Note: The quantitative difference resulting from the choice of a discount factor at an annual frequency rather than a discount rate at a monthly frequency is insignificant. If the monthly frequency of the PV of $1 factor for 7 years @ 13% (0.404499) had been used in the above example, the adjusted sale price would have come to $99,000 (rounded). Errors in discounting are generally attributable to the choice of the discount rate, not the frequency of that rate.

Alternatively, the outstanding mortgage balance at the end of seven years can be calculated. Although these methods require more calculation, they are preferable because they reflect the typical holding period more accurately. Either set of calculations can be handled easily with a financial calculator or computer.

Transactions involving mortgage assumptions can be adjusted to cash equivalency with the same method applied to seller-financed transactions. However, the appraiser should be certain that the existing loan was assumed, not paid off. Other atypical mortgage terms include payments of interest only, followed by payments that include the repayment of the principal. This type of mortgage can also be adjusted to its cash equivalent value using the adjustment procedure described here. The present values of the payments (monthly, quarterly, semi-annual, or annual) at the market rate, year by year, are derived using present value factors. If balloon payments are involved, present value factors may be applied to isolate the contributory market value of the unpaid balance of the mortgage.

Conditions of Sale

If the influence of differences in the conditions of sale of comparable properties is not addressed in an adjustment for atypical financing, the appraiser may be able to estimate an adjustment through paired sales analysis or through interviews with market participants. For example, if the sale of a comparable property was a 1031 tax exchange involving a buyer anxious to meet the deadline of the exchange program, that transaction can be compared to typical sales of similar properties in the market and an indication estimated of the premium paid by the buyer under an extraordinary motivation.

Making direct comparisons is more difficult when the motivations of market participants are atypical. If the buyer is related to the seller, the sale price paid may not reflect the price that would be paid on the open market. Likewise, if a seller needs the proceeds of the sale quickly to avoid bankruptcy, a shrewd buyer may be able to purchase the property for less than what it would bring if it were on the market for a typical exposure time, allowing more potential buyers to participate in negotiations.

Interviewing the participants involved in the transaction may provide an indication of the magnitude of the adjustment, but sometimes the direction of an adjustment for conditions of sale may be all that can be determined. In the case of a distressed seller, an upward adjustment would probably be necessary to reflect the value the seller is not recapturing by accepting an expedient offer. The direction of a conditions of sale adjustment in transactions involving related parties may be more difficult to determine. Parents may accept a below-market price for a property to help their children pay for their first home, which would necessitate an upward adjustment if that sale were used as a comparable, or younger members of a family may offer to purchase a property belonging to an older relative at a price higher than the market level so that they can keep the property in the family, which would suggest a downward adjustment is necessary. If the details of the transaction are too difficult to verify, an adjustment for conditions of sale may not be usable.

Expenditures Made Immediately After Purchase

Generally an adjustment for expenditures made immediately after purchase is simple to quantify when transaction data is being verified with the market participants. For example, consider a 150,000-sq.-ft. warehouse that is comparable to the property being appraised and was recently sold for $850,000. The new owner-occupant expected to spend $65,000 to install an additional door and loading dock, which was a market-driven decision. In an interview with the new owner of the comparable property, the appraiser learns that the demolition and new construction actually cost $105,000. The value indication for that comparable would be $915,000 ($850,000 + $65,000) rather than $955,000 ($850,000 + $105,000), though, because the $65,000 expenditure anticipated by the buyer was deducted from the price the property would command in the market if no expenditures were necessary. If the actual cost of the renovation had been $40,000, the buyer would have enjoyed a $25,000 savings ($65,000 − $40,000) from the expected cost, but those savings would not be reflected in the price the buyer was willing to pay, which is already an established fact.

Adjustments for deferred maintenance can be handled similarly, but the appraiser should make sure that the buyer was aware of any items needing immediate repair. If the seller was not required to disclose that the roof of the warehouse had a leak and needed repairs, the buyer may not have anticipated those expenditures after the purchase, and there would be no adjustment to the recorded sale price for that item of deferred maintenance.

Other items that a buyer may need to budget expenses immediately after purchase for include

- Cost of obtaining entitlements
- Demolition and removal costs
- Environmental remediation costs

In sales comparison analysis, costs incurred by the new owners of comparable properties are reflected as positive adjustments to the sale prices of those properties. If the subject property requires some expenditure immediately after the purchase to reach its full utility, the adjustment is subtracted from the value indication for the subject.

Market Conditions

Consider a 10,000-sq.-ft. strip shopping center that sold five years ago for $300,000 and then sold again recently for $345,000. The indicated average annual appreciation of the shopping center would be $9,000

([$345,000 – $300,000]/5), or $0.900 per square foot per year. In the same market area, a 12,000-sq.-ft. shopping center with similar characteristics sold for $323,000 five years ago, and another 12,000-sq.-ft. property sold last year for $365,000. The average annual change per unit for those comparable properties is $0.875 per square foot per year ([($365,000 – $323,000)/4]/$12,000 = 0.875). The results of additional calculations made using sale and resale data and paired sales of comparable properties can be reconciled to support the estimate of the market conditions adjustment. The transactions used in these additional calculations all have similar markets, comparable land-to-building value ratios, and other elements of comparability.

The appreciation or depreciation of average sale prices in a market does not have to follow a linear pattern. Changes in sale price can also be irregular or stepped, or they can increase or decrease on a compounded basis. Statistical tools such as regression analysis and extrapolation, which may be necessary if the effective date of the appraisal is after the last sale, are useful in determining precise mathematical relationships, but any statistical model generated from the available data must reflect market thinking to be useful in the adjustment process.

Sorting and plotting sale and resale or paired sales data on a graph is another way to determine patterns of change. If sales data is not available for comparable properties, other evidence of shifting market conditions may include changes in

- The ratio between sale prices and listing prices or between lease contracts and lease offering rates
- Exposure time
- Listing prices
- Trends in rents
- The number of offers a seller receives and the frequency of backup offers
- The proportion of accepted offers that actually close
- The number of foreclosures
- The number of available properties
- The number of building permits issued and their aggregate value
- Terms of available institutional financing
- Use of seller financing
- Changing market demographic patterns
- Demolition and new construction

Location

Consider an interior vacant lot being appraised and two sales of vacant lots similar to the subject in most respects except for location. Comparable A, a corner lot with frontage on two streets, was sold for $12.00 per square foot. Comparable B, an interior lot with frontage on only one street, was sold for $9.00 per square foot. The adjustment for location can be extracted by comparing the prices of the comparable on the corner lot with the comparable on the interior lot.

$$\$9.00/\$12.00 = 0.75$$

It can therefore be concluded that an interior lot is worth only 75% of the value of a corner lot. To bring the value of Comparable A, the corner lot, in line with the value of the interior subject lot, a percentage adjustment of 75% is applied to the unit price of Comparable A.

$$\text{Value of the subject} = \$12.00 \text{ per square foot} \times 0.75$$
$$= \$9.00 \text{ per square foot}$$

The sale price of Comparable A, adjusted downward for its corner location, indicates a value of $9.00 per square foot for the subject interior lot. This relationship could also be expressed in terms of the complement of the value of Comparable A, i.e., the value of the subject equals the value of Comparable A less 25% of that value.

$$\text{Value of the subject} = \$12.00 - (0.25 \times \$12.00) = \$9.00$$

Physical Characteristics

Consider an apartment complex with both one-bedroom and two-bedroom units. Average monthly rents for competitive apartment properties are shown below.

Comparable	One-Bedroom Unit	Two-Bedroom Unit	Incremental Rent for Second Bedroom
A	$650	$700	$50
B	$675	$728	$53
C	$700	$752	$52
D	$710	$760	$50
E	$714	$766	$52
F	$720	$771	$51

If the comparable apartment buildings are essentially the same, the incremental rent attributable to a second bedroom could be reconciled at $51 per month. Given a 5% annual vacancy and collection loss, operating expenses of 35% of rent collections, and a market-derived overall capitalization rate of 9%, the value of a second bedroom is calculated as follows:

Rent per month	$51
Gross income per year ($51 × $12)	$612
Less 5% vacancy and collection loss	− 31
Subtotal	$581
Less operating expenses (35%)	− 203
Annual income attributable to second bedroom	$378
Capitalized @ 9%	$4,200

Based on this analysis an adjustment could be applied to sales of comparable properties with unit mixes that differ from the subject property.

Economic Characteristics

Paired data analysis may provide the only persuasive support for adjustments for differences in the attributes of a property that affect its income such as operating expenses, management quality, tenant mix, rent concessions, and other characteristics. Some of these characteristics may already be reflected in the adjustment for location. For example, a warehouse in a municipality with low property tax rates may have a higher value than a comparable warehouse in a neighboring community with higher tax rates, but the difference in value attributable to the tax rates will likely already be reflected in the adjustment for location.

Some appraisers analyze net operating income per unit to account for differences in economic characteristics, but the technique is not widely used because it essentially duplicates the techniques used in direct capitalization (see Chapter 22). Thus, errors are duplicated in two of the three approaches and these errors will be hard to identify in the final reconciliation of the value indications.[2]

Use/Zoning

To qualify as comparable properties, the highest and best use of the properties in question should be the same as that of the subject property. Although it would be impossible to support an adjustment for different highest and best uses of otherwise comparable sites, market data can be used to support an adjustment for different intensities of use allowed by zoning. For example, consider a 100,000-sq.-ft. office building on a 3.0-acre site where the current zoning allows for a maximum floor area ratio (FAR) of 0.50. The existing improvements predate a zoning change and are a legal nonconforming use. The zoning regulations allow for improvements of equal size to be built if the existing improvements are razed or destroyed. Most of the comparable properties are in areas zoned for a maximum FAR of 1.0.

A quantitative adjustment would be difficult to calculate using paired data analysis, but if a strong relationship between the zoning and sale price can be determined, the comparable sales can still be analyzed. The following recent land sales in the subject's market area are already adjusted for other elements of comparison:

Sale	Size (in acres*)	Size (in sq. ft.)	Sale Price	Maximum FAR
A	0.77	33,541	$738,000	1.0
B	0.95	41,382	$450,000	0.5
C	1.40	60,984	$690,000	0.5
D	2.30	100,188	$2,100,000	1.0
E	3.23	140,699	$2,810,000	1.0

* 1 acre = 43,560 square feet

---

2. For further discussion of the limitations of net operating income multiplier analysis, see Mark W. Galleshaw, "Appropriate Uses of Economic Characteristics in the Sales Comparison Approach," *The Appraisal Journal* (January 1992): 91–98, and the letters to the editor in the July 1992 issue of *The Appraisal Journal.*

The prices per square foot in ascending order are

Sale	Price per Square Foot of Land
B	$10.87
C	$11.31
E	$19.97
D	$20.96
A	$22.00

The prices per square foot of the land sales range widely, but the prices per square foot of building area allowed by the zoning indicate a much tighter range, suggesting a stronger relationship:

Sale	Price per Square Foot of Allowable Building Area (or $/FAR)
E	$19.97
D	$20.96
B	$21.74
A	$22.00
C	$22.62

The indications of price per square foot of allowable building area can be reconciled to $21.50 per square foot of allowable building area. With a floor area ratio of 0.76, the value of the subject site could be estimated to be worth $16.34 per square foot (21.50 × 0.76), or $2,135,000.

Non-realty Components of Value

Components of the subject property or sale properties that are not real property must be considered in the comparison of those properties. Realty and non-realty items must be separated. Sometimes the component may be included in the development of an opinion of market value—for example, the furniture, fixtures, and equipment in a hotel. At other times, non-realty components may be excluded—for example, the business enterprise value component of a regional mall.

Considerations for Multiple Adjustments

Adjustment considerations such as those demonstrated in this chapter are examples of many that may be important in comparison processes, but a function of market research is to determine which factors, if any, are important in a given market circumstance. Not all properties are perfect, and to create a theoretically perfect property by making every conceivable adjustment may go as far beyond the applicable market as failing to consider the important adjustments may fall short of the market. Thus, adjustments must be defensible not only individually but collectively as well.

When many adjustments are applied by the appraiser and when their individual and collective amounts are substantial, the appraiser must ask, "Is the comparable property really comparable?" The greater the amount of collective adjustment, the more the appraiser may reduce the weight placed on a given comparable, or the appraiser may determine that it is not sufficiently comparable to be used at all. When a sale property is considered to offer important market evidence but finding the means to make quantitative adjustments is lacking, the appraiser may turn to the other major sales comparison technique, qualitative analysis.

Qualitative Analysis Techniques

The property being appraised is a five-year-old, multitenant office building with 36,000 square feet of gross building area and 31,800 square feet of rentable area (88% of GBA). Its occupancy rate is 90%, which is considered stable in the subject market. The amount of space occupied by individual tenants ranges from 2,500 square feet to 7,000 square feet. The building is of average construction quality and is in average condition. The ratio of rentable area to gross building area is low in comparison to the average for the subject market area, which is approximately 93%. The site is appropriately landscaped. The open-space parking provided is both adequate and in compliance with the zoning code. The location, which may also be considered average, is an interior site accessed from a major arterial highway.

Current base rents range from $12 per square foot to $13 per square foot of rentable area. Rent for the overall building averages $12.60 per square foot and the quality of the tenants is good. With the exception of telephone service, the landlord pays all expenses, including janitorial and electrical. Operating expenses are typical for the market. The leases have three- and four-year terms; they contain an option to renew for three more years at the then-current market rent. All leases are less than 18 months old, and the rents and terms they specify are standard for the current market. Leasehold positions in the subject property do not have any particular advantage. The leased fee interest in the property is the interest to be appraised.

Five comparable sales are used in the analysis. All the comparables are mid-rise, multitenant office properties located in the subject's market area and all were financed at market rates with conventional loan-to-value ratios. All the transactions involved the sale of a leased fee estate. The unit of comparison employed in this analysis is price per square foot of rentable area. The five comparables are described below (as of the date of sale) and summarized in Table 19.1.

- Sale A was sold five months ago for $2,930,000. It is six years old and in average condition. The building contains 40,000 square feet of gross building area and 37,600 square feet of rentable area (94% of GBA). The indicated price per square foot of rentable area is $77.93. Average rent is $12.80 per square foot of rentable area. The landlord pays all expenses and occupancy is 87%. The rents, lease terms, and expenses of the property are at market levels. The site is located at the intersection of a

Table 19.1   **Market Data Grid for Relative Comparison Analysis**

Element of Comparison	Subject	Sale A	Sale B	Sale C	Sale D	Sale E
Sale price	–	$2,930,000	$2,120,000	$2,450,000	$2,160,000	$2,470,000
Price/sq. ft. of rentable area	–	$77.93	$71.38	$76.09	$80.90	$73.08
Property interest	Leased fee	Leased fee	Leased fee	Leased fee	Leased fee	Leased fee
Age	5 years	6 years	4 years	5 years	6 years	4 years
Sq. ft. of GBA	36,000	40,000	32,000	35,000	30,000	38,000
Sq. ft. of rentable area	31,800	37,600	29,700	32,200	26,700	33,800
Rental area ratio	88%	94%	93%	92%	89%	89%
Occupancy rate	90%	87%	85%	90%	95%	90%
Construction quality and condition	Average	Average	Average	Average	Average	Average
Ratio of parking spaces to rental area	Good	Similar	Similar	Similar	Inferior	Similar
Average rent per sq. ft. of rentable area	$12.60	$12.80	$11.80	$12.60	$13.00	$12.30
Location	Average	Superior	Inferior	Similar	Superior	Inferior
Expense ratio	Market norm	Similar	Similar	Higher	Similar	Similar
Overall comparability	–	Superior	Inferior	Superior	Superior	Inferior

major arterial highway and a collector road. Parking is adequate. The ratio of parking spaces to rentable area in Sale A is approximately the same as that of the subject.

- Sale B was sold four months ago for $2,120,000. The building is four years old and contains 32,000 square feet of gross building area and 29,700 square feet of rentable area (93% of GBA). Its unit price is calculated to be $71.38 per square foot of rentable area. Site improvements are average, and the ratio of parking area to rentable area is similar to that of the subject property. The property is in average condition. The leases provide tenants with full services. Occupancy is 85% and the average base rent is $11.80 per square foot of rentable area, which is slightly below market levels. The lengths of the leases and property expenses are considered to be at market levels. The property is located on an interior site accessed from a major collector street. Parking is adequate.

- Sale C was sold nine months ago for $2,450,000. The building contains 35,000 square feet of gross building area and 32,200 square feet of rentable area (92% of GBA). Its unit price is $76.09 per square foot of rentable area. The improvements were constructed five years ago and are in average condition. Rent averages $12.60 per square foot of rentable area. All tenant services are provided by the landlord. The building has an occupancy rate of 90%, and all rents and lease terms are at market levels. The total expenses for the building are slightly higher than is typical for the market because two tenants who occupy 15% of the total space use excessive electricity; they do not pay additional rent to compensate for the extra expense. The property's location is an interior site accessed from a major arterial highway. The property has a parking ratio similar to that of the subject.

- Sale D was sold two months ago for $2,160,000. The building is six years old and in average condition. It contains 30,000 square feet of gross building area and 26,700 square feet of rentable area (89% of GBA). The unit price is $80.90 per square foot of rentable area. The rent averages $13.00 per square foot of rentable area, and the lease terms and building expenses are at market levels. The occupancy rate is 95%. The site is located at the intersection of two major arterial highways in a district zoned for higher-density development than is permitted in the subject district. Thus, the ratio of parking area to rentable area is lower than that of the subject property.

- Sale E was sold six months ago for $2,470,000. The building was constructed four years ago and is in average condition. It contains 38,000 square feet of gross building area and 33,800 square feet of rentable area (89% of GBA). Its unit price is $73.08 per square foot of rentable area. The location is an interior site accessed by a major collector street. The occupancy rate for the building is 90%. Rents average $12.30 per square foot of rentable area. Full tenant services are provided by the landlord. Rents, lease terms, and property expenses are at market levels. The property has adequate parking, and the parking ratio is similar to that of the subject property.

Qualitative analysis recognizes the inefficiencies of real estate markets and the difficulty in expressing adjustments with mathematical precision. It is essential, therefore, that the appraiser explain the logic applied in arriving at the adjustments so that readers of the appraisal report will understand how they were derived.

The appraiser first analyzes the market data and determines that all of the office building sales involved the transfer of a leased fee interest. Thus, no adjustment for differences in property rights conveyed is necessary. (The below-market rent of Sale B will be considered subsequently.) All sales were transacted with market financing, so no adjustment for this element of comparison is required either. Because all of the transactions were conducted at arm's length, there is no adjustment for conditions of sale. The comparables used were recent transactions, all occurring within nine months of the date of valuation. There have been no significant changes in rent levels and occupancy, so no adjustments are warranted for market conditions. The relative comparison analysis of dissimilar elements is described below.

- Sale A has an indicated unit price of $77.93 per square foot of rentable area. Its location at the intersection of a major arterial highway and a collector road is superior to the location of the subject property. The building has an average rentable area ratio, but it is a more efficient building than the subject. The building occupancy rate for Sale A is slightly lower than the subject's and lower than the rate considered typical for stabilized occupancy in the market. In short, Sale A has more superior than inferior attributes and these attributes are considered more significant. This sale indicates a unit value for the subject property of less than $77.93 per square foot of rentable area.

- Sale B has an indicated unit price of $71.38 per square foot of rentable area. Effective contract rent is lower than market rent. The location of this property on a major collector street is inferior to the subject property's location on a major arterial highway. Sale B has a superior rentable area ratio, indicating that the property will yield a higher net income. The occupancy rate for the comparable is below the market rate for stabilized occupancy. In all, more of the attributes of Sale B are inferior than superior and these inferior factors are also considered more significant. In this particular case, the difference in the rentable area ratios may be considered to have the least impact on value. Therefore, the analysis of Sale B indicates that the subject should have a unit value greater than $71.38 per square foot of rentable area.

- Sale C has a unit price of $76.09 per square foot of rentable area. The location of the comparable is similar to that of the subject, but the comparable has a superior rentable area ratio. The expense ratio for the property is slightly higher than typical, resulting in a lower net income. Since a higher rentable area ratio usually has a greater effect on value than a higher expense ratio, Sale C is superior to the subject and the value for the subject should be less than $76.09 per square foot of rentable area.

- Sale D indicates a unit price of $80.90 per square foot of rentable area. Because it is situated at the intersection of two major arterial highways, the property has a significantly superior location compared to that of the subject. The availability of parking is more limited. Sale D has a higher occupancy rate than the stabilized occupancy rate that characterizes the market for this type of property. The superior location and higher occupancy outweigh the limited parking. Overall, this comparable is superior to the subject and an appropriate value for the subject would be less than $80.90 per square foot of rentable area.

- Sale E has an indicated unit price of $73.08 per square foot of rentable area. The location of the property on a major collector street is inferior to that of the subject. The property is similar to the subject in all other elements of comparison. Since Sale E has an inferior location, the price of the subject should be greater than $73.08 per square foot of rentable area.

The value indications derived from the comparable sales are reconciled into a single value indication by arranging the five sales in an array relative to the subject (Table 19.2).

Table 19.2	Bracketing the Subject Property	
Sale	**Price Per Square Foot**	**Overall Comparability**
D	$80.90	superior
A	$77.93	superior
C	$76.09	superior
Subject	–	–
E	$73.08	inferior
B	$71.38	inferior

Sales A, C, and D have unit values greater than that of the subject; Sales B and E have unit values less than that of the subject. The lowest value indication in the first group is $76.09 per square foot of rentable area for Sale C. The higher value indication in the second group was $73.08 per square foot of rentable area for Sale E. Therefore, the bracket for the value of the subject is between $73.08 and $76.09 per square foot of rentable area. Sale E is the property most similar to the subject and therefore may be accorded the greatest weight. Based on the indicated range of value and the weight placed on Sale E, a single point estimate of $74.00 per square foot of rentable area may be concluded.

A total value indication for the subject property may then be calculated by multiplying the unit value of $74.00 per square foot of rentable area by the 31,800 square feet of rentable area, resulting in a value indication of $2,353,200, which may be rounded to $2,350,000.

In relative comparison analysis, reliable results can usually be obtained by bracketing the subject between comparables that are superior and inferior to it. If the comparables are either all superior or all inferior, only a lower or upper limit is set and no range of possible values for the subject can be defined. In this case the only conclusion the appraiser can draw for the subject is either that its value is more than the highest comparable indication (if all that comparable's qualitative factors are inferior) or less than the lowest comparable indication (if all that comparable's qualitative factors are superior). The appraiser must search the market diligently to obtain and analyze sufficient pertinent data to bracket the value of the subject property. If the available comparable sales do not bracket the subject's value, the appraiser should consider employing other analytical techniques to establish such a bracket. Quantitative adjustments to the comparables can often serve this purpose. An example illustrating the combined use of quantitative adjustments and qualitative analysis is provided later in the chapter.

A value indication derived with qualitative analysis will usually require more narrative explanation in an appraisal report than an indication derived with quantitative adjustments will. In applying either technique, the appraiser must ensure that his or her reasoning is clear and adequately explained. The extent of narrative explanation required depends on the complexity of the property being appraised. The more complex the property, the more factors that must be considered.

Comparative Analysis

In everyday appraisal practice, available market data may allow the appraiser to make quantitative adjustments for some elements of comparison and to analyze qualitatively the factors that cannot be quantified. When these techniques are combined they should be consistently applied for each element of comparison. In other words, the appraiser should not make a quantitative adjustment for change in market conditions for some comparables and perform a qualitative analysis of market conditions for others. Quantitative adjustments should be made first. Qualitative analysis is subsequently applied to an adjusted sale or unit price. The following combined application of quantitative adjustments and qualitative analysis makes use of paired data and relative comparison analyses.

Comparative Analysis of a Warehouse

The property being appraised is a 15-year-old warehouse containing 25,000 square feet of gross building area and 2,500 square feet of finished office area. The ceiling height is 18 feet. The quality of construction is good and the building's condition is average.

The five comparable sales described below were used in the analysis. All of the comparables are warehouses located in the subject property's market area.

- Sale A was sold one year ago for $622,000. The seller provided advantageous financing that resulted in the buyer paying $63,000 more than if the buyer had paid cash. The property is a 28,000-sq.-ft. warehouse with an 18-ft. ceiling height and 2,250 square feet of finished office area. It was 14 years old at the time of the sale. The quality of construction is good, but at the time of sale the warehouse exhibited excessive deferred maintenance. The buyer budgeted for expenses of $35,000 to upgrade the property.
- Sale B was sold six months ago for $530,000 in a cash payment to the seller. This 27,000-sq.-ft. warehouse has 18-ft. ceilings and 2,200 square feet of finished office area. It was 13 years old. The quality of construction and condition are average.
- Sale C is a current sale transacted for $495,000. The buyer assumed an existing loan at below market rates. This favorable financing resulted in the buyer paying $9,000 more than he would have paid if the buyer had obtained market terms. This 22,000-sq.-ft. warehouse has 17-ft. ceilings and 3,000 square feet of finished office area. The property is 13 years old. The quality of construction is good and its condition is average. This warehouse is subject to a long-term lease at below-market levels so its purchase price was set at $25,000 below market prices.
- Sale D was sold three months ago for $554,000. This 25,000-sq.-ft. warehouse has a 17-ft. ceiling height and 2,500 square feet of finished office area.

It is 16 years old. The quality of construction is good and the condition is excellent.

- Sale E is a current sale for $626,000 paid in cash to the seller. This 26,000-sq.-ft. warehouse has 19-ft. ceilings and 2,100 square feet of finished office area. It is 16 years old. The quality of construction is good and its condition is average. The property is subject to a long-term lease that is above market levels. The purchase price of the warehouse was consequently set at $80,000 above market prices.

Quantitative Adjustments

The quantitative adjustment procedure is described below and summarized in Table 19.3.

Property rights conveyed. Sales C and E were sold subject to long-term leases, so both require an adjustment for property rights conveyed. Sale C

Table 19.3	Quantitative Adjustments					
	Subject	**Sale A**	**Sale B**	**Sale C**	**Sale D**	**Sale E**
Price		$622,000	$530,000	$495,000	$554,000	$626,000
Area in square feet	25,000	28,000	27,000	22,000	25,000	26,000
Ceiling height	18 ft.	18 ft.	18 ft.	17 ft.	17 ft.	19 ft.
Age	15 years	14 years	13 years	13 years	16 years	16 years
Construction quality	Good	Good	Average	Good	Good	Good
Office area	2,500	2,250	2,200	3,000	2,500	2,100
Property rights	Fee simple	Fee simple	Fee simple	Leased fee	Fee simple	Leased fee
Adjustment		0	0	+$25,000	0	-$80,000
Adjusted price		$622,000	$530,000	$520,000	$554,000	$546,000
Financing terms	Cash	Carryback		Cash Loan assumption	Cash	Cash
Adjustment		-$63,000	0	-$9,000	0	0
Adjusted price		$559,000	$530,000	$511,000	$554,000	$546,000
Conditions of sale	Arm's-length	Arm's-length	Arm's-length	Arm's-length	Arm's-length	Arm's-length
Market conditions	Current	One year	Six months	Current	Three months	Current
Adjustment		× 1.04	× 1.02	0	× 1.01	0
Adjusted price		$581,360	$540,600	$511,000	$559,540	$546,000
Deferred maintenance (condition)	Average	Excessive	Average	Average	None	Average
Adjustment		+$35,000	0	0	-$10,000	0
Adjusted price		$616,360	$540,600	$511,000	$549,540	$546,000
Adjusted price per sq. ft.		$22.01	$20.02	$23.23	$21.98	$21.00

requires an upward adjustment of $25,000 because it is leased at below-market contract rent. Sale E requires a downward adjustment of $80,000 because it is leased at above-market contract rent.

Financing. Sales A and C require adjustment for financing terms. The seller of Sale A provided advantageous financing that resulted in the buyer paying $63,000 more than the buyer would have paid in a cash transaction. Therefore, a downward adjustment of $63,000 is made to Sale A. The buyer of Sale C assumed an existing, below-market loan. The buyer paid a $9,000 premium above the price that would have been paid under market terms, so a downward adjustment of $9,000 is made to Sale C.

Conditions of sale. Because all the comparables were arm's-length transactions, none requires an adjustment for conditions of sale.

Market conditions. The sales occurred over a 12-month period. Properties in this market have been appreciating at 4% annually. Sales A, B, and D require an upward adjustment for change in market conditions.

Condition of improvements. Sale A suffered from excessive deferred maintenance. At the time of sale, the buyer anticipated spending $35,000 upgrading the building to average condition. The subject property is in average condition. Therefore, Sale A is adjusted upward by $35,000 to bring it in line with the subject's average condition. Sale D had no deferred maintenance and was in excellent condition. Therefore, it requires a downward adjustment of $10,000 to bring it in line with the subject's average condition.

Adjusted unit prices. After applying all known quantitative adjustments, the comparables indicate a value range from $20.02 to $23.23 per square foot.

Qualitative Analysis

After quantitative adjustments are exhausted, the sales must be analyzed to determine if the market evidence supports qualitative adjustments. The following data array shows a value trend within the comparables for percentage of office area to building area. The properties with a higher percentage of office space had a higher average unit price than did the properties with a smaller percentage of office space. A qualitative adjustment for the amount of office space is supported by the comparable sales.

Percentage of Office Area to Building Area

Sale	8%	10%	14%
A	$22.01		
B	$20.02		
C			$23.23
D		$21.98	
E	$21.00		
Mean	$21.01	$21.98	$23.23
Subject		10%	
Adjustment	Inferior	Similar	Superior

This analysis recognizes that the comparable sales unit prices are affected to some degree by other elements of comparison. A similar data array would be done for each of the elements. If the data does not show discernible trends for an element, then no adjustment is warranted. Care must be taken not to duplicate adjustments. The data array in the example is the same for size and percentage of office area to building area. A decision must be made as to which adjustment is most relevant. Within the data set, to use both would be a duplication and would distort the analysis. If it is determined that the office space ratio was more market-reactive than size, no adjustment for size will be made. For example, no adjustments are supported within the data set for age. The data arrays for the adjustment elements within the data set support the adjustments summarized in Table 19.4.

Table 19.4   **Qualitative Adjustment Summary Chart**

	Sale A	Sale B	Sale C	Sale D	Sale E
Adj. price/sq. ft.	$22.01	$20.02	$23.23	$21.98	$21.00
Const. quality	Similar	Inferior	Similar	Similar	Similar
Age	Superior	Inferior	Superior	Inferior	Inferior
Ceiling height	Similar	Similar	Superior	Superior	Similar
% office space	Inferior	Inferior	Superior	Similar	Inferior
Overall adj.	Similar	Inferior	Superior	Similar	Inferior

Sale	Inferior	Similar	Superior
A		$22.01	
B	$20.02		
C			$23.23
D		$21.98	
E	$21.00		

The value range of the comparables has been narrowed to the most similar sales, which indicate values of $21.98 to $22.01 per square foot. If the bracket of values were broader—for example if the adjusted unit prices of Sales A and D had ranged from $19.00 to $23.00—the appraiser could do further analysis to determine if the subject is more similar to the sales in the upper or lower levels of the bracket. Also, the range of adjusted unit prices for inferior or superior sales may overlap the range set by sales of different overall comparability—for example, if Sale D had an adjusted unit price of $20.50 per square foot, which is less than the unit price of Sale E, an "inferior" comparable. In this situation the appraiser should address the causes for the overlapping and refine the value bracket. Comparing the ranges of inferior, similar, and superior comparables can help the appraiser identify statistical outliers—i.e., observations that are extreme and often evidence of an error. An outlier may have an inordinate effect on a statistical model if the reason for its departure from the typical range cannot be explained.

FURTHER READING

Akerson, Charles B. *The Appraiser's Workbook.* 2d ed. Chicago: Appraisal Institute, 1996.

PART

V

INCOME CAPITALIZATION ANALYSIS

Part V of the text deals with the variety of techniques real estate appraisers use to capitalize an income stream into an indication of value. **Chapter 20, The Income Capitalization Approach,** discusses the fundamentals of the income capitalization approach and defines the myriad terms used in describing rents, rates, multipliers, and future benefits of ownership. **Chapter 21, Income and Expense Analysis,** delves into the various forms of income a property can generate, the expenses that must be considered in the successful operation of a property, and the compilation of a reconstructed operating statement using that data. **Chapter 22, Direct Capitalization,** examines the simplest form of capitalization, using an overall capitalization rate and a single year's income to calculate the value of a property. **Chapter 23, Yield Capitalization—Theory and Basic Applications** introduces the consideration of income streams that remain constant or change in various ways over a holding period, which complicates the application of capitalization rates and the analysis of property value. **Chapter 24, Discounted Cash Flow Analysis and Special Applications in Income Capitalization,** discusses a powerful and increasingly common form of appraisal analysis, discounted cash flow analysis, as well as other sophisticated techniques for analyzing income streams.

THE INCOME CAPITALIZATION APPROACH

Income-producing real estate is typically purchased as an investment, and from an investor's point of view earning power is the critical element affecting property value. One basic investment premise holds that the higher the earnings, the higher the value, provided the amount of risk remains constant. An investor who purchases income-producing real estate is essentially trading present dollars for the expectation of receiving future dollars. The income capitalization approach to value consists of methods, techniques, and mathematical procedures that an appraiser uses to analyze a property's capacity to generate benefits (i.e., usually the monetary benefits of income and reversion) and convert these benefits into an indication of present value.

The analysis of cost and sales data is often an integral part of the income capitalization approach, and capitalization techniques are frequently employed in the cost and sales comparison approaches. Capitalization techniques are commonly used to analyze and adjust sales data in the sales comparison approach; in the cost approach, obsolescence is often measured by capitalizing an estimated income loss. The income capitalization approach is described here as part of the systematic valuation process, but the various methods, techniques, and procedures used in the approach are general-purpose analytical tools applicable in the valuation and evaluation of income-producing properties.

This chapter provides a broad overview of the income capitalization approach and discusses the rationale and methods behind it. Chapters 21 through 24 continue this discussion with detailed explanations of the specific methods, techniques, and procedures used to project and capitalize future benefits.

> In the **income capitalization approach,** an appraiser analyzes a property's capacity to generate future benefits and capitalizes the income into an indication of present value. The principle of anticipation is fundamental to the approach. Techniques and procedures from this approach are used to analyze comparable sales data and to measure obsolescence in the cost approach.

Relationship to Appraisal Principles
Anticipation and Change
Anticipation is fundamental to the income capitalization approach. All income capitalization methods, techniques, and procedures attempt to consider anticipated future benefits and estimate their present value. This may involve either forecasting the anticipated future income or estimating a capitalization rate that implicitly reflects the anticipated pattern of change in income over time.

The approach must also consider how change affects the value of income-producing properties. To provide sound value indications, the appraiser must carefully address and forecast investors' expectations of changes in income levels, the expenses required to ensure income, and probable increases or decreases in property value. The defined income of a real estate investment may differ according to the type of investor. The ongoing securitization and globalization of real estate investment has brought new participants into the market. The income streams that real estate investment trusts (REITs) and pension funds look to are different from the net incomes on which more traditional investors have focused.[1]

The capitalization process must reflect the possibility that actual future income, expenses, and property value may differ from those originally anticipated by an investor on the date of appraisal. The more uncertainty there is concerning the future levels of these variables, the riskier the investment. Investors expect to earn a higher rate of return on investments that are riskier. This should be reflected in the support for the discount rate and capitalization rate obtained from market research.

Supply and Demand

The principles of supply and demand and the related concept of competition are particularly useful in forecasting future benefits and estimating rates of return in the income capitalization approach. Both income and rates of return are determined in the market. The rents charged by the owners of a motel, a shopping center, an office building, an apartment building, or any income-producing property usually do not vary greatly from those charged by owners of competing properties.

If the demand for a particular type of space exceeds the existing supply, owners may be able to increase rents. Vacancy rates may fall and developers may find new construction profitable. Property values may increase until supply satisfies demand. On the other hand, if the demand for space is less than the existing supply, rents may decline and vacancy rates may increase. Therefore, to estimate rates of return and forecast future benefits, appraisers consider the demand (both present and anticipated) for the particular type of property and how the demand relates to supply.

Applicability and Limitations

Any property that generates income can be valued using the income capitalization approach. When more than one approach to value is used to develop an opinion of value for an income-producing property, the value indication produced by the income capitalization approach might be given greater weight than that of the other approaches in the final reconciliation of value indications.

---

1.   For a discussion of how pension fund managers and other institutional investors analyze income and cash flow to property, see the section of Chapter 6 on the securitization of real estate markets.

INTERESTS TO BE VALUED

Income-producing real estate is usually leased, which creates legal estates of the lessor's interest (i.e., the leased fee) and the lessee's interest (i.e., the leasehold). There are also hybrid situations involving partially leased buildings. Federal or state law often requires appraisers to value leased properties as fee simple estates, not leased fee estates (e.g., for eminent domain and ad valorem taxation).

When an appraisal assignment involves the valuation of the fee simple interest in a leased property (whether due to government regulations or the desires of the client), the valuation of the entire bundle of rights may or may not require the valuation of the separate parts. The value of a leasehold estate may be positive, zero, or negative, depending on the relationship of market rent and contract rent, as explained in Chapter 5, and the difference between the market rent and contract rent may be capitalized at an appropriate rate to produce an indication of leasehold value, if any, without consideration of the value of the leased fee estate.

Although the market values of leased fee and leasehold positions are often said to be "allocated" between the two (or more) interests, each interest must be valued on its own merit. The results can then be compared with the valuation of an unencumbered fee simple interest. This comparison is particularly important when contract benefits or detriments are substantial.

Appraisers should not necessarily conclude that leasehold and leased fee values are additive and always equal fee simple value. It is possible that both the leaseholder and the leased fee owner are disadvantaged because of the terms of the lease. Also, there may be an apparent advantage of one party over the other when compared with other leases. However, the fact of the advantage may result in problems that outweigh its benefits and ultimately serve to the disadvantage of that party.

Like all contracts, the real estate lease depends on the actual performance of all parties to the contract. A weak tenant with the best of intentions may still be a high risk. The same is true for a financially capable tenant who is litigious and is willing to ignore lease terms or to break a lease and defy lawsuits. If the tenant defaults or does not renew a lease, the value of the underlying property does not change, but the value of the leased fee may be seriously affected.

Because a leasehold or a leased fee is based upon contract rights, the appraiser needs special training and experience to differentiate between what is generally representative of the market and other elements of a contract that are not typical of the market. An understanding of risks associated with the parties and the lease arrangement is also required. A lease never increases the market value of real property rights to the fee simple estate. Any potential value increment in excess of a fee simple estate is attributable to the particular lease contract, and even though the rights may legally "run with the land," they constitute contract rather than real property rights. Conversely, detrimental aspects of a lease may result in a situation in which either or both of the parties to the lease, and their corresponding value positions, may be diminished.

Income capitalization can be used to simulate investor motivations. For example, investors in small residential income properties might typically purchase on the basis of effective gross income multipliers (*EGIM*s). Thus, the appraiser could develop an opinion of the value of a subject property using *EGIM*s. Similarly, investors in large office buildings with numerous tenants might project future cash flows by analyzing each lease, considering the impact of lease renewals and the anticipated sale of the property at the end of a holding period. Thus, the appraiser could simulate this process by conducting a similar discounted cash flow analysis for the subject property.

Income capitalization techniques do not always rely on comparable sales, but some appropriate form of market support is needed. Yield capitalization does require selection or development of an appropriate "yield" rate. The yield rate should reflect what investors expected to earn on comparable sales as well as other real estate investment alternatives currently available in the market with similar risk.

Definitions

The income capitalization approach employs more specialized terminology than any of the other approaches to value, and the meanings of the various terms sometimes overlap. Table 20.1 shows the relationships between different rates used in the approach and the real property interests that can be valued. Table 20.2 lists synonymous terms and symbols commonly used in income capitalization.

Table 20.1   Rates, Ratios, and Relationships

Property Interest	Net Income or Cash Flow	Forecast Reversion	Capitalization Rate	Yield Rate
Total property (V_O)	Net operating income (NOI or I_O)	Proceeds of resale (PR), property reversion	Overall capitalization rate (R_O)	Risk rate, discount rate (Y_O)
Debt, mortgage loan (V_M)	Debt service (I_M), monthly—DS, annual—ADS	Balance, balloon, book value (b)	Mortgage capitalization rate (R_M)	Yield rate to mortgage (Y_M), interest rate
Equity (V_E)	Equity dividend (I_E)	Equity reversion (ER)	Equity capitalization rate (R_E)	Equity yield rate (Y_E)
Land, site (V_L)	NOI to land (NOI_L or I_L)	Land reversion (LR)	Land capitalization rate (R_L)	Land yield rate (Y_L)
Building, improvements (V_B)	NOI to building (NOI_B or I_B)	Building reversion (BR)	Building capitalization rate (R_B)	Building yield rate (Y_B)
Leased fee (V_{LF})	NOI to lessor (NOI_{LF} or I_{LF})	Property reversion (PR) or proceeds of resale	Leased fee capitalization rate (R_{LF})	Leased fee yield rate (Y_{LF})
Leasehold (V_{LH})	NOI to lessee (NOI_{LH} or I_{LH})	None or proceeds of resale of leasehold estate	Leasehold capitalization rate (R_{LH})	Leasehold yield rate (Y_{LH})

Table 20.2	Terms and Synonyms Used in the Income Capitalization Approach	
Category	**Preferred Term**	**Synonym/Symbol**
Lease	Flat rental lease	Level payment lease
	Variable rental lease	Index lease
	Step-up or step-down lease	Graduated rental lease
	Revaluation lease	
	Lease with an annual increase	
	Percentage lease	
Rent	Contract rent	
	Market rent	Economic rent
	Scheduled rent	
	Pro forma rent	
	Effective rent	
	Excess rent	
	Deficit rent	
	Percentage rent	
	Overage rent	
Future benefits	Potential gross income	PGI
	Effective gross income	EGI
	Net operating income	NOI or I_O*
	Equity dividend	Income to equity (I_E)
	Reversion	Reversionary benefits, resale value, property reversion
Operating expenses	Fixed expense	
	Variable expense	
	Replacement allowance	Replacement reserve
Rates of return	Overall capitalization rate	R_O
	Equity capitalization rate	Cash flow rate, cash on cash return, equity dividend rate, R_E
	Terminal capitalization rate	Residual capitalization rate, R_N
	Land capitalization rate	R_L
	Building capitalization rate	R_B
	Discount rate	Risk rate
	Safe rate	Riskless rate, relatively riskless rate
	Internal rate of return	IRR
	Overall yield rate	Property yield rate, Y_O
	Equity yield rate	Y_E
	Mortgage capitalization rate	Mortgage constant, annual loan constant, R_M
Income multipliers	Potential gross income multiplier	$PGIM$
	Effective gross income multiplier	$EGIM$

* The traditional abbreviation *NOI* is commonly used in accounting, finance, economics, and other professional disciplines. The abbreviation I_O is used in Appraisal Institute educational materials to maintain a consistent set of variables and subscripts throughout income capitalization calculations. The abbreviations can be used interchangeably.

MARKET VALUE AND INVESTMENT VALUE

An important distinction is made between market value and investment value. Investment value is the value of a certain property use to a particular investor. Investment value may coincide with market value, which was defined in Chapter 2, if the client's investment criteria are typical of investors in the market. In this case, the two opinions of value may be the same number, but the two types of value and their concepts are not interchangeable.

Market value is objective, impersonal, and detached; investment value is based on subjective, personal parameters. To develop an opinion of market value with the income capitalization approach, the appraiser must be certain that all the data and forecasts used are market-oriented and reflect the motivations of a typical investor who would be willing to purchase the property at the time of the appraisal. A particular investor may be willing to pay a price different from market value, if necessary, to acquire a property that satisfies other investment objectives unique to that investor.

> **investment value:** The specific value of an investment to a particular investor or class of investors based on individual investment requirements; distinguished from market value, which is impersonal and detached.

Leases

The income to various lease interests is generally derived through the conveyance and operation of leases. A lease is a written[2] document in which the rights to use and occupy land or structures are transferred by the owner to another for a specified period of time in return for a specified rent. An appraiser begins the income capitalization approach by studying all existing and proposed leases that apply to the subject property. These leases provide information on the base rent, any other income, and the division of expenses between the landlord and the tenant.

Although a lease can be drawn to fit any situation, most leases[3] fall into one of several broad classifications:

> **lease:** A written document in which the rights to use and occupy land or structures are transferred by the owner to another for a specified period of time in return for a specified rent.
>
> **base rent:** The minimum rent stipulated in a lease.

- Flat rental
- Variable rental
- Step-up or step-down
- Revaluation
- Annual increase
- Percentage

> **Lease types** include gross rental, net rental, flat rental, variable rental, step-up or step-down, revaluation, level with an annual increase, and percentage leases.

Leases may be negotiated on a gross rental basis, with the lessor paying most or all the operating expenses of the real estate, or on a net rental basis, with the tenant paying all expenses. When leases

---

2.   Most states require a written lease only when the term is greater than one year.

3.   Other lease types are defined in accounting practice, e.g., capital or financing leases and operating or service leases. These leases often involve equipment.

GROSS, MODIFIED GROSS, NET, DOUBLE NET, AND TRIPLE NET LEASES

The terms *gross lease, modified gross lease, net lease, single net lease, double net lease,* and *triple net lease* do not always mean the same thing in different markets. The expenses that are included in each type of rent vary from market to market. In general, the following distinctions can be made:

- Gross lease—tenant pays rent, and landlord pays expenses.
- Modified gross lease (sometimes *semi-gross*)—tenant and landlord share expenses.
- Single net lease—tenant pays utilities and taxes or insurance, and landlord pays structural repairs, property maintenance, and property taxes or insurance.
- Double net lease—tenant pays utilities and taxes and insurance, and landlord pays structural repairs and property maintenance.
- Triple net lease—tenant pays utilities, taxes, insurance, and maintenance, and landlord pays for structural repairs only.

Sometimes real estate professionals will refer to an *absolute net lease* (or simply a net lease, without a modifier for the term net) in which the landlord pays nothing toward maintaining the property.

Lease Type	Who pays for:				
	Utilities	Property Taxes	Insurance	Property Maintenance	Structural Repairs
Gross	Landlord	Landlord	Landlord	Landlord	Landlord
Modified gross	Tenant and landlord share expenses				
Single net	Tenant	Tenant or landlord pays one or the other		Landlord	Landlord
Double net	Tenant	Tenant	Tenant	Landlord	Landlord
Triple net	Tenant	Tenant	Tenant	Tenant	Landlord
Absolute net	Tenant	Tenant	Tenant	Tenant	Tenant

In the analysis of income and expenses based on market observation, the appraiser must understand how these terms are used in the market and clearly communicate that information to the client in the appraisal report. Furthermore, the appraiser must consistently account for the same expenses in the analysis of the income generated by a certain type of lease. For example, the available market data for five comparable office properties supports an estimate of market rent in the range of $27.50 to $31.00 per square foot, all quoted on a "net" rental basis. The rents for four of the properties range from $27.50 to $29.00 per square foot, and the tenants in those buildings pay for all expenses. The owner of the fifth comparable property, where "net" rents are quoted at $31.00 per square foot, actually pays for insurance—i.e., that owner defines "net" rent differently than the other property owners. Consequently, the "net" rent of the fifth property, which would be equivalent to "single net" rent in the other buildings, is noticeably higher.

are negotiated on a modified gross rental basis, lease terms fall between these extremes and specify the division of expenses between the lessor and the lessee. Leases can also be categorized by their terms of occupancy:

- Month-to-month
- Short-term (of five years or less)
- Long-term (of more than five years)

Flat Rental Lease

A flat rental lease specifies a level of rent that continues throughout the duration of the lease. In a stable economy, this type of lease is typical and acceptable. This type of lease is also prevalent in net rent situations where changes in expenses are the responsibility of the tenant(s). In a changing economy, however, leases that are more responsive to fluctuating market conditions are preferred. When flat rental leases are used in inflationary periods, they tend to be short-term such as apartment leases. Some assignments for the federal government require the appraiser to express the estimate of market rent on a "leveled" basis. This requires forecasting any increase in market rent over a holding period and converting the total income generated by that lease over the holding period into an annual level equivalent.

> **flat rental lease:** A lease with a specified level of rent that continues throughout the lease term; also called *level payment lease.*
>
> **index lease:** A lease, usually for a long term, that provides for periodic rent adjustments based on the change in an economic index, e.g., a cost-of-living index (CPI).

Variable Rental Lease

A variable rental lease is quite common, particularly when an owner anticipates periodic changes in rent. Sometimes this type of lease may specify a periodic percentage change; at other times the change may be tied into a specific index such as a nationally published index like the Consumer Price Index. (Often those leases are called *index leases.*) At other times the lease may specify that the rent change would be the higher or lower of the two—the period percentage or the index. This is particularly prevalent in gross and modified gross leases where an owner needs periodic income adjustments to offset increases in expenses.

Step-up or Step-down Rental Lease

Step-up or step-down leases (also known as *graduated rental leases*) provide for specified changes in the amount of rent at one or more points during the lease term. A step-up lease, which allows for smaller rent payments in the early years, can be advantageous to a tenant establishing a business in a new location. This type of lease can also be used to recognize tenant expenditures on a property that are effectively amortized during the early years of the lease. Long-term ground leases may include provisions for increasing the rent to reflect the expectation of future increases in property value and protect the purchasing power of the landlord's investment. Because property value is usually expected to increase, tenants are expected to pay commensurately higher rents.

> **step-up (step-down) lease:** A lease that provides for a certain rent for an initial period, followed by an increase (or decrease) in rent over stated periods.
>
> **revaluation lease:** A lease that provides for periodic rent adjustments based on a revaluation of the real estate under prevailing market rental conditions.

Step-down leases are less common than step-up leases. They are generally used to reflect unusual circumstances associated with a particular property such as the likelihood of reduced tenant appeal in the future or capital recapture of interior improvements during the early years of a long-term lease. Also, a step-down lease may be used when initial tenant improvements are recaptured over the first lease period by the landlord and when the second lease period has a lower income level.

Lease With an Annual Increase

One of the most common types of leases is neither a flat rental lease nor a variable or graduated rental lease that changes based on an index or percentage or according to a schedule of increases over the lease term. Rather, this type of lease increases annually by a dollar amount specified in the lease.

Revaluation Lease

Revaluation leases provide for periodic rent adjustments based on revaluation of market rent under prevailing market conditions. Although revaluation leases tend to be long-term, some are short-term with renewal option rents based on revaluation of market rent when the option is exercised. When the parties to a lease cannot agree on the value or rent, revaluation through appraisal or arbitration may be stipulated in the lease.

Percentage Lease

In percentage leases some or all of the rent charged is based on a specified percentage of the volume of business, productivity, or use achieved by the tenant. Percentage leases may be short- or long-term and are most frequently used for retail properties. A straight percentage lease may have no minimum rent, but most specify a guaranteed minimum rent and an overage rent, which is defined in the next section.

Rent

The income to investment properties consists primarily of rent. Different types of rent affect the quality of property income. Several categories are used by appraisers to analyze rental income.

> **Fundamental categories of rent** analyzed include market rent, contract rent, effective rent, excess rent, deficit rent, percentage rent, and overage rent.

- Market rent
- Contract rent
- Effective rent

- Excess rent
- Deficit rent
- Percentage rent
- Overage rent

Market Rent

Market rent is the rental income a property would probably command in the open market. It is indicated by the current rents that are either paid or asked for comparable space with the same division of expenses as of the date of the appraisal. Market rent is sometimes referred to as *economic rent*.

Rent for vacant or owner-occupied space is usually estimated at market rent levels and distinguished from contract rent in the income analysis. In fee simple valuations, all rentable space is estimated at market rent levels. Any rent attributed to specific leases is disregarded in the income analysis. In a leased fee analysis, current contract rents defined by any existing leases are used for leased space, and income for vacant space is estimated at market rent. In developing market rent and expense estimates, the appraiser should make sure that property management is competent.

> **market rent:** The rental income a property would probably command in the open market; indicated by the current rents that are either paid or asked for comparable space as of the date of the appraisal.
>
> **contract rent:** The actual rental income specified in a lease; may be a combination of base rent, percentage rents, and expense reimbursements.

Market data usually provides evidence of a range of market rents. For example, if the market for industrial space shows a rent range of $4.00 to $5.00 per square foot of gross building area on a gross rental basis and the subject property is leased for $3.00 per square foot of gross building area, the appraiser could conclude that the actual rent is below market levels. However, if the actual rents were $3.90, $4.50, or $5.05 per square foot of gross building area, it would be reasonable to conclude that those rents are consistent with market rents. If market rents are on a gross rental basis and the subject is leased on a net rental basis, it may be difficult to compare market and contract rent.

Contract rent and market rent are typically not the same, but it is possible that they will generate about the same level of income over time. In this case the leased fee value and fee simple value of the property would be about the same.

Contract Rent

Contract rent is the actual rental income specified in a lease. It is the rent agreed on by the landlord and the tenant and may be higher than, less than, or equal to market rent. Also, it is important to compare rents of properties with similar division of expenses, similar lease terms, and/or a similar level of finished space provided.

Effective Rent

In markets where concessions take the form of free rent, above-market tenant improvements, or atypical allowances, the true effective rent must be quantified. Effective rent (or actual occupancy cost) is an analytical tool used as a common

> **effective rent:** The rental rate net of financial concessions such as periods of no rent during the lease term; may be calculated on a discounted basis, reflecting the time value of money, or on a simple, straight-line basis.

denominator to compare leases with different provisions and develop an estimate of market rent. Effective rent may be defined as the total of base rent, or minimum rent stipulated in a lease, over the specified lease term minus rent concessions—e.g., free rent, excessive tenant improvements, moving allowances, lease buyouts, cash allowances, and other leasing incentives.

Effective rent may be estimated on the basis of rental income from existing leases at contract rates or rental income from leases at market rates. In calculating effective rent, an appraiser must allow for rent concessions in effect at the time of the appraisal, discounts, or other benefits that may have prompted a prospective tenant to enter into a lease.

The timing of the rent concessions may make analysis of effective rent a moot point. For example, consider a 10,000-sq.-ft. industrial property with a five-year lease at $4,000 per month, four months of rent concessions (the first two months of the first two years), and a date of value at the beginning of the third year of the lease. The concessions granted in the first two years of the lease are not an issue in the analysis of the income generated in the third year, and the actual and effective rent would be the same on the date of value.

Effective rent can be calculated as the average, annual rent net of rent concessions or as an annual rent that produces the same present value as the actual annual rents net of rent concessions. While these two methods are considered interchangeable, they do not produce the same results. The first method is a mathematical average, whereas the second is a discounting procedure where the rent concessions are accounted for in the years that they actually occur.

As a simple example of effective rent calculations, consider a lease on a 10,000-sq.-ft. industrial building where the rent is specified as $4,000 per month (or $48,000 per year) for a five-year term with level income throughout the lease term. When the lease was negotiated, the tenant received free rent for the first month of each year as a concession. The contract rent is $4.80 per square foot. However, the effective rent is only $4.40 per square foot:

$4,000 per month × 11 months = $44,000
$44,000 / 10,000 square feet = 4.40 per square foot

There are options for the treatment of tenant improvement costs. Some practitioners deduct all tenant improvements, while others deduct only the excess of actual tenant improvement costs over a market standard.

excess rent: The amount by which contract rent exceeds market rent at the time of the appraisal; created by a lease favorable to the landlord (lessor) and may reflect a locational advantage, unusual management, unknowledgeable parties, or a lease execution in an earlier, stronger rental market. Due to the higher risk inherent in the receipt of excess rent, it may be calculated separately and capitalized at a higher rate in the income capitalization approach.

Excess Rent

Excess rent is the amount by which contract rent exceeds market rent at the time of the appraisal. Excess rent is created by a lease that is favorable to the lessor and may reflect superior management or a lease that was negotiated in a stronger rental market. Excess rent may be expected to continue for the remainder of the lease (if the relationship of contract rent and market rent is expected to remain the same for the duration of the lease), but, due to the higher risk associated with the receipt of excess rent, it is often calculated separately and capitalized or discounted at a higher rate. Because excess rent is a result of the lease contract rather than the income potential of the underlying real property on the valuation date, the incremental value created by a lease premium can result in a leased fee value that exceeds the fee simple value. Such a situation is known as a *negative leasehold*.

The existence of excess rent does not automatically signal that an additional non-realty value is present. Small tenants may not be able to succeed because of the rent disadvantage. Higher risk may also be present for a large, financially capable company with the power to break the lease.

Deficit Rent

Deficit rent is the amount by which market rent exceeds contract rent at the time of the appraisal. It is created by a lease favorable to the tenant and may reflect uninformed parties, inferior management, or a lease executed in a weaker rental market. Similarly, when leased fee value is less than fee simple, taxes may be based on the higher fee simple value. A leased fee value that is less than the fee simple value results in a *positive leasehold interest* for the tenant's position in the property. When there is a positive leasehold interest for a financially strong tenant, there is likely a reduced risk for the leased fee owner. This may reduce the capitalization rate that is appropriate for the leased fee position.

Percentage Rent

Percentage rent is rental income received in accordance with the terms of a percentage clause in a lease. Percentage rent is typically derived from retail tenants

percentage rent: Rental income received in accordance with the terms of a percentage lease; typically derived from retail store tenants and based on a certain percentage of their retail sales.

and is based on a certain percentage of their sales revenue. It is usually paid at the end of each year and is more difficult to collect than other forms of rent paid on a more regular basis. Therefore, percentage rent involves more risk than other forms of rent and may be capitalized or discounted separately or at a different rate.

> **overage rent:** The percentage rent paid over and above the guaranteed minimum rent or base rent; calculated as a percentage of sales in excess of a specified breakeven sales volume.

The emergence of new competition in the area or the departure of an anchor tenant from a shopping center may reduce or eliminate anticipated percentage rent. Also, as for excess rent, the conditions that create percentage rent may not extend for the duration of the lease. Furthermore, calculation of a store's sales revenue can be impacted by transactions involving a "virtual" or Internet component.

Overage Rent

Overage rent is percentage rent paid over and above the guaranteed minimum rent or base rent. As mentioned previously, the level of sales at which a percentage clause is activated is specified in a lease and called a *breakpoint*. The *natural breakpoint* is the level of sales at which the percentage rent exactly equals the base rent.

The breakpoint in a percentage lease does not necessarily have to be the natural breakpoint. For example, if the annual base rent was set in the lease at $400,000 and the percentage of retail sales specified in the lease was 20%, then the natural breakpoint would be a sales volume of $2,000,000—i.e., $2,000,000 × 0.20 = $400,000. The breakpoint specified in the lease could be set at a sales volume of $2,250,000; in this case the tenant would pay the base rent of $400,000 until the percentage clause is activated, and the percentage rent jumps to $450,000 ($2,250,000 × 0.20 = $450,000). The breakpoint could also be set lower than the natural breakpoint—say, at a sales volume of $1,750,000—but the actual rent paid is usually the higher of the two, base rent or percentage rent.

Overage rent should not be confused with excess rent. Overage rent is a contract rent; it may be market rent, part market and part excess rent, or excess rent only.

> An income capitalization analysis may consider the following **components of future property benefits**: potential gross income (*PGI*), effective gross income (*EGI*), net operating income (*NOI*), equity dividend, and the resale value or reversion.

Future Benefits

The benefits of owning specific rights in income-producing real estate include the right to receive all cash flows accruing to the real property over the holding or study period (i.e., the term of ownership) plus any proceeds from disposition of the property at the termination of the investment.[4]

> **potential gross income (*PGI*):** The total income attributable to real property at full occupancy before operating expenses and vacancy and collection losses are deducted.

---

4. The *holding period* is a more broadly defined, market-oriented measure of how long investors typically retain ownership of real property, whereas the *study period* is used in investment analysis to forecast the term of ownership given the reasonable expectation of certain market events occurring in the future.

Various measures of future benefits are considered in the income capitalization approach. Commonly used measures include

- Potential gross income
- Effective gross income
- Net operating income
- Equity dividend
- Reversionary benefits

Potential Gross Income

Potential gross income (*PGI*) is the total potential income attributable to the real property at full occupancy before operating expenses are deducted. It may refer to the level of rental income prevailing on the date of the appraisal or expected during the first full month or year of operation, or to the periodic income anticipated during the holding period.

Effective Gross Income

Effective gross income (*EGI*) is the anticipated income from all operations of the real property adjusted for vacancy and collection losses. This adjustment covers losses incurred due to unoccupied space, turnover, and nonpayment of rent by tenants.

Net Operating Income

Net operating income (*NOI* or I_O) is the actual or anticipated net income remaining after all operating expenses are deducted from effective gross income. Net operating income is customarily expressed as an annual amount. In certain income capitalization applications, a single year's net operating income may represent a steady stream of fixed income that is expected to continue for a number of years. In other applications, the income may represent the starting level of income that is expected to change in a prescribed pattern over the years. Still other applications may require that net operating income be estimated for each year of the analysis.

Equity Dividend

Equity dividend (I_E) is the portion of net operating income that remains after debt service is paid. Like net operating income, a single year's equity dividend may

effective gross income (*EGI*): The anticipated income from all operations of the real property after an allowance is made for vacancy and collection losses.

net operating income (*NOI* or I_O): The actual or anticipated net income that remains after all operating expenses are deducted from effective gross income, but before mortgage debt service and book depreciation are deducted; may be calculated before or after deducting replacement reserves.

equity dividend: The portion of net operating income that remains after total mortgage debt service is paid but before ordinary income tax on operations is deducted.

reversion: A lump-sum benefit an investor receives or expects to receive upon the termination of an investment; also called *reversionary benefit.*

Table 20.3	**Summary of Incomes and Reversions Associated with Various Real Property Interests in Income-Producing Property**

Fee Simple

Income	Net operating income based on market rents (NOI or I_O)
Reversion	Net proceeds of disposition (V_N)

Mortgagee (Lender's Position)

Income	Mortgage debt service (I_M)
Reversion	Balance if paid prior to maturity or balloon payment if paid at maturity; none if loan amortizes fully (V_M)

Equity

Income	Cash flow (I_E) or equity dividend
Reversion	Net equity proceeds of disposition (V_E)

Leased fee

Income	Net operating income based on contract rents
Reversion	Property reversion or net proceeds of disposition of leased fee estate

Leasehold

Income	Rental advantage when contract rent is below market rent; rental disadvantage when contract rent is above market rent
Reversion	None if held to end of lease or net proceeds of resale of leasehold estate

represent a steady stream of fixed income, the starting level of a changing income stream, or the equity income for a particular year of the analysis.

Reversion

Reversion is a lump-sum benefit an investor receives upon termination of an investment or at an intermediate analysis period during the term of an investment (especially for appraisals). The reversionary benefit may be calculated before or after the mortgage balance is deducted. For example, the reversionary benefits for fee simple and leased fee estates are the net proceeds expected to result from resale of the property at the end of the investment holding period. For a mortgagee or lender, reversion consists of the balance of the mortgage when it is paid off or forecast to be paid off. Table 20.3 shows several possible investment positions in an income-producing property and identifies the income streams and reversions associated with each interest.

> **operating expenses:** The periodic expenditures necessary to maintain the real property and continue production of the effective gross income, assuming prudent and competent management.

Reversionary benefits are usually estimated as anticipated dollar amounts or as relative changes in value over the presumed holding period. A dollar estimate of the reversion might be based on a lessee's option to purchase the property at the end of the lease. Alternatively, the value of the reversion at the end of the holding period might be estimated by applying a capitalization rate to the income that a buyer expects to receive at

reconstructed operating statement:
A statement prepared by an appraiser that represents his or her opinion of the probable future net operating income of an investment property. In preparing reconstructed operating statements, appraisers may consult accountants' financial balance sheets and auditors' statements.

fixed expenses: Operating expenses that generally do not vary with occupancy and which prudent management will pay whether the property is occupied or vacant.

variable expenses: Operating expenses that generally vary with the level of occupancy or the extent of services provided.

replacement allowance: An allowance that provides for the periodic replacement of building components that wear out more rapidly than the building itself and must be replaced during the building's economic life.

the time of resale (or expected resale). Reversionary benefits may or may not require separate measurement, depending on the purpose of the analysis and the method of capitalization employed.

Operating Expenses

In the income capitalization approach, a comprehensive analysis of the annual expenses of property operation is essential whether the value indication is derived from estimated net operating income or equity dividend. Operating expenses are the periodic expenditures necessary to maintain the real property and continue the production of the revenue.

An operating statement that conforms to this definition of operating expenses is used for appraisal purposes; this reconstructed operating statement may differ from statements prepared for an owner or an accountant because these often include non-cash expenses such as depreciation or interest expenses. Operating statements are prepared on either a cash or accrual basis, and the appraiser must know the accounting basis used in the operating statements for the property being appraised. Operating statements provide valuable factual data and can be used to identify trends in operating expenses.

Operating expenses comprise three categories:

1. Fixed expenses
2. Variable expenses
3. Replacement allowance

These classifications have been used for a long time, but there are other valid systems that an appraiser can employ and different property types may require different formats.

Fixed Expenses

Fixed expenses are operating expenses that generally do not vary with occupancy and have to be paid whether the property is occupied or vacant. Real estate taxes and building insurance costs are typically considered fixed expenses. Although these expenses rarely remain constant, they generally do not fluctuate widely from year to year, do not vary in response to changing occupancy levels, and are not subject to management control. Therefore, an appraiser can usually identify a trend and accurately estimate these expense items.

Variable Expenses

Variable expenses are operating expenses that generally vary with the level of occupancy or the extent of services provided, though most variable expenses have some minimal fixed component regardless of occupancy. Specific expense items of this type may vary greatly from year to year, but similar types of property often reflect a reasonably consistent pattern of variable expenses in relation to gross income. Because fewer services are provided to the tenants of freestanding retail and industrial properties, these properties usually have a much lower ratio of expenses to gross income than apartment and office buildings do.

Replacement Allowance

A replacement allowance provides for the periodic replacement of building components that wear out more rapidly than the building itself and must be replaced periodically during the building's useful life.

Rates of Return

In applying the income capitalization approach, an appraiser assumes that the investor ultimately seeks a total return greater than or equal to the amount invested. Therefore, the investor's expected return consists of two components:

1. Full recovery of the amount invested, i.e., the return *of* capital
2. A reward for the assumption of risk, i.e., a return *on* invested capital

Because the returns from real estate may take a variety of forms, many rates, or measures of return, are used in capitalization. All measures of return can be categorized as either *income rates,* such as an overall capitalization rate (R_O) or equity capitalization rate (R_E), or *discount rates,* such as an effective interest rate (the rate of return on debt capital), yield rate (the rate used to convert future payments into present value, Y_O), or internal rate of return (*IRR*).

---

income rate: A rate that reflects the ratio of one year's income to the value of the property; includes the overall capitalization rate (R_O), the equity capitalization rate (R_E), and the mortgage capitalization rate (R_M); also called *cash flow rate.*

discount rate: An interest rate used to convert future payments or receipts into present value; a general term used to refer to any rate used to convert future cash flows into a present value. The *IRR* and Y_O are examples of discount rates that require all benefits be allowed to enter the calculation of the rate.

yield rate (Y): A rate of return on capital for a specific time period, usually expressed as a compound annual percentage rate. A yield rate considers all expected property benefits, including the proceeds from sale at the termination of the investment. Yield rates include, and are calculated in the same manner as, the interest rate, internal rate of return (*IRR*), overall yield rate (Y_O), and equity yield rate (Y_E).

An investor's **total expected return** includes the return of capital (recapture of capital) and a return on capital (compensation for use of capital until recapture). **Rates of return** may be income rates (ratios of annual income to value that are used to convert income into value) or yield rates (rates of return on capital).

The term *discount rate* describes any rate used to convert future cash flows over time into a present value. Because investors expect their total return to exceed the amount invested, the present value of a prospective benefit is less than the expected future worth of that benefit—thus the "discount."[5] A *yield rate,* a specific type of discount rate, is the rate of return on capital. It considers all expected property benefits, including a reversion.

Under certain conditions, the yield rate for a property may be numerically equivalent to the corresponding income rate; nevertheless, the rates and their concepts are not the same, nor are they interchangeable. An income rate is the ratio of one year's income to value.[6] A yield rate is applied to a series of individual incomes to obtain the present value of each and is calculated in the same way as an internal rate of return.

In the income capitalization approach, both income rates and yield rates can be derived for, and applied to, any component of real property rights or the underlying physical real estate. For example, an appraiser may analyze total property income in terms of income to the land and income to the building or in terms of income to the mortgage and equity interests in the property. Similarly, an appraiser may seek the total investment yield or analyze the separate yields to the land and the building or to the mortgage and the equity interests. Finally, an appraiser may want to know the value of the unencumbered fee simple, the leased fee, or the leasehold interest. (Practical examples of these applications and the relevant symbols, formulas, and procedures are presented in Chapters 21 through 23.)

Return on and Return of Capital

The notion that an investor anticipates a complete recovery of invested capital—plus a payment for the use of capital—prevails in the real estate market just as it does in other markets. The term *return of capital* refers to the recovery of invested capital; the term *return on capital* refers to the additional amount received as compensation for use of the investor's capital until it is recaptured. Investors are concerned with both types of return. The rate of return on capital is analogous to the yield rate or the interest rate earned or expected. A typical example is the mortgage loan calculation in which return of and return on are considered in the level mortgage payment over time.

> **return of capital:** The recovery of invested capital, usually through income and/or reversion.
>
> **return on capital:** The additional amount received as compensation (profit or reward) for the use of an investor's capital until it is recaptured. The rate of return on capital is analogous to the yield rate or the interest rate earned or expected.

---

5. For a thorough discussion of discounting, see Charles Akerson, *Capitalization Theory and Techniques: Study Guide,* 2d ed. (Chicago: Appraisal Institute, 2000).

6. The rate is usually calculated with the income for the first year, although the income for the previous year may be used. In rare cases the incomes for several years might be averaged to obtain a representative income figure.

In real estate investments, capital may be recaptured in many ways.[7] Investment capital may be recaptured through annual income, or it may be recaptured all or in part through disposition of the property at the termination of the investment. It may also be recaptured through a combination of both. If the property value does not change between the time the initial investment is made and the time the property is sold, the investor can recapture all the initial capital invested at property resale at the end of the holding period. Thus, when initial value is equivalent to resale value, the annual income can all be attributed to the return on capital. If the income has remained level (or constant), the indicated income rate (i.e., the overall capitalization rate) will equal the return on capital.

In yield capitalization the distinction between the return on and the return of capital is more explicit. The yield rate estimated for cash flows determines a specified return on capital. Direct capitalization, on the other hand, uses income rates such as overall capitalization rates, which must implicitly allow for both the return on and return of capital. When the capitalization rate is applied to the subject property's income, the indicated value must represent a price that would allow the investor to earn a market rate of return on the capital invested along with the recapture of the capital. Thus, the capitalization rate estimated and applied to value property must reflect or consider a market level of return of and return on the initial investment in one calculation.

Income Rates

An income rate expresses the relationship between one year's income and the corresponding capital value of a property.

Overall capitalization rate. An overall capitalization rate (R_O) is an income rate for a total property that reflects the relationship between a single year's net operating income and the total property price or value. It is used to convert net operating income into an indication of overall property value. An overall capitalization rate is not a rate of return on capital or a full measure of investment performance. It may be more than, less than, or equal to the expected yield on the capital invested, depending on projected income and value changes.

> **overall capitalization rate (R_O):** An income rate for a total real property interest that reflects the relationship between a single year's net operating income and the total property price or value; used to convert net operating income into an indication of overall property value $(R_O = I_O/V_O)$.
>
> **equity capitalization rate (R_E):** An income rate that reflects the relationship between a single year's cash flow expectancy and the equity investment; used to convert equity dividend into an equity value indication; also called the *cash on cash rate, cash flow rate,* or *equity dividend rate.* $(R_E$ = equity dividend/ equity invested.)

---

7.   The term *recapture* was coined at a time when investors assumed that property values could only decline due to depreciation from physical or functional causes. Today appraisers use the term when some income provision must be made to compensate for the loss of invested capital.

Equity capitalization rate. An equity capitalization rate (R_E) is an income rate that reflects the relationship between a single year's equity cash flow expectancy and the equity investment. When used to capitalize the subject property's cash flow after debt service into equity value, the equity capitalization rate is often referred to in the real estate market as the *cash flow rate, cash on cash return,* or *equity dividend rate.* Like the overall capitalization rate, the equity capitalization rate is not a rate of return on capital; it may be more than, less than, or equal to the expected equity yield rate, depending on projected changes in income, value, and amortization of the loan.

Discount Rates

Various sorts of discount rates are used to discount cash flows applicable to a specific position or interest in defined real estate. Discount rates may or may not be developed in the same way as internal rates of return and *may not* necessarily consider all expected property benefits.

Yield rate. A yield rate is a rate of return on capital. It is usually expressed as a compound annual percentage rate. The yield rate considers all expected property benefits (both positive and negative over time), including the proceeds from disposition at the termination of the investment, if any. The term *interest rate* usually refers to the yield rate for debt capital, not equity capital.

Internal rate of return. An internal rate of return (*IRR*) is the yield rate that is earned for a given capital investment over the period of ownership. The internal rate of return for an investment is the yield rate that equates the present value of the future benefits of the investment to the amount of capital invested. The internal rate of return applies to all expected benefits, including the net proceeds from disposition at the investment's termination. It can be used to measure the return on any capital investment, before or after income taxes.

Overall yield rate. An overall yield rate (Y_O), or *property yield rate,* is a rate of return on the total capital invested. It considers all changes in income over the investment holding period as well as the reversion at the end of the holding period. It does not, however, consider the effect of debt financing. Rather, it is calculated as if the property were purchased with no debt capital.

The overall yield rate can be viewed as the combined yield on both the debt and equity capital. It is calculated in the same way the internal rate of return is calculated.

> **overall yield rate (Y_O):** The rate of return, or internal rate of return, on the total capital invested, including both debt and equity. The Y_O considers all changes in net income over the investment period and net reversion at the end of the holding period; it is applied to cash flow before debt service. Also called *property yield rate.*

Equity yield rate. An equity yield rate (Y_E) is a rate of return on equity capital. It may be distinguished from a rate of return on debt capital, which is usually referred to as an *effective mortgage interest rate.* The equity yield rate is the equity investor's internal rate of return; it is affected by the amount of financial leverage employed in securing mortgage debt.

Estimating Rates

Whether it is an income rate or a yield rate, the conversion of income into property value should represent the annual rate of return the market indicates is necessary to attract investment capital. This rate is influenced by many factors:

- The degree of perceived risk
- Market expectations regarding future inflation
- The prospective rates of return for alternative investments
- The rates of return earned by comparable properties in the past
- Availability of debt financing
- The prevailing tax law

To the extent that the rates of return used in the income capitalization approach represent prospective rates, not historical rates, the market's perception of risk and changes in purchasing power are particularly important. Generally, higher overall capitalization rates $(R_O s)$ are associated with less desirable properties, and lower overall capitalization rates with more attractive properties.

The suitability of a particular rate of return cannot be proved with market evidence, but the rate estimated should be consistent with the data available. Rate estimation requires appraisal judgment and knowledge of prevailing market attitudes and economic indicators.

Typically, investors expect to receive a return on capital that represents the time value of money with an appropriate adjustment for perceived risk. The time value of money underlies the accrual of interest on investments. The minimum rate of return for invested capital is sometimes referred to as the *safe, riskless,* or *relatively riskless rate*—e.g., the prevailing rate on insured savings accounts or guaranteed government securities.[8] Theoretically, the difference between the total rate of return on capital and the safe rate may be considered a

time value of money: The concept underlying compound interest, which holds that $1 received today is worth more than $1 received in the future due to opportunity cost, inflation, and the certainty of payment.

risk rate: The annual rate of return on capital that is commensurate with the risk assumed by the investor; the rate of interest or yield necessary to attract capital.

safe rate: The minimum rate of return on invested capital. Theoretically, the difference between the total rate of return and the safe rate is considered a premium to compensate the investor for risk, the burden of management, and the illiquidity of the capital invested; also called *riskless rate* or *relatively riskless rate.*

---

8. For example, federal statutes prescribe certain U.S. securities rates as a means of compensating for the time value of money on an essentially risk-free basis while accounting for inflation. See 40 U.S.C. § 1961 and the amendment contained in Public Law No. 106-554, effective December 21, 2000.

> The **rate of return** on investment combines a safe rate with a premium to compensate the investor for risk and the illiquidity of invested capital. The rate of return on capital may incorporate inflationary expectations and should reflect the competition for capital among alternative investments of comparable risk.

premium to compensate the investor for risk, the illiquidity of invested capital, and other investment considerations.

A discount rate reflects the relationship between income and the value that a market will attribute to that income. The financial and economic concepts implicit in a discount rate are complex and have been the subject of significant analysis for more than a century. Although four key components can be identified within a discount rate—the safe rate plus considerations of illiquidity, management, and various risks—a discount rate that is constructed by adding allowances for these components can be misleading or inaccurate. The band-of-investment concept can be helpful in understanding these components, especially in differentiating marginal risk considerations, but the band-of-investment methodologies should not be represented as developing a market discount rate.

Risk

The anticipation of receiving future benefits creates value, but the possibility of not receiving or losing future benefits reduces value and creates risk. Higher rewards are required in return for accepting higher risk. To a real estate investor, risk is the chance of incurring a financial loss and the uncertainty of realizing projected future benefits. Most investors try to avoid excessive risk; they prefer certainty to uncertainty and expect a reward for taking a risk. Appraisers must recognize investors' attitudes in analyzing market evidence, projecting future benefits, and applying capitalization procedures. The appraiser must be satisfied that the income rate or yield rate used in capitalization is consistent with market evidence and reflects the level of risk associated with receiving the anticipated benefits.

Inflation

Appraisers should be aware of the difference between inflation and appreciation in real value. Inflation is an increase in the volume of money and credit, a rise in the general level of prices, and the consequent erosion of purchasing power. Appreciation in real value results from an excess of demand over supply, which increases property values beyond typical levels of inflation.

The amount of inflation expected affects the forecast of future benefits and the estimation of an appropriate income or yield rate. If inflation is anticipated, the desired nominal rate of return on invested capital will likely increase to compensate for lost purchasing power. The required nominal rate, then, will increase to offset the expected inflation. Most investors try to protect the real rate of return over time.

A distinction must be made between expected inflation and unexpected inflation. Expected inflation refers to changes in price levels that are expected at the time the investment is made or when the property is being appraised.

However, actual inflation may differ from what was anticipated at the time the investment was made. Depending on how the investment responds to the actual change in price levels, its value may fluctuate over time at a different rate than originally anticipated. If the return on the investment does not increase with unexpected inflation, the investor's real rate of return will be less than originally projected.

> The **two methods of income capitalization** are direct capitalization, in which a single year's income is divided by an income rate or multiplied by an income factor to reach an indication of value, and yield capitalization, in which future benefits are converted into a value indication by discounting them at an appropriate yield rate (DCF analysis) or applying an overall rate that reflects the income pattern, value change, and yield rate.

Procedure

The income capitalization approach supports two basic methodologies: direct capitalization, which uses the relationship of one year's income to conclude a value, and yield capitalization, which considers a series of cash flows over time together with any reversion value or resale proceeds.

As an initial step, both methods require a comprehensive study of historical income and expenses for the subject property. This study is combined with an analysis of typical income and expense levels for comparable properties. A reconstructed operating statement is developed for the subject property. This statement must reflect the purpose of the appraisal, especially with respect to the property interest being appraised. Leased fee value will reflect current leases and the associated expense structure, while fee simple value starts with an income basis using market rent.

Yield capitalization will require a consideration of probable income and expenses over the designated holding period, anywhere from five to ten years. When this method is used, the appraiser must forecast income and expenses over time together with the eventual reversion or resale value of the property. Direct capitalization, on the other hand, requires a one-year cash flow estimate (date of valuation plus next 12 months) to use for application of an overall rate to estimate value. This method inherently relies upon sales of properties with similar income characteristics including future expectations.

Although there are various income capitalization techniques available to the appraiser, certain steps are essential in applying the income capitalization approach. Before applying any capitalization techniques, an appraiser must work down from potential gross income to net operating income. To do this, the appraiser will

1. Research the income and expense data for the subject property and comparables.
2. Estimate the potential gross income of the property by adding the rental income and any other potential income.
3. Estimate the vacancy and collection loss.

4. Subtract vacancy and collection loss from total potential gross income to arrive at the effective gross income of the subject property.

5. Estimate the total operating expenses for the subject by adding fixed expenses, variable expenses, and a replacement allowance (where applicable).

6. Subtract the estimate of total operating expenses from the estimate of effective gross income to arrive at net operating income.

7. Apply one of the direct or yield capitalization techniques to this data to generate an estimate of value via the income capitalization approach.

Direct Capitalization, Yield Capitalization, and Discounting

Direct capitalization makes use of a single year's income and a market-derived factor or overall capitalization rate. Initially, the process appears rather simple. The practitioner need only estimate the income and the factor or overall capitalization rate. In this analysis, the most important consideration is choosing sales with similar income and expense expectations over time. In contrast, the application of yield capitalization requires the practitioner to set forth explicit forecasts of income, expenses, and changes in vacancy levels and expenditures over the holding period. The net sale price of the property at the end of the holding period must also be estimated. The concluded yield rate is then applied to convert anticipated economic benefits into present value. Yield rates must be derived from properties with similar characteristics.

Practitioners who use direct capitalization must recognize that while an overall capitalization rate is only applied to one characteristic of the property (i.e., to a single year's net operating income), the overall capitalization rate is valid only if it accounts for all other characteristics of the property. For example, assume that annual increases of 3% are forecast in the net rent of a sale property over the holding period and annual increases of 2% are forecast in the net rent for the subject. Applying the sale property's 10% overall capitalization rate to the subject's income would be a misapplication of the approach and would overstate the subject's value.

In yield capitalization, the practitioner must draw specific conclusions about changes in net income, cash flow, and property value over the holding period. These conclusions are set forth in forecasts of future income and property reversion. The reader of the appraisal report can review the forecasts and examine each component of the future income and property value.

Also, specific investment goals for the return on and of invested capital can be considered in yield capitalization. The property's projected income and reversion are capitalized into a present value by applying the investor's anticipated yield rate in the present value procedure. Yield rates can be derived with formulas and factors obtained from financial tables or calculated and applied with hand-held financial calculators or personal computers. Various software programs for personal computers can also be used to discount cash flows.

Both direct capitalization and yield capitalization are market-derived, and when applied correctly each should result in similar value indications for a subject property. In applying the income capitalization approach, the appraiser need not be limited to a single capitalization method. With adequate information and proper use, direct and yield capitalization methods should produce similar value indications. If differences arise, the appraiser should check that the various techniques are being applied correctly and consistently.

FURTHER READING

Akerson, Charles B. *The Appraiser's Workbook.* 2d ed. Chicago: Appraisal Institute, 1996.

___. *Capitalization Theory and Techniques: Study Guide.* 2d ed. Chicago: Appraisal Institute, 2000.

American Institute of Real Estate Appraisers. *Forecasting: Market Determinants Affecting Cash Flows and Reversions.* Research Series Report 4. Chicago, 1989.

___. *Readings in the Income Capitalization Approach to Real Property Valuation,* Volume II. Chicago, 1985.

Burton, James H. *Evolution of the Income Approach.* Chicago: American Institute of Real Estate Appraisers, 1982.

Fisher, Clifford E., Jr. *Rates and Ratios Used in the Income Capitalization Approach.* Chicago: Appraisal Institute, 1995.

CHAPTER 21

INCOME AND EXPENSE ANALYSIS

To apply any capitalization procedure, a reliable estimate of income expectancy must be developed. Although some capitalization procedures are based on the actual level of income at the time of the appraisal, all must eventually consider a projection of future income. An appraiser must consider the future outlook both in the estimate of income and expenses and in the selection of the appropriate capitalization methodology to use. Failure to consider future income would contradict the principle of anticipation, which holds that value is the present worth of future benefits.

Historical income and current income are significant, but the ultimate concern is the future. The earning history of a property is important only insofar as it is accepted by buyers as an indication of the future. Current income is a good starting point, but the direction and expected pattern of income change are critical to the capitalization process.

Four types of first-year income can be converted into value estimates for different property interests in direct capitalization:

- Potential gross income (*PGI*)
- Effective gross income (*EGI*)
- Net operating income (*NOI* or I_O)
- Equity dividend (I_E)

In yield capitalization, various cash flows and appropriate reversion values can be used to estimate the value of different property interests:

- *NOI* and property reversion over a holding period for a fee simple interest value
- I_E and equity reversion over a holding period for a fee simple interest value
- Cash flow considering tenant improvements (TIs) and leasing commissions, and property reversion over the study period

When using either direct or yield capitalization, reliable projections of income are important. Significant value differences can result when the same overall capitalization rate or potential gross income multiplier is used to convert different income estimates into value. If, for example, a potential gross income multiplier of 6.0 is applied to potential gross income estimates of $50,000 and $55,000, values of $300,000 and $330,000 result. A $5,000 difference in potential gross income produces a $30,000 difference in value.

In the direct capitalization approach, **four income streams** may be analyzed: potential gross income (*PGI*), effective gross income (*EGI*), net operating income (*NOI* or I_O), and equity dividend.

Similarly, when an overall capitalization rate of 10.0% is applied to net operating income estimates of $35,000 and $40,000, values of $350,000 and $400,000 result. In this example a $5,000 difference in net operating income results in a $50,000 value difference. Thus, income forecasting is a sensitive and crucial part of income capitalization.

An appraiser may estimate income for a single year or series of years depending on the data available and the capitalization method employed. The analysis can be based on

- The actual level of income at the time of the appraisal
- A forecast of income for the first year of the investment
- A forecast of income over a specified holding period
- A stabilized, average annual income over a specific holding period

line item: An individual income or expense category considered in an analysis.

If an opinion of market value is sought, the income forecast should reflect the expectations of market participants. In an assignment to develop an opinion of investment value, the appraiser may base the income forecasts on the specific ownership or management requirements of the investor.

If an investment in a partial interest, e.g., an equity interest in a fee simple or leased fee estate, is being valued, the equity dividend may be used. In this case the equity income is determined by deducting annual mortgage debt service from net operating income to calculate equity dividend. Sometimes debt service is based on an existing mortgage and the amount is specified; in other cases, debt service must be estimated based on the typical mortgage terms indicated by current market activity and the property type being appraised.

Table 21.1 lists the key elements to investigate in developing income and expense estimates for various property types. The specific line items involved in the generation of income and the allocation of expenses may vary for different property types.

Estimating and Adjusting Market Rent

An investigation of market rent levels starts with the subject property. By examining financial statements and leases and interviewing selected tenants during property inspection, an appraiser can verify the subject property's current rent schedule. Further verification may be necessary if the owner's or manager's information is in doubt. The sum of current rents may be compared with previous totals using operating statements for the past several years. Statements of rents, including the rent paid under percentage leases or

Table 21.1	**Characteristic Income and Expenses of Principal Property Types**
Industrial Buildings	
Lease and income	Medium- to long-term net lease; contract rent.
Expenses	Tenants pay most operating expenses and sometimes prorated property taxes, insurance, and exterior maintenance; landlord pays management fees; tenant improvement allowance sometimes provided by landlord; leasing commissions paid by landlord to agent or broker.
Retail Properties	
Major (anchor) tenants	
Lease and income	Long-term net lease; base and percentage (overage) rent.
Expenses	Tenants pay utilities, interior maintenance, and common area maintenance (such expense recoveries are prorated); tenants may share in advertising and management costs; tenant improvement allowance provided by landlord; leasing commissions paid by landlord to agent or broker; tenant improvements and leasing commissions are typically treated as below-the-line items.
Smaller (local) tenants	
Lease and income	Short- to medium-term net lease; base and percentage (overage) rent.
Expenses	Same as above.
Multifamily Residential	
Lease and income	One-year or less; modified gross lease; contract rent.
Expenses	Tenants pay own utility expenses; landlord pays property taxes, insurance, management, maintenance and common area maintenance; replacement allowance treated as an above-the-line item; no tenant improvement allowance or leasing commissions.
Office Buildings	
Lease and income	Medium- to long-term; base rent may be adjusted upward on an escalation basis according to an index or, for retail tenants, as a percentage of sales.
Expenses	Under a gross lease, landlords pay all operating expenses; under a net lease, tenants pay all expenses; leases may contain provisions to pass through any increase in certain expenses, over a specified base amount and customarily on a per square foot basis. Tenant improvement allowance provided by landlord; leasing commissions paid by landlord to agent or broker.

Note: The treatment of expenses described here is typical of many, but not all, markets.

escalation clauses, should be examined for all building tenants. After analyzing the existing rent schedule for the subject property, the appraiser reduces all rents to a unit basis for comparison. All differences in rents within the property are described and explained. Then rental data for comparable space in the market is assembled so that equivalent market rents can be estimated, if necessary, and reduced to a unit of comparison.

When a market rent estimate for the subject property is required, the appraiser gathers, compares, and adjusts comparable rental data. The parties

INTERESTS

To a certain extent, the interest being appraised determines how rents are analyzed and estimated. The valuation of fee simple interests in income-producing real estate is based on the market rent the property is capable of generating. Therefore, to value proposed projects without actual leases, properties with unleased space, and owner-occupied properties, market rent estimates are used in the income capitalization approach.

To value the leased fee estate, the appraiser considers contract rent for leased space, which may or may not be at market levels, and market rent for vacant and owner-occupied space. When discounted cash flow analysis is used, future market rent estimates are required to estimate income after existing leases expire. It should be emphasized that the discounting of contract rents usually does *not* result in an opinion of the market value of the fee simple interest; it results in an opinion of market value of the leased fee interest, or the fee simple interest subject to the existing lease.

> The discounting of contract rents usually does not result in an opinion of the market value of the **fee simple interest.**

To value a leased fee interest in a recently completed, income-producing property that has not achieved stabilized occupancy, an appropriate vacancy and collection loss must be forecast over an appropriate absorption or lease-up period. In appraising the value of a fee simple interest in a newly completed, 100% owner-occupied property, it may be appropriate to make a deduction in the forecast time for the market to achieve 100% use and occupancy of the building. (This is analogous to the lease-up time needed to achieve stabilized occupancy in tenanted properties.) Appraisals of proposed properties for lending purposes often require value estimates at different stages in the property's development:

- As is
- When completed
- At stabilization

The "as is" value is typically the current value of the vacant land. The other two values are prospective values as of the completion of construction (value considering lease-up) and when the property actually achieves stabilized occupancy.

to each lease should be identified to ensure that the party held responsible for rent payments is actually a party to the lease or, by endorsement, the guarantor. It is also important to ascertain that the lease represents a freely negotiated, arm's-length transaction. A lease that does not meet these criteria, such as a lease to an owner-tenant or a sale-leaseback (financing lease), may not provide a reliable indication of market rent.

The rents of comparable properties can provide a basis for estimating market rent for a subject property once they have been reduced to the same unit basis applied to the subject property. Comparable rents may be adjusted just as the transaction prices of comparable properties are adjusted in the sales comparison approach. Recent leases relating to the subject property may be a good indication of market rent, but lease renewals or extensions negotiated with existing tenants should be used with caution. Existing tenants may be willing to pay above-market rents to avoid relocating. Alternatively, a landlord may offer existing tenants lower rent to avoid vacancies and the expense of obtaining new tenants.

The elements of comparison considered in rental analysis are

Real property rights being leased and conditions of rental	Rentals that do not reflect arm's-length negotiations most likely will have to be eliminated as comparables.
Market conditions	Economic conditions change, so leases negotiated in the past may not reflect current prevailing rents.
Location	Time-distance linkages and unit-specific location in project.
Physical characteristics	Size, height, interior finish, functional layout, site amenities, etc.
Division of expenses stipulated in the lease and other lease terms	Were concessions made? Who pays operating expenses?
Use of the property	Market rents might have to be adjusted for the intended use or level of build-out of the subject property when it differs from that of the comparable.
Non-realty components	For example, if a leasing or management company is involved, the income of a hotel that is part of a national chain may be higher than that of a hotel not in a chain. The higher income stems from the value associated with the name of the hotel franchise, not from any difference in the income potential of the real property.

The amount of data needed to support a market rent estimate for a subject property depends on the complexity of the appraisal problem, the availability of directly comparable rentals, and the extent to which the pattern of adjusted rent indications derived from the comparables differs from the income pattern of the subject property. When sufficient, closely comparable rental data is not available, the appraiser should include other data, preferably data that can be adjusted. If an appraiser uses proper judgment in making adjustments, a reasonably clear pattern of market rents should emerge.

Income and Expense Data

To derive pertinent income and expense data, an appraiser investigates comparable sales and rentals of competitive income-producing properties of the same type in the same market. For investment properties, current and recent incomes are reviewed, and vacancy and collection losses and typical operating expenses are studied. Published and electronic information on property values for several consecutive years can suggest the pattern of appreciation or depreciation applicable to various property types. Interviews with owners and tenants in the area can provide lease and expense data. Lenders may be contacted for information on available financing terms.

Appraisers try to obtain all income and expense data from the income-producing properties used as comparables. This data is tabulated in a reconstructed operating statement and filed by property type. (A suggested format for reconstructed operating statements is illustrated later in this chapter.)

> An income and expense forecast begins with **lease analysis.**

Like expense data, rental information is difficult to obtain. Therefore, appraisers should take every opportunity to add rents to their rental databases. Long-term leases may be filed in public records. A separate county index may cite the parties to recorded leases and the volume and page where leases are recorded. Sometimes this information is listed with deeds and mortgages, but it is usually coded for easy identification. In certain cities, abstracts of recorded leases are printed by private publishing services. Classified ads may also provide rental information. Many appraisers periodically check advertised rentals and recorded rental information by property type or area. It is convenient to file rental data under the same property use classifications used for sales data.

Income and expense comparables should be filed chronologically and by property type so they can be retrieved easily and used to estimate the expenses for a similar type of property. Income and expense figures should be converted to appropriate units of comparison for analysis. For example, income may be reported in terms of rent per apartment unit, per room, per hospital bed, or per square foot. Expenses for insurance, taxes, painting, decorating, and other required maintenance can be expressed in the same units of comparison used for income, or they can be expressed as a percentage of the effective gross income. The unit of comparison selected must be used consistently throughout the analysis for the subject property and the rental database information.

Rental property data may show vacancy rates as a percentage of potential gross income and operating expenses as a percentage of effective gross income. This data is essential in valuing income-producing property.

Lease Data

If written leases exist and the income estimate is based on the continuation of lease income, the appraiser examines lease provisions that could affect the quantity, quality, and durability of property income. The appraiser may either read the leases or rely on the client or another authorized party to disclose all pertinent lease provisions through lease summaries or briefs. In any case, the source of information and level of verification should be described in the scope of work section of the appraisal report. The appraiser also analyzes the leases of competitive properties to estimate market rent and other forms of income applicable to the market for competitive space.

Typical lease data includes

- Date of the lease
- Reference information, if the lease is recorded
- Legal description or other identification of the leased premises
- Name of lessor—i.e., owner or landlord
- Name of lessee—i.e., tenant
- Lease term

- Occupancy date
- Commencement date for rent payment
- Rent amount, including any percentage clause, graduation, and payment terms
- Rent concessions, including any discounts or benefits
- Landlord's covenants—i.e., items such as taxes, insurance, and maintenance for which the owner or landlord is responsible
- Tenant's covenants—i.e., items such as taxes, insurance, maintenance, utilities, and cleaning expenses for which the tenant is responsible
- Right of assignment or right to sublet—i.e., whether the leasehold, or tenant's interest, may be assigned or sublet, under what conditions, and whether assignment relieves the initial tenant of future liability
- Option(s) to renew, including the date of required notice, term of renewal, rent, and other renewal provisions
- Expense caps and expense stops, escalation rent, and expense recoveries
- Options to purchase and any accompanying conditions
- Escape clauses, cancellation clauses, and kick-out clauses
- Continued occupancy contingency
- Security deposits, including advance rent, bond, or expenditures by the tenant for items such as leasehold improvements
- Casualty loss—i.e., whether the lease continues after a fire or other disaster and on what basis
- Lessee's improvements, including whether they can be removed when the lease expires and to whom they belong
- Noncompete and exclusive use clauses
- Condemnation, including the respective rights of the lessor and the lessee if all or any part of the property is appropriated by a public agency
- Revaluation clauses
- Special provisions

Special attention should be paid to lease data on rent, rent concessions, the division of expenses, renewal options, escalation clauses, purchase options, escape clauses, and tenant improvements.

A sample form for analyzing a typical office lease is shown in Figure 21.1.

Rent

The amount of rent to be paid by the tenant is basic lease data. An appraiser considers rent from all sources, which may include base, or minimum, rent, contract rent, percentage rent, and escalation rent. The sources of rental income should be clearly identified.

Figure 21.1	**Office Space Rental Worksheet**

Building: _____

Lessor: _____

Lessee: _____

Premises: Floor_____ Rentable area _____ Usable area _____ Loss factor _____

Term: Commencement _____ Expiration _____

Base rent: _____ CPI escalation   ❏   Yes   ❏   No

Graduations: _____

Escalations:

    Real estate taxes_____

    Operating expenses_____

    Energy_____

Work letter (costs): _____

Special provisions—e.g., repainting, etc.:_____

Who pays:	Lessor	Lessee	Stop	Stop Amount per Sq. Ft.	Cap	Cap Amount per Sq. Ft.
Fixed expenses						
Real estate taxes	❏	❏	❏	—	❏	—
Property insurance (Fire, storm, vandalism)	❏	❏	❏	—	❏	—
Variable expenses						
Tenant electric	❏	❏	❏	—	❏	—
Building electric	❏	❏	❏	—	❏	
Tenant HVAC	❏	❏	❏	—	❏	—
Building HVAC	❏	❏	❏	—	❏	—
Tenant space cleaning (Janitorial service)	❏	❏	❏	—	❏	—
Public space cleaning (Janitorial service)	❏	❏	❏	—	❏	—
Fuel	❏	❏	❏	—	❏	—
Repairs and maintenance						
Exterior	❏	❏	❏	—	❏	—
Interior	❏	❏	❏	—	❏	—
Management	❏	❏	❏	—	❏	—

Renewal options: _____

How many: _____ Years each _____

New rent: _____

New escalation (and base year):_____

New rentable area or loss factor:_____

New work letter: _____

Occupancy (or status) of building when lease was originally signed:_____

Comments: _____

Rent Concessions

When real estate markets are oversupplied, landlords may give tenants concessions such as free rent for a specified period of time or extra tenant improvements. In shopping center leases, retail store tenants are sometimes given rent credit for interior store improvements. All rent concessions result from market conditions and the relative negotiating strengths of the landlord and the tenant. It is not unusual for free rent concessions to be given outside of the lease term so that the concessions do not appear on the written lease contract. In these situations appraisers must still consider the lease concessions when calculating the effective rent being paid.

> **rent concession:** A discount or other benefit offered by a landlord to induce a prospective tenant to enter into a lease; usually in the form of one or more months of free rent, but it may be expressed in extra services to the tenant or some other consideration; also called *rent offset*.

Lessor/Lessee Division of Expenses

Most leases outline the obligations of the lessor and the lessee to delineate specifically who must pay for taxes, insurance, utilities, heat, janitorial service (if any), repairs, unit owner's or common area (CAM) expenses, and other expenses required to maintain and operate the leased property. The appraiser should identify the division of expenses in each lease analyzed and compare the rents and estimated rental value of the subject space to those of comparable space. Any required adjustments in the division of expenses in comparable properties should reflect the same lease terms and division of expenses as the subject property.

Renewal Options

Renewal options that allow a tenant to extend the lease term for one or more prescribed periods of time are frequently included in leases. A typical renewal option requires that the tenant provide advance notice of the intention to renew. The tenant also must identify the length of the renewal period and the rent or method of determining the rent to be paid. The extension period rent may be set at the original rent or at a level determined when the lease was negotiated. Or, it may be calculated with a procedure or formula specified in the lease when the option is exercised. Renewal options are binding on the lessor but allow the tenant to make a decision based on the circumstances at the time of renewal. Thus, renewal options tend to favor the tenant, not the lessor.

If the terms of the renewal option are favorable to the tenant, then this fact should be noted in the appraisal report, and the appraiser would probably be justified in concluding that the tenant would exercise the option to renew. If the terms of the renewal option are not favorable to the tenant, however, this fact should still be pointed out, and the appraiser could reasonably conclude that the tenant would not exercise the option to renew. This is particularly important in discounted cash flow analysis and yield capitalization, where it might have a significant impact on the appraiser's projection of a holding period as well as projections of tenant improvements and leasing commissions.

Expense Cap and Expense Stop Clauses

Leases often include clauses that limit the expenses that either the landlord or the tenant will pay. With an expense cap, operating expenses are borne by the tenant to a specified level above which the landlord picks up additional expenses. The cap defines the tenant's maximum obligations and limits the tenant's exposure to the risk of increasing expenses. With an expense stop, the landlord meets defined operating expenses to a specified level above which increases in operating expenses become the responsibility of the tenant or lessee. This allows the landlord to pass through any increases above the specified level over time and protects the landlord against unforeseen increases in expenses. Often the level of expenses incurred during the first year of the lease is specified as the level of the stop, although a stated amount per square foot is sometimes used.

Expense stop clauses are often added to traditional gross or flat rental leases. In multitenant office buildings, increased expenses are usually prorated among the tenants in proportion to the area they occupy or on some other equitable basis. The prorated shares are then added to the tenants' rents; the expenses allocated to vacant space are normally paid by the owner.

Sometimes a single stop provision is used to cover all the expenses to be passed through to the tenants. Alternatively, an expense stop might be specified for individual expense items. For example, tax stop clauses provide that any increases in taxes over a specified level be passed on to the tenant.

Escalation Clauses

Escalation payments are frequently based on changes in a local wage rate or index such as the Consumer Price Index (CPI). In New York City, for example, the porter wage escalation formula is frequently used. Each one-cent increase in the porter wage rate—i.e., the hourly wage paid to office workers who are members of the porters' union—produces a one- to one and one-half-cent increase in expense charges per square foot of space. An escalation clause helps the landlord offset increases in operating expenses, which are passed on to tenants on a pro rata basis. Some escalation clauses are drawn so broadly that the lease is almost applied on a net rental basis.

expense cap: A clause in a lease that limits an anchor tenant's share of common area maintenance expenses.

expense stop: A clause in a lease that limits the landlord's expense obligation because the lessee assumes any expenses above an established level.

escalation clause: A clause in an agreement that provides for the adjustment of a price or rent based on some event or index, e.g., a provision to increase rent if operating expenses increase; also called *expense recovery clause.*

Expense Recovery Clauses

An expense recovery clause stipulates that some or all operating expenses paid by the landlord are recoverable from the tenant. In different parts of the country, expense recoveries are known as *reimburseables, billables,* or *pass-throughs.* Some of these items, e.g., common area maintenance charges, may be considered under operating expenses, while others may be considered under replacement allowance. Recoverable expenses are deducted as expenses (or were already deducted in previous years), and recoveries are treated as separate revenue items in income and expense statements.

Purchase Options

Certain leases include a clause granting the lessee an option to purchase the leased property. In some cases this option must be exercised on the lease termination date or at some point or points during the lease term; in other cases this option may be available at any time. The option price may be fixed or it may change periodically based on an empirical formula, depreciated book value, or revaluation of the property. In industrial and office build-to-suit situations, the option price may be the cost to construct improvements plus the interest through the option period. A purchase option may only give the lessee the right to purchase the property or make an offer if an offer to purchase is made by a third party. This provision is referred to as a *right of first refusal.* A purchase option can restrict marketability. Also, unless the property is being appraised in fee simple, the option price, if stated, may represent a limit on the market value of the leased fee estate.

Escape and Kick-Out Clauses

An escape clause permits a tenant to cancel a lease under circumstances that would not ordinarily be considered justification for lease cancellation. For example, a condemnation or casualty clause might allow the tenant to cancel the lease if the condemnation or casualty loss hinders operations. A casualty clause may stipulate that the lessor be allowed a reasonable amount of time to make necessary repairs and provide for appropriate abatement of rent in the interim. A landlord might include a demolition clause in a lease to preserve the prospects for sale or redevelopment of the site. This type of escape clause can affect rent levels and market value.

A kick-out clause written into a shopping center lease allows a lessee to cancel a long-term lease (of five to ten years or more) if sales have not achieved a specified level after the first, second, or third year. Another type of kick-out clause allows the tenant to cancel the lease if the landlord fails to replace a departing anchor within a specified period of time. Kick-out clauses may create risk and warrant discount rate adjustments.

Continued Occupancy Clauses

Multitenant properties may be subject to leases that condition the continued occupancy of one tenant on the occupancy of another tenant. An anchor tenant's

escape clause: A provision that allows a tenant to cancel a lease.

decision to vacate during the lease term can precipitate the departure of other tenants as well. In appraising shopping centers, the probability of an anchor tenant leaving at or before expiration of the current lease must be carefully analyzed. This is true whether or not the satellite stores have leases conditioning their occupancy on the continued occupancy of the anchor tenant. Small stores are often unable to continue operation if the anchor leaves the center.

Tenant Improvements

Extensive tenant improvements can influence contract rent or they may be built into the asking rent as a tenant improvement allowance. Consideration of tenant improvements is usually addressed in yield capitalization and discounted cash flow analysis because the costs accrued can be incorporated into the analysis at the appropriate points of the holding period. Ignoring the impact of TIs in direct capitalization may be a mistake. Stabilized *NOI* should recognize the tenant improvements made to a property that are appropriate for the market.

When capital expenditures not accounted for in the asking rent are made by the lessor, reimbursement may be accomplished through marginally higher rent that amortizes the lessor's expenditures over all or part of the lease period. If capital expenditures are made by the tenant, the lessor may reduce the tenant's rent for all or part of the lease term as compensation for such tenant expenditures. In many retail environments, the rents vary directly with the level of build-out provided to the tenant. When using these leases as comparable data, the level of build-out supplied with the rent is an important element of comparison.

Tenant improvements are driven by the market—i.e., they are only done if the market dictates it. Also, tenant improvements do not apply to all property types. The standard maintenance and upkeep of an apartment unit before renting the unit to a new tenant is not usually a tenant improvement, unless the cleaning and refurbishment exceed the typical levels needed to maintain the property's competitiveness in the market. Furthermore, tenant improvements on a new building are usually capital expenditures while TIs in an existing space being retenanted are usually an expense. When TIs occur during the economic lifespan of a building dictates how they are treated and impact *NOI*—i.e., if they directly impact *NOI* and are recorded above the *NOI* line item in a reconstructed operating statement, they are considered *above-the-line expenses,* while at other times they are *below the line.*

A developer or owner may be responsible for a certain level of build-out or tenant improvements and that will be reflected in

continued occupancy clause: A lease provision that conditions the continued occupancy of one tenant upon the occupancy of another, usually an anchor tenant in a multitenant retail center.

tenant improvement allowance: A dollar amount or allowance provided to the tenant by the landlord for the construction of tenant improvements, which may or may not equal the full cost of construction or remodeling.

the rent. Costs in excess of that level are the responsibility of tenants, are not reflected in the rent, and are usually amortized over the lease term. The level of build-out may be different for new space and for retrofitting an existing space, and the level of tenant improvements may be different for a renewal tenant and a new tenant.

Noncompete and Exclusive Use Clauses

Leases may contain a provision that prohibits both parties from operating a nearby business that competes with either party. For example, a tenant who sells sporting goods may agree not to open another, competing sporting goods facility near the shopping center. If sufficient data is available, the value of the additional income resulting from a noncompete clause may be estimated and discounted over the term of the lease.

above-the-line expense: An expense that is recorded "above" the net operating income line in a reconstructed operating statement and therefore is considered part of the total operating expenses for the property.

below-the-line expense: An expense that is recorded "below" the net operating income line in a reconstructed operating statement and therefore is not considered part of the total operating expenses for the property; tenant improvements and leasing concessions are the most common line items recorded below the net operating income line.

exclusive use clause: A provision that limits the landlord from leasing to any other tenants in the property or in a defined area who are conducting a similar business.

An exclusive use clause may be written into a lease by a landlord who wishes to control the retail mix of the shopping center. Such a clause may also be sought by a tenant who wants to achieve some degree of monopoly status.

Developing Reconstructed Operating Statements

Assessing the earning power of a property means reaching a conclusion regarding its net operating income expectancy. The appraiser estimates income and expenses after researching and analyzing the following:

- The income and expense history of the subject property
- Income and expense histories of competitive properties
- Recently signed leases, proposed leases, and asking rents for the subject and competitive properties
- Actual vacancy levels for the subject and competitive properties
- Management expenses for the subject and competitive properties
- Published operating expense data and operating expenses at the subject and competitive properties
- Forecast changes in taxes, energy costs, and other operating expenses

Appraisers often present this information in tabular form to assist the reader of the report. Income and expenses are generally reported in annual or monthly dollar amounts and analyzed in terms of nominal dollar amounts, dollars and cents per unit of rentable area, or dollars and cents based on another unit of comparison. To show how historical and forecast data on operating expenses is commonly arrayed, Table 21.2 summarizes the operating expense history of a downtown office building with 60,000 rentable square feet of space. Table 21.3 summarizes the operating expenses of five comparable properties in the same market area and allows for easy comparison of the subject property and the comparables. It is obvious that the total operating expenses of the subject, at $14.79 per square foot, for the year being studied are significantly higher than those of the comparables, which range from $12.65 to $13.92 per square foot. For most of the operating expenses listed, the per-unit expenses for the subject fall within the ranges set by the comparable properties, but the expenses for electricity, at $4.14 per square foot, and cleaning, at $2.28 per square foot, are higher than for any of the comparables. In the income and expense analysis, the appraiser will have to investigate the reasons for the higher cost of electricity and cleaning for the subject property.

After thoroughly analyzing property and lease data for the subject and comparable properties, the appraiser develops a net operating income estimate for the subject property. If the appraiser is focusing on the benefits accruing to the equity investment, the equity dividend is also estimated.

Table 21.2   **Subject Property Operating Expense History**

	Year 1 Actual		Year 2 Actual		Year 3 Actual		Year 4 Budget	
	Dollars	Per Square Foot	Dollars	Per Square Foot	Dollars	Per Square Foot	Dollars	Per Square Foot
Fixed expenses								
Real estate taxes	$232,812	$3.88	$272,378	$4.54	$314,433	$5.24	$323,400	$5.39
Insurance	2,378	0.04	2,350	0.04	6,625	0.11	6,700	0.11
Variable expenses								
Electricity	$200,390	$3.34	$216,632	$3.61	$211,789	$3.53	$248,350	$4.14
Steam heat	79,211	1.32	71,390	1.19	72,675	1.21	85,250	1.42
Cleaning	117,102	1.95	109,775	1.83	128,987	2.15	136,750	2.28
Payroll	8,432	0.14	10,208	0.17	11,386	0.19	12,600	0.21
Repairs and maintenance	17,388	0.29	30,688	0.51	38,875	0.65	52,825	0.88
Water and sewer	3,010	0.05	3,030	0.05	2,412	0.04	4,800	0.08
Administrative, legal, and accounting	1,180	0.02	1,778	0.03	10,856	0.18	10,850	0.18
Management fees	4,757	0.08	4,930	0.08	5,010	0.08	5,350	0.09
Miscellaneous	3,031	0.05	88	0.001	610	0.01	600	0.01
Total operating expenses	$669,691	$11.16	$723,247	$12.05	$803,658	$13.39	$887,475	$14.79

Note: Figures have been rounded.

Table 21.3   Analysis of Operating Expense Comparables

	Subject Property Pro Forma	A 130 Main Street	B 110 Second Avenue	C 717 Fourth Avenue	D 133 Third Avenue	E One Commerce Plaza
				Comparables		
Operating year	2003	2002	2002	2002	2002	2002
Year built	1996	1996	1985	1978	1981	1995
Rentable area in square feet	60,000	75,000	49,411	56,411	52,000	66,000
Operating Expenses*						
Fixed expenses						
Real estate taxes	$5.39	$5.51	$5.48	$5.01	$5.47	$5.35
Insurance	0.11	0.06	0.09	0.10	0.17	0.09
Variable expenses						
Electricity	$4.14	$4.03	$3.47	$3.31	$3.25	$3.45
Steam heat	1.42	1.25	1.60	1.35	1.75	1.55
Cleaning	2.28	1.61	1.38	1.27	1.28	1.30
Payroll	0.21	0.25	0.32	0.78	0.73	0.21
Repairs and maintenance	0.88	0.45	0.63	0.98	0.99	0.38
Water and sewer	0.08	0.08	0.08	0.08	0.09	0.10
Administrative, legal, and accounting	0.18	0.19	0.19	0.26	0.08	0.11
Management fees	0.09	0.08	0.08	0.08	0.09	0.10
Miscellaneous	0.01	0.02	0.01	0.02	0.02	0.01
Total operating expenses	$14.79	$13.53	$13.33	$13.24	$13.92	$12.65

* Per square foot

Potential Gross Income

Appraisers usually analyze potential gross income on an annual basis. Potential gross income comprises

- Rent for all space in the property— e.g., contract rent for current leases, market rent for vacant or owner-occupied space, percentage and overage rent for retail properties
- Rent from escalation clauses
- Reimbursement income
- All other forms of income to the real estate—e.g., income from services supplied to the tenants, such as switchboard service, antenna connections, storage, garage space, and income from coin-operated equipment and parking fees

> **Income estimates are developed by** analyzing information on the subject and competitive properties, i.e., individual income and expense histories, recent transactional data (signed leases, rents asked and offered), vacancy levels, and management expenses; published operating data, tax assessment policies, projected utility rates, and market expectations should also be investigated.

Because service-derived income may or may not be attributable to the real property, an appraiser might find it inappropriate to include this income in the property's potential gross income. The appraiser may treat such income as business income or as personal property income, depending on its source. If a form of income is subject to vacancy and collection loss, it should be incorporated into *PGI*, and the appropriate vacancy and collection charge should be made to reflect effective gross income.

Vacancy and Collection Loss

Vacancy and collection loss is an allowance for reductions in potential gross income attributable to vacancies, tenant turnover, and nonpayment of rent or other income. This line item considers two components:

- Physical vacancy as a loss in income
- Collection loss caused by concessions or default by tenants

The rents collected each year are typically less than annual potential gross income, so an allowance for vacancy and collection loss is usually included in the appraisal of income-producing property. The allowance is usually estimated as a percentage of potential gross income, which varies depending on the type and characteristics of the physical property; the quality of its tenants; the type and level of income streams; current and projected market supply and demand conditions; and national, regional, and local economic conditions.

> **vacancy and collection loss:** An allowance for reductions in potential gross income attributable to vacancies, tenant turnover, and nonpayment of rent; also called *vacancy and credit loss* or *vacancy and contingency loss*.

Published surveys of similar properties under similar conditions may indicate an appropriate percentage allowance for vacancy and collection loss. An appraiser should survey the local market to support the vacancy estimate. The conclusion in the income capitalization approach may differ from the current vacancy level indicated by primary or secondary data because the estimate reflects typical investor expectations for the subject property only over the projected holding period. Other methods of measuring vacancy and collection loss include comparing potential gross income at market rates against the subject property's actual collected income.

Effective Gross Income

Effective gross income is calculated as the potential gross income minus the vacancy and collection loss allowance.

Operating Expenses

Operating expenses may be recorded in categories selected by the property owner. The records also may follow a standard system of accounting established by an association of owners or by accounting firms that serve a particular segment of the real estate market. Generally, operating expenses are divided into three categories:

1. Fixed expenses
2. Variable expenses
3. Replacement allowance

However operating expenses are organized, an appraiser analyzes and reconstructs expense statements to develop an estimate of the typical operating expense forecast for the property on an annual cash basis.

Fixed Expenses

Most reconstructed operating statements contain line items for real estate taxes and building insurance costs. Tax data can be found in public records, and the assessor's office may provide information about projected changes in assessments or rates and their probable effect on future taxes. If a property is assessed unfairly, the real estate tax expense may need to be adjusted in the reconstructed operating statement. If the subject property is subject to an unusually low assessment compared to other, similar properties or appears to deviate from the general pattern of taxation in the jurisdiction, the most probable amount and trend of future taxes must be considered. Any past changes in the assessment of the subject property should be studied. If the assessment is low, the assessor is required by law to raise it. If the figure is high, however, a reduction may not be easily obtained. In projecting real estate taxes, an appraiser tries to anticipate tax assessments based on past tax trends, present taxes, the municipality's future expenditures, and the perceptions of market participants.

For proposed properties or properties that are not currently assessed, appraisers can develop operating statement projections without including real estate taxes. The resulting estimate is net operating income before real estate taxes, and a provision for real estate taxes is included in the capitalization rate used to convert this net income into property value. For example, assume that real estate taxes are typically 2% of market value and net operating income after real estate taxes would normally be capitalized at 11% to derive an opinion of market value for the subject property. In this case the estimated net operating income before real estate taxes could be capitalized at 13% (11% + 2%) to derive a property value indication. Alternatively, the appraiser may choose to estimate real estate taxes for a proposed project based on building costs or the taxes paid by recently constructed, competitive properties. Any unusual, unpaid special assessments or other mandatory, one-time expenses should be addressed as a lump-sum adjustment at the end of the analysis, if that is what the market would do.

operating expenses: The periodic expenditures necessary to maintain the real property and continue production of the effective gross income, assuming prudent and competent management.

fixed expenses: Operating expenses that generally do not vary with occupancy and that prudent management will pay for whether the property is occupied or vacant.

variable expenses: Operating expenses that generally vary with the level of occupancy or the extent of services provided.

replacement allowance: An allowance that provides for the periodic replacement of building components that wear out more rapidly than the building itself does and must be replaced during the building's economic life.

An owner's operating expense statement may show the insurance premiums paid on a cash basis. If the premiums are not paid annually, they must be adjusted to a hypothetical annual cash expense before they are included in the reconstructed operating statement. Fire, extended coverage, and owner's liability insurance are typical insurance items; depending on the type of property, elevators, boilers, plate glass, or other items may also be insured. The appraiser must determine the amount of insurance and, if it is inadequate or superadequate, adjust the annual cost to indicate appropriate coverage for the property.

Insurance on business inventory, business liability, and other business property is the occupant's responsibility and therefore should not be charged to the operation of the real estate. When questions concerning co-insurance or terms of coverage arise, an appraiser might need to obtain professional insurance counsel.

Variable Expenses

Operating statements for large properties frequently list many types of variable expenses such as the following:

- Management charges
- Leasing fees
- Utilities—e.g., electricity, gas, water, and sewer
- Heat
- Air-conditioning
- General payroll
- Cleaning
- Maintenance and repair of structure
- Decorating
- Grounds and parking area maintenance
- Miscellaneous—e.g., security, supplies, rubbish removal, and exterminating

Management charges. Management services may be contracted or provided by the property owner. The expense of management is usually expressed as a percentage of effective gross income and conforms to the local pattern of such charges for typical management.[1]

---

1. Actual property management should be distinguished from asset management. Large, investment-grade properties are often held as part of a portfolio that includes both securities and real estate. The managers of these portfolios make critical decisions concerning when to acquire a real estate asset, how to finance or when to refinance, and when to reposition a property in the market. Though their roles are distinct, the functions of a property manager and an asset manager may sometimes be intertwined. Asset management fees should not be included among the items enumerated as operating expenses for real property. See *The Office Building: From Concept to Investment Reality*, John Robert White, ed. (Chicago: Counselors of Real Estate, Appraisal Institute, and Society of Industrial and Office Realtors, 1993), 488–489, 529–530.

The operation of multitenant properties requires a considerable amount of supervision, accounting, and other services. Larger properties may have on-site offices or apartments for resident managers and corresponding expenses for their maintenance and operation. Other management expenses may include the cost of telephone service, clerical help, legal or accounting services, printing and postage, and advertising and promotion. Management fees may occasionally be included among recoverable operating expenses for some property types.

In some markets standard retail leases contain a provision for levying administrative charges as a percentage of common area maintenance charges. These charges are typically treated as a mark-up to tenant reimbursements and are distinct from, and unrelated to, the management fee.

Leasing commissions. Leasing commissions are paid to agents for negotiating and securing tenants. When these commissions are spread over the term of a lease or lease renewal, they are included in the operating statement. If they are not projected to occur in the next year, they are not likely to be listed in the reconstructed operating statement for direct capitalization. However, initial leasing commissions, which may be extensive in a new shopping center or other large development, are usually treated as part of the capital expenditure for developing the project. These initial leasing commissions are not included as ongoing periodic expenses. When a net income or equity dividend forecast is developed, leasing fees can be deducted in the year they are payable or spread over the lease term, depending on local practice.

> **leasing commission:** Fees paid to an agent for leasing tenant space. When leasing fees are spread over the term of a lease or lease renewal, they are treated as a variable operating expense. Initial leasing fees usually fall under capital expenditures for development and are not included among periodic expenses.

A blended rate can be developed to reflect leasing commission costs for both existing leases and new leases. For example, if the tenant renewal ratio for a property is 70%, the leasing commission for existing tenants is 2.5%, and the leasing commission for new tenants is 6%, a blended rate can be developed as follows:

$$0.70 \times 0.025 = 0.0175$$
$$0.30 \times 0.060 = \underline{0.0180}$$
$$\text{Blended rate} = \underline{0.0355} \text{ (3.6\% rounded)}$$

This blended rate is then applied to existing tenant leases as they expire.

Utilities. Utility expenses for an existing property are usually projected based on an analysis of past charges and current trends. The subject property's utility requirements can be compared with known utility expenses per unit of measure—e.g., per square foot, per room, per apartment unit—for similar properties to estimate probable future utility expenses. Hours of tenant operation may prove to be significant in the analysis. For example, the number of nights per week that a shopping center is open and the hours of after-dark operation will directly affect electricity consumption and may also affect expenses for maintenance and garbage removal. In analyzing utility expenses, appraisers recognize local circumstances and the current and expected future cost of all applicable types of energy.

Although the cost of electricity for leased space is frequently a tenant expense, and therefore not included in the operating expense statement, the owner may be responsible for lighting public areas and for the power needed to run elevators and other common building equipment. These expenses may or may not be recouped as part of common area reimbursements.

Gas. When used for heating and air-conditioning, gas can be a major expense item that is either paid by the tenant or paid by the property owner and reflected in the rent.

Water. The cost of water is a major consideration for industrial plants that use processes that depend on water and for multifamily projects, in which the cost of sewer service is usually tied to the amount of water used. It is also an important consideration for laundries, restaurants, taverns, hotels, and similar operations. The leases for these properties may stipulate that the tenant pay this expense. If the owner typically pays for water, this charge should be included in the expense statement.

Sewer. In municipalities with sewerage systems, a separate charge for use of the system may be paid by the tenant or the owner of the real estate. When the property owner is responsible, the total expense may be substantial, particularly for hotels, motels, recreation facilities, apartments, and office buildings.

Heat. The cost of heat is generally a tenant expense in single-tenant properties, industrial or retail properties, and apartment or office projects with individual heating units. It is a major expense item shown in operating statements for office buildings and centrally heated apartment properties. The fuel consumed may be coal, oil, gas, electricity, or public steam. Heating supplies, maintenance, and workers' wages are included in this expense category under certain accounting methods.

Public steam suppliers and gas companies maintain records of fuel consumption and corresponding degree days from year to year. (One degree day is equal to the number of degrees, during a 24-hour day, that the mean temperature falls below 65° Fahrenheit, which is the base temperature in the United States.) An appraiser can use these records and fuel cost data to compare the property's heating expense for the most recent years with a typical year. Probable changes in the cost of the fuel used should be reflected in the appraiser's projection.

Air-conditioning. Air-conditioning expenses may be charged under the individual categories of electricity, gas, water, payroll, and repairs, or heating and air-conditioning may be combined under the category of heating, ventilation, and air-conditioning (HVAC). The cost of air-conditioning varies substantially with local climatic conditions and the type of system installed. A projection of this expense may be based on typical unit charges for the community or the property type. Most office buildings and many apartment buildings have central HVAC systems, and operating expenses are included in their annual statements. Most retail properties and some apartment buildings have individual heating and air-conditioning units that are operated by the tenants. The maintenance and repair of these units, particularly in apartments, may continue to be the property owner's obligation.

General payroll. General payroll expenses include payments to all employees whose services are essential to property operation and management but whose salaries are not included in other specific expense categories. In some areas the cost of custodial or janitorial service is based on union wage schedules; in others the charge is negotiated based on local custom and practice. If a custodian or manager occupies an apartment as partial payment for his or her services, the apartment's rental value may be included as income and an identical amount deducted as an expense. In certain properties additional expenses are incurred to pay the salaries of security personnel, porters, and elevator operators. Unemployment and social security taxes for employees may be included under general payroll expenses or listed in a separate expense category.

Cleaning. In office buildings the cost of cleaning or janitorial services is a major expense and usually includes two elements: cleaning costs and cleaning supplies. It is usually estimated in terms of cost per square foot of rentable area, whether the work is done by payroll personnel or by an outside cleaning firm. This expense is equivalent to maid service or housekeeping in hotels and furnished apartments. In hotels and motels, cleaning expenses are attributed to the rooms department and may be estimated as a percentage of the department's gross income. The percentage established reflects the property's previous experience and industry standards. Cleaning may be an owner or tenant expense, depending on the property type and lease provisions.

Maintenance and repair of structure. Maintenance and repair expenses are incurred during the year to maintain the structure and its major components and to keep them in good working order. These expenses may cover roof repair; window caulking; tuckpointing; exterior painting; and the repair of heating, lighting, and plumbing equipment. Typically, under triple net leases, maintenance costs are paid by the tenants and repair costs by the owners. There may be a contract for elevator maintenance and repair, and often owners are still responsible for maintenance of the roof, HVAC system, and general structure. However, the comprehensiveness of these contracts varies, and the appraiser must determine any additional operating expenses not covered by the maintenance contract. A contract covering air-conditioning equipment, for example, would probably be included in the air-conditioning expense category.

Alterations, including major replacements, modernization, and renovation, may be considered capital expenditures and therefore are not included as a periodic expense under repair and maintenance. If the lessor makes alterations in the rented space, the expense may or may not be amortized by additional rental; in some cases the tenant may pay for alterations.

The total expense for property maintenance and repair is affected by the extent to which building component and equipment replacements are covered in the replacement allowance as well as the age, condition, and functional utility of the property. If an extensive replacement allowance is included in the reconstructed operating statement, annual maintenance and repair expenses may be reduced. Similarly, if an owner cures items of deferred maintenance, the annual maintenance and repair expenses may be reduced.

For some properties, historical expense records may include typical repairs and even capital expenses in an overall category called *repairs and maintenance.* If this is the case, the reconstructed operating statement will need to show an adjustment to the historical data, especially where separate replacement allowances are included. The goal of the analysis is to consider all appropriate expenses over time together with a replacement allowance to ensure the ongoing repair of major building components. Also, there may be some crossover in the tenant improvement category and the replacement allowance and/or repair category. The same methodology should be applied to any comparable sales information to ensure an underlying consistency for extracting the various rates and ratios and then applying them to the subject property.

Decorating. Decorating expenses may include the cost of interior painting, wallpapering, or wall cleaning in tenant or public areas. Lease provisions may stipulate that the owner is only responsible for decorating vacant space to attract new tenants. Decorating expenditures may vary with local practice and the supply and demand for space.

Grounds and parking area maintenance. The cost of maintaining grounds and parking areas can vary widely depending on the type of property and its total site area. The cost of snow removal may be substantial in northern states, particularly for properties with outdoor parking in addition to sidewalks and driveways. Hard-surfaced public parking areas with drains, lights, and marked car spaces are subject to intensive wear and can be expensive to maintain. These expenses may be entirely or partly compensated with an increment added to the rents of tenants served by the facility. In this case both the added income and the added expenses are included in the appraiser's reconstructed operating statement. Landscape and lawn maintenance are also covered by this expense category.

Security. Certain types of buildings in some areas may require security provisions, the cost of which will vary according to the number of employees needed to control entry and exit and to circulate through the property. Maintenance and energy expenses may also be incurred if security provisions include electric alarm systems, closed circuit television, or flood lighting.

Supplies. The cost of cleaning materials, office supplies, and miscellaneous items not covered elsewhere may be included under supplies.

Rubbish removal and exterminating. Garbage and pest control services are usually contracted and their cost is included in the expense statement.

Miscellaneous. Expenses for miscellaneous items vary with property type. If this expense category represents a significant percentage of effective gross income, however, it may be wise to explain individual expense items or reallocate them to specific categories.

Replacement Allowance

The annual replacement allowance for each component of a property is usually estimated as the anticipated cost of its replacement prorated over its total useful life, provided this does not exceed the total useful life of the structure. Some appraisers use simple averaging (with or without calculating a sinking fund payment), while others prefer to show the actual cost and timing of these replacements. New elevators or other components that are expected to have useful lives that equal or exceed the remaining useful life of the structure do not require an allowance for replacement, unless making replacements or installing new equipment increases the remaining useful life of the structure beyond that of the long-lived items. (Examples of building components that may require a replacement allowance are listed in Table 21.4.)

The scope of items to be covered in a replacement allowance is a matter of appraisal judgment based on market evidence; however, the magnitude and coverage of the replacement allowance is based on the annual repair and maintenance expenses of the property for the specific components considered in the allowance. Historical operating statements prepared on a cash basis may include periodic replacement expenses under repair and maintenance. If comprehensive provisions for replacement are made in the reconstructed operating statement, these charges may be duplicated unless the annual maintenance expense estimate is reduced.

In certain real estate markets, space is rented to a new tenant only after substantial interior improvements are made. If this work is performed at the

Table 21.4	**Building Components Requiring Replacement Allowance**

Roof covering
Carpeting
Kitchen, bath, and laundry equipment
Compressors, elevators, and boilers
Specific structural items and equipment that have limited economic life expectancies
Sidewalks
Driveways
Parking areas
Exterior painting

landlord's expense and is required to achieve market rent, the expense of these improvements should be included in the reconstructed operating statement as part of the replacement allowance or in a separate "tenant improvements" category.

A total expense estimate that provides for all items of repair, maintenance, and replacement may exceed the actual expenditures shown in the owner's operating statements for recent years. This is particularly common when the building being appraised is relatively new and the owner has not incurred many capital or repair expenses. In preparing a reconstructed operating statement for a typical year, an appraiser recognizes that replacements must be made eventually and that replacement costs affect operating expenses; these costs can be reflected in increased annual maintenance costs or, on an accrual basis, in an annual replacement allowance.

The appraiser must know whether or not a replacement allowance is included in any operating statement used to derive a market capitalization rate for use in the income capitalization approach. It is essential that the income statements of comparable properties be compatible. Otherwise, adjustments will be required. A capitalization rate derived from a comparable sale property is valid only if it is applied to the subject property on the same basis. Consequently, a rate derived from a sale with an expense estimate that does not provide for a replacement allowance should not be applied to an income estimate for a subject property that includes such an allowance without an adjustment that reflects the difference.

Total Operating Expenses

Total operating expenses are the sum of fixed and variable expenses and the replacement allowance cited in the operating expense estimate.

Net Operating Income

After total operating expenses are deducted from effective gross income, the remainder is the net operating income.

Additional Calculations

After the appraiser reaches a value for net operating income, further calculations may be needed to determine

- Mortgage debt service
- Equity dividend
- Expense and income ratios

Mortgage Debt Service

Mortgage debt service is the annual sum of all mortgage payments. Mortgage debt service is deducted from net operating income to derive equity dividend, which is used in certain capitalization procedures. The definition of market value assumes financing terms compatible with those found in the market.

EXCLUSIONS FROM RECONSTRUCTED OPERATING STATEMENTS

The operating statements prepared for real estate owners typically list all expenditures made during a specific year. An owner's statement may include nonrecurring items that should not be included in an expense estimate intended to reflect typical annual expenses. Such a statement may also include items of business expense or costs associated with the specific circumstances of ownership.

A reconstructed operating statement represents an opinion of the probable future net operating income of an investment.* Certain items included in operating statements prepared for property owners should be omitted in reconstructed operating statements prepared for appraisal purposes. These items include

- Book depreciation
- Depletion allowances or other special tax considerations
- Income tax
- Special corporation costs
- Additions to capital
- Mortgage interest
- Below-the-line tenant improvements or leasing commissions

Book Depreciation

The book depreciation for the improvements on a parcel of real estate is based on historical cost or another previously established figure that may have no relation to current market value. Moreover, book depreciation may be based on a formula designed for tax purposes. The capitalization method and procedure selected provide for the recapture of invested capital, so including depreciation in the operating expense statement would be redundant.

Depletion Allowances or Other Special Tax Considerations

A depletion allowance is an accounting process that allows for lower taxation of revenue generated by extracting natural resources from a property because there is less oil, coal, natural gas, or other minerals left in the ground. The concept of depletion is similar to the depreciation of assets, and including the depletion allowance in the operating expenses would be redundant for the same reasons given for book depreciation.

Income Tax

The amount of income tax varies with the type of property ownership—i.e., the property may be held by a corporation, a partnership, a public utility, or an individual. The income tax obligation of the owner is not an operating expense of the property; it is an expense of ownership.

Special Corporation Costs

The expenses attributable to corporate operation also pertain to the type of ownership. Corporate expenses are not part of a reconstructed operating statement developed for appraisal purposes.

Additions to Capital

Expenditures for capital improvements usually do not recur annually and therefore should not be included in an estimate reflecting the typical annual expenses of operation. Capital improvements may enhance value by increasing the annual net operating income or economic life of the property, but the capital expenditure is not a periodic operating expense.

> **capital expenditures:** Investments of cash or the creation of liability to acquire or improve an asset, e.g., land, buildings, building additions, site improvements, machinery, equipment; as distinguished from cash outflows for expense items that are normally considered part of the current period's operations.

EXCLUSIONS FROM RECONSTRUCTED OPERATING STATEMENTS *(continued)*

The exclusion of capital expenditures is specific to reconstructed operating statements, which are used to calculate net operating income. An average annual expectation may be included in the replacement reserve. When cash flows are estimated for a discounted cash flow analysis, capital expenditures may be deducted from the net operating income in the year the expenditure is expected to occur and not averaged on an annual basis. This is particularly important when the property's future net operating income is based on the assumption that the capital expenditure will be made. In this case, failure to account for the capital expenditure could result in an overstatement of value. Similarly, value may be understated if capital improvements are presumed to have been "written off" without appropriately considering their contribution to value or their additions to the total capital invested.

Mortgage Interest

Mortgage interests can include periodic payments, such as monthly interest payments or annual debt service, and the reversionary interest in the mortgage—i.e., the balance of the loan if paid prior to maturity or a balloon payment if paid at maturity. The reversionary interest is not a periodic expense and debt service is not included in the calculation of *NOI*, so neither form of mortgage interest is included in a reconstructed operating statement.

Below-the-Line Tenant Improvements and Leasing Commissions

If tenant improvements and leasing commissions are considered initial capital expenditures instead of ongoing operating expenses, then they will not be included in the calculation of *NOI* in a reconstructed operating statement.

---

*　Some practitioners use the term *pro forma* synonymously with reconstructed operating statement. Technically, a pro forma is a financial statement—e.g., a balance sheet or income statement used by a business developed "according to form." In appraisal practice, a *reconstructed operating statement* is developed to conform to the appraiser's definition of net operating income, which generally differs from the definition of income used by accountants. Thus, a reconstructed operating statement drawn up by an appraiser will usually differ from a typical pro forma income statement prepared by an accountant.

Thus, in estimating market value, the mortgage debt service to be deducted from the net operating income must be based on market terms. In some cases the appraiser may be asked to develop an opinion of the value of the equity investor's position based on existing financing. Here the debt service would reflect the terms specified in the existing mortgage(s).

Equity Dividend

Equity dividend is the income that remains after all mortgage debt service is deducted from net operating income.

Expense and Income Ratios

The ratio of total operating expense to effective gross income is the operating expense ratio (*OER*). The complement of this ratio is the net income ratio (*NIR*), which is the ratio of net operating income to effective gross income. These ratios tend to fall within ranges for specific categories of property. Experienced appraisers recognize appropriate ratios, so they can identify statements that deviate from typical patterns and require further analysis.

Nationwide studies of apartment and office building properties conducted by the Institute of Real Estate Management (IREM) and the Building Owners and Managers Association (BOMA) can often be used as general guides in assessing the reasonableness of operating expense ratios. Similar studies are also available for hotels, industrial properties, and mini-warehouses. Sometimes local BOMA or IREM chapters or real estate appraisal organizations and their chapters conduct and publish studies of operating expenses that can be used as market indicators. Published studies are useful, but the appraiser must still develop operating expense ratios from comparable properties in the subject property's market or verify the applicability of published ratios to this market.

> **operating expense ratio (OER):** The ratio of total operating expenses to effective gross income (*TOE/EGI*); the complement of the net income ratio, i.e., OER = 1 − NIR.
>
> **net income ratio (NIR):** The ratio of net operating expenses to effective gross income (*NOI/EGI*); the complement of the operating expense ratio, i.e., NIR = 1 − OER.

> **Operating expense ratios and net income ratios** are used to identify income and expense statements that are not typical or to confirm those that are typical.

Sample One-Year Income and Expense Forecast

The property being appraised, Southside Apartments, is a three-year-old, 55-unit apartment project with total annual rent collections of $367,200 at 100% occupancy. Additional information needed for the income and expense forecast follows.

- Open parking is included in the rent.
- Additional income from coin-operated equipment averages about $1,380 per year, so the total, annual potential gross income at 100% occupancy is $368,580.
- Annual vacancy and collection loss is estimated at 4% and local management services are available for 5% of rent collections.
- The building superintendent receives an annual salary of $16,800, including fringe benefits.
- Last year's tax bill was $17,875, but taxes are expected to be $18,700 by the end of this year.
- The owner carries $1 million in fire and extended coverage insurance and pays an annual premium of $1,567. The appraiser believes that this coverage should be increased to $1,200,000 with a premium of $1,880 (1.2 × $1,567 = $1,880). The additional expense for other insurance coverage is $770 per year and is a typical requirement.
- The cost to cover site maintenance and snow removal averages $5,900 per year.
- Trash removal costs $45 per month and supplies are estimated at $325 per year.
- Pest control costs are $65 per month and miscellaneous expenditures are projected at $325 per year.

- Building tenants pay their own utilities, including gas and electricity for individual apartment heating and air-conditioning units. Based on the expenses of the comparables and anticipated rate changes, the electricity for public space is expected to cost $2,200 in the coming year. Expenses for other utilities, including water, consistently run about $1,000 each year.
- Historically, repair and maintenance expenses have ranged from $12,000 to $13,000 per year, including some capital expenditures.
- The appraiser anticipates that capital replacement will accelerate, and the reconstructed operating statement should include a separate replacement allowance for such capital items in addition to normal repair and maintenance expenses.
- Exterior painting, which is estimated to cost $4,650 in the present market, is scheduled to be done every three years.
- Most of the apartments are rented on one-year leases, with a typical redecorating cost of $200 per apartment every third year.
- Public space is minimal, and redecorating this space costs about $240 every third year.
- All the apartments have electric stoves, refrigerators, dishwashers, garbage disposals, and exhaust fans, so a replacement allowance of $1,300 per apartment is required. The economic lives of these items vary, but they are estimated to average 10 years.
- The replacement of carpeting costs the owner about $900 per unit, and the average economic life of carpeting is six years.
- The roof is considered to have a 20-year life and a replacement cost of $18,000.

The operating statement shown in Table 21.5 reflects these estimates. The precision of each entry is approximate, and in most cases the appraiser is rounding to the closest $5 or $10, which is well within the estimated accuracy of the data.

Sample Multiyear Income and Expense Forecast

The analysis that follows (Table 21.6) is based on a six-year forecast of the income and expenses generated by the apartment building described in the preceding example. All the techniques described in this chapter are used to develop a net operating income estimate for the first year of the forecast. Estimates for the other years are based on existing lease provisions and expected forecasts regarding lease renewals and growth rates applied to other income and operating expenses. The following assumptions are made.

- Market rents are anticipated to increase 3% annually as are the receipts from the coin-operated equipment in the property.

Table 21.5   Southside Apartments: Reconstructed Operating Statement

Income

Potential gross annual income

Rents	11 units @ $500/mo.	$66,000
	12 units @ $525/mo.	75,600
	16 units @ $575/mo.	110,400
	16 units @ $600/mo.	115,200
		$367,200

Other income		+ 1,380
Total potential gross income @ 100% occupancy		$368,580
Less vacancy and collection loss @ 4%		− 14,743
Effective gross income		$353,837

Operating expenses

Fixed

Real estate taxes	$18,700
Insurance	
Fire and extended coverage	1,880
Other	770
Subtotal	$21,350

Variable

Management ($352,512 × 0.05)	$17,625
Superintendent	16,800
Site maintenance and snow removal	5,900
Electricity	2,200
Other utilities	1,000
Repair and maintenance	12,500
Trash removal ($45 × 12)	540
Pest control ($65 × 12)	780
Supplies	325
Other	325
Subtotal	$57,995

Replacement allowance

Interior decorating*	$3,750
Exterior paint ($4,650/3)	1,550
Kitchen and bath equipment ($1,300 × 55)/10	7,150
Carpeting ($900 × 55)/6	8,250
Roof ($18,000/20 years)	900
Subtotal (6.1% of EGI)	$21,600

Total operating expenses	− $100,945
Operating expense ratio ($100,945/$353,837) = 28.53%	
Total expenses per unit ($100,945/55) = $1,835 per unit	
Net operating income	$252,892
Net operating income ratio ($252,892/$353,837) = 71.47%	

* 55 units × $200 = $11,000; $11,000 + $240 = $11,240; $11,240/3 = $3,750 (rounded).

Table 21.6   **Income and Expense Analysis (Multiyear Forecast)**

	Year 1	Year 2	Year 3	Year 4	Year 5	Year 6
Income						
Potential gross income	$367,200	$378,216	$389,562	$401,249	$413,286	$425,685
Other income	1,380	1,420	1,465	1,505	1,550	1,600
Vacancy and collection loss	(14,743)	(15,129)	(15,582)	(16,050)	(16,531)	(17,027)
Effective gross income	$353,837	$364,507	$375,445	$386,704	$398,305	$410,258
Operating expenses						
Fixed expenses						
Real estate taxes	$18,700	$18,700	$18,700	$18,700	$18,700	$18,700
Insurance						
Fire and extended coverage	1,880	1,880	1,880	1,880	1,880	1,880
Other	770	770	770	770	770	770
Variable expenses						
Leasing commissions	$10,575	10,890	11,220	11,555	11,900	12,260
Tenant improvements	0	0	0	0	0	0
Management	17,625	18,155	18,700	19,260	19,840	20,435
Superintendent	16,800	17,640	18,520	19,450	20,420	21,440
Site maintenance and snow removal	5,900	5,900	5,900	5,900	5,900	5,900
Electricity	2,200	2,365	2,540	2,735	2,730	3,160
Other utilities	1,000	1,000	1,000	1,000	1,000	1,000
Repair and maintenance	12,500	12,500	12,500	12,500	12,500	12,500
Trash removal	540	540	540	540	540	540
Pest control	780	780	780	780	780	780
Supplies	325	325	325	325	325	325
Other	325	325	325	325	325	325
Replacement allowance						
Interior decorating	$3,750	$3,750	$3,750	$3,750	$3,750	$3,750
Exterior painting	1,550	1,550	1,550	1,550	1,550	1,550
Kitchen and bath equipment	7,150	7,150	7,150	7,150	7,150	7,150
Carpeting	8,250	8,250	8,250	8,250	8,250	8,250
Roof	900	900	900	900	900	900
Total operating expenses	$111,520	$113,370	$115,300	$117,315	$119,420	$121,615
Operating expense ratio	31.52%	31.10%	30.71%	30.34%	29.98%	29.64%
Total expenses per unit	$2,028	$2,061	$2,096	$2,133	$2,171	$2,211
Net operating income	$242,317	$251,137	$260,145	$269,389	$278,885	$288,643

- For simplicity in this example, most of the operating expenses are forecast to remain level over the study period, with the exception of the superintendent's salary, which will increase an average of 5% per year, and the cost of electricity for common areas, which is expected to increase 7.5% annually. (More detailed examples of yield capitalization techniques and discounted cash flow analysis are shown in Chapters 23 and 24.)

- Note that leasing commissions and tenant improvements are included as a variable expense in the multiyear forecast for the apartment building. Leasing commissions are estimated at 3% of rent collections on average, while no tenant improvements are anticipated for the six-year study period.

FURTHER READING

Akerson, Charles B. *The Appraiser's Workbook.* 2d ed. Chicago: Appraisal Institute, 1996.

____. *Capitalization Theory and Techniques: Study Guide.* 2d ed. Chicago: Appraisal Institute, 2000.

American Institute of Real Estate Appraisers. *Forecasting: Market Determinants Affecting Cash Flows and Reversions.* Research Series Report 4. Chicago, 1989.

____. *Readings in the Income Capitalization Approach to Real Property Valuation,* Volume II. Chicago, 1985.

Fisher, Clifford E., Jr. *Rates and Ratios Used in the Income Capitalization Approach.* Chicago: Appraisal Institute, 1995.

Sources of Operating Costs and Ratios

Only a few of the many published sources are cited below.

Robert Morris Associates. *Sources of Composite Financial Data—A Bibliography.* 3d ed. Philadelphia, 1971.
An annotated list of 98 nongovernment sources, arranged in manufacturing, wholesaling, retail, and service categories. Subject index to specific businesses. Publishers' names and addresses included for each citation.

Building Owners and Managers Association International. *Downtown and Suburban Office Building Experience Exchange Report.* Washington, D.C.
Published annually since 1920. Includes analysis of expenses and income quoted in cents per square foot as well as national, regional, and selected city averages.

Dun & Bradstreet, Inc. *Key Business Ratios in 125 Lines.* New York.
Published annually. Contains balance sheet and profit-and-loss ratios.

Institute of Real Estate Management. *Income/Expense Analysis: Apartments, Condominiums & Cooperatives.* Chicago.
Published annually since 1954. Data arranged by building type, then by national, regional, metropolitan, and selected city groupings. Operating costs listed per room, per square foot, etc. Formerly *Apartment Building Experience Exchange.*

____. *Income/Expense Analysis: Suburban Office Buildings.* Chicago.
Published annually since 1976. Data analyzed on the basis of gross area and gross and net rentable office areas. Includes dollar-per-square-foot calculations; national, regional, and metropolitan comparisons; and detailed analyses for selected cities.

FURTHER READING *(continued)*

National Institute of Real Estate Brokers. *Percentage Leases.* 13th ed. Chicago, 1973.
Based on reports of 3,100 leases for 97 retail and service categories in seven U.S. regions. Data broken down by type of operation, area, center, and building. Regional and store averages given for average minimum rent, rent per square foot, average gross leasable areas, and sales per square foot.

National Retail Merchants Association, Controllers' Congress. *Department Store and Specialty Store Merchandising and Operating Results.* New York.
Published annually since 1925. Merchandise classification base used since 1969 edition (1968 data). Includes geographical analysis by Federal Reserve districts. Known as the "MOR" report.

___. *Financial and Operating Results of Department and Specialty Stores.* New York.
Published annually since 1963. Data arranged by sales volume category. Known as the "FOR" report.

Pannell Kerr Forster. *Clubs in Town & Country.* Houston.
Published annually since 1953. Lists income-expense data and operating ratios for city and country clubs. Geographical data broken down into four U.S. regions.

___. *Trends in the Hotel Industry.* Houston.
Published annually since 1937. Lists income-expense data and operating ratios for transient and resort hotels and motels. Geographical data broken down into five U.S. regions.

Urban Land Institute. *Dollars and Cents of Shopping Centers.* Washington, D.C., 2000.
First issued in 1961 and revised every three years. Includes income and expense data for neighborhood, community, and regional centers as well as statistics for specific tenant types.

CHAPTER

22 | DIRECT CAPITALIZATION

Direct capitalization is a method used in the income capitalization approach to convert a single year's income expectancy into a value indication. This conversion is accomplished in one step, either by dividing the income estimate by an appropriate income rate or by multiplying it by an appropriate income factor.

Direct capitalization is widely used when properties are already operating on a stabilized basis and there is an ample supply of comparable sales with similar risk levels, incomes, expenses, physical and locational characteristics, and future expectations. This methodology may be less useful for properties going through an initial lease-up or when income and/or expenses are expected to change in an irregular pattern over time. Comparables with similar future expectations may not be available in these cases and one of the yield capitalization techniques may be more appropriate. The advantages of direct capitalization are that it is simple to use, easy to explain, often expresses market thinking, and provides strong market evidence of value when adequate sales are available.

Direct capitalization is divided into two basic methodologies:

- Applying an overall capitalization rate to relate value to the entire property income (i.e., net operating income)

- Using residual techniques that consider components of a property's income and the use of market-derived capitalization rates for each component analyzed

Direct capitalization is distinct from yield capitalization, which is discussed in Chapters 23 and 24, in that the former does not directly consider the individual cash flows beyond the first year. Although yield capitalization explicitly calculates year-by-year effects of potentially changing income patterns, changes in the original investment's value, and other considerations, direct capitalization processes a single year's income into an indication of value. Either direct capitalization or yield capitalization may correctly produce a

The **basic formulas** for direct capitalization are:

$$I = R \times V \qquad R = I / V \qquad V = I / R$$
$$V = I \times F \qquad I = V / F \qquad F = V / I$$

where I is income, R is capitalization rate, V is value, and F is factor.

direct capitalization

1. A method used to convert an estimate of a single year's income expectancy into an indication of value in one direct step, either by dividing the income estimate by an appropriate rate or by multiplying the income estimate by an appropriate factor.

2. A capitalization technique that employs capitalization rates and multipliers extracted from sales. Only the first year's income is considered. Yield and value change are implied but not identified.

Table 22.1	Income Streams, Rates, and Factors for Direct Capitalization	
Income Streams	**Income Rates**	**Income Factors**
Potential gross income	Overall (property) capitalization rate,	Potential gross income
Effective gross income	fee simple (R_O)	multiplier ($PGIM$)
Net operating income	Mortgage capitalization rate (R_M)	Gross rent multiplier (GRM)
Equity income	Equity capitalization, or equity dividend,	Effective gross income
Mortgage income	rate (R_E)	multiplier ($EGIM$)
Land income	Land capitalization rate (R_L)	
Building income	Building capitalization rate (R_B)	
Income to the landlord's	Capitalization rate for the leased fee	
leased fee interest	position (R_{LF})	
Income to the tenant's	Capitalization rate for the leasehold	
leasehold interest	position (R_{LH})	

supportable indication of value when based on relevant market information derived from comparable properties, which should have similar income-expense ratios, land value-to-building value ratios, risk characteristics, and future expectations of income and value changes over a typical holding period. A choice of capitalization method does not produce a different indication of value under this circumstance.

Direct capitalization may be based on various income flows and use various income rates and factors. Table 22.1 lists the sorts of information an appraiser will need to apply the income capitalization approach. The list is not all-inclusive.

Derivation of Overall Capitalization Rates

Any interest in real estate that is capable of generating income can be valued by direct capitalization. For owner-occupied properties or properties not subject to a lease, it is most common to appraise the fee simple interest. However, if a property is subject to a lease, then the appropriate interest to appraise is the leased fee interest.[1] The direct capitalization formula that applies to these types of valuation assignments is

$$\text{Value} = \frac{\text{Net operating income}}{\text{Overall capitalization rate}}$$

Overall capitalization rates can be estimated with various techniques; the techniques used depend on the quantity and quality of data available.[2] When supported by appropriate market data, accepted techniques include

- Derivation from comparable sales
- Derivation from effective gross income multipliers and net income ratios

---

1. There are specific exceptions to appraisals of leased fee interests, such as assignments relating to real estate taxes.

2. Surveys of overall capitalization rates based on the market expectations of lenders and owners are available, but such data should be rigorously scrutinized.

- Band of investment—mortgage and equity components
- Band of investment—land and building components
- The debt coverage formula
- Yield capitalization techniques such as the general yield and change formula (R_O = yield – change in income and value) and the Ellwood method[3]

> **Overall capitalization rates may be derived** from comparable sales, effective gross income multipliers and net income ratios, band-of-investment or weighted-average techniques (based on mortgage and equity components with R_M and R_E or land and building components with R_L and R_B), debt coverage ratios (*DCR*s), and yield capitalization techniques.

The debt coverage formula and yield capitalization techniques can be used to estimate an overall rate or support rates derived from market sales. They are not primary methods of direct capitalization.

Derivation of R_O from Comparable Sales

Deriving capitalization rates from comparable sales is the preferred technique when sufficient data on sales of similar, competitive properties is available. Data on each property's sale price, income, expenses, financing terms, and market conditions at the time of sale is needed. In addition, the appraiser must make certain that the net operating income of each comparable property is calculated and estimated in the same way that the net operating income of the subject property is estimated; often the operating data available for comparable sale properties is from the year that ended just prior to the date of value, so the appraiser may have to explain (or adjust for) the time difference. Both the income and expense data (on the date of valuation plus the next 12 months) and the structure of expenses in terms of replacement allowances and other components should be similar to those of the subject. Moreover, neither non-market financing terms nor different market conditions should have affected the prices of the comparables. If the objective of the appraisal is to value the fee simple interest, incomes for the comparables analyzed must be at or around the level of market rent or adjustments will be necessary. If the value of the leased fee interest is being sought, the comparables must be leased in the same manner as the subject property or again adjustments will be required.

The overall level of risk associated with each comparable should be similar to that of the subject property. Risk can be analyzed by investigating the credit rating of the property's tenants, market conditions for the particular property, the stability of the property's income stream, and the property's upside or downside potential.

When these requirements are met, the appraiser can estimate an overall rate by dividing each property's net operating income by its sale price. Table

---

3. Readers interested in reviewing Ellwood mortgage-equity analysis may consult Appendix C or Charles B. Akerson, *Capitalization Theory and Techniques: Study Guide*, 2d ed. (Chicago: Appraisal Institute, 2000).

Table 22.2	Derivation of Overall Capitalization Rates From Comparable Sales

	Sale A	Sale B	Sale C	Sale D
Price	$368,500	$425,000	$310,000	$500,000
Net operating income	$35,000	$40,000	$30,500	$48,500
Indicated R_o	0.0950	0.0941	0.0984	0.0970

22.2 illustrates this procedure using data from four comparable sales. If all four transactions are equally reliable and comparable, the appraiser might conclude that an overall rate of 0.0941 to 0.0984 should be applied to the subject property. The final rate concluded depends on the appraiser's judgment as to how comparable each sale is to the subject property. For example, if Sales A and D are the most comparable, the rate chosen might be about 9.6%.

If there are differences between a comparable property and the subject property that could affect the overall capitalization rate concluded, the appraiser must account for these differences. In such cases the appraiser must decide whether the rate concluded for the subject property should be higher or lower than the rate indicated by a specific sale or group of sales. Appraisal judgment is also needed to determine whether the rate selected for the subject should fall within the range established by the sales or, as in certain cases, be set above or below the range. If there are wide differences between a comparable property and the subject property that could affect the overall capitalization rate, the appraiser must explain the market behavior or property characteristics that account for these differences.

When rates derived from comparable sales are used, the overall capitalization rate is applied to the subject property in a manner consistent with its derivation. In other words, if the market-derived capitalization rates are based on the properties' net operating income expectancies for the first year—i.e., date of sale through next 12 months—the capitalization rate for the subject property should be applied to its anticipated net operating income for the first year of operation.

The net income to be capitalized may be estimated before or after an annual allowance for specific replacement categories, e.g., the allowance for furniture, fixtures, and equipment for hotel properties and the replacement allowance for office properties.[4] Again, it is imperative that the appraiser analyze comparable sales and derive their capitalization rates in the same manner used to analyze the subject property and capitalize its income.

The following examples illustrate the importance of deriving and applying rates consistently. In the first example, the replacement allowance for the subject property is estimated to be $2,500. The overall rate indicated by comparable sales, in which a replacement allowance is not deducted as an

---

4.   In some markets, practitioners no longer deduct a replacement allowance as an above-the-line item in direct capitalization. Whenever this expense item is implicit in the capitalization rate, it should not be deducted in estimating the net operating income for a subject property.

operating expense, was 0.0850. In the second example, the replacement allowance is deducted as an operating expense, and the indicated overall rate becomes 0.0825. In the first calculation, the allowance is not included as an expense item for the subject property, so the net operating income there is $2,500 higher than in the second calculation. The valuation conclusions produced by the two calculations are identical.

With an Allowance for Replacements	
Net operating income	85,000
Overall rate	0.0850
Capitalization: $85,000/0.0850	$1,000,000

Without an Allowance for Replacements	
Net operating income	$82,500
Overall rate	0.0825
Capitalization: $82,500/0.0825	$1,000,000

Whether net operating income is estimated with or without an allowance for replacements, the overall capitalization rate is calculated by dividing net operating income by a comparable property's sale price. An overall capitalization rate provides compelling evidence of value when a series of conditions are met:

1. Data must be drawn from properties that are physically similar to the property being appraised and from similar (preferably competing) markets. Where significant differences exist for a given comparable, its indications are afforded less weight or may be discarded entirely.
2. Sale properties used as sources for calculating overall capitalization rates should have current (date of sale) and future market expectations, including income and expense patterns and likely value trends, that are comparable to those affecting the subject property.
3. Income and expenses must be estimated on the same basis for the subject property and all comparables properties.
4. The comparable property's price must reflect market terms, or an adjustment for cash equivalency must be possible.
5. If adjustments are considered necessary for differences between a comparable and the subject property, they should be made separately from the process of calculating the overall capitalization rate and should be based on market evidence.

Derivation of R_o from Effective Gross Income Multipliers

Sometimes an overall capitalization rate cannot be derived directly because the stringent data requirements cannot be met, but reliable transaction data and gross income data can be obtained from several comparable sales. In such cases an effective gross income multiplier can be derived and used in conjunction with a net income ratio (*NIR*) to produce an overall capitalization rate. The *NIR* is the complement of the operating expense ratio (*OER*); thus, *NIR* = 1 − *OER*. (The derivation of income multipliers is discussed later in this chapter.)

The net income ratio is the ratio of net operating income to effective gross income. Although effective gross income multipliers can be based on annual or monthly income, annual income is used unless otherwise specified. Monthly income is primarily used for single-family or small multifamily properties. Frequently, an appraiser can obtain marketwide averages of operating expense ratios as well as the effective gross income multipliers indicated by comparable sales. If a comparable is truly comparable to the subject, it may be appropriate to use the subject's net income ratio and the comparable's effective gross income multiplier to develop the rate.

The formula for deriving an overall capitalization rate from a net income ratio and an effective gross income multiplier is

$$R_o = \frac{NIR}{EGIM}$$

Returning to Table 22.2, consider Sale A, which was recently sold for $368,500. Assume the potential gross income of the property is $85,106 and its effective gross income is $80,000. The operating expense ratio of the property is 56.25%, so its operating expenses are $45,000 and its *NOI* is $35,000. The effective gross income multiplier is 4.6063 ($368,500/$80,000) and the net income ratio is 0.4375 ($35,000/$80,000). The overall capitalization rate extracted from the effective gross income multiplier of Sale A is

$$R_o = \frac{0.4375}{4.6063}$$
$$R_o = 0.09497, \text{ or } 9.5\%$$

After this calculation is performed for all the comparables, an estimated overall capitalization rate can be reconciled from the overall capitalization rate indications derived.

Derivation of R_o by Band of Investment—Mortgage and Equity

Because most properties are purchased with debt and equity capital, the overall capitalization rate must satisfy the market return requirements of both investment positions. Lenders must anticipate receiving a competitive interest rate commensurate with the perceived risk of the investment or they will not make funds available. Lenders generally require that the loan principal be repaid through periodic amortization payments. Similarly, equity investors must anticipate receiving a competitive equity cash return commensurate with the perceived risk, or they will invest their funds elsewhere.

The mortgage capitalization rate (R_M) is the ratio of the annual debt service to the principal amount of the mortgage loan. The rate established at the inception of a mortgage is commonly called the *mortgage constant*. The *annual mortgage constant* for a new loan is calculated by multiplying each period's payment by the number of payments per year and then dividing this amount by the amount of the loan. A *current mortgage constant* may also be calculated on the basis of the outstanding mortgage amount once debt service payments have been made. It should be noted that the mortgage capitalization rate (R_M) differs from the mortgage interest rate (Y_M). The mortgage interest rate, or *yield rate to the mortgage,* is the internal rate of return that equates the present value of the mortgage payments with the principal balance of the loan—i.e., the rate used to calculate the mortgage payment.

The mortgage capitalization rate is a function of the interest rate, the frequency of amortization, and the amortization term of the loan. It is the sum of the interest rate and the sinking fund factor. When the loan terms are known, the mortgage cap rate can be calculated using a financial calculator or any of a variety of computer software programs. (Mortgage capitalization rates can also be found in financial tables, but in everyday practice appraisers generally use calculators or computer software to perform such operations.)

The equity investor also seeks a systematic cash return. The rate used to capitalize equity income is called the *equity capitalization rate* (R_E). It is the ratio of annual equity dividend to the amount of equity investment. The equity capitalization rate may be more or less than the expected equity yield rate (Y_E) because the latter takes into account the effect of debt financing on the income received by the equity investor. For appraisal purposes, a property's equity capitalization rate is the anticipated cash

band of investment: A technique in which the capitalization rates attributable to components of a capital investment are weighted and combined to derive a weighted-average rate attributable to the total investment.

mortgage capitalization rate (R_M): The capitalization rate for debt; the ratio of the annual debt service to the principal amount of the mortgage loan. A mortgage capitalization rate may be calculated based on the initial mortgage amount or the outstanding mortgage amount. Also known as *annual constant.* (R_M = debt service/mortgage principal)

equity capitalization rate (R_E): An income rate that reflects the relationship between a single year's equity dividend and the initial equity investment; used to convert equity dividend into an equity value indication; also called the *cash on cash rate, cash flow rate,* or *equity dividend rate.* (R_E = equity dividend/equity invested)

equity yield rate (Y_E): A rate of return on equity capital as distinguished from the rate of return on debt capital (the interest rate); the equity investor's internal rate of return. The equity yield rate considers the effect of debt financing on the cash flow to the equity investor.

loan-to-value ratio (M): The ratio between a mortgage loan and the value of the property pledged as security, usually expressed as a percentage.

equity ratio (E): The ratio between the equity investment on a property and its total price; the fraction of the investment that is unencumbered by debt.

weighted average: An average in which each component is adjusted by a factor that reflects its relative importance to the whole; obtained by multiplying each component by its assigned weight, adding the products, and dividing the sum of the products by the sum of the weights.

flow to the equity investor divided by the initial equity investment, usually for the first year of the holding period.

The overall capitalization rate must satisfy both the mortgage capitalization rate requirement of the lender and the equity dividend requirement of the equity investor. For mortgage-equity analysis, it can be viewed as a composite rate, weighted in proportion to the total property investment represented by debt and equity. The overall capitalization rate is a weighted average of the mortgage capitalization rate (R_M) and equity capitalization rate (R_E). The loan-to-value ratio (M) represents the loan or debt portion of the property investment; the equity ratio (E) represents the equity portion of the property investment. The sum of E and M is 1, i.e., 100%. Typical mortgage terms and conditions may be obtained by surveying lenders active in the market area. Equity capitalization rates are derived from comparable sales by dividing the annual equity dividend of each sale by the equity investment. The equity capitalization rate used to capitalize the subject property's equity dividend ultimately depends on the appraiser's judgment as to how individual investors perceive the relationship between market value and investment value, especially in a market with fluctuating mortgage interest rates.

When the mortgage and equity capitalization rates are known, an overall rate may be derived with the band-of-investment, or weighted-average, technique using the following formulas:

Mortgage component	$M \times R_M =$ _____
Equity component	$E \times R_E = +$ _____
	$R_O =$ _____

To illustrate how the overall capitalization rate is calculated with the band-of-investment technique, assume that the following characteristics describe the subject property.

Available loan	75% ratio, 10.0% interest, 25-year amortization period (monthly payment), 0.1090 mortgage capitalization rate (R_M)
Equity capitalization rate	6.5% (derived from comparable sales)

The overall rate is calculated as follows:

$$R_O = (0.75 \times 0.1090) + (0.25 \times 0.0650)$$
$$= 0.0818 + 0.0163$$
$$= 0.0981$$

Although this technique can be used to derive overall capitalization rates, appraisers should be extremely careful when using it for this purpose. The technique is only applicable when sufficient market data is available to extract equity capitalization rates and when equity dividends are the primary investment criteria used by buyers and sellers. Typically, where sufficient market data is available, the R_O can be calculated directly, reducing the underlying usefulness of this technique. A capitalization rate used to develop an opinion of market value should be justified and supported by market data, but such data often is not available. When available market data is scarce or less reliable, mortgage-equity techniques may be used to test capitalization rates but not to develop them. Appraisers may develop information through interviews with market participants and from their own records, which can be pieced together for such tests. These indirect analyses are not substitutes for market data, but they can lead to valuable insights and understandings. The mortgage yield rate (Y_M) should not be used in place of the mortgage capitalization rate (R_M), nor should an equity yield rate (Y_E) be substituted for an equity capitalization rate (R_E).

Derivation of R_O by Band of Investment—Land and Building

A band of investment formula can also be applied to the physical components of property—i.e., the land or site and the buildings. Essentially this methodology is the same as the mortgage-equity technique, except that the elements are the physical property components. Just as weighted rates are developed for mortgage and equity components in mortgage-equity analysis, weighted rates for the land and buildings can be developed if accurate rates for these components can be estimated independently and the proportion of total property value represented by each component can be identified. The formula is

$$R_O = L \times R_L + B \times R_B$$

where L = land value as a percentage of total property value, R_L = land capitalization rate, B = building value as a percentage of total property value, and R_B = building capitalization rate.

Assume that the land represents 45% of the value of a property and the building represents the other 55%. The land capitalization rate derived from comparable sales data is 0.1025; the building capitalization rate is 0.1600. The indicated R_O is calculated as follows:

$$R_O = (0.45 \times 0.1025) + (0.55 \times 0.1600)$$
$$= 0.0461 + 0.0880$$
$$= 0.1341$$

Land and building capitalization rates may be extracted by applying residual analysis to improved properties. (Land and building residual techniques are illustrated later in this chapter.)

land capitalization rate (R_L)
1. The rate used to convert land income into an indication of land value when certain residual or band-of-investment techniques are applied.
2. The ratio of land income to land value.

building capitalization rate (R_B)
1. The rate used in certain residual techniques or in a band of investment to convert building income into an indication of building value.
2. The ratio of building income to building value.

Debt Coverage Formula

In addition to the traditional terms of lending—i.e., the interest rate, loan-to-value ratio, amortization term, maturity, and payment period—real estate lenders sometimes use another judgment criteria: the debt coverage ratio (*DCR*). This is the ratio of net operating income to annual debt service (I_M), or the payment that covers interest on and retirement of the outstanding principal of the mortgage loan:

$$DCR = \frac{NOI}{I_M}$$

The debt coverage ratio is frequently used by institutional lenders, who are generally fiduciaries who manage and lend the money of others, including depositors and policyholders. Because of their fiduciary responsibility, institutional lenders are particularly sensitive to the safety of loan investments, especially the safety of principal. They are concerned with safety and profit and are anxious to avoid default and possible foreclosure. Consequently, when they underwrite loans on income-producing property, institutional lenders try to provide a cushion so that the borrower will likely be able to meet the debt service obligations on the loan even if building income declines.

> **debt coverage ratio (DCR):** The ratio of net operating income to annual debt service ($DCR = NOI / I_M = I_O / I_M$); measures the ability of a property to meet its debt service out of net operating income; also called *debt service coverage ratio* (*DSCR*).
>
> **debt service (I_M):** The periodic payment that covers the interest on, and retirement of, the outstanding principal of the mortgage loan; also called *mortgage debt service*.

To estimate an overall rate, the debt coverage ratio can be multiplied by the mortgage capitalization rate and the loan-to-value ratio. The method should only be applied, however, if the property is at stabilized occupancy. Lenders sometimes refer to overall capitalization rates derived by this method as *in-house capitalization rates*. The formula is

$$R_O = DCR \times R_M \times M$$

For a property with net operating income of $50,000 and annual debt service of $43,264, the debt coverage ratio is calculated as

$$DCR = \frac{\$50,000}{\$43,264}$$
$$= 1.1557$$

If R_M equals 0.1090 and M is 0.75, R_O is estimated as

$$R_O = 1.1557 \times 0.1090 \times 0.75$$
$$= 0.0945$$

With this method lenders can use market data to check on the reasonableness of capitalization rates derived from comparables and internal evaluation guidelines.

Residual Techniques

Residual techniques are based on the same basic premises as those that apply to direct capitalization rates. However, while an overall rate processes the entire net operating income into a value indication, the residual techniques separate net operating income into various components. These include the income attributable to physical components (land and building residuals) and financial components (mortgage and

> **residual techniques:** Procedures used to capitalize the income allocated to an investment component of unknown value after all investment components of known values have been satisfied; may be applied to a property's physical components (land and building), financial interests (mortgage and equity), or legal estates (leased fee and leasehold).

equity residuals). Although these components can be appraised by applying yield capitalization techniques, in direct capitalization only the first year's net operating income for each component is included in the analysis. The application of residual techniques is only justified if the inferences on which the techniques are based can be made reasonably.

Regardless of which known and unknown (residual) components of the property are being analyzed, the appraiser starts with the value of the known items and the net operating income, as shown in Table 22.3. The appraiser

1. Applies an appropriate capitalization rate to the value of the known component to derive the annual income needed to support the investment in that component

Table 22.3   **Known and Unknown Variables in Residual Calculations**

Residual Technique	Known	Unknown
Land residual	Net operating income (*NOI*) Building value (V_B) Building capitalization rate (R_B) Land capitalization rate (R_L)	Land or site value (V_L)
Building residual	Net operating income (*NOI*) Land or site value (V_L) Land capitalization rate (R_L) Building capitalization rate (R_B)	Building value (V_B)
Mortgage residual	Net operating income (*NOI*) Amount of equity (V_E) Equity capitalization rate (R_E) Mortgage capitalization rate (R_M)	Mortgage amount (V_M)
Equity residual	Net operating income (*NOI*) Mortgage amount (V_M) Mortgage capitalization rate (R_M) Equity capitalization rate (R_E)	Amount of equity (V_E)

2.   Deducts the annual income needed to support the investment in the known component from the net operating income to derive the residual income available to support the investment in the unknown component

3.   Capitalizes the residual income at a capitalization rate appropriate to the investment in the residual component to derive the present value of this component

4.   Adds the values of the known component and the residual component to derive a value indication for the total property

Residual techniques allow an appraiser to capitalize the income allocated to an investment component of unknown value after other investment components of known value have been satisfied. They can be applied to the physical components of a property (land and building) or to the financial components of a property (mortgage and equity). Residual techniques are based on specific assumptions. If these assumptions are unreasonable, application of the residual technique is not justified. The usefulness of the building residual and mortgage residual techniques is extremely limited.

Prior to the publication of *The Ellwood Tables* in 1959, the physical residual techniques (land and building) were the dominant methods for valuing real estate. L. W. Ellwood's contribution to the income capitalization approach changed the practice of appraisal in several ways:

- Prior to *The Ellwood Tables*, appraisers generally considered all market value transactions to reflect cash transfers between the buyer and the seller with no provision for financing. Ellwood recognized that most market transactions involved cash to the seller but were financed in part with some form of debt or other financial consideration on the part of the buyer. His view was that each component—mortgage and equity— could be analyzed separately in the context of a given property.

- Ellwood promoted the simple understanding that choosing an alternate method—direct capitalization or yield capitalization—did not produce a different result; as long as market rates appropriate to the method were applied, the same result would be produced.

- Ellwood emphasized that the concept of the present worth of anticipated future benefits provides that if it is possible to construct a cash flow statement for any given time horizon, it is possible to use some form of discounting in the capitalization process. This realization permitted appraisers and investors to consider more precisely the anticipated benefits of a given property and to avoid using direct capitalization to analyze a single year's income, which might be less precise. Ellwood said, "Two years are better than just one," and that even a five-year analysis was feasible for most income-producing properties.

- Until *The Ellwood Tables*, most appraisers focused on land and building components (or at times on leases and the analysis of natural resources).

Ellwood added the consideration of mortgage and equity components, not as a substitute, but to provide another dimension to the analysis.

- Ellwood did not limit his concept to market value alone. Instead he provided an analytical framework in which specific anticipations or specific assumptions could be tested and the results applied to either opinions of market value or other aspects of property financial analysis.

- Although Ellwood is most often credited with adding new consider-ations to real property appraisal analysis, he also clarified, refocused, and brought new understanding to the fundamental appraisal methods and techniques that had been applied for many years. In this way, he helped overcome errors and abuses in traditional practices while adding new techniques.

The development of computerized discounted cash flow analyses in professional appraisal practice has largely supplanted the use of residual techniques, except when the data needed to apply more sophisticated tech-niques is not available. Today residual techniques are used primarily in specialized situations—e.g., in highest and best use analysis as a test of financial feasibility. Nevertheless, residual analysis remains a fundamental component of appraisal theory with which a well-rounded appraiser should be familiar.

Building Residual Technique

An appraiser who applies the building residual technique assumes that land or site value can be estimated independently. The technique is especially applicable when data on land values and land rents is available to establish land capitaliza-tion rates. The appraiser applies the land capitalization rate to the known land value to obtain the amount of annual net income needed to support the land value. Then this amount is deducted from the net operating income to derive the residual income available to support the investment in the building(s). The appraiser capitalizes this residual income at the building capitalization rate to derive an indication of the present value of the building(s). Finally, the land value and the building value are added to derive an indication of total property value. The land and building capitalization rates derived from the market are then applied to the subject property.

For example, consider a small ware-house with an estimated land value of $200,000. Analysis of several sales of comparable sites reveals a land capitalization rate of 9% and an 11% building capitaliza-

building residual technique: A capitalization technique in which the net operating income attributable to improvements is isolated and capitalized by the building capitalization rate (R_B) to indicate the improvements' contribu-tion to total property value. When the improvements' value is added to land value, a total property value estimate is produced.

land residual technique: A method of estimating land value in which the net operating income attributable to the land is isolated and capitalized to produce an indication of the land's contribution to the total property.

tion rate. (Techniques for calculating capitalization rates for residual components are illustrated later in the chapter.) The net operating income of the subject property is estimated to be $65,500. Using the building residual technique, the value of the subject property is calculated as follows:

Estimated land value		$200,000
Net operating income	$67,500	
Less income attributable to land		
Land value × R_L ($200,000 × 0.09)	− 18,000	
Residual income to building	$49,500	
Building value (capitalized: $49,500 / 0.11)		+ 450,000
Indicated property value		$650,000

This technique is simple, but its applicability and usefulness are limited. Depending on the particular market, the building residual technique may or may not reflect the way purchaser-investors regard investment real estate. It is also extremely difficult to apply when the income projection is shorter than the remaining economic life of the improvements, and the reversion consequently represents more than simply the value of the site.

When the required data is available, the building residual technique can be used to value properties with improvements that have suffered substantial depreciation. In fact, current reproduction or replacement cost minus the present value of the improvements provides an estimate of total depreciation. In addition, the building residual technique directly measures the contribution of the improvements to total property value, so it can help an appraiser determine when demolition or major renovation of property improvements is economically feasible or, if appropriate, help establish the tax basis for depreciation of the improvements.

Land Residual Technique

The land residual technique assumes that the value of the building (or buildings) can be estimated separately. In land residual applications, an appraiser will often consider a new highest and best use assuming a building that does not exist. Thus, building value is usually estimated as the current cost to construct a new building that represents the highest and best use of the land or site.

The building capitalization rate is applied to the building value to obtain the amount of annual net income needed to support the value of the building. This amount is then deducted from net operating income to indicate the residual income available to support the investment in the land. The residual income is capitalized at the land capitalization rate to derive an indication of the value of the land. Finally, the building value is added to the land value to derive an indication of total property value.

Using the same data as in the building residual example but assuming that building value rather than land value is known, the problem is calculated from the opposite viewpoint. The land and building capitalization rates derived from the market are applied to the subject property as follows:

Estimated building value		$450,000
Net operating income	$67,500	
Less income attributable to the building		
Building value × R_B ($450,000 × 0.11)	− 49,500	
Residual income to land	$18,000	
Land value (capitalized: $18,000 / 0.09)		+ 200,000
Indicated property value		$650,000

The land residual technique allows an appraiser to estimate land values when recent data on land sales is not available. In practice, the technique is used often as a test of the highest and best use of the land or site for proposed construction. It can also be used to provide a value indication for new structures that do not suffer from depreciation. However, the land residual technique is not as applicable when the cost to produce a new building is inconsistent with the amount of value such a building would contribute to property value.

Equity Residual Technique

To apply the equity residual technique, an appraiser deducts annual debt service from net operating income to obtain the residual income to the equity interest. An appraiser who uses this technique must be able to obtain mortgage loan terms from the market and estimate the dollar amount of the debt. To derive a market equity capitalization rate, the appraiser may apply the following process:

Sale property net operating income	$60,000
Less mortgage debt service	
$375,000 loan, 10% interest, 25-year term	
$375,000 × 0.10904* =	− 40,890
Residual income to equity	$19,110
Equity investment	$212,333
Equity capitalization rate	
$19,110 / $212,333	0.09, or 9%

* Annual constant R_M for monthly loan payment from precomputed tables; a financial calculator or computer can also be used to calculate the present value of annual debt service.

For a similar property with comparable characteristics, the 9% equity capitalization rate can be divided into the equity income to develop an indication of equity value. When added to the mortgage amount, an indication of property value is produced.

Mortgage Residual Technique

When the mortgage residual technique is applied, the amount of available equity is the known component and the mortgage amount or value is unknown. The income needed to satisfy the equity component at the equity capitalization rate is deducted from the net operating income to obtain the residual income to the mortgage component. The residual mortgage income is then capitalized into value at the mortgage capitalization rate. The preceding example on equity residual capitalization can be approached from the opposite side of the equation to illustrate mortgage residual technique calculations:

Available equity		$212,333
Net operating income	$60,000	
Equity × R_E ($212,333 × 0.09)	− 19,110	
Residual income to mortgage	$40,890	
Mortgage value		
(capitalized: $40,890 / 0.10904)		+ 375,000
Indicated property value		$587,333

The mortgage residual technique works as a mathematical process, but it does not follow the customary logic of market participants. Its most common use is in determining the amount of mortgage available and the associated value requirement. However, the technique assumes that the amount of funds the equity investor is willing to invest in the property has already been determined and that the investor requires a specified equity dividend rate from the property. This implies that the loan amount depends on the residual cash flow available for mortgage debt service and the mortgage capitalization rate. Lenders are generally unwilling to make a loan unless net operating income exceeds the mortgage debt service by a specified amount. Also, once the loan is made, the lender has the legal right to receive the agreed-upon debt service, but any residual cash flow goes to the equity investor. Even with below-market loans, the equity investor gets income remaining after payment of the contract interest. Thus, the mortgage residual technique does not reflect market behavior and would not normally be appropriate for estimating the value of a property subject to a specific mortgage.

Deriving a Building Capitalization Rate

The appraiser must find support for one or more of the rates used in each of residual techniques and then must solve for the unknown rate. Consider the following examples of extracting a building capitalization rate:

Example 1. A nearby property with the same use recently sold for $750,000. The land was purchased for $230,000 and the improvements were constructed within the past year. Based on its design and construction materials, the improvements are expected to have a remaining economic life of 50 years. First-year net operating income is expected to be $77,900. Rate extraction is performed as follows:

Sale price	$750,000
Less land value	− 230,000
Indicated building value	$520,000
Annual recapture with 50-year economic life	× 2%
Annual recapture in dollars	$10,400
Net operating income	$77,900
Less annual recapture	− 10,400
Annual interest earnings	$67,500
Interest rate on land and building investment	
$67,500 / $750,000 =	0.09, or 9%
Building capitalization rate	
0.09 + 0.02 =	0.11, or 11%

Example 2. A similar property in the same area just sold in a sale-leaseback transaction. After acquiring land and constructing a building for their own use, the sellers sold the completed property to a buyer who then leased the property to its original owners for a 25-year term with options to renew. The land was acquired for $200,000 and a $400,000 building was constructed. The buyer paid $600,000 for the property and leased it back to the sellers for $59,000 per year, with the tenant paying all taxes, insurance, maintenance, and other costs. In the market, land leases of similar sites typically require an 8.5% rent rate for 25-year terms. The building is expected to have a 50-year economic life. Rate extraction is performed as follows:

Total rent		$59,000
Less land rent ($200,000 × 8.5%)		− 17,000
Indicated annual building rent		$42,000
Less indicated annual building recapture		
$400,000 × 2%		− 8,000
Indicated annual building income		$34,000
Annual land rent	$17,000	
Plus indicated annual building income	+ 34,000	
Total annual interest earnings		$51,000
Annual interest rate on land and building investment		
$51,000 / $600,000 =		0.085, or 8.5%

Note that the appraiser must recognize that this procedure is actually a lease analysis, not an analysis of the land and building alone. For example, the lease calls for a renewal in 25 years. If there is no renewal, the buyer will receive an additional "income" in the amount of the value of the property in 25 years. If there is a renewal, the buyer will receive additional benefits that depend on the terms of the renewal. Thus, the 8.5% annual interest rate is actually a return on the terms of the lease contract and, in this instance, will probably underestimate the land and building rates. Although this calculation does not produce land and building rates for capitalization purposes, it may be used as an additional consideration in conjunction with more definitive market data.

Example 3. A five-year-old building constituting leasehold improvements just sold. The property is nearby and has a similar use to the property being appraised. The improvements at the time of construction had an expected remaining economic life of 50 years, and there have been no significant market changes or building alterations over the past five years. Market data indicates that if the property were owned by a single owner, it would likely have a market value of $700,000. An overall capitalization rate of 10.5% would apply to the land and building combined. The improvements sold for $485,000 at the same time that the business operating on the property was sold. The new owner must pay land rent of $19,350. Rate extraction is performed as follows:

Indicated property value		$700,000
Less sale price of the improvements		− 485,000
Indicated land value		$215,000
Sale price of the improvements		$485,000
Remaining economic life	45 years	
Recapture rate	1 / 45 =	× 0.022
Annual recapture in dollars		$10,670
Indicated property value		$700,000
Overall capitalization rate		× 0.105
Indicated property income		$73,500
Less annual recapture in dollars		− 10,670
Annual interest on land and building		$62,830
Interest rate of land and improvements		
$62,830 / $700,000 =		0.09, or 9%
Building capitalization rate		
0.09 + 0.022 =		0.112, or 11.2%

The **application of income multipliers** is also a direct capitalization procedure. In developing an income or rent multiplier, it is essential that the income or rent of the properties used to derive the multiplier is comparable to that of the subject and that the specific multiplier derived be applied to the same income base.

gross income multiplier (GIM): The relationship or ratio between the sale price or value of a property and its gross income from rent and other income sources.

potential gross income multiplier (PGIM): The ratio between the sale price of a property and its potential gross income ($PGIM = V / PGI$).

effective gross income multiplier (EGIM): The ratio between the sale price (or value) of a property and its effective gross income; a single year's EGI expectancy or an annual average of several years' EGI expectancies ($EGIM = V / EGI$).

Gross Income Multipliers

Gross income multipliers (*GIM*s) are used to compare the income-producing characteristics of properties. Potential or effective gross income may be converted into an opinion of value by applying the relevant gross income multiplier. This method of capitalization is mathematically related to direct capitalization because rates are the reciprocals of multipliers or factors. Therefore, it is appropriate to discuss the derivation and use of multipliers under direct capitalization.

To derive a gross income multiplier from market data, sales of properties that were rented at the time of sale or were anticipated to be rented within a short time must be available. The ratio of the sale price of a property to its annual gross income at the time of sale or projected over the first year of ownership is the gross income multiplier.

Appraisers who attempt to derive and apply gross income multipliers for valuation purposes must be careful for several reasons. First, the properties analyzed must be comparable to the subject property and to one another in terms of physical, locational, and investment characteristics. Properties with similar or even identical multipliers can have very different operating expense ratios and, therefore, may not be comparable for valuation purposes.

Second, the term *gross income multiplier* is used because some of the gross income from a property or type of property may come from sources other than rent. A *gross rent multiplier* applies to rental income only.

Third, the appraiser must use similar income data to derive the multiplier for each transaction. For example, *GIM*s extracted from full-service rentals would not be applied to a subject property leased on a net basis. The sale price can be divided by either the potential or effective gross income, but the data and measure must be used consistently throughout the analysis to produce reliable results. Different income measures may be used in different valuation studies and appraisals, however. The income measure selected is dictated by the availability of market data and the purpose of the analysis.

To illustrate the difference between various gross income multipliers, the following calculations are made using data for Sale A in Table 22.2. Note that in the discussion following Table 22.2, potential gross income was assumed to be $85,106 and the effective gross income was $80,000.

$$\text{Potential gross income multiplier} = \frac{\text{sale price}}{\text{potential gross income}}$$

$$= \frac{\$368,500}{\$85,106}$$

$$= 4.33 \text{ (rounded)}$$

$$\text{Effective gross income multiplier} = \frac{\text{sale price}}{\text{effective gross income}}$$

$$= \frac{\$368,500}{\$80,000}$$

$$= 4.61 \text{ (rounded)}$$

After the gross income multiplier is derived from comparable market data, it must be applied on the same basis it was derived. In other words, an income multiplier based on effective gross income can only be applied to the effective gross income of the subject property; an income multiplier based on potential gross income can only be applied to the potential gross income of the subject property. The timing of income also must be comparable. If sales are analyzed using next year's income expectation, the multiplier derived must be applied to next year's income expectation for the subject property.

FURTHER READING

Akerson, Charles B. *The Appraiser's Workbook.* 2d ed. Chicago: Appraisal Institute, 1996.

____. *Capitalization Theory and Techniques: Study Guide.* 2d ed. Chicago: Appraisal Institute, 2000.

American Institute of Real Estate Appraisers. *Forecasting: Market Determinants Affecting Cash Flows and Reversions.* Research Series Report 4. Chicago, 1989.

____. *Readings in the Income Capitalization Approach to Real Property Valuation,* Volume II. Chicago, 1985.

Fisher, Clifford E., Jr. *Rates and Ratios Used in the Income Capitalization Approach.* Chicago: Appraisal Institute, 1995.

Mason, James J., ed. and comp. *AIREA Financial Tables.* Chicago: American Institute of Real Estate Appraisers, 1981.

CHAPTER 23

Yield Capitalization— Theory and Basic Applications

Yield capitalization is the second fundamental method used in the income capitalization approach to value. Various techniques are available within this methodology for converting a series of future cash flows over time into an opinion of value.

Yield capitalization is used to convert future benefits into an indication of present value by applying an appropriate yield rate. To select an appropriate yield rate for a market value appraisal, an appraiser analyzes market evidence of the yields anticipated by typical investors and/or supported by market sales data. When investment value is sought, the yield rate used should reflect the individual investor's requirements, which may differ from the requirements of typical investors in the market.

To perform yield capitalization, an appraiser

1. Selects an appropriate holding or study period
2. Forecasts all future cash flows or cash flow patterns (including the reversion)
3. Chooses an appropriate yield rate
4. Converts future benefits into present value by discounting each annual future benefit or by developing an overall rate that reflects the income pattern, value change, and yield rate using one of the various yield formulas

The application of capitalization rates that reflect an appropriate yield rate, the use of present value factors, and discounted cash flow analysis are all yield capitalization procedures. Mortgage-equity formulas and yield rate or value change formulas may be used to derive overall capitalization rates.

Like direct capitalization, yield capitalization should reflect market behavior. To apply the discounting procedure, the appraiser must be familiar with the following concepts and techniques:

*   Income patterns
*   Capital return concepts
*   The mathematics of the discounting process

> **Yield capitalization** is used to convert future benefits, typically a periodic income stream and reversion, into present value by discounting each future benefit at an appropriate yield rate or by applying an overall rate (extracted using one of the yield methods) that explicitly reflects the investment's income pattern, change in value, and yield rate.

In yield capitalization, an appraiser 1) selects an appropriate **holding period**; 2) forecasts all future **cash flows** or cash flow patterns (including the reversion); 3) selects the appropriate **yield rate**; and 4) converts **future benefits** into present value by discounting each annual future benefit or applying an overall rate that reflects the income pattern, value change, and yield rate ($R_O = Y_O - \Delta a$).

yield capitalization: The capitalization method used to convert future benefits into present value by discounting each future benefit at an appropriate yield rate or by developing an overall rate that explicitly reflects the investment's income pattern, value change, and yield rate.

discounting: A procedure used to convert periodic incomes, cash flows, and reversions into present value; based on the concept that benefits received in the future are worth less than the same benefits received now.

- Investor requirements or expectations—i.e., holding period, anticipated market growth, and inflation
- The appropriateness of the selected yield rate

Discounting

Discounting is a general term used to describe the process of converting future cash flows into a present value. The discount rate is the interest rate used for the discounting process and may be the discount rate, property yield rate, equity yield rate, or some other defined rate. In real estate appraisal practice, the most common total bundle of rights methodology used is the property yield rate (Y_O).

In the discounting process, periodic incomes and the final reversion are converted into present value through discounting, a procedure based on the concept that benefits received in the future are worth less than the same benefits received today. The return on an investment compensates the investor for foregoing present benefits—i.e., the immediate use of capital—and accepting future benefits and risks. This return is usually called *interest* by lenders and *yield* by equity investors. The discounting procedure includes the expectation that the return of capital will be accomplished through periodic income, the final reversion, or a combination of the two.

An investor seeks a total return that exceeds the amount invested. The present value of a prospective benefit must be less than its expected future benefits. A future payment is discounted to present value by calculating the amount that, if invested today, would grow with compound interest at a

THE NATURE OF ANNUITIES

Although the word *annuity* means an annual income, it is used to refer to a program or contract specifying regular payments of stipulated amounts. Payments need not be annual, but the interval between payments is usually regular. An annuity can be level, increasing, or decreasing, but the amounts must be scheduled and predictable. Income characterized as an annuity is expected at regular intervals and in predictable amounts. Obviously real estate income or rental income can have the characteristics of an annuity. Monthly mortgage payments are perhaps the best example of an annuity. The pattern of income expected from a real estate investment may be regular or irregular. Various capitalization techniques have been developed to apply to a wide range of income patterns.

satisfactory rate to equal the future payment. In other words, discounting of a future benefit uses the reciprocal of the growth of compound interest. The standard formula for discounting future value to present value is

$$\text{Present value} = \frac{\text{Future value}}{(1+i)^n}$$

where i is the rate of return on capital per period (or the discount rate) that will satisfy the investor and n is the number of periods that the payment will be deferred. If a series of future payments is expected, each payment is discounted with the standard formula, and the present value of the payments is the sum of all the present values. The yield formula is expressed as

$$PV = \frac{CF_1}{1+Y} + \frac{CF_2}{(1+Y)^2} + \frac{CF_3}{(1+Y)^3} + \ldots + \frac{CF_n}{(1+Y)^n}$$

where PV = present value; CF = the cash flow for the period specified; Y = the appropriate periodic yield rate; and n = the number of periods in the projection. This standard discounting procedure is the foundation for all present value calculations.[1]

The amount deposited or received can be in the form of a single lump sum, a series of periodic installments such as rental income, or a combination of both. When amounts are compounded or discounted, the rate used is the effective interest rate; on an annual basis, this rate is identical to the nominal interest rate. If amounts are compounded or discounted more often than annually—e.g., semiannually or monthly—the nominal interest rate is divided by the number of compounding or discounting periods. For example, a nominal rate of 12% is an effective rate of 6% for semiannual conversion periods, or an effective rate of 1% for monthly conversions. Standard tables of factors or financial calculators can be used to facilitate the application of factors, but the user must select the appropriate conversion frequency—i.e., monthly, quarterly, or annually.

All present value problems consider the following:

1. The initial starting cost, value, or investment
2. The periodic cash flows over time
3. The reversion or resale value
4. The yield rate that equates the cash flows and reversion to the initial starting value

effective interest rate (*i*): Interest per dollar per period; the nominal annual interest rate divided by the number of conversion periods per year; also, the lender's yield to maturity, which in many instances is equivalent to the lender's internal rate of return; also called *effective rate.*

nominal interest rate (*I*): A stated or contract rate; an interest rate, usually annual, that does not necessarily correspond to the true or effective rate of growth at compound interest; e.g., a true or effective 1% monthly interest rate may be called a nominal annual interest rate of 12%, although true growth with monthly compounding amounts to slightly more than 12.68% per year.

1. For formulas, tables, and sample applications of the six functions of $1, see Appendix C.

discounted cash flow (DCF) analysis:
The procedure in which a discount rate is applied to a set of projected income streams and a reversion. The analyst specifies the quantity, variability, timing, and duration of the income streams as well as the quantity and timing of the reversion and discounts each to its present value at a specified yield rate. DCF analysis can be applied with any yield capitalization technique and may be performed on either a lease-by-lease or aggregate basis.

cash flow: The periodic income attributable to the interests in real property.

Because each individual cash flow is considered separately, a discounted cash flow (DCF) analysis can be used to solve any present value problem when three of the four factors are known.

In DCF analysis the quantity, variability, timing, and duration of cash flows are specified. *Cash flow* refers to the periodic income attributable to the interests in real property. Each cash flow is discounted to present value and all the present values are totaled to obtain the value of the real property interest being appraised. The future value of that interest, the reversion, is forecast at the end of the study period—i.e., the holding period or remaining economic life—and is also discounted. The cash flows discounted with the DCF process may be the net operating income to the entire property or the cash flows to specific interests—e.g., the cash flows to the equity interest (equity dividends), or debt service for the mortgage interest.

With the DCF process an appraiser can discount each payment of income and the reversion separately and add all the present values together to obtain the present value of the property interest being appraised. The formula treats the reversion as a cash flow that can be valued separately from the income stream. The formula can be used to develop opinions of

- Total property value (V_O)
- Loan value (V_M)
- Equity value (V_E)
- Leased fee value (V_{LF})
- Leasehold value (V_{LH})
- The value of any other interest in real property

Any series of periodic incomes, with or without a reversion, can be valued with the basic DCF formula. A wide range of formulas are available for valuing level annuities and increasing and decreasing annuities, which are introduced later in this chapter. These formulas have two benefits. First, they can be used as shortcuts to solve for property value, although if used as shortcuts they may be harder for the appraiser to explain and for the client to understand. More importantly, they provide a systematic methodology to evaluate real estate and the interactions of current value, income flows, and future value in a single problem-solving framework.

Most often financial calculators or computer spreadsheets are used to solve discounting problems mathematically. Each precomputed factor has specific, built-in investment expectations (level income, etc.) that are implied when the table is used or the factor is calculated. Therefore, the appraiser must identify the expectations applicable to the subject property and use the factor table or yield formula that corresponds to these expectations. Thus, to apply compounding or discounting procedures, the appraiser must know

- The basic formulas
- How the various factors relate to one another
- How they may be used or combined to apply yield capitalization and derive an indication of value

Spreadsheets and standardized tables and factors are useful in solving various yield capitalization problems. However, in the final analysis, an opinion of value and conclusions about time, amount, and yield reflect the appraiser's judgment based on appropriate research of the subject property and the relevant market data.

Estimation of a Yield Rate for Discounting

The estimation of an appropriate yield rate is critical to DCF analysis. To select an appropriate rate an appraiser must verify and interpret the attitudes and expectations of market participants, including buyers, sellers, advisers, and brokers. Although the actual yield or internal rate of return on an investment cannot be calculated until the investment is sold, an investor may set a target yield for the investment before or during ownership. Historical yield rates derived from comparable sales may be relevant, but they reflect past, not future, benefits in the mind of the investor and may not be reliable indicators of current yield. Therefore, the estimation of yield rates for discounting cash flows should focus on the prospective or forecast yield rates anticipated by typical buyers and sellers of comparable investments. An appraiser can verify investor expectations directly, by interviewing the parties to comparable sales transactions, or indirectly, by estimating the income expectancy and likely reversion for a comparable property and deriving a prospective yield rate.

The appraiser narrows the range of indicated yield rates and selects an appropriate rate by comparing the physical, economic, financial, and risk characteristics of the comparable properties with the property being appraised and assessing the competition for capital in other rival investments. In some situations there may be reason to select a yield rate above or below the indicated range. The final estimation of a yield rate requires judgment, just as an appraiser uses judgment to select an overall rate or equity capitalization rate from the range indicated by comparable sales. In selecting a yield rate, the appraiser should analyze current conditions in capital and real estate markets and the actions, perceptions, and expectations of real estate investors.

Different Rates

Yield rates are primarily a function of perceived risks. Different portions of forecast future income may have different levels of risk and therefore different yield rates.[2] In lease valuation, for example, one rate might be applied to discount the series of net rental incomes stipulated in the lease and a different rate might be applied to discount the reversion. One rate reflects the creditworthiness of the tenant as well as the benefits, constraints, and limitations of the lease contract, while the other is subject to free, open-market conditions. The decision to apply a single yield rate to all benefits or to apply different rates to different benefits should be based on investors' actions in the market and the methodology used to extract the yield rate. In all cases the rate should be applied in the same way it was extracted.

Income Stream Patterns

After specifying the amount, timing, and duration of the cash flows to the property interest being appraised, the appraiser should identify the pattern that the income stream is expected to follow during the holding period. These patterns may be grouped into the following basic categories:

- Variable annuity (irregular income pattern)
- Level annuity
- Increasing or decreasing annuity

Variable Annuity: Nonsystematic Change

In a variable annuity, payment amounts may vary in each period. To value a variable annuity, the present value of each income payment is calculated separately and these values are totaled to obtain the present value of the entire income stream. This procedure is discounted cash flow analysis.

> **Rental income** is similar to an **annuity**. Real estate income streams may conform to the pattern of 1) a variable annuity, 2) a level annuity, or 3) a regularly increasing or decreasing annuity reflecting either a) levels of step-up/step-down change, b) straight-line change per period, or c) exponential-curve change per period.

Any income stream can be valued as if it were a variable annuity. Level annuities and annuities that change systematically are subsets or regular patterns of income that can also be handled with special formulas that reflect the systematic pattern of the income stream. These shortcut formulas can save time and effort in certain cases, but

---

2.   When future events that could profoundly impact the income-producing potential of a property may or may not occur, probability analysis may be appropriate. Probability analysis is frequently required when properties are subject to potential environmental hazards and compliance with environmental regulations is pending. For example, a site may require an undetermined level of environmental remediation, the remediation required may or may not be completed within a given time frame, or the environmental regulation(s) governing the remediation may be modified. In such situations, probability analysis can help an appraiser develop a yield rate.

valuing an income stream as a variable annuity with a calculator or computer program may be just as easy and will result in the same conclusion.

Level Annuity

A level annuity is an income stream in which the amount of each payment is the same; it is a level, unchanging flow of income over time. The payments in a level annuity are equally spaced and regularly scheduled. There are two types of level annuities:

- Ordinary annuities
- Annuities payable in advance

> **variable annuity:** An income stream in which the payment amounts vary per period. A variable annuity is characteristic of one kind of income model and one kind of property model.
>
> **level annuity:** An income stream in which the amount of each payment is the same; a level, unchanging flow of income over time.
>
> **ordinary annuity:** A common type of level annuity in which income payments are received at the end of each period.
>
> **annuity payable in advance:** A type of level annuity; similar to an ordinary annuity except that payments are received at the beginning of each period.

Ordinary Annuity

An ordinary annuity, which is the most common type of level annuity, is distinguished by income payments that are received at the end of each period. Standard fixed-payment mortgage loans, many corporate and government bonds, endowment policies, and certain lease arrangements are ordinary annuities.

Annuity Payable in Advance

An annuity payable in advance is a level annuity in which the payments are received at the beginning of each period. A lease that requires payments at the beginning of each month, such as most apartment leases, creates an annuity payable in advance. Level annuities can be discounted in the same manner as variable annuities. However, compound interest tables simplify the calculation for level income patterns, while providing an identical result.

Increasing or Decreasing Annuity

An income stream that is expected to change in a systematic pattern is either an increasing annuity or a decreasing annuity. Appraisers encounter three basic patterns of systematic change:

1. Step-up and step-down annuities
2. Straight-line (constant-amount) change per period annuities
3. Exponential-curve (constant-ratio) change per period annuities

> **increasing or decreasing annuity:** An income stream of evenly spaced, periodic payments that is expected to increase in a systematic pattern.
>
> **step-up or step-down annuity:** A type of increasing or decreasing annuity, usually created by a lease contract that calls for a succession of level annuities of different amounts to be paid in different periods of the lease term.

Step-Up and Step-Down Annuities

A step-up or step-down annuity is usually created by a lease contract that calls for a succession of level annuities of different amounts to be paid in different periods of the lease term. For example, a lease might call for monthly payments of $500 for the first three years, $750 for the next four years, and $1,200 for the next six years. Over the 13-year term of the lease, there are three successive level annuities—one for three years, one for four years, and one for six years.

> **straight-line (constant-amount) change per period:** Refers to a type of annuity or income/property model that increases by a fixed amount per period; also called *constant amount change per period.*
>
> **exponential-curve (constant-ratio) change per period:** Refers to a type of annuity or income/property model that increases or decreases at a constant ratio and, as a result, the increases or decreases are compounded.

Straight-Line (Constant-Amount) Change per Period Annuity

An income stream that increases or decreases by a fixed amount each period fits the pattern of a straight-line (constant-amount) change per period annuity. These income streams are also called *straight-line increasing* or *straight-line decreasing annuities.* For example, a property may have an estimated first-year net operating income of $100,000 that is forecast to increase by $7,000 per year. Thus, the second year's net operating income will be $107,000, the third year's net operating income will be $114,000, and so forth. Similarly, the income stream of a straight-line decreasing annuity is expected to decrease by a constant amount each period.

Exponential-Curve (Constant-Ratio) Change per Period Annuity

An income stream with an exponential-curve (constant-ratio) change per period is also referred to as an *exponential annuity.* This type of income stream increases or decreases at a constant ratio and therefore the increases or decreases are compounded. For example, a property with an estimated first-year equity dividend of $100,000 that is forecast to increase 7% per year over each preceding year's cash flow will have an equity dividend in the second year of $107,000 ($100,000 × 1.07). However, the third year's equity dividend will be $114,490 ($107,000 × 1.07) and the fourth year's cash flow will be $122,504 ($114,490 × 1.07).

Reversion

As mentioned previously, income-producing properties typically provide two types of financial benefits—periodic income and the future value obtained from sale of the property or reversion of the property interest at the end of the holding period. The length of the holding period usually may be determined by reviewing the property's lease expiration date(s). The length of the holding period and the discount rate are interactive. Generally, the longer the holding period, the greater the risk and the higher the discount rate. This future cash flow is called a *reversion* because it represents the anticipated return of a capital sum at the end of the investment.

There are several ways to estimate a resale price or property reversion at the end of the holding period. A capitalization rate can be applied to the appropriate income for the last year of the forecast or the year following the end of the forecast. When an overall capitalization rate is used to estimate a resale price, it is called a *terminal, coming-out,* or *residual capitalization rate* (R_N). The rate is different from the *going-in capitalization rate*—i.e., the overall capitalization rate found by dividing a property's net operating income for the first year after purchase by the present value of the property. The terminal or residual capitalization rate forecast is generally, though not necessarily, higher than the going-in capitalization rate. The terminal capitalization rate must reflect the reduction in the remaining economic life of the property and the greater risk associated with estimating *NOI* at the end of the holding period. The balance of the mortgage could then be deducted to calculate the owner's net sale proceeds, or equity reversion, if an equity yield analysis is being performed.

proceeds of resale: The net difference between the transaction price and the selling expenses of a property; refers to the property's reversion.

terminal capitalization rate (R_N): The rate used to convert income—e.g., *NOI,* cash flow—into an indication of the anticipated value of the subject real property at the end of the holding period. The terminal capitalization rate is used to estimate the resale value of the property using direct capitalization. Also called *residual capitalization rate.*

balloon payment: The outstanding balance due at the maturity of a balloon mortgage.

A single property may include one or more property interests that have their own streams of periodic benefits and reversions. For example, a property may have an equity interest with equity dividend as the periodic benefit and the equity reversion--i.e., property reversion minus the mortgage balance at loan maturity or property resale—as the reversionary benefit. The same property could have a mortgage with debt service as the periodic benefit and the mortgage balance (called a *balloon payment*) as the reversionary interest. A single property also comprises both building and land components. In situations involving long-term ground leases where the objective is to value the leasehold estate in the building, annual ground rent should be deducted before capitalizing *NOI* attributable to the leasehold estate.

The reversion is often a major portion of the total benefit to be received from an investment in income-producing property. If the investor's capital is not recaptured through some combination of cash flow and reversion proceeds, the effective rate of return on the investment will always be negative or zero. For certain investments, all capital recapture is accomplished through the reversion, indicating higher risk; for other investment properties, part of the recapture is provided by the reversion and part is provided by the investment's income stream.

To judge how much of the return of an investment will be provided by the reversion, an appraiser acknowledges that three general situations could result from the original investment.

1. The property may increase in value over the holding period.
2. The property's value may not change—i.e., the value of the property at the end of the holding period or remaining economic life may be equal to its value at the beginning of the period.
3. The property may decline in value over the period being analyzed.

Because these possible outcomes affect the potential yield of the investment and the amount of income considered acceptable, yield capitalization requires the appraiser to determine market expectations as to the change, if any, that will occur in the original investment or the property value over the holding period. (For leveraged investments, equity build-up may also occur through periodic debt service payments that include amortization.)

When a property is expected to be sold, the appraiser projects the reversion amount and considers the net proceeds of resale. The term *net proceeds of resale* refers to the net difference between the transaction price and the selling expenses, which may include brokerage commissions, legal fees, closing costs, transfer taxes, and possibly penalties for the prepayment of debt. The transaction price should be carefully analyzed to determine if costs of repair, capital improvements, and environmental remediation costs, if any, have been appropriately reflected. The transaction price may have to be adjusted to reflect extraordinary costs incurred by either party.

An appraiser establishes the likely value of the reversion in light of the expectations of investors in the market for the type of property being appraised. The appraiser may ask:

- Do investors expect a change in the value of this type of property in this particular locale?
- By how much will values change and in which direction?

The appraiser analyzes and interprets the market and estimates the value of the future reversion based on the direction and the amount or percentage of change that investors expect. The use of personal computers and software to perform lease-by-lease analysis allows appraisers to make more accurate forecasts of future cash flows, which help establish or estimate the reversion.

Discounting Models

The present value of any increasing, level, or decreasing income stream or of any irregular income stream can be calculated with DCF analysis. Specific valuation models, or formulas, categorized as either income models or property models have been developed for application to corresponding patterns of projected benefits. Income models are based on broad trends and require fewer specific cash flow inputs. When these models fit specific property expectations, they may be applied as shortcuts in place of more detailed DCF analysis and provide the same results.

> Specific valuation formulas, called **income and property models,** have been developed to solve and explain specific patterns of benefits without the need for a comprehensive DCF calculation.

Income models can be applied only to a stream of income. The present value of an expected reversion or any other benefit not already included in the income stream must be added to obtain the investment's total present value. When a property model is used, an income stream and a reversion are valued in one operation. Other present value models employ discounted cash flow analysis, which is discussed in Chapter 24.

Income Models

Valuation models can be applied to the following patterns of income:

- Variable or irregular income
- Level income
- Straight-line (constant-amount) change per period income
- Exponential-curve (constant-ratio) change per period income

These models are not necessarily real estate- or property-specific, but they can be used to solve a variety of asset valuation problems including real estate.

Variable or Irregular Income

As mentioned previously, the discounting process or formula can be used to solve any present value problem. The present value of an uneven stream of income is the sum of the discounted benefits treated as a series of separate payments or reversions. This model simply totals all present values using the standard discounting formula. The routine can be applied as a property valuation model as well as an income valuation model because it can be adapted to include the final reversion as part of the final cash flow expected at the end of the last, or *n*th, period.

Level Income

When a lease provides for a level stream of income or when income can be projected at a stabilized level, one or more capitalization procedures may be appropriate depending on the investor's assumptions with respect to capital recovery. Capitalization can be accomplished using capitalization in perpetuity. In the past, the present worth of an income stream was also calculated using

> **income model:** A formula developed to project a pattern of periodic income. Income models can be applied to level income with no change in value, level income with changing value, income and value that change by fixed amounts per period (straight-line), income and value that change at a constant ratio (exponential-curve), and variable or irregular income with changing value.

capitalization in perpetuity: Capitalization in which the discount rate equals the overall cap rate. Capitalization in perpetuity is applicable when a property is expected to generate level net operating income for a finite period and then be resold at the original purchase price.

compound interest: The continuous and systematic additions to a principal sum over a series of successive time periods so that previously earned interest earns interest.

the Inwood premise or the Hoskold premise, which are discussed in Appendix C.[3]

Capitalization in perpetuity can be considered a property valuation model or an income valuation model. If, for example, a property is expected to generate level net operating income for a finite period of time and then be resold for the original purchase price, the property could be valued with capitalization in perpetuity simply by dividing the expected periodic income by an appropriate discount rate. In this model the discount rate and the overall capitalization rate are the same because the original investment is presumed to be recovered at the termination of the investment.

Straight-Line (Constant-Amount) Change per Period in Income

When income is expected to increase or decrease by a fixed amount per period, the periodic income over time can be graphically portrayed as a straight line. Hence the term *straight-line* is used to describe this type of income pattern.

The formula for valuing straight-line income patterns should not be confused with direct capitalization with straight-line recapture. Although direct capitalization with straight-line recapture may be seen as a model for valuing a particular income stream, the procedure can also be applied to properties in which the expected change in value is commensurate with the expected change in income. Therefore, direct capitalization with straight-line recapture and related concepts are discussed with property models later in this chapter. Again, the formula applies to income streams only. Special tables of present value factors based on the formula are available.[4]

Exponential-Curve (Constant-Ratio) Change per Period in Income

The constant-ratio model represents an income pattern that increases or decreases at the same rate per period. Many times real estate income streams will increase with a pattern close to the constant-ratio premise, although

---

3. Over time, the Hoskold premise has become less popular and rarely reflects the thinking of real estate investors. It is now considered appropriate only for certain types of investments, e.g., in calculating the replacement allowance for leasing equipment or personal property. A Hoskold capitalization rate can be easily constructed by adding the speculative rate to the sinking fund factor for the safe rate, e.g., the prevailing rate for insured savings accounts or government bonds.

4. See James J. Mason, ed. and comp., *American Institute of Real Estate Appraisers Financial Tables*, rev. ed. (Chicago: American Institute of Real Estate Appraisers, 1982), Table No. 5, Ordinary Annuities Changing in Constant Amount.

typically on a short-term basis. Portrayed graphically, this type of income stream follows an exponential curve rather than a straight line. This income pattern is sometimes referred to as changing at a compound rate. Analysis of exponential-curve change is primarily done on computers.

Property Models

When both property value and income changes are expected to follow a regular or predictable pattern, one of the yield capitalization models for property valuation may be applicable. The common yield capitalization models employ a capitalization rate, R, which is also used in direct capitalization. There is a difference, however, between direct capitalization and yield capitalization. In direct capitalization R is derived directly from market data, without directly addressing the expected rate of return on capital or the means of recapture; in yield capitalization R cannot be determined without taking into account the income pattern, the antici-pated rate of return on capital, and the timing of recapture. This does not mean that yield capitalization procedures are not market-oriented. On the contrary, for some property types yield capitalization procedures may repre-sent the most realistic simulation of decision making in the marketplace.

property model: A formula developed to project the benefit pattern of a given property by considering the periodic income stream and the reversion in one operation. Property models describe properties with level income and no change in value, properties with level income and changing value, properties with income and value changing by fixed amounts per period (straight-line), properties with income and value changing at a constant ratio (exponen-tial-curve), and properties with income and value changing in a variable or irregular pattern.

Real estate investors are greatly influenced by expectations of change in property values. When an investor looks forward to property appreciation as a component of the eventual investment yield, that investor is anticipating that the total yield rate will be higher than the expected rate of income—i.e., the overall capitalization rate. The total yield rate is a complete measure of performance that includes any property appreciation. The general formula for this relationship is:

$$Y = R + A$$

where Y is the yield rate, R is the capitalization rate, and A is the adjustment rate that reflects the total change or growth in income and value.

Thus, the capitalization rate for an appreciating property equals the total yield rate minus an adjustment for expected growth:

$$R = Y - A$$

Similarly, the capitalization rate for a depreciating property can be seen as the yield rate plus an adjustment for expected loss:

$$R = Y - (-A) \text{ or } R = Y + A.$$

Because A is often expressed as a function of the total relative change in property income and value, the Greek letter *delta* (Δ) is used to denote change. To calculate A it is usually necessary to multiply Δ by a conversion factor, such as an annual sinking fund factor or an annual recapture rate, to convert the total relative change in income and value into an appropriate periodic rate of change. The symbol for the annualizer is a. The general formula for R may be expressed as

$$R = Y - \Delta\, a$$

where R is the capitalization rate, Y is the yield rate, Δ is the total relative change in income and value over the study period, and a is the annualizer or conversion factor.

This general formula for the capitalization rate can be adapted for use with typical income/value patterns for the property as a whole or for any property components. In the general formula, R, Y, and Δ apply to the total property and are expressed without subscripts. However, if there is a possibility of confusing the total property with any of its components, subscripts should be used for clarification. Once the appropriate capitalization rate has been determined, an indication of property value can be obtained by applying the following universal valuation formula:

$$\text{Value} = \frac{\text{Income}}{\text{Cap rate}} \text{ or } V = \frac{I}{R}$$

Level Income

Level income with no change in value. When both income and value are expected to remain unchanged, a property may be valued by capitalization in perpetuity, which was explained in the discussion of income models. According to the general formula, $R = Y - \Delta\, a$, the capitalization rate (R) becomes the yield rate (Y) when there is no change in value because Δ equals zero.

delta (Δ): The mathematical symbol for percent of change; used in yield and change formulas to represent the expected percentage of change in the value or income of a total property or a specified interest in property over a projection period.

conversion factor (a): An element in yield and change formulas that converts the total change in capital value over the projection period into an annual percentage; varies with the pattern of the income stream and may be an annual sinking fund factor or an annual recapture rate; also called the *annualizer*.

Level income with change in value. When level income with a change in value is projected over a period of n years, the general formula for R is adapted by substituting the sinking fund factor at rate Y over n years in place of the conversion factor (a). For example, consider a commercial property that will generate a stable *NOI* of $25,000 per year for the next eight years. Total property appreciation of 40% is expected during this eight-year period. The appraiser is asked to value the property to yield 15%. To solve this problem, the formula $R = Y - \Delta\, a$ is used with the sinking fund factor for 15% over eight years as *a*. According to the tables, the sinking fund factor is 0.072850, so *R* is calculated as follows:

$$R = 0.15 - (0.40 \times 0.072850) = 0.12086$$

$$\text{Value} = NOI / R$$

$$\text{Value} = \$25,000/0.12086 = \$206,851$$

Property models used in solving for value can also be used to manipulate or explain a given set of market data to determine other unknowns. For example, in the problem above only the *NOI* and rate of change or appreciation in property value are known. While DCF analysis may be used as proof of the solution, it is not feasible to apply DCF analysis to solve the problem. This is because only the rate of appreciation is known from the market, and the dollar amount of the future reversion and the current present value are unknown and interdependent. This illustrates the greatest benefits of the property models—i.e., the ability to make value decisions based on broad trends as well as the ability to explain market behavior.

Straight-Line (Constant-Amount) Changes in Income and Value

When income and value are expected to increase or decrease by fixed amounts per period according to the standard, straight-line pattern, property value can be estimated using direct capitalization with straight-line recapture. The general formula for the capitalization rate (*R*) can be adapted for use with the standard, straight-line income/value pattern by using the straight-line recapture rate as the conversion factor (*a*). The straight-line recapture rate is simply the reciprocal of the projection period. For example, if income is projected over a period of 25 years, the annual, straight-line recapture rate is 1/25, or 4%. Depreciation of 100% would indicate that the projection period is equal to the property's remaining economic life. The concept of a limited remaining economic life does not apply to appreciating properties, but 100% appreciation would indicate a projection period equal to the amount of time required for the property to double in value.

Classic straight-line recapture. The straight-line capitalization procedure has historically been used to value wasting or waning assets, i.e., investments whose income is declining as their asset base wanes. This classic procedure has limited applicability due to its underlying expectations, but it should be thoroughly understood to ensure its proper use. The classic straight-line procedure is based on the expectation that capital will be recaptured in equal dollar amounts during the investment's economic life and that net income always consists of a fixed amount that represents the return of capital plus a declining return on the capital remaining in the investment. Total income, therefore, diminishes until the asset is worthless and all capital has been recovered.

The presumption that value and income will decline steadily is frequently inconsistent with market behavior; nevertheless, the procedure has important uses. Straight-line recapture is appropriate whenever the projection of income and value in an investment corresponds with the expectations implicit in the procedure. Classic straight-line recapture is most easily understood when it is applied to an investment in a wasting asset such as a perishable structure, a stand of timber, or a mineral deposit. The procedure is inappropriate for valuing an investment in land or another asset that can sustain value indefinitely.

For example, consider an investment in a partial interest in real estate such as a leasehold in which all improvements must be written off during the term of the lease. Assume that $50,000 is invested in a 10-year leasehold to earn 8% per year as a yield on capital. What flow of income to the investor would be required to return the entire amount of the investment on a straight-line basis during the 10-year period and, in addition, yield 8% per year to the investor?

Yearly recapture would, of course, be one-tenth of $50,000, or $5,000. The investor is entitled to a return on unrecaptured capital amounting to 8% of $50,000 in the first year, 8% of $45,000 in the second year, 8% of $40,000 in the third year, and so forth (see Table 23.1). The income flow starts at $9,000 the first year and drops $400 each year after that. The total income payable at the end of the tenth and final year would be $5,400, of which $5,000 would be the last installment of the return of capital and the other $400 would be the interest due on the capital remaining in the investment during the tenth year. Thus, the investor achieves 100% capital recovery plus an 8% return on the outstanding capital, assuming non-level income.

Note that the recapture rate amounts to 10% of the original investment and is simply the reciprocal of the economic life. Also, all income is presumed to be payable at the end of each year, and the yields are always computed at the end of the year on the amount of capital outstanding during the year. Based on the starting income, the capitalization rate in this example would be

Table 23.1   **Periodic Return of and Return on Capital**

End of Year	Invested Capital	Return of Capital	Return on Capital	Total Return	% of Previous Year's Invested Cap. at 8%
0	$50,000	—	—	—	—
1	45,000	$5,000	$4,000	$9,000	18.00%
2	40,000	5,000	3,600	8,600	19.11
3	35,000	5,000	3,200	8,200	20.50
4	30,000	5,000	2,800	7,800	22.29
5	25,000	5,000	2,400	7,400	24.67
6	20,000	5,000	2,000	7,000	28.00
7	15,000	5,000	1,600	6,600	33.00
8	10,000	5,000	1,200	6,200	41.33
9	5,000	5,000	800	5,800	58.00
10	0	5,000	400	5,400	108.00

$9,000/$50,000, or 18%. The 18% capitalization rate could also be calculated by adding the 10% recapture rate to the 8% yield rate.

The straight-line capitalization procedure reflects some useful mathematical relationships:

first period return on investment = original value × yield rate
periodic change in value = original value × periodic rate of change
periodic change in income = periodic change in value × yield rate

When the decline in income and value reflects these relationships, the periodic rate of change is the recapture rate and the reciprocal of the recapture rate is the economic life.

Expanded straight-line concept. The traditional concept of straight-line recapture can be expanded to remove some of its theoretical constraints and facilitate a broader range of practical applications. The expectation of a predictable decline in income can be expanded to include any predictable change, which allows the appraiser to consider growing assets as well as wasting assets. A predictable rate of change within the foreseeable future can also eliminate the need to consider the full economic life of a property. Although there are significant theoretical differences, the expanded straight-line concept corresponds mathematically to classic straight-line recapture.

Under both the expanded and classic straight-line concepts, changes in value and income are presumed to occur on a straight-line basis. The basic requirements for a satisfactory return on, and complete recovery of, invested capital are also preserved. However, the expanded concept does not require that capital be recaptured in annual installments throughout the economic life of a property. Rather, the property could be resold for a predictable amount at some point during its economic life, thereby providing for partial or complete return of the invested capital at the time of resale.

The straight-line capitalization rate is simply a combination of the yield rate and the straight-line rate of change, which is expressed in the general formula $R = Y - \Delta a$, where Δ is the relative change in value in n periods and a is $1/n$. For example, consider a leasehold that will produce I_{LH} of $19,000 the first year. This I_{LH} is expected to decline thereafter in the standard straight-line pattern and value is expected to fall 25% in 10 years. The anticipated income pattern must match up with the lease contract. To appraise the leasehold to yield 12%, use the formula $R_{LH} = Y_{LH} - \Delta_{LH} a$, where the subscript LH denotes the leasehold.

$$R_{LH} = 0.12 - (-0.25 \times 0.1) = 0.145$$
$$\text{Value} = I_{LH} / R_{LH}$$
$$\text{Value} = \$19,000 / 0.145 = \$131,034$$

The classic and expanded straight-line concepts are popular because they are simple and do not require the use of compound interest tables. However, straight-line concepts have theoretical and practical limitations. The straight-line premise is not always a realistic reflection of investor expectations of changing income and value.

Exponential-Curve (Constant-Ratio) Changes in Income and Value

When both income and value are expected to change at a constant ratio, the capitalization rate can be determined without tables using the general formula

$$R = Y - \Delta a$$

where Δa is the relative change in value and income for one period. Thus, Δa can be replaced with the periodic compound rate of change (CR). The formula then becomes

$$R = Y - CR$$

where Y is the yield rate per period and CR is the rate of change per period. An expected loss is treated as a negative rate of change, and the formula becomes

$$R = Y - (-CR)$$

or

$$R = Y + CR$$

    If both income and value are expected to change at the same rate, the capitalization rate is expected to remain constant. Therefore, this pattern of growth or decline is sometimes referred to as the *frozen cap rate pattern.* For example, assume an income-producing property is expected to produce *NOI* of $50,000 for the first year. Thereafter both *NOI* and value are expected to grow at a constant ratio of 2% per year. In other words, 2% is the expected ratio of the increase in income for any year to the income for the previous year; the ratio of the increase in value for any year to the value for the previous year is also 2%. To appraise the property to yield 11%, the formula is

$$R_o = Y_o - CR_o$$
$$R_o = 0.11 - 0.02 \ = 0.09$$
$$\text{Value} = \$50,000/0.09 = \$555,556$$

The elements in the above equation can be transposed so that:

$$Y_o = R_o + CR_o$$

The overall yield rate, therefore, is equal to the overall capitalization rate plus the periodic adjustment, provided the rate of appreciation is anticipated to continue at the same rate into the foreseeable future. Property models based on an exponential pattern of change in income and value often reflect the thinking of investors in the market.

Variable or Irregular Income and Value Changes

When income and value are not expected to follow a regular pattern of change, the present value of a property can be obtained by applying the standard discounting formula separately to each projected benefit, including the final reversion. This is often done by discounted cash flow analysis rather than by using an income or property model. Examples of applications of discounted cash flow analysis are provided in the following chapter.

FURTHER READING

Akerson, Charles B. *The Appraiser's Workbook.* 2d ed. Chicago: Appraisal Institute, 1996.

____. *Capitalization Theory and Techniques: Study Guide.* 2d ed. Chicago: Appraisal Institute, 2000.

American Institute of Real Estate Appraisers. *Forecasting: Market Determinants Affecting Cash Flows and Reversions.* Research Series Report 4. Chicago, 1989.

____. *Readings in the Income Capitalization Approach to Real Property Valuation,* Volume II. Chicago, 1985.

Fisher, Clifford E., Jr. *Rates and Ratios Used in the Income Capitalization Approach.* Chicago: Appraisal Institute, 1995.

Mason, James J., ed. and comp. *AIREA Financial Tables.* Chicago: American Institute of Real Estate Appraisers, 1981.

CHAPTER 24

DISCOUNTED CASH FLOW ANALYSIS AND SPECIAL APPLICATIONS IN INCOME CAPITALIZATION

Discounted cash flow (DCF) analysis is appropriate for any pattern of regular or irregular income.[1] In many markets DCF analysis is the technique investors prefer. Basic computer technology makes DCF analysis a practical tool for everyday appraisal work.

Applicability of DCF Analysis

Discounted cash flow analysis can be used both to estimate present value and to extract a yield rate from a comparable sale. Generally, DCF analysis is used to solve for present value given the rate of return or for the rate of return given the purchase price. In typical appraisal work, the appraiser begins by developing detailed spreadsheets with computer software. These spreadsheets show itemized incomes, expenses, and cash flows year by year, or occasionally month by month, over the presumed period of ownership or other study period. The cash flows, including the net resale price, are then discounted at a rate (or rates) to derive an indication of present value. In this way the appraiser can account for all cash flows in and out of the real property interest being appraised and estimate the timing of these cash flows so that the time value of money is properly recognized in the analysis.

Critics point out that projections not warranted by market evidence can result in unsupported market values and that the results of the analysis can be subtly affected by minor leaning. These problems, like those problems associated with the Ellwood formula,[2] reflect misuse by individual appraisers; they do not undermine the technique's soundness. Other

> **Discounted cash flow (DCF) analysis** is a procedure in which a yield rate is applied to a set of projected income streams and a reversion to determine whether the investment property will produce a required yield given a known acquisition price. If the rate of return is known, DCF analysis can be used to solve for the present value of the property. If the property's purchase price is known, DCF analysis can be applied to find the rate of return.

---

1. Statement on Appraisal Standards No. 2 of the Uniform Standards of Professional Appraisal Practice addresses criteria for proper DCF analysis as well as unacceptable practices.

2. The specialized yield capitalization formula once used for DCF analysis (i.e., the Ellwood formula) has generally been replaced by the use of computer programs. Readers interested in reviewing Ellwood mortgage-equity analysis may consult Appendix C or Charles Akerson, *Capitalization Theory and Techniques: Study Guide,* 2d ed. (Chicago: Appraisal Institute, 2000).

critics object to the uncertainty of forecasting financial results five or ten years into the future and cite this as a reason for not using or relying on the DCF technique. However, this argument ignores the reality of the real estate marketplace. Investors do make forecasts and rely on DCF analysis, particularly in regard to investment-grade, multitenant properties such as shopping centers and office buildings.

In keeping with the principle of anticipation, market-supported forecasting is the essence of valuation. Hence, it must be approached in the same way that all market data extractions are accomplished—i.e., with diligent research and careful verification. Discounted cash flow analysis can only provide accurate results if the forecasts developed are based on accurate, reliable information. Rather than attempt to forecast peaks and troughs over the holding period, a level of precision that is virtually impossible to achieve, appraisers reflect market expectations as to how the subject property will perform over time.

Forecasting

In making forecasts an appraiser employs the same procedure applied by investors who use DCF analysis in their decision making. The procedural steps typically include forecasting income, vacancy, operating and capital expenses, and equity dividend (if appropriate) over ownership periods of 5 to 15 years. In some markets, 10 years is cited as an average or standard study period or typical ownership period; in others, the forecast period may be shorter or longer. When appropriate, debt service and after-tax cash flow may also be forecast. The residual income from the sale of the property at the end of the forecast period is also estimated.

Typical forecast categories to be addressed in DCF analysis include:

forecasting: Predicting a future happening or condition based on past trends and the perceptions of market participants, tempered with analytical judgment concerning the continuation of these trends and the realization of these perceptions in the future.

Forecasts typically include data on potential gross income, vacancy and collection losses, effective gross income, operating expenses, net operating income, debt service (where appropriate), equity cash flow over the holding period, and residual income from the sale of the property at the end of the forecast period.

- Current market rental rates and expected rate changes
- Existing base rents and contractual base rent adjustments
- Renewal options
- Existing and anticipated expense recovery (escalation) provisions
- Tenant turnover
- Re-leasing assumptions including new lease terms, vacancy loss and sometimes rent concessions at existing lease expirations, tenant space preparation costs, and leasing commissions

- Operating expenses
- Net operating income
- Reversion and any selling or transaction costs
- Discount rate(s)

Applications

The two DCF analyses that follow concern a 10,000-sq.-ft. shopping center. The first example provides an overview of the procedures used to forecast and discount cash flows into value. The second example shows how to extract a yield rate from a comparable sale.

Forecasting and Discounting Cash Flows into Value

The property being appraised is the leased fee ownership of a small strip shopping center consisting of five units of 2,000 square feet each. The following information is gathered for the DCF analysis:

- Market rents are currently $8.00 per square foot per year and are increasing at a compound rate of 4% per year.
- The lease on Store A will run for two more years at a rent of $825 per month. The tenant will re-lease at market rent when the lease expires.
- Store B has a 10-year lease with six years remaining. The rent is currently $1,223 per month and will increase at a rate of 5% per year or one-half the change in the Consumer Price Index (CPI), whichever is greater. The CPI is expected to increase 4% per year over the next five years.
- Stores C, D, and E were recently leased for 10 years. These leases and all new leases are set at market rent with provisions to keep the rents at market rates throughout the projection period.
- The landlord is responsible only for real estate taxes and exterior maintenance; tenants are responsible for all other expenses.
- Taxes are currently $7,000 per year. The tax assessor reviews and reassesses properties every three years. The subject property was reviewed one year ago and taxes are expected to increase by about $800 with each subsequent review.
- General exterior maintenance, including cleanup and landscaping, costs $100 per month; this expense is expected to increase each year by $10 per month.
- Management fees are set at 5% of the rents collected.
- A nominal collection loss of $250 per year is anticipated.
- The roof should be replaced during the second year at a cost of $12,500, but no other exterior repairs or replacements are expected during the projection period.
- Income for the sixth year of the investment is forecast to estimate the

resale price of the property at the end of the five-year projection period. The income for Year 6 of this forecast is the income for the first year of operation under the new owner. The net resale price of the property in five years is expected to be approximately $655,700 (*NOI* for Year 6 capitalized at 12% minus 3% sales expense).

The appraiser has determined that a leased fee yield rate of 15% is proper and is using the five-year discounted cash flow analysis shown in Table 24.1 to estimate the value of the leased fee estate.

Table 24.1   **Five-Year DCF Analysis of a Shopping Center**

	Year 1	Year 2	Year 3	Year 4	Year 5	Year 6
Income						
Store A	$9,900	$9,900	$17,306	$17,999	$18,718	$19,467
Store B	14,676	15,410	16,180	16,989	17,839	18,730
Store C	16,000	16,640	17,306	17,999	18,718	19,467
Store D	16,000	16,640	17,306	17,999	18,718	19,467
Store E	16,000	16,640	17,306	17,999	18,718	19,467
Subtotal	$72,576	$75,230	$85,404	$88,985	$92,711	$96,598
Expenses						
Taxes	$7,000	$7,000	$7,800	$7,800	$7,800	$8,600
Maintenance	1,200	1,320	1,440	1,560	1,680	1,800
Management	3,629	3,762	4,270	4,449	4,636	4,830
Collection loss	250	250	250	250	250	250
Replacement	0	12,500	0	0	0	0
Subtotal	$12,079	$24,832	$13,760	$14,059	$14,366	$15,480
NOI	$60,497	$50,398	$71,644	$74,926	$78,345	$81,118

Present value of income stream

Cash Flow		PV of $1 @ 15%*		Present Value
$60,497	×	0.869565	=	$52,606
$50,398	×	0.756144	=	$38,108
$71,644	×	0.657516	=	$47,107
$74,926	×	0.571753	=	$42,839
$78,345	×	0.497177	=	$38,951
Subtotal			=	$219,611

Present value of net resale price

(Year 6 *NOI* capitalized at a terminal capitalization rate of 12% less a sales expense of 3% of sale price)

$655,700	×	0.497177	=	$325,999

Total leased fee present value indication $545,610

*   The present value of $1 factor is not needed when discounted cash flow calculations are performed with a financial calculator or computer.

Extracting a Yield Rate from a Comparable Sale

In the subject property's market area, a 12,000-sq.-ft. strip shopping center with four tenants was sold for $453,000 five years prior to the date of value of the subject and then sold again for $506,000 shortly before the date of value. Table 24.2 compiles historical income and expense data at stabilization for the comparable property for five years plus the next 12 months.

Table 24.2   Historical Income and Expenses of Comparable Shopping Center

	Year 1	Year 2	Year 3	Year 4	Year 5	Year 6*
Income						
Store 1	$10,000	$10,400	$10,816	$11,249	$11,699	$12,165
Store 2	17,676	18,210	18,888	19,453	19,941	20,835
Store 3	13,151	13,677	14,224	14,793	15,385	16,000
Store 4	19,726	20,515	21,348	22,189	23,077	24,000
Subtotal	$60,553	$62,802	$65,276	$67,684	$70,102	$73,000
Expenses						
Taxes	$6,600	$6,600	$6,600	$7,200	$7,200	$7,200
Maintenance	810	875	953	1,060	1,108	1,210
Management	3,020	3,133	3,256	3,374	3,515	3,625
Collection loss	300	257	243	240	264	250
Replacement	0	0	5,200	0	5,200	0
Subtotal	$10,730	$10,865	$16,252	$11,874	$17,287	$12,285
NOI	$49,823	$51,937	$49,024	$55,810	$52,815	$60,715

* Budget for the first year under new ownership.

At the end of the holding period, the shopping center has a terminal capitalization rate of 12% ($506,000/$60,715), which is equivalent to the terminal capitalization rate of the subject property. Solving for a yield rate involves a mathematical trial-and-error process in which various overall yield rates are tested against the known sale price and cash flows. In practice, these repetitive calculations are handled by special functions of financial calculators and spreadsheet software, not calculated by hand.

Present value of income stream

Cash Flow		PV of $1 @ 15%		Present Value
$49,823	×	0.869565	=	$43,324
$51,937	×	0.756144	=	$39,272
$49,024	×	0.657516	=	$32,234
$55,810	×	0.571753	=	$31,910
$52,815	×	0.497177	=	$26,258
Subtotal			=	$172,998
Present value of resale price				
$490,820	×	0.497177	=	$244,024
Total leased fee present value indication				$417,022

Choosing a 15% yield rate produces a total present value significantly less than the $453,000 originally paid for the property. The analyst would next try a lower overall yield rate—say, 10%.

Present value of income stream

Cash Flow		PV of $1 @ 10%		Present Value
$49,823	×	0.909091	=	$45,294
$51,937	×	0.826446	=	$42,923
$49,024	×	0.751315	=	$36,832
$55,810	×	0.683013	=	$38,119
$52,815	×	0.620921	=	$32,794
Subtotal			=	$195,962
Present value of resale price				
$490,820	×	0.620921	=	$304,760
Total leased fee present value indication				$500,722

The total present value indication of $500,722 is greater than $453,000, so the 10% yield rate chosen is too low. The analyst would continue testing yield rates between 10% and 15%, slowly narrowing the range of rates chosen until the correct yield rate is discovered. These repetitive calculations are no longer necessary in appraisal practice because financial calculators and computers can solve for the unknown variable (Y_O) quickly and easily given the necessary inputs.

In this example, solving for the overall yield rate with a financial calculator produces a rate of 12.7% (rounded), which is noticeably less than the 15% yield rate selected in the valuation of the subject property. The yield rate extracted from the comparable sale is based on historical data, whereas the yield rate chosen for the subject property is based on the owner's anticipated return on the investment at the end of the holding period. The higher yield rate for the subject property may reflect the increased risk of that investment or the investor's expectations of an improving market over the holding period. As an additional check, other comparable sales could be analyzed and the resulting yield rates reconciled to provide additional market support for the overall yield rate estimate.

Investment Analysis

In addition to developing an opinion of value or extracting a yield rate from comparable sales, discounted cash flow analysis techniques are often used to test the performance of real estate investments at a desired rate of return. Measures of investment performance include

- Net present value
- Internal rate of return
- Payback period
- Profitability index (or cost/benefit ratio)
- Time-weighted rate

These measures are not individually perfect, but as a collection of tools they have proven their effectiveness. They reflect a common market understanding and are useful in typical real estate applications.

Net Present Value and the Internal Rate of Return

Net present value (*NPV*) and the internal rate of return (*IRR*) are two discounted cash flow models widely used to measure investment performance and develop decision-making criteria. Net present value (dollar reward) is the difference between the present value of all positive cash flows and the present value of all negative cash flows, or capital outlays. When the net present value of the positive cash flows is greater than the net present value of the negative cash flows or capital outlays, an investment is deemed viable. If the reverse relationship exists, the investment is not considered feasible.[3]

A net present value of zero indicates that the present value of all positive cash flows equals the present value of all negative cash flows or capital outlays. The rate of discount that makes the net present value of an investment equal zero is the internal rate of return. In other words, the *IRR* discounts all returns from an investment, including returns from its termination, to a present value equal to the original investment.

Applicability and Limitations of NPV

A number of decision rules for applying the *NPV* can be established. For example, assume that a property with an anticipated present value of $1,100,000 for all investment returns over a 10-year holding period can be purchased for $1,000,000. If one investor's *NPV* goal is zero, this investment exceeds that criterion. It also meets a second investor's goal for an *NPV* of $100,000, but it would not qualify if the goal were $150,000.

> Net present value (*NPV*) and the internal rate of return (*IRR*) are two discounted cash flow models widely used for **measuring investment performance**.

net present value (NPV): The difference between the present value of all expected investment benefits, or positive cash flows, and the present value of capital outlays, or negative cash flows. For purposes of real property valuation, negative cash flows include the initial cash outlay required to purchase the property. Generally, when *NPV* is positive, the investment is acceptable; if *NPV* is zero, the investment is marginally acceptable; and when *NPV* is negative, the investment is unacceptable. Also called *dollar reward.*

internal rate of return (IRR): The annualized yield rate or rate of return on capital that is generated or capable of being generated within an investment or portfolio over a period of ownership. The *IRR* is the rate of discount that makes the net present value of the investment equal to zero. The *IRR* discounts all returns from the investment, including returns from its termination, to equal the original capital outlay. This rate is similar to the equity yield rate. As a measure of investment performance, the *IRR* is the rate of discount that produces a profitability index of one and a net present value of zero. It is often used to measure profitability after income taxes, i.e., the after-tax equity yield rate.

---

3. Net present value does not explicitly consider the time value of money, nor does it adequately deal with the problem of risk. Each is implicit in the discount rate.

The *IRR* has notable **limitations.** Unusual combinations of cash flows may produce more than one *IRR.* The *IRR* must be viewed with suspicion when net cash flows to an investment at a zero rate of return have a negative cumulative value. A negative *IRR* may be interpreted as a rate of loss but is theoretically meaningless. Moreover, as a measure of return on invested capital, the *IRR* is not valid for investments that are "financed out" and require little or no equity capital.

Net present value does consider the time value of money, and different discount rates can be applied to different investments to account for general risk differences. However, this method cannot handle different required capital outlays. It cannot differentiate between an *NPV* of $100,000 on a $1,000,000 capital outlay and the same *NPV* on a $500,000 capital outlay. Therefore, this technique is best used in conjunction with other measures.

Limitations and Pitfalls of the IRR

By understanding the limitations and pitfalls appraisers may encounter using the *IRR*, practitioners can avoid wasted effort and false conclusions. The search for a single *IRR* within a plausible range is not always successful. Unusual combinations of cash flows may produce strange results, and more than one *IRR*, or in rare cases no *IRR*, may be indicated.

More than one *IRR*. Consider a real estate investment with the cash flows set forth in Table 24.3. Assuming that the investor borrows $10,000 and pays 10% interest only, with the principal to be repaid in a lump sum at the end of 10 years, the investor's net cash flows can be tabulated.

The *IRR* for the net cash flows after financing can be obtained through graphic analysis. Net present values are calculated for even discount rates

Table 24.3   Net Cash Flow

Year	Cash Flow Before Loan/Interest	Loan	Interest	Net Cash Flow
0	−$12,300*	$10,000	$0	−$2,300
1	$2,000	0	−$1,000	$1,000
2	$2,000	0	−$1,000	$1,000
3	$2,000	0	−$1,000	$1,000
4	$2,000	0	−$1,000	$1,000
5	$1,000	0	−$1,000	0
6	$1,000	0	−$1,000	0
7	$1,000	0	−$1,000	0
8	$1,000	0	−$1,000	0
9	$1,000	0	−$1,000	0
10	$9,000†	−$10,000	−$1,000	−$2,000

*   Initial cash outlay

†   Income and proceeds from sale

between 0% and 24% and plotted on a graph. Table 24.4 and Figure 24.1 indicate not one, but two, *IRR*s. Using a computer, the two *IRR*s are calculated as 4.50839% and 18.3931%.

Multiple rates like these are interesting theoretically, but it is difficult to accept more than one *IRR* as a useful measure of performance. In real estate investment analysis, the presence of multiple *IRR*s usually suggests that some other measure of performance would be more appropriate or that the cash flows or time frame should be adjusted to permit a more meaningful analysis. Close examination of the example presented here reveals some characteristics of the *IRR* that may not be apparent in more typical examples.

Table 24.4   **Table of Net Present Values**

Discount Rate	Net Present Value
0	-$300
2	-$133
4	-$21
6	$48
8	$86
10	$99
12	$93
14	$74
16	$45
18	$8
20	-$34
22	-$80
24	-$128

Figure 24.1   **Graphic Solution to Example**

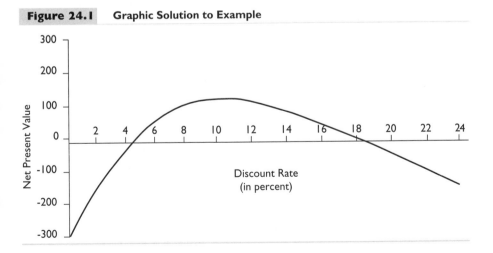

Negative net present value at zero rate of return. The cumulative value of the net cash flows in Table 24.3 is negative. Negative net cash flows total $4,300, while positive net cash flows total $4,000. Therefore, the net present value— i.e., the difference between the present value of expected benefits, or positive cash flows, and the present value of capital outlays, or negative cash flows— with no discounting or at a zero discount rate is -$300 (see Figure 24.1). This should be a warning sign to the analyst.

Under these conditions, the *IRR* cannot be positive unless the mixture of positive and negative cash flows over time is such that the net present value increases with increases in the discount rate until the net present value reaches zero. The preceding example illustrates this phenomenon. This type of reverse discounting is mathematically valid, but it is contrary to the practical notion of reducing net present value by increasing the discount rate. It is not surprising that the *IRR* in such cases is difficult to comprehend and of questionable use.

Negative IRR. If the net present value of an investment at a 0% rate of return is negative, a negative *IRR* may be indicated. A negative *IRR* may be interpreted as a rate of loss, but the *IRR* is generally understood to be a positive rate of return. Any prospective rate of loss will normally discourage capital investment.

The concept of a negative *IRR* has theoretical, as well as practical, limitations. A glance at the *IRR* equation reveals that a negative *IRR* of 100% or more has no meaning because it involves division by zero or powers of a negative number.

Little or no equity. Because the *IRR* is a measure of the return on invested capital, it cannot be used to measure the performance of opportunities that require no investment of capital. Some investments can be "financed out"— i.e., financed with loans that cover 100% or more of the capital required. If the projected net cash flows are all positive, there is no *IRR*. Obviously, no discount rate can make a series of exclusively positive benefits equal zero.

The same rationale can be applied to investments calling for very low equity or a very small down payment in relation to expected returns. For example, a profit of $1 on an investment of $1 amounts to a 100% rate of return; a return of $100 on an investment of $1 indicates a 10,000% rate of return. When the investment is very small, slight changes in income can cause astronomical changes in the rates of return and loss. The *IRR* is an impractical yardstick for such investments.

However, the *IRR* can be a valuable indicator in analyzing investments that are 100% financed at the start and expected to operate at a loss for a period of time. In these arrangements, the early negative cash flows may represent a significant investment of equity capital and the prospective *IRR* may be the best measure of performance. It may also be useful to compare the prospective *IRR* before financing with an interest rate that reflects the cost of capital. The difference can be used as a measure of prospective leverage.

Reinvestment Concepts

The *IRR* is an internal rate of return on the capital within an investment. It can be applied to a single property or to an entire investment portfolio. No assumption is made as to how the investor actually employs funds that are received during the investment's ownership. The income from a real estate investment may be reinvested in another project at another rate of return, stored in a vault, or spent, but the *IRR* is not affected. Regardless of whether or not an investor in fact reinvests capital withdrawn from the investment at any given rate, a defining characteristic of the *IRR* is that it is mathematically consistent with reinvestment at the same rate of interest as the *IRR*. This establishes a framework for distinguishing between the *IRR* and other measures of investment return that make explicit reinvestment assumptions.

Incorporating a reinvestment concept in investment analysis is useful when viewing returns within the context of overall portfolio performance. It is a fundamental concept of finance that to calculate a rate of return on an investment and to compare two or more alternative investments, all of the dollars in an investment must be considered over the entire period of analysis. Although it is entirely possible to calculate the actual return in hindsight by considering what all of the dollars in the original investment produced over the analysis period, appraisers generally consider the opportunity returns of anticipated future cash flows. Income-producing real estate typically generates both a return on and a return of invested capital over the life of the investment. The rate of return can differ with various reinvestment assumptions. Although there are potential problems with the concept of an *IRR*, its use does not force any particular reinvestment assumptions, even though it is consistent with reinvestment at the same rate as the *IRR*.

One of several problems associated with the *IRR* is that certain situations can produce mathematical results that support more than one *IRR*. A different rate of return concept with a specific reinvestment premise is sometimes used to avoid multiple *IRR*s. Although the assumption of a specific reinvestment rate other than the *IRR* does not result in an *IRR*, reinvestment assumptions are applied to a number of rate of return concepts that make up a family of *IRR*-related measures.

IRR with reinvestment. This variation of the *IRR* is based on the expectation that all income from a project can be immediately reinvested at a specified rate and left to grow at that rate until the end of the investment holding period. The combined results of the investment's earnings and reinvestment are then reflected in one overall rate of return. The *IRR* with reinvestment traces the expected total performance of the original capital sum at work in more than one investment, rather than ignoring what occurs with the portions

Reinvestment concepts may be incorporated into *IRR* analysis. The adjusted or modified *IRR* (*AIRR* or *MIRR*) is an *IRR* with reinvestment. The financial management rate of return (*FMRR*) is an *IRR* with a specified borrowing rate.

of the capital investment during the ownership period. This measure can also be used to prevent multiple solutions to the *IRR* equation. The *IRR* with reinvestment is often called the *adjusted* or *modified IRR* (*AIRR* or *MIRR*). The formula for the *MIRR* appears in Appendix C.

IRR with a specified borrowing rate. The *IRR* with a specified borrowing rate is another variation of the *IRR* that can be used to prevent multiple rates. It is sometimes called the *IRR for investment* or *financial management rate of return* (*FMRR*). The *IRR* for investment or *FMRR* specifies an interest rate for the borrowed funds needed during the period when the investment is producing negative cash flows. As with other rates derived from the *IRR*, it recognizes that there are different risks and potential earnings that apply to the funds withdrawn from the original investment. The concept of financial management is that lower rates will be paid on borrowings and risk management will permit the eventual earning of a higher rate of return on the real estate investment. And again, as is the case with other rates that assume reinvestment (*AIRR* and *MIRR*), to derive the *FMRR* the entire amount of invested capital is analyzed over the life of the real estate investment.

Conclusion

The *IRR* can be as important to the real estate investor as the interest rate is to the mortgage lender; in fact, the two measures are equivalent. The interest rate on a mortgage is the same as the mortgagee's yield, or the *IRR*, unless points are involved. The *IRR* is not a meaningful measure of all investments and, even when it is meaningful, it is not the only possible criterion. It is, however, a fundamental and pure measure of a particular investment's financial performance. In general, the *IRR* is a valuable analytical tool if the decision maker understands its attributes and limitations and has access to complementary or alternative analytical techniques.

Other Measures of Performance

Popular alternative measures of financial performance or profitability include

- Payback period
- Profitability index or cost/benefit ratio
- Time-weighted rate

These yardsticks do not measure performance or profit on the same scale or under the same assumptions as the *IRR*. Their usefulness depends on the situation and the user's preferences. Neither the *IRR* nor any alternative measure is superior in all situations.

Payback Period

As a measure of investment return, the payback period is seldom used alone; it is commonly employed in conjunction with other measures. The payback period (*PB*) is defined as the length of time required for the stream of net cash flows produced by an investment to equal the original cash outlay. The breakeven point is reached when the investment's cumulative income is equal to its cumulative loss. The payback period can be calculated from either before- or after-tax cash flows, so the type of cash flow selected should be identified. The equation for payback period may be expressed as follows:

$$PB = \frac{\text{equity capital outlay}}{\text{annual net equity cash flows}}$$

This measure of performance is used by investors who simply want to know how long it will take them to recapture the dollars they have invested. In theory, an investment with a payback period of three years would be preferable to one

> **payback period (PB):** The length of time required for the stream of cash flows produced by the investment to equal the original cash outlay.

with a payback period of five years, all else being equal. Similarly, an investment that will return the investor's capital in six years would be unacceptable to an investor who seeks investment payback within four years.

For an equity investment that is expected to produce equal cash flows, the payback period is simply the reciprocal of the equity capitalization rate (or equity dividend rate):

$$PB = \frac{1}{R_E}$$

If annual equity cash flows are not expected to be equal over the payback period, the equity cash flows for each year must be added until the sum equals or exceeds the equity capital outlay; this point indicates the year in which payback occurs.

Although the payback period is simple and easily understood, it has a number of drawbacks. First, it measures the amount of time over which invested money will be returned to the investor, but it does not consider the time value of the money invested. A five-year investment payback for a $100,000 investment that pays $10,000 in Year 1 and $90,000 in Year 5 is not distinguished from the payback for a $100,000 investment that pays $90,000 in Year 1 and $10,000 in Year 5. The time value of money allows the first investment to use an additional $80,000 (i.e., the difference between the $90,000 paid in the second investment and the $10,000 paid in the first investment) from the second year through the fifth.[4]

---

4. A more sophisticated, but less popular, measure is the discounted payback period, which recognizes the time value of money at a stipulated rate of return. In this context the payback period is the amount of time required for the discounted benefits to equal the discounted costs.

> **profitability index (PI):** The present value of anticipated investment returns (benefits) divided by the present value of the capital outlay (cost); also called *cost/benefit ratio.*

Another shortcoming of the payback period is that it does not consider the effect of any gain or loss of invested capital beyond the breakeven point and does not specifically account for investment risks. An investment with a three-year payback may be far riskier than another investment with a five-year payback, but the shorter period generally appears preferable. Thus this measure of performance should only be used to compare investments with similar investment characteristics or in conjunction with other performance measures in carefully weighted applications.

Profitability Index

Although measuring the investment proceeds per dollar invested is too imprecise for general use, a refinement of this technique is commonly applied. The profitability index *(PI)*, which is also called the *cost/benefit ratio,* is defined as the present value of the anticipated investment returns (benefit) divided by the present value of the capital outlay (cost). The formula is

$$PI = \frac{\text{present value of anticipated investment returns}}{\text{present value of capital outlay}}$$

This measure employs a desired minimum rate of return or a satisfactory yield rate. The present value of the anticipated investment returns and the present value of the capital outlay are calculated using the desired rate as the discount rate. If, for example, the present value of the capital outlay discounted at 10% is $12,300 and the present value of the benefits is $12,399, the profitability index, based on a satisfactory yield rate of 10%, is $12,399/$12,300 = 1.008.

A profitability index greater than 1.0 indicates that the investment is profitable and acceptable in light of the chosen discount rate. A profitability index of less than 1.0 indicates that the investment cannot generate the desired rate of return and is not acceptable. A profitability index of exactly 1.0 indicates that the opportunity is just satisfactory in terms of the desired rate of return and, coincidentally, the chosen discount rate is equal to the anticipated *IRR.* The discount rate used to compute the profitability index may represent a minimum desired rate, the cost of capital, or a rate that is considered acceptable in light of the risks involved.

This refined measure of investment performance considers the time value of money, which is not considered in calculating the proceeds per dollar invested. A profitability index is particularly useful in comparing investments that have different capital outlay requirements, different time frames for receiving income or other investment returns, and different risk characteristics. A profitability index is commonly used in conjunction with other measures, particularly with net

> **time-weighted rate:** The average of all actual, instantaneous rates over a period of time; also called *unit-method rate* or *share-accounting rate.*

present value. When combined, these measures provide special insights into the investments under consideration.

Time-Weighted Rate

A time-weighted rate is technically an average of all actual, instantaneous rates over a period of time. It is similar to the rate of growth for capital invested in a mutual fund in which all dividend income is automatically reinvested. The time-weighted rate, which is also known as the *unit-method rate* or the *share-accounting rate,* is used primarily to measure the performance of a portfolio manager, not the performance of the portfolio itself.

Analysis of Office Building Investment

The analysis that follows is based on a 10-year forecast of the future benefits from an office building investment. Both net operating income and equity dividend are estimated for each year. The proceeds from resale of the property at the end of the tenth year are also estimated.

Property Analysis

- The subject property is a 50,000-sq.-ft. site improved with a 50-year-old, 25-story office building in a secondary location north of the downtown commercial district.
- The rentable area totals 951,049 square feet of office and retail space.
- The retail space consists of 13,293 square feet and is covered by five leases.
- The office space is fully occupied by 19 tenants under 21 leases. Many of the leases are old and will expire soon. The leases for approximately 58.4% of the building's rentable area will expire and be available for renewal or releasing in Year 3 and Year 4. The last existing lease will expire in Year 22. (Lease expiration and subsequent re-leasing is referred to as *lease rollover.*) The property's lease expiration profile is summarized in Table 24.5.
- The current average gross rent is $8.57 per square foot of rentable area. Appraisers estimate current average market rents at $18 per square foot for office space and $25 per square foot for retail space. The weighted-average market rent is estimated to be $18.10 per square foot. Therefore, the market differential—i.e., the difference between potential gross income at market rent and existing contract rent—is $9.53 per square foot ($18.10 – $8.57), and the total actual rent is 47.35% of market rent.
- The market for office space is in balance and there is above-average demand for space in this building. Although the building is old, it has been remodeled, and extensive capital expenditures have been made to improve its mechanical systems and maintain its competitive position. It is located in a good secondary area and is ideally suited to back-office, computer, bookkeeping, or storage operations that require a large, contiguous space.

Table 24.5   **Subject Property Lease Expiration Profile**

Year	No. of Expiring Leases	Rentable Area in Sq. Ft.	Percent of Total Area Available for Leasing (Cumulative)
1	0	0	—
2	0	0	—
3	7	268,458	28.2
4	6	286,706	58.4
5	2	51,302	63.8
6	2	22,730	66.2
7	1	7,930	67.0
8	1	45,979	71.8
9–10	0	0	71.8
11	1	924	71.9
12–21	0	0	71.9
22	1	267,020	100.0
Total	21	951,049	

Rationale for the Forecast

The appraiser determines that investors in office buildings similar to the subject property typically forecast net operating incomes or equity dividends over a 10-year holding period. To establish a purchase price that will justify the risk inherent in the proposed investment, the forecast net operating incomes or equity dividends and the reversion are discounted at an appropriate yield rate.

To simulate typical investor analysis, the appraiser

1. Analyzes current income, establishes the market rent level for each tenant's space, and forecasts future income for each year of a 10-year period based on existing leases, probable lease renewal at market rent, and expected vacancy experience.

2. Forecasts other income, including income from escalation clauses contained in existing leases and expected escalation provisions in new leases.

3. Forecasts future property expenses after analyzing historical operating expenses, the experience of competitive properties, and the current budget for the property.

4. Estimates *NOI*.

5. Estimates property reversion.

6. Forecasts mortgage debt service based on existing or proposed financing terms.

7. When appropriate, estimates the equity dividends to be generated by the property in each year of the forecast holding period.

8. Estimates the reversionary benefits to be received at the end of the forecast holding period (in this case, Year 11 *NOI* using an 11% terminal cap rate).

If a significant capital expenditure or change in leases in the 11th year—i.e., the year of reversion—is expected, the study period may be extended to incorporate this event. This will ensure that the analysis is not impacted by an unusual event in the reversion year used to calculate the reversion value.

In a market value appraisal, these steps must be applied in a manner that reflects the thinking of market participants. In this sample application, the appraiser begins by assembling pertinent information on comparable office buildings in the same market as the subject property. To verify the data, the appraiser interviews one of the participants, usually the buyer, to determine the *NOI* (or equity dividend) forecast associated with each comparable. Table 24.6, which lists information on Comparable 1, illustrates the type of detailed information that should be sought for each comparable.

Forecasts for the Subject Property

- **Holding period.** The forecasts are based on an expected 10-year holding period beginning on the date of valuation. A 10-year forecast is typical in this market and for this property type. This forecast considers the effects of re-leasing 71.9% of the building space; a lease for the other 28.1% of the building is held by one major tenant and does not expire until Year 17.

- **Existing rents.** Contract rents and rent adjustments are forecast in light of existing leases and escalation provisions.

- **Escalation income.** Escalation income is calculated in accordance with the specific terms of existing leases. For anticipated new leases, escalation income is based on a pro rata share of the amount by which operating expenses and real estate taxes exceed these expenses in the base year. The base year is defined as the year of lease commencement. By local custom, escalation income is reported for the year after it accrues.

    Although specific escalation provisions vary, the appraiser's analysis reveals that prospective investors use a combination of escalation provisions that, taken together, increase tenant collections annually so that total collections in any given year do not lag far behind market rents.

- **Renewal options.** It is anticipated that the renewal options contained in existing leases, all of which specify new contract rents or escalation provisions, will be exercised; the income specified under these renewals is incorporated into the forecast. One lease has a seven-year renewal option beginning in Year 2 that specifies an annual rent that is less than the expected market rent for that year (market rent of $18.00 per square foot compared with contract rent of $13.00 per square foot). Other renewal options that do not specify contract rent or escalation provisions are also anticipated to be exercised; in these cases market rental rates and new escalation provisions are applied.

- **Tenant turnover.** Approximately 35% of the space in the building is occupied by three major corporations that are likely to remain. It is anticipated that this space will be re-leased to the existing tenants. Another 50% of the

Table 24.6   **Comparable Sale Data**

Comparable No.	I
Address	I 10 Main St.
	Subject city, subject state
Date of sale	June 2001
Sale price	$60 million
Seller	XYZ Investment Co.
Purchaser	I 10 Main Street Co.
Description	A 32-story, multitenant office building that was built in 1969 and contains 748,701 square feet of area on floors that range in size from 8,100 square feet to 30,600 square feet situated on a 32,609-sq.-ft. plot
Comments	The property was sold on an all-cash basis; the buyer expects above-average increases in net income.
Sale price per sq. ft.	$80.14
Average contract rent per sq. ft. at sale date	$12.44
Anticipated financial data for Year 1 (buyer's estimate):	
Average market rent per square foot	$18.00
Average contract rent per square foot	$12.44
Fixed expenses per square foot	$2.67
Variable expenses per square foot	$4.79
Replacement allowance per square foot	$0.50
Net operating income per square foot	$4.98
Overall capitalization rate*	6.2%
Equity capitalization rate	6.2%
Market 10-year yield (*IRR*) requirement	13.5%

Purchaser's forecast:	
Market rent rate	Averages $18 per square foot in Years 1 and 2, increasing 5% per year thereafter.
Escalation income	Typical total rent will closely approximate market rent rates.
Expense increases	Real estate taxes assumed to increase 2% per year; energy expenses assumed to increase 5% per year; other operating expenses assumed to increase 4% per year.
Re-leasing	All space assumed to be re-leased for successive 5-year terms.
Vacancy	75% of space being re-leased assumed to be vacant for 3 months.
Leasing commissions†	Standard commission schedule payable in first year of lease.
Interior improvements to tenant space	$20.00 per square foot for new leases; $7.50 per square foot for renewal of existing leases.
Resale	Computed by applying a 10% overall capitalization rate to the net operating income in Year 11 and deducting 2.5% for selling expenses.

---

*   Because the property is not mortgaged, the equity capitalization rate is the same as the overall capitalization rate. The occupancy level for this building is 100%.

†   It is imperative that the appraiser consider leasing commission costs for both new tenants and existing tenants as well as probable tenant renewal/turnover ratios. To account for these factors, the appraiser develops a blended rate by means of weighting.

building is estimated to be re-leased to other existing tenants; the remaining 15% will be leased to new tenants. These parameters are consistent with comparable sales data, given the character of the property and its tenants.

- **New lease terms.** When the existing leases and any renewal options expire, all space is projected to be re-leased for successive 10-year terms. In this market 10-year leases are customary for this type of space.

- **Market rental rates:**

  Office space: For two years beginning January 1, Year 1, rent will average $18 per square foot; the market rate is anticipated to increase 5% per year thereafter.

  Retail space: For the year beginning on January 1, Year 1, average rent will be $25 per square foot; the market rate is estimated to increase 5% per year.

  The office rental rate forecasts are supported by an analysis of actual leases for office space in competitive buildings over time and the probable supply and demand outlook for the subject submarket area. Expectations of rate increases are consistent with the assumptions or allocations made by the buyers of all but one of the comparable sales (see Table 24.7).

- **Vacancy and collection loss.** Fifteen percent of the building space is being leased to new tenants and will probably remain vacant for an average of four months. The other 85% is assumed to be re-leased by existing tenants, so no vacancy is anticipated. The appraiser has considered the income loss associated with vacancies by not accruing contract

Table 24.7   Analysis of Growth Rate Information Derived from Office Building Data

		Market Rent Growth Rates					Expense Growth Rates		
		1st Period		2nd Period		Thereafter			Real Estate
Sale			No. of		No. of		Variable		Taxes and
No.	Date	%	Years	%	Years		Operating	Energy	Insurance
1	9/00	0.0	2	—	—	5.0%	4.0%	5.0%	2.0%
2	9/00	4.0	—	—	—	4.0	4.5	4.5	3.0
3	6/00	0.0	2	4.0	2	5.0	4.5	5.0	3.0
4	7/99	0.0	3	—	—	5.0	4.0	4.0	4.0
5	3/00	0.0	2	4.0	2	5.0	4.0	5.0	4.0
6	3/00	0.0	3	—	—	5.0	4.0	4.0	4.0
7	4/99	5.0	—	—	—	5.0	5.0	5.0	4.0
8	4/99	0.0	2	—	—	5.0	4.5	4.5	4.0
9	7/99	5.0	—	—	—	5.0	5.0	6.0	5.0
10	10/99	0.0	3	—	—	5.0	4.0	5.0	4.0
11	8/00	0.0	2	4.0	2	5.0	4.0	4.0	5.0

rent or escalation income for the space for a four-month period beginning at the expiration of each lease. Accordingly, vacancy windows—i.e.,
periods of anticipated vacancy—are included in the gross income estimate
resulting in a forecast that reflects some level of vacancy and hence
effective gross income. Furthermore, an additional allowance for the
underlying level of vacancy and collection loss not already reflected in the
income estimate for multitenant office buildings in this market is estimated at 0.5% of total gross revenue, as indicated by comparable sales data.

- **Real estate taxes and insurance.** Real estate taxes and insurance are
estimated at $998,000, or $1.05 per square foot of rentable area, for the
end of fiscal Year 1. The combined real estate tax and insurance expense
is assumed to increase at a rate of 4% per year thereafter.

- **Management.** For this property, management fees are estimated at
$75,000 for Year 1 and are expected to increase 4.5% each subsequent
year. Although the building is large, the small number of tenants and the
significant leasing activity scheduled for the near term should attract
competent management at this rate. In many cases management is
calculated as a percentage of effective gross income.

- **Leasing commissions.** To estimate leasing commissions, the appraiser
applies a weighted-average leasing commission rate of 17.15% of the first
year's base rent to all re-leasing activities. This estimate is based on
expectations that 35% of the space will be re-leased to the three major
tenants at a commission rate of 14% of the first year's contract rent; 50%
of the space will be re-leased to existing tenants at a commission rate of
14% of the first year's contract rent; and 15% of the space will be leased
to new tenants at a commission rate of 35% of the first year's contract
rent. Commissions are assumed to be paid in full upon occupancy and are
deducted from income. This commission schedule is consistent with the
typical rates obtained by local real estate brokers and is usually reflected
after the *NOI* line—i.e., "below the line"—in the analysis summary table.

- **Variable operating expenses.** Variable operating expenses, excluding
leasing commissions and management, which have been treated separately, are estimated to be $2,161,000 in Year 1, or $2.27 per square foot
of rentable area (see Table 24.8). The expense estimates are supported by
an analysis of the recent operating histories of competitive buildings. The
HVAC estimate is decreased from Year 0 to Year 1 because the building
is being converted from steam to oil heat (see Table 24.8). Expenses for
energy-related items are expected to increase 5% per year, and other
expenses are estimated to increase 4.5% per year. These rate increases are
based on the expense rate increase projections supported by comparable
sales. Expenses for tenant electricity and the cleaning of tenant space are
not included because existing tenants pay for their own cleaning and
electricity. This is typical in the leasing of back-office space, and the
market rent estimate of $18 per square foot is based on this practice.

Table 24.8	Estimate of Variable Operating Expenses for Subject Property*	
	Previous Year's Budget	**Year 1 Estimate**
HVAC	$500,000	$400,000†
Payroll	154,000	175,000
Repairs and maintenance	385,000	440,000
Building electricity	600,000	660,000
Security	175,000	200,000
Cleaning public areas	25,000	30,000
Garbage collection	5,000	6,000
Administrative and general	185,000	200,000
Water and sewer	44,000	50,000
Total	$2,073,000	$2,161,000
Total per rentable square foot	$2.18	$2.27

* Excluding management expenses and leasing commissions, which are estimated separately

† Reflects conversion to oil heat for part of year

- **Replacement allowance.** The cost to replace building improvements—e.g., roof and HVAC equipment—is forecast at $100,000 for Year 1, increasing 4.5% each following year. This analysis treats the replacement reserve allowance essentially as an average expectation over time. In most cases it may be more appropriate to account for the entire expenditure in the specific year when it is forecast to occur.

- **Tenant improvements.** Tenant improvements (TIs) consist of the cost of preparing tenant space. The forecast for the TIs begins the third and fourth years out with seven leases expiring in Year 3 and six leases in Year 4 (see Table 24.5). All space being leased to new tenants is anticipated to require decorating at a cost of $20.00 per square foot. Space being re-leased to existing tenants is assumed to incur decorating or tenant improvement expenses of $7.50 per square foot.

- **Reversion.** The resale price is forecast by applying a 10% overall capitalization rate to the net operating income for the year after the projection period (Year 11). The net operating income for Year 11 represents the projected income for Year 1 under the next owner. In this application sales expenses of 2.5% are deducted to determine the net resale price.

Forecast Results

Mathematical calculations based on the forecasts set forth in this sample application are shown in Table 24.9.

The Investor's Desired Rate of Return

The value of the property can be estimated by calculating the present value of the *NOI* for each year of the 10-year holding period and adding the present value of the cash flow from the sale of the property in Year 11 (the net resale price). Suppose the typical investor requires an overall yield rate (Y_O) of 13%.

Table 24.9 Income and Expense Estimates

	Year 1	Year 2	Year 3	Year 4	Year 5	Year 6	Year 7	Year 8	Year 9	Year 10	Year 11†
Income											
Contract and market rents*	$8,149,802	$8,149,802	$8,986,591	$12,645,178	$15,241,645	$16,035,714	$16,485,322	$17,432,668	$19,487,680	$20,291,478	$20,291,478
Escalation income	153,078	283,867	360,523	528,617	625,906	772,808	1,074,136	1,455,791	1,816,841	2,061,857	2,336,857
Vacancy and collection loss	(40,749)	(40,749)	(44,933)	(63,226)	(76,208)	(80,179)	(82,427)	(87,163)	(97,438)	(101,457)	(101,457)
Effective gross income	$8,262,131	$8,392,920	$9,302,181	$13,110,569	$15,791,343	$16,728,343	$17,477,031	$18,801,296	$21,207,083	$22,251,878	$22,526,878
Operating expenses											
Fixed expenses											
Real estate taxes	$926,671	$963,738	$1,002,287	$1,042,379	$1,084,074	$1,127,437	$1,172,534	$1,219,436	$1,268,213	$1,318,942	$1,371,699
Insurance	71,329	74,182	77,149	80,235	83,445	86,783	90,254	93,864	97,619	101,523	105,584
Variable expenses											
HVAC 400,000	420,000	441,000	463,050	486,203	510,513	536,038	562,840	590,982	620,531	651,558	684,136
Payroll 175,000	182,875	191,104	199,704	208,691	218,082	227,896	238,151	248,868	260,067	271,770	284,000
Repair and maintenance	440,000	459,800	480,491	502,113	524,708	548,320	572,994	598,779	625,724	653,882	683,307
Electricity	660,000	693,000	727,650	764,033	802,234	842,346	884,463	928,686	975,121	1,023,877	1,075,070
Security 200,000	209,000	218,405	228,233	238,504	249,236	260,452	272,172	284,420	297,219	310,594	324,571
Cleaning 30,000	31,350	32,761	34,235	35,776	37,385	39,068	40,826	42,663	44,583	46,589	48,686
Garbage removal	6,000	6,270	6,552	6,847	7,155	7,477	7,814	8,165	8,533	8,917	9,318
Water/sewer	50,000	52,250	54,601	57,058	59,626	62,309	65,113	68,043	71,105	74,305	77,648
Administrative and general	200,000	209,000	218,405	228,233	238,504	249,236	260,452	272,172	284,420	297,219	310,594
Management	75,000	78,375	81,902	85,587	89,439	93,464	97,670	102,065	106,658	111,457	116,473
Replacement allowance	100,000	104,500	109,203	114,117	119,252	124,618	130,226	136,086	142,210	148,609	155,297‡
Total operating expenses	$3,334,000	$3,484,340	$3,641,510	$3,805,824	$3,977,611	$4,157,206	$4,344,974	$4,541,285	$4,746,536	$4,961,131	$5,185,501
Operating expense ratio	40.35%	41.52%	39.15%	29.03%	25.19%	24.85%	24.86%	24.15%	22.38%	22.30%	23.02%
Net operating income	$4,928,131	$4,908,580	$5,660,671	$9,304,745	$11,813,732	$12,571,137	$13,132,057	$14,260,011	$16,460,547	$17,290,747	$17,341,377
Tenant improvements	0	0	1,399,740	1,562,261	292,114	135,266	49,309	298,771	312,216	326,266	6,851
Leasing commissions	0	0	870,166	976,026	183,356	85,293	31,239	190,196	0	0	4,424
Net income from operations	$4,928,131	$4,908,580	$3,390,765	$6,766,458	$11,338,262	$12,350,578	$13,051,509	$13,771,044	$16,148,331	$16,964,481	$17,330,102

* Reflects added vacancy associated with lease rollovers, as discussed under vacancy and collection loss.

† For calculation of residual value or reversion in Year 10.

‡ In some models, a replacement allowance is not deducted as an expense item in the NOI estimate for the last year of the forecast. The NOI estimate for that year (which comes to $17,496,674 without deduction of the replacement allowance) would be capitalized to arrive at the reversion. Whether or not it is appropriate to deduct a replacement allowance for that year is a function of the terminal or residual capitalization rate applied to the NOI.

Table 24.10	**Discounting of Income Streams and Reversion for Office Building**				
Year	**NOI***		**PV of $1 factor (13%)†**		**Discounted Value**
1	$4,928,131	×	0.884956	=	$4,361,179
2	$4,908,580	×	0.783147	=	$3,844,140
3	$5,660,671	×	0.693050	=	$3,923,128
4	$9,304,745	×	0.613319	=	$5,706,777
5	$11,813,732	×	0.542760	=	$6,412,021
6	$12,571,137	×	0.480319	=	$6,038,156
7	$13,132,057	×	0.425061	=	$5,581,925
8	$14,260,011	×	0.376160	=	$5,364,046
9	$16,460,547	×	0.332885	=	$5,479,469
10	$17,290,747	×	0.294588	=	$5,093,647
					$51,804,488
Reversion (based on *NOI* in Year 11)					$173,413,770
Less sales expenses @ 2.5%					− 4,335,344
					$169,078,426
Discounted at 0.294588					$49,808,426
Value of office building as of January 1, Year 1					$101,612,963

* *NOIs* from Table 24.9.

† The present value of $1 factor is not needed when discounted cash flow calculations are performed with a financial calculator or computer.

At a 13% discount rate, the present value of the *NOI* and reversion is $101,612,963 (see Table 24.10). This means that the investor would expect to earn a 13% rate of return if $101,612,963 is paid for the property.

Additional Analysis

Although property value was estimated by discounting the projected cash flow for each year rather than by applying a formula to develop an overall capitalization rate, an overall capitalization rate is implied in the solution. In this case the overall capitalization rate (R_O) for Year 1 is 4.8% ($4,928,131/ $101,612,963). This overall capitalization rate is considerably lower than the 10% capitalization rate applied to the estimated *NOI* for Year 11 to estimate the resale price. The difference is attributable to the fact that the *NOI* for Year 1 in this example is relatively low due to the impact of existing leases. The overall capitalization rate of 4.8% implied by a value estimate of $101,612,963 was calculated using only the *NOI* for Year 1. In this example, many of the existing leases specify a contract rate that is below market rate. As these leases are renewed at market levels during the 10-year holding period, the *NOI* is projected to increase. By the end of the holding period, most of the leases will have been renewed. Thus, the projected increase in *NOI* from Year 11 onward should closely parallel changes in the market rental rate, and the 10% capitalization rate used to estimate the resale price would reflect this assumption.

For example, if *NOI* is projected to increase 3% per year from Year 11 onward and the desired discount rate remains 13%, then the exponential-curve property model discussed in Chapter 23, which implies a capitalization rate of 10%, would be appropriate. In addition, all else being equal, terminal capitalization rates (R_Ns) are usually, though not necessarily, higher than first-year capitalization rates. This is due to the reduction in the remaining economic life of the property over the forecast period (as the property loses its competitive position in the market) and the increased risk associated with projecting income several years into the future.[5] Recapture requirements for older properties are generally also higher because of shorter remaining economic lives and greater associated risks.

The estimated present value of the property in this example, $101,612,963, reflects the projected increase in *NOI* due to lease renewals and increases in the market rental rate and the estimated resale price. The resulting value estimate for the property is high relative to the *NOI* for the first year, which explains the relatively low overall capitalization rate of 4.8%. Although many investors base their purchase decisions on the total expected yield, most have a limited amount of time to achieve an acceptable return, typically within five to ten years.

The long-term projections of income and expenses developed by appraisers will almost always differ from actual property income and expenses. However, rather than attempt to forecast the peaks and troughs that will occur during an anticipated holding period, appraisers simulate how market participants expect the property to perform.

This example illustrates the need to consider carefully the anticipated pattern of *NOI* when selecting an overall capitalization rate to be used in direct capitalization or a property model for yield capitalization. Capitalization rates can differ significantly for properties with different patterns of *NOI* beyond the first year and different resale potential. The absence of a regular income pattern does not necessarily mean that detailed DCF analysis is the only method that should be considered. The appraiser may discover that one of the standard valuation models can be adjusted to compensate for a deviation from the regular income pattern or that a special valuation model can be devised to solve the problem at hand.

---

5.   See D. Richard Wincott, "Terminal Capitalization Rates and Reasonableness," *The Appraisal Journal* (April 1991): 253–260. If, over the holding period, a substantial capital expenditure is allocated for the refurbishment or renovation of an aging property, R_N may equal or be less than R_O. Such a relationship between R_N and R_O is also likely when current income exceeds market levels.

FURTHER READING

Akerson, Charles B. *The Appraiser's Workbook.* 2d ed. Chicago: Appraisal Institute, 1996.

___. *Capitalization Theory and Techniques: Study Guide.* 2d ed. Chicago: Appraisal Institute, 2000.

American Institute of Real Estate Appraisers. *Forecasting: Market Determinants Affecting Cash Flows and Reversions.* Research Series Report 4. Chicago, 1989.

___. *Readings in the Income Capitalization Approach to Real Property Valuation,* Volume II. Chicago, 1985.

Fisher, Clifford E., Jr. *Rates and Ratios Used in the Income Capitalization Approach.* Chicago: Appraisal Institute, 1995.

Greer, Gaylon E. *Investment Analysis for Real Estate Decisions.* 4th ed. Chicago: Dearborn Financial Publishing, 1997.

Mason, James J., ed. and comp. *AIREA Financial Tables.* Chicago: American Institute of Real Estate Appraisers, 1981.

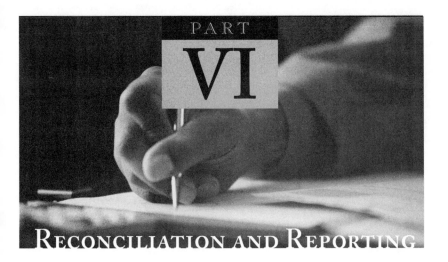

PART

VI

RECONCILIATION AND REPORTING

Part VI explores the essential tasks of resolving discrepancies between the value indications produced by the individual approaches to value and then communicating the appraiser's conclusions to the client in an appraisal report. **Chapter 25, Reconciling Value Indications,** covers the penultimate step of the valuation process in which an appraiser applies professional judgment and experience to render a supportable opinion of the defined value. **Chapter 26, The Appraisal Report,** discusses the means through which the conclusions of the appraisal analysis are delivered to the client, either in a written appraisal report or some form of oral communication of the value conclusions.

RECONCILING VALUE INDICATIONS

In the valuation process, more than one approach to value is usually applied, and each approach typically results in a different indication of value. If two or more approaches are used, the appraiser must reconcile at least two value indications. Moreover, several value indications may be derived in a single approach. In the sales comparison approach, for example, the analysis of each comparable sale produces an adjusted sale price, which is an indication of value for the subject property. The various units of comparison applied to sales may also produce different value indications—e.g., apartment properties may be analyzed in terms of price per unit or price per room and office buildings in terms of price per square foot of gross building area (GBA) or price per square foot of rentable area. In an analysis of income, different indications of value can result from applying income multipliers to specific types of income, directly capitalizing net income, and discounting cash flows.

The appraiser often resolves multiple value indications derived within a single approach as part of the application of that approach. At times, however, an appraiser may choose to resolve these differences after reexamining the purpose and use of the appraisal, the relevancy and adequacy of the data available and gathered, and all work previously performed in the appraisal. In either case, the integrity of each approach is maintained. Resolving the differences among various value indications is called *reconciliation*. Although the result of the final reconciliation process is usually the ultimate value conclusion, the reconciliation analysis may indicate that more research is needed or that new analyses must be performed. For example, if each of the three approaches is performed independently reconciliation may reveal conflicts or unresolved questions. Thus, reconciliation provides an integral quality control assessment of the valuation process prior to the final opinion of value and also helps identify key factors that must be cited and explained in the appraisal report.

The final value opinion does not simply represent the average of the different value indications derived. No mechanical formula is used to select one indication over the

> **reconciliation:** The last phase of any valuation assignment in which two or more value indications derived from market data are resolved into a final value opinion, which may be either a final range of value or a single point estimate.
>
> **final opinion of value:** The range of values or single dollar figure derived from the reconciliation of value indications and stated in the appraisal report.

> Appraisal judgment, experience, and proper application of appraisal techniques are **critical in final reconciliation.**

others, rather, final reconciliation relies on the proper application of appraisal techniques and the appraiser's judgment and experience. Table 25.1 illustrates the types of questions an appraiser asks in the final reconciliation process.

Table 25.1 **Questions Asked in Final Reconciliation**

Regarding land valuation:
- Are there an adequate number of sales?
- Are the sales comparable?
- Are the sales competitive?
- Is there market support for the adjustments that were made?
- Were those factors that could not be supported by quantitative adjustment dealt with using qualitative analysis in the reconciliation?
- Is the range of adjusted sale or unit prices in the range exhibited in the market?

Regarding the cost approach:
- Is the land value well supported?
- Are the cost estimates reliable?
- Do the cost estimates account for all of the costs?
- Are the sales used to extract depreciation from the market reliable?
- Was the depreciation allocated between the components accurately?
- Are the conclusions of the approach consistent with the conclusions in the other approaches?

Regarding the sales comparison approach:
- Are there an adequate number of sales?
- Are the sales comparable?
- Are the sales competitive?
- Is there market support for the adjustments that were made?
- Were those factors that could not be supported by quantitative adjustment dealt with using qualitative analysis in the reconciliation?
- Is the range of adjusted sale or unit prices in the range exhibited in the market?
- Are the conclusions of the approach consistent with the conclusions in the other approaches?

Regarding the income capitalization approach:
- Are there an adequate number of rental comparables?
- Are the comps comparable?
- Is there market support for the adjustments that were made?
- Were those factors that could not be supported by quantitative adjustment dealt with using qualitative analysis in the reconciliation?
- Is there historical expense information available? If so, how reliable is it?
- Do the owner's income and expense statements include all income?
- Do the owner's income and expense statements include all expenses?
- Do the owner's income and expense statements include any expenses that are not typical?
- Are the expense projections in line with market estimates?
- Is there market support for the capitalization method?
- Is there market support for the capitalization or discount rate?
- Does the method of capitalizing income reflect market patterns?
- Does the approach reflect market thinking?
- Are the conclusions of the approach consistent with the conclusions in the other approaches?

Reevaluation

To prepare for reconciliation the appraiser reconsiders the entire appraisal, making sure that the data available and the analytical techniques and logic applied have led to consistent judgments. The appraiser checks the data to ensure that it is authentic, pertinent, and sufficient. The value definition, the identified property rights, and the qualifying conditions imposed are carefully reconsidered to ascertain whether the procedures used in the analysis specifically address each of these items. The appraiser should examine the differences in the conclusions derived from the various approaches, apply tests of reasonableness to these primary conclusions, and resolve any inconsistencies.

At this stage of the valuation process, the appraiser asks a variety of questions:

- Is the effective age of the property used in the cost approach consistent with the physical condition reported?
- Is the same physical condition assumed in making adjustments to rent comparables, expense comparables, and sales comparables in the income and sales comparison approaches?
- Are the results of all the approaches consistent with the appraiser's conclusion of highest and best use?
- Do the indications derived from the approaches applied reflect the same defined value? For example, a value indication derived from income capitalization that is higher than an indication based on the cost approach may or may not include a non-realty or business enterprise value component.

All mathematical calculations should be checked, preferably by someone other than the person who performed them originally. Significant errors can lead to incorrect value indications, but even minor errors can diminish the client's confidence in the appraisal. Finally, the logic employed throughout the valuation process should be scrutinized, and the appraiser should ask these additional questions:

- Do the approaches and methods applied consider all the available data and systematically lead to meaningful conclusions that relate directly to the intended use of the appraisal?
- Does the appraisal provide the information required to solve the client's problem? For example, if the client wants to establish a depreciation basis to compute federal income tax, does the appraisal allocate separate values to the improvements and the land? A client who contemplates remodeling will want information on

> In reconciliation, the appraiser **reexamines the entire appraisal** to check for inconsistencies among the approaches applied (comparables used and adjustments calculated), the highest and best use conclusions upon which each approach is based, the defined value estimated in each approach, and the real property interests being appraised.

the costs and benefits of this plan. If the client is considering whether to accept an offer to purchase, the appraiser must adequately analyze the terms of the proposed contract.

> The appraiser uses **reconciliation criteria** to form a meaningful, defensible, and credible final value conclusion. The appropriateness of the approaches, the accuracy of the data and calculations, and the quantity or sufficiency of the evidence presented are considered relative to the specific appraisal problem.

Reconciliation Criteria

Reexamining an appraisal helps ensure its accuracy, its consistency, and the logic leading to the value indications. An appraiser relies more on professional experience and judgment in reconciliation than in any other part of the valuation process. The appraiser weighs the relative significance, applicability, and defensibility of each value indication and relies most heavily on the approach that is most appropriate to the nature of the appraisal problem.

Reconciliation requires appraisal judgment and a careful, logical analysis of the procedures that lead to each value indication. Appropriateness, accuracy, and quantity of evidence are the criteria with which an appraiser forms a meaningful, defensible final opinion of value.

Appropriateness

The appropriateness of an approach to the intended use of the appraisal is usually directly related to property type. For example, an appraisal to develop an opinion of the market value of a 30-year-old community shopping center will ordinarily employ procedures associated with the income capitalization approach, such as the derivation of an income multiplier, net income capitalization, or the discounting of cash flows. The cost approach might not be useful in valuing obsolete improvements, but it may be useful in an analysis of highest and best use to determine whether demolition of all or part of the improvements is appropriate. Where income data is scarce, in a market dominated by owner-occupants, the sales comparison approach can be used to obtain value information of a property.

Although the final value opinion is based on the approach or approaches that are most applicable, the final value opinion need not be identical to the value produced by the most applicable approach. If two approaches are applicable, the final opinion of value may be closer to one value indication than to the other. For example, the value indication derived from the income capitalization approach may be lower than the value indication derived from the sales comparison approach. If market participants are primarily interested in income-earning potential, the final opinion of value may be closer to the conclusion derived from income capitalization than from sales comparison. If the property is an owner-occupied dwelling, however, the sales comparison approach would likely be of primary relevance.

Accuracy

The accuracy of an appraisal is measured by the appraiser's confidence in the accuracy of the data and the adjustments made to each comparable property analyzed. For example, how confident is the appraiser of the adjustments made to each cost comparable, each sale comparable, and each rent comparable? Similarly, how reliable is the data supporting depreciation and cost estimates, estimates of income and expenses, and the capitalization rate selected? An appraiser may have more confidence in the accuracy of the data and calculations used in one approach than another.

The number of comparable properties, the number of adjustments, and the gross and net dollar amounts of adjustments may suggest the relative accuracy of a particular approach. If a large number of comparable properties are available for one approach and they seem to suggest a reasonably uniform pattern of market activity, greater accuracy may be indicated and the appraiser may place more reliance on this approach. For example, if there are many rental properties competitive with the appraised property, an appraiser may be able to extract current income, expense, and capitalization rate data from these properties and attribute greater accuracy and confidence to the income capitalization approach. If the appraiser finds several recently developed properties similar to the property being appraised, comparable data supporting land values and development costs may lend authority to the cost approach. Recent sales of similar properties may provide the data, needed to estimate accurate unit values by sales comparison.

Quantity of Evidence

Appropriateness and accuracy affect the quality and relevance of the value indication derived from a comparable or an approach. Although these criteria are considered separately in reconciliation, both must be studied in relation to the quantity of evidence provided by a particular comparable or approach. Even accurate and appropriate data can be weakened by a scarcity of evidence.

For example, consider an appraiser who is attempting to extract an overall capitalization rate from three comparable sales. The properties are considered appropriate in terms of their physical and locational characteristics and the similarity of the transactions. The available data for each sale is verified and considered reliable, and it appears that each comparable could produce an accurate estimate of the overall capitalization rate. However, the available data for one comparable includes a detailed capital budget and an operating statement of the property's expenses and income for the preceding three years. The data on the two other comparables is less detailed. Only total gross and net income data for three years is available for one comparable; for the other, detailed data is available for only one year. Because more data is available for the first comparable, the appraiser will have greater confidence in the capitalization rate obtained from this sale than in the rates obtained from the other two sales. In statistical terms, the confidence interval in which the

confidence interval: In statistics, the specification of a zone within a population, based on a sample mean and its standard error, within which the true mean most probably lies.

true value lies may be narrowed by the additional data. Regardless of the quantity of evidence available, the responsibility of the appraiser goes beyond the manipulation of numbers. It is the appraiser's duty to provide a supported value opinion consistent with the definition of value used in the assignment.

Finally, although the evidence from comparable sales may be accurate and appropriate, this data may relate to events that took place well before the effective date of the appraisal. Improved property sales, land sales, rentals, expenses, construction and development costs, and vacancy and absorption rates may significantly precede the date of value. Such data is relevant only insofar as it helps the appraiser estimate the future anticipated benefits of the property and the present value of these benefits. Market data is important, but it must help, not hamstring, the appraiser's analyses.

Final Opinion of Value

In an appraisal report, the final opinion of value may be stated as a single figure, as a range of values, or in relation to a benchmark amount (e.g., "not more than" or "not less than"). Traditionally an opinion of value is reported as a single dollar amount called a *point estimate*. A point estimate is required for many purposes:

- Real estate taxation
- Calculating depreciation deductions for federal income tax
- Estimating compensation in casualty, liability, and condemnation cases
- Determining value-based rent
- Making property transfer decisions

Because of legal or other requirements, most clients require a point estimate of value.

A point estimate should be rounded to reflect the degree of precision the appraiser can associate with the particular opinion of value. Often the manner in which the figure is rounded is a matter of convention—e.g., to two or three significant digits. For example, if the final value estimate is a six-digit number, the figure will likely be rounded to the nearest thousand or ten thousand dollars; if it is a seven-digit number, it will likely be rounded to the nearest ten thousand or hundred thousand dollars. In some instances, when market data is more diverse the range may be wider.

Even a rounded figure may imply greater precision than is warranted. Because an appraised value is an opinion, it implies a range in which the property value may fall. That value range usually reflects the range of value conclusions derived from two or more approaches, but the final value opinion need not fall within this range. For example, an appraiser may report an opinion of value of $9,400,000 to represent a conclusion drawn from two approaches with preliminary indications of $9,390,000 and $9,380,000. In this case the conclusion of $9,400,000 is not statistically derived. It is outside the range indicated by the two approaches, but it may reasonably reflect the market value of the property based on the two approaches. In addition to the point value estimate, the appraiser might report the value range as "between $9,300,000 and $9,400,000."

When reporting a range, the appraiser indicates that the value is no lower than the low end and no higher than the high end of the range. A wide range may be of no use to a client, but a narrow range may imply precision that is not warranted. When provided with a value range, clients might see the extreme that suits their purposes as a virtual guarantee. Accordingly, appraisers must take care to report their final value conclusions in a manner that does not mislead clients.

Aside from a range of value, an appraiser may report a probability range to suggest the confidence level associated with the opinion of value. The evidence considered in each approach should allow for such variation. For example, an appraiser may consider a more aggressive and a less aggressive market rent schedule for a proposed shopping center. Different capitalization rates may be applied to the two income streams along with different discount rates and income multipliers. Any value differences resulting from the higher and lower projected rents in the income capitalization approach should be correlated with different levels of risk-related entrepreneurial incentive in the cost approach.

> The final opinion of value may be stated as a **single figure** (point estimate), as a **range of value**, or in relation to a **benchmark amount** (e.g., "not more than" or "not less than").

> **point estimate:** A final value indication reported as a single dollar amount. A point estimate is typically regarded as the most probable number, not the only possible number, and is often required for revenue and compensation purposes.
>
> **range of value:** The range, or confidence interval, in which the final opinion of market value may fall; usually stated as a variable amount between a high and low value limit.
>
> **probability range:** The confidence level associated with a specific value estimate or set of value estimates.
>
> **rounding:** Expressing an amount as an approximate number—i.e., exact only to a specific decimal place. An appraisal conclusion may be rounded to reflect the lack of precision associated with the value opinion.

FURTHER READING

Emerson, Ralph III. "Proper Reconciliation in Narrative Reports Favors Substance Over Form." *The Appraisal Journal* (January 1998).

Roberts, Joe R., and Eric Roberts. "The Myth About Appraisals." *The Appraisal Journal* (April 1991).

Spence, Mark T., and James A. Thorson. "The Effect of Expertise on the Quality of Appraisal Services." *Journal of Real Estate Research*, vol. 15, no. 1/2 (1998).

26 | THE APPRAISAL REPORT

The conclusions reached by appraisers in valuation analysis are communicated to the client in an appraisal report. An appraisal report leads the reader from the definition of the appraisal problem through analysis and relevant descriptive data to a specific conclusion. In a self-contained or summary appraisal report, the appraiser must present all facts, reasoning, and conclusions clearly and succinctly. The length, type, and content of appraisal reports are dictated by the intended use and purpose of the appraisal, the nature and complexity of the problem to be solved, and the information needs of the intended user (or users).

Standards for Written Reports

Each analysis, opinion, or conclusion that results from an appraisal must be communicated in a manner that is meaningful to the intended user and will not be misleading. Professional appraisers are required to conduct their appraisal activities in compliance with the requirements of the Uniform Standards of Professional Appraisal Practice (USPAP). Appraisal Institute members must also adhere to the organization's Code of Professional Ethics, Supplemental Standards, and Guide Notes.

The Preamble to the Uniform Standards of Professional Appraisal Practice states, "It is essential that professional appraisers develop and communicate their analyses, opinions, and conclusions to intended users of their services in a manner that is meaningful and not misleading." Standard 2 of USPAP sets forth the requirements for reporting an appraisal of real property.

Standards Rule 2-1 states that each written or oral real property appraisal report must:

(a) clearly and accurately set forth the appraisal in a manner that will not be misleading;

(b) contain sufficient information to enable the intended users of the appraisal to understand the report properly; and

> **appraisal report:** The written or oral communication of an appraisal; the document transmitted to the client upon completion of an appraisal assignment. Reporting requirements are set forth in the Standards Rules relating to Standard 2 of the Uniform Standards of Professional Appraisal Practice.

> Professional appraisers are required to conduct their appraisal activities in **compliance with the requirements** of the Uniform Standards of Professional Appraisal Practice.

(c) clearly and accurately disclose any extraordinary assumption, hypothetical condition, or limiting condition that directly affects the appraisal and indicate its impact on value.

Standards Rule 2-2 requires that each written appraisal report be prepared under one of the following three options, which must be prominently stated in the report:

- Self-contained appraisal report
- Summary appraisal report
- Restricted use appraisal report

The essential difference between the three reporting options is the level of detail required in certain areas of presentation and the accompanying work file. Figure 26.1 compares the reporting options and indicates which elements may be abbreviated in summary and restricted use appraisal reports. The Standards are revised periodically, so practitioners must always refer to the most current revision of USPAP for more detailed explanation.

Types of Reports

An appraisal report may be oral or written.[1] Written communications prepared under one of the three reporting options may be form or narrative reports. Usually a report is presented in the format requested by the intended user. However, even if a client asks for a report that does not include detailed documentation, the appraiser must undertake the analysis required by the assignment as set by the scope of work. In such a case all material, data, and working papers used to prepare the appraisal are kept in the appraiser's permanent file. Although the appraiser may never need to provide written substantiation for an opinion that is submitted in abbreviated form, he or she may be asked to explain or defend the opinion at a later time.

The extent of file documentation depends on the type of report prepared. A less detailed report will require more file documentation, while a more detailed report will require little external documentation. At one end of the spectrum is the self-contained appraisal report, which includes detailed descriptions of the data, reasoning, and analyses used to arrive at the value conclusion. At the other end of the spectrum is the restricted use appraisal report, which contains virtually none of this information. In the middle of the range is the summary appraisal report, which contains some, but not all, of the descriptive information gathered in the appraiser's analysis.

The discussion of some topics may be less extensive in a summary or restricted use appraisal report, but the report still must conform to USPAP and contain sufficient information to lead the reader to the appraiser's

---

1. An appraisal report sent to a client via e-mail or some other electronic medium qualifies as a written appraisal report. USPAP provides direction on the electronic transmission of reports in Statement on Appraisal Standards No. 8 (SMT-8).

conclusions. In the case of an oral report, the appraiser who prepares a restricted use appraisal report must keep all notes and data on file with a complete synopsis of the analysis, conclusions, and value opinion.

> Regardless of how a report is conveyed, all data and notes as well as a summary of the analysis and conclusions should be kept in the **work file** unless that information is in the report itself—i.e., the information should either be in the report or in the file.

Oral Reports

An appraiser may make an oral report when the circumstances or the needs of the intended user do not permit or warrant a written report. Expert testimony presented in a deposition or in court is considered an oral report. In other situations oral reports are communicated to the intended user in person or by telephone. Standards Rule 2-4 states that an oral report must address, at a minimum, the substantive matters set forth for

> **oral report:** An unwritten appraisal report that includes a property description as well as all facts, assumptions, conditions, and reasoning on which the value conclusion is based. The reporting requirements for oral reports, which are the same as those applied to written reports, are set forth in the Standards Rules relating to Standard 2 of the Uniform Standards of Professional Appraisal Practice.

a summary appraisal report in Standards Rule 2-2(b). Each oral report must include the underlying bases of the appraisal, especially any extraordinary assumptions or hypothetical conditions used. After communicating an oral report, the appraiser must keep on file all notes and data relevant to the assignment so that if asked at a later date (i.e., any time during the required record retention period) the appraiser could produce a report that would meet the minimum requirements for a summary appraisal report.

The organization and composition of the appraiser's work file may vary so long as the file contents are retrievable by the appraiser during the required record retention period. The work file can reference information that is located elsewhere—e.g., stored electronically on a computer, in another file, or at some other location.

Form Reports

Most form reports may be classified as summary appraisal reports, depending on the level of detail and the quantity of supporting documentation. Form reports often meet the needs of financial institutions, insurance companies, and government agencies. They are required for the purchase and sale of most homes and existing mortgages on residential properties in the secondary mortgage market created by government agencies and private organizations. Because these intended users review many appraisals, using a standard report form is both efficient and convenient. When a form is used, those responsible for reviewing the appraisal know exactly where to find each category or item of data in the report. By completing the form, the appraiser ensures that no item required by the reviewer is overlooked. Figure 26.2 shows a Uniform

Figure 26.1 Comparison of Report Types

Self-contained Appraisal Report	Summary Appraisal Report	Restricted Use Appraisal Report
i. **State** the identity of the client and any intended users, by name or type.	i. **State** the identity of the client and any intended users, by name or type.	i. **State** the identity of the client, by name or type.
ii. **State** the intended use of the appraisal.	ii. **State** the intended use of the appraisal.	ii. **State** the intended use of the appraisal.
iii. **Describe** information sufficient to identify the real estate involved in the appraisal, including the physical and economic property characteristics relevant to the assignment.	iii. **Summarize** information sufficient to identify the real estate involved in the appraisal, including the physical and economic property characteristics relevant to the assignment.	iii. **State** information sufficient to identify the real estate involved in the appraisal.
iv. **State** the real property interest appraised.	iv. **State** the real property interest appraised.	iv. **State** the real property interest appraised.
v. **State** the purpose of the appraisal, including the type and definition of value and its source.	v. **State** the purpose of the appraisal, including the type and definition of value and its source.	v. **State** the purpose of the appraisal, including the type of value, and **refer** to the definition of value pertinent to the purpose of the assignment.
vi. **State** the effective date of the appraisal and the date of the report.	vi. **State** the effective date of the appraisal and the date of the report.	vi. **State** the effective date of the appraisal and the date of the report.
vii. **Describe** sufficient information to disclose to the client and any intended users of the appraisal the scope of work used to develop the appraisal.	vii. **Summarize** sufficient information to disclose to the client and any intended users of the appraisal the scope of work used to develop the appraisal.	vii. **State** the extent of the process of collecting, confirming, and reporting data or **refer** to an assignment agreement retained in the appraiser's work file that describes the scope of work to be performed.
viii. **State** all assumptions, hypothetical conditions, and limiting conditions that affected the analyses, opinions, and conclusions.	viii. **State** all assumptions, hypothetical conditions, and limiting conditions that affected the analyses, opinions, and conclusions.	viii. **State** all assumptions, hypothetical conditions, and limiting conditions that affect the analyses, opinions, and conclusions.

Figure 26.1   Comparison of Report Types *(continued)*

Self-contained Appraisal Report	Summary Appraisal Report	Restricted Use Appraisal Report
ix. **Describe** the information analyzed, the appraisal procedures followed, and the reasoning that supports the analyses, opinions, and conclusions.	ix. **Summarize** the information analyzed, the appraisal procedures followed, and the reasoning that supports the analyses, opinions, and conclusions.	ix. **State** the appraisal procedures followed, state the value opinion(s) and conclusion(s) reached, and reference the work file.
x. **State** the use of the real estate existing as of the date of value and the use of the real estate reflected in the appraisal; and, when the purpose of the assignment is market value, **describe** the support and rationale for the appraiser's opinion of the highest and best use of the real estate.	x. **State** the use of the real estate existing as of the date of value and the use of the real estate reflected in the appraisal; and, when the purpose of the assignment is market value, **summarize** the support and rationale for the appraiser's opinion of the highest and best use of the real estate.	x. **State** the use of the real estate existing as of the date of value and the use of the real estate reflected in the appraisal; and, when the purpose of the assignment is market value, **state** the appraiser's opinion of the highest and best use of the real estate.
xi. **State** and explain any permitted departures from specific requirements of Standard 1 and the reason for excluding any of the usual valuation approaches.	xi. **State** and explain any permitted departures from specific requirements of Standard 1 and the reason for excluding any of the usual valuation approaches.	xi. **State** and explain any permitted departures from specific requirements of Standard 1; **state** the exclusion of any of the usual valuation approaches; and **state** a prominent use restriction that limits use of the report to the client and warns that the appraiser's opinions and conclusions set forth in the report cannot be understood properly without additional information in the appraiser's work file.
xii. Include a signed certification in accordance with Standards Rule 2-3.	xii. Include a signed certification in accordance with Standards Rule 2-3.	xii. Include a signed certification in accordance with Standards Rule 2-3.

Note the use of the terms *describe, summarize,* and *state* to specify the level of detail required.

No comment sections are included in this chart; the chart is prepared for discussion purposes only.

Source: Uniform Standards of Professional Appraisal Practice, 2001 edition. Consult the most recent edition of USPAP for more detailed explanation.

Figure 26.2 Uniform Residential Appraisal Report Form and Statement of Limiting Conditions and Appraiser's Certification (Fannie Mae Form 1004 and 1004B)

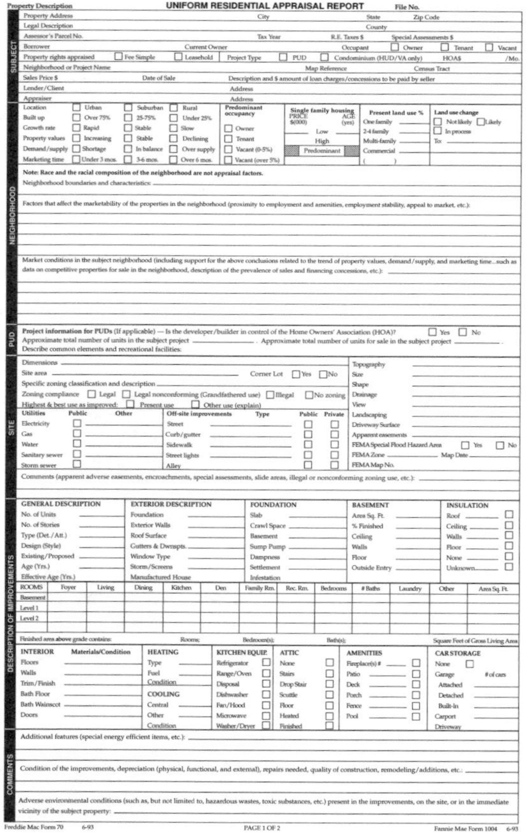
Property Description UNIFORM RESIDENTIAL APPRAISAL REPORT File No.

SUBJECT
Property Address City State Zip Code
Legal Description County
Assessor's Parcel No. Tax Year R.E. Taxes $ Special Assessments $
Borrower Current Owner Occupant: Owner Tenant Vacant
Property rights appraised: Fee Simple Leasehold | Project Type: PUD Condominium (HUD/VA only) HOA$ /Mo.
Neighborhood or Project Name Map Reference Census Tract
Sales Price $ Date of Sale Description and $ amount of loan charges/concessions to be paid by seller
Lender/Client Address
Appraiser Address

NEIGHBORHOOD
Location: Urban Suburban Rural
Built up: Over 75% 25-75% Under 25%
Growth rate: Rapid Stable Slow
Property values: Increasing Stable Declining
Demand/supply: Shortage In balance Over supply
Marketing time: Under 3 mos. 3-6 mos. Over 6 mos.
Predominant occupancy: Owner Tenant Vacant (0-5%) Vacant (over 5%)
Single family housing: PRICE $(000) AGE (yrs) Low High Predominant
Present land use %: One family 2-4 family Multi-family Commercial ( )
Land use change: Not likely Likely In process To:
Note: Race and the racial composition of the neighborhood are not appraisal factors.
Neighborhood boundaries and characteristics:
Factors that affect the marketability of the properties in the neighborhood (proximity to employment and amenities, employment stability, appeal to market, etc.):
Market conditions in the subject neighborhood (including support for the above conclusions related to the trend of property values, demand/supply, and marketing time — such as data on competitive properties for sale in the neighborhood, description of the prevalence of sales and financing concessions, etc.):

PUD
Project information for PUDs (If applicable) — Is the developer/builder in control of the Home Owners' Association (HOA)? Yes No
Approximate total number of units in the subject project. Approximate total number of units for sale in the subject project
Describe common elements and recreational facilities:

SITE
Dimensions
Site area Corner Lot Yes No
Specific zoning classification and description
Zoning compliance: Legal Legal nonconforming (Grandfathered use) Illegal No zoning
Highest & best use as improved: Present use Other use (explain)
Utilities: Public Other — Electricity, Gas, Water, Sanitary sewer, Storm sewer
Off-site improvements: Type Public Private — Street, Curb/gutter, Sidewalk, Street lights, Alley
Topography, Size, Shape, Drainage, View, Landscaping, Driveway Surface, Apparent easements
FEMA Special Flood Hazard Area Yes No
FEMA Zone Map Date
FEMA Map No.
Comments (apparent adverse easements, encroachments, special assessments, slide areas, illegal or nonconforming zoning use, etc.):

DESCRIPTION OF IMPROVEMENTS
GENERAL DESCRIPTION: No. of Units, No. of Stories, Type (Det./Att.), Design (Style), Existing/Proposed, Age (Yrs.), Effective Age (Yrs.)
EXTERIOR DESCRIPTION: Foundation, Exterior Walls, Roof Surface, Gutters & Dwnspts., Window Type, Storm/Screens, Manufactured House
FOUNDATION: Slab, Crawl Space, Basement, Sump Pump, Dampness, Settlement, Infestation
BASEMENT: Area Sq. Ft., % Finished, Ceiling, Walls, Floor, Outside Entry
INSULATION: Roof, Ceiling, Walls, Floor, None, Unknown

ROOMS	Foyer	Living	Dining	Kitchen	Den	Family Rm.	Rec. Rm.	Bedrooms	# Baths	Laundry	Other	Area Sq. Ft.
Basement												
Level 1												
Level 2												

Finished area above grade contains: Rooms; Bedroom(s); Bath(s); Square Feet of Gross Living Area
INTERIOR Materials/Condition: Floors, Walls, Trim/Finish, Bath Floor, Bath Wainscot, Doors
HEATING: Type, Fuel, Condition; COOLING: Central, Other, Condition
KITCHEN EQUIP.: Refrigerator, Range/Oven, Disposal, Dishwasher, Fan/Hood, Microwave, Washer/Dryer
ATTIC: None, Stairs, Drop Stair, Scuttle, Floor, Heated, Finished
AMENITIES: Fireplace(s) #, Patio, Deck, Porch, Fence, Pool
CAR STORAGE: None, Garage # of cars, Attached, Detached, Built-In, Carport, Driveway
Additional features (special energy efficient items, etc.):

COMMENTS
Condition of the improvements, depreciation (physical, functional, and external), repairs needed, quality of construction, remodeling/additions, etc.:
Adverse environmental conditions (such as, but not limited to, hazardous wastes, toxic substances, etc.) present in the improvements, on the site, or in the immediate vicinity of the subject property:

Freddie Mac Form 70 6-93 PAGE 1 OF 2 Fannie Mae Form 1004 6-93

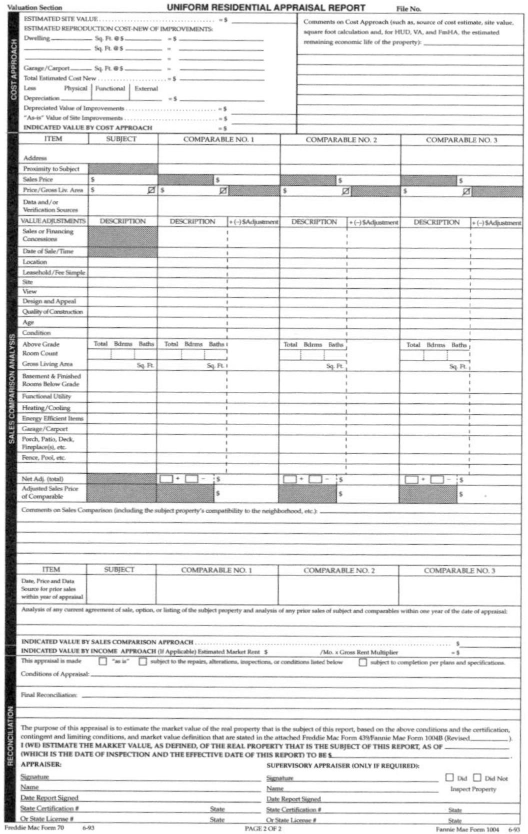
Valuation Section UNIFORM RESIDENTIAL APPRAISAL REPORT File No.

COST APPROACH
ESTIMATED SITE VALUE = $
ESTIMATED REPRODUCTION COST-NEW OF IMPROVEMENTS:
Dwelling Sq. Ft. @ $ = $
Sq. Ft. @ $ =
Garage/Carport Sq. Ft. @ $ =
Total Estimated Cost New = $
Less Physical Functional External
Depreciation = $
Depreciated Value of Improvements = $
"As-is" Value of Site Improvements = $
INDICATED VALUE BY COST APPROACH = $
Comments on Cost Approach (such as, source of cost estimate, site value, square foot calculation and, for HUD, VA, and FmHA, the estimated remaining economic life of the property):

SALES COMPARISON ANALYSIS

ITEM	SUBJECT	COMPARABLE NO. 1		COMPARABLE NO. 2		COMPARABLE NO. 3	
Address							
Proximity to Subject							
Sales Price	$	$		$		$	
Price/Gross Liv. Area	$ Ø	$ Ø		$ Ø		$ Ø	
Data and/or Verification Sources							
VALUE ADJUSTMENTS	DESCRIPTION	DESCRIPTION	+(-)$Adjustment	DESCRIPTION	+(-)$Adjustment	DESCRIPTION	+(-)$Adjustment
Sales or Financing Concessions							
Date of Sale/Time							
Location							
Leasehold/Fee Simple							
Site							
View							
Design and Appeal							
Quality of Construction							
Age							
Condition							
Above Grade Room Count	Total Bdrms Baths	Total Bdrms Baths		Total Bdrms Baths		Total Bdrms Baths	
Gross Living Area	Sq. Ft.	Sq. Ft.		Sq. Ft.		Sq. Ft.	
Basement & Finished Rooms Below Grade							
Functional Utility							
Heating/Cooling							
Energy Efficient Items							
Garage/Carport							
Porch, Patio, Deck, Fireplace(s), etc.							
Fence, Pool, etc.							
Net Adj. (total)		+ -	$	+ -	$	+ -	$
Adjusted Sales Price of Comparable			$		$		$

Comments on Sales Comparison (including the subject property's compatibility to the neighborhood, etc.):

ITEM	SUBJECT	COMPARABLE NO. 1	COMPARABLE NO. 2	COMPARABLE NO. 3
Date, Price and Data Source for prior sales within year of appraisal				

Analysis of any current agreement of sale, option, or listing of the subject property and analysis of any prior sales of subject and comparables within one year of the date of appraisal:

RECONCILIATION
INDICATED VALUE BY SALES COMPARISON APPROACH $
INDICATED VALUE BY INCOME APPROACH (If Applicable) Estimated Market Rent $ /Mo. x Gross Rent Multiplier = $
This appraisal is made "as is" subject to the repairs, alterations, inspections, or conditions listed below subject to completion per plans and specifications.
Conditions of Appraisal:
Final Reconciliation:
The purpose of this appraisal is to estimate the market value of the real property that is the subject of this report, based on the above conditions and the certification, contingent and limiting conditions, and market value definition that are stated in the attached Freddie Mac Form 439/Fannie Mae Form 1004B (Revised).
I (WE) ESTIMATE THE MARKET VALUE, AS DEFINED, OF THE REAL PROPERTY THAT IS THE SUBJECT OF THIS REPORT, AS OF (WHICH IS THE DATE OF INSPECTION AND THE EFFECTIVE DATE OF THIS REPORT) TO BE $
APPRAISER: Signature, Name, Date Report Signed, State Certification # State, Or State License # State
SUPERVISORY APPRAISER (ONLY IF REQUIRED): Signature, Name, Date Report Signed, State Certification # State, Or State License # State — Did Did Not Inspect Property

Freddie Mac Form 70 6-93 PAGE 2 OF 2 Fannie Mae Form 1004 6-93

In 1986 Fannie Mae and Freddie Mac introduced the Uniform Residential Appraisal Report (URAR). The URAR form was the first form to be adopted by all the major governmental and quasi-governmental agencies (Fannie Mae, Freddie Mac, the Department of Housing and Urban Development, the Department of Veterans Affairs, and the Federal Home Administration) involved in mortgage activities. Since the form was introduced, these agencies have required an appraisal presented on the URAR form as the basis for all mortgages they issue that may eventually be sold in the secondary mortgage market.

A revised URAR form was released in 1993. The government agencies that use the form worked with The Appraisal Foundation, the Appraisal Institute, and other appraisal organizations on the revisions to improve the reporting of essential information and reflect changes in industry requirements and standards.

Figure 26.2 Uniform Residential Appraisal Report Form and Statement of Limiting Conditions and Appraiser's Certification (Fannie Mae Form 1004 and 1004B) (continued)

CONTINGENT AND LIMITING CONDITIONS: The appraiser's certification that appears in the appraisal report is subject to the following conditions:

1. The appraiser will not be responsible for matters of a legal nature that affect either the property being appraised or the title to it. The appraiser assumes that the title is good and marketable and, therefore, will not render any opinions about the title. The property is appraised on the basis of it being under responsible ownership.

2. The appraiser has provided a sketch in the appraisal report to show approximate dimensions of the improvements and the sketch is included only to assist the reader of the report in visualizing the property and understanding the appraiser's determination of its size.

3. The appraiser has examined the available flood maps that are provided by the Federal Emergency Management Agency (or other data sources) and has noted in the appraisal report whether the subject site is located in an identified Special Flood Hazard Area. Because the appraiser is not a surveyor, he or she makes no guarantees, express or implied, regarding this determination.

4. The appraiser will not give testimony or appear in court because he or she made an appraisal of the property in question, unless specific arrangements to do so have been made beforehand.

5. The appraiser has estimated the value of the land in the cost approach at its highest and best use and the improvements at their contributory value. These separate valuations of the land and improvements must not be used in conjunction with any other appraisal and are invalid if they are so used.

6. The appraiser has noted in the appraisal report any adverse conditions (such as, needed repairs, depreciation, the presence of hazardous wastes, toxic substances, etc.) observed during the inspection of the subject property or that he or she became aware of during the normal research involved in performing the appraisal. Unless otherwise stated in the appraisal report, the appraiser has no knowledge of any hidden or unapparent conditions of the property or adverse environmental conditions (including the presence of hazardous wastes, toxic substances, etc.) that would make the property more or less valuable, and has assumed that there are no such conditions and makes no guarantees or warranties, express or implied, regarding the condition of the property. The appraiser will not be responsible for any such conditions that do exist or for any engineering or testing that might be required to discover whether such conditions exist. Because the appraiser is not an expert in the field of environmental hazards, the appraisal report must not be considered as an environmental assessment of the property.

7. The appraiser obtained the information, estimates, and opinions that were expressed in the appraisal report from sources that he or she considers to be reliable and believes them to be true and correct. The appraiser does not assume responsibility for the accuracy of such items that were furnished by other parties.

8. The appraiser will not disclose the contents of the appraisal report except as provided for in the Uniform Standards of Professional Appraisal Practice.

9. The appraiser has based his or her appraisal report and valuation conclusion for an appraisal that is subject to satisfactory completion, repairs, or alterations on the assumption that completion of the improvements will be performed in a workmanlike manner.

10. The appraiser must provide his or her prior written consent before the lender/client specified in the appraisal report can distribute the appraisal report (including conclusions about the property value, the appraiser's identity and professional designations, and references to any professional appraisal organizations or the firm with which the appraiser is associated) to anyone other than the borrower; the mortgagee or its successors and assigns; the mortgage insurer; consultants; professional appraisal organizations; any state or federally approved financial institution; or any department, agency, or instrumentality of the United States or any state or the District of Columbia; except that the lender/client may distribute the property description section of the report only to data collection or reporting service(s) without having to obtain the appraiser's prior written consent. The appraiser's written consent and approval must also be obtained before the appraisal can be conveyed by anyone to the public through advertising, public relations, news, sales, or other media.

Freddie Mac Form 439 6-93   Page 1 of 2   Fannie Mae Form 1004B 6-93

APPRAISER'S CERTIFICATION: The Appraiser certifies and agrees that:

1. I have researched the subject market area and have selected a minimum of three recent sales of properties most similar and proximate to the subject property for consideration in the sales comparison analysis and have made a dollar adjustment when appropriate to reflect the market reaction to those items of significant variation. If a significant item in a comparable property is superior to, or more favorable than, the subject property, I have made a negative adjustment to reduce the adjusted sales price of the comparable and, if a significant item in a comparable property is inferior to, or less favorable than the subject property, I have made a positive adjustment to increase the adjusted sales price of the comparable.

2. I have taken into consideration the factors that have an impact on value in my development of the estimate of market value in the appraisal report. I have not knowingly withheld any significant information from the appraisal report and I believe, to the best of my knowledge, that all statements and information in the appraisal report are true and correct.

3. I stated in the appraisal report only my own personal, unbiased, and professional analysis, opinions, and conclusions, which are subject only to the contingent and limiting conditions specified in this form.

4. I have no present or prospective interest in the property that is the subject to this report, and I have no present or prospective personal interest or bias with respect to the participants in the transaction. I did not base, either partially or completely, my analysis and/or the estimate of market value in the appraisal report on the race, color, religion, sex, handicap, familial status, or national origin of either the prospective owners or occupants of the subject property or of the present owners or occupants of the properties in the vicinity of the subject property.

5. I have no present or contemplated future interest in the subject property, and neither my current or future employment nor my compensation for performing this appraisal is contingent on the appraised value of the property.

6. I was not required to report a predetermined value or direction in value that favors the cause of the client or any related party, the amount of the value estimate, the attainment of a specific result, or the occurrence of a subsequent event in order to receive any compensation and/or employment for performing the appraisal. I did not base the appraisal report on a requested minimum valuation, a specific valuation, or the need to approve a specific mortgage loan.

7. I performed this appraisal in conformity with the Uniform Standards of Professional Appraisal Practice that were adopted and promulgated by the Appraisal Standards Board of The Appraisal Foundation and that were in place as of the effective date of this appraisal, with the exception of the departure provision of those Standards, which does not apply. I acknowledge that an estimate of a reasonable time for exposure in the open market is a condition in the definition of market value and the estimate I developed is consistent with the marketing time noted in the neighborhood section of this report, unless I have otherwise stated in the reconciliation section.

8. I have personally inspected the interior and exterior areas of the subject property and the exterior of all properties listed as comparables in the appraisal report. I further certify that I have noted any apparent or known adverse conditions in the subject improvements, on the subject site, or on any site within the immediate vicinity of the subject property of which I am aware and have made adjustments for these adverse conditions in my analysis of the property value to the extent that I had market evidence to support them. I have also commented about the effect of the adverse conditions on the marketability of the subject property.

9. I personally prepared all conclusions and opinions about the real estate that were set forth in the appraisal report. If I relied on significant professional assistance from any individual or individuals in the performance of the appraisal or the preparation of the appraisal report, I have named such individual(s) and disclosed the specific tasks performed by them in the reconciliation section of this appraisal report. I certify that any individual so named is qualified to perform the tasks. I have not authorized anyone to make a change to any item in the report; therefore, if an unauthorized change is made to the appraisal report, I will take no responsibility for it.

SUPERVISORY APPRAISER'S CERTIFICATION: If a supervisory appraiser signed the appraisal report, he or she certifies and agrees that: I directly supervise the appraiser who prepared the appraisal report, have reviewed the appraisal report, agree with the statements and conclusions of the appraiser, agree to be bound by the appraiser's certifications numbered 4 through 7 above, and am taking full responsibility for the appraisal and the appraisal report.

ADDRESS OF PROPERTY APPRAISED: _____

APPRAISER:	SUPERVISORY APPRAISER (only if required):
Signature:	Signature:
Name:	Name:
Date Signed:	Date Signed:
State Certification #:	State Certification #
or State License #:	or State License #:
State:	State:
Expiration Date of Certification or License:	Expiration Date of Certification or License:
	☐ Did ☐ Did Not Inspect Property

Freddie Mac Form 439 6-93   Page 2 of 2   Fannie Mae Form 1004B 6-93

Residential Appraisal Report form with the appropriate certification and limiting conditions.

Form reports, like all appraisal reports, must comply with Standard 2 of USPAP. Some forms currently in use do not address all of the information required by professional standards. Such forms may be used only if they are augmented with supplemental information so that they meet Standard 2. In addition, most forms in use do not contain a certification statement that meets Appraisal Institute's Supplemental Standards. (The Supplemental Standards are shown in Appendix A.) Appraisal Institute members must therefore attach supplemental material when they use these forms.

Guide Note 3 to the Uniform Standards addresses the use of form reports in the appraisal of residential property. Forms are increasingly being used for appraisals of both residential and nonresidential properties, e.g., apartment, commercial, and industrial properties.[2] Current market trends indicate that the use of form reports for all kinds of properties is likely to continue.

Appraisers must be very careful to ensure that a report form does not dictate the appraisal process. The methodology employed in a valuation is determined by the nature of the specific appraisal problem, not by the type of report. If a report form does not provide for adequate presentation and discussion of all the analysis and data that the appraiser believes to be pertinent, that information must be added as a supplement.

> **form report:** An appraisal report presented on a form, as opposed to one written in narrative style. Some standard forms include those required by financial institutions, insurance companies, and government agencies. The reporting requirements for form reports, which are the same as for other types of reports, are set forth in the Standards Rules relating to Standard 2 of the Uniform Standards of Professional Appraisal Practice and the Appraisal Institute's Guide Note 3.
>
> **Uniform Residential Appraisal Report (URAR):** A standardized appraisal form developed jointly by the Federal National Mortgage Association, the Federal Home Loan Mortgage Corporation, the Federal Housing Administration, the Veterans Administration, and the Farmers' Home Administration and used to communicate valuations of one- to four-family residential properties; Fannie Mae, Freddie Mac, HUD, VA, and FHA require the use of the URAR form as the basis for all mortgages they issue that may be sold in the secondary mortgage market.

Narrative Appraisal Report Format

Narrative appraisal reports give appraisers the opportunity to support and explain their opinions and conclusions fully and to convince the reader of the soundness of the final opinion of value. In preparing a

---

2. For an in-depth discussion of appraisal form reports, see the following guidebooks from the *Communicating the Appraisal* series: Arlen C. Mills and Dorothy Z. Mills, *The Uniform Residential Appraisal Report*, 2d ed. (Chicago: Appraisal Institute, 1994); Arlen C. Mills and Dorothy Z. Mills, *The Individual Condominium Unit Appraisal Report*, 2d ed. (Chicago: Appraisal Institute, 1995); Arlen C. Mills and Dorothy Z. Mills, *The Small Residential Income Property Appraisal Report*, 2d ed. (Chicago: Appraisal Institute, 1995); and Joseph L. Minnich III, *Fannie Mae Desktop Underwriter™ Quantitative Analysis Appraisal Report Form 2055 and Qualitative Analysis Appraisal Report Form 2065* (Chicago: Appraisal Institute, 1997).

narrative appraisal report, the appraiser should keep descriptive sections separate from analysis and interpretation. Factual and descriptive data is usually presented in early sections of the report so that subsequent analysis and interpretation may refer to these facts and indicate how they influence the final opinion of value. Repetition and unnecessary duplication should be avoided, but the presentation of data may depend on the nature and length of the report.

The research presented in a well-prepared appraisal report can be very detailed, and the report should exhibit logical organization and sound reasoning. These basic attributes are enhanced by good composition, a fluid writing style, and clear expression. The use of technical jargon and slang should be avoided. To communicate with the reader effectively, the contents of the report should be set forth as succinctly as possible.[3]

The appraiser may not be present when the report is reviewed or examined, so the report is his or her representative. A good report creates a favorable impression of the appraiser's professional competence. The following suggestions may help appraisers make a good impression:

- The paper, cover, and binding of the report should be of good quality.
- The size and style of the type used should be attractive and readable. Graphics such as photographs and charts should be carefully prepared. The style of headings and subheadings should be appropriate to the subject matter.
- Ideally, illustrations should be integrated within the text or presented on pages that face the material being discussed. For example, a photograph of the subject property may be placed on the page facing the identification of the property. A neighborhood map could be included on a page facing the neighborhood description to show the location of the subject property. Charts and graphs should be presented where they are discussed, but illustrations that are not directly related to the narrative should be placed in the addenda.
- The contents of the report should be presented in clearly labeled sections that are identified in the table of contents.
- Advances in desktop publishing technology should allow appraisers to print attractive, high-quality reports in their offices.

General Outline

Narrative appraisal reports will vary in content and organization, but they all contain certain elements. Essentially, a narrative appraisal report follows the order of the valuation process.

Most narrative appraisal reports have four major parts. The contents of each section may be formally divided with subheadings or presented in a continuous narrative. In either case, the major divisions of the report should

---

3. For further discussion of effective appraisal report writing, see Alan Blankenship, *The Appraisal Writing Handbook* (Chicago: Appraisal Institute, 1998).

A **narrative appraisal report** generally has four parts (introduction, premises of the appraisal, presentation of data, and analysis of data and conclusions) and an addenda.

be identified with individual headings. The four basic parts of a report are the introduction, the premises of the appraisal, the presentation of data, and the analysis of data and conclusions. Many reports have a fifth section, the addenda, which includes supplemental information and illustrative material that would interrupt the text. The organization of narrative reports varies, but the outline in Figure 26.3 can be used as a general guide.

The arrangement of items in this outline is flexible and can be adapted to almost any appraisal assignment and any type of real property. In practice, this outline would be adapted to the particular requirements of the assignment and to suit the personal preference of the appraiser and, more importantly, the client. Appraisals of certain types of property may require revisions in or additions to the basic framework presented here.

Part One—Introduction

Title Page

The title page lists the property address, the date of value, the name and address of the appraiser, and the name and address of the client.

Letter of Transmittal

The letter of transmittal formally presents the appraisal report to the client. It should be drafted in proper business style and be as brief as the character and nature of the assignment permit. A suitable letter of transmittal may include the following elements:

- Date of letter and salutation
- Street address of the property and a brief description, if necessary
- Statement identifying the interest in the property being appraised
- Statement that the property inspection and all necessary investigation and analyses were made by the appraiser
- Reference that the letter is accompanied by an appraisal report of a specified number of pages and identification of the type of appraisal and report format
- Type of value developed in the appraisal report
- Effective date of the appraisal
- Opinion of value[4]

---

4.   Detaching of the letter of transmittal from the report can mislead the intended user of the report. If the appraiser deems it appropriate to include the opinion of value or another conclusion in the letter of transmittal, the conclusion should be qualified with a statement such as the following:

>   This letter must remain attached to the report, which contains *n* pages plus related exhibits, for the value opinion set forth to be considered valid.

See Guide Note 10 of the Appraisal Institute's Guide Notes to the Standards of Professional Appraisal Practice for further information.

Figure 26.3   **General Outline of Narrative Appraisal Report**

Part One—Introduction

Title page

Letter of transmittal

Table of contents

Certification

Summary of important conclusions

Part Two—Premises of the Appraisal

Identification of type of appraisal and type of report

Extraordinary assumptions and hypothetical conditions

General assumptions and limiting conditions

Purpose and intended use of the appraisal

Definition of value and date of opinion of value

Property rights appraised

Scope of work

Part Three—Presentation of Data

Identification of the property, legal description

Identification of any personal property or other items that are not real property

History, including prior sales and current offers or listings

Market area, city, neighborhood, and location data

Land description

Improvement description

Taxes and assessment data

Marketability study, if appropriate

Part Four—Analysis of Data and Conclusions

Highest and best use of the land as though vacant

Highest and best use of the property as improved

Land value

Cost approach

Sales comparison approach

Income capitalization approach

Reconciliation and final opinion of value

Estimate of exposure time

Qualifications of the appraiser

Addenda

Detailed legal description, if not included in the presentation of data

Detailed statistical data

Leases or lease summaries

Other appropriate information

Secondary exhibits

- Any extraordinary assumptions and hypothetical conditions
- Appraiser's signature

Table of Contents

The various sections of the report are customarily listed in order in the table of contents. The major divisions of the report and any subheadings used in the report should be shown here.

Certification

The certification may follow the final opinion of value or be combined with it. The signature of the appraiser and the date may then be added. The certification states that the appraiser has personally conducted the appraisal in an unbiased, objective manner in accordance with USPAP. Figure 26.4 shows what information must be included in an appraiser's certification.

certification of value: A part of the introduction to an appraisal report in which the appraiser certifies that the statements of fact presented are correct to the best of his or her knowledge; that the analysis and conclusions are limited only by the reported assumptions and conditions; that the appraiser has no interest (or the specified interest) in the subject property; that the appraiser's compensation is not contingent upon any aspect of the report; that the appraisal was performed in accordance with the Code of Professional Ethics and Standards of Professional Practice of the Appraisal Institute, which may review the report; that the appraiser has (or has not) satisfied continuing education requirements; that the appraiser has (or has not) made a personal inspection of the property; and that no one, except those specified, has provided assistance in preparing the report.

Whether the certification is included as part of the introduction or presented on a separate, signed page, certification is important because it establishes the appraiser's position, thereby protecting both the appraiser's integrity and the validity of the appraisal.

Summary of Important Conclusions

When an appraisal report is long and complex, a summary of the major points and important conclusions in the report may be useful. Such a statement, which is sometimes called an *executive summary,* is convenient for readers of the report and allows the appraiser to stress the major points considered in reaching the final opinion of value. The following list indicates the type of material that is frequently included in a summary; however, all of the following items do not apply to every appraisal assignment:

- Brief identification of the property
- Identification of the type of appraisal and report format
- Any extraordinary assumptions or hypothetical conditions
- Determinations of the highest and best use of the land as though vacant and of the property as improved
- Age of improvements
- Land value opinion

Figure 26.4   Certification

According to Standards Rule 2-3, the certification must be similar in content to the following:

I certify that, to the best of my knowledge and belief:

- the statements of fact contained in this report are true and correct.
- the reported analyses, opinions, and conclusions are limited only by the reported assumptions and limiting conditions and are my personal, impartial, and unbiased professional analyses, opinions, and conclusions.
- I have no (or the specified) present or prospective interest in the property that is the subject of this report and no (or the specified) personal interest with respect to the parties involved.
- I have no bias with respect to the property that is the subject of this report or to the parties involved with this assignment.
- my engagement in this assignment was not contingent upon developing or reporting predetermined results.
- my compensation for completing this assignment is not contingent upon the development or reporting of a predetermined value or direction in value that favors the cause of the client, the amount of the value opinion, the attainment of a stipulated result, or the occurrence of a subsequent event directly related to the intended use of this appraisal.
- my analyses, opinions, and conclusions were developed, and this report has been prepared, in conformity with the Uniform Standards of Professional Appraisal Practice.
- I have (or have not) made a personal inspection of the property that is the subject of this report. (If more than one person signs this certification, the certification must clearly specify which individuals did and which individuals did not make a personal inspection of the appraised property.)
- no one provided significant real property appraisal assistance to the person signing this certification. (If there are exceptions, the name of each individual providing significant real property appraisal assistance must be stated.)

The Appraisal Institute's Supplemental Standards require Appraisal Institute members to include statements similar in content to the following:

- the reported analyses, opinions, and conclusions were developed, and this report has been prepared, in conformity with the requirements of the Code of Professional Ethics and the Standards of Professional Appraisal Practice of the Appraisal Institute.
- the use of this report is subject to the requirements of the Appraisal Institute relating to review by its duly authorized representatives.

Also, one of the following statements must be included in any report prepared by a designated member of the Appraisal Institute (according to Supplemental Standards Rule 1-3):

Either

As of the date of this report, I (or Designated Member's name or Designated Members' names) have/has completed the continuing education program of the Appraisal Institute.

or

As of the date of this report, I (or Designated Member's name or Designated Members' names) have not/has not completed the continuing education program of the Appraisal Institute.

- Value indication from the cost approach
- Value indication from the sales comparison approach
- Value indication from the income capitalization approach
- Final opinion of defined value

Part Two—Premises of the Appraisal

Identification of Type of Appraisal and Report Format

The type of appraisal (i.e., limited or complete) and the report format (i.e., self-contained, summary, or restricted use) must be stated.

Extraordinary Assumptions and Hypothetical Conditions

Limiting conditions or assumptions affecting the opinion of value or conclusion are an important part of a report and should be stated clearly. When a value opinion is subject to an extraordinary assumption or hypothetical condition, such as a pending lease agreement, atypical financing, or a known but not yet quantified environmental issue, the appraiser must state that condition in the report so that its effect on the value opinion or conclusion is clear.

General Assumptions and Limiting Conditions

General assumptions and limiting conditions may be stated in the letter of transmittal, but they are usually included as separate pages in the report because the letter of transmittal is not technically part of the report. These statements are used to help protect the appraiser and to inform the client and other intended users of the report. The general assumptions found in a typical appraisal report deal with issues such as legal and title considerations, liens and encumbrances, property management, information furnished by others (e.g., engineering studies, surveys), concealment of hazardous substances on the property, and compliance with zoning regulations and local, state, and federal laws. General assumptions and limiting conditions are not boilerplate for the report. Neither are they a means of avoiding research or issues that are pertinent to a given appraisal. Each assumption or condition must be reasonable and supportable in the context of the appraisal and must not conflict with the appraiser's other responsibilities such as the identification of extraordinary assumptions or hypothetical conditions. (See Figure 26.5 for examples of typical general assumptions and limiting conditions.)

Purpose and Intended Use of the Appraisal

The purpose of an appraisal report is the question for which the client and intended users seek an answer. The intended use is the reason the client needs the appraisal—for example, to make a purchase, sale, or lending decision.

Definition of Value and Date of Opinion of Value

An acceptable definition of the value being appraised is included in the report to eliminate any confusion in the mind of the intended user or other readers of the report. (Definitions of various types of value are cited in Chapter 2.)

Figure 26.5 General Assumptions and Limiting Conditions

Appraisers need to consider the applicability of general assumptions and limiting conditions on a case-by-base basis. The following assumptions and limiting conditions are commonly found in appraisal reports, but the specific wording of the items and the inclusion of a specific item may not be applicable to every assignment:

This appraisal report has been made with the following general assumptions:

1. No responsibility is assumed for the legal description provided or for matters pertaining to legal or title considerations. Title to the property is assumed to be good and marketable unless otherwise stated.
2. The property is appraised free and clear of any or all liens or encumbrances unless otherwise stated.
3. Responsible ownership and competent property management are assumed.
4. The information furnished by others is believed to be reliable, but no warranty is given for its accuracy.
5. All engineering studies are assumed to be correct. The plot plans and illustrative material in this report are included only to help the reader visualize the property.
6. It is assumed that there are no hidden or unapparent conditions of the property, subsoil, or structures that render it more or less valuable. No responsibility is assumed for such conditions or for obtaining the engineering studies that may be required to discover them.
7. It is assumed that the property is in full compliance with all applicable federal, state, and local environmental regulations and laws unless the lack of compliance is stated, described, and considered in the appraisal report.
8. It is assumed that the property conforms to all applicable zoning and use regulations and restrictions unless a nonconformity has been identified, described, and considered in the appraisal report.
9. It is assumed that all required licenses, certificates of occupancy, consents, and other legislative or administrative authority from any local, state, or national government or private entity or organization have been or can be obtained or renewed for any use on which the opinion of value contained in this report is based.
10. It is assumed that the use of the land and improvements is confined within the boundaries or property lines of the property described and that there is no encroachment or trespass unless noted in the report.
11. Unless otherwise stated in this report, the existence of hazardous materials, which may or may not be present on the property, was not observed by the appraiser. The appraiser has no knowledge of the existence of such materials on or in the property. The appraiser, however, is not qualified to detect such substances. The presence of substances such as asbestos, urea-formaldehyde foam insulation, and other potentially hazardous materials may affect the value of the property. The value estimated is predicated on the assumption that there is no such material on or in the property that would cause a loss in value. No responsibility is assumed for such conditions or for any expertise or engineering knowledge required to discover them. The intended user is urged to retain an expert in this field, if desired.

This appraisal report has been made with the following general limiting conditions:

1. Any allocation of the total value estimated in this report between the land and the improvements applies only under the stated program of utilization. The separate values allocated to the land and buildings must not be used in conjunction with any other appraisal and are invalid if so used.
2. Possession of this report, or a copy thereof, does not carry with it the right of publication.
3. The appraiser, by reason of this appraisal, is not required to give further consultation or testimony or to be in attendance in court with reference to the property in question unless arrangements have been previously made.
4. Neither all nor any part of the contents of this report (especially any conclusions as to value, the identity of the appraiser, or the firm with which the appraiser is connected) shall be disseminated to the public through advertising, public relations, news, sales, or other media without the prior written consent and approval of the appraiser.

Figure 26.5   **General Assumptions and Limiting Conditions** *(continued)*

An appraisal report might contain these additional assumptions and limiting conditions:

1. Any opinions of value provided in the report apply to the entire property, and any proration or division of the total into fractional interests will invalidate the opinion of value, unless such proration or division of interests has been set forth in the report.

2. Only preliminary plans and specifications were available for use in the preparation of this appraisal; the analysis, therefore, is subject to a review of the final plans and specifications when available.

3. Any proposed improvements are assumed to have been completed unless otherwise stipulated, so any construction is assumed to conform with the building plans referenced in the report.

4. The appraiser assumes that the reader or user of this report has been provided with copies of available building plans and all leases and amendments, if any, that encumber the property.

5. No legal description or survey was furnished, so the appraiser used the county tax plat to ascertain the physical dimensions and acreage of the property. Should a survey prove this information to be inaccurate, it may be necessary for this appraisal to be adjusted.

6. The forecasts, projections, or operating estimates contained herein are based on current market conditions, anticipated short-term supply and demand factors, and a continued stable economy. These forecasts are, therefore, subject to changes with future conditions.

7. The Americans with Disabilities Act (ADA) became effective January 26, 1992. The appraiser has not made a specific compliance survey or analysis of the property to determine whether or not it is in conformity with the various detailed requirements of ADA. It is possible that a compliance survey of the property and a detailed analysis of the requirements of the ADA would reveal that the property is not in compliance with one or more of the requirements of the act. If so, this fact could have a negative impact upon the value of the property. Since the appraiser has no direct evidence relating to this issue, possible noncompliance with the requirements of ADA was not considered in estimating the value of the property.

An appraisal assignment may call for one of the following:

- An opinion of current value
- An opinion of retrospective value
- An opinion of prospective value

It is essential to report the date as of which the value conclusion is applicable. Commonly, the date of the opinion of value and the date of the inspection of the property are the same, especially for appraisals of current market value. If the date of inspection differs from the date of the opinion of value, then both dates should be noted in the appraisal report.

Property Rights Appraised

In identifying the subject property, the appraiser must state and should define the particular rights or interests being valued. A thorough discussion is warranted in appraisals of partial interests in property, limited rights such as surface or mineral rights, fee simple estates subject to long-term leases, and leasehold interests. Other encumbrances such as easements, mortgages, and special occupancy or use requirements should also be identified and explained in relation to the defined value to be developed.

Scope of Work

A clear and accurate description of the scope of work appropriate to the appraisal assignment is desirable to protect those persons whose reliance on the appraisal may be affected. The term *scope of work* refers to the amount and type of information researched and the analysis applied in an assignment. The standards clearly impose a responsibility on the appraiser to determine the appropriate scope of work to develop the value opinion and prepare the report. By describing the scope of work, the appraiser signifies acceptance of this responsibility.

The appraisal report should prominently disclose the degree of precision attributable to the value opinion given the defined scope of work. When the purpose of the appraisal requires the appraiser to narrow the scope of work, the value opinion may be less precise than in a more typical assignment and the value opinion is only appropriate and reliable for the intended use of the appraisal. Discussing the scope of work in the appraisal report helps an appraiser clarify why the conclusions are valid only for the intended use agreed upon by the client and the appraiser.

Part Three—Presentation of Data

Identification of the Property

The subject real estate is identified so that it cannot be confused with any other parcel of real estate. This can be achieved by including a full legal description of the property in the report. When a copy of the official plat or an assessment map is used, the appraiser may refer to it at this point and present it on a facing or following page. If the official plat is unavailable, the appraiser can describe the property by name, specifying the side of the street on which the property fronts, the street address, and the lot and block number. A photograph of the subject property on a facing page can enhance this section of the report. Personal property and other items that are not real property should be identified.

History

The Uniform Standards require that prior sales of the subject property (within one year for one- to four-family residential properties and within three years for all other properties) be analyzed and addressed in the appraisal report.[5] For properties other than single-family residences, recent changes in the property's operating profile should be addressed. Historical property data may include information on the following:

- Original assemblage, acquisition, or construction costs
- Expenditures for capital additions or modernization
- Financial data or transfers of ownership
- Casualty loss experience

5.   Other jurisdictional standards such as the *Uniform Appraisal Standards for Federal Land Acquisitions* (Washington, D.C.: Interagency Land Acquisition Conference, 2000) require sales transacted within 10 years to be reported.

- History and type of occupancy
- Any other facts that may pertain to or affect the computations, estimates, or conclusions presented in the report

Market Area, City, Neighborhood, and Location Data

All facts about a city and its surroundings that the appraiser considers pertinent to the appraisal problem should be included in the market data. (The use and reliability of different types of data, in relation to various classifications of property and specific appraisal problems are discussed in Chapters 7 and 8.) An appraiser weighs and considers all pertinent factors in data analysis, but the report should discuss only the data that is found to be significant to the problem at hand. Both positive and negative aspects of the market area should be discussed. If the appraiser only provides data in support of either positive or negative factors, the report will be misleading.

If a considerable amount of supporting statistical data (e.g., population figures, cost of living indexes, family income figures) is needed, the appraiser may choose to incorporate this data into the body of the report or present it in tabular form on facing pages and reference it in the discussion. A separate section for market data is not needed in many reports. In fact, market data is often combined with neighborhood data.

The amount of neighborhood and location data required depends on the appraisal assignment and the intended user. For example, when an appraisal is prepared for an out-of-town client who is unfamiliar with the property and the community, it may be wise to include more community and neighborhood data than would be needed by a local client. If the appraisal concerns an important business property that derives its income from the purchasing power of the surrounding area, the appraiser should provide a detailed description of the neighborhood and discuss how the population and its purchasing power affect the value of the subject property.

An appraiser should also note the presence of special amenities or detrimental conditions in the neighborhood and provide reasons or data to support any conclusions about these factors. For example, if the appraiser states that the market area is growing, actual growth figures or building projections should be included in the report. If a report states that a neighborhood is in decline due to abnormal deterioration or poor maintenance, the appraiser might refer to specific properties that exhibit these detrimental conditions or use photographs to illustrate neighborhood conditions.

Land Description

Pertinent facts about the subject site belong in the land description section. Land description involves three different aspects of the subject property's site:

- Physical characteristics
- Legal characteristics
- Economic characteristics

Physical characteristics. Relevant physical site data may include descriptions of the following:

- The property's frontage, depth, site area, and shape
- Soil and subsoil conditions
- Utilities
- Any improvements that benefit or harm the site

In the land description section of an appraisal report, the appraiser should offer a conclusion as to the utility or adaptability of the site for existing or proposed improvements.

Legal characteristics. When significant to the appraisal problem, zoning and private restrictions (such as easements) should be discussed in detail. The appraiser should provide sufficient land use data to help the reader understand the limitations that zoning regulations place on the use or development of the site. If appropriate, the appraiser may explore the possibility of a zoning change. Other existing public and private restrictions such as floodplain regulations, scenic easements, and wetland restrictions should be discussed and their effect on the utility and value of the property described.

Economic characteristics. Economic characteristics of a property that may have an effect on its value and should be discussed in the appraisal report include

- Real estate taxes
- Special assessments
- Development bonds
- Facilities benefits districts or other public encumbrances affecting the site

These economic encumbrances differ from legal encumbrances such as easements and encroachments. The former are related to the governmental power of taxation whereas the latter arise from police power.

Improvement Description

In the description of improvements section, all building and improvement data relevant to the appraisal problem is presented and discussed. Although an appraiser considers and processes much data in the course of an appraisal, only significant property characteristics that influence the value conclusion are presented in the report. These characteristics may include the following:

- Actual and effective building age
- Building size
- Number and size of units
- Structural and construction details
- Mechanical equipment
- Physical condition
- Functional utility or inutility

Property information may be supported with drawings, photographs, floor plans, and elevations. If the description of structural details and mechanical equipment is long, an outline may be used in the body of the report to emphasize the important items.

Tax and Assessment Data

Current assessed values and ad valorem tax rates should be reported and a calculation of the current annual tax load of the subject property should be included. Existing assessment trends or prospective changes in tax rates should be analyzed. It may be appropriate to discuss the tax assessment or tax load on the subject in relation to the taxes on other properties, particularly if the difference is significant.

Marketability Study

In the appraisal of income-producing properties such as office buildings, shopping centers, and apartment buildings, a marketability study may be performed to find out how the subject property fits into the overall market in terms of rent levels and absorption rates. A marketability study is usually directly related to the conclusions presented in the appraisal report. Such a study may examine the following:

*   The specific real estate market or submarket
*   The supply of existing properties (e.g., inventory of space, construction trends, vacancy patterns, and absorption rates)
*   The demand forecast (e.g., projected expansion or shrinkage)
*   The current balance of supply and demand
*   Competitive rent levels

Part Four—Analysis of Data and Conclusions

Highest and best use should be expressed in terms of the property's most probable and profitable use. Typically, the four criteria—legal permissibility, physical possibility, financial feasibility (market support), and maximum productivity—are discussed in relation to the subject property. Land use patterns in the area, zoning regulations, and the profitability of existing or proposed improvements should also be discussed.

Highest and Best Use of the Land as Though Vacant

The highest and best use on which the appraiser bases the value estimate of the land as though vacant should be clearly stated in the report. The character and amount of data presented and analyzed in this section are dictated by the purpose and intended use of the appraisal.

Highest and Best Use of the Property as Improved

After briefly discussing the theory and related principles of highest and best use in the report and presenting the analysis of the highest and best use of the site as though vacant in the level of detail appropriate to the assignment, the appraiser must explain the logic of the analysis of the highest and best use of the property as improved. A discussion of the economics of any alternative uses will lead to the appraiser's conclusions regarding whether the existing improvements should be retained, replaced, or removed. The appraiser may then suggest a possible course of action such as rehabilitation, improved maintenance, or better property management.

Land Value

In the land value section of an appraisal report, market data is presented along with an analysis of the data and reasoning that lead to the land value opinion. The factors that influence land value should be presented in a clear and precise manner. The narrative should lead the reader to the land value opinion.

Approaches to Value

An appraiser develops the approaches applicable to the assignment and derives indications of value. The application of each approach is described and the factual data, analysis, and reasoning leading to the value indication are presented in the report.

Many intended users are not familiar with the mechanics of the three approaches to value, so the appraiser may want to explain the procedures applied briefly. The extent of explanation required depends on the circumstances of the assignment. Simple statements that describe what is included in each of the three approaches (such as those provided in Figure 26.6) can help the reader better understand the report.

The three approaches are seldom completely independent. An appraisal is composed of a number of integrated, interrelated, and inseparable procedures that have a common objective: a convincing, reliable opinion of value.

Figure 26.6   **Descriptions of the Approaches to Value**

The approaches to value could be described in an appraisal report as follows:

In the sales comparison approach, properties similar to the subject property that have been sold recently or for which listing prices or offers are known are compared to the subject. Data from generally comparable properties is used and comparisons are made to demonstrate a probable price at which the subject property would sell if offered on the market.

In the cost approach, an estimated reproduction or replacement cost of the building and land improvements as of the date of appraisal is developed (including an estimate of entrepreneurial profit or incentive), and an estimate of the losses in value that have taken place due to wear and tear, design and plan deficiencies, or neighborhood influences is subtracted. An estimate of the value of the land is then added to this depreciated building cost estimate. The total represents the value indicated by the cost approach.

In the income capitalization approach, the rental income of the property is calculated and deductions are made for vacancy and collection loss and expenses. The prospective net operating income of the property is then estimated. To support this estimate, operating statements for the subject property in previous years and for comparable properties are reviewed. An applicable capitalization method and appropriate capitalization rates are developed and used in computations that lead to an indication of value.

Reconciliation of Value Indications

The reconciliation of value indications should lead the reader logically to the final opinion of value. The final opinion of defined value may be stated in many ways. The following is a simple example:

As a result of my investigation and analysis, it is my opinion that the market value of the identified interest in the property, as of July 20, 2001, was:

$400,000

Note that the date on which the value opinion is applicable may differ from the date of the letter of transmittal.

When the appraiser chooses to allocate the opinion of value among property components, a breakdown may be presented after the final opinion of value. In this case, the value opinion may be allocated as follows:

Land	$90,000
Improvements	$310,000
Personal property and other items	+ $0
Total	$400,000

Exposure Time

Most definitions of market value presuppose a transaction that occurs after "reasonable exposure in the market." The Uniform Standards of Professional Appraisal Practice states that, when the purpose of an assignment is to develop an opinion of market value, the appraiser must also develop an opinion of the reasonable exposure time linked to the value opinion, which should be stated in the report. Exposure time can be defined as the estimated length of time the property interest being appraised would have been offered on the market prior to the hypothetical consummation of a sale at market value on the effective date of the appraisal.

According to Statement on Appraisal Standards No. 6 in USPAP:

> The discussion of reasonable exposure time should appear in an appropriate section of the appraisal report, one that presents the discussion and analysis of market conditions, and also be referenced at the statement of the value definition and value conclusion.

Even though USPAP only requires an opinion of exposure time, many clients also request an opinion of marketing time.[6]

---

6.   The concept of marketing time is distinct from exposure time. Many appraisal clients, including most financial institutions, require that appraisals consider the "reasonable marketing period" for the property at the concluded value. Advisory Opinion 7 of USPAP states:

> Marketing time occurs after the effective date of the market value opinion and the marketing time opinion is related to, yet apart from, the appraisal process. Therefore, it is appropriate for the section of the appraisal report that discusses marketing time and its implications to appear toward the end of the report after the market value conclusion. The request to provide a reasonable marketing time opinion exceeds the normal information required for the appraisal process and should be treated separately from that process.

Qualifications of the Appraiser

The appraiser's qualifications are usually included in the report as evidence of the appraiser's competence to perform the assignment. These qualifications may include facts concerning the following:

- Professional experience
- Educational background and training
- Business, professional, and academic affiliations and activities
- Clients for whom the appraiser has rendered professional services, the types of properties appraised, and the nature of the appraisal assignments undertaken

The use of such a statement of qualifications is so widespread that many appraisers find it expedient to insert a printed statement of their qualifications in each appraisal report. Misrepresentation of qualifications or presenting misleading information regarding qualifications would, of course, be a breach of professional ethics.

Addenda

Depending on the size and complexity of the appraisal assignment, supplementary material may be added to the report to present information that would interrupt the narrative. The following items may be included in the addenda, if they have not already been incorporated into the body of the report:

- Plot plan
- Plans and elevations of buildings
- Photographs of properties referred to in the report
- City, neighborhood, and other maps
- Charts and graphs
- Historical income and expense data
- Building specifications
- Detailed estimates of the reproduction or replacement costs of buildings
- Sales and listing data
- Leases and lease abstracts
- Marketability analysis data (e.g., information on construction trends, vacancy trends, and competitive rent levels)

FURTHER READING

Blankenship, Alan. *The Appraisal Writing Handbook*. Chicago: Appraisal Institute, 1998.

Craft, J. L. "Logic and Rhetoric in Appraisal Reporting." *The Appraisal Journal* (April 1995).

Eaton, J. D. "FRCP: The Other Appraisal Report Standard." *Valuation Insights & Perspectives*, vol. 4, no. 2 (Second Quarter 1999).

Horevitz, Ann Marie. "Appraisal Writing, Aristotle, and the Art of Persuasion." *The Appraisal Journal* (July 1997).

Mills, Arlen C., and Dorothy Z. Mills. *Communicating the Appraisal: The Uniform Residential Appraisal Report*. 2d ed. Chicago: Appraisal Institute, 1994.

Minnich, Joseph L., III. *Communicating the Appraisal: Fannie Mae Desktop Underwriter™ Quantitative Analysis Appraisal Report Form 2055 and Qualitative Analysis Appraisal Report From 2065*. 2d ed. Chicago: Appraisal Institute, 1997.

Rex, Charles W., III, and Susan Motycka Rex. "Market Analysis in Appraisal Reports: Vitalizing Key Data Sections." *Valuation Insights & Perspectives*, vol. 1, no. 4 (Fall 1996).

Tardiff, Frank D. "Using an Engagement Letter to Minimize Discrepancies Between Appraised Value and Transaction Price." *The Appraisal Journal* (January 1994).

Wilson, L. Deane. "Are Appraisal Reports Logical Fallacies?" *The Appraisal Journal* (April 1996).

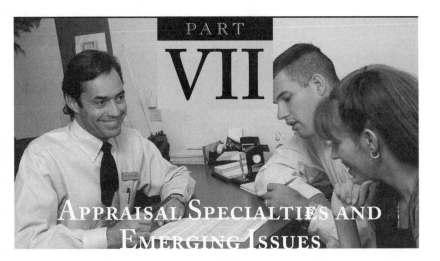

PART

VII

APPRAISAL SPECIALTIES AND EMERGING ISSUES

Part VII of the text covers specialized topics in appraisal practice that will require further investigation and study by readers of this text. **Chapter 27, Appraisal Specialties and Emerging Issues,** discusses emerging issues in the appraisal of real property, such as the treatment of business enterprise value and public interest value, as well as traditional appraisal specialties, such as consulting, appraisal review, and litigation work.

27 APPRAISAL SPECIALTIES AND EMERGING ISSUES

Real estate appraisers are required to have extensive education, training, and experience before they are recognized as professionals. The importance of their services to the public as well as the client, the high ethics and standards requirements they must adhere to, and the application of a body of knowledge based on economics, legal, and other important foundations are all reasons that appraisal itself is recognized as a profession. Professional appraisers commonly have special skills in various disciplines that overlap appraisal, including economics, statistics, mathematics, finance, construction, planning, and others. Thus, an appraiser's skills have value in a wide range of activities outside traditional appraisal services.

The majority of appraisal assignments focus on market value and follow the procedures outlined in the valuation process. At some point in their careers, however, most appraisers will encounter an appraisal situation or receive a request for a valuation-related service outside their normal range of activities, many of which require specialized knowledge and skills. Some appraisers create profitable niche businesses out of these specialized assignments, but additional study and experience in these areas is required.

The specialized appraisal topics covered in this chapter include

- Consulting
- Appraisal review
- International valuation
- Business enterprise value
- Personal property appraisal
- Litigation work
- Public interest value

Some of these topics are emerging areas in the discipline of appraisal. Appraisers are entering all these areas to diversify their practices, and opinions and interpretations of proper methodologies may diverge. The scope of this text does not allow for a comprehensive discussion of each issue. This chapter will define the issues and explain the arguments offered in any ongoing debates. Sources for additional information are included to facilitate further study of these topics.

Consulting

A real estate appraiser may be engaged in an assignment that differs from a traditional appraisal assignment in that the objective is to provide advice, recommendation, or a conclusion other than value. Such assignments are broadly categorized as consulting assignments.

Professional appraisers are asked to provide consulting services because they have the market knowledge and expertise needed to help clients solve a variety of real estate problems. Given this recognition, appraisers must be particularly careful when approached about such services to properly identify the client's problem to be solved and to ascertain whether they have the requisite competency to solve it.

Appraisal Consulting

Appraisal consulting, as defined by the Uniform Standards of Professional Appraisal Practice, is the development of an analysis, recommendation, or opinion to solve a problem, where an opinion of value is a component of the analysis leading to the assignment results. Appraisal consulting involves developing an opinion of value, though reporting that opinion of value is not the object of the client's question.

An example of a common appraisal consulting assignment is a feasibility study. The appraiser must develop opinions of value for various alternative uses of a property to test the feasibility of a proposed use. However, the objective of this type of assignment is not to develop value, but rather to draw a conclusion about feasibility.

Standards 4 and 5 of USPAP address the development and reporting of appraisal consulting assignments. Advisory Opinion 21 (AO-21), which was approved in 2000, gives further guidance on when USPAP applies to valuation-related services.

> **appraisal consulting:** The act or process of developing an analysis, recommendation, or opinion to solve a problem, where an opinion of value is a component of the analysis leading to the assignment results. (USPAP, 2001 ed.)

Other Types of Consulting Services

Consulting services that do not involve developing an opinion of value are not addressed by USPAP. Some common assignments that are likely to fall under the broader category of *consulting* include

- Land utilization studies
- Market studies
- Marketability studies
- Due diligence for a client's acquisition or sale decision
- Operations audits
- Absorption analyses
- Risk analysis
- Portfolio analyses
- Adaptive reuse analyses—i.e., analysis of an existing property's proposed change of use

- Property inspections
- Capital market analyses
- Studies that provide support for litigation

Several of these examples may call for the development of an opinion of value—e.g., marketability studies, absorption studies, portfolio analysis, risk analysis, litigation support—and would therefore be categorized as *appraisal consulting* assignments, subject to USPAP. Other services—e.g., property inspections, market studies—generally do not require the development of an opinion of value.

Consulting frequently involves consideration of the specific needs and objectives of the client, not the generalized, composite market perspective that characterizes market value appraisal assignments. In both appraisal and consulting assignments, appraisers must at all times maintain their objectivity and support their findings with facts extracted from competent research. By their nature, consulting assignments frequently draw on the appraiser's own opinions, not those of the marketplace, rendering them more subjective than valuation assignments. Therefore, a practitioner who undertakes a consulting assignment must identify and evaluate both facts and judgments and then relate his or her findings to the financial decisions under consideration.

Competency Issues

The Competency Rule of USPAP states that appraisers must disclose any lack of knowledge or experience necessary to complete an assignment *before* accepting the assignment. As appraisers diversify their professional activities and enter new areas, they may not have sufficient experience to recognize the requirements of certain consulting assignments. A clear understanding of the client's problem to be solved is imperative. Then the appraiser must determine if the assignment is an appraisal, appraisal consulting, or appraisal review assignment, as defined in USPAP, or some other type of assignment that is not covered by USPAP. Either way, the appraiser must be sure that he or she is capable of completing the assignment in a competent manner.

FURTHER READING

Standards 4 and 5, Uniform Standards of Professional Appraisal Practice. Washington, D.C.: The Appraisal Foundation, current edition.

Appraisal Review

Appraisal review is a quality control or auditing function. Appraisers may formally or informally review the work of one another before submitting their reports to managers or clients. To meet the defined objectives of the review, the reviewer will examine the data, reasoning, analyses, and conclusions developed by the appraiser. Most appraisal reviews are performed to determine the reliability of

appraisal review: The act or process of developing and communicating an opinion about the quality of another appraiser's work. (USPAP, 2001 ed.)

the value conclusion and the adequacy of the supporting evidence provided. The reasonableness of any hypothetical conditions, extraordinary assumptions, or general limiting conditions is also considered.

Appraisal reviews are performed by appraisers, clients, and other users of appraisal services. The type and extent of a review may vary with the training of the reviewer, the specific needs of the client, and other circumstances. The review requirements of lenders may be tailored to their specific policies and procedures, which include compliance with the requirements of federal agencies. Mortgage insurers have unique appraisal requirements, as do federal and quasi-federal agencies that conduct appraisal reviews as a normal part of their audit procedures. State and local government agencies such as highway departments conduct reviews in conjunction with the acquisition of rights of way and have specific appraisal requirements for condemnation proceedings. Review appraisers also serve the corporate and private sectors by facilitating decisions pertaining to the buying, selling, and leasing of property as well as decisions relating to the management of properties as fixed assets.

Like those who prepare appraisals, review appraisers must disclose the nature and extent of their work and carefully detail the contingent or limiting conditions that apply. If an appraiser accepts an assignment to conduct a third-party review of an appraisal prepared by another appraiser, it may be wise for the review appraiser to inform the client of the different levels of appraisal reviews available and to recommend the type of review appropriate to the client's needs. The review appraiser should clearly disclose the nature and extent of the review performed to avoid any misunderstanding or abuse of the review comments.

The function of the review appraiser is not to appraise the subject property but to examine the contents of the appraisal report and form an opinion as to its adequacy and appropriateness. In some instances a review appraiser may be called upon to form an opinion of property value based on the information contained in the appraisal report. When this occurs, the review appraiser "changes hats," becomes an appraiser, and is subject to all the requirements that apply to developing an appraisal.

Usually a review appraiser identifies and judges the reasoning and logic that underlie another appraiser's work but does not substitute his or her own judgment for the judgment of that appraiser. The reviewer appraiser's task is to analyze the total work product of the appraiser in an impartial and objective manner. Review appraisers violate rules of fairness and objectivity when they level undue criticism against an appraisal report. If an appraisal review contains factual errors or substitutes a review appraiser's judgment for that of the appraiser, it may result in a breach of ethics. Also, the review appraiser must keep the opinion of value and the judgment of the appraiser confidential.

The appraisal review function should be understood as something different from activities limited to factual verifications of work performed by an appraiser. Appraisers are sometimes asked to verify or to comment on the accuracy of only a portion of the work of another appraiser. In many instances the verification work may not even permit access of the verifier to the original report. This is an important and necessary adjunct to due diligence studies that frequently relate to the information in an appraisal rather than the conclusions of value. To avoid confusion or misrepresentation or the abuse of the verification product, the appraiser's report must identify the scope of work as something different than an appraisal review (which determines the reliability of the value conclusion and the adequacy of the supporting evidence provided). As a further example, in some states an investigation of possible USPAP violations is specifically identified as an activity that does not constitute an appraisal review and is frequently performed by non-appraisers.

Technical and Administrative Reviews

Advisory Opinion 6 to USPAP distinguishes between two categories of appraisal reviews:

1. Technical reviews
2. Administrative reviews

A technical review is performed by an appraiser in accordance with Standard 3 of USPAP to form an opinion as to whether the analyses, opinions, and conclusions in the report under review are appropriate and reasonable.

The review appraiser who conducts a technical review renders a written opinion to accept, reject, or modify the conclusions contained in the report. In drafting this opinion, the review appraiser generally

- Checks the appraisal file on the subject property or project to discover the purpose of the appraisal, the scope of work of the appraisal assignment, and the contractual obligations under which the appraisal was performed.

- Analyzes the contents of the appraisal report. If the review appraiser has received more than one appraisal report on the same property, he or she may compare the reports at this point to uncover any inconsistencies.

technical review: Performed by an appraiser in accordance with Standard 3 of the Uniform Standards to form an opinion as to whether the analyses, opinions, and conclusions of the report under review are appropriate and reasonable.

administrative review: A preliminary review of an appraisal to check the calculations and determine whether the appraisal report complies with basic content specifications. The compliance reviewer notes any discrepancies or omissions of items specified in the appraisal contract. Generally performed by a client or user of appraisal services to exercise due diligence in making a business decision, e.g., underwriting, purchase, sale. May be performed by an appraiser to assist a client with these functions. Also known as a *compliance review.*

- Conducts a thorough field inspection if necessary. In some offices most reports are subject to a desk review, and field inspections are performed only for a representative sampling.

An administrative review is performed by a client or user of appraisal services to exercise due diligence in making a business decision (e.g., underwriting, purchase, sale). On occasion an appraiser may perform an administrative review to assist a client with these functions. An appraiser or consultant may become a user of the appraisal, particularly when the report contains information that might not be available from other sources. An administrative review is sometimes called a *compliance review*. While the outline provided by Standard 3 may be helpful to the parties who perform administrative reviews, they are not required to observe Standard 3, as an appraiser who conducts a technical review is.

The review appraiser must clearly distinguish between a difference of opinion with the appraiser who prepared the report and an objective review of the report itself. When a review appraiser makes a judgment or forms an opinion concerning the analysis or conclusions in the appraisal, the review appraiser's conduct must conform to Standard 3 of USPAP.

Limitations of Appraisal Reviews

The distinction between an appraisal review and a second opinion of value is critical. An appraisal review does not lead to an alternative value conclusion. The review appraiser may disagree with the value opinion or the analytical process presented in the report and may even recommend that another appraisal be commissioned.

Also, the review appraiser must distinguish between the review process and appraisal process. A review appraiser who suggests an alternative opinion of value has assumed the role of an appraiser and is no longer acting as a review appraiser. To avoid any confusion concerning these different functions in the minds of market participants, appraisers who review appraisal reports should not sign the appraisal reports under review. A review appraiser who signs an appraisal report becomes fully responsible for the contents of that report.

USPAP GUIDANCE ON APPRAISAL REVIEW

The following sections of the Uniform Standards of Professional Appraisal Practice provide guidance on the development and reporting of an appraisal review:

Standard 3	Real Property and Personal Property Appraisal Review, Development and Reporting
Advisory Opinion 6 (AO-6)	The Appraisal Review Function
Advisory Opinion 20 (AO-20)	An Appraisal Review Assignment that Includes the Reviewer's Own Opinion of Value
Advisory Opinion 21 (AO-21)	When Does USPAP Apply in Valuation Services?

Appraisal Review Procedures

The appraisal review procedures applied vary with the scope or nature of the assignment, the requirements of the client, and the complexity of the property appraised. The distinction between a technical and an administrative review, which was discussed earlier, involves the purpose of the review and the observance of Standard 3.

There are two basic types of review procedures:

1. Desk reviews
2. Field reviews

Both are acceptable procedures for checking the thoroughness and consistency of appraisals, but the desk review is more common.

Desk Review

A desk review is completed without a field inspection and is usually limited to the data presented in the report. The data in the appraisal report may or may not be independently confirmed and additional market data is typically not researched. The review appraiser often uses a customized checklist.

- Mathematical calculations are checked.
- The appraiser's methodology is reviewed for appropriateness.
- The appraisal is reviewed to ascertain that it was completed in accordance with the client's guidelines, appraisal policy requirements, regulatory requirements, and USPAP.

Field Review

In addition to the tasks performed in a desk review, a field review may include

- Inspection of the exteriors of comparable properties
- Limited or full verification of market data
- Independent research to gather additional market data
- Verification of results obtained with electronic spreadsheet software and software used in lease-by-lease analysis

Many variations exist in desk reviews, field reviews, and combinations of the two. Review policies should be flexible enough to allow review appraisers to exercise due

desk review: An appraisal review that is limited to the data presented in the report, which may or may not be independently confirmed. A desk review is generally performed using a customized checklist of items. The reviewer checks the accuracy of the calculations, the reasonableness of the data, and the appropriateness of the methodology as well as compliance with client guidelines, regulatory requirements, and professional standards.

field review: An appraisal review that includes inspection of the exterior and sometimes the interior of the subject property and possibly inspection of the comparable properties to confirm the data provided in the report. A field review is generally performed using a customized checklist that covers the items examined in a desk review and may also include confirmation of market data, research to gather additional information, and verification of the software used in preparing the report.

diligence in each case. The extent of the review process is usually a function of the complexity of the property and the transaction value involved.

FURTHER READING

Richard C. Sorenson. *Appraising the Appraisal: The Art of Appraisal Review.* Chicago: Appraisal Institute, 1998.

International Valuation

The end of the Cold War introduced an entirely new concept of economics and provided new opportunities for worldwide economic cooperation that could not have been attempted a decade ago. Yet, at the same time that international markets opened up, the global economy demonstrated that it cannot allow the collapse of an important economic segment. Global powers must aid struggling economies, just as the United States government came to the aid of major corporations like Continental Illinois Bank and Chrysler when they faced possible financial ruin. In the late 1990s, currency crises in Mexico, Russia, and Southeast Asia illustrated the increasing interdependence of national economies and how failure in one country affects the whole world. Had these situations not been addressed by the global financial community, including entities such as the International Monetary Fund, there could have been a critical economic problem in every part of the world. Thus, we now recognize international economic dependency and see the broad implications of relationships that were previously viewed as regional or domestic.

As American investors expand their overseas activities, appraisers based in the United States are increasingly called upon to prepare appraisal reports in foreign countries for American clients. Domestic investors are accustomed to receiving comprehensive appraisal reports that include discussion of subjects such as local market dynamics, the analysis of comparable sales, and the supportability of market rent estimates. While the thought process and level of analysis undertaken by valuation experts in the United Kingdom and other European countries may be comparable, their reports often do not contain the same level of documentation.

To ensure the correct analysis of data in overseas markets, American appraisers usually find it necessary to consult with local appraisers (frequently called *valuers*). Although the same principles are applied in valuation assignments throughout the world, local customs and institutions vary significantly. For example, in many of the countries of Eastern Europe and the former Soviet Union, the definition of property rights is still evolving. Ownership may mean "the right to use" rather than possession of the full bundle of rights and interests associated with real property. In some Latin American countries, actual transaction prices may not be recorded because of high transfer taxes, or sale records may not be maintained in a single location. The American appraiser should be aware of the impact of local leasing practices, which may affect the selection of an appropriate valuation technique. In countries where office space is rented under long-term net leases, direct capitalization may be more appropriate than discounted cash flow analysis. In many European countries (e.g., France), sales commissions are often factored in at the beginning, not the end, of the holding period.

Most businesspeople overseas have a working knowledge of English as a second language, so language does not generally pose a problem. While security can be a concern in some countries, American appraisers on assignment abroad can generally expect a warm reception from their foreign colleagues, who recognize the advanced state of valuation practice in the United States and are eager to learn our valuation techniques.

International Valuation Standards

The United States, represented by the Appraisal Institute, joined with many other nations in 1981 to form the International Valuation Standards Committee (IVSC). The first international statement of valuation standards was issued in 1984 and these standards were recognized as world standards by the United Nations in 1985. Today the IVSC includes representatives of more than 50 nations and is recognized as the principal body for establishing international valuation standards.

International valuation standards are developed by the IVSC after review of domestic standards for each country, recognition of the appraisal principles that are reflected in these standards, review of appraisal practices worldwide, and interaction with other standards bodies such as the International Accounting Standards Committee and the International Federation of Accountants. The committee holds dialogs with international organizations such as the World Bank and the Organisation for Economic Co-operation and Development (OECD), regulatory organizations of the more developed countries, and many others involved with the use or provision of appraisal services throughout the world. The IVSC is a non-governmental organization (NGO) member of the United Nations.

From its inception the IVSC has recognized that international commerce demands that differences in appraisal procedures, terminology, and other valuation-related matters be resolved. Differing premises of market value, highest and best use, real property, personal property, value in use, going-concern value, and other important concepts can have significant adverse effects on entire economies as well as individual transactions. As a result, international standards are periodically revised to incorporate explanations and responses to issues that arise from international commerce or from domestic referrals.

When initially formed, the IVSC concentrated on standards of valuations performed in support of financial reporting. Market value has been a standard for reporting asset values (as contrasted with a depreciated historical cost basis) in many countries of the world. The IVSC and many nations determined that market value reporting of assets provided a basis for clear understanding in international commerce and for reasonable financial comparisons and decisions when accompanied by unequivocal international valuation standards. The concept has grown in importance over the past 25 years and is expanding today.

As is true of other international standards bodies, the IVSC does not establish standards for individual countries, although a number of countries have adopted the international standards as their domestic standards. By promulgating internationally accepted standards and by developing their standards only after public disclosure, debate among nations, and liaison with other international standards bodies, the IVSC offers objective, unbiased, and well-researched standards that are a source of agreement among nations and provide guidance for domestic standards. Recognizing that laws, customs, and other conditions may prevent a given country from full implementation of international standards, the IVSC also compiles lists of countries whose domestic standards are different from the international standards and makes this information publicly available.

In 2000 the IVSC published the third edition of international valuation standards, *International Valuation Standards 2000*. This edition marks the first major public accomplishment of the IVSC Standards Project, which plans to publish a set of even more comprehensive and robust international standards by 2002. The most recent edition reflects several of the most important discoveries that have been produced by the IVSC's work:

1. There is virtually unanimous agreement among the countries of the world as to valuation principles.

2. Despite the revision of standards, valuation principles do not change from edition to edition because they are well established and market-supported.

3. Many international (and domestic) misunderstandings are fostered by imprecise or confusing language; valuation standards are instrumental in recognizing these problems and offer precise understandings within the standards and in supplemental commentaries.

The goals of the IVSC Standards Project, which are explained on the IVSC's Web site (http://www.ivsc.org), include

- To facilitate cross-border transactions and contribute to the viability of international property markets by promoting transparency in financial reporting as well as the reliability of valuation performed to secure loans and mortgages, for transactions involving transfers of ownership, and for settlements in litigation or tax matters.

- To serve as a professional benchmark, or beacon, for valuers around the world, thereby enabling them to respond to the demands of international property markets for reliable valuations and to meet the financial reporting requirements of the global business community.

- To provide standards of valuation and financial reporting that meet the needs of emerging and newly industrialized countries[1]

The IVSC document includes two standards, one on the market value basis of valuation and the other covering valuation bases other than market value, along with applications of these standards, explanatory guidance notes, and a glossary of terms.

FURTHER READING

Gelbtuch, Howard C., and David Mackmin, with Michael R. Milgrim. *Real Estate Valuation in Global Markets*. Chicago: Appraisal Institute, 1997.

International Valuation Standards 2000. London: International Valuation Standards Committee, 2000.

Business Enterprise Value

The existence of a residual intangible personal property component in certain properties has been widely recognized for years. Among the many terms used to describe this phenomenon, *business enterprise value* (BEV) is the most widely used. The issue has attracted attention primarily through assessment, condemnation, and damage claim assignments, which require that an estimate of the value of the real estate component be separated from the market value of the total assets of the business (MVTAB).

These assignments necessarily involve an allocation among the component parts of real property and tangible and intangible personalty. The latter can include what has traditionally been called *business enterprise value* but more recently has become known as *capitalized economic profit* (CEP). CEP is defined as the present worth of an entrepreneur's economic (pure) profit expectation. In other words, CEP is the value of a residual claim that is subordinate to the opportunity cost claims of all agents of production employed by the business (e.g., land, labor, and/or capital).

Hotels were among the first property types for which CEP was analyzed. Other owner-operated business enterprises followed suit, including health care facilities, restaurants (especially fast-food chains), manufacturing plants, and bowling alleys. As awareness spread that CEP could be part of the total assets of a business, arguments emerged supporting its existence in nearly all property types, including leased proper-

> **capitalized economic profit (CEP):** The present worth of an entrepreneur's economic (pure) profit expectation from being engaged in the activity of acquiring an asset or collection of assets at a known price and then selling or being able to sell the same asset or collection of assets at a future uncertain price.

---

1. The International Valuation Standards Committee can be contacted at:

    International Valuation Standards Committee
    12 George Street
    London
    United Kingdom SW1P3AD

ties such as regional malls. Frequently such claims were not adequately supported or developed. They were also countered by other claims that questioned the extent of its applicability, suggesting that it was just a misallocated increment attributable to entrepreneurial incentive or a situs advantage or location premium.

Definitions

Because of inconsistent definitions of the various terms related to the topic among assessors, business and real estate appraisers, and the courts, a new lexicon has been developed. In discussing business enterprise value, the term *going concern*, for example, has been replaced with *total assets of the business* (TAB). TAB includes

- Real property
- Tangible personal property
- Intangible personal property

The personal property is broken down into

- Furniture, fixtures, and equipment (FF&E)
- Inventory

The intangibles are made up of

- Contracts
- Name
- Patents
- Copyrights
- An assembled work force
- Cash
- Other residual intangibles

CEP is included in the residual intangible category.

Arguments For and Against

Three arguments are commonly made to support the recognition of capitalized economic profit:

1. A residual intangible component of personal property exists.
2. It can be measured.
3. It is the beneficiary of any residual or surplus income generated by the operating enterprise or leased investment.

Evidence that intangible asset values—including CEP—might be present includes the following:

- The expected sale price is greater than reproduction or replacement cost less deprecation plus land value (i.e., the value indication by the cost approach).

- Net income of the business is derived primarily from the sale of a product or service.
- Net income is based primarily or exclusively on percentage rentals.
- Net income is persistently above market levels.
- New ownership or management consistently and perceptibly increases revenues (i.e., who the owner-operator is matters as does the identity of the tenants or occupants).
- Goodwill exists.

In assignments involving the market value of the total assets of the business, the cost approach offers little insight. Valuation by sales comparison is reasonably straightforward (although difficult adjustments are unavoidable), and the income capitalization approach is relatively manageable, especially if the subject facility has an operating history. In the cost approach, however, all the costs associated with the tangible and intangible personalty must be estimated and added. These might include FF&E, business start-up costs, franchise costs, and similar expenses. Even when the client is interested only in the market value of the total assets of the business, which is often the case, the Uniform Standards of Professional Appraisal Practice still requires that the appraiser include a separate valuation when the value of a non-realty item or combination of such items is significant to the overall value (see Standards Rule 1-4[g]).

When the appraiser is asked to value the real estate component only, use of the cost approach is relatively straightforward, although quantifying depreciation can be an obstacle. In contrast, the sales comparison and income capitalization approaches involve complex analysis. In sales comparison, any sales are most likely transfers of TAB, and all tangible and intangible personal property must be removed in order to isolate the contribution of the real estate to the sale price. (These are the same items that are added on in the cost approach when estimating MVTAB.) In the income capitalization approach, because the capitalized income stream will most likely reflect income to TAB, all components of net operating income not attributable to the real estate must be removed. The difficulty of these assignments does not relieve the appraiser of the responsibility to treat the tangible and intangible

SIGNIFICANT DECISIONS RELATING TO BUSINESS ENTERPRISE VALUE

Darcel Inc. v. Manitowoc Board of Review, 137 Wis. 2d 623, 405 N.W. 2d 344 (Wis. 1987).

State ex rel. N/S Associates v. Board of Review, 473 N.W. 2d 554 (Wis. App. 1991).

Equitable Life Assurance Society of the United States v. County of Hennepin, 1995 WL 702527 (Minn. Tax 1995).

Merle Hay Mall v. City of Des Moines Board of Review, 564 N.W. 2d 419 (Iowa 1997).

See also Marsha Kleffman, "Multi-State Survey: Update on 'Business Enterprise Value'," paper presented at the International Association of Assessing Officers' 20th Legal Seminar, Chicago, Ill., November 18–19, 1999, in *A Business Enterprise Anthology* (Chicago: Appraisal Institute, 2001), 369–379.

personalty properly. Not to do so produces either use value or the value of TAB; neither is the market value of the fee simple estate in real property.

Arguments against the existence of residual intangibles often point to the lack of universal acceptance of the various theories, especially in the courts. This is particularly true in the analysis of regional shopping malls. Another argument frequently advanced is that the theoretical increment labeled as intangible is instead a location premium awarded by the market, which therefore belongs with the real estate. A final argument against the existence of a residual intangible (and CEP) is that there can be none unless it can be sold or transferred to another location and is recognized as a separate item in the negotiations.

Most appraisal clients want to know the market value of the total assets of the business. Allocation of that value among component parts is often not requested or desired. Thus, appraisers who make such allocations are imposing that requirement on themselves. USPAP, among other authorities, mandates that appraisers analyze the effect that non-realty components have on value. Most state appraiser laws incorporate these standards by reference. For these reasons business enterprise value remains one of the most important and controversial topics confronting appraisers.

FURTHER READING

Lennhoff, David C., editor. *A Business Enterprise Value Anthology.* Chicago: Appraisal Institute, 2001.

personal property: Identifiable tangible objects that are considered by the general public as being "personal"—for example, furnishings, artwork, antiques, gems and jewelry, collectibles, machinery and equipment; all tangible property that is not classified as real estate. Also known as *personalty.*

Personal Property Appraisal

Just as real estate appraisers are called on to separate the value of a business enterprise from the market value of the accompanying real estate, practitioners may be required to develop an opinion of value of the personal property related to an appraised property. Common assignments involving the appraisal of personal property include

- Insurable value
- Estate tax
- Damage claims
- Donation of personal property
- Sale of a business (transfer tax)
- Dissolution of marriage and equitable distribution of personal property

The distinction between real property and personal property can be important in property tax assessment because often personal property is not taxed at the same rate as real property (or personal property may not be taxed at all). Also, the distinction between personal property and fixtures may be important. For example, in state condemnation cases personal property on the premises is generally not included in the calculation of just compensation for the taking of a parcel of real estate, but the fixtures attached to the real estate are included. There are exceptions, such as Michigan and Iowa, which have allowed compensation for personal property. Appraisers should investigate local regulations. In federal condemnation cases, the court will generally be guided by state law in differentiating between personal property and realty.

Personal property is often a consideration in the valuation of property types for which business enterprise value is also a concern, particularly hotels. The value of the furniture, fixtures, and equipment (FF&E) of a hotel, which are essential to the operation of a lodging facility, must be separated from the value of the real estate in some appraisals such as those for property tax assessments and for loans when the lender does not have personal property as collateral.[2] The items making up FF&E are often heavily capitalized and thus are not included in a hotel's operating statement, even though they do affect the cash flow. Hotel operating statements often include a replacement reserves line item for short-lived assets, which includes FF&E.

FURTHER READING

Hennessey, Sean F. "Myths About Hotel Business and Personalty Values." *The Appraisal Journal* (October 1993).

Lesser, Daniel H., and Karen E. Rubin. "Understanding the Unique Aspects of Hotel Property Tax Valuation." *The Appraisal Journal* (January 1993).

Standards 7 and 8. Uniform Standards of Professional Appraisal Practice. Washington, D.C.: The Appraisal Foundation, current edition.

Litigation Work

Litigation work is often considered a subcategory of appraisal consulting, but this niche business has grown to encompass various services including

- Serving as an expert witness
- Condemnation appraisal
- Property tax assessment appeals
- Appraisal review and other services for litigation support

While traditional appraisal services are in less demand, in an increasingly litigious environment opportunities exist for appraisers to diversify their practices by taking advantage of skills professional appraisers have already acquired and extending them into new areas.

Valuation for litigation is often called *forensic appraisal*, meaning belonging to the courts of justice, because it is the application of the principles and practices of appraisal to the clarification of questions before courts of law. In

---

2. The development and reporting of value opinions using mass appraisal techniques are covered in Standard 6 of USPAP.

TEN COURTROOM COMMANDMENTS FOR APPRAISERS

   I. Thou shalt not lie nor be evasive.

  II. Thou shalt not exaggerate the "highest and best use."

 III. Thou shalt not testify to a dictated appraisal.

  IV. Thou shalt carefully examine and evaluate all comparable sales.

   V. Thou shalt be wary of capitalizing hypothetical income on vacant land.

  VI. Thou shalt be judicious in the exercise of thy right to explain thy answer.

 VII. Thou shalt not clothe thyself in the garments of infallibility.

VIII. Thou shalt remember that thou art an impartial witness and not an advocate.

  IX. Thou shalt so live with thyself that thy testimony would be the same if appearing for the opposing party.

   X. Thou shalt always remember to control thy temper on cross-examination and retain a sense of humor.

Source: John P. Horgan, "Ten Courtroom Commandments for Appraisers," *Right of Way* (October 1959), reprinted in *The Appraisal Journal* (January 1960).

some instances this may include the investigation of statistical, financial, and economic data in search of misleading or fraudulent data relating to an event in the past. Forensic appraisers must be highly skilled and confident of their abilities. The litigation environment is commonly an adversarial one in which an appraiser's opinion of value will undoubtedly be challenged along with the appropriateness of the methodologies employed to arrive at that opinion. The potential for client pressure to produce a certain opinion of value may be greater than in traditional appraisal assignments for lending purposes, particularly if the appraiser relies on word-of-mouth and personal referrals for this type of business. The credibility of appraisers as expert witnesses is based on their objectivity and independence, which may put appraisers at odds with attorneys, who are advocates for their clients and are often paid on a contingency basis. Appraisers who are involved in litigation work must clearly define the scope of work required by the assignment to avoid confusion as to whether an attorney is explaining a point of law or expressing an opinion regarding a value premise.

Generally, the responsibility of an appraiser to a client ends upon delivery of the appraisal report. However, in litigation work the appraiser's professional responsibility continues until the case has been settled, which is usually after the appraiser has delivered a report or given testimony in court.

Condemnation Appraising

Eminent domain is the power of government to take private property for public use upon payment of just compensation. In recent years, city, state, and federal governments (and public service companies such as utilities and telephone companies that have been granted the power of eminent domain) have been acquiring vast amounts of land for highway improvements, conservation, fiber optic corridor easements, and tax increment financing districts among other purposes. The bulk of potential appraisal work is related to the acquisition activities of governments; only about 10% of governments acquisition require the exercise of the right of eminent domain, and many condemnation cases are not contested but are brought simply to clear title to the property.

Appraisers may be hired by either the condemnor—i.e., the government agency—or the condemnee—i.e., the owner of the property involved in the taking. The Uniform Relocation Assistance and Real Property Acquisition Act of 1970 (P.L. 91-646, as amended, 42 U.S.C. 4601, et seq.) and the corresponding legislation adopted by all 50 states requires agencies to have an appraisal of a property made before the agency can make an offer to purchase private lands. Historically, these appraisals were done by the agencies themselves, but in the 1990s much of that work was contracted out to private fee appraisers.

When a condemnation case goes to court, the definition of market value used in the proceeding must be acceptable to the court where the trial will be held. *Market value* and *just compensation* are not synonymous though. The distiction is a legal issue rather than an appraisal matter. An appraiser's opinion of market value is a tool used by the court in making a determination of just compensation. A property is generally valued before and after a partial taking to determine the just compensation. Most appraisals used for litigation purposes follow a similar procedure. An opinion of the contested loss in market value is developed by comparing market value of the property at different times or under different conditions.

Property Tax Assessment Appeals

Another litigation niche for appraisers is property tax assessment appeals. Property taxes can be the largest line item operating expense for a property. When property owners seek to ease their tax burden by challenging the assessed value of their real estate, they (or their attorneys) employ appraisers to provide an independent opinion of value, which may differ from the assessed value of the property. If the cycle between assessments is long (up to 10 years in some jurisdictions), changes in market conditions in the interim can affect value, either positively or negatively, without being reflected in the assessed value of the individual property.

Differences among property tax jurisdictions are important for appraisers involved in tax appeal work. Jurisdictions may differ in

> **assessed value:** The value of a property according to the tax rolls in ad valorem taxation. May be higher or lower than market value or based on an assessment ratio that is a percentage of market value.

- The definition of value sought
- Requirements or restrictions on valuation methodologies[3]

---

3. Standards Rule 1-2(e) of USPAP requires an appraiser to "identify the characteristics of the property that are relevant to the purpose and intended use of the appraisal, including: ...

(iii) any personal property, trade fixtures, or intangible items that are not real property but are included in the appraisal; ..."

- Length of the cycle for reviews and appeals
- The inclusion of personal property in assessed value

The mass appraisal techniques used by assessors' offices (often based on the cost approach) can be a point of contention. Appraisers have historically pointed to three inadequacies in the valuation models used for ad valorem taxation purposes:

- Incorrect methodology, such as a canned statistical package
- Inaccurate data
- Inaccurate applications

Assessors pioneered the use of automated valuation models (AVMs) to compensate for the limited budget, time, and staff that assessors' offices had to devote to the analysis of property data. The increasing sophistication and flexibility of AVMs has diminished the lack of reliability in assessed values. Also, in the last 10 years assessors' offices have made efforts to "clean up" historical data and improve data collection and storage efficiency, improving the quality of the value estimates derived from that data. Appraisers still believe that mass appraisal techniques are inappropriate valuation tools for situations involving special-use properties, properties whose current uses differ from their highest and best uses, and properties suffering from substantial obsolescence not reflected in the model.

mass appraisal: The process of valuing a universe of properties as of a given date utilizing standard methodology, employing common data, and allowing for statistical testing. (USPAP, 2001 ed.)

Appraisal Review for Litigation Support

Most attorneys are unfamiliar with appraisal reports and therefore need professional assistance in evaluating these documents to prepare a case. An appraiser might review appraisals prepared at the request of the attorney who engaged the appraiser or at the request of opposing counsel. Related services include

- Advising an attorney on matters of standards of practice, professional codes of ethics, market data sources, and industry trends
- Helping frame questions for appraisal experts on either side of the case at depositions and during trial testimony
- Case management

Further Reading

Eaton, James D. *Real Estate Valuation in Litigation,* 2d ed. Chicago: Appraisal Institute, 1995.

Expert Witness Testimony

Boothe, Russell H. "The Factual Basis of an Appraiser's Testimony." *The Appraisal Journal* (April 1995).

Dorchester, John D., Jr. "The Federal Rules of Evidence and Daubert: Evaluating Real Property Valuation Witnesses." *The Appraisal Journal* (July 2000).

Friedman, Jack P., and Nicholas Ordway. "Appraisal Review in a Litigation Support Role." *The Appraisal Journal* (January 2000).

Grover, Michael. R. "Expert Witness: Preparing Reports for Court." *Canadian Appraiser,* vol. 44, no. 3 (Fall 2000).

Roddewig, Richard J. "Junk Science, Environmental Stigma, Market Surveys, and Proper Appraisal Methodology: Recent Lessons from the Litigation Trenches." *The Appraisal Journal* (October 1999).

Condemnation Appraising

Shepard, Richard C. "Real Estate Counseling in Litigation: Illustrated by Eminent Domain." *Real Estate Issues,* vol. 24, no. 3 (Fall 1999).

Uniform Appraisal Standards for Federal Land Acquisitions. Washington, D.C.: Interagency Land Acquisition Conference, 2000.

Property Tax Assessment Appeals

McErlean, Matthew N. "Find a Lucrative Niche Market in Property Tax Assessment Appeals Work." *Valuation Insights & Perspectives,* vol. 1, no. 3 (Summer 1996).

Standard on Property Tax Policy. Chicago: International Association of Assessing Officers, 1997. Available online at: http://www.iaao.org/standard.htm.

Public Interest Value

Public interest value is a general term covering a family of non-market value concepts that relate the highest and best use of property to non-economic uses such as conservation or preservation. The term originated in the 1970s in federal legislation relating to federal lands (i.e., private-public exchanges of federal lands deemed to be in the public interest) and federal income taxes (i.e., tax deductions for certain types of donations or dedications of private land for public purposes). The issue of public interest value has also come up in determining the just compensation required in land acquisitions by federal agencies.

Huge amounts of public funds are involved in what has become a highly controversial subject. The United States General Accounting Office criticized the use of public interest value in valuations within the Arctic National Wildlife Refuge and blocked proposed acquisitions of lands applying public interest concepts as early as the late 1980s. There have been a number of attempts to apply the same concepts since then, but most have been called *market value* even though they apply the same concepts and rationales.[4] The Appraisal Institute has officially stated that public interest value concepts are

---

4. United States General Accounting Office. *Federal Land Management: Consideration of Proposed Alaska Land Exchanges Should Be Discontinued.* GAO/RCED-88-179. Washington, D.C., September 1988.

not to be applied when the purpose of the appraisal is to estimate market value.[5] The federal Interagency Appraisal Task Force has spoken clearly on the issue, stating a conclusion that is consistent with that of the Appraisal Institute and pointing out the possible violation of federal laws that can be involved with transgressions. The American Society of Farm Managers and Rural Appraisers issued an unequivocal statement that follows the same theme as the statements by the Appraisal Institute and the Interagency Appraisal Task Force.

Public interest value remains a contentious and divisive issue, and appraisers valuing conservation easements, view easements, wetlands, historic sites, and similar properties must be aware of both the history of the debate and any current rulings or positions taken by the parties involved.

FURTHER READING

Dorchester, John D., Jr. "Market Value is Not an Ideology: The Attack on Market Value Continues Through Public Interest Value and its Family." Paper presented at a national seminar on public interest value issues in Sacramento, Calif., in April 1999. Available from author.

Fellows, James. "The Legal Doctrine of Regulatory Takings: An Evolving Issue." *The Appraisal Journal* (October 1996).

Hanson, Woodward S. "Public Interest Value and Non-Economic Highest and Best Use: The Appraisal Institute's Position." *Valuation Insights & Perspectives*, vol. 1, no. 2 (Spring 1996).

Interagency Land Conference. "Position Paper: On the Issue of Whether a Non-economic Highest and Best Use Can Be a Proper Basis for the Estimate of Market Value." Washington, D.C.: 1995, cited in Robertson, Jerry D. "Tradition or Stagnation? In Defense of Non-Economic Highest and Best Use." *The Appraisal Journal* (April 1997).

Lowe, Timothy R. "Discussion Paper on Valuation Methodology: Public Interest Value and Market Value" in *Viewpoints: A Collection of Papers Presented at the Appraisal Institute's 1997 National Summer Conference*. Chicago: Appraisal Institute, 1997.

Lusvardi, Wayne C. "A Critique of the Position Papers on the Valuation of Land Suitable for Habitat Preservation or Mitigation." *Right of Way* (November/December 1996).

____. "The Flawed Logic of Sales Substitution in the Appraisal of Land Suitable for Habitat Preservation or Mitigation." *Right of Way* (May/June 1997).

Mundy, Bill, and William N. Kinnard, Jr. "The New Non-Economics: Public Interest Value, Market Value, and Economic Use." *The Appraisal Journal* (April 1998). See also letters to the editor in the January 1999 issue of *The Appraisal Journal*.

Wilson, Donald C. "Highest and Best Use: Preservation of Environmentally Significant Real Estate." *The Appraisal Journal* (January 1996).

Wilson, Donald C., and Craig D. Hungerford. "Toward Just and Feasible Solutions: The Economic Preservation Use Debate Rages On." *Right of Way* (January/February 1997).

---

5. Woodward S. Hanson, "Public Interest Value and Non-Economic Highest and Best Use: The Appraisal Institute's Position," *Valuation Insights & Perspectives*, vol. 1, no. 2 (Spring 1996): 27–29, 48. See also "Taking Issue with Public Interest Value Article," Letter to the Editor, *Valuation Insights & Perspectives*, vol. 1, no. 4 (Fall 1996): 42 and Woodward S. Hanson, "Public Interest Value Debate Continues," *Valuation Insights & Perspectives*, vol. 2, no. 1 (First Quarter 1997): 3, 42.

APPENDIX A PROFESSIONAL PRACTICE AND LAW

A profession is distinguished from a trade or service industry by a combination of the following factors:

- High standards of competence in a specialized field
- A distinct body of knowledge that is continually augmented by the contributions of members and can be imparted to future generations
- A code of ethics and standards of practice and members who are willing to be subject to peer review

Professional appraisal practice is founded upon an established body of knowledge. In solving most appraisal problems, however, the final conclusions depend to a great extent on the ability, judgment, and integrity of individual appraisers. To form a sound conclusion, relevant data must be available and the appraiser must be committed to finding and analyzing the data. A valid analysis also depends on the skillful application of appraisal techniques. Because appraisal is an inexact science, appraisers must reach their conclusions in an impartial, objective manner, without bias or any desire to accommodate their own interests or the interests of their clients. Professional appraisers have the requisite knowledge and the ability to apply it capably and objectively.

The Appraisal Institute was formed for three purposes.

1. To establish criteria for selecting and recognizing individuals with real estate valuation skills who were committed to competent and ethical practice
2. To develop a system of education to train new appraisers and sharpen the skills of practicing appraisers
3. To formulate a code of professional ethics and standards of professional practice to guide real estate appraisers and serve as a model for other practitioners

The heart of the Appraisal Institute's commitment to professionalism is contained in the five canons of the Code of Professional Ethics and in the

The Standards-related material in this appendix is continuously revised by the appropriate organizations. Appraisers should consult the most recent editions of any publications referenced in this appendix.

Standards of Professional Appraisal Practice, which include the Uniform Standards of Professional Appraisal Practice, the Supplemental Standards, and the Guide Notes.

Code of Professional Ethics
Canon 1
A Member must refrain from conduct that is detrimental to the Appraisal Institute, the appraisal profession and the public.

Canon 2
A Member must assist the Appraisal Institute in carrying out its responsibilities to the users of appraisal services and the public.

Canon 3
In the performance of an assignment, a Member must develop and communicate each analysis and opinion without being misleading, without bias for the client's interest and without accommodation of his or her own interests.

Canon 4
A Member must not violate the confidential nature of the appraiser-client relationship.

Canon 5
A Member must use care to avoid advertising or solicitations that are misleading or otherwise contrary to the public interest.

Uniform Standards of Professional Appraisal Practice
Standard 1   Real Property Appraisal, Development
In developing a real property appraisal, an appraiser must identify the problem to be solved and the scope of work necessary to solve the problem, and correctly complete research and analysis necessary to produce a credible appraisal.

Standard 2   Real Property Appraisal, Reporting
In reporting the results of a real property appraisal, an appraiser must communicate each analysis, opinion, and conclusion in a manner that is not misleading.

Standard 3   Real Property and Personal Property Appraisal Review, Development and Reporting
In reviewing an appraisal review assignment involving a real property or personal property appraisal, an appraiser acting as a reviewer must develop and report a credible opinion as to the quality of another appraiser's work and must clearly disclose the scope of work performed in the assignment.

Standard 4   Real Property Appraisal Consulting, Development

In developing a real property appraisal consulting assignment, an appraiser must identify the problem to be solved and the scope of work necessary to solve the problem, and correctly complete the research and analysis necessary to produce credible results.

Standard 5   Real Property Appraisal Consulting, Reporting

In reporting the results of a real property appraisal consulting assignment, an appraiser must communicate each analysis, opinion, and conclusion in a manner that is not misleading.

Standard 6   Mass Appraisal, Development and Reporting

In developing a mass appraisal, an appraiser must be aware of, understand, and correctly employ those generally accepted methods and techniques necessary to produce and communicate credible appraisals.

Standard 7   Personal Property Appraisal, Development

In developing a personal property appraisal, an appraiser must identify the problem to be solved and the scope of work necessary to solve the problem and correctly complete research and analysis necessary to produce a credible appraisal.

Standard 8   Personal Property Appraisal, Reporting

In reporting the results of a personal property appraisal, an appraiser must communicate each analysis, opinion, and conclusion in a manner that is not misleading.

Standard 9   Business Appraisal, Development

In developing a business or intangible asset appraisal, an appraiser must identify the problem to be solved and the scope of work necessary to solve the problem and correctly complete the research and analysis steps necessary to produce a credible appraisal.

Standard 10   Business Appraisal, Reporting

In reporting the results of a business or intangible asset appraisal, an appraiser must communicate each analysis, opinion, and conclusion in a manner that is not misleading.

Standards 7 through 10 will not be enforced by the Appraisal Institute. Two supplemental standards follow. These standards apply only to Members of the Appraisal Institute.

Supplemental Standards

Supplemental Standard 1

The form of certification used by a Member in a written report must include:

1. A statement indicating compliance with the Code of Professional Ethics and Standards of Professional Appraisal Practice; and

2. A statement advising the client and third parties of the Appraisal Institute's right to review the report; and

3. A statement indicating the current status of the Designated Member under the Appraisal Institute's continuing education program.

Supplemental Standard 2

The Uniform Standards of Professional Appraisal Practice contains an Ethics Rule. The language in this Ethics Rule is very broad and the Appraisal Institute has interpreted this Ethics Rule to apply to appraisal conduct only. The Appraisal Institute has an existing Code of Professional Ethics that is adequate to carry out the intent of the Ethics Rule. Therefore, the Appraisal Institute will enforce its own Code of Professional Ethics under its existing enforcement procedures as the proper means of enforcing the Ethics Rule of the Uniform Standards of Professional Appraisal Practice.

USPAP Definitions

The following definitions are taken from the Uniform Standards of Professional Appraisal Practice (USPAP), 2001 edition:

Advocacy: representing the cause or interest of another, even if that cause or interest does not necessarily coincide with one's own beliefs, opinions, conclusions, or recommendations.

Appraisal: (noun) the act or process of developing an opinion of value; an opinion of value. (adjective) of or pertaining to appraising and related functions such as appraisal practice or appraisal services.

> **Complete Appraisal:** the act or process of developing an opinion of value or an opinion of value developed without invoking the Departure Rule.

> **Limited Appraisal:** the act or process of developing an opinion of value or an opinion of value developed under and resulting from invoking the Departure Rule.

> *Comment:* An appraisal must be numerically expressed as a specific amount, as a range of numbers, or as a relationship (e.g., not more than, not less than) to a previous value opinion or numerical benchmark (e.g., assessed value, collateral value).

Appraisal Consulting: the act or process of developing an analysis, recommendation, or opinion to solve a problem, where an opinion of value is a component of the analysis leading to the assignment results.

Comment: An appraisal consulting assignment involves an opinion of value but does not have an appraisal or an appraisal review as its primary purpose.

Appraisal Practice: valuation services including, but not limited to, appraisal, appraisal review, and appraisal consulting, performed by an individual as an appraiser.

Comment: Appraisal practice is provided only by appraisers, while valuation services are provided by a variety of professionals and others. The terms appraisal, appraisal review, and appraisal consulting are intentionally generic and not mutually exclusive. For example, an opinion of value may be required as part of an appraisal review and is required as a component of the analysis in an appraisal consulting assignment. The use of other nomenclature for an appraisal, appraisal review, or appraisal consulting assignment (e.g., analysis, counseling, evaluation, study, submission, or valuation) does not exempt an appraiser from adherence to the Uniform Standards of Professional Appraisal Practice.

Appraisal Review: the act or process of developing and communicating an opinion about the quality of another appraiser's work.

Comment: The subject of an appraisal review assignment may be all or part of an appraisal report, workfile, or a combination of these.

Appraiser: one who is expected to perform valuation services competently and in a manner that is independent, impartial, and objective.

Comment: Such expectation occurs when individuals, either by choice or by requirement placed upon them or upon the service they provide by law, regulation, or agreement with the client or intended users, represent that they comply.

Appraiser's Peers: other appraisers who have expertise and competency in the same or a similar type of assignment.

Assignment: a valuation service provided as a consequence of an agreement between an appraiser and a client.

Assignment Results: an appraiser's opinions and conclusions developed specific to an assignment.

Comment: Assignment results include an appraiser's:

* opinions or conclusions developed in an appraisal assignment, such as value;

* opinions of adequacy, relevancy, or reasonableness developed in an appraisal review assignment; or

* opinions, conclusions, or recommendations developed in an appraisal consulting assignment.

Assumption: that which is taken to be true.

Bias: a preference or inclination, used in the development or communication of an appraisal, appraisal review, or appraisal consulting assignment, that precludes an appraiser's impartiality.

Binding Requirement: all or part of a Standards Rule of USPAP from which departure is not permitted. (See Departure Rule.)

Business Enterprise: an entity pursuing an economic activity.

Business Equity: the interests, benefits, and rights inherent in the ownership of a business enterprise or a part thereof in any form (including, but not necessarily limited to, capital stock, partnership interests, cooperatives, sole proprietorships, options, and warrants).

Cash Flow Analysis: a study of the anticipated movement of cash into or out of an investment.

Client: the party or parties who engage an appraiser (by employment or contract) in a specific assignment.

Comment: The client identified by the appraiser in an appraisal, appraisal review, or appraisal consulting assignment (or in the assignment work file) is the party or parties with whom the appraiser has an appraiser-client relationship in the related assignment, and may be an individual, group, or entity.

Confidential Information: information received from a client, not available from any other source, which the client identifies as confidential when providing it to an appraiser.*

Comment: Information available to the appraiser from other sources does not become confidential when given to the appraiser by the client.

> * *Privacy Notice:* Due to the passage of the Gramm-Leach-Bliley Act in November 1999, numerous regulatory agencies (e.g., OTS, OCC, FDIC, FTC, FRB) have new privacy regulations. These regulations, as well as others, may supersede the minimum requirements put forth in the 2001 USPAP.

Cost: the amount required to create, produce, or obtain a property.

Comment: Cost is either a fact or an estimate of fact.

Extraordinary Assumption: an assumption, directly related to a specific assignment, which, if found to be false, could alter the appraiser's opinions or conclusions.

Comment: Extraordinary assumptions presume as fact otherwise uncertain information about physical, legal, or economic characteristics of the subject property; or about conditions external to the property, such as market conditions or trends; or about the integrity of an economic endeavor.

Feasibility Analysis: a study of the cost-benefit relationship of an economic endeavor.

Hypothetical Condition: that which is contrary to what exists but is supposed for the purpose of analysis.

Comment: Hypothetical conditions assume conditions contrary to known facts about physical, legal, or economic characteristics of the subject property; or about conditions external to the property, such as market conditions or trends; or about the integrity of data used in an analysis.

Intangible Property (Intangible Assets): nonphysical assets, including but not limited to franchises, trademarks, patents, copyrights, goodwill, equities, mineral rights, securities, and contracts, as distinguished from physical assets such as facilities and equipment.

Intended Use: the use or uses of an appraiser's reported appraisal, appraisal review, or appraisal consulting assignment opinions and conclusions, as identified by the appraiser based on communication with the client at the time of the assignment.

Intended User: the client and any other party as identified, by name or type, as users of the appraisal, appraisal review, or appraisal consulting report, by the appraiser on the basis of communication with the client at the time of the assignment.

Investment Analysis: a study that reflects the relationship between acquisition price and anticipated future benefits of a real estate investment.

Market Analysis: a study of market conditions for a specific type of property.

Market Value: a type of value, stated as an opinion, that presumes the transfer of a property (i.e., a right of ownership or a bundle of such rights), as of a certain date, under specific conditions set forth in the definition of the term identified by the appraiser as applicable in an appraisal.

Comment: Forming an opinion of market value is the purpose of many real property appraisal assignments, particularly when the client's intended use includes more than one intended user. The conditions included in market value definitions establish market perspectives for development of the opinion. These conditions may vary from definition to definition but generally fall into three categories:

1. the relationship, knowledge, and motivation of the parties (i.e., seller and buyer);

2. the terms of sale (e.g., cash, cash equivalent, or other terms); and

3. the conditions of sale (e.g., exposure in a competitive market for a reasonable time prior to sale).

Appraisers are cautioned to identify the exact definition of market value, and its authority, applicable in each appraisal completed for the purpose of market value.

Mass Appraisal: the process of valuing a universe of properties as of a given date using standard methodology, employing common data, and allowing for statistical testing.

Mass Appraisal Model: a mathematical expression of how supply and demand factors interact in a market.

Personal Property: identifiable portable and tangible objects that are considered by the general public as being "personal"—for example, furnishings, artwork, antiques, gems and jewelry, collectibles, machinery and equipment; all property that is not classified as real estate.

Price: the amount asked, offered, or paid for a property.

Comment: Once stated, price is a fact, whether it is publicly disclosed or retained in private. Because of the financial capabilities, motivations, or special interests of a given buyer or seller, the price paid for a property may or may not have any relation to the value that might be ascribed to that property by others.

Real Estate: an identified parcel or tract of land, including improvements, if any.

Real Property: the interests, benefits, and rights inherent in the ownership of real estate.

Comment: In some jurisdictions, the terms real estate and real property have the same legal meaning. The separate definitions recognize the traditional distinction between the two concepts in appraisal theory.

Report: any communication, written or oral, of an appraisal, appraisal review, or appraisal consulting service that is transmitted to the client upon completion of an assignment.

Comment: Most reports are written and most clients mandate written reports. Oral report guidelines (see the Record Keeping section of the Ethics Rule) are included to cover court testimony and other oral communications of an appraisal, appraisal review, or appraisal consulting service.

The types of written reports listed below apply to real property, personal property, and business valuation appraisal assignments, as indicated.

Appraisal Report: a written report prepared under Standards Rule 10-2(a).

Self-Contained Appraisal Report: a written report prepared under Standards Rule 2-2(a) or 8-2(a).

Summary Appraisal Report: a written report prepared under Standards Rule 2-2(b) or 8-2(b).

Restricted Use Appraisal Report: a written report prepared under Standards Rule 2-2(c) or 8-2(c).

Scope of Work: the amount and type of information researched and the analysis applied in an assignment. Scope of work includes, but is not limited to, the following:

- the degree to which the property is inspected or identified;
- the extent of research into physical or economic factors that could affect the property;
- the extent of data research; and
- the type and extent of analysis applied to arrive at opinions or conclusions.

Signature: personalized evidence indicating authentication of the work performed by the appraiser and the acceptance of the responsibility for content, analyses, and the conclusions in the report.

Comment: A signature can be represented by a handwritten mark, a digitized image controlled by a personalized identification number, or other media, where the appraiser has sole personalized control of affixing the signature.

Specific Requirements: all or part of a Standards Rule of USPAP from which departure is permitted under certain limited conditions. (See Departure Rule.)

Supplemental Standard: an assignment performance requirement that adds to the requirements in USPAP.

Value: the monetary relationship between properties and those who buy, sell, or use those properties.

Comment: Value expresses an economic concept. As such, it is never a fact but always an opinion of the worth of a property at a given time in accordance with a specific definition of value. In appraisal practice, value must always be qualified; for example, market value, liquidation value, or investment value.

Valuation Services: services pertaining to aspects of property value.

Comment: Valuation services pertain to all aspects of property value and include services performed both by appraisers and by others.

Workfile: documentation necessary to support an appraiser's analysis, opinions, and conclusions.

Federal Legislation Affecting the Appraisal Profession*

Truth in Lending Act of 1968 (15 U.S.C. 41)

Simplified and reformed as part of the Depository Institutions Deregulations and Monetary Control Act of 1980

Areas of appraisal affected

Requires a copy of an appraisal be made available to all consumers

Government agencies subject to specific legislation

Federal Reserve Board, Department of Transportation (DOT), Veterans Administration, Department of Housing and Urban Development (HUD), Federal Home Loan Bank Board, and National Credit Union Administration (The last two are independent agencies.)

Uniform Relocation Assistance and Real Properties Acquisition Act of 1970 (Public Law 91-646, Titles II & III)

Amended in the Surface Transportation Bill (1987)[†]

Areas of appraisal affected

Just compensation for displaced owners and tenants affected by land acquisitions for federally funded projects

Government agencies subject to specific legislation

Department of Agriculture; Department of the Interior—National Park Service; DOT (A total of 14 agencies are affected.)

Real Estate Settlement Procedures Act of 1974 (12 U.S.C. 2601)

Areas of appraisal affected

Requires lenders to give a borrower an estimate of closing costs within three business days of applying for a loan

Government agencies subject to specific legislation

HUD; Office of Thrift Supervision (OTS) and Office of Comptroller of the Currency (OCC), both under the Treasury Department; Federal Reserve Board; Federal Deposit Insurance Corporation (FDIC); and the National Credit Union Administration (The last three are independent agencies.)

---

* Appraisal policies and procedures may also be established by means other than regulatory legislation. Memoranda and banking or examining circulars and executive orders are noteworthy examples. Several federal agencies (OCC, FDIC, OTS) issue circulars that specify the definition of value they require, e.g., fair value, net realizable value (see 12 CFR 7.3024 and the two other banking/examining circulars cited in this chart and the second note on the next page). Also note Executive Order 12630.

† Uniform appraisal standards for land acquisition, developed in the Yellow Book of 1973, were revised and published in 1992 and again in 2000 as *Uniform Appraisal Standards for Federal Land Acquisitions* by the Interagency Land Acquisition Conference (Washington, D.C.: U.S. Government Printing Office, 2000).

Federal Legislation Affecting the Appraisal Profession

Competitive Equality Banking Act of 1987 (CEBA) (Public Law 100-86)	CEBA was the foundation for FIRREA‡
Areas of appraisal affected	Appraisals done for the five Federal Financial Institutions Regulatory Agencies (FFIRAs) Brought appraisals for S&Ls under the same policies and procedures as those for commercial banks
Government agencies subject to specific legislation	OTS (since 1989) and OCC, both under the **Treasury Department; Federal Reserve Board, FDIC,** and **National Credit Union Administration**
Federal Land Exchange Facilitation Act of 1988 (Public Law 101-17)	
Areas of appraisal affected	Valuation of parcels involved in exchanges between federal and state agencies
Government agencies subject to specific legislation	**Department of Agriculture—U.S. Forestry Service; Department of the Interior—Bureaus of Land Management** (public land) and **Mines**
Financial Institutions Reform, Recovery and Enforcement Act of 1989 (FIRREA) (Public Law 101-73, Title XI) (8/8/89)	Each of the five FFIRAs plus the RTC was directed to draft preliminary and final rules (within a year) to give substance to this legislation‖ Title XI was amended 11/27/91
Areas of appraisal affected	Appraisals done for the five Federal Financial Institutions Regulatory Agencies (FFIRAs) Appraisals for all federal and state S&Ls and banking institutions
Government agencies subject to specific legislation	**OTS** (superseding the FHLBB) and **OCC,** both under **Treasury; Federal Reserve Board, FDIC,** and **National Credit Union Administration;** and the **Resolution Trust Corporation (RTC),** a quasi-independent agency set up to oversee the liquidation of insolvent S&Ls (The RTC became defunct in 1995.)

‡ In response to **CEBA,** the Federal Home Loan Bank Board (FHLBB) adopted **Regulation 563.17-1a** and **Statement of Policy 563-1b** (12/12/87).

‖ Pursuant to FIRREA, banking/examining circulars were issued by the federal banking agencies. The dates when these circulars were published are shown below; all became effective between 8/9/90 and 9/21/90:

Office of Comptroller of the Currency, 12 CFR Part 34, Subpart C "Real Estate Appraisals" (8/24/90)
Federal Reserve Board, 12 CFR Parts 208 and 225 (7/28/90)
Federal Deposit Insurance Corporation, 12 CFR Part 323 (8/20/90)
Resolution Trust Corporation, 12 CFR Part 1608 (8/22/90)
Office of Thrift Supervision, 12 CFR Parts 506, 545, 563, 564, 571 (8/23/90)
National Credit Union Administration, 12 CFR Parts 701, 722, 741 (7/25/90)

Federal Legislation Affecting the Appraisal Profession

Homeowners Protection Act of 1998 (Pub. L. 105-216)

Areas of appraisal affected
Provides for the cancellation of private mortgage insurance

Appraisals done for residential mortgage transactions[#]

Government agencies subject to specific legislation
OTS (superseding the FHLBB) and OCC, both under **Treasury, Federal Reserve Board, FDIC**, and the **National Credit Union Administration**

Gramm-Leach-Bliley Act of 1999 (Pub. L. 106-102)[**]
Repeals Section 20 (12 U.S.C. §377) and Section 32 (12 U.S.C. §78) of the Glass-Steagall Act, which restrict banks and their affiliates from being affiliated with companies engaged in the business of underwriting and dealing in securities, and creates a major new exception to Section 4(a) of Bank Holding Company Act of 1956, which prohibits a bank holding company from acquiring interests in companies other than banks.

Areas of appraisal affected
Sets requirements for use of non-public personal information by lending institutions and third parties

Government agencies subject to specific legislation
Federal Reserve Board, Federal Trade Commission (FTC), and OCC

Cabin User Fee Fairness Act of 2000 (Pub. L. 106-291)

Areas of appraisal affected
Appraisals done in determining fair and reasonable fees to the federal government for the use and occupancy of National Forest System land under the recreation residence program

Government agencies subject to specific legislation
U.S. Forestry Service, Department of Agriculture

[#] Exceptions include government mortgage insurance (i.e., FHA loans) and lender-paid mortgage insurance.

[**]Section 504 of the Act requires the Federal Trade Commission and other federal regulatory agencies to issue regulations as may be necessary to implement notice requirements and restrictions on a financial institution's ability to disclose nonpublic personal information about consumers to nonaffiliated third parties.

Federal Regulations Affecting the Appraisal Profession

12 CFR 7.3025 "Other Real Estate Owned" (8/28/79)	Amended 3/28/84
Areas of appraisal affected	Appraisals done for commercial banks
Government agencies subject to specific legislation	Office of Comptroller of the Currency (OCC), under the Treasury Department
Internal Revenue Service Regulation Section 1.170A-13 (1986)	
Areas of appraisal affected	Reporting requirements established for appraisals done for income tax purposes (specifically dealing with charitable contributions)
Government agencies subject to specific legislation	Internal Revenue Service (Treasury Department)
Executive Order 12630 (1988)	
Areas of appraisal affected	Requires all agencies to determine whether an action will result in a taking
Government agencies subject to specific legislation	All federal agencies
Circular A-129 of 1988 (updated in 2000)	The Federal Interagency Real Property Appraisal Committee (FIRPAC) is made up of various federal agencies with an interest in appraisal issues. FIRPAC, which is headed by OMB, was established to develop and revise Circular A-129. It includes many agencies not bound by FIRREA.
Areas of appraisal affected	Appraisals done for any federal credit agency under the Office of Management and Budget (OMB) (Does not apply to land acquisition agencies; mandates hiring of certified appraisers.)
Government agencies subject to specific legislation	Office of Management and Budget (OMB) (an executive agency)

Banking/Examining Circulars Affecting the Appraisal Profession

Examining Circular 234 "Troubled Real Estate Loans" (10/30/85) and **Supplement No. 1 "Guidelines for Troubled Real Estate Loans Clarified"** (7/10/87)

Areas of appraisal affected
Appraisals done for commercial banks

Government agencies subject to specific legislation
Office of Comptroller of the Currency (OCC), under the Treasury Department

Banking Circular 225 "Guidelines for Real Estate Appraisal Policies and Review Procedures" (12/7/87) and **"Clarification of Guidelines for Real Estate Appraisal Policies and Review Procedures"** (9/8/88)

Areas of appraisal affected
Appraisals done for commercial banks

Government agencies subject to specific legislation
Federal Reserve Board, Federal Reserve Board; Federal Deposit Insurance Corporation (FDIC), and OCC

For further insights on the development of appraisal legislation, see Alison K. Bailey Seas, "Evolution of Appraisal Reform and Regulation in the United States," *The Appraisal Journal* (January 1994): 26-46 and Thomas A. Dorsey, "The Influence of Government Regulations on Market Value," *Valuation Insights & Perspectives*, vol. 3, no. 1 (First Quarter 1998): 16-18, 20-21.

B | MATHEMATICS AND STATISTICS IN APPRAISING

Appraisers use a wide variety of mathematical techniques ranging from simple arithmetic and algebraic formulas to the statistical techniques of multiple regression analysis. Addition, subtraction, multiplication, and division can be done manually or with a simple calculator, but more sophisticated calculators may be needed to solve algebraic formulas and to perform linear regression analyses. Computers are required for nearly all stepwise multiple regression analyses.

With the general availability of calculators and personal computers, the use of sophisticated techniques is increasing in appraisal practice. This section provides a review of the mathematical procedures and terminology used by appraisers. Familiar processes are illustrated and the rules that apply to each process are discussed.

Basic Arithmetic for Data Processing

Data collected in the market is analyzed in the valuation process to derive an opinion of value. This data may include building dimensions, population figures, reproduction and replacement costs, rents, and sale prices. Processing this data ultimately leads to conclusions and final value indications, which are expressed numerically. The mathematical relationships represented by rates and factors are usually stated as decimals rather than fractions.

Rates

Rates are percentages expressed in terms of a specific time period. For example,

> $8 interest per year on $100 principal = 8% interest per year
> $0.50 interest per month on $100 = 0.005 or 0.5% interest per month

A rate reflects the relationship between one quantity and another. In the first example, the 8% rate relates the $8 of interest returned to the $100 of principal invested. In appraising, an unknown capital amount can be determined when only the rate and the amount of annual return are known.

Reciprocals

The reciprocal of a number is 1 divided by that number. For example, the reciprocal of 4 is $1/4$, which may be expressed as 0.25. When two numbers have a reciprocal relationship, 1 divided by either number equals the other number. Reciprocal relationships exist between some financial factors, which are explained in Appendix C. For example, the present value of $1 per period factor and the partial payment factor are reciprocals. These annual factors in the 10% tables for 10 periods are 6.144567 and 0.162745, respectively. Because they are reciprocals,

$$\frac{1}{6.144567} = 0.162745$$

and

$$\frac{1}{0.162745} = 6.144567$$

When a reciprocal relationship exists, multiplication by one of the numbers is equivalent to division by the other.

Factors

Factors are the reciprocals of rates and may be used to express relationships between income and capital value. Using *I, R,* and *V* to represent income, rate, and value, and *F* to represent a factor, the relationships may be expressed as

$$I = V \times R \qquad\qquad\qquad\qquad I = \frac{V}{F}$$

$$R = \frac{I}{V} \qquad\qquad\qquad\qquad F = \frac{V}{I}$$

$$V = \frac{I}{R} \qquad\qquad\qquad\qquad V = I \times F$$

These relationships, which are commonly referred to as IRV and VIF, may be shown as follows.

$$\frac{I}{R \mid V} \qquad\qquad \text{and} \qquad\qquad \frac{V}{I \mid F}$$

The formula for any single component is represented by the horizontal or vertical relationship of the remaining two components as one multiplied by, or divided by, the other.

Basic Statistics

Statistics can be applied to interpret available data and to support a value conclusion. In the language of statistics, a *population* is defined as all the items in a specific category. If, for example, the category is houses in Boston, the population consists of all the houses in Boston. However, data pertaining to an entire population is rarely available and conclusions often must be developed from incomplete data.

Using statistical concepts, conclusions about a population can be derived and evaluated from sample data. A *sample* is part of a population. The quality of conclusions based on a sample will vary with the quality and extent of the sample.

One item in a population is called a *variate.* In appraising, statistics can be used to identify the attributes of the typical variate in a population. When observations about a population can be measured, the analysis may be quantitative; when these observations cannot be measured, the analysis is qualitative—i.e., it reflects the attributes of the population.

A variate is discrete when it can assume a limited number of values on a measuring scale and continuous when it can assume an infinite number of values. A typical population of attributes for house types might include one-story, two-story, and split-level houses. It is usually impractical to display or identify a population of variates because there are many.

One common problem in statistics is how to describe a population in universally understandable terms. For example, how does one describe all the houses in a community that have sold in the past year without describing each sale individually? One possible solution is to use a single number called a *parameter* to describe the whole population. When one parameter is used to describe a population, it is called an *aggregate,* which is the sum of all the variates. For example, all the house sales in a community in a given year can be described by the total dollar amount of all the sales. In statistical language this is written as

$$\Sigma = \text{sigma or sum of}$$
$$X = \text{variate}$$
$$\Sigma X = \text{aggregate (sum of the variates)}$$

Measures of Central Tendency

Three common statistical measures are the mean, the median, and the mode. All three measure central tendency and are used to identify the typical variate in a population or sample. Measures that refer to a population are called *parameters,* while similar measures in a sample are called *statistics.*

The mean, which is commonly called the *average,* is by far the most commonly used parameter. It is obtained by dividing the sum of all the variates in a population by the number of variates. In real estate appraising, the mean may represent an average sale price, an average number of days on the market, an average apartment rent, or an average cost per square foot.

When the mean is used to describe a population, it can be distorted by extreme variates. Consider the following list of 36 house sales in a neighborhood. From these figures, the mean of the population can be calculated. (The list indicates the median and the mode of the population, which are discussed next.)

$72,000	
74,600	
76,000	
77,200	
78,000	
79,000	
79,800	
79,800	
82,000	
82,000	
84,000	
85,600	
85,800	
86,000	
87,000	
87,200	
87,400	
87,800	← median = $87,800
87,800	
87,800	
88,000	
89,800	
90,000	
90,000	mode = $90,000
90,000	
90,000	
90,600	
91,000	
91,000	
93,800	
93,800	
96,600	
97,000	
97,200	
97,200	
98,800	
$3,131,600	

$$\text{Mean} = \bar{X} = \frac{\Sigma X}{N} = \frac{\$3,131,600}{36} = \$86,989$$

where ΣX = sum of the variates and N = number of variates.

The same procedure can be performed with grouped data. To group the data, the frequency (f) with which a given sale price occurs must be identified and its contribution must be effectively weighted. Given the same data, identical results are produced.

X	f	fX
$72,000	1	$72,000
74,600	1	74,600
76,000	1	76,000
77,200	1	77,200
78,000	1	78,000
79,000	1	79,000
79,800	2	159,600
82,000	2	164,000
84,000	1	84,000
85,600	1	85,600
85,800	1	85,800
86,000	1	86,000
87,000	1	87,000
87,200	1	87,200
87,400	1	87,400
87,800	3	263,400
88,000	1	88,000
89,800	1	89,800
90,000	4	360,000
90,600	1	90,600
91,000	2	182,000
93,800	2	187,600
96,600	1	96,600
97,000	1	97,000
97,200	2	194,400
98,800	1	98,800
	$N = 36$	$\Sigma fX = \$3,131,600$

$$\text{Mean} = \overline{X} = \frac{\Sigma fX}{N} = \frac{\$3,131,600}{36} = \$86,989$$

The average, or mean, price in this example might not accurately represent the population of houses that have been sold at prices outside the indicated range.

The median is another measure used to describe a population, a sample, or an average variate. The median divides the variates of a population or sample into equal halves. To find the median, the variates are arranged in numerical order like the list of sale prices in the example. If the total number of variates is odd, the median is the middle variate. If the total number of variates is even, as in the example, the median is the arithmetic mean of the two middle variates.

In the list of 36 house sales, the middle two variates are $87,800 and $87,800. The mean of these two variates is $87,800, which is the median of the 36 sales. The same number of sales occur above the median as below it.

Like the median and the mean, the mode is a parameter used to describe the typical variate of a population. The mode is the variate or attribute that appears most frequently in a population. Of the 36 house sales, four were sold at $90,000. No other sale price occurs with this frequency, so the mode in this sample is $90,000. If two variates occur with equal frequency, both are modes and the sample is bimodal.

To illustrate, consider the following population of the types of condominium apartments available in a nine-unit complex:

efficiency
efficiency
efficiency
town house
town house
town house } mode (the most frequent attribute)
town house
town house
multibedroom

One of the problems in using statistics is selecting the appropriate measure of central tendency to describe a population. The following numbers could be used to describe the 36 variates in the group of house sales:

$\bar{X}$ = $86,989 (the mean of all the sales)
Median = $87,800 (the median of the sales)
Mode = $90,000 (the mode of the sales)

The mean is often used to describe a sample or population because this measure is widely understood and amenable to further statistical analysis.

Measures of Variation

The parameters of mean, median, and mode are used to describe the central tendencies of a population. Other sets of parameters can provide more information about the population being described. Measures of variation, or measures of dispersion, describe the disparity among the values of the variates that make up the population. They indicate the degree of uniformity among the variates and reflect the quality of the data as a basis for a conclusion.

Range

One way to measure the disparity between the variates is with a range (R). The range is the difference between the highest and the lowest variates.

$$R = \text{maximum variate} - \text{minimum variate}$$

The range for the 36 house sales is calculated as

$$R = \$98,800 - \$72,000 = \$26,800$$

As a measure of variation, the range has limited usefulness because it considers only the variation between the highest and lowest values, not the variation in the remaining values. Furthermore, a range does not lend itself to further statistical analysis.

Average Deviation

Another parameter used to measure the variation in a population is the average deviation, which is also known as the *average absolute deviation* because positive and negative signs are ignored. The average deviation is a measure of how much the actual values of a population or sample deviate from the mean. It is the mean of the sum of the absolute differences of each of the variates from the mean of the variates.

The average deviation of the 36 sales can be calculated from ungrouped or grouped data.

	Ungrouped Data
X Sale Price	$\|X - \bar{X}\|$ **Absolute Deviation Between Each Variate and the Mean Sale Price of $86,989**
$72,000	$14,989
74,600	12,389
76,000	10,989
77,200	9,789
78,000	8,989
79,000	7,989
79,800	7,189
79,800	7,189
82,000	4,989
82,000	4,989
84,000	2,989
85,600	1,389
85,800	1,189
86,000	989
87,000	11
87,200	211
87,400	411
87,800	811
87,800	811
87,800	811
88,000	1,011
89,800	2,811
90,000	3,011
90,000	3,011
90,000	3,011
90,000	3,011
90,600	3,611
91,000	4,011
91,000	4,011
93,800	6,811
93,800	6,811
96,600	9,611
97,000	10,011
97,200	10,211
97,200	10,211
98,800	11,811
$3,131,600 Total of sale prices	$192,088 Total deviation from mean $\Sigma \|X - \bar{X}\|$

Grouped Data

X	$|X - \bar{X}|$	f	$f|X - \bar{X}|$
$72,000	$14,989	1	$14,989
74,600	12,389	1	12,389
76,000	10,989	1	10,989
77,200	9,789	1	9,789
78,000	8,989	1	8,989
79,000	7,989	1	7,989
79,800	7,189	2	14,378
82,000	4,989	2	9,978
84,000	2,989	1	2,989
85,600	1,389	1	1,389
85,800	1,189	1	1,189
86,000	989	1	989
87,000	11	1	11
87,200	211	1	211
87,400	411	1	411
87,800	811	3	2,433
88,000	1,011	1	1,011
89,800	2,811	1	2,811
90,000	3,011	4	12,044
90,600	3,611	1	3,611
91,000	4,011	2	8,022
93,800	6,811	2	13,622
96,600	9,611	1	9,611
97,000	10,011	1	10,011
97,200	10,211	2	20,422
98,800	11,811	1	11,811
		36	$192,088 Total deviation from mean $\Sigma f|X - \bar{X}|$

$$\text{A.D. (ungrouped data)} = \frac{\Sigma|X - \bar{X}|}{n} = \frac{\$192,088}{36} = \$5,336$$

$$\text{A.D. (grouped data)} = \frac{\Sigma f|X - \bar{X}|}{n} = \frac{\$192,088}{36} = \$5,336$$

A.D. = average deviation

Σ = sum of

f = frequency

X = observed value

$|\ |$ = absolute value (ignore whether the difference is positive or negative)

n = number of observations in sample

$\bar{X}$ = mean of sample

These calculations indicate that the average deviation of the individual values in the population from the mean is $5,336, or about 6%. This relatively small variation suggests that the mean is an acceptable representation of the population.

Like the range, the average deviation does not lend itself to further statistical calculations.

Standard Deviation

The standard deviation is a way to describe a sample or a population that does lend itself to further mathematical treatment. When this measure is used, the rules of probability can be applied to draw inferences from samples concerning the attributes of the population. The square of the difference between each observation and the mean of the observations is used in lieu of the absolute deviation. In this way the effects of extreme variance from the mean are magnified.

In the example the mean house sale price is $86,989; for an $82,000 sale, the standard deviation is $4,989 squared, or $24,890,121.

When the standard deviation of an entire population is being calculated, it is symbolized by the lowercase sigma (σ). The formula may be expressed verbally as follows:

> The standard deviation of a population is the square root of the sum of the squared differences between each observation and the mean of all the observations in the population, divided by the number of observations in the population.

When the standard deviation of a sample of a population is being calculated, it is symbolized by the lowercase letter *s*. Expressed verbally, the formula is:

> The standard deviation of a sample is the square root of the sum of the squared differences between each observation and the mean of all the observations in the sample, divided by the number of observations in the sample minus one.

One is subtracted from the number of observations in a sample to adjust for the one degree of freedom that is lost when the mean is calculated. (See the discussion of simple linear regression analysis that is presented later in this appendix.) A set of data starts with as many degrees of freedom as there are observations; each time a statistic is calculated directly from the data, one degree of freedom is lost.

Formulas for calculating the standard deviations follow.
For a population:

Ungrouped

$$\sigma = \sqrt{\frac{\Sigma(X - \bar{X})^2}{N}}$$

Grouped

$$\sigma = \sqrt{\frac{\Sigma f(X - \bar{X})^2}{N}}$$

For a sample:

Ungrouped

$$s = \sqrt{\frac{\Sigma(X - \bar{X})^2}{n - 1}}$$

Grouped

$$s = \sqrt{\frac{\Sigma f(X - \bar{X})^2}{n - 1}}$$

Samples are typically used in real estate appraising, so the second formula is usually applicable. The standard deviation for the 36 house sales as grouped data is calculated in Table B.1.

Table B.1		Standard Deviation for 36 House Sales		
X	f	(X – X̄)	(X – X̄)²	f(X – X̄)²
$72,000	1	$14,989	$224,670,000	$224,670,000
74,600	1	12,389	153,487,000	153,487,000
76,000	1	10,989	120,758,000	120,758,000
77,200	1	9,789	95,824,500	95,824,500
78,000	1	8,989	80,802,100	80,802,100
79,000	1	7,989	63,824,100	63,824,100
79,800	2	7,189	51,681,700	103,363,000
82,000	2	4,989	24,890,100	49,780,200
84,000	1	2,989	8,934,120	8,934,120
85,600	1	1,389	1,929,320	1,929,320
85,800	1	1,189	1,413,720	1,413,720
86,000	1	989	978,121	978,121
87,000	1	11	121	121
87,200	1	211	44,521	44,521
87,400	1	411	168,921	168,921
87,800	3	811	657,721	1,973,160
88,000	1	1,011	1,022,120	1,022,120
89,800	1	2,811	7,901,720	7,901,720
90,000	4	3,011	9,066,120	36,264,500
90,600	1	3,611	13,039,300	13,039,300
91,000	2	4,011	16,088,100	32,176,200
93,800	2	6,811	46,389,700	92,779,400
96,600	1	9,611	92,371,300	92,371,300
97,000	1	10,011	100,220,000	100,220,000
97,200	2	10,211	104,265,000	208,530,000
98,800	1	11,811	139,500,000	139,500,000
				$1,631,755,444
			Rounded	$1,631,760,000

The standard deviation is a useful way to describe the dispersion of a population or sample. It indicates how well the mean represents the whole sample or population by describing a standard measure of variation. The standard deviation is used and understood in many disciplines and it can be calculated easily with an electronic calculator. It will undoubtedly be more widely used by appraisers in the future.

The standard deviation can also indicate what percentage of the sample of a population may be expected to fall within selected ranges of confidence intervals. (Confidence levels are discussed later in this appendix.) Approximately 68.26% of the sample or population will generally fall within plus or minus one standard deviation from the mean, provided the data meets the tests of normal distribution, which are explained later. Many types of real estate data conform to the pattern of a normal distribution when they are developed with appropriate sampling techniques.

Assuming this is a normal distribution, 68.26% of the house sales in the population will fall between $80,161 ($86,989 − $6,828) and $93,817 ($86,989 + $6,828). Approximately 95.44% of the sales should fall within two standard deviations from the mean and approximately 99.74% should fall within three standard deviations from the mean.

Because the standard deviation lends itself to further mathematical calculations, it can be used for analytical purposes as well as to describe a population.

$$s = \sqrt{\frac{\Sigma f(X - \bar{X})^2}{n - 1}}$$

Mean: $86,989

$$s = \sqrt{\frac{\$1,631,760,000}{36 - 1}}$$

$$s = \sqrt{\$46,621,714}$$

$$s = \$6,828$$

Statistical Inference

Statistical inference is based on the assumption that past market actions provide a valid basis for forecasting present or future market actions. In the example, past sale prices are used to estimate current sale prices. The same technique can be used to forecast rents, costs, depreciation, and other amounts using the rules of probability.

A normal curve is produced when a normal distribution is plotted on a graph to illustrate a distribution of data. Although the original data may not be normally distributed, the results of repeated random samples may approximate a normal distribution. Sales are often treated as though they were normally distributed in competitive, open-market situations.

A normal curve often takes the form of a bell curve. One major characteristic of a bell curve is its symmetry. Both halves of the curve have the same shape and contain the same number of observations. The mean, median, and mode are the same value and fall at the midpoint, or apex, of the curve.

Figure B.1 is a bell curve that illustrates the 36 house sales. It shows that 68.26% of the observations will fall within the range of the mean, plus or minus one standard deviation; 95.44% will fall within plus or minus two standard deviations; and 99.74% will fall within plus or minus three standard deviations. The figure depicts an analysis of the probable population distribution for the 36 sales, assuming a normal distribution.

Under the bell curve, the ranges for one, two, and three standard deviations are shown. The percentage of the population that will fall within a given distance from the mean or within any specified range can be calculated. For example, the percentage of sales included within a range of $91,989 to $81,989 (i.e., the mean of $86,989 plus or minus $5,000) may be estimated by calculating the Z value for this range with the formula presented below and then consulting a table of areas under the normal curve for the calculated value of Z.

Z = the deviation of X from the mean measured in standard deviations

$$Z = \frac{X - \text{mean}}{\text{standard deviation}}$$

$$Z = \frac{\$91,989 - \$86,989}{\$6,828} = 0.73$$

This formula shows that $91,989 and $81,989 each deviate from the mean of $86,989 by 0.73 standard deviations.

Figure B.1   **Area Under the Normal Curve for 36 House Sales**

50% of sales under $86,989

50% of sales over $86,989

68.26% of the sales between $80,161 and $93,817

95.44% of the sales between $73,333 and $100,645

99.74% of the sales between $66,505 and $107,473

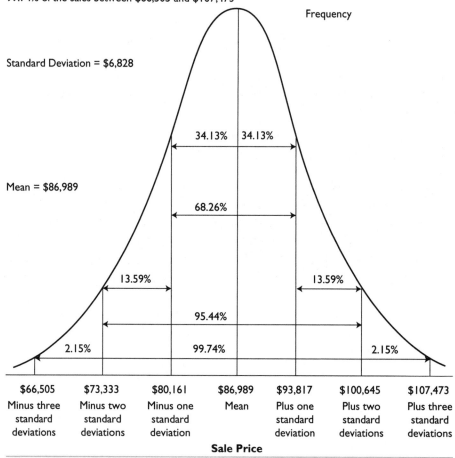

$66,505	$73,333	$80,161	$86,989	$93,817	$100,645	$107,473
Minus three standard deviations	Minus two standard deviations	Minus one standard deviation	Mean	Plus one standard deviation	Plus two standard deviations	Plus three standard deviations

Sale Price

The percentage of sales within this Z range of plus or minus 0.73 standard deviations can be found by locating 0.7 in the Z column of Table B.2 and then looking across the top of the table for the next digit—i.e., 0.03. The table indicates that 26.73% of the sales fall between $86,989 and $91,989 or between $86,989 and $81,989; therefore, 53.46% of the sales will fall between $91,989 and $81,989.

The probability of a randomly selected sale falling within a given range can also be determined with the Z value. Using the sample of 36 house sales, which has a mean of $86,989 and a standard deviation of $6,828, the prob-

Table B.2 Areas Under the Normal Curve

Z	.00	.01	.02	.03	.04	.05	.06	.07	.08	.09
0.0	0.0000	0.0040	0.0080	0.0120	0.0160	0.0199	0.0239	0.0279	0.0319	0.0359
0.1	0.0398	0.0438	0.0478	0.0517	0.0557	0.0596	0.0636	0.0675	0.0714	0.0753
0.2	0.0793	0.0832	0.0871	0.0910	0.0948	0.0987	0.1026	0.1064	0.1103	0.1141
0.3	0.1179	0.1217	0.1255	0.1293	0.1331	0.1368	0.1406	0.1443	0.1480	0.1517
0.4	0.1554	0.1591	0.1628	0.1664	0.1700	0.1736	0.1772	0.1808	0.1844	0.1879
0.5	0.1915	0.1950	0.1985	0.2019	0.2054	0.2088	0.2123	0.2157	0.2190	0.2224
0.6	0.2257	0.2291	0.2324	0.2357	0.2389	0.2422	0.2454	0.2486	0.2517	0.2549
0.7	0.2580	0.2611	0.2642	0.2673	0.2704	0.2734	0.2764	0.2794	0.2823	0.2852
0.8	0.2881	0.2910	0.2939	0.2967	0.2995	0.3023	0.3051	0.3078	0.3106	0.3133
0.9	0.3159	0.3186	0.3212	0.3238	0.3264	0.3289	0.3315	0.3340	0.3365	0.3389
1.0	0.3413	0.3438	0.3461	0.3485	0.3508	0.3531	0.3554	0.3577	0.3599	0.3621
1.1	0.3643	0.3665	0.3686	0.3708	0.3729	0.3749	0.3770	0.3790	0.3810	0.3830
1.2	0.3849	0.3869	0.3888	0.3907	0.3925	0.3944	0.3962	0.3980	0.3997	0.4015
1.3	0.4032	0.4049	0.4066	0.4082	0.4099	0.4115	0.4131	0.4147	0.4162	0.4177
1.4	0.4192	0.4207	0.4222	0.4236	0.4251	0.4265	0.4279	0.4292	0.4306	0.4319
1.5	0.4332	0.4345	0.4357	0.4370	0.4382	0.4394	0.4406	0.4418	0.4429	0.4441
1.6	0.4452	0.4463	0.4474	0.4484	0.4495	0.4505	0.4515	0.4525	0.4535	0.4545
1.7	0.4554	0.4564	0.4573	0.4582	0.4591	0.4599	0.4608	0.4616	0.4625	0.4633
1.8	0.4641	0.4649	0.4656	0.4664	0.4671	0.4678	0.4686	0.4693	0.4699	0.4706
1.9	0.4713	0.4719	0.4726	0.4732	0.4738	0.4744	0.4750	0.4756	0.4761	0.4767
2.0	0.4772	0.4778	0.4783	0.4788	0.4793	0.4798	0.4803	0.4808	0.4812	0.4817
2.1	0.4821	0.4826	0.4830	0.4834	0.4838	0.4842	0.4846	0.4850	0.4854	0.4857
2.2	0.4861	0.4864	0.4868	0.4871	0.4875	0.4878	0.4881	0.4884	0.4887	0.4890
2.3	0.4893	0.4896	0.4898	0.4901	0.4904	0.4906	0.4909	0.4911	0.4913	0.4916
2.4	0.4918	0.4920	0.4922	0.4925	0.4927	0.4929	0.4931	0.4932	0.4934	0.4936
2.5	0.4938	0.4940	0.4941	0.4943	0.4945	0.4946	0.4948	0.4949	0.4951	0.4952
2.6	0.4953	0.4955	0.4956	0.4957	0.4959	0.4960	0.4961	0.4962	0.4963	0.4964
2.7	0.4965	0.4966	0.4967	0.4968	0.4969	0.4970	0.4971	0.4972	0.4973	0.4974
2.8	0.4974	0.4975	0.4976	0.4977	0.4977	0.4978	0.4979	0.4979	0.4980	0.4981
2.9	0.4981	0.4982	0.4982	0.4983	0.4984	0.4984	0.4985	0.4985	0.4986	0.4986
3.0	0.4987	0.4987	0.4987	0.4988	0.4988	0.4989	0.4989	0.4989	0.4990	0.4990

ability of a randomly selected sale falling between $86,989 and $88,989 is calculated as follows:

$$Z = \frac{X - \text{mean}}{\text{standard deviation}} = \frac{\$88,989 - \$86,989}{\$6,828} = 0.29$$

The table of areas under the normal curve, Table B.2, shows that a Z value of 0.29 corresponds to 0.1141. This indicates that there is an 11.41% chance that the sale will fall within $2,000 above the mean. Because the curve of a normal distribution is symmetrical, there is the same probability that a sale will fall within $2,000 below the mean.

Probability a sale will fall between $88,989 and $86,989	11.41%
Probability a sale will fall between $84,989 and $86,989	11.41%
Probability a sale will fall between $84,989 and $88,989	22.82%

If the range in this example is expanded to $4,000 plus or minus the mean of $86,989—i.e., between $82,989 and $90,989—the probability of a randomly selected sale falling within this range is increased.

$$Z = \frac{X - \text{mean}}{\text{standard deviation}} = \frac{\$90,989 - \$86,989}{\$6,828} = 0.59$$

According to Table B.2, a Z value of 0.59 corresponds to 0.2224.

Probability a sale will fall between $90,989 and $86,989	22.24%
Probability a sale will fall between $82,989 and $86,989	22.24%
Probability a sale will fall between $82,989 and $90,989	44.48%

In these examples the range being tested has been equally distributed above and below the mean sale price. However, the probability of a randomly selected sale falling within any selected range in the population can also be tested. For example, the probability of a sale falling between $80,000 and $100,000 can be calculated as follows:

$$Z \text{ area}_1 = \frac{X_1 - \text{mean}}{\text{standard deviation}} = \frac{\$80,000 - \$86,989}{\$6,828} = 1.02$$

$$Z \text{ area}_2 = \frac{X_2 - \text{mean}}{\text{standard deviation}} = \frac{\$100,000 - \$86,989}{\$6,828} = 1.91$$

A Z value of 1.02 in Table B.2 indicates a probability of	0.3461
A Z value of 1.91 in Table B.2 indicates a probability of	0.4719
Probability	0.8180

There is an 81.8% chance that a randomly selected sale in this sample will fall between $80,000 and $100,000.

Confidence Level

Using statistical inference and the laws of probability for a normal distribution, the previous examples have shown how confidence intervals can be constructed for a sample when a normal distribution of data has been assumed or approximated. These calculations may be valuable in loan administration, housing development, appraising, and other decision-making situations involving real estate.

The examples have illustrated that, with 36 sales as a sample, an appraiser can state with a 95% degree of confidence that any sale randomly selected from the population will fall between $73,333 and $100,645. Similarly, there is a 68% level of confidence that a given sale will fall between $80,161 and $93,817.

These measures may be meaningful when used in conjunction with other statistical conclusions. However, they depend on how accurately the estimated mean represents the true population mean, so some confidence in the reliability of the mean must be established. Regardless of the size of the population, there is a specific sample size that will permit a certain level of confidence in the estimated mean.

For the 36 house sales, the standard deviation for price has been calculated as $6,828. The arithmetic mean is $86,989, or approximately $87,000. If an appraiser wants to be 95% certain that the true mean is within $1,000 of the estimated mean of $86,989—i.e., between $86,000 and $88,000—the necessary sample size can be calculated with the following formula:

$$n = \frac{z^2 s^2}{e^2}$$

$$n = \frac{(1.96)^2 \, (\$6,828)^2}{(\$1,000)^2} = 179 \text{ sales}$$

where
- n = sample size required
- z = Z statistic at 95% confidence level
- s = standard deviation of the sample
- e = required maximum difference in the mean

Thus, with a sample of 179 sales, the required level of confidence could be met. Similarly, for a confidence interval of not more than $1,500, the calculations would be

$$n = \frac{(1.96)^2 \, (\$6,828)^2}{(\$1,500)^2} = 80 \text{ sales}$$

Using the original sample of 36 sales, an appraiser may want to know the limits within which the true population mean may fall at a 95% confidence level. By substitution

$$e^2 = \frac{z^2 s^2}{n}$$

and

$$e^2 = \frac{(1.96)^2 \, (\$6,828)^2}{36} = \$4,975,041$$

$$e = \sqrt{\$4,975,041} = \$2,230$$

Thus, the appraiser can be 95% certain that the true population mean falls between $84,759 and $89,219.

Although calculations such as these may not seem to be directly related to day-to-day appraising, professional appraisers have a continuing interest in obtaining adequate data and understanding the markets in which they appraise. Statistical calculations can be useful in quantifying change and performing the neighborhood analyses that are essential to value estimation. Many appraisers routinely analyze the inferences that can be drawn from measures such as the standard deviations of raw and adjusted sale or rental data. These calculations are also applied in appraisal review, loan underwriting, and other analyses.

Regression Analysis

Regression analysis is another technique used by appraisers to analyze market data. It can be applied to estimate value and to isolate and test the significance of specific value determinants.

Simple Linear Regression Analysis

To estimate a probable sale price in the market, it is seldom sufficient to develop a sample of sales, calculate the standard deviation, and base an estimate on this evidence. In most cases the range of values at the confidence level required is too broad to be useful. However, the accuracy of an estimate can be substantially increased by considering one or more characteristics of the sale properties in addition to their sale prices.

In simple linear regression analysis, one independent variable, or property characteristic, is used to reflect a relationship that changes on a straight-line basis. In other words, a change in the independent variable is reflected in the same proportion in the dependent variable, which is unknown. The basic regression equation is

$$Y_c = a + bX$$

where Y_c is the predicted value of the dependent variable; a is the constant; b is the coefficient, or multiplier, for the independent variable; and X is the value of the variable. If, for example, the independent variable is the square foot area of a building and the dependent variable is its sale price, the simple linear regression equation $Y_C = 10,000 + 45X$ means that the sale price of the building is predicted to be $10,000 plus $45 times its square foot area.

To find the constant, a, the data for this regression must be graphed. Increasing square foot areas are indicated along the horizontal axis of the graph and increasing sale prices are indicated along the vertical axis. Then a number of sales are plotted on the graph and a line that evenly divides these points is drawn. This is the regression line, and its slope is the b coefficient. The point on the vertical axis of the graph at which the regression begins is the intercept, or the constant symbolized as a. In other words, this is a base value that represents all positive and negative factors that are not explained by the equation and to which the coefficients, or adjustment factors, are added.

Another important statistic that results from a simple linear regression is the coefficient of determination, r^2. This statistic represents the approximate percentage of variation in the dependent variable, which is explained by the equation and is one measure of the efficacy of the regression. When a regression is performed on an electronic, handheld calculator, the coefficient of determination given is unadjusted for degrees of freedom (i.e., the number of observations minus the number of variables). This adjustment should be applied to the resulting coefficient of determination:

$$r^2_{adj} = 1 - (1 - r^2)\,[(n - 1)/(n - 2)]$$

The standard error of the estimate is another measure of how well the regression fits. It is expressed as S_{yx} and represents the remaining dispersion in the data after the regression equation is applied. The equation for arriving at the standard error of the estimate is

$$S_{yx} = S_y \sqrt{1 - r^2}$$

The b coefficient also has a t value. The t value is the coefficient expressed as a ratio to its standard deviation; it is a measure of the significance of the coefficient. The precise degree of significance represented by a particular t value depends on several factors and must be calculated. As a general rule, however, coefficients with t values greater than 2 are usually significant at a reasonably high confidence level.

Simple regression analysis is particularly useful when one element is overwhelmingly important in determining a property's sale price. Furthermore, this technique allows appraisers to analyze the relationships between real estate values and the significance of their various components.

Example of Simple Linear Regression

Using the 36 house sales analyzed earlier, simple linear regression can be used to demonstrate the apparent relationship between the sale price of a property and its living area in square feet. The gross living area (GLA) of each of the 36 houses is shown in Table B.3. Most appraisers would only analyze properties with the same approximate square foot area as the subject property and disregard the other sales.

The appraiser is valuing a 1,375-sq.-ft. dwelling, so Sales 1, 2, and 3 are most similar in terms of size. Their prices are reported as $57.53, $64.14, and $55.95 per square foot, respectively. The other sales may provide a clue to the "right answer," but they do little to resolve the discrepancy between these figures. Adjustments could be made for other differences in the properties, but complications would develop if multiple adjustments produced overlapping effects.

Sales 1, 2, and 3 indicate a price range of $55.95 to $64.14 per square foot; when these figures are applied to the 1,375-sq.-ft. area of the subject property, a value range of $76,931 to $88,192 is indicated. (These figures would be rounded in the appraiser's report.) The remaining market informa-

Table B.3	Comparable Sales Data Set for Simple Regression Analysis		
Sale	GLA in Square Feet	Sale Price	Price per Square Foot GLA
1	1,321	$76,000	$57.53
2	1,372	88,000	64.14
3	1,394	78,000	55.95
4	1,403	74,600	53.17
5	1,457	85,800	58.89
6	1,472	87,400	59.38
7	1,475	84,000	56.95
8	1,479	85,600	57.88
9	1,503	72,000	47.90
10	1,512	77,200	51.06
11	1,515	82,000	54.13
12	1,535	79,000	51.47
13	1,535	87,800	57.20
14	1,577	91,000	57.70
15	1,613	90,000	55.80
16	1,640	79,800	48.66
17	1,666	91,000	54.62
18	1,681	79,800	47.47
19	1,697	87,200	51.38
20	1,703	87,000	51.09
21	1,706	89,800	52.64
22	1,709	90,600	53.01
23	1,709	93,800	54.89
24	1,720	93,800	54.53
25	1,732	82,000	47.34
26	1,749	97,200	55.57
27	1,771	97,200	54.88
28	1,777	86,000	48.40
29	1,939	87,800	45.28
30	1,939	90,000	46.42
31	1,939	90,000	46.42
32	1,939	90,000	46.42
33	1,939	96,600	49.82
34	1,940	87,800	45.26
35	2,014	98,800	49.06
36	2,065	97,000	46.97

tion cannot be used effectively in traditional appraisal analysis except perhaps to reinforce the appraiser's judgment.

With simple linear regression, however, more of the market data can be analyzed. To apply the formula $Y_c = a + bX$, the 36 sales were analyzed with a calculator, which produced the following figures:

$$a = \$49,261$$
$$b = \$22.59$$
$$r = 0.6599 \text{ (simple correlation coefficient)}$$
$$r^2 = 0.4354$$
$$r^2_{adj} = 1 - (1 - 0.4354)\,[(36 - 1)/(36 - 2)]$$
$$= 0.4188 \text{ (adjusted coefficient of determination)}$$

Thus, for the 1,375-sq.-ft. property being appraised

$$Y_c = \$49,261 + \$22.59 \times 1,375$$
$$= \$80,322, \text{ or } \$58.42 \text{ per square foot}$$

The 36 sales are plotted on the graph shown in Figure B.2 and the calculated regression line is indicated. The graph also shows the standard error of the estimate, which allows the appraiser to construct confidence intervals around the regression line. The calculations in this example produce a standard error estimate of $5,205. When this figure is applied to the property being appraised, the appraiser can state that 36 sales in the market support a value indication of $80,300 for the appraised property, based only on a comparison of their square foot area. Moreover, at a 68% confidence level, the market price should fall between $80,300 ± $5,205—i.e., from $75,095 to $85,505. At a 95% confidence level, the price should fall between $80,300 ± 2 × $5,205, or from $69,890 to $90,710.

Although other statistical measures such as the standard error of the forecast (Sf) may be used, most appraisers would consider this analysis to be sufficient and reasonably representative of most single-family market situations. Although a more refined analysis of this data could be performed, this example illustrates a simple application of a regression technique. The standard error of the forecast for the appraised property could be calculated as follows:

$$Sf = S_{yx}\sqrt{1 + \frac{1}{n} + \frac{(X_K - \bar{X})^2}{(X - \bar{X})^2}}$$
$$Sf = 5,205\sqrt{1 + \frac{1}{36} + \frac{(1,720 - 1,670)^2}{1,469,045}}$$
$$Sf = 5,281$$

Applying this adjustment to the standard error makes only a small change because the measure of value (i.e., square footage) of the subject property is quite close to the mean square footage of the sample data. The greater the difference between the appraised property and the mean of the sample in regard to any property attribute, the more this distortion affects the standard error as a measure of variation in the regression prediction.

Figure B.2   Plot of Sales, Regression Line, and Standard Error for 36 Sales

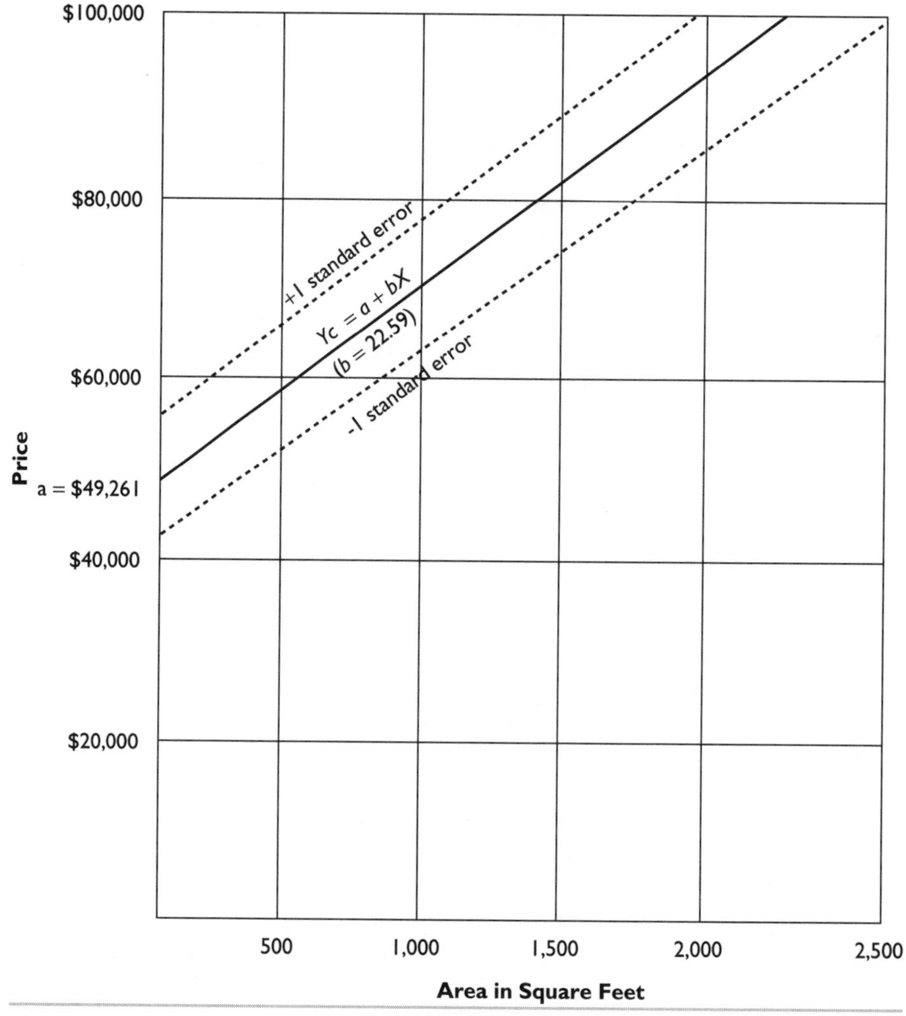

Multiple Regression Analysis

Multiple regression analysis is performed with the same basic methods as simple linear regression, but the analysis is expanded to include more than one independent variable. Some handheld calculators are preprogrammed or can be programmed to perform regressions using two or three independent variables, but multiple regressions are generally performed on a computer. Stepwise regression is an improvement on the standard regression procedure because variables can be added or removed from the regression equation depending on their degree of explanatory power. This type of regression produces an optimum combination of variables by retaining only the most significant.

Curvilinear Regression Analysis

Most appraisal data does not reflect straight-line relationships, but appraisers often deal with short segments of a curve so tools such as linear regression and correlation can be used. However, inferences can be distorted when linearity is assumed for a set of data that is clearly curvilinear. Fortunately, many sets of curvilinear data may also be transformed rather easily and processed as if they were linear.

APPENDIX

C | Financial Formulas

Basic Formulas
Symbols

I = income	**Subscript:**
R = capitalization rate	O = overall property
V = value	M = mortgage
M = mortgage ratio	E = equity
DCR = debt coverage ratio	L = land
F = capitalization factor (multiplier)	B = building
GIM = gross income multiplier	LF = leased fee
$EGIM$ = effective gross income multiplier	LH = leasehold
NIR = net income ratio	

Basic Income/Cap Rate/ Value Formulas

$$I = R \times V$$
$$R = I/V$$
$$V = I/R$$

Basic Value/Income/ Factor Formulas

$$V = I \times F$$
$$I = V/F$$
$$F = V/I$$

Adaptations for Mortgage/Equity Components

Band of investment (using ratios)

$$R_O = M \times R_M + [(1 - M) \times R_E]$$
$$R_E = (R_O - M \times R_M)/(1 - M)$$

Equity residual

$$V_O = [(I_O - V_M \times R_M)/R_E] + V_M$$
$$R_E = (I_O - V_M \times R_M)/V_E$$

Mortgage residual

$$V_O = [(I_O - V_E \times R_E)/R_M] + V_E$$

Debt coverage ratio

$$R_O = DCR \times M \times R_M$$
$$DCR = R_O/(M \times R_M)$$
$$M = R_O/(DCR \times R_M)$$

Cap Rate/Factor Relationships
$$R = 1/F$$
$$R_O = NIR/GIM$$
$$R_O = NIR/EGIM$$

Note: NIR may relate to scheduled gross or effective gross income; care should be taken to ensure consistency.

Adaptations for Land/Building Components

Land residual

$$V_O = [(I_O - V_B \times R_B)/R_L] + V_B$$
$$R_L = (I_O - V_B \times R_B)/V_L$$

Building residual

$$V_O = [(I_O - V_L \times R_L)/R_B] + V_L$$
$$R_B = (I_O - V_L \times R_L)/V_B$$

Discounted Cash Flow Analysis Formulas

Symbols

PV = present value	**Subscript:**
CF = cash flow	n = projection periods
Y = yield rate	O = overall property
R = capitalization rate	I = income
Δ = change	
a = annualizer	
$1/S_{\overline{n}\vert}$ = sinking fund factor	
1/n = 1/projection period	
CR = compound rate of change	
V = value	

Discounted Cash Flows/Present Value (DCF/PV)

$$PV = \frac{CF_1}{1+Y} + \frac{CF_2}{(1+Y)^2} + \frac{CF_3}{(1+Y)^3} + \ldots + \frac{CF_n}{(1+Y)^n}$$

Basic Cap Rate/Yield Rate/Value Change Formulas

$$R = Y - \Delta a$$
$$Y = R + \Delta a$$
$$\Delta a = Y - R$$
$$\Delta = (Y - R)/a$$

Adaptations for Common Income/Value Patterns

Pattern	Premise	Cap Rate (R)	Yield Rate (Y)	Value Change (Δ)
Perpetuity	$\Delta = O$	$R = Y$	$Y = R$	
Level annuity*	$a = 1/S_{\overline{n}\vert}$	$R = Y - \Delta 1/S_{\overline{n}\vert}$	$Y = R + \Delta 1/S_{\overline{n}\vert}$	$\Delta = (Y - R)/1/(S_{\overline{n}\vert})$
Straight-line change	$a = 1/n$	$R = Y - \Delta 1/n$	$Y = R + \Delta 1/n$	$\Delta = (Y - R)/(1/n)$
Exponential change	$\Delta a = CR$	$R_O = Y_O - CR$	$Y_O = R_O + CR$	$\Delta = (1 + CR)^n - 1$

* Inwood premise: $1/S_{\overline{n}\vert}$ at Y rate; Hoskold premise: $1/S_{\overline{n}\vert}$ at safe rate

Straight-Line Change* in Income	Straight-Line Change* in Value	Compound Rate of Change
$\$\Delta_I = V \times \Delta 1/n \times Y$	$\$\Delta 1/n = \$\Delta_I/Y$	$CR = \sqrt[n]{(FV/PV - 1)}$
$\Delta_I = (Y \times \Delta 1/n)/(Y - \Delta 1/n)$	$\Delta 1/n = (Y \times \Delta_I)/(Y + \Delta_I)$	$CR = Y_O - R_O$

* In these formulas Δ_I is the ratio of one year's change in income to the first year's income.

Six Functions of $1

The following formulas may be used to convert the annual constant (R_M) for a monthly payment loan to the corresponding monthly functions.

Function for Monthly Frequency	Formula
Amount of $1	$S^n = R_M/(R_M - I)$
Amount of $1 per month	$S^n = 12/(R_M - I)$
Sinking fund factor	$1/S_{\overline{n}} = (R_M - I)/12$
Present value of $1	$1/S_{\overline{n}} = (R_M - I)/R_M$
Present value of $1 per month	$a_{\overline{n}} = 12/R_M$
Partial payment	$1/a_{\overline{n}} = R_M/12$

In these formulas, I = nominal interest rate.

Present Value of Level Annuities

The Inwood Premise

The Inwood premise applies to income that is an ordinary level annuity. It holds that the present value of a stream of income is based on a single discount rate. Each installment of income is discounted with a single discount rate, and the total discounted values of the installments are accumulated to obtain the present value of the income stream. The present value of a series of $1 payments can be found in compound interest tables for a given rate and a given period of time. It is assumed that the income will be sufficient to return all investment capital to the investor and to pay the specified return on the investment.

In most mortgages the amount of interest declines gradually over the holding period and is calculated as a specified percentage of the unrecaptured capital. Any excess over the required interest payment is considered a return of capital and reduces the amount of capital remaining in the investment. Because the installments are always the same amount, the principal portion of the payments increases by the same amounts that the interest portion of the payments decreases. It is also valid, but not customary, to see the interest payments as constant, always amounting to the specified return on the original investment, with any excess over the required, fixed-interest payments credited to a hypothetical sinking fund that grows with interest at the same rate to repay the original investment.

An Inwood capitalization rate can be constructed by adding the interest rate to a sinking fund factor $(1/S_{\overline{n}})$ that is based on the same interest rate and duration as the income stream. The resulting capitalization rate is simply the reciprocal of the ordinary level annuity (present value of $1 per period) factor found in financial tables. Thus, the Inwood premise is consistent with the use of compound interest tables to calculate the present value of the income stream.

The Inwood premise applies only to a level stream of income. Therefore, the present value of any expected reversion or other benefit not included in the income stream must be added to obtain the total present value of the investment. For example, assume that the NOI of a property is $10,000 per year for five years. What is the value of the property assuming an overall yield rate (Y_O) of 10% under the Inwood premise?

Solution 1

Apply the PV of $1 per period (ordinary level annuity) factor to the NOI:

$$3.79079 \times \$10,000 = \$37,908 \text{ (rounded)}$$

Solution 2

The general yield capitalization formula can also be used for a level income with a percentage change in value:

$$R_O = Y_O - \Delta_O \ 1/S_{\overline{n}}$$

Because there is no reversion, the property will lose 100% of its value. Δ_O is thus -1.0 and the yield capitalization formula becomes

$$R_O = Y_O + 1/S_{\overline{n}}$$

With appropriate inputs, this equation represents the Inwood premise. By substituting the data given in the example, R_O can be solved for as follows:

$$R_O = 0.10 + 0.163797$$
$$R_O = 0.263797$$

The value of the property may be estimated using the basic valuation formula:

$$V_O = NOI / R_O$$
$$= \$10,000 / 0.263797$$
$$= \$37,908 \text{ (rounded)}$$

Note that the sinking fund factor $(1/S_{\overline{n}})$ is based on a 10% discount rate, which implies that a portion of the NOI could be reinvested at 10% to replace the investment. It can be said that Y_O represents the return on capital and $1/S_{\overline{n}}$ represents the return of capital.

The Inwood premise assumes a constant rate of return on capital each year with the return of capital being reinvested in a sinking fund at the same yield rate as Y_O. The amount accumulated in this sinking fund can be used to replace the asset at the end of its economic life. Using the assumptions applied in the preceding example, the NOI for the first year may be allocated as follows:

NOI	$10,000.00
Return on capital (10% of $37,908)	− $3,790.80
Return of capital	$6,209.20

If the return of capital ($6,209.20) is placed in a sinking fund earning 10%, the fund will accumulate to $37,908 over five years. The sinking fund accumulation factor (future value of $1 per period), $S_{\overline{n}}$, is applied to the return of capital:

$$6.1051 \times \$6,209.20 = \$37,908$$

This is the exact amount required to replace the asset.

The Hoskold Premise

The Hoskold premise differs from the Inwood premise in that it employs two separate interest rates:

- A speculative rate, representing a fair rate of return on capital commensurate with the risks involved
- A safe rate for a sinking fund, designed to return all the invested capital to the investor in a lump sum at the termination of the investment

In contrast to the Inwood premise, the Hoskold premise assumes that the portion of NOI needed to recover or replace capital (the return of capital) is reinvested at a "safe rate"—e.g., the prevailing rate for insured savings accounts or government bonds—which is lower than the "speculative" yield rate (Y_O) used to value the other portion of NOI. Like the Inwood premise, the Hoskold technique was designed to be applied when the asset value of the investment decreases to zero over the holding period. However, Hoskold assumed that funds would have to be set aside at a lower, safe rate to replace the asset at the end of the holding period. Hoskold suggested that this technique might be appropriate for valuing wasting assets such as a mine where the value is reduced to zero as minerals are extracted; thus funds have to be set aside to invest in a new mine once the minerals are totally depleted—i.e., the reversion equals zero.

Using the same NOI, yield, and term set forth in the previous example, assume that a portion of NOI has to be set aside at a 5% safe rate to allow for the recovery of capital at the end of every five-year period. All other assumptions remain the same. This problem may be solved with the same yield capitalization formula applied in the Inwood calculation, but the sinking fund factor $(1/S_{n|})$ is based on the safe rate of 5% rather than the yield rate of 10%. Thus, the overall rate is calculated as follows:

$$R_O = Y_O + 1/S_{n|}$$
$$= 0.10 + 0.180975$$
$$= 0.280975$$

Because the sinking fund factor $(1/S_{n|})$ is calculated at a 5% rate rather than the 10% rate, the capitalization rate is higher and the value is lower. The value is calculated as:

$$V_O = NOI / R_O$$
$$= \$10,000 / 0.280975$$
$$= \$35,590 \text{ (rounded)}$$

The lower value is a result of setting aside the portion of NOI earning 5% to allow for the recovery of capital ($35,590) at the end of five years. The income allocation for the first year can be shown as follows:

NOI	$10,000
Return on capital (10% of $35,590)	− 3,559
Return of capital	$6,441

To find the future value of $6,441 at 5% for five years, apply the sinking fund accumulation factor (future value of $1 per period), $S_{\overline{n}|}$, to the return of capital:

$$5.525631 \times \$6,441.00 = \$35,590$$

The result is the exact amount required to recover the capital invested.

Present Value of Increasing/Decreasing Annuities

Straight-Line Changes

To obtain the present value of an annuity that has a starting income of d at the end of the first period and *increases h dollars* per period for n periods:

$$PV = (d + h\,n)\, a_{\overline{n}|} - \frac{h\,(n - a_{\overline{n}|})}{i}$$

To obtain the present value of an annuity that has a starting income of d at the end of the first period and *decreases h dollars* per period for n periods, simply make h negative in the formula.

Exponential-Curve (Constant-Ratio) Changes

To obtain the present value of an annuity that starts at $1 at the end of the first period and increases each period thereafter at the rate x for n periods:

$$PV = \frac{1 - (1 + x)^n / (1 + i)^n}{i - x}$$

where i is the periodic discount rate and x is the ratio between the increase in income for any period and the income for the previous period.

To obtain the present value of an annuity that starts at $1 at the end of the first period and *decreases each period* thereafter at rate x, simply make x negative in the formula.

Rates of Return

Symbols

PV = present value

NPV = net present value

CF = cash flow   **Subscript:**

i = discount rate (in NPV formula) 0 = at time zero

n = projection period 1 = end of 1st period

IRR = internal rate of return 2 = end of 2nd period

PI = profitability index 3 = end of 3rd period

$MIRR$ = modified internal rate of return n = end period of series

$FVCFj$ = future value of a series of cash flows

i = reinvestment rate (in MIRR formula)

Net Present Value (NPV)

$$NPV = CF_0 + \frac{CF_1}{1 + i} + \frac{CF_2}{(1 + i)^2} + \frac{CF_3}{(1 + i)^3} + \ldots + \frac{CF_n}{(1 + i)^n}$$

Internal Rate of Return (IRR)

$$\text{Where } NPV = 0; IRR = i$$

Profitability Index (PI)

$$PI = PV/CF_0$$

Modified Internal Rate of Return (MIRR)

$$MIRR = \sqrt[n]{\frac{FVCFj}{CF_0}} - 1$$

$$MIRR = \sqrt[n]{\frac{CF_1(1+i)^{n-1} + CF_2(1+i)^{n-2} + CF_3(1+i)^{n-3} + \ldots + CF_n}{CF_0}} - 1$$

Note: In these formulas individual CFs may be positive or negative for PV and NPV solutions; however, CF_0 is treated as a positive value for PI and MIRR solutions.

Mortgage Interests

Mortgage investments have a great impact on real property value and equity yield rates. Because yield is a significant consideration in the lender's decision to invest in a mortgage interest in real estate, the lender's yield must be understood and often calculated. In the absence of points and any participation or accrual feature, the lender's yield equals the interest rate.

Mortgage information used to value income-producing properties may include

1. The monthly or periodic payments and annual debt service on a level-payment, fully amortized loan
2. The accompanying partial payment factors and annual constants (R_M)
3. The balance outstanding (B) on an amortized loan at any time before it is fully amortized, expressed as a dollar amount or a percentage of the original loan amount
4. The percentage or proportion of the principal amount paid off before full amortization (P)

Mortgage Components

Periodic (Monthly) Payment

The monthly payment factor for a fully amortized, monthly payment loan with equal payments is the direct reduction loan factor, or monthly constant, for the loan, given the interest rate and amortization term. Thus, the monthly payment factor for a 30-year, fully amortized, level monthly payment loan at 15.5% interest is 0.013045. This number can be obtained from a direct reduction loan table or by solving for the monthly payment (PMT) on a financial calculator, given the number of periods (n), the interest rate (i), and the principal loan amount.

If the loan had an initial principal amount of $160,000, the monthly payment required to amortize the principal over 30 years and provide interest at the nominal rate of 15.5% on the outstanding balance each month would be

$$\$160,000 \times 0.013045 = \$2,087.20$$

Annual Debt Service and Loan Constant

Cash flows are typically converted to an annual basis for real property valuation, so it is useful to calculate the amount of annual debt service as well as the monthly payments. For the 30-year, fully amortized, level monthly payment loan of $160,000 at a 15.5% interest rate, the annual debt service is

$$\$2,087.20 \times 12 = \$25,046.40$$

The annual loan constant is simply the ratio of annual debt service to the loan principal. (The annual loan constant, often called the *mortgage constant*, describes a rate although it is actually the annual debt service per dollar of mortgage loan outstanding, which may be expressed as a dollar amount.) The annual loan constant is expressed as R_M to signify that it is a capitalization rate for the loan or debt portion of the real property investment. For the loan mentioned, the annual loan constant can be calculated as follows:

$$R_M = \frac{\text{annual debt service}}{\text{loan principal}}$$
$$= \frac{\$25,046.40}{\$160,000.00}$$
$$= 0.156540$$

The annual loan constant can also be obtained when the amount of the loan principal is not known. In this case the monthly payment factor is simply multiplied by 12.

$$R_M = \text{monthly payment factor} \times 12$$
$$= 0.013045 \times 12$$
$$= 0.156540$$

Although these figures are rounded to the nearest cent, in actual practice most loan constants are rounded up to make sure that the loan will be repaid during the stated amortization period.

Outstanding Balance

Properties are frequently sold, or loans may be refinanced, before the loan on the property is fully amortized. Furthermore, loans often mature before the completion of loan amortization. In such cases there is an outstanding balance or balloon payment due on the note; from the lender's point of view, this is the loan or debt reversion to the lender.

The outstanding balance (B) on any level-payment, amortized loan is the present value of the debt service over the remaining amortization period discounted at the interest rate. Thus, at the end of 10 years, the balance for the 30-year note discussed above would be the present value of 20 years of remaining payments. The balance is calculated by multiplying the monthly payment by the present value of $1 per period factor (monthly) for 20 years at the interest rate. The balloon payment, or future value, may be calculated.

$$B = \$2{,}087.20 \times 73.861752$$
$$= \$154{,}164.25$$

Similarly, the outstanding balance at the end of 18 years would be equal to the monthly payment times the present value of $1 per period factor (monthly) for 12 years at the interest rate.

$$B = \$2{,}087.20 \times 65.222881$$
$$= \$136{,}133.20$$

The outstanding balance on a loan can also be expressed as a percentage of the original principal. This is useful, and sometimes necessary, if dollar amounts are not given or are unavailable. For a 10-year projection with 20 years remaining on the note, the outstanding balance is

$$B = \frac{\$154{,}164.25}{\$160{,}000.00}$$
$$= 0.963527$$

For an 18-year projection with 12 years remaining on the note, the balance is

$$B = \frac{\$136{,}133.20}{\$160{,}000.00}$$
$$= 0.850833$$

A percentage balance can also be calculated as the ratio of the present value of $1 per period factor for the remaining term of the loan at the specified interest rate divided by the present value of $1 per period factor for the full term of the loan at the interest rate. This can be expressed as

$$B = \frac{PV\ 1/P\ \text{remaining term}}{PV\ 1/P\ \text{full term}}$$

In the case of the 30-year, 15.5% loan, the balance for a 10-year projection with 20 years remaining is calculated as

$$B = \frac{73.861752}{76.656729}$$
$$= 0.963539$$

For an 18-year projection with 12 years remaining, the balance would be

$$B = \frac{65.222881}{76.656729}$$
$$= 0.850844$$

These results are similar to those obtained using dollar amounts.

Percentage of Loan Paid Off

It is often necessary to calculate the percentage of the loan paid off before full amortization over the projection period, especially in Ellwood mortgage-equity analysis. The percentage of the loan paid off is expressed as P and is most readily calculated as the complement of B.

$$P = I - B$$

For the 30-year note, P is calculated as follows:

$$P_{10} = I - 0.963539$$
$$= 0.036461$$
$$P_{18} = I - 0.850844$$
$$= 0.149156$$

The percentage of the loan paid off prior to full amortization over the projection period (P) can also be calculated directly. There are many different procedures for this operation and they are not all presented here. Calculator users are advised to consult their manuals on the AMORT function.

The simplest, most direct procedure is to calculate P as the ratio of the sinking fund factor for the full term (monthly) divided by the sinking fund factor for the projection period (monthly).

$$P = \frac{I/S_{\overline{n}|}}{I/S_{\overline{n}|p}}$$

For the 30-year monthly payment note at 15.5%, the calculations are

$$P_{10} = \frac{0.000129}{0.003524}$$
$$= 0.036606$$
$$P_{18} = \frac{0.000129}{0.000862}$$
$$= 0.149652$$

Any differences are due to rounding.

Lender's Yield

To illustrate how the lender's yield on a mortgage loan investment is calculated, consider a mortgage loan with the following characteristics.

Loan amount	$100,000
Interest rate	13.5%
Term	25 years
Payment	Monthly
Balance in five years	$96,544
Points	3
Other costs	Borrower to pay all other costs

If the mortgage runs full term, the yield can be obtained using a calculator.

n = 300
PMT = $1,165.65
PV = $97,000 ($100,000 less 3 points, or $3,000)*
i = 13.97%

* Each point is equal to 1% of the loan amount: $100,000 × 0.01 = $1,000.

The lender's yield is greater than the nominal interest rate because of the points paid by the borrower. In effect, the lender only loaned $97,000 ($100,000 – $3,000) but receives a stream of debt service payments based on $100,000. If the mortgage is paid off in five years, the lender's yield is calculated with these figures.

n = 60
PMT = $1,165.65
PV = $97,000
FV = $96,544
i = 14.36%

If there were no points in either of these examples, the yield to the lender would be 13.5% in each case. Points or any other monetary payments that reduce the lender's investment are important considerations in calculating the lender's yield. The lender's yield may be supplemented through the syndication process.

In some depressed markets, lenders may find that the property securing the loan has declined in value to the point that the loan balance exceeds the property's value. In this case there is no longer any equity interest in the property, and the value of the loan may often be calculated based on the actual cash flows to the property rather than the cash flows projected when the loan contract was obtained. To do otherwise would be to estimate the value of the mortgage interest as greater than the value of the property.

Mortgage/Equity Formulas
Symbols

r = basic capitalization rate
Y = yield rate
M = mortgage ratio
C = mortgage coefficient
P = ratio paid off—mortgage
$1/S_{\overline{n}|}$ = sinking fund factor
R = capitalization rate
$S_{\overline{n}|}$ = future value of $1 per period
Δ = change
J = J factor (changing income)
n = projection period
NOI = net operating income
B = mortgage balance
I = nominal interest rate

Subscript:
E = equity
M = mortgage
P = projection
O = overall property
I = income
1 = 1st mortgage
2 = 2nd mortgage

Basic Capitalization Rate (r)

$r = Y_E - MC$

$r = Y_E - (M_1 C_1 + M_2 C_2)$

$C = Y_E + P\, 1/S_{\overline{n}|} - R_M$

$P = (R_M - I)/(R_{Mp} - I)$

$P = 1/S_{\overline{n}|} \times S_{\overline{n}|} P$

Capitalization Rates (R)

Level income

$$R = Y_E - MC - \Delta \, I/S_{\overline{n}}$$

$$R = r - \Delta \, I/S_{\overline{n}}$$

J-factor changing income

$$R_O = \frac{Y_E - MC - \Delta_O \, I/S_{\overline{n}}}{1 + \Delta_I J}$$

$$R_O = \frac{r - \Delta_O \, I/S_{\overline{n}}}{1 + \Delta_I J}$$

Required Change in Value (Δ)

Level income

$$\Delta = \frac{r - R}{I/S_{\overline{n}}}$$

$$\Delta = \frac{Y_E - MC - R}{I/S_{\overline{n}}}$$

J-factor changing income

$$\Delta_O = \frac{r - R_O(1 + \Delta_I J)}{I/S_{\overline{n}}}$$

$$*\Delta_O = \frac{r - R_O}{R_O J + I/S_{\overline{n}}}$$

Note: For multiple mortgage situations, insert M and C for each mortgage.

*   This formula assumes value and income change at the same ratio.

Equity yield (Y_E)

Level income

$$Y_E = R_E + \Delta_E \, I/S_{\overline{n}}$$

J-factor changing income

$$Y_E = R_E + \Delta_E \, I/S_{\overline{n}} + \frac{[R_O \, \Delta_I] J}{1 - M}$$

Change in equity

$$\Delta_E = (\Delta_O + MP) / (1 - M)$$
$$\Delta_E = [V_O(1 + \Delta_O) - B - V_E] / V_E$$

Assumed mortgage situation

Level income

$$V_O = \frac{NOI + BC}{Y_E - \Delta_O \, I/S_{\overline{n}}}$$

J-factor changing income

$$V_O = \frac{NOI(1 + \Delta_I J) + BC}{Y_E - \Delta_O \, I/S_{\overline{n}}}$$

Mortgage/Equity Without Algebra Format

Loan ratio × annual constant	=	_____
Equity ratio × equity yield rate	=+	_____
Loan ratio × paid off loan ratio × SFF	=−	_____
Basic rate (r)	=	_____
+ Dep or − App × SFF	=±	_____
Cap rate (R)	=	_____

Note: SFF is sinking fund factor at equity yield rate for projection period. Dep/App is the change in value from depreciation or appreciation during the projection period.

Mortgage-Equity Analysis

L.W. Ellwood was the first to organize, develop, and promulgate the use of mortgage-equity analysis in yield capitalization for real property valuation. He theorized that mortgage money plays a major role in determining real property prices and values. Ellwood saw real property investments as a combination of two components—debt and equity—and held that the return requirements of both components must be satisfied through income, reversion, or a combination of the two. Thus, Ellwood developed an approach for estimating property value that made explicit assumptions as to what a mortgage lender and an equity investor would expect from the property.

In general, mortgage-equity analysis involves estimating the value of a property on the basis of both mortgage and equity return requirements. The value of the equity interest in the property is found by discounting the equity dividends available to the equity investor. The equity yield rate (Y_E) is used as the discount rate. The total value of the property is equal to the present value of the equity position plus the value of the mortgage. This is true whether the value is found using discounted cash flow analysis or yield capitalization formulas that have been developed for mortgage-equity analysis.

Applications

Mortgage-equity analysis can facilitate the valuation process in many ways. It may be used

1. To compose overall rates
2. To analyze and test the capitalization rates obtained with other capitalization techniques
3. As an investment analysis tool to test the values indicated by the sales comparison and cost approaches
4. To analyze a capitalization rate graphically

Given a set of assumptions concerning the NOI, mortgage (amount, rate, and term), reversion (rate of appreciation or depreciation), equity yield rate, and projection period, mortgage-equity analysis may be employed to estimate the present value of the equity and to arrive at the total property value. The following example illustrates a general approach to mortgage-equity analysis.

Given:

Annual NOI (level)	$25,000
Projection period	10 years
Loan amount	$168,000
Loan terms*	
Interest rate	9%
Amortization term (monthly payments)	25 years
Estimated reversion	$201,600
Equity yield rate	15%

* Contract terms are at current market rates.

Using these assumptions, cash flow to the equity investor can be projected as follows:

Annual Cash Flow from Operations—Years 1–10	
Annual net operating income	$25,000
Annual debt service	16,918
Equity dividend	$8,082
Cash Flow from Reversion—Year 10	
Estimated resale price	$201,600
Mortgage balance	139,002
Cash flow from reversion	$62,598

Using the present value factor for a 15% yield rate and a 10-year holding period, we may calculate the present value of the cash flows to the equity investor as follows:

Years	Cash Flow	Present Value Factor	Present Value
1–10	$8,082	5.018769*	$40,562
10	$62,598	0.247185†	15,473
Present value of equity			$56,035

* Ordinary level annuity (present value of $1 per period) factor
† Reversion (present value of $1) factor

The total property value can now be found by adding the present value of the equity to the present value of the loan.[1]

Present value of the equity	$56,035
Present value of the loan	168,000
Total value	$224,035

This example illustrates a fairly straightforward application of mortgage-equity analysis. The present value of the equity was easily calculated by discounting the dollar estimates of the cash flows. The assumptions in this example were simplified in several ways. First, the income was assumed to be level. In a more complex situation, income may be expected to change over the holding period. Second, the loan amount was specified in dollars.[2] If the loan amount were assumed to be based on a loan-to-value ratio, the dollar amount of the loan would depend on the property value being calculated. In such a case the cash flows to the equity investor could not be specified in dollars and discounted as they were in the example. Third, the resale price was specified in dollars.[3] Investors often assume that property values will

1. Because the loan is assumed to be at current market rates, the face amount of the loan is equal to the value of the loan to the lender.

2. This might be the case if the property were being valued subject to an existing loan. Such a situation is illustrated later in this appendix. Alternatively, the dollar amount may have resulted from a separate calculation of the maximum amount that could be borrowed to meet a minimum debt coverage ratio.

3. This situation might occur if there is a purchase option in a lease that the appraiser believes will be exercised. Alternatively, a dollar estimate may be the result of a separate estimate of the resale price calculated by applying a capitalization rate to the income at the end of the holding period.

change by a specified percentage amount over the holding period (see Chapter 23). Thus, the resale price depends on the property value being calculated. Finally, in the preceding example the total property value is greater than the loan amount. If the opposite were true, the value of the loan could not exceed the combined debt and equity interests in the property.

When either the loan amount or the resale price depends on the value of the property, the cash flows cannot be projected in dollar amounts and discounted. An alternative procedure must be used to solve for the present value. One such alternative is to use a yield capitalization formula that has been developed to solve this type of problem.[4] This is what L.W. Ellwood did when he developed the Ellwood equation, which is illustrated in the following section.

Mortgage-Equity Formula

The general mortgage-equity formula is:

$$R_O = \frac{Y_E - M\ [Y_E + P\ 1/S_{\overline{n}|} - R_M] - \Delta_O\ 1/S_{\overline{n}|}}{1 + \Delta_I\ J}$$

where:

R_O = overall capitalization rate

Y_E = equity yield rate

M = loan-to-value ratio

P = percentage of loan paid off

$1/S_{\overline{n}|}$ = sinking fund factor at the equity yield rate

R_M = mortgage capitalization rate or mortgage constant

Δ_O = change in total property value

Δ_I = total ratio change in income

J = J factor (This symbol is discussed later in this appendix.)

The part of the formula represented as $Y_E - M\ [Y_E + P\ 1/S_{\overline{n}|} - R_M]$ can be referred to as the *basic capitalization rate* (r). It satisfies the lender's requirement and adjusts for amortization. It also satisfies the investor's equity yield requirement before any adjustment is made for income and value changes. Therefore, the basic rate starts with an investor's yield requirement and adjusts it to reflect the effect of financing. The resulting basic capitalization rate is a building block from which an overall capitalization rate can be developed with additional assumptions.

If level income and no change in property value are anticipated, the basic rate will be identical to the overall capitalization rate. The last part of the numerator, $\Delta_O\ 1/S_{\overline{n}|}$, allows the appraiser to adjust the basic rate to reflect an expected change in overall property value. If the value change is positive, referred to as property appreciation, the overall capitalization rate is reduced

---

4.   A computer can be programmed to handle this type of valuation problem. For a discussion of this proceudure, see Jeffrey D. Fisher, "Using Circular Reference in Spreadsheets to Estimate Value," *The Quarterly Byte*, vol. 5, no. 4 (Fourth Quarter 1989).

to reflect this anticipated monetary benefit; if the change is negative, referred to as depreciation, the overall capitalization rate is increased.

Finally, the denominator, $1 + \Delta_I J$, accounts for any change in income. The J factor is always positive. Thus, if the change in income is positive, the denominator will be greater than one and the overall rate will be reduced. If the change in income is negative, the overall rate will be increased. For level-income applications, $\Delta = 0$, so the denominator is $1 + 0$, or 1.

Akerson Format

The mortgage-equity procedure developed by Charles B. Akerson substitutes an arithmetic format for the algebraic equation in the Ellwood formula.[5] This format is applicable to level-income situations; when modified with the J or K factor, it can also be applied to changing-income situations.

The Akerson format for level-income situations is

Loan ratio × annual constant	= _____
Equity ratio × equity yield rate	=+ _____
Loan ratio × % paid off in projection period × $1/S_{\overline{n}}$	=− _____
Basic rate (r)	= _____
+ dep or − app × $1/S_{\overline{n}}$	=± _____
Overall capitalization rate	= _____

where $1/S_{\overline{n}}$ is the sinking fund factor at the equity yield rate for the projection period and dep/app denotes the change in value from property depreciation or appreciation during the projection period.

Level-Income Applications

Mortgage-equity analysis can be used to value real property investments with level income streams or variable income streams converted to level equivalents using overall capitalization rates and residual techniques.

Use of Overall Capitalization Rates

In the simplest application of the mortgage-equity formula and the Akerson format, a level income and a stable or changing overall property value are assumed. The following example illustrates the application of the mortgage-equity formula using an overall capitalization rate applied to a level flow of income.

NOI (level)	$25,000
Projection period	10 years
Loan terms	
Interest rate	9%
Amortization term (monthly payments)	25 years
Loan-to-value ratio	75%
Property value change	20% gain
Equity yield rate	15%

5. The format was first presented by Charles B. Akerson in "Ellwood without Algebra," *The Appraisal Journal* (July 1970).

The overall rate is calculated as follows:

$$R_o = \frac{Y_E - M\,[Y_E + P\,1/S_{\overline{n}} - R_M] - \Delta_o\,1/S_{\overline{n}}}{1 + \Delta_I J}$$

$$R_o = \frac{0.15 - 0.75\,(0.15 + 0.1726 \times 0.04925 - 0.1007) - (0.20 \times 0.04925)}{1 + 0 \times J}$$

$$R_o = \frac{0.15 - 0.75\,(0.057801) - 0.009850}{1}$$

$$R_o = \frac{0.15 - 0.043350 - 0.009850}{1}$$

$$R_o = \frac{0.096800}{1}$$

$$R_o = 0.0968 \text{ (rounded)}$$

The capitalized value of the investment is $25,000/0.0968 = $258,264.

Using the same data and assumptions, an identical value can be derived by applying the Akerson format:

0.75×0.100704	$= \quad 0.075528$
0.25×0.15	$= + 0.037500$
$-0.75 \times 0.172608 \times 0.049252$	$= - 0.006376$
Basic rate (r)	$= \quad 0.106652$
0.20×-0.049252	$= - 0.009850$
R_o	$= \quad 0.098602$
The capitalized value is $25,000/0.0986	$= \quad $258,264$

The answer derived in this example is virtually the same as the answer that would be derived using DCF analysis. In fact, it is possible to check the answer found with the Ellwood formula by discounting the implied cash flows. This is true because the dollar amount of the loan and resale price are approximately the same in both examples. That is, the implied amount of the loan is 75% of $224,014, or approximately $168,000, and the implied resale price is 90% of $224,014, or approximately $201,600. It is important to realize, however, that this was not known until the problem was solved. The examples were designed to produce the same answer to demonstrate that both problems are based on the same concepts of discounted cash flow analysis.

Use of Residual Techniques

Land and building residual techniques can be applied with land and building capitalization rates based on mortgage-equity procedures. The general mortgage-equity formula or the Akerson format is applied to derive a basic rate, which is used to develop land and building capitalization rates.

For example, assume that a commercial property is expected to produce level annual income of $15,000 per year over a 10-year term. Mortgage financing is available at a 75% loan-to-value ratio, and monthly payments at 11% interest are made over an amortization term of 25 years. The land is currently valued at $65,000 and is forecast to have a value of $78,000 at the end of the projection period, indicating a 20% positive change in land value.

The building is expected to have no value at the end of the projection period and the equity yield rate is 15%.

The first step in valuing this property is to derive the basic rate (r) using the Ellwood Formula:

$$r = Y_E - M\ (Y_E + P\ 1/S_{\overline{n}} - R_M)$$
$$r = 0.15 - 0.75\ (0.15 + 0.137678 \times 0.049252 - 0.117614)$$
$$= 0.15 - 0.029375$$
$$= 0.120625$$

The Akerson format can also be used to derive the basic rate:

0.75×0.117614	=	0.088211
0.25×0.15	=	0.037500
$0.75 \times 0.137678 \times 0.049252$	=	− 0.005086
Basic capitalization rate (r)	=	0.120625

Next, the land and building capitalization rates are calculated. To solve for the land capitalization rate, R_L, the calculations are

$$R_L = r - \Delta_L\ 1/S_{\overline{n}}$$
$$= 0.120625 - (0.20 \times 0.049252)$$
$$= 0.120625 - 0.009850$$
$$= 0.110775$$

The building capitalization rate, R_B, is calculated as follows:

$$R_B = r - \Delta_B\ 1/S_{\overline{n}}$$
$$= 0.120625 - (-1.0 \times 0.049252)$$
$$= 0.120625 + 0.049252$$
$$= 0.169877$$

These rates can be used to value the property with the building residual technique:

NOI	$15,000	
Land income		
$(V_L \times R_L) = \$65,000 \times 0.110775$	7,200	
Residual income attributable to building	$7,800	
Capitalized value of building		
$(I_B \div R_B) = \$7,800/0.169877$		$45,916
Plus land value		+ 65,000
Indicated property value		$110,916

When the rates are used in the land residual technique, a similar property value is indicated:

NOI	$15,000
Building income	
$(V_B \times R_B) = \$46,000 \times 0.169877$	7,814
Residual income attributable to land	$7,186
Capitalized value of land	
$(I_L \div R_L) = \$7,186/0.110775$	$64,870
Plus building value	+ 46,000
Indicated total property value	$110,870

Changing-Income Applications

The general mortgage-equity formula can be applied to income streams that are forecast to change on a curvilinear or exponential-curve (constant-ratio) basis by using a J factor for curvilinear change or a K factor for constant-ratio change. The J factor, used in the stabilizer $(1 + \Delta_I J)$, may be obtained from precomputed tables or calculated with the J-factor formula.[6] The K factor, an income adjuster or stabilizer used to convert a changing income stream into its level equivalent, can be calculated with the K-factor formula.[7]

Use of the J Factor

The J-factor formula for curvilinear income reflects an income stream that changes from time zero in relation to a sinking fund accumulation curve. The formula is

$$J = 1/S_{\overline{n}|} \times \left[\frac{n}{1 - 1/(1+Y)^n} \right] - \frac{1}{Y}$$

where:

$1/S_{\overline{n}|}$ = sinking fund factor at equity yield rate

n = projection period

Y = equity yield rate

Consider the facts set forth in the level annuity example, but assume a 20% increase in income. Note that the J factor is applied to the income in the year prior to the first year of the holding period.

---

6. Before the advent of financial calculators, present value and future value problems were solved using precomputed tables of compound interest factors. Although the tables are no longer used in everyday practice, they remain useful for checking results of calculations made with calculators and computers and in teaching the mathematics of finance. See James J. Mason, ed., comp., *American Institute of Real Estate Appraisers Financial Tables*, rev. ed. (Chicago: American Institute of Real Estate Appraisers, with tables computed by Financial Publishing Company, 1982), 461-473.

7. Charles B. Akerson, *Capitalization Theory and Techniques: Study Guide*, 2d ed. (Chicago: Appraisal Institute, with tables computed by Financial Publishing Company, 2000), T-47 to T-52.

$$R_o = \frac{0.15 - 0.75\,(0.15 + 0.172608 \times 0.049252 - 0.100704) - (0.20 \times 0.049252)}{1 + (0.20 \times 0.3259)}$$

$$= \frac{0.15 - 0.043348 - 0.009850}{1 + 0.0652}$$

$$= \frac{0.096802}{1.0652}$$

$$= 0.09088$$

The capitalized value is $25,000/0.09088 = $275,088.

The net operating incomes for the projection period that are implied by the curvilinear J-factor premise are calculated in the following table.

Period	1st Year Adjustment*		$S_{\overline{n}}$		Periodic Adjustment		Base NOI†		NOI
1	$246.26	×	1/1.000000	=	$246	+	$25,000	=	$25,246
2	$246.26	×	1/0.465116	=	$529	+	$25,000	=	$25,529
3	$246.26	×	1/0.287977	=	$855	+	$25,000	=	$25,855
4	$246.26	×	1/0.200265	=	$1,230	+	$25,000	=	$26,230
5	$246.26	×	1/0.148316	=	$1,660	+	$25,000	=	$26,660
6	$246.26	×	1/0.114237	=	$2,156	+	$25,000	=	$27,156
7	$246.26	×	1/0.090360	=	$2,725	+	$25,000	=	$27,725
8	$246.26	×	1/0.072850	=	$3,380	+	$25,000	=	$28,380
9	$246.26	×	1/0.059574	=	$4,134	+	$25,000	=	$29,134
10	$246.26	×	1/0.049252	=	$5,000	+	$25,000	=	$30,000

* This adjustment was derived by multiplying the NOI ($25,000) by the assumed increase in the NOI (20%); the resulting figure ($5,000) was then multiplied by the sinking fund factor for the anticipated 15% equity yield rate over the 10-year projection period ($1/S_{\overline{n}} = 0.049252$).

† The base NOI is the income for the year prior to the beginning of the projection period.

Mathematical proof of the example is provided below.

Valuation of Equity

Period	NOI		Debt Service		Cash to Equity		PVF at 15%		PV
1	$25,246	−	$20,772	=	$4,474	×	0.869565	=	$3,890
2	$25,529	−	$20,772	=	$4,757	×	0.756144	=	$3,597
3	$25,855	−	$20,772	=	$5,083	×	0.657516	=	$3,342
4	$26,230	−	$20,772	=	$5,458	×	0.571753	=	$3,121
5	$26,660	−	$20,772	=	$5,888	×	0.497177	=	$2,927
6	$27,156	−	$20,772	=	$6,384	×	0.432328	=	$2,760
7	$27,725	−	$20,772	=	$6,953	×	0.375937	=	$2,614
8	$28,380	−	$20,772	=	$7,608	×	0.326902	=	$2,487
9	$29,134	−	$20,772	=	$8,362	×	0.284262	=	$2,377
10	$30,000	−	$20,772	=	$9,228	×	0.247185	=	$2,281
					$159,400*	×	0.247185	=	$39,401

Value of equity at 15% = $68,797
Check: $275,088 × 0.25 = $68,772

* The reversion is calculated as follows:
Resale ($275,088 × 1.20) = $330,106
Loan balance ($275,088 × 0.75)(1 − 0.1726) = 170,706
Equity proceeds = $159,400

Use of the K Factor

The K-factor formula, which is applied to income that changes on an exponential-curve (constant-ratio) basis, is expressed as

$$K = \frac{1 - (1 + C)^n / S^n}{(Y - C) a_{\overline{n}|}}$$

where:

K = factor
C = constant-ratio change in income
S^n = future value factor
Y = equity yield rate
$a_{\overline{n}|}$ = present value factor for ordinary level annuity

When the general mortgage-equity formula is used to derive an overall capitalization rate applicable to an income expected to change on a constant-ratio basis, K is substituted for the denominator $(1 + \Delta_I J)$. The following example is based on the same property used for the level-income and J-factor examples, but it assumes that NOI will increase by 2% per year, on a compound basis. This property can be valued using the K factor in the mortgage-equity formula.

$$R_O = \frac{Y_E - M [Y_E + P \, 1/S_{\overline{n}|} - R_M] - \Delta_O \, 1/S_{\overline{n}|}}{K}$$

$$= \frac{0.15 - 0.75 \, (0.15 + 0.172608 \times 0.049252 - 0.100704) - (0.20 \times 0.049252)}{1.070877}$$

$$= 0.090395$$

The capitalized value of the investment is $25,000/0.090395 = $276,564.

Note that the indicated values based on the J-factor and K-factor premises are very close, i.e., $275,088 and $276,564. The indicated value based on a level-income assumption is much lower, i.e., $238,264. This is because all of the yield has to occur on resale, not in increased income.

Based on the income data in Table C.1, J-factor and K-factor income patterns are plotted on the graph in Figure C.1. Both examples assume a 20% increase in overall property value. In the J-factor example, income is projected to increase by 20%. In the K-factor example, income is projected to increase at a constant ratio of 2% per year. Under the J-factor assumption, the value of the property is $275,088 and the R_O is 9.088%. Under the K-factor assumption, the value of the property is $276,569, and the R_O is 9.039%.

Solving for Equity Yield

Given an actual or proposed equity sale price and a forecast of equity benefits, an equity yield rate can be estimated. When level income is forecast, a formula is used. The calculations can be performed by iteration or with the financial functions of a calculator. When income is expected to change on a curvilinear basis or a constant-ratio basis, formulas must be used to solve for

Table C.1   **J-Factor Income Pattern and K-Factor Income Pattern**

	J Factor	K Factor
Year 1	$25,246	$25,000
Year 2	$25,529	$25,500
Year 3	$25,855	$26,010
Year 4	$26,230	$26,530
Year 5	$26,660	$27,060
Year 6	$27,156	$27,602
Year 7	$27,725	$28,154
Year 8	$28,380	$28,717
Year 9	$29,134	$29,291
Year 10	$30,000	$29,877

Figure C.1   **J-Factor and K-Factor Income Pattern Curves**

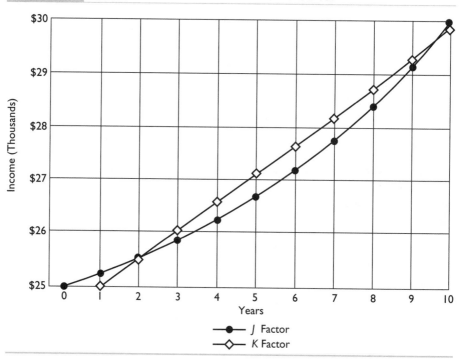

the yield. A calculator cannot be used to solve the problem conveniently, and the iteration technique is too time-consuming.

Level-Income Example

Consider a property that is purchased for $250,000. The net operating income is forecast to remain level at $35,000 per year and the buyer believes that property value will decline 15% over a five-year ownership period. The mortgage amount is $200,000 and monthly payments are at 10% interest with an amortization term of 20 years. The investment forecast is outlined below:

Purchase		Holding Period	
Sale price	$250,000	NOI	$35,000
Mortgage	− 200,000	Debt service	− 23,161*
Equity	$50,000	Equity dividend	$11,839

Resale After 5 Years	
Sale price	$212,500
Mortgage balance	$179,605†
Equity reversion	$32,895
Original equity	$50,000
Equity change	-$17,105

* $200,000 × 0.115803 mortgage constant

† Unamortized portion of $200,000 mortgage at end of 5-year projection period

$$R_E \text{ (equity capitalization rate)} = \frac{\$11,839}{\$50,000} = 0.236780$$

$$\Delta_E \text{ (equity change)} = \frac{-\$17,105}{\$50,000} = -0.342100$$

The equity yield rate may now be computed through iteration or by using the formula and interpolation. Iteration is performed using the formula

$$Y_E = R_E + \Delta_E \; 1/S_{\overline{n}|}$$

Because the sinking fund factor for five years at the Y_E rate cannot be identified without knowing Y_E, a trial-and-error procedure must be used to develop Y_E. Without discounting, the 34.21% equity decline over the five-year holding period would subtract 6.84% each year from the equity capitalization rate of 23.67%. Consequently, Y_E will be less than 23.67% and more than 16.83% (23.67% − 6.84%).

The first computation is performed with a Y_E of 18%. When the correct equity yield rate is applied, the equation will balance.

Estimated Y_E	R_E	+	Δ_E	×	$1/S_{\overline{n}|}$	=	Indicated Y_E
0.1800	0.2368	+	(-0.3425)	×	0.139778	=	0.1889
0.2000	0.2368	+	(-0.3425)	×	0.134380	=	0.1908
0.1900	0.2368	+	(-0.3425)	×	0.137050	=	0.1899

Therefore, $Y_E = 0.1900$, or 19.0%.

This procedure for computing Y_E is correct because Y_E is defined as the rate that makes the present value of the future equity benefits equal to the original equity. The future benefits in this case are the equity dividend of $11,839 per year for five years and the equity reversion of $32,895 at the end of the five-year period.

If Y_E is 19%, the present value of the two benefits can be computed.

$$\$11,839 \times 3.057635 = \quad \$36,199$$
$$\$32,895 \times 0.419049 = + \underline{\ 13,785}$$
$$\$49,984$$

Thus, the equity yield rate has been proven to be 19.0%. Precision to 0.03% represents a level of accuracy in keeping with current practice and the normal requirements of the calculation. This example is based on level income, but the same procedure can be applied to changing income streams by incorporating J and K factors into the formula.

J-Factor Premise Example

Consider the information set forth in the previous example, but assume that income is expected to decline 15% according to the J-factor premise.

$$R_O = \$35,000/\$250,000 = 0.14, \qquad M = \$200,000/\$250,000 = 0.80$$

$$Y_E = R_E + \frac{\Delta_E}{S_{\overline{n}|}} + \frac{R_O \Delta}{1 - M}J$$

Try 15%,

$$0.2368 + \text{-}0.3421 \times 0.1483 + \frac{0.14 \times \text{-}0.15}{0.2} \times 0.4861 = 0.135$$

Try 12%,

$$0.2368 + \text{-}0.3421 \times 0.1574 + \frac{0.14 \times \text{-}0.15}{0.2} \times 0.5077 = 0.130$$

Try 13%,

$$0.2368 + \text{-}0.3421 \times 0.1543 + \frac{0.14 \times \text{-}0.15}{0.2} \times 0.5004 = 0.131472$$

Therefore, $Y_E = 13.15\%$ (rounded).

K-Factor Premise Example

Consider the same information, but assume that income is expected to decrease at a compound rate of 3% per year, indicating a constant-ratio change in income.

$$Y_E = R_E + \Delta_E \ 1/S_{\overline{n}|} + \frac{R_O (K - 1)}{1 - M}$$

Try 13%,

$$0.2368 + \text{-}0.3421 \times 0.1543 + \frac{0.14 \times (0.9487 - 1)}{0.2} = 0.148$$

Try 15%,

$$0.2368 + \text{-}0.3421 \times 0.1483 + \frac{0.14 \times (0.9497 - 1)}{0.2} = 0.151$$

Therefore, $Y_E = 15.1\%$.

Rate Analysis

Rate analysis allows an appraiser to test the reasonableness of the value conclusions derived through the application of overall capitalization rates. Once an overall capitalization rate has been developed with mortgage-equity analysis or another technique, its reliability and consistency with market expectations of equity yield and value change can be tested using Ellwood graphic analysis.

To create a graph for rate analysis, the appraiser chooses equity yield rates that cover a realistic range of rates expected and demanded by investors. It is often wise to include a rate that is at the low end of the range of market acceptance as well as a rate at the high end of the range. For the analysis to be useful to the client, the range of yield rates chosen should be in line with investors' perceptions of the market.

In most real estate investments, there is no assurance that the investment can be liquidated at the convenience of the equity investor or on the terms dictated by the investor. For example, in the early 1990s most liquidity evaporated from the market. Moreover, in negotiating a purchase price, the prospects for profit within a plausible range of possibilities may be greater than the chance of achieving a specific equity yield rate, which cannot be determined until the property is resold. However, the appraiser's value judgments can easily be subjected to realistic tests. The appraiser should ask the following questions:

- What resale prices correspond to various yield levels?
- Can the property suffer some loss in value and still produce an acceptable profit?
- How sensitive is the equity yield rate to possible fluctuations in value?
- What percentage of the investor's return is derived from annual cash flows, and what percentage comes from the reversion? (Reversion is generally considered riskier.)
- What prospective equity yield rates can be inferred from the overall capitalization rates found in the marketplace?

Many of these questions focus on the relationship between the change in property value and the equity yield rate. The unknown variable in rate analysis is the change in property value (Δ_o). The formula for the required change in property value in a level-income application is

$$\Delta_o = \frac{r - R_o}{1/S_{\overline{n}|}}$$

Level-Income Example

Consider an investment that will generate stable income and has an overall capitalization rate of 10%. The purchase can be financed with a 75% loan at 10% interest amortized over 25 years with level monthly payments. If the investment is held for 10 years, what levels of depreciation or appreciation should be expected with equity yield rates of 9%, 12%, and 15%?

To solve this problem the appraiser must first find the basic rate (r) and the sinking fund factor for each equity yield rate. The Ellwood Tables[8] are the source of the following figures:

Y_E	r	$1/S_{\overline{n}|}$
9%	0.096658	0.065820
12%	0.105185	0.056984
15%	0.113584	0.049252

When the difference between *r* and the overall rate (R_O) is divided by the corresponding sinking fund factor, the result is the expected change in property value. If r is greater than R_O, a value increase is indicated; if *r* is less than R_O, value loss is indicated. Analysis of the 10% overall capitalization rate is shown below:

$$Y_E = \frac{r - R_O}{1/S_{\overline{n}|}}$$

9%	-0.0508 (5.1% depreciation)
12%	0.0910 (9.1% appreciation)
15%	0.2758 (27.6% appreciation)

The formula produces answers consistent with the notion that a loss is negative and a gain is positive. In some texts the numerator in this formula is expressed as $R_O - r$. Use of this formula results in a change of sign—i.e., positive answers indicate depreciation and negative answers indicate appreciation.

J-Factor Premise

A similar analysis can be performed when income is presumed to change commensurately with value according to the J-factor premise. In this case the expected change in overall property value is calculated by dividing $(r - R_O)$ by $(R_O J + 1/S_{\overline{n}|})$.

Graphic Rate Analysis

Various systems have been developed to employ mortgage-equity concepts in graphic rate analysis. The graphic analysis of capitalization rates is a helpful analytical tool used by practicing appraisers and investment analysts. Rate analysis in graphic or tabular form is particularly useful in interpreting market data. Although analyzing a market-oriented overall capitalization rate cannot reveal a property's eventual equity yield rate or resale price, the analysis can reveal combinations of Y_E and Δ_O implicit in the overall rate. Thus, an appraiser can use rate analysis to decide whether a particular combination of Y_E and Δ_O is consistent with market behavior.

The accompanying figures illustrate two types of graphic analysis. Figure C.2 shows Ellwood-style graphic analysis, with time on the horizontal axis and the percentage change in property value on the vertical axis. Figure C.3 illustrates another type of graphic analysis with the equity yield rate on the horizontal axis and the percentage change in value on the vertical axis.

---

8.   L.W. Ellwood, *Ellwood Tables for Real Estate Appraising and Financing*, 4th ed. (Cambridge, Mass.: Ballinger Publishing Co., 1977).

Figure C.2   **Ellwood-style Graphic Analysis**

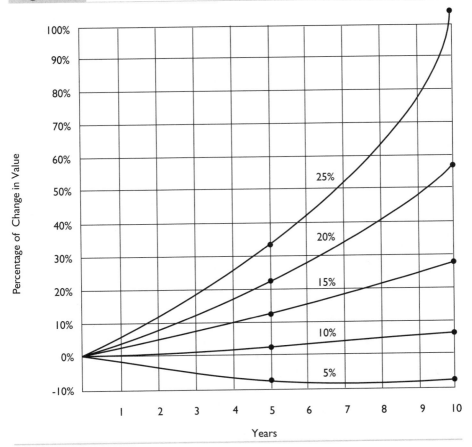

Graphs like these can be constructed manually by plotting three or more key points and connecting the points with a smooth curve; they can also be constructed using a computer.

The graph in Figure C.2 shows change in value and income under the J-factor premise with respect to time for equity yield rates of 5%, 10%, 15%, 20%, and 25%. It is assumed that $R_O = 0.11$, $I = 0.125$, $R_M = 0.135$, $M = 0.7$, and $\Delta_O = \Delta_I$.

The graph in Figure C.3 shows the change in value and income under the J-factor premise for equity yield rates ranging from 5% to 25% over a 10-year holding period. Again, it is assumed that $R_O = 0.11$, $I = 0.125$, $R_M = 0.135$, $M = 0.7$, and $\Delta_O = \Delta_I$.

After a graph is created, it must be interpreted by the appraiser. Usually the appraiser determines the range of property value changes (Δ_O) anticipated

Figure C.3   Alternative Graphic Analysis

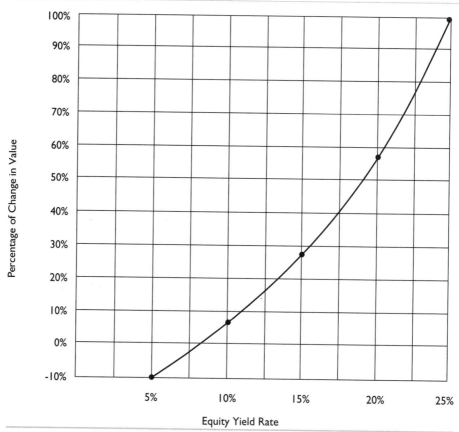

by the market and then forms an opinion as to the reasonableness of the overall capitalization rate. If the value changes are in line with the expectations of market participants and there is nothing unusual about the subject property, the overall rate being tested may be reasonable. If the value changes are not within the range expected by the marketplace, the overall capitalization rate should either be considered unreasonable and in need of further analysis or must be explained and accounted for.

Rate Extraction

Rate extraction is a technique that allows an appraiser to infer the market's expectation of yield and change in property value from a market-oriented overall capitalization rate. The key is to determine what assumptions about the yield rate and the change in property value are consistent with the overall capitalization rates derived from comparable sales. Although a specific yield rate or change in value cannot be identified using this approach, an analyst can determine what change in property value is needed to produce a given yield rate. That is, for each assumed yield rate, there is only one assumption about the change in property value that can be used with that rate to obtain the overall capitalization rate implied by comparable sales.

The following example illustrates this technique. The subject property is an apartment complex. Data on three comparable properties is given.

Factual Data on Three Apartment Complexes

	Sale 1	Sale 2	Sale 3
Number of units	240	48	148
Sale price	$4,678,000	$811,000	$3,467,000
Cash down payment	$1,300,000	$462,145	$1,370,000
Gross income	$594,540	$126,240	$507,120
NOI	$368,600	$71,500	$293,400

Comparative Factors

	Sale 1	Sale 2	Sale 3
Price per unit	$19,492	$16,896	$23,426
Gross income per unit			
Annually	$2,477	$2,638	$3,426
Monthly	$206	$219	$285
Gross income multiplier (GIM)	7.870	6.420	6.830
Overall capitalization rate (R_O)	0.079	0.088	0.085
Loan-to-value ratio (M)	0.722	0.430	0.605
Mortgage constant (R_M)	0.107	0.127	0.136
Percent paid off (P)	-0.125	0.016	0.032
Equity capitalization rate (R_E)	0.006	0.059	0.006
Debt coverage ratio (DCR)	1.021	1.610	1.030

Using the mortgage-equity J-factor formula, pairs of Y_E and Δ_O can be extracted for each comparable sale. The formula for change in income and value is

$$\Delta_{O=1} = \frac{Y_E - MY_E + (P\ 1/S_{\overline{n}|} - R_M) - R_O}{R_O\ J + 1/S_{\overline{n}|}}$$

The overall rate for each of the sales can be used in this formula to solve for the combinations of Y_E and Δ_O that would produce that overall capitalization rate. This data is shown in the following table:

Calculated Required Changes for the Three Sales (Five-Year Projection)   % $\Delta_{O=1}$

%Y_E	Sale 1	Sale 2	Sale 3
10	19.9	10.7	16.1
12	23.2	16.8	20.8
14	26.7	23.3	25.7
16	30.5	30.3	31.0
18	34.5	37.8	36.6
20	38.8	45.8	42.7
22	43.4	54.3	49.1
24	48.3	63.4	55.9
26	53.7	73.2	63.2
28	59.0	83.4	70.9
30	64.9	94.6	79.2

Note that the rate of change in property value is assumed to equal the rate of change in income. This reflects the appraiser's belief that this assumption is consistent with market perceptions. The relationship between equity yield and change in value and income can now be graphed (see Figure C.4).

Once the graph is completed, the appraiser can draw certain conclusions. If the sales used accurately reflect market perceptions, every pair of equity yield rate and change in property value is a perfect pair. When the figures are

Figure C.4   Relationship Between Equity Yield and Total Change in Value and Income

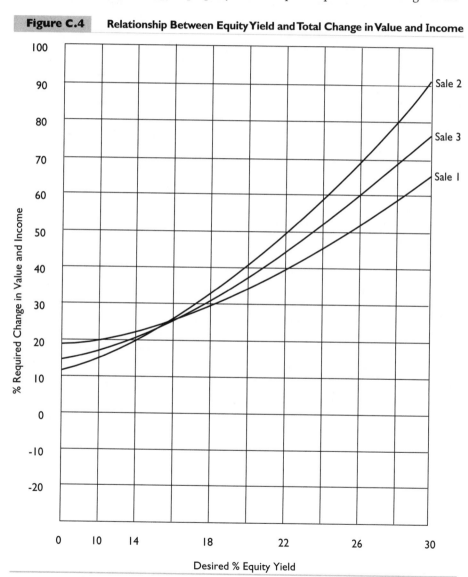

inserted into the mortgage-equity formula to derive an overall capitalization rate, the resulting value estimate will be market-oriented.

In this case any pair of Y_E and Δ_O that does not coincide with the lines on the graph is not market-oriented. The lines have different slopes and cross at some point because each sale has a different loan-to-value ratio (M). Furthermore, because of the differences in the loan-to-value ratios, we would expect some variation in the yield rate that equity investors would require for each of the sales. For example, Sale 1 had the highest loan-to-value ratio and, therefore, probably had the highest required yield rate because of its greater risk. The curves indicate reasonable assumptions about yield rates and changes in value that are consistent with the prices paid for comparable sales and the manner in which they were financed.

The graph can also be used to reflect the most likely pair of Y_E and Δ_O for developing an overall capitalization rate. By verifying current investor perceptions of the yield anticipated for the type of property being appraised, the appraiser can determine the necessary property value change. Then, with the mortgage-equity formula, the overall capitalization rate can be calculated. This overall rate will reflect typical investor assumptions for both yield and change in property value.

Compound Interest (Future Value of $1)

This factor reflects the amount to which an investment or deposit will grow in a given number of time periods, including the accumulation of interest at the effective rate per period. It is also known as the *amount of one*.

$$S^n = (1 + i)^n$$

where:
S^n = future value factor
i = effective rate of interest
n = number of compounding periods

and
$$S^n = (e)^{in} \text{ for continuous compounding}$$
where:
S^n = future value factor
i = nominal rate of interest
n = number of years
e = 2.718282

This factor is used to solve problems dealing with compound growth.

When money is invested or deposited at the beginning of a period in an account that bears interest at a fixed rate, it grows according to the interest rate and the number of compounding (conversion) periods that it remains in the account. To illustrate how and why this growth occurs, consider an investment of $1.00, a nominal interest rate of 10% with annual compounding, and an investment holding period of five years.

Original investment	$1.00
Interest, first year at 10%	0.10
Accumulation, end of 1 year	$1.10
Interest, second year at 10%	0.11
Accumulation, end of 2 years	$1.21
Interest, third year at 10%	0.121
Accumulation, end of 3 years	$1.331
Interest, fourth year at 10%	0.1331
Accumulation, end of 4 years	$1.4641
Interest, fifth year at 10%	0.14641
Accumulation, end of 5 years	$1.61051

One dollar grows to $1.61051 in five years with interest at 10%, so the future value of $1 factor at 10% annually for five years is 1.610510; $1,000 would grow 1,000 times this amount to $1,610.51 over the same five years at the same 10% annual rate. When interest is not collected or withdrawn as it is earned, it is added to the capital amount and additional interest accumulates in subsequent periods. This process is called *compounding*.

The results of compounding can be calculated with the formula $(1 + i)^n$, where n is the number of compounding periods and i is the interest rate per period.

n

1	$1.10 \times 1 = 1.10^1$	$= 1.10$
2	$1.10 \times 1.10 = 1.10^2$	$= 1.21$
3	$1.10 \times 1.10 \times 1.10 = 1.10^3$	$= 1.331$
4	$1.10 \times 1.10 \times 1.10 \times 1.10 = 1.10^4$	$= 1.461$
5	$1.10 \times 1.10 \times 1.10 \times 1.10 \times 1.10 = 1.10^5$	$= 1.61051$

Thus, the factors in Figure C.5, the amount of one or the future value of $1, reflect the growth of $1.00 accumulating at interest for the number of compounding periods shown at the left and right sides of each page of tables. For example, the 10% annual column reveals a factor of 2.593742 for 10 periods. This means that $1.00 deposited at 10% interest compounded annually for 10 years will grow to $1.00 × 2.593742, or just over $2.59. In other words, $1.10^{10} = 2.593742$. The factors for seven and eight years indicate that $1.00 (or any investment earning 10% per year) will double in value in approximately 7.5 years. Similarly, an investment of $10,000 made 10 years ago, earning no periodic income during the 10-year holding period, must be liquidated in the current market at $10,000 × 2.593742, or $25,937.42, to realize a 10% return on the original investment.

This factor reflects the growth of the original deposit measured from the beginning deposit period. Thus, at the end of the first period at a rate of 10%, the original $1.00 has grown to $1.10 and the factor is 1.100000, as shown above.

Figure C.5   Compound Interest Table for 10%

10% RATE i / n	1 AMOUNT OF $1 — The amount to which $1 will grow with compound interest	2 AMOUNT OF $1 PER PERIOD — The amount to which $1 per period will grow with compound interest	3 SINKING FUND FACTOR — The amount per period which will grow with compound interest to $1	4 PRESENT WORTH OF $1 — What $1 due in the future is worth today	5 PRESENT WORTH OF $1 PER PERIOD — What $1 payable periodically is worth today	6 PARTIAL PAYMENT — The installment to repay $1 with interest	10% RATE i / n
1	1.100 000	1.000 000	1.000 000	.909 091	.909 091	1.100 000	1
2	1.210 000	2.100 000	.476 190	.826 446	1.735 537	.576 190	2
3	1.331 000	3.310 000	.302 115	.751 315	2.486 852	.402 115	3
4	1.464 100	4.641 000	.215 471	.683 013	3.169 865	.315 471	4
5	1.610 510	6.105 100	.163 797	.620 921	3.790 787	.263 797	5
6	1.771 561	7.715 610	.129 607	.564 474	4.355 261	.229 607	6
7	1.948 717	9.487 171	.105 405	.513 158	4.868 419	.205 405	7
8	2.143 589	11.435 888	.087 444	.466 507	5.334 976	.187 444	8
9	2.357 948	13.579 477	.073 641	.424 098	5.759 024	.173 641	9
10	2.593 742	15.937 425	.062 745	.385 543	6.144 567	.162 745	10
11	2.853 117	18.531 167	.053 963	.350 494	6.495 061	.153 963	11
12	3.138 428	21.384 284	.046 763	.318 631	6.813 692	.146 763	12
13	3.452 271	24.522 712	.040 779	.289 664	7.103 356	.140 779	13
14	3.797 498	27.974 983	.035 746	.263 331	7.366 687	.135 746	14
15	4.177 248	31.772 482	.031 474	.239 392	7.606 080	.131 474	15
16	4.594 973	35.949 730	.027 817	.217 629	7.823 709	.127 817	16
17	5.054 470	40.544 703	.024 664	.197 845	8.021 553	.124 664	17
18	5.559 917	45.599 173	.021 930	.179 859	8.201 412	.121 930	18
19	6.115 909	51.159 090	.019 547	.163 508	8.364 920	.119 547	19
20	6.727 500	57.274 999	.017 460	.148 644	8.513 564	.117 460	20
21	7.400 250	64.002 499	.015 624	.135 131	8.648 694	.115 624	21
22	8.140 275	71.402 749	.014 005	.122 846	8.771 540	.114 005	22
23	8.954 302	79.543 024	.012 572	.111 678	8.883 218	.112 572	23
24	9.849 733	88.497 327	.011 300	.101 526	8.984 744	.111 300	24
25	10.834 706	98.347 059	.010 168	.092 296	9.077 040	.110 168	25
26	11.918 177	109.181 765	.009 159	.083 905	9.160 945	.109 159	26
27	13.109 994	121.099 942	.008 258	.076 278	9.237 223	.108 258	27
28	14.420 994	134.209 936	.007 451	.069 343	9.306 567	.107 451	28
29	15.863 093	148.630 930	.006 728	.063 039	9.369 606	.106 728	29
30	17.449 402	164.494 023	.006 079	.057 309	9.426 914	.106 079	30
31	19.194 342	181.943 425	.005 496	.052 099	9.479 013	.105 496	31
32	21.113 777	201.137 767	.004 972	.047 362	9.526 376	.104 972	32
33	23.225 154	222.251 544	.004 499	.043 057	9.569 432	.104 499	33
34	25.547 670	245.476 699	.004 074	.039 143	9.608 575	.104 074	34
35	28.102 437	271.024 368	.003 690	.035 584	9.644 159	.103 690	35
36	30.912 681	299.126 805	.003 343	.032 349	9.676 508	.103 343	36
37	34.003 949	330.039 486	.003 030	.029 408	9.705 917	.103 030	37
38	37.404 343	364.043 434	.002 747	.026 735	9.732 651	.102 747	38
39	41.144 778	401.447 778	.002 491	.024 304	9.756 956	.102 491	39
40	45.259 256	442.592 556	.002 259	.022 095	9.779 051	.102 259	40
41	49.785 181	487.851 811	.002 050	.020 086	9.799 137	.102 050	41
42	54.763 699	537.636 992	.001 860	.018 260	9.817 397	.101 860	42
43	60.240 069	592.400 692	.001 688	.016 600	9.833 998	.101 688	43
44	66.264 076	652.640 761	.001 532	.015 091	9.849 089	.101 532	44
45	72.890 484	718.904 837	.001 391	.013 719	9.862 808	.101 391	45
46	80.179 532	791.795 321	.001 263	.012 472	9.875 280	.101 263	46
47	88.197 485	871.974 853	.001 147	.011 338	9.886 618	.101 147	47
48	97.017 234	960.172 338	.001 041	.010 307	9.896 926	.101 041	48
49	106.718 957	1057.189 572	.000 946	.009 370	9.906 296	.100 946	49
50	117.390 853	1163.908 529	.000 859	.008 519	9.914 814	.100 859	50
51	129.129 938	1281.299 382	.000 780	.007 744	9.922 559	.100 780	51
52	142.042 932	1410.429 320	.000 709	.007 040	9.929 599	.100 709	52
53	156.247 225	1552.472 252	.000 644	.006 400	9.935 999	.100 644	53
54	171.871 948	1708.719 477	.000 585	.005 818	9.941 817	.100 585	54
55	189.059 142	1880.591 425	.000 532	.005 289	9.947 106	.100 532	55
56	207.965 057	2069.650 567	.000 483	.004 809	9.951 915	.100 483	56
57	228.761 562	2277.615 625	.000 439	.004 371	9.956 286	.100 439	57
58	251.637 719	2506.377 186	.000 399	.003 974	9.960 260	.100 399	58
59	276.801 490	2758.014 905	.000 363	.003 613	9.963 873	.100 363	59
60	304.481 640	3034.816 395	.000 330	.003 284	9.967 157	.100 330	60

$$S^n = (1+i)^n \qquad S_{\overline{n}} = \frac{S^n - 1}{i} \qquad \frac{1}{S_{\overline{n}}} = \frac{i}{S^n - 1} \qquad \frac{1}{S^n} = \frac{1}{(1+i)^n} \qquad a_{\overline{n}} = \frac{1 - 1/S^n}{i} \qquad \frac{1}{a_{\overline{n}}} = \frac{i}{1 - 1/S^n}$$

$$S = 1 + i$$

The use of precomputed tables of loan factors has largely been supplanted by the use of financial calculators and computer applications. The tables remain useful to illustrate the mathematical of finance, particularly the relative rates of change of loan factors over time for different interest rates.

Tables for additional interest rates can be found in various publications:

- Charles B. Akerson, *The Appraiser's Workbook*, 2d ed. (Chicago: Appraisal Institute, 1996).

- Charles B. Akerson, *Capitalization Theory and Techniques: Study Guide*, 2d ed. (Chicago: Appraisal Institute, with tables computed by Financial Publishing Company, 2000).

- L. W. Ellwood, *Ellwood Tables for Real Estate Appraising and Financing*, 4th ed. (Cambridge, Mass.: Ballinger Publishing Co., 1977).

- James J. Mason, ed., comp., *American Institute of Real Estate Appraisers Financial Tables*, rev. ed. (Chicago: American Institute of Real Estate Appraisers, with tables computed by Financial Publishing Company, 1982), 461–473.

Reversion Factors (Present Value of $1)

This factor is the present value of $1 to be collected at a given future time discounted at the effective interest rate for the number of periods between now and the date of collection. It is the reciprocal of the corresponding compound interest factor.

$$1/S^n = \frac{1}{(1+i)^n}$$

where:
$1/S^n$ = present value factor
i = effective rate of interest
n = number of compounding periods

and
$$1/S^n = \frac{1}{(e)^{in}}$$ for continuous compounding

where:
$1/S^n$ = present value factor
i = nominal rate of interest
n = number of years
$e = 2.718282$

This factor is used to solve problems that involve compound discounting.

As demonstrated in the discussion of future value, $1.00 compounded annually at 10% will grow to $1.610151 in five years. Accordingly, the amount that will grow to $1.00 in five years is $1.00 divided by 1.61051, or $0.62092. In the 10% table, the present value of $1 factor for five years is 0.620921. In other words, $1.00 to be collected five years from today has a present value of $0.620921 when discounted at 10% per year. And $10,000 to be collected five years from today, discounted at the same 10% annual rate, has a present value of $10,000 × 0.620921, or $6,209.21. The $10,000 sum to be received in five years is a reversion.

Ordinary Level Annuity (Present Value of $1 per Period)

This factor represents the present value of a series of future installments or payments of $1 per period for a given number of periods discounted at an effective interest rate. It is commonly referred to as the *Inwood coefficient*.

$$a_{\overline{n}|} = \frac{1 - 1/S^n}{i}$$

where:
$a_{\overline{n}|}$ = level annuity factor
$1/S^n$ = present value factor
i = rate of interest yield

This factor is used in solving problems that deal with the compound discounting of cash flows that are level or effectively level.

Finding the present value of a future income stream is a discounting procedure in which future payments are treated as a series of reversions. The present value of a series of future receipts may be quickly ascertained using the precomputed present value of $1 per period factors for the selected discount rate provided the receipts are all equal in amount, equally spaced over time, and receivable at the end of each period.

If, for example, 10% per year is a fair rate of interest or discount, it would be justifiable to pay $0.909091 (i.e., the annual present value of $1 at 10%) for the right to receive $1.00 one year from today. Assuming that the cost of this right is $0.909091, the $1.00 received at the end of the year could be divided between principal and interest as follows.

Return of principal	$0.90909
Interest on principal for one year @ 10%	0.09091
Total received	$1.00000

If approximately $0.091 is the present value of the right to receive $1.00 of income one year from today at 10% interest, the present value of the right to receive $1.00 two years from today is less. According to the present value formula, the present value of $1.00 to be received two years from today is $0.826446. The present value of $1.00 payable at the end of two years can be confirmed with these calculations.

Return on principal	$0.82645*
Interest for first year at 10% on $0.82645	0.08264
	$0.90909
Interest for second year at 10% on $0.90909	0.09091
Total principal repayment + interest received	$1.00000

*Present value factor, 0.826446 × $1.00 = $0.82645 (rounded).

Similarly, the present value of the right to receive $1.00 at the end of three years is $0.751315, at the end of four years it is $0.683013, and at the end of the fifth year it is $0.620921. The present value of these rights to receive income at one-year intervals for five years is accumulated as the present value of $1.00 per year. This is known as the *compound interest valuation premise,* also referred to as the *ordinary annuity factor.* Therefore, the sum of the five individual rights to receive $1.00 each year, payable at the end of the year, for five years is $3.790787 (i.e., the 10% annual present value of $1 per period factor for five years).

Sum of Individual Present Values of $1.00 Payable at the End of the Period	
Present value of $1.00 due in 1 year	$0.909091*
Present value of $1.00 due in 2 years	0.826446*
Present value of $1.00 due in 3 years	0.751315*
Present value of $1.00 due in 4 years	0.683013*
Present value of $1.00 due in 5 years	0.620921*
Total present value of $1.00 per year for 5 years	$3.790786**

* 10% present value of $1 factor.
** 10% present value of $1 per period factor is 3.790787; the difference is due to rounding.

The present value of $1 per period table for five annual discounting periods ($n = 5$) gives a factor that represents the total of the present values of a series of periodic amounts of $1.00, payable at the end of each period. The calculation presented above is unnecessary because multiplying $1.00 by the factor for the present value of $1 per year for five years produces the same present value ($1.00 × 3.790787 = $3.790787).

For appraisal purposes, the present value of $1 per period factor may be multiplied by a periodic income with the characteristics of an ordinary annuity to derive the present value of the right to receive that income stream. The future payments of income provide for recapture of, and interest on, this present value. Present value factors are multipliers and perform the same function as capitalization rates.

The 10% ordinary annuity factor for five years, 3.790787, represents the present value of each $1.00 of annual end-of-year collection based on a nominal annual discount rate of 10%. Tables and formulas for semiannual, quarterly, and monthly payments are also available. The ordinary annuity factor for semian-nual payments in the 10% nominal annual rate table is 7.721735. If payment continues for five years, each $1.00 of semiannual payment represents $10.00 received but reflects only $7.72 of the discounted present value of monthly payments for five years. In the table for a 10% nominal rate, the monthly factor is 47.065369, indicating that the present value of an ordinary annuity income stream of 60 monthly payments of $1.00 each discounted at a nominal rate of 10% is 47.065369 × $1.00, or about $47.065.

Based on a 10% nominal rate, semiannual payments would involve an effective rate of 5%. In the 5% annuity table, the factor for 10 periods is 7.721735; this is the same factor shown in the 10% semiannual table for a five-year period. Thus, annuity factors for more frequent payment periods can be derived using nominal annual rate tables. Preprogrammed financial calculators can be used to facilitate these calculations.

In computing the present value of an annuity income stream, it may be desirable to assume that periodic payments are made at the beginning rather than the end of each payment period. The present value of an annuity payable in advance is equal to the present value of an ordinary annuity in arrears multiplied by the base (i.e., 1 plus the effective interest rate for the discount-ing period: $1 + i$). Thus, the present value of semiannual payments in advance over a five-year period discounted at a nominal rate of 10% becomes $1.00 × 7.721735 × 1.05 = $8.107822, or $8.11, compared to $7.72 as computed for payments received at the end of each payment period.

Ordinary Annuities Changing in Constant Amounts

Present Value of Annual Payments Starting at $1 and Changing in Constant Amounts

$$PVF = (1 + h\,n)\,a_{\overline{n}|} - \frac{h\,(n - a_{\overline{n}|})}{i}$$

where:

PVF = present value factor

h^* = annual increase or decrease after first year

n = number of years

$a_{\overline{n}|}$ = PVF for ordinary level annuity

i = rate of interest yield

* h is positive for an increase and negative for a decrease

This factor is used to solve problems dealing with the compound discounting of cash flows that are best represented by a straight-line pattern of change.

This factor is similar to the ordinary level annuity table, but the annual receipts are converted into constant dollar amounts. For instance, assume that the amount to be received one year from today is $10,000, additional future receipts are expected to increase $1,000 per year for the next nine years, and 15% per year is a fair rate of interest. According to the 15% annual present value of $1 factor, it would be justifiable to pay $67,167 for the right to receive $10,000 one year from today and nine additional payments growing at $1,000 per year for nine additional years. The table for 15% indicates that the factor to be applied to the initial receipt is 6.7167.

Proof:

Year	Income	×	Present Value Factor	=	Present Value
1	$10,000	×	0.869565	=	$8,695.65
2	11,000	×	0.756144	=	8,317.58
3	12,000	×	0.657516	=	7,890.19
4	13,000	×	0.571753	=	7,432.79
5	14,000	×	0.497177	=	6,960.48
6	15,000	×	0.432328	=	6,484.92
7	16,000	×	0.375937	=	6,014.99
8	17,000	×	0.326902	=	5,557.33
9	18,000	×	0.284262	=	5,116.72
10	19,000	×	0.247185	=	4,696.52
Present value					$67,167.17

$$\frac{\text{Present value}}{\text{Initial receipt}} = \text{Factor}$$

$$\frac{\$67,167.17}{\$10,000.00} = 6.7167$$

Ordinary Annuities Changing in Constant Ratio
Present Value of Annual Payments Starting at $1 and Changing in Constant Ratio

$$PVF = \frac{1 - (1 + x)^n/(1 + i)^n}{i - x}$$

where:
PVF = present value factor
x^* = constant ratio change in income
n = number of years
i = rate of interest or yield

* x is positive for an increase and negative for a decrease

This factor is used to solve problems dealing with the compound discounting of cash flows that are best represented by an exponential-curve pattern of change.

Sinking Fund Factors
Periodic Payment to Grow to $1

This factor represents the level periodic investment or deposit required to accumulate to $1 in a given number of periods including interest at the effective rate. It is commonly known as the *amortization rate* and is the reciprocal of the corresponding sinking fund accumulation factor.

$$1/S_{\overline{n}|} = \frac{i}{S^n - 1}$$

where:
$1/S_{\overline{n}|}$ = sinking fund factor
i = effective rate of interest
n = number of compounding periods
S^n = future value factor

This factor is used to solve problems that involve calculating required sinking fund deposits or providing for the change in capital value in investment situations where the income or payments are level.

When deposits are made at the end of each compounding period, sinking fund factors reflect the fractional portion of $1.00 that must be deposited periodically at a specified interest rate to accumulate to $1.00 by the end of the series of deposits.

If $10,000 is to be accumulated over a 10-year period and annual deposits are compounded at 10% interest, the factor shown on the 10-year line of the annual column in the 10% sinking fund table indicates that each annual deposit must amount to $10,000 × 0.062745, or $627.45.

Sinking Fund Accumulation Factors
Future Value of Periodic Payments of $1

This factor represents the total accumulation of principal and interest on a series of deposits or installments of $1 per period for a given number of periods with interest at the effective rate per period. It is also known as the *amount of one per period.* It is the reciprocal of the corresponding sinking factor.

$$S_{\overline{n}|} = \frac{S^n - 1}{i}$$

where: $S_{\overline{n}|}$ = sinking fund accumulation factor
    i = effective rate of interest
    S^n = future value factor

This factor is used to solve problems that involve the growth of sinking funds or the calculation of capital recovery in investment situations where the income or payments are level.

Sinking fund accumulation factors are similar to the future value of $1 (amount of one) factors except that deposits are periodic (in a series) and are assumed to be made at the end of the first compounding period and at the end of each period thereafter. Thus, the initial deposit, which is made at the end of the first period, has earned no interest and the factor for this period is 1.000000.

If compounding at 10% per year for 10 years is assumed, a factor of 15.937425 reveals that a series of 10 deposits of $1.00 each made at the end of each year for 10 years will accumulate to $1.00 × 15.937425, or almost $15.94.

Direct Reduction Loan Factors
Monthly Payment and Annual Constant per $1 of Loan

Payment:

$$1/a_{\overline{n}|} = \frac{i}{1 - 1/S^n}$$

Annual constant: $R_M = 12/a_{\overline{n}|}$

where: $1/a_{\overline{n}|}$ = direct reduction loan factor
     $1/S^n$ = present value factor
      i = effective rate of interest
     R_M = annual constant

Part paid off:

$$P = \frac{R_M - 12i}{R_{Mp} - 12i}$$

where: R_M = actual annual constant
     R_{Mp} = annual constant for projection period
      i = effective rate of interest

This factor is used to solve problems dealing with monthly payment, direct reduction loans. Payments and constants for quarterly, semiannual, and annual payment loans can be obtained by calculating the reciprocals of the present value of $1 per period factors.

These factors, which are known as *mortgage constants for loan amortization,* reflect the amount of ordinary annuity payment that $1.00 will purchase. They indicate the periodic payment that will extinguish the debt and pay interest on the declining balance of the debt over the life of the payments. The mortgage constant may be expressed in terms of the periodic payments. A mortgage constant related to a monthly payment is the ratio of the monthly payment amount to the original amount of the loan. Whether payments are monthly, semiannual, or annual, the mortgage constant is usually expressed in terms of the total payments in one year as a percentage of the original loan amount. This is called the *annual constant* and is represented by the symbol R_M. As the loan is paid off and the outstanding balance is reduced, a new annual mortgage constant can be calculated as the ratio of total annual payments to the unpaid balance of the loan at that time.

A loan of $10,000 to be amortized in 10 annual end-of-year payments at a mortgage interest rate of 10% would require level annual payments of $10,000 × 0.162745, the 10% direct reduction annual factor for 10 years. If monthly payments were made at 10% over 10 years, the amount of each payment would be $132.15 (i.e., $10,000 × 0.013215). The annual mortgage constant in this case would be 0.158580, or 12 × 0.013215.

Direct reduction factors consist of the interest rate plus the sinking fund factor at the specific point in time. They are reciprocals of the corresponding ordinary level-annuity factors.

Interrelationships Among the Factors

Note that mathematical relationships exist among the formulas for the various factors. These relationships can be useful in understanding the factors and solving appraisal problems. For example, appraisers should know that the factors in the ordinary level annuity and direct reduction loan tables are reciprocals; the factors in the ordinary level annuity table can be used as multipliers instead of using the direct reduction loan factors as divisors.

Reciprocals

The factors in some of the tables are reciprocals of those in other tables. This is indicated by their formulas.

Future Value of $1 and Reversion Factors

$$S^n \text{ and } \frac{1}{S^n}$$

The reversion factor at 12% for 10 years with annual compounding is 0.321973, which is the reciprocal of the future value of $1 factor.

$$0.321973 = 1/3.105848$$

Sinking Fund Accumulations and Sinking Fund Factors

$$S_{\overline{n}|} \text{ and } 1/S_{\overline{n}|}$$

The sinking fund factor at 12% for 10 years with annual compounding is 0.056984, which is the reciprocal of the sinking fund accumulation factor.

$$0.056984 = 1/17.548735$$

Ordinary Level Annuity and Direct Reduction Loan Factors

$$a_{\overline{n}|} \text{ and } 1/a_{\overline{n}|}$$

The direct reduction loan factor at 12% for 10 years with annual compounding is 0.176984, which is the reciprocal of the ordinary level annuity factor.

$$0.056984 = 1/17.548735$$
$$0.176984 = 1/5.650223$$

Summations

Ordinary Level Annuity Factors

An ordinary level annuity factor represents the sum of the reversion factors for all periods up to and including the period being considered. For example, the ordinary level annuity factor for five years at 12% with annual compounding is 3.604776, which is the sum of all the reversion factors for Years 1 through 5.

$$
\begin{array}{r}
0.892857 \\
0.797194 \\
0.711780 \\
0.635518 \\
0.567427 \\
\hline
3.604776
\end{array}
$$

Direct Reduction Loan Factors

A direct reduction loan factor represents the sum of the interest, yield, or discount rate stated at the top of the table and the sinking fund factor. For example, the direct reduction loan factor at 12% for 10 years with monthly compounding is 0.1721651, which is the sum of 0.12 plus the monthly sinking fund factor of 0.0043471 times 12 (0.12 + 0.0521651 = 0.1721651).

Conversely, the sinking fund factor can be obtained by subtracting the interest rate from the direct reduction loan factor. The sinking fund factor at 12% for 10 years with monthly compounding is 0.1721651 − 0.12 = 0.0521651. In addition, the interest rate can be obtained by subtracting the sinking fund factor from the direct reduction loan factor. Given a mortgage constant of 0.1721651 with monthly compounding for 10 years, the interest rate is 0.1721651 − 0.0521651 = 0.12000, or 12.0%.

BIBLIOGRAPHY

Selected Readings and Information Sources

Books

Abrams, Charles. *The Language of Cities: A Glossary of Terms.* New York: Viking Penguin, Inc., 1972.

Albritton, Harold D. *Controversies in Real Property Valuation: A Commentary.* Chicago: American Institute of Real Estate Appraisers, 1982.

American Association of State Highway Officials. *Acquisitions for Right of Way.* Washington, D.C., 1962.

American Institute of Real Estate Appraisers. *Appraisal Thought: A 50-Year Beginning.* Chicago, 1982.

American Society of Farm Managers and Rural Appraisers and Appraisal Institute. *The Appraisal of Rural Property.* 2d ed. Denver and Chicago, 2000.

Andrews, Richard B. *Urban Land Economics and Public Policy.* New York: Free Press, 1971.

Andrews, Richard N.L. *Land in America.* Lexington, Mass.: D.C. Heath, 1979.

Appraisal Institute. *Appraising Residential Properties.* 3d ed. Chicago, 1999.

___. *The Dictionary of Real Estate Appraisal.* 3d ed. Chicago, 1993.

Appraisal Institute and American Society of Farm Managers and Rural Appraisers. *The Appraisal of Rural Property.* 2d ed. Chicago and Denver, 2000.

Arnold, Alvin L., and Jack Kusnet. *The Arnold Encyclopedia of Real Estate.* 2d ed. Boston: Warren, Gorham & Lamont, Inc., 1993.

Babcock, Frederick M. *The Valuation of Real Estate.* New York: McGraw-Hill, 1932.

Barlowe, Raleigh. *Land Resource Economics.* 4th ed. Englewood Cliffs, N.J.: Prentice-Hall, 1986.

Bierman, Harold, Jr., and Seymour Smidt. *The Capital Budgeting Decision: Economic Analysis of Investment Projects.* New York: Macmillan, 1993.

Bloom, George F., Arthur M. Weimer, and Jeffrey D. Fisher. *Real Estate.* 8th ed. New York: John Wiley & Sons, Inc., 1982.

Bonright, James C. *The Valuation of Property.* Vol. 1. New York: McGraw-Hill, 1937.

Brueggeman, William B., Jeffrey D. Fisher, and Leo D. Stone. *Real Estate Finance.* 8th ed. Homewood, Ill.: Richard D. Irwin, 1989

Burton, James H. *Evolution of the Income Approach.* Chicago: American Institute of Real Estate Appraisers, 1982.

Byrne, Therese E. *A Guide to Real Estate Information Sources.* Therese E. Byrne, 1980.

Carn, Neil, Joseph Rabianski, Maury Seldin, and Ron Racster. *Real Estate Market Analysis: Applications and Techniques.* Englewood Cliffs, N.J.: Prentice-Hall, 1988.

Cartwright, John M. *Glossary of Real Estate Law.* Rochester, N.Y.: The Lawyers Co-Operative Publishing Co., 1972.

Counselors of Real Estate (American Society of Real Estate Counselors). *Real Estate Counseling.* 2d ed. Chicago, 1988.

Davies, Pearl Janet. *Real Estate in American History.* Washington, D.C.: Public Affairs Press, 1958.

Desmond, Glenn M., and Richard E. Kelley. *Business Valuation Handbook.* Llano, Calif.: Valuation Press, 1988.

Dilmore, Gene. *Quantitative Techniques in Real Estate Counseling.* Lexington, Mass.: D.C. Heath, 1982.

Dum, Mary. *The Computerized Appraisal Office.* Chicago: Appraisal Institute, 1996.

Eaton, James D. *Real Estate Valuation in Litigation.* 2d ed. Chicago: Appraisal Institute, 1995.

Fanning, Stephen F., Terry V. Grissom, and Thomas D. Pearson. *Market Analysis for Valuation Appraisals.* Chicago: Appraisal Institute, 1994.

Financial Accounting Standards Board. FASB Statement No. 66, Accounting for Sales of Real Estate, and FASB Statement No. 67, Accounting for Costs and Initial Rental Operations of Real Estate Projects. Norwalk, Conn.: FASB, 1982.

Fisher, Clifford E., Jr. *Mathematics for Real Estate Appraisers.* Chicago: Appraisal Institute, 1996.

Friedman, Jack P., et al. *Dictionary of Real Estate Terms.* 5th ed. New York: Barron, 2000.

Friedman, Edith J., ed. *Encyclopedia of Real Estate Appraising.* 3d ed. Englewood Cliffs, N.J.: Prentice-Hall, 1978.

Graaskamp, James A. *Graaskamp on Real Estate.* Stephen P. Jarchot, ed. Washington, D.C.: Urban Land Institute, 1991.

___. *A Guide to Feasibility Analysis.* Chicago: Society of Real Estate Appraisers, 1973.

Greer, Gaylon E. *The Real Estate Investment Decision.* Lexington, Mass.: D.C. Heath, 1980.

Gross, Jerome S., comp. *Webster's New World Illustrated Encyclopedia Dictionary of Real Estate.* 3d ed. New York: Prentice-Hall, 1987.

Harris, Cyril M. *Dictionary of Architecture and Construction.* New York: McGraw-Hill, 1975.

Heilbroner, Robert L. *The Worldly Philosophers.* Rev. ed. New York: Simon and Schuster, 1964.

Hoover, Edgar M. *The Location of Economic Activity.* New York: McGraw-Hill, 1966.

International Association of Assessing Officers. *Property Appraisal and Assessment Administration.* Chicago, 1990.

Jevons, W. Stanley. *The Theory of Political Economy.* 5th ed. New York: Augustus M. Kelley, 2001.

Kahn, Sanders A., and Frederick E. Case. *Real Estate Appraisal and Investment.* 2d ed. New York: Ronald Press, 1977.

Kinnard, William N., Jr., and Byrl N. Boyce. *Appraising Real Property.* Lexington, Mass: D.C. Heath, 1984.

Kinnard, William N., Jr., Stephen D. Messner, and Byrl N. Boyce. *Industrial Real Estate.* 4th ed. Washington, D.C.: Society of Industrial Realtors®, 1984.

Klink, James J. *Real Estate Accounting and Reporting: A Guide for Developers, Investors and Lenders.* New York: John Wiley & Sons, Inc., 1995.

Levine, Mark Lee. *Real Estate Appraisers' Liability.* New York: Clark Boardman Callaghan, 1991.

Mason, James J., ed. and comp. *AIREA Financial Tables.* Chicago: American Institute of Real Estate Appraisers, 1981.

R.S. Means, Inc. *Means Illustrated Construction Dictionary.* New unabr. ed. Kingston, Mass.: R.S. Means, Inc., 2000.

North, Lincoln W. *The Concept of Highest and Best Use.* Winnipeg, Manitoba: Appraisal Institute of Canada, 1981.

Noyes, C. Reinold. *The Institution of Property.* London: Longmans, Green and Company, 1936.

Olin, Harold B., John L. Schmidt, and Walter H. Lewis. *Construction—Principles, Materials & Methods.* 7th ed. Chicago: Institute of Financial Education and Interstate Printers and Publishers, 2001.

O'Mara, Paul W. *Residential Development Handbook.* Washington, D.C.: Urban Land Institute, 1978.

Perin, Constance. *Everything in Its Place: Social Order and Land Use in America.* Princeton, N.J.: Princeton University Press, 1979.

Ratcliff, Richard U. *Modern Real Estate Valuation: Theory and Application.* Madison, Wis.: Democrat Press, 1968.

___. *Urban Land Economics.* New York: Greenwood, 1972.

Reilly, John W. *The Language of Real Estate.* 5th ed. Chicago: Real Estate Education Co., 2000.

Ring, Alfred A., and James H. Boykin. *The Valuation of Real Estate.* 4th ed. Englewood Cliffs, N.J.: Prentice-Hall, 1993.

Ring, Alfred A., and Jerome Dasso. *Real Estate Principles and Practices.* 11th ed. Englewood Cliffs, N.J.: Prentice-Hall, 1989.

Roca, Ruben A. *Market Research for Shopping Centers.* New York: International Council of Shopping Centers, 1980.

Rohan, Patrick J., and Melvin A. Reskin. *Condemnation Procedures and Techniques; Forms.* Albany, N.Y.: Matthew Bender, 1968 (looseleaf service).

Roll, Eric. *A History of Economic Thought.* 3d ed. Englewood Cliffs, N.J.: Prentice-Hall, 1964.

Rosenberg, Jerry M. *Dictionary of Banking and Finance.* New York: John Wiley & Sons, Inc., 1982.

Sackman, Julius L., and Patrick J. Rohan. *Nichols' Law of Eminent Domain.* 3d rev. ed. Albany, N.Y.: Matthew Bender, 1973 (looseleaf service).

Samuelson, Paul A., and William D. Nordhaus. *Economics.* 13th ed. New York: McGraw-Hill, 1989.

Schmutz, George L. *The Appraisal Process.* North Hollywood, Calif.: the author, 1941.

___. *Condemnation Appraisal Handbook,* rev. and enl. by Edwin M. Rams. Englewood Cliffs, N.J.: Prentice-Hall, 1963.

Seldin, Maury, and James H. Boykin. *Real Estate Analyses.* Homewood, Ill.: American Society of Real Estate Counselors and Dow Jones-Irwin, 1990.

Shenkel, William M. *Modern Real Estate Appraisal.* New York: McGraw-Hill, 1978.

Shlaes, Jared. *Real Estate Counseling in a Plain Brown Wrapper.* Chicago: Counselors of Real Estate, 1992.

Sirmans, C.F., and Austin J. Jaffe. *The Complete Real Estate Investment Handbook: A Professional Investment Strategy.* 4th ed. New York: Prentice-Hall, 1988.

Smith, Halbert C., and Jerry D. Beloit. *Real Estate Appraisal.* 3d ed. Columbus, Ohio: Century VII Publishing Company, 1995.

Smith, Halbert C., Carl J. Tschappat, and Ronald L. Racster. *Real Estate and Urban Development.* 3d ed. Homewood, Ill.: Richard D. Irwin, 1981.

Talamo, John. *The Real Estate Dictionary.* 6th ed. Boston: Laventhal & Horwath/ Financial Publishing Co., 1998.

Vane, Howard R., and John L. Thompson. *Monetarism—Theory, Evidency and Policy.* New York: Halsted, 1979.

Ventrolo, William L., and Martha R. Williams. *Fundamentals of Real Estate Appraisal.* 5th ed. Chicago: Real Estate Education Co., 1990.

Wendt, Paul F. *Real Estate Appraisal Review and Outlook.* Athens, Ga.: University of Georgia Press, 1974.

Werner, Raymond J., and Robert Kratovil. *Real Estate Law.* 10th ed. Englewood Cliffs, N.J.: Prentice-Hall, 1993.

West, Bill W., and Richard L. Dickinson. *Street Talk in Real Estate.* Alameda/Sacramento, Calif.: Unique Pub., 1987.

Wolf, Peter. *Land in America: Its Value, Use, and Control.* New York: Pantheon, 1981.

Periodicals

American Council of Life Insurance Investment Bulletins. American Council of Life Insurance, Washington, D.C.
> Annual and quarterly reports on the lending activities and holdings of life insurance companies.

American Right of Way Proceedings. American Right of Way Association, Los Angeles.
> Annual. Papers presented at national seminars.

Appraisal Institute Magazine. Appraisal Institute of Canada, Winnipeg, Manitoba.
> Quarterly. General and technical articles on appraisal and expropriation in Canada. Includes information on institute programs, news, etc.

The Appraisal Journal. Appraisal Institute, Chicago. Quarterly.
> Oldest periodical in the appraisal field, published since 1932. Includes technical articles on all phases of real property appraisal and regular feature on legal decisions. Bibliographies for 1932–1969, 1970–1980, 1980–1987, and 1988–1993 are available.

Appraiser News In Brief. Appraisal Institute, Chicago.
> Published eight times a year. News bulletin covering current events and trends in appraisal practice.

Buildings. Stamats Communications, Inc., Cedar Rapids, Iowa.
> Monthly. Journal of building construction and management. http://www.buildings.com

Crittenden Report on Real Estate Financing. Crittenden Publishing, Inc., Novato, Calif.
Weekly. Real estate finance information. http://www.crittendenonline.com

Editor and Publisher Market Guide. Editor and Publisher, New York.
Annual. Standardized market data for more than 1,500 areas in the United States
and Canada, including population estimates for trading areas. List of principal
industries, transportation, climate, chain store outlets, etc.
http://www.mediainfo.com

Emerging Trends in Real Estate. Real Estate Research Corp., Atlanta and New York.
Annual. http://www.pwcglobal.com

Journal of the American Society of Farm Managers and Rural Appraisers. Denver.
Semiannual. Includes appraisal articles.

Journal of Property Management. Institute of Real Estate Management, Chicago.
Bimonthly. Covers a broad range of property investment and management issues.

Journal of Real Estate Literature. American Real Estate Society, Cleveland, Ohio.
Semiannual. Contains review articles, case studies, doctoral dissertations, and
reviews of technical literature, data sets, computer applications, and software.

Journal of Real Estate Portfolio Management. American Real Estate Society, Cleveland,
Ohio.
Semiannual. Contains the results of applied research on real estate investment and
portfolio management.

Journal of Real Estate Research. American Real Estate Society, Cleveland, Ohio.
Quarterly. Publishes the results of applied research on real estate development,
finance, investment, management, market analysis, marketing, and valuation.

Just Compensation: A Monthly Report on Condemnation Cases. Sherman Oaks, Calif.
Monthly.

Land Economics. University of Wisconsin, Madison, Wis.
Quarterly. Journal devoted to the study of economics and social institutes.
Includes reports on university research and trends in land utilization. Frequently
publishes articles on developments in other countries.

Korpacz Real Estate Investor Survey. Peter Korpacz, Frederick, Md.
Quarterly. Survey of a cross-section of the major participants in real estate equity
markets.
http://www.pwcreval.com/cgi-bin/webc/pwcreval/home.html?sid=1e6dT6FW

MarketSource. Appraisal Institute, Chicago.
Quarterly. Published since 1991. Data on key rates, economic trends, and real
estate financing and market conditions.

National Real Estate Review. National Association of Realtors®, Chicago
  Annual. Includes information on office, industrial, retail, multifamily, and hotel real estate.

NCREIF Quarterly Real Estate Performance Report. National Council of Real Estate Investment Fiduciaries, which maintains the NCREIF Classic Property Index (formerly the Russell-NCREIF Property Index).
  Quarterly. Tracks the performance of properties acquired on behalf of tax-exempt institutions, on an unleveraged basis, and held in fiduciary trusts. The index is calculated on the basis of four different rates of return (total return, income return, capital appreciation return, and annual/annualized return). http://www.ncreif.org/sub_i_reports.htm

PREA Quarterly. Pension Real Estate Association, Glastonbury, Conn.
  Quarterly. Contains articles and information areas such as real estate securities, legislative issues, capital flows and market research, as well as articles exploring issues and trends of importance to institutional real estate investors. http://www.prea.org/education/quarterly.html

Property Tax Journal. International Association of Assessing Officers, Chicago.
  Quarterly. Includes articles on property taxation and assessment administration.

Real Estate Capital Markets Report. Institutional Research, Inc., Walnut Creek, Calif.
  Quarterly. Contains articles and information on the financial markets and the availability, cost, and flow of capital.

Real Estate Economics, formerly *Journal of the American Real Estate and Urban Economics Association.* Bloomington, Ind.
  Quarterly. Focuses on research and scholarly studies of current and emerging real estate issues.

Real Estate Information Standards: 1995. Joint Task Force of the National Association of Real Estate Investment Managers (NAREIM), the National Council of Real Estate Investment Fiduciaries (NCREIF), and the Pension Real Estate Association (PREA).
  Includes standards for investment and asset information, valuation information, and performance measurement as well as the NCREIF market value accounting policy manual and appendices on terminology, computation methodology, prior initiatives and existing regulations, and reference source contacts. http://www.ncreif.com/pdf/reis2000.pdf

Real Estate Issues. American Society of Real Estate Counselors, Chicago.
  Semiannual.

Real Estate Law Journal. Warren, Gorham and Lamont, Inc., Boston.
  Quarterly. Publishes articles on legal issues and reviews current litigation of concern to real estate professionals.

Real Estate Market Forecast. Landauer Real Estate Counselors, New York. Annual.

Real Estate Report. Real Estate Research Corp., Atlanta and New York. Quarterly.

Right of Way. American Right of Way Association, Los Angeles.
  Bimonthly. Articles on all phases of right of way activity—e.g., condemnation, negotiation, pipelines, electric power transmission lines, and highways. Includes association news.

Small Business Reporter. Bank of America, San Francisco.
  Irregular. Each issue devoted to a specific type of small business—e.g, coin-operated laundries, greeting card shops, restaurants.

Survey of U.S. Industrial and Commercial Buying Power. Sales Management, New York.
  Annual. Includes population totals and characteristics and income and consumption data presented in national, regional, metropolitan area, county, and city categories. Separate section for Canadian information. Population estimates between decennial censuses.

Survey of Current Business. U.S. Bureau of Economic Analysis, U.S. Department of Commerce, Washington, D.C.
  Monthly. Includes statistical and price data. Biennial supplement, *Business Statistics.*

Valuation. American Society of Appraisers, Washington, D.C.
  Three issues per year. Articles on real property valuation and the appraisal of personal and intangible property. Includes society news.

Valuation Insights & Perspectives. Appraisal Institute, Chicago.
  Published quarterly. Provides timely, practical information and ideas to assist real estate appraisers in conducting their businesses effectively.

Valuation Strategies. RIA, New York.
  Published bimonthly. Includes technical articles, case studies, and research on all aspects of real estate valuation.

Index

cash flow, 552

See also discounted cash flow analysis

cash flow rate. *See* equity capitalization rates

cash on cash rate. *See* equity capitalization rates

CBDs. *See* central business districts

CDs. *See* certificates of deposit

ceilings and ceiling heights

in commercial buildings, 256

in warehouses, 260–261

census data. *See* data collection and analysis

central business districts, 180, 182

certificates of deposit, 106

certification of value

in appraisal reports, 616–617

chambers of commerce

as source of general data, 148

change, 34–36

and land valuation, 331–332

in market area analysis,165–168

changing income

and yield capitalization, 554–556

chattel fixtures. *See* trade fixtures

chimneys, 233

See also fireplaces

chronological age. *See* actual age

Clean Air Acts of 1963 and 1990, 208 fn. 2

Clean Water Act of 1977, 203–204

cleaning

as variable expense, 517

climate

and agricultural land, 217

CMOs. *See* collateralized mortgage obligations

coal heat, 246

cogeneration, 245–246

collateralized mortgage obligations (CMOs), 126

columns, 229, 243

commercial banks, 122–123

commercial districts, 177–178

See also central business districts; community shopping centers; neighborhood shopping centers; regional shopping centers; specialty shopping centers

commercial mortgage-backed securities (CMBSs), 126

commercial paper, 106–107

commercial properties, 254–258

common area maintenance (CAM), 76–77

common level ratio, 145–146

communications technology, 257–259

community shopping centers, 181

comparability of data, 157–160

comparable properties, 58

comparative analysis, 429–430, 464–467

See also paired data analysis; relative comparison analysis

comparative-unit method of cost estimating, 371–375

comparison. *See* elements of comparison; sales comparison approach; units of comparison

compatibility, 252

Competency Rule, 633

competition, 38

competitive supply, 275–276

competitive supply and demand data, 144

sources of, 152–157

competitive supply inventory, 144

complementary properties, 163–164

complete appraisals, 11, 13

compliance review, 635–636

compound interest, 550–552

computers, 145–149, 151–157

condemnation appraising, 646–647

condition. *See* quality and condition survey

conditions of appraisal, 56

conditions of sale

in sales comparison approach, 433, 453–454

pipe, 243–244

See also drainage

platform construction, 230

plots, 190

plottage, 197–198

plumbing fixtures, 243–244

plumbing systems, 243–244

POB. *See* point of beginning

point estimate, 602–603

point of beginning

in metes and bounds land description, 191

police power, 70

pollution. *See* environmental liabilities

pollution rights, 208

population. *See* demographics

post and beam framing, 230

potential gross income (PGI), 484, 511–512

definition of, 483–484

potential gross income multiplier (PGIM), 546–547

powers of government, 70

preliminary analysis and data collection, 57–58

present value factors, 560

preservation easements, 86

price, 19–20

primary data, 135

prime rates, 105–106

principal meridians, 191–192

private debt, 93

private equity, 93

probability range, 603

production, agents of, 33–34

profitability index (PI), 582–583

progression, principle of, 42

property damage, 402

property inspection, 221–223

property interests

types of, 79–90

See also air rights; easements; fee interests; leased fee interests; leasehold interests; life estates; partial interests; subsurface rights; transferable development rights; vertical interests

property models, 561–567

exponential-curve changes, 566

level income, 562–563

straight-line changes, 563–566

variable or irregular changes, 566–567

Property Observation Checklist, 210–213

property rights. *See* real property rights

property taxes, 141–142

assessment appeals, 647–648

as operating expense, 477, 486, 513

prospective value. *See* date of value opinion

proposed properties, 367

public amenities, 170–172

public controls. *See* government regulations

public debt, 93

public equity, 93

public interest value, 649–650

public records

as source of specific data, 150–151

public utilities, 204, 206

purchase-money mortgages, 111

quadrangles

in Geodetic Survey System, 199, 201

qualitative analysis, 445–448, 459–464, 466–467

See also ranking analysis; relative comparison analysis

quality and condition survey, 264–267

quantitative adjustments, 438–445

quantitative analysis, 445–446, 449–459, 465–466

See also graphic analysis; paired data analysis; trend analysis

DISCARD

For Reference
Not to be taken from this room

DISCARD